CIVIL WAR
MAPS

"In every house & shop, an American map has been unrolled, & daily studied." *

*Ralph Waldo Emerson writing in 1865 on the benefits of the Civil War. See *The Journals and Miscellaneous Notebooks of Ralph Waldo Emerson.* Vol. XV, 1860–1866. Edited by Linda Allardt, David W. Hill and Ruth H. Bennett (Cambridge, Mass. and London, Eng.: The Belknap Press of Harvard University Press, 1982), p. 64.

CIVIL WAR MAPS

An Annotated List of Maps and Atlases in the Library of Congress

Second Edition

Compiled by
RICHARD W. STEPHENSON
Geography and Map Division

LIBRARY OF CONGRESS
Washington · 1989

Library of Congress Cataloging-in-Publication Data

Library of Congress. Geography and Map Division.
    Civil War maps.

    Includes indexes.
    Supt. of Docs. no. : LC 1.12/2:C49
    1. United States—History—Civil War, 1861–1865—
Maps—Bibliography—Catalogs. 2. Library of Congress.
Geography and Map Division—Catalogs. I. Stephenson,
Richard W., 1930–   . II. Title.
Z6027.U5L5   1989   [GA405.5]   016.9737   88–600031
ISBN 0–8444–0598–1

The paper used in this publication meets the requirements
for permanent printing papers.

Designed by William Chenoweth

For sale by the Superintendent of Documents
U.S. Government Printing Office, Washington, D.C. 20402

Contents

Preface

This is the second edition of the cartobibliography *Civil War Maps,* initially published a quarter of a century ago by the Library of Congress to commemorate the centennial of that war. This greatly expanded edition includes descriptions of 2240 maps and charts and 76 atlases and sketch books, chiefly in the custody of the Geography and Map Division. Also included are a selection of 162 maps from 28 collections of papers in the Library's Manuscript Division and a few atlases that accompany volumes of text housed in the Library's general book collections.

The maps, charts, and atlases described in this bibliography depict troop positions and movements, engagements, and fortifications. Also included are reconnaissance maps, sketch maps, coastal charts, and theater of war maps. An introductory essay traces the development of mapping during the Civil War, with special reference to maps and atlases in the Geography and Map Division.

The bibliography not only includes descriptions of printed, photoreproduced, annotated, and hand-drawn maps made between 1861 and 1865, but also maps made later to illustrate or explain specific events, movements, and battles of the war. The vast majority of the maps were prepared by Federal forces or by commercial firms in the North, but there are also a substantial number by Confederate military authorities and a few by Southern publishers. The largest group among the Confederate works are the 341 manuscript maps and sketchbooks that make up the Hotchkiss Map Collection. Assembled by Maj. Jedediah Hotchkiss, who served as topographic engineer with the Army of Northern Virginia, this remarkable collection was acquired by the Library of Congress in 1948 from Hotchkiss's granddaughter, Mrs. R. E. Christian of Deerfield, Virginia. The entries for the collection, described in a separate section, were prepared in 1951 by Clara Egli LeGear and were originally published by the Library of Congress under the title *The Hotchkiss Map Collection: A List of Manuscript Maps, Many of the Civil War Period, Prepared by Major Jedediah Hotchkiss, and Other Manuscript and Annotated Maps in His Possession.* References to numerous other printed maps and photocopies owned by Hotchkiss are scattered throughout the bibliography and may be accessed through the general index under his name.

As in the previous edition, the bibliography begins with maps of the United States or large portions thereof, arranged either by date of content or by publishing date, and subdivided by authority. Included here are maps of the whole United States, maps of major regions such as the Eastern or Southern States, maps showing all or parts of more than two states, and maps of the Mississippi River. State maps follow, with maps of specific battles, cities and towns, and natural features listed alphabetically under each state. This section concludes with the description of one map of the English Channel showing the sinking of the Confederate ship *Alabama* off Cherbourg, France. The next two sections describe in detail the contents of the Hotchkiss Map Collection and the Sherman Map Collection. The latter collection, consisting of 210 maps and 3 atlases belonging to Gen. William Tecumseh Sherman, was formed by the Library of Congress from three separate accessions. The first, received in 1912, numbered some fifty-eight maps that were included among the papers presented to the Library of Congress by Sherman's son, Philemon Tecumseh Sherman. A second segment was obtained in 1942 from the general's granddaughter, Miss Eleanor Sherman Fitch. The final group of maps was obtained in 1955 from the William L. Clements Library, Ann Arbor, Michigan, in exchange for a copy of Joseph F. W. Des Barres's *The Atlantic Neptune* (London, 1774–1781). The collection includes a significant number of maps used by the general and his staff during the march on Atlanta in 1864, other maps of the Civil War period, tracings of the detailed district maps in Robert Mills's *Atlas of the State of South Carolina* (Baltimore, 1825), and a few maps and atlases owned by Sherman either before or after the war. In the previous edition, only those maps in the Sherman Collection that depicted fortifications and troop positions and movements were described. These citations have been removed from the general geographical section and, in the new edition, have been placed in their proper position in the comprehensive list of the Sherman Collection. Cross references, however, are provided from the old entry number to the number in the Sherman Collection.

Whenever possible, individual entries include the author's name (i.e., the person, agency, unit, or firm responsible for preparing or drawing the map), the full title, the imprint, a color notation, the natural scale, and the size of the map image. In keeping with modern library convention, sizes are given in centimeters rather than in inches as was done in the previous edition. Vertical measurements are given first, followed by horizontal measurements. The name of the lithographic establishment is indicated in the same form as that which appears on the map, except for the omission of the street address. Most of the entries include a brief paragraph describing the contents of the map, but no attempt has been made to analyze it completely or to evaluate it critically.

Two indexes complete the bibliography. The first includes short titles and the second lists battles, places, subjects, personal names, cartographers, surveyors, engravers, lithographers, publishers, and printers. The numbers following index terms refer to the bibliographical entries and not to pages. The entry numbers used in the first edition have been retained and new entries have been interfiled in their proper order by the use of decimal numbers. Numbers used in the previous edition, therefore, are still valid. All entries in the Hotchkiss Map Collection are prefixed by the letter "H," and all entries in the Sherman Map Collection by the letter "S."

Facsimile reproductions of Civil War maps are not stocked for sale by the Library of Congress. Black-and-white photoreproductions, color slides, and color transparencies of specific maps may be ordered from the Library of Congress, Photoduplication Service, Washington, D.C. 20540. Civil War battle maps frequently distinguish between opposing forces by the use of red and blue coloring. The color differentiation is lost, however, in a black-and-white photocopy.

The Library actively seeks to enrich its cartographic collections and would welcome information that may lead to the acquisition of maps and atlases of the American Civil War not already included in its holdings.

RICHARD W. STEPHENSON
Geography and Map Division

Introduction

W ar, like necessity, has been called the mother of invention. The same might be said of cartography, for with every war there is a great rush to produce maps to aid in understanding the nature of the land over which armies will move and fight, to plan engagements and the deployment of troops, and to record victories for posterity to study and admire. The American Civil War is a classic example of the effect that was has had on cartography.

PREWAR MAPPING

On the eve of the Civil War, few detailed maps existed of areas in which fighting was likely to occur. Uniform, large-scale topographic maps, such as those produced today by the U.S. Geological Survey, did not exist and would not become a reality for another generation. In most cases, the best medium-scale, published maps available in 1861 were those sponsored by various state legislatures.

In the Eastern theater (i.e., southern Pennsylvania, Maryland, and Virginia) both Union and Confederate military authorities initially relied on several maps: that of Pennsylvania (scale 5 miles to 1 inch) published in 1860 by Rufus L. Barnes of Philadelphia; Fielding Lucas, Jr.'s map of Maryland (scale 5½ miles to 1 inch) published in Baltimore in 1852; and the nine-sheet map of Virginia by Herman Böÿe (scale 5 miles to 1 inch), revised by Ludwig von Buchholtz and published in Richmond in 1859. Each was actually a revision of a map published long before the Civil War: the Pennsylvania map was originally compiled and published by John Melish in 1822; the map of Maryland was first issued by Lucas in 1841; and the map of Virginia was first copyrighted by the state in 1826 and offered for sale in 1827.

The most detailed maps available in the 1850s were of selected counties. Published at about the scale of one inch to a mile, these commercially produced wall maps showed roads, railroads, towns and villages, rivers and streams, mills, forges, taverns, dwellings, and the names of residents.[1] The few maps of selected counties in Virginia, Maryland, and southern Pennsylvania that were available were eagerly sought by military commanders on both sides. In his communication to the American Philosophical Society in March 1864, map publisher Robert Pearsall Smith told how, on the eve of the invasion of Pennsylvania in 1863, Confederate soldiers in advance of the main army confiscated all the maps of Franklin, Cumberland, and Adams counties that they could find:

> For a day or two, not a map of the seat of war was to be obtained at Harrisburg for the use of the Governor and his staff. General Couch had but a single copy at his headquarters. An order on Philadelphia could only be filled by sending out a special agent, who succeeded, at great personal risk, in procuring one or two of each county. Judge Watts, of Carlisle, informed me that the maps were torn hastily from the walls of the farmers' houses, and sent with the horses and other valuables for safety, over the North Mountain, into the Juniata Valley. The rebel visitation was very complete; he thought it likely that not a single house had been overlooked. . . .
>
> A rebel general is understood to have made a reconnoissance of these counties previous to the invasion under the guise of a map-peddler, and while selling some of a more general character, no doubt bought up county maps to be used in the invasion.[2]

Interest in county maps was substantiated by Confederate cavalry officer Lt. Col. William W. Blackford who wrote:

> At Mercersburg I found that a citizen of the place had a county map and of course called at the house for it, as these maps had every road laid down and would be of the greatest service to us. Only the females of the family appeared, who flatly refused to let me have the map, or to acknowledge that they had one; so I was obliged to dismount and push by the infuriated ladies, rather rough specimens, however, into the sitting room where I found the map hanging on the wall. Angry women do not show to advantage, and the language and looks of these were fearful, as I coolly cut the map out of its rollers and put it in my haversack.[3]

UNION MAPPING

Federal military authorities were keenly aware that they were unprepared to fight a war on American soil. Any significant campaign into the seceding states could be successfully carried out only after good maps, based on reliable data

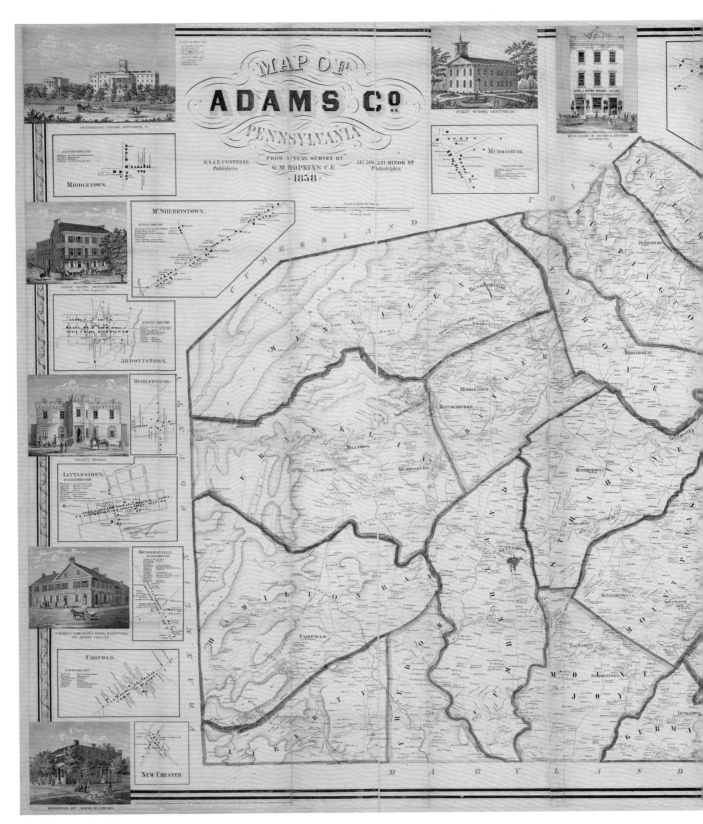

The most detailed maps available for some areas in southern Pennsylvania, Maryland, and Virginia were commercially produced county wall maps. Griffith M. Hopkins's 1858 map of Adams County, Pennsylvania, for example, was used by both Union and Confederate authorities during the Gettysburg Campaign of 1863.

2

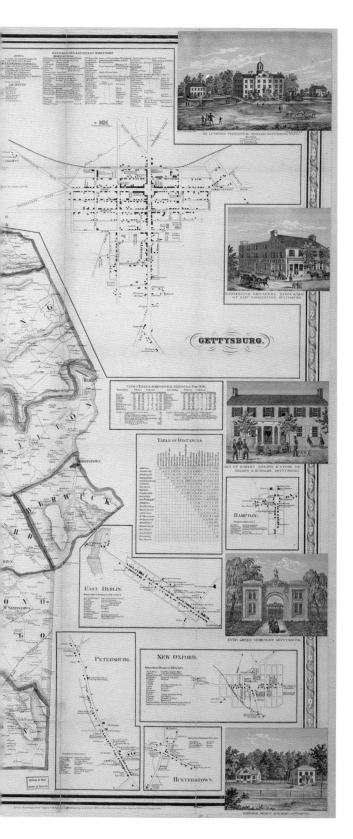

from the field, had been prepared. Existing Federal mapping units, such as the Army's Corps of Topographical Engineers and Corps of Engineers, the Treasury Department's Coast Survey, and the Navy's Hydrographic Office, therefore, were considered of immense importance to the war effort and were given full support to expand and carry out their missions.[4] Although Federal authorities were unprepared to fight a war, they had one great advantage over the Confederacy: they were able to build upon an existing organizational structure, which included equipment and trained personnel.

Mapping of Washington, D.C.

As the war began, perhaps the most vulnerable area of the Union was the nation's capital. Situated on the banks of the Potomac River, Washington, D.C., was located between the Commonwealth of Virginia which ratified the ordinance of secession on April 17, 1861, and Maryland, which initially wavered, but remained a part of the Union. On the evening of May 23, as soon as sufficient troops were on hand in the nation's capital, Federal regiments crossed the Potomac into Virginia and began occupying the strategic approaches to the city. Within the next two months efforts were concentrated on the preparation of earthen fortifications to defend the city from an attack from the South. Throughout the war the defenses of Washington were extended, strengthened, and modified. Entrusted with this important task was Bvt. Maj. Gen. John G. Barnard of the Corps of Engineers. General Barnard served as Chief Engineer of the Army of the Potomac, 1861 to 1862, Chief Engineer of the Department of Washington from 1861 to 1864, and then as Chief Engineer of the armies in the field from 1864 to 1865. In his *Report on the Defenses of Washington* published after the war, Barnard noted with some pride that:

> From a few isolated works covering bridges or commanding a few especially important points, was developed a connected system of fortification by which every prominent point, at intervals of 800 to 1,000 yards, was occupied by an inclosed field-fort every important approach or depression of ground, unseen from the forts, swept by a battery for field-guns, and the whole connected by rifle-trenches which were in fact lines of infantry parapet, furnishing emplacement for two ranks of men and affording covered communication along the line, while roads were opened wherever necessary, so that troops and artillery could be moved rapidly from one point of the immense periphery to another, or under cover, from point to point along the line.[5]

Of the numerous maps depicting the defenses of Washington, D.C., the detailed map compiled by the U.S. Army Corps of Engineers showing the entire interlinking network

3

of fortifications is of particular importance. Measuring 132 by 144 cm., this remarkable map was made to accompany General Barnard's official report on the defenses of the nation's capital. Albert Boschke's notable 1861 printed map of Washington, D.C., was used as the base, and to it army mapmakers added, by hand, cultural data on Virginia, a new map title, forts, batteries, and rifle pits, as well as the military roads built to link them (entry no. 676).

Mapping of Northern Virginia

Occupancy of key positions in Virginia enabled Federal officials to begin the first major mapping project of the war. In June 1861, on orders from Winfield Scott, General in Chief of the Army, two field parties made up of U.S. Coast Survey personnel and under the direction of H. L. Whiting, the survey's "most experienced field assistant,"[6] began a 38-square-mile plane table survey of the secured part of northern Virginia. Transportation and protection were provided by army detachments, and the actual map itself was compiled in the Topographical Engineers Office at the Division Headquarters of Gen. Irvin McDowell at Arlington, Virginia. This cooperative undertaking involving both Coast Survey and army personnel was to be the pattern followed throughout the war. Coast Survey assistants provided valuable service to armies in the field as well as to the naval squadrons blockading Southern bays, harbors, and ports.

Work on the map was interrupted in July when Federal troops in northern Virginia suffered a jolting defeat at Manassas, Virginia (Bull Run). The need for an accurate map of northern Virginia was reinforced by the Union disaster only a few miles from the capital city. Work was quickly resumed on this key map and, under orders from Gen. George McClellan, who had assumed command of the armies around Washington, the area covered by the survey was significantly expanded. The first edition of the map was "engraved on stone" and issued on January 1, 1862.

A second edition incorporating corrections "from recent surveys and reconnaissances under direction of the Bureau of Topographical Engineers" was published on August 1, 1862, only 28 days before the second Battle of Manassas, Virginia.

Published at the scale of one inch to one mile (1:63,360), field assistant Whiting commented that "The detailed survey shows all the important topographical features of the country which it embraces; the main roads, by-roads, and bridle-paths; the woods, open grounds, and streams; houses, out-buildings, and fences; with as close a sketch of contour as the hidden character of the country would allow—producing in all a map by which any practicable military movement might be studied and planned with perfect reliability."[7] This was the first detailed map of northern Virginia to be compiled and published, and it remains today an essential cartographic tool for the study of that region at midnineteenth century (entry no. 466–470).

Field Reconnaissance

Federal authorities used every means at their disposal to gather accurate information on the location, number, movement, and intent of Confederate armed forces. Army cavalry parties were constantly probing the countryside in search of the enemy's picket lines; travelers and peddlers were interrogated; Southerners sympathetic to the Union were contacted and questioned; and spies were dispatched into the interior to obtain information. The army also turned to a new device for gathering information, the stationary observation balloon. Early in the war a balloon corps under the direction of Thaddeus Lowe was established and attached to the Army of the Potomac. Although used chiefly for observing the enemy's position in the field, the balloon was also successfully employed for the making of maps and sketches. Aeronaut John La Montain made one of the earliest sketches from the platform of a balloon. Dated August 10, 1861, the simple sketch shows the location of Confederate tents and batteries at Sewall's Point, Virginia (entry no. 654).

The Geography and Map Division has an interesting reconnaissance map prepared during the crucial Seven Days' battles of the Peninsula Campaign. It was compiled under the alias of E. J. Allen, by the famous nineteenth-century detective Allan Pinkerton, with the assistance of one of his operatives, John C. Babcock. Pinkerton, who earlier had established the U.S. Secret Service in Washington, served as McClellan's chief of intelligence during the Peninsula Campaign. Based in part on the prewar map of Henrico County by James Keily, Pinkerton and Babcock's map includes a wealth of up-to-date military information, such as Confederate batteries, Federal lines, and Federal cavalry and infantry pickets. The faded sunprint in the Geography and Map Division was initially prepared on May 31, 1862, corrected on June 20, and again on July 22 (entry no. 620).

Another badly faded issue of this map is preserved in the Library's Manuscript Division.[8] This photocopy, dated June 6, 1862, is particularly noteworthy because it has been annotated in red and black inks to show information obtained from two tethered balloons (entry no. 619.5). A note written by Thaddeus Lowe at the bottom of the map reads as follows:

Balloon Camp, June 14th 1862.

The red lines represent some of the most important earth works seen this morning & are located as near as possible, as is also the camps in black ink. As soon as I can get an observation from the Mechanicsville Balloon I can make many additions to this map.

[Signed] T. S. C. Lowe

Map Production

Field and harbor surveys, topographic and hydrographic surveys, reconnaissances, and road traverses by Federal mappers led to the preparation of countless thousands of manuscript maps and the publication of maps and charts in unprecedented numbers. The Superintendent of the Coast Survey in his annual report for 1862 noted that "upwards of forty-four thousand copies of printed maps, charts, and sketches have been sent from the office since the date of my last report—a number more than double the distribution in the year 1861, and upwards of five times the average annual distribution of former years. This large and increasing issue of charts within the past two years has been due to the constant demands of the Navy and War Departments, every effort to supply which still continues to be made."[9] By 1864, the number of maps and charts printed during the year reached 65,897, of which more than 22,000 were military maps and sketches.[10] Large numbers of maps also were compiled and printed by the Army's Corps of Engineers. The Chief Engineer reported that in 1864, 20,938 map sheets were furnished to the armies in the field, and in the final year of the war this figure grew to 24,591.[11]

The great demand for maps and charts could not have been met were it not for the introduction of two lithographic presses in the Coast Survey office in 1861. Previously, the Survey, like most other Federal mapping agencies, was dependent upon the laborious and time-consuming process of printing maps from engraved copper plates. Because of the ease in transferring manuscript data to stone, the versatility of the process, and the speed of the lithographic presses, reliance on lithography grew rapidly during the war. By 1863, the Superintendent reported that "Two lithographic presses have been kept in constant operation throughout the year, and such has occasionally been the pressure on the division that it has been found necessary to employ other lithographic establishments in the execution of special jobs."[12] To help satisfy the Federal government's printing demands, commercial firms such as Julius Bien and Company in New York, and Bowen and Company in Philadelphia were hired to print the needed maps.

The development and growing sophistication of the Union mapping effort was apparent in 1864 when it became possible for Coast Survey officials to compile a uniform, ten-mile-to-the-inch base map described by the Superintendent as "the area of all the States in rebellion east of the Mississippi river, excepting the back districts of North and South Carolina, and the neutral part of Tennessee and to southern Florida, in which no military movements have taken place."[13] Moreover, as the Superintendent noted, the map was placed on lithographic stones so that "any limits for a special map may be chosen at pleasure, and a sheet issued promptly when needed in prospective military move-

ments."[14] During the final two years of the conflict, numerous regional base maps at ten miles to the inch and showing boundaries, relief, place names and lines of transportation were issued by the Coast Survey. Some were printed without map titles, such as the map of eastern Tennessee and environs (entry no. 75.8), while others bore map titles, such as the map of "North Carolina & South Carolina" (entry no. 305a.4).

Relief Representation

Throughout the war military publishing authorities continued to favor the use of hachures to depict relief on published maps. Although contour lines or "horizontal curves," as they were sometimes called, were used increasingly by topographic engineers in their field surveys, the technique apparently was not considered satisfactory for the finished or published map. Col. William E. Merrill, for example, submitted to the Engineer Department a topographic survey of the battlefield of Chickamauga, Georgia, on which relief is represented by contour lines at 20-foot intervals and layer tints. In an explanatory note, Merrill wrote that "This map was prepared as a guide to the draughtsman who might be employed to prepare the complete map of the battle of Chicamauga [sic]. By carefully studying the contour lines and tints on this map an accurate map with hachures may be made of the ground" (entry no. 157.4).

The map of the "Approaches to Grand Gulf. From a Topographical & Hydrographical Survey by F. H. Gerdes" is an example of a printed map in which the publisher favored hachures over contours to depict the topography of the area. On file in the Geography and Map Division is a photocopy of a preliminary version of the Grand Gulf map with annotations in ink and pencil (entry no. 271). Believed to be Gerdes's field copy, it shows that he elected to indicate relief by contour lines rather than by hachures. By the time the map was issued, however, the publisher had converted this information into the more conventional hachure technique with which the nonexpert was more familiar (entry no. 270).

CONFEDERATE MAPPING

The Confederate Army had difficulty throughout the war in supplying its field officers with adequate maps. The situation in the South was acute from the beginning of hostilities because of the lack of established government mapping agencies capable of preparing large-scale maps, and the inadequacy of printing facilities for producing them. The situation was further complicated by the almost total absence of surveying and drafting equipment, and the lack of trained military engineers and mapmakers to use the equipment that was available.

Their ignorance of the land about them during the Seven Days' battles in 1862 was bitterly described by Gen. Richard Taylor. "The Confederate commanders," he wrote, "knew no more about the topography of the country than they did about Central Africa. Here was a limited district, the whole of it within a day's march of the city of Richmond, capital of Virginia and the Confederacy, almost the first spot on the continent occupied by the British race, the Chickahominy itself classic by legends of Captain John Smith and Pocahontas; and yet we were profoundly ignorant of the country, were without maps, sketches,. or proper guides, and nearly as helpless as if we had been suddenly transferred to the banks of the Lualaba [Congo River]." [15]

Confederate officers, of course, were not alone in their lack of adequate maps. During the Peninsula Campaign which culminated in the Seven Days' battles, Union Army commanders were also hard pressed to obtain reliable maps. Gen. George B. McClellan, commander of the Army of the Potomac, lamented that "Correct local maps were not to be found, and the country, though known in its general features, we found to be inaccurately described, in essential particulars, in the only maps and geographical memoirs or papers to which access could be had; erroneous courses to streams and roads were frequently given, and no dependence could be placed on the information thus derived. This difficulty has been found to exist with respect to most portions of the State of Virginia, through which my military operations have extended. Reconnoisances [sic], frequently under fire, proved the only trustworthy sources of information." [16]

On assuming command of the Army of Northern Virginia from the wounded Joseph E. Johnston on June 1, 1862, Gen. Robert E. Lee, a former army engineer himself, took prompt action to improve the Confederate mapping situation. Five days after his appointment, Lee assigned Captain (later Major) Albert H. Campbell to head the Topographical Department. Within a few days, two or three field parties were organized and dispatched into the countryside around Richmond to collect the data for an accurate map of the environs of the Confederate capital. "The field work was mapped as fast as practicable," Campbell wrote, "but as the army soon changed its location, more immediate attention was given to other localities. Therefore, this map in question was dated 1862–3: it was not available as complete until the spring of 1863." [17]

As quickly as possible, other survey parties were formed and sent into Virginia counties in which fighting was likely to occur. Based on the new information, Confederate engineers under the direction of Campbell and Maj. Gen. Jeremy F. Gilmer, Chief of Engineers, prepared detailed maps of most counties in eastern and central Virginia. The maps were drawn in ink on tracing linen and filed in the Topographical Department in Richmond.

Prepared most often on a scale of 1:80,000, with a few at 1:40,000, each county map generally indicated boundaries, villages, roads, railroads, relief (by hachures), mountain passes, woodland, drainage, fords, ferries, bridges, mills, houses, and names of residents. These maps today are sometimes referred to as the Gilmer-Campbell maps or the "Lost War Maps of the Confederates," the latter term being applied because their whereabouts was unknown until many years after the war. This was also the title of Albert Campbell's revealing article published in the January 1888 issue of *Century Magazine*.[18]

Lt. C. S. Dwight's "Map of Albemarle County from Surveys and Reconnaissances" is typical of the maps made by Confederate engineers in Virginia. This well-executed map, drawn in ink on a sheet of tracing linen measuring 80 by 68 cm. was approved by Albert H. Campbell on June 15, 1864 (entry no. 520a.8).

Introduction of Photography

Initially, when requests were received in the Topographical Department for maps of a particular area, a draftsman was assigned to make a tracing of the file copy. But, "So great was the demand for maps occasioned by frequent changes in the situation of the armies," Campbell noted, "that it became impossible by the usual method of tracings to supply them. I conceived the plan of doing this work by photography, though expert photographers pronounced it impracticable, in fact impossible. . . . Traced copies were prepared on common tracing-paper in very black India ink, and from these sharp negatives by sun-printing were obtained, and from these negatives copies were multiplied by exposure to the sun in frames made for the purpose. The several sections, properly toned, were pasted together in their order, and formed the general map, or such portions of it as were desired; it being the policy, as a matter of prudence against capture to furnish no one but the commanding general and corps commanders with the entire map of a given region." [19] Jedediah Hotchkiss, Topographic Engineer with the Second Corps, Army of Northern Virginia, received from the Confederate Topographical Engineers Office the following formula and instructions for photocopying maps:

Formula of Sanxay used in copying maps in Topl.
  Eng. Office, C.S.A. (from Sanxay)
Formula for Capt. Hotchkiss
Silver Bath
Nit. Silver 60 gr to 1 oz water
Con Amonia 1 drop to the oz of water
  float the paper on the Silver Solution then dry,
    after printing

Wash the print about 15 minutes in fair water,
  then immerse in Toning Bath
Bi Carb Soda Saturate Solution
Cloride Gold 15 gr to 1 oz water
nutralize [sic] gold solution with soda solution
  (try with litmus paper)
Wash prints in fair water 15 minuets [sic] and then
  immerse in Fixing Solution
Hypo Soda 1 lb to 1 gal water about 15 minuets [sic]
Wash in running water about 12 hours, dry and the
  prints are finished.

Take the map to be copied and lay it on a glass in printing frame the back of map to the glass. Place the sencitised [sic] paper face to face on the map. Put the back in the frame and wedge it up tight. Expose it to the sun and make a *dark* print (that is very intense). Tone & fix, that will be the negative. Print in the same way from the negative to make the positive.[20]

By 1864, therefore, the Confederate Topographical Department was capable of supplying field officers with photo-reproductions and thereby able to avoid making time-consuming tracings or costly lithographic prints. The resulting photocopies, although crude by today's standards, were quite legible and were frequently cut and mounted in sections on cloth to fold to a convenient size to fit an officer's pocket or saddle bag. Because of the lack of printing presses and paper, maps remained in relatively short supply. The manuscript and photoreproduced copies that were available, however, were the equal in quality to the more numerous maps by Federal authorities. Campbell's "Map of the Vicinity of Richmond and Part of the Peninula" is typical of the maps prepared by the Confederate engineers for the use of the field commanders. Prepared in 1864, the map was photographed, hand colored, sectioned, and mounted on cotton muslin to fold to 16 by 13 cm. (entry no. 624–626).

All the maps used by the Federal and Confederate forces of course were not compiled and produced at headquarters in Washington or Richmond. On both sides, armies, corps, and divisons in the field had topographical engineers assigned to their staffs whose role was to gather information for the preparation of maps. Many significant reconnaissance maps were compiled in the field, detailed battlefield maps were prepared, and base maps supplied by headquarters were vastly improved as new information was collected.

FIELD MAPPING

Although all successful field commanders realized the necessity of clearly understanding the lay of the land over which they were moving or fighting, some placed a higher value on mapping activities than others. Two eminent com-

manders that fall in this category are Generals William T. Sherman and Thomas J. "Stonewall" Jackson.

General William Tecumseh Sherman

On March 18, 1864, Sherman became Commanding General of the Military Division of the Mississippi, succeeding Ulysses S. Grant, who became General in Chief of the Armies of the United States. Grant immediately ordered Sherman "to move against Johnston's army, to break it up, and to get into the interior of the enemy's country as far as you can, inflicting all the damage you can against their war resources."[21] Sherman, with more than one hundred thousand men under his command from the Armies of the Cumberland, Tennessee, and the Ohio, immediately began preparations for what became known as the Atlanta Campaign.

The Topographical Department of the Army of the Cumberland, under the direction of Col. William E. Merrill, was chiefly responsible for providing the maps necessary for the Atlanta Campaign. Thomas B. Van Horne in his *History of the Army of the Cumberland* (1875) notes that "The army was so far from Washington that it had to have a complete map establishment of its own. Accordingly, the office of the chief topographical engineer contained a printing press, two lithographic presses, one photographic establishment, arrangements for map-mounting, and a full corps of draughtsmen and assistants."[22]

The lithographic presses were invaluable for quickly providing multiple copies of a map. However, the weight of the presses and stones made transporting them difficult, necessitating that they remain in a central depot near the front lines. As Van Horne points out, the topographic engineers in the field had available to them a mobile "fac-simile photoprinting device invented by Captain Margedant, chief assistant. This consisted of a light box containing several india-rubber baths, fitting into one another, and the proper supply of chemicals. Printing was done by tracing the required map on thin paper and laying it over a sheet coated with nitrate of silver. The sun's rays passing through the tissue paper blackened the prepared paper except under the ink lines, thus making a white map on black ground. By this means copies from the drawing-paper map could be made as often as new information came in, and occasionally there would be several editions of a map during the same day. The process, however, was expensive, and did not permit the printing of a large number of copies; therefore these maps were only issued to the chief commanders."[23] The map of the environs of Resaca, Georgia, is an example of a quickly made field map produced by the Margedant photoreproduction process. Printed on May 13, 1864, it shows the critical position of the Army of the Tennessee at Snake Creek Gap, Georgia (entry no. S102).

In preparation for the coming campaign, the Topographical Department began the compilation of an accurate campaign map of northern Georgia. The best available map was enlarged to the scale of an inch to the mile.[24] According to Van Horne, this was then "elaborated by cross-questioning refugees, spies, prisoners, peddlers, and any and all persons familiar with the country in front of us. It was remarkable how vastly our maps were improved by this process. The best illustration of the value of this method is the fact that Snake Creek Gap, through which our whole army turned the strong positions at Dalton and Buzzard Roost Gap, was not to be found on any printed map that we could get, and the knowledge of the existence of this gap was of immense importance to us."[25]

Two days before the Atlanta Campaign began, the Topographical Department was informed of the date of advance. As Van Horne notes, the single copy of the map of northern Georgia over which the Topographical Department had been laboring "was immediately cut up into sixteen sections and divided among the draughtsmen, who were ordered to work night and day until all the sections had been traced on thin paper in autographic ink. As soon as four adjacent sections were finished they were transferred to one large stone, and two hundred copies were printed. When all the map had thus been lithographed the map-mounters commenced their work. Being independent of sunlight the work was soon done—the map-mounting requiring the greatest time; but before the commanding generals left Chattanooga, each had received a bound copy of the map, and before we struck the enemy, every brigade, division, and corps commander in the three armies had a copy."[26] Entitled "Map of Northern Georgia made under the direction of Capt. W. E. Merrill, Chief Topl. Engr.," the finished map measures 94 by 88 cm. It is lightly hand colored and indicates below the title and scale that it was "Lith. and printed at Topl. Engr. Office, Dept. Cumbd., Chattanooga, Tenn. May 2d, 1864." For ease of carrying in the field, the map was cut into 24 sections and mounted on cloth to fold to 16 by 23 cm. Pasted to the cloth mounting were cardboard covers to protect the map when folded (entry no. S29–S30).

In addition to the standard edition of the campaign map lithographed on paper, it was also printed directly on muslin and issued in three parts. Van Horne points out that this was mainly for the convenience of the cavalry, "as such maps could be washed clean whenever soiled and could not be injured by hard service."[27] Each section of the cloth map is entitled "Part of Northern Georgia" and was printed from one of the lithographic stones used for the standard campaign map. The superb work of the Topographic Department, Army of the Cumberland, led Van Horne to conclude "that the army that General Sherman led to Atlanta was the best supplied with maps of any that fought in the Civil War"[28] (entry nos. 129.75, S22, and S31).

Preserved in the Geography and Map Division, Library of Congress, is a collection of 210 maps and three atlases belonging to Gen. William T. Sherman. This important cartographic collection, brought together from three separate acquisitions by the Library, includes both printed and manuscript maps, as well as contemporary photocopies. Many of the items were used by the general and his staff during the march on Atlanta in 1864. Represented are small-scale regional maps, maps indicating troop positions and fortifications, and reconnaissance maps. The latter were issued to topographical engineers on field assignment who were then required to plot new data and directed to return the reconnaissance maps to headquarters as soon as possible. Annotations were usually made in red to show additional roads, railroads, fortifications, and dwellings. One such reconnaissance map made as the army moved toward Atlanta is entitled "Part of De Kalb and Fulton County, Ga." (entry no. S77). The base map was compiled and printed in Marietta, Georgia, on July 5, 1864, by the Topographical Engineer's Office, Department of the Cumberland. Instructions on the map direct topographical engineers "to return as soon as possible one copy of this land map with all the information they are able to obtain, to this office. Corps Engineers will cause a speedy compilation." The copy of the map in Sherman's possession has annotations apparently made by Lt. Harry C. Wharton, an engineer in the Army of the Cumberland.

Also issued to field parties during the campaign was a similar printed base map covering the area south of Atlanta. The lithographed copy preserved as number 24 in the Sherman Map Collection has been revised by the use of an overlay covering the East Point-Rough and Ready area. The overlay has a significant number of revisions of the original base map, including the realignment of lines of communication and the repositioning of the towns of East Point and Rough and Ready. In addition, numerous names of residents and some relief have been added. By the use of this simple expediency, the Topographical Engineer's Office was able to get the revised data to the field parties without having to redraft and print the entire map.

Gen. Thomas J. Jackson

After distinguishing himself in June 1861 at the first battle of Manassas where he earned the nickname "Stonewall," Thomas J. Jackson was promoted to major general and assumed command of the Confederate forces protecting the Shenandoah Valley. The valley was of immense strategic importance to the Confederate cause because it provided needed agricultural products for the South and a natural transportation route for invading the North. Jackson's defense of the valley provides an excellent example of the significance of skilled field mapping.

At the beginning of March 1862, a schoolmaster from Staunton, Virginia, named Jedediah Hotchkiss joined Jackson's staff as topographical engineer. Realizing his need for a better understanding of his surroundings, Jackson ordered Hotchkiss to "make me a map of the Valley, from Harper's Ferry to Lexington, showing all the points of offence and defence in those places."²⁹ The resulting comprehensive map, drawn on tracing linen at the scale of 1:80,000 and measuring 254 by 111 cm., was of significant value to Jackson and his staff in planning and executing the Valley Campaign in May and June 1862 (entry no. H89). Conducted against numerically superior forces, the Valley Campaign is considered "one of the most brilliant operations of military history."³⁰ The success of his actions and movements so disturbed Federal planning that large numbers of troops were withheld from General McClellan's advance on Richmond. Conceivably, without the aid of superior maps, Jackson's diversionary efforts would not have succeeded and McClellan's movement on Richmond would have had a different ending.

The map of the Shenandoah Valley constructed for Jackson is preserved with the rest of Jedediah Hotchkiss's map collection in the Library's Geography and Map Division.³¹ This is one of the finest collections of Confederate maps in existence today. In addition to the master map, there are countless sketches, reconnaisance maps, county maps, regional maps, and battle maps. Of particular interest is his sketchbook with over one hundred pages of drawings recording roads and distances, topographic features, and the location of dwellings and names of occupants (entry no. H1). Much of the information recorded in the sketchbook was later transferred to his finished maps. Hotchkiss annotated the cover of the sketchbook as follows:

This volume is my field sketch book that I used during the Civil War. Most of the sketches were made on horseback just as they now appear. The colored pencils used were kept in the places fixed on the outside of the other cover.

These topographical sketches were often used in conferences with Generals Jackson, Ewell and Early.

The cover of this book is a blank Federal commission found in Gen. Milroy's quarters at Winchester.

[signed] Jed Hotchkiss.

OFFICIAL BATTLEFIELD MAPS

When time permitted, topographical engineers in both armies were called upon to prepare accurate, detailed maps of the fields of battle. Cultural and topographic features were carefully shown and the position of troops and batteries was depicted in detail. Many of these maps were used to illustrate official reports of the field commanders or were sent back to headquarters in Washington and Richmond for

placement in the official files. Excellent examples of maps made to accompany an official account are those prepared by Hotchkiss to illustrate the "Report of the Camps, Marches & Engagements, of the Second Corps, A.N.V., Army of the Valley Dist. and of the Department of Northern Va., during the Campaign of 1864." Both the handwritten narrative and the accompanying manuscript atlas containing 59 campaign and battle maps are preserved in the Hotchkiss Map Collection. The maps were carefully executed in pen and ink and watercolors by Hotchkiss and his assistant Sampson B. Robinson between November 1864 and March 1865 (entry no. H8).

Federal mapping authorities, aware of the need for good public relations, made an occasional attempt to inform the populace on the progress of the war. In May 1862, for example, the U.S. Coast Survey issued the first of at least four editions of a "Historical Sketch of the Rebellion," which depicted the "limits of loyal states in July, 1861," the "limits occupied by United States forces March 1st 1862," and the "limits occupied by United States forces May 15th 1862" (entry no. 34). For the most part, however, the responsibility for keeping the public informed as the war unfolded rested with the private sector and not the government.

COMMERCIAL MAPPING

Throughout the American Civil War, commercial publishers in the North and to a lesser extent in the South produced countless maps for an eagerly awaiting public in need of up-to-date geographical information. Few families were without someone in the armed forces serving in a little-known place in the American South. Maps, therefore, were not only important sources of information, but also satisfied the patriotic impulses of the populace. Publishers in New York, Philadelphia, Washington, and Boston quickly became aware of this profitable market and began to issue maps in quantities undreamed of before the war.

Northern Publishers

One of the earliest maps, copyrighted by M. H. Traubel of Philadelphia less than a month after the bombardment of Fort Sumter on April 12, 1861, is entitled "Pocket Map of the Probable Theatre of the War." The compiler of the map, civil engineer G. A. Aschbach, accurately anticipated that the principal seat of war in the East would be Virginia, Maryland, and Pennsylvania. To assist the map user, Aschbach underlined camps and forts in red and prominent places in blue (entry no. 1).

Many of the early maps were little more than general maps depicting railroads, rivers, state boundaries, cities and

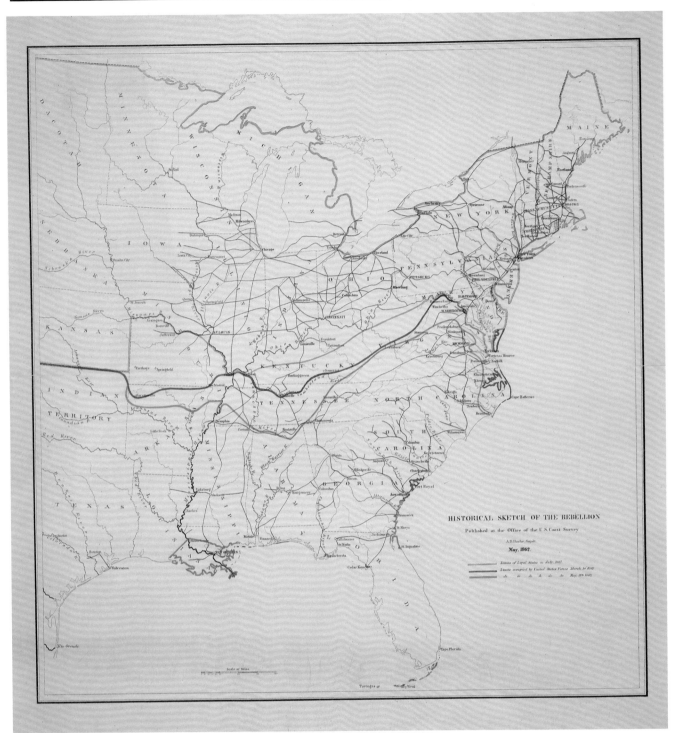

The U.S. Coast Survey published this map, entitled "Historical Sketch of the Rebellion," at least four times during the war. In this edition dated May 1862, it shows by colored lines the "limits of loyal states in July, 1861," the "limits occupied by United States forces March 1st 1862," and the "limits occupied by United States forces May 15, 1862." Maps such as this were valuable in informing the general public about the progress of the war. (See entry no. 34.)

towns, and perhaps a few well-known forts. "Lloyd's Map of the Southern States" for example, produced and sold by James T. Lloyd, publisher of *Lloyd's American Railroad Weekly,* was very popular and was issued in each of the first three years of the war. Although Lloyd included little specific information about the war on his map, he issued it after July 12, 1861, with an extensive "gazetteer of the Southern States" printed on the verso.[32]

Lloyd's maps are especially interesting today for the informative advertisements and testimonials that the publisher unabashedly included on them. One advertisement, for example, called attention to Lloyd's "$100,000 Topographical Map of the State of Virginia," priced at 25 cents a copy, and about which the publisher noted, "we intend to sell 3,000,000 copies of this great map" (entry no. 14.25).

Although it is doubtful that Lloyd sold so many copies, his map of Virginia was indeed popular with the public with editions appearing in 1861, 1862, and 1863. Lloyd based his first edition on the Wood-Böye nine-sheet map of Virginia initially published in 1826 (mistakenly cited by Lloyd as 1828) and revised in 1859 by Ludwig von Buchholtz. To enhance his map over his competitors, Lloyd called his the "official map" and included a note on the 1861 edition that "This is the only map used to plan campaigns in Virginia by Gen. Scott." (entry no. 450).

The 1862 edition announced that it had been "corrected from surveys made by Capt. W. Angelo Powell, of the U.S. Topographical Engineers." Since the aged Gen. Winfield Scott had been forced into retirement by then, Lloyd now noted that "This is the only map used to plan campaigns in Virginia by Gen. McClellan." (entry no. 465.1).

During the war, James Lloyd carried on an acrimonious dispute with another New York publisher, H. H. Lloyd and Company. On his map of the Mississippi River issued in 1863, James Lloyd cautioned the public "against another 'Lloyd' by which name he hopes to deceive the public with spurious 'Lloyd Maps.' This man's maps are engraved coarsely on wood and very erroneous. He follows us with an imitation of every map we issue." H. H. Lloyd's map of the Mississippi River, engraved on wood by Waters and Company (entry no. 37.2), is indeed inferior in appearance and content to James Lloyd's very detailed, nicely lithographed map (entry no. 41). It is difficult to determine, however, whether or not the former purposely traded on the name of the latter.

While it is true that H. H. Lloyd's maps are somewhat coarse, they are good examples of wood-engraved maps, and they are generally clear and easy to read. The 1865 edition of his "New Military Map of the Border & Southern States," for example, emphasizes battlefields by red underlining, and strategic places by red dots. Furthermore, it effectively delineates in red the "territory held by Rebels April 1st, 1865," in yellow, the "territory gained from Rebels since January

1st, 1862," and in blue, "Sherman's march from Chattanooga" (entry no. 71).

To enhance sales, some publishers went to great lengths to make their maps as distinctive from those of their competitors as possible. For instance, Prang and Company of Boston conceived the idea of publishing a "War Telegram Marking Map" on which one could follow the events of the war. This popular map, issued in at least six editions, was published on a large scale to permit the marking of "change of position of the Union forces in red pencil and the rebel forces in blue on the receipt of every telegram from the seat of war." The map was accompanied by colored pencils which the publisher noted "should be used with a light hand to enable obliterating the marks with the aid of a little soft bread, if found necessary. These peculiarities combined with extreme cheapness will make this map a welcome companion to every person interested in the pending struggle of our nation." (entry no. 465.75).

Prang's map, primarily designed for the use of the citizen back home, included an advertisement for "Agents wanted to sell this map in all parts of the country." Some Northern publishers also aimed their maps at the lucrative market comprising the officers and enlisted men serving in the Union armed forces. Boston publisher John H. Bufford's map of Georgia and South Carolina, entitled "Genl. Sherman's Campaign War Map," and his map of the environs of Richmond, Virginia, entitled "Genl. Grant's Campaign War Map," both carried notes that "Agents wanted in all the camps and throughout the loyal states to sell this map, pictures & photographs of every description." (entry nos. 124 and 623). Bufford's maps are particularly interesting because of their use of a letter-number grid reference system, described by the publisher as follows:

> The horizontal and upright lines [of the map grid] represent five miles square. By referring to the number on the left and to the letter on the base, any point may be found to show the locality of the Union armies. By this method those in the army are enabled to inform their friends of the movements of their companies and their location and will also serve as a journal to each soldier.

As another means of maximizing sales, publishers sometimes combined various kinds of illustrative data. In 1861, for example, H. H. Lloyd published a brightly colored wood engraving featuring "Military Portraits, Map of the Seat of War, Uniforms, Arms, &c." Here the map of the "Western Border Lands" occupied only a third of the printed sheet and definitely was of secondary importance to the portraits of the war heroes (entry no. 12.7).

Other publishers depended on bold titles emblazoned across the sheet to catch the citizen's attention and hopefully to sell the map. The title to the W. H. Forbes and Company's unimaginative map of Central Virginia certainly "sells" the

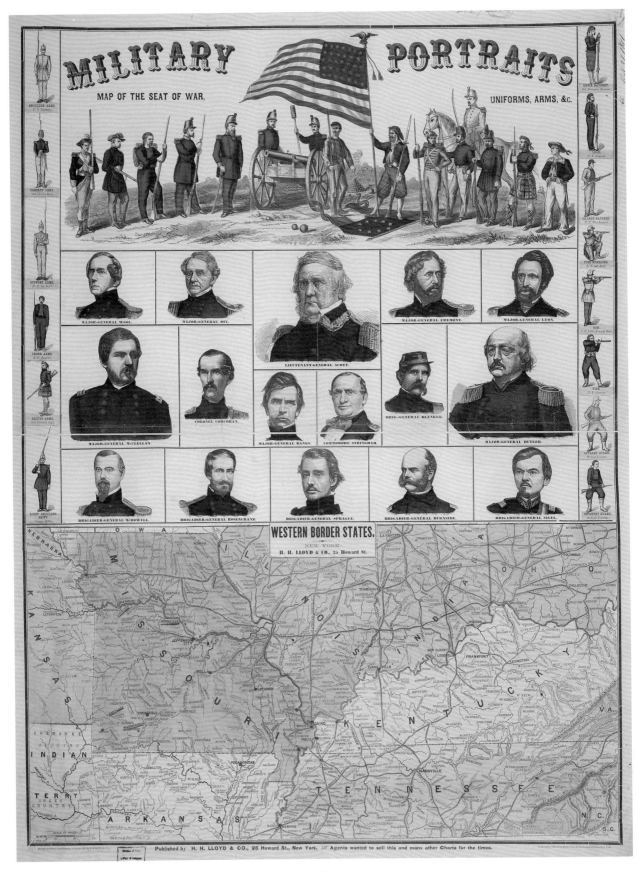

map. It reads in part: "Theatre of the War: A Complete Map of the Battle Ground of Hooker's Army!!" (entry no. 479.5).

The New York and Washington publisher Charles Magnus sold his popular map of "One Hundred & Fifty Miles Around Richmond" separately and as part of a "Half Dollar Portfolio." Included with the map in this "Glorious Union Packet," as the publisher called it, was a "Mirror of Events [i.e., list of battles], 2 illustrated Notesheets, 1 Song Notesheet, 3 illustrated Envelopes, 6 Portraits of Army and Navy Officers, 4 plain Notesheets, 4 plain Envelopes, Penholder, [and] Pen and Lead-pencil" (entry no. 632.4).

Southern Publishers

Compared to those in the North, publishers in the South produced few maps for the general public, and those that did appear were issued in small numbers. Printing presses and paper, as well as lithographers and wood engravers, were in short supply. The few maps published for sale to the public were invariably simple in construction, relatively small in size, and usually devoid of color. The Confederate imprint, "Map of the Seat of War in Virginia," is representative. Lithographed and published by Blanton Duncan in Columbia, South Carolina, it is dated December 1, 1862, and measures only 37 by 24 cm. (entry no. 457).

British Publishers

The broad interest among the British in the American Civil War is evidenced by the number of maps produced by some of the major contemporary map publishers of Great Britain—James Wyld, George Philip, Edward Stanford, Bacon and Company in London, and John Bartholomew in Edinburgh. The leading English publisher and seller of maps of the American Civil War was Bacon and Company. By 1862, this firm had published a series of six maps that were known collectively as the "Shilling War Maps." In an advertisement, the firm described the maps as being a "complete series, just published, compiled from authentic sources, and corrected to the present time—showing the railways, forts, and fortifications, population, area, &c, and designating in three colors the boundaries of the Federal, Confederate, and Border Slave States."[33] An example of one of the shilling war maps is "Bacon's Military Map of the United States Shewing the Forts & Fortifications" (entry no. 24). Published in August 1862, it delineates by color the "Free or Non-Slaveholding States," the "Border Slave

States," and the "Seceded or Confederate States." In addition to publishing maps, Bacon also served as agent in Britain for "Colton's Maps of America, and Complete Series of War Maps." Joseph H. Colton was described by the firm as being for "30 years the largest American Map Publisher."[34]

Propaganda Maps

Although propaganda maps are better known from their use during World Wars I and II, an occasional map of this type was published during the Civil War. Such works are designed to have a maximum psychological impact on the user of the map. The commercial publisher J. B. Elliott of Cincinnati published a cartoon map in 1861 entitled "Scott's Great Snake" which pictorially illustrates Gen. Winfield Scott's plan to crush the South both economically and militarily. His plan called for a strong blockade of the Southern ports and a major offensive down the Mississippi River to divide the South. The press ridiculed this as the "Anaconda Plan," as shown on this map, but this general scheme contributed greatly to the Northern victory (entry no. 11).

Another propaganda map more subtle in appearance, but perhaps just as effective, was Edmund and George Blunt's "Sketch of the Atlantic and Gulf Coasts of the United States." The Blunts depicted the "loyal part" of the coast with a heavy (strong) line and the "rebel part" with a thin (weak) line. "This sketch was prepared to show at a glance," explains George Blunt, "the difference in extent of the coasts of the U. States occupied by the loyal men and rebels; its circulation it is believed will have the effect of counteracting the exertions of traitors at home as well as those abroad. Persons having correspondents in Europe would do well to send copies of this sketch to them for circulation" (entry no. 25).

Battlefield Maps

Countless large-scale maps of battlefields, sieges, and fortifications were produced by commercial firms. Maps of those places and events in the news, particularly those perceived to be victories, guaranteed the publisher a quick profit from a grateful public. To give authenticity to their products, publishers based their maps on "reliable" eyewitness accounts, including those of active participants. For example, the "Map of the Battlefield of Antietam," lithographed by the Philadelphia firm of Duval and Sons, was prepared by Lt. William H. Willcox, Topographical Officer and Additional Aide-de-camp on the staff of Brig. Gen. Abner Doubleday, commander of a Union Division at the Battle of Antietam (although better known today as the inventor of baseball). It is interesting to note that this particular copy is inscribed in longhand, "Obtained from Washing-

---

H. H. Lloyd and Company of New York City attractively combined a map of the "Western Border States" with portraits of leading Union generals, uniforms, and arms. The overall effect of the hand-colored sheet is striking and probably sold well to the public. (See entry no. 12.7.)

1ˢ BACON'S MILITARY MAP

Bacon and Company of London, England, published a series of six maps that were known collectively as the "Shilling War Maps." One map in this series is "Bacon's Military Map of the United States Shewing the Forts & Fortifications" published in 1862. Colors are used to differentiate between "Free or Non-Slaveholding States," "Border Slave States," and "Seceded or Confederate States." (See entry no. 24.)

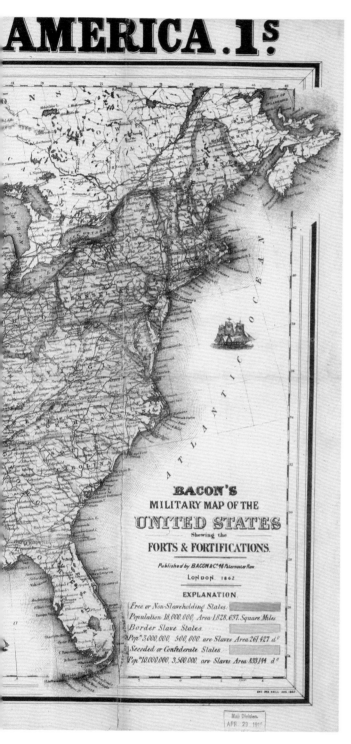

son and the surrounding batteries" (entry no. 240). Theodore Ditterline went further, supplementing his unusually shaped oval map of the "Field of Gettysburg" with a 24-page pamphlet describing the battle in detail (entry no. 331).

Panoramic Maps

Perhaps the finest and most attractive battle map produced during the war was John B. Bachelder's "Gettysburg Battle-Field" (entry nos. 321–324). Bachelder, an experienced prewar maker of city views, copyrighted his stunning perspective drawing of the field of battle in 1863. In the opening sentence to the accompanying key, Bachelder invited the viewer of his panorama to "Imagine yourself in a balloon, two miles east of the town of Gettysburg, Pa." Not only was the map an artistic success, its accuracy was attested to by no less an authority than the commanding general of the Army of the Potomac at Gettysburg, George G. Meade. Reproduced in facsimile below the map, Meade's handwritten endorsement reads, "I am perfectly satisfied with the accuracy with which the topography is delineated and the position of the troops laid down." The signatures of other field commanders attesting to the "accuracy of our respective commands" are also reproduced in the bottom margin.

Bachelder subsequently became one of the directors of the Gettysburg Battlefield Memorial Association and Superintendent of Legends and Tablets. He was responsible for the compilation and publication in 1876 of a very detailed three-sheet map of the battlefield which still is widely used today (entry no. 325). For his base map, Bachelder used the survey conducted in 1868 and 1869 under the direction of Gen. Gouverneur K. Warren, U.S. Army Corps of Engineers and revised in 1873 by P. M. Blake (entry no. 353.5).

The panoramic map in fact became a popular and effective technique for conveying information about the Civil War. Early in 1861, the skillful artist and lithographer John Bachmann of New York City conceived the idea of producing a series of bird's-eye views of the likely theaters of war. These visually attractive panoramas were easily understood and perhaps more meaningful to a public largely unskilled in map reading. Between 1861 and 1862, Bachmann drew and lithographed at least eight panoramas of the seats of war in Virginia and Maryland, Richmond, North and South Carolina, Florida and part of Georgia, the confluence of the Ohio and Mississippi Rivers, Kentucky and Tennessee, the Gulf Coast in the vicinity of the Mississippi delta, and Texas and part of Mexico (entry nos. 1.5–3, 23.5, 117.2, 304.5–304.6, 446.8, and 621).

The panoramic map or bird's-eye view also lent itself to colorful depictions of fortifications, hospitals, prisons, and military camps. Excellent representative examples of these are the Baltimore artist and lithographer Edward Sachse's

ton & presented to Gen. R. E. Lee by J. E. B. Stuart" (entry no. 253).

To further expand on the information depicted cartographically, some compilers and publishers added descriptive text to their battle maps. Boston publisher George W. Tomlinson, for example, printed beside his "New Map of Port Hudson" (1863), a one-column "Sketch of Port Hud-

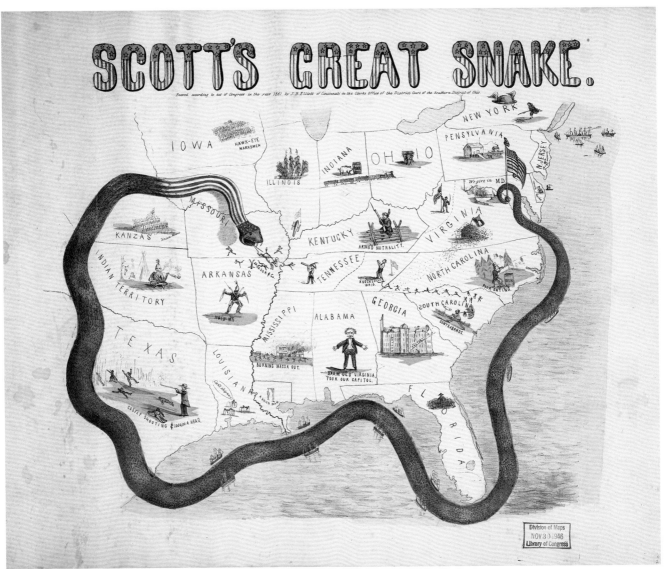

bird's-eye view of Fortress Monroe, Virginia, published and sold in 1861 by Casimir Bohn of Washington, D.C., and Charles Magnus of New York City (entry nos. 547 and 547.1); "Point Lookout, Md. View of Hammond Genl. Hospital & U.S. Genl. Depot for Prisoners of War," also lithographed by Edward Sachse & Company, and copyrighted in 1864 by George Everett (entry no. 257); and Albert Ruger's "Bird's eye view of Camp Chase, near Columbus, Ohio" (entry no. 318).

The commercial success of bird's-eye views contributed to the widespread adaptation of the technique after the war for the depiction of American and Canadian cities and towns.[35] Albert Ruger, mentioned above, was the first successful postwar artist to produce urban panoramas.[36] His earliest extant drawings were made during the war and are of military camps (entry nos. 318, 319.5 and 660).

This cartoon map published by J. B. Elliot, Cincinnati, Ohio, in 1861, illustrates Gen. Winfield Scott's plan to blockade Southern ports and to mount a major offensive down the Mississippi. As demonstrated in this map, the press ridiculed Scott's proposal as the "Anaconda Plan." (See entry no. 11.)

Popular items for sale to the public were maps of battles, particularly those perceived to be victories. Especially popular were those based on eye witness accounts such as Lt. William H. Willcox's "Map of the Battlefield of Antietam." This particular copy was "obtained from Washington & presented to Gen. R. E. Lee by J. E. B. Stuart." The Library of Congress acquired it in 1948 with the purchase of the papers and maps of Confederate topographic engineer Jedediah Hotchkiss. (See entry no. 253.)

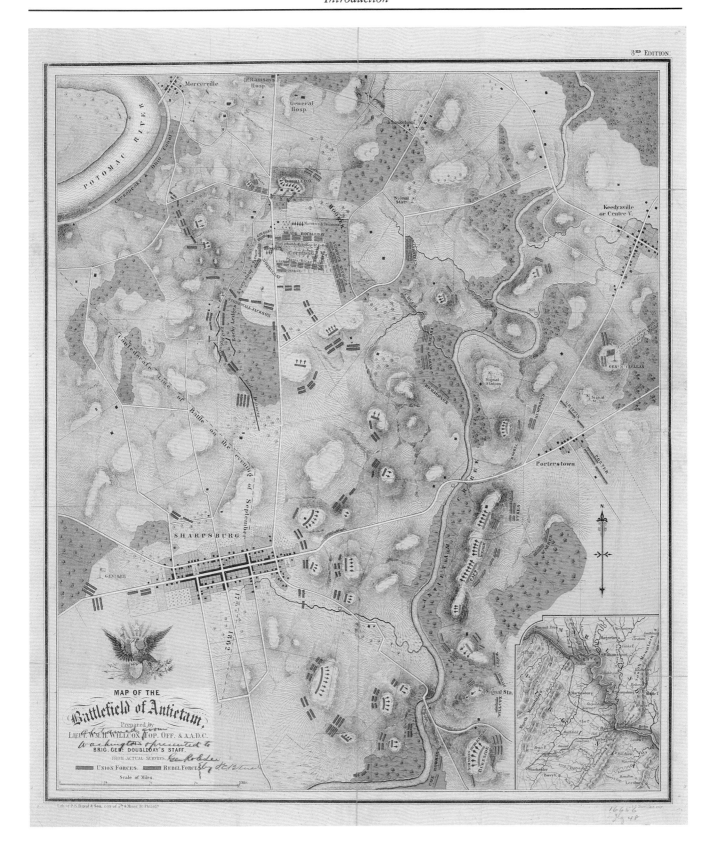

City Plans

Commercial publishers also issued an occasional city plan, usually to depict seige or defensive positions. A fine example is civil engineer E. G. Arnold's well-executed map of Washington, D.C., showing the ring of fortifications built to defend the nation's capital from Confederate attack. Because of the sensitive information that Arnold's map contained, the Federal government suppressed its sale shortly after it was published (entry nos. 674–674.1).

Maps in Newspapers and Journals

Another readily available, yet inexpensive source for maps were the major newspapers and pictorial journals of the day. Maps had occasionally appeared in journals or newspapers since the seventeenth century, but in North America it was not until the American Civil War that they were published with any regularity. At that time, all types of illustrations had reached a new level of popularity. One authority has noted that "*Harper's, Leslie's* and their lesser rival, the *New York Illustrated News* . . . employed twenty-seven 'special' or combat artists during the war, and also used the work of more than three hundred identified amateurs as well as of a great many photographers. All together, these three northern weeklies printed nearly six thousand war pictures."[37] Since no inventory or bibliography of maps in newspapers and journals has been compiled, it is not known if any of the combat artists and amateurs also supplied their publishers with sketch maps.

Most newspaper and journal illustrations were printed from woodcuts. This form of reproduction, albeit crude, was inexpensive, reasonably quick to execute, and the woodblocks could be inserted into pages of text and printed on newspaper presses without difficulty. A close-grained hardwood, usually boxwood, cut against the grain, was employed to make the wood engraving. Usually the blocks consisted of several parts tightly bolted together from the rear, a technique invented in England and pioneered in this country by Frank Leslie. After the image was drawn on the block, the parts were separated and distributed among several wood engravers to be worked on simultaneously. Once the carving was completed, place names cast in type metal from a mold (stereotype) were cemented into place, the parts bolted together again, and the whole retouched to insure uniformity. An electrotype metal copy of the woodcut was made and the illustration was ready for printing on the ro-

John B. Bachelder's "Gettysburg Battle-field" was one of the most stunning and popular battle maps produced during the war. In describing this perspective drawing of the field of battle he suggested to the reader to "Imagine yourself in a balloon, two miles east of the town of Gettysburg, Pa." (See entry no. 322.)

MAP OF THE
BATTLE FIELD OF GETTYSBURG.
JULY 1ST 2ND 3RD 1863.
Published by authority of the Hon. the SECRETARY OF WAR.
Office of the CHIEF OF ENGINEERS U.S. Army.
1876.

tary press. The entire process required approximately two weeks to complete from the time the sketch was received by the publisher.

The public was enthralled by pictorial representations of the war, and pictures did much to shape their image and opinion of events and people in the news. Although sometimes lacking the timeliness and artistic merit found in many of the "on the spot" depictions from the battle fronts and military camps, maps nevertheless provided valuable information on the location of places in the news.

Included in the collections of the Library of Congress is a rare example of a woodblock that was used to print a panoramic map published in the March 22, 1862, edition of the *New York Illustrated News.* Entitled "Scene of the late naval fight and the environs of Fortress Monroe, and Norfolk and Suffolk, now threatened by General Burnside," it was printed from a 25 by 36 cm woodblock composed of 12 separate parts bolted together, each part measuring 13 by 6 cm. The woodblock is now imperfect, with the lower right and left corners missing and some of the individual parts beginning to separate due to age (entry no. 558.7).

From the bombardment of Fort Sumter on April 12, 1861, to the end of the war, maps were occasionally used to illustrate major events or situations. On June 17, 1861, for example, the *New York Herald* published a timely map entitled "The Seat of War in Virginia" (entry no. 451.3). This simple woodcut, published a little more than a month before the Union's disastrous defeat at the first Battle of Manassas, depicts strategic cities and towns, transportation routes, fortified positions, and the location and number of Confederate troops at several locations. The map noted, for example, that there were "15,000 troops at Manassas Junction and 15,000 more on the Manassas Gap Railroad" nearby. Executed by Waters and Son, Engravers, New York, it is typical of the maps that appeared throughout the war in newspapers and weekly journals. With minor variations the map was used again on July 27 by the *New York Herald.* This time, however, it served as the lead map in a special supplement of 34 maps entitled "War Maps and Diagrams" (entry no. 14.65).

The *New-York Daily Tribune,* not to be outdone by its rival, published "The Tribune War Maps" as a supplement to its daily paper issued on July 30, 1861 (entry no. 6.2). This section of 17 maps was compiled and engraved on wood by the well-known New York map publisher, George Woolworth Colton. One of the maps in this section that contained

some noteworthy strategic information is entitled "Baltimore and Its Points of Attack and Defence." The accompanying explanation notes that "The above drawing, which has been kindly furnished for *The Tribune* by an officer of the United States Engineers, exhibits very clearly the points in Baltimore which might be held by military forces whether for purposes of attack or of occupation merely."

In the November 9, 1861, issue of *Harper's Weekly* a "Map of the Southern States" was published which depicted, among other things, "the harbors, inlets, forts and position of blockading ships" (entry no. 14.55). An accompanying article entitled "Our War Map" described the map and offered suggestions on its use:

> We break through our usual habits in this number, and devote four pages to the publication of a large WAR MAP of the Southern States. Without intending to disparage any of the maps in existence, we think this will be found more reliable, and more useful to the student of the war, than any other we have seen. . . .
>
> Such of our readers as wish to keep "posted" on the progress of the war will do well to paste or otherwise fasten this map on a large board against a wall. A series of pins, alternately black and white, should be inserted at the various points occupied by the National and the Rebel forces, and shifted as often as authentic accounts of movements are received. Care should be taken, however, not to confound newspaper rumors with authentic intelligence. The adoption of this simple expedient will render the otherwise confused accounts of the war in Missouri and Kentucky perfectly intelligible, and will shed a flood of light on the newspaper narratives of current events.
>
> We may refer, in this connection, with a feeling of pride, to the large series of war maps published in this journal. They constitute already a valuable atlas—such a one as would cost, if purchased separately, more than the whole price of *Harper's Weekly.*[38]

POSTWAR MAPPING

At the conclusion of the Civil War, the U.S. War Department published numerous detailed battlefield maps and atlases to document significant military engagements such as those at Antietam, Manassas, Gettysburg, and Atlanta, to name a few. The premier cartographic work of the postwar years, however, is the U.S. War Department's *Atlas to Accompany the Official Records of the Union and Confederate Armies* (entry no. 99). Initially issued in 37 parts between 1891 and 1895, it includes 178 plates and constitutes the most detailed atlas yet published on the Civil War. The maps present an especially well-balanced cartographic record of the war because both Union and Confederate sources were used in their compilation. Confederate topographic engi-

---

After years of research and study, John B. Bachelder compiled and published in 1876 a three-sheet map of Gettysburg battlefield showing in detail the deployment of troops. For his base map, Bachelder employed the survey of the battlefield conducted under the direction of Brevet Major General Gouverneur K. Warren. Depicted here is the "Second Day's Battle." (See entry no. 325.)

46A

1. Light house,	7. Chapel,	13. Ward E.
2. Dining room & kitchen,	8. Reservoir,	14. E. L. Donnellys Stores,
3. Hospital Headquarters,	9. Circle of wards,	15. Dead house,
4. Baggage house,	10. Ward C.	16. Sisters' quarters,
5. Reading room,	11. „ D.	17. Wharf & Post-Com. buildings,
6. Half Diet kitchen,	12. „ F.	18. Ice house.

POINT LOOKOUT, M

VIEW OF HAMMOND GENL HOSPITAL & U.S. GENL DEPOT FO

34. Line dividing Hospt. fr. Military.	40. Office of Com. of Musters	45. Contraband quarters.
35. Qurs. of Capt. Loras, C. S.	41. Office of Capt. Patterson Provost	46. Star Spangled Masonic Lodge,
36. „ of Mr Tompkins q. m. Clark,	Marshal,	47. Murphy's farm house,
37. Qurs. of Capt. Cook C. S.	42. Brig. Gen. Marstons Headquarters,	48. Hospital 2nd N. H. V.
38. „ of Lt. Sargant Ord. officer,	43. 2nd Wisconsin battery,	49. Qurs. of Dr. Morrow, Sur. 2nd.
39. „ of Capt. Godfrey, Q. M.	44. Cluster of stables,	N. H. V.

50. Qurs. of Col. Bailey 2nd, N. H. V.	54. Qurs. of Union recruits from rebel
51. Camp of 2nd, N. H. V.	prisoners.
52. „ of 12th, N. H. V.	55. Guard house,
53. Qurs. of Major Langley, Com'g,	56. Rebel Camp,
12th, N. H. V.	57. Camp 5th, N. H. V.
	58. Qurs. of Col. Cross, 5th, N. H. V.

neer Jedediah Hotchkiss, for example, supplied the editors with 123 maps for this atlas. Although the original edition of the *Atlas to Accompany the Official Records* is no longer available for sale from the U.S. Government Printing Office, complete facsimile editions were published in 1958 by Thomas Yoseloff of New York City and in 1978 by Arno Press and Crown Publishers, Inc., New York. The Yoseloff edition was published under the title *The Official Atlas of the Civil War* and includes an introduction by the noted historian Henry Steel Commager (entry no. 101). The Arno Press/Crown Publishers edition is entitled *The Official Military Atlas of the Civil War,* with an introduction by archivist-historian Richard Sommers (entry no. 101.2).

Clearly, the war created an urgent need for maps that cartographers on both sides worked tirelessly for four years to satisfy. Field survey methods were improved; the gathering of intelligence became more sophisticated; faster, more adaptable printing techniques were developed; and photoreproduction processes became an important means of duplicating maps. The result was that thousands of manuscript, printed, and photoreproduced maps of unprecedented quality were prepared of areas where fighting erupted or was likely to occur. Rarely could an officer have cause to be ignorant of his surroundings, as if he "had been suddenly transferred to the banks of the Lualaba." [39] After peace came in the spring of 1865, another fourteen years were to pass before Congress established the beginnings of a national topographic mapping program with the creation of the U.S. Geological Survey. It was many years, therefore, before modern topographic maps became available to replace those created by war's necessity. The maps of the Civil War are splendid testimony to the skill and resourcefulness of Union and Confederate mapmakers and commercial publishers in fulfilling their responsibilities.

References

1. For a list of county maps in the Library of Congress, see Richard W. Stephenson, *Land Ownership Maps* (Washington: Library of Congress, 1967), 86 pp.

2. Robert Pearsall Smith, "Communication . . . Respecting the Published County Maps of the United States," American Philosophical Society, *Proceedings* 9 (March 1864): 350.

3. William W. Blackford, *War Years with Jeb Stuart* (New York: Charles Scribner's Sons, 1945), p. 165.

4. The Corps of Topographical Engineers was incorporated into the Corps of Engineers on March 3, 1863.

The panoramic map or bird's-eye view became a popular and effective technique for conveying information about the Civil War. In this view lithographed by Edward Sachse of Baltimore and published in 1864 by George Everett of Point Lookout, Maryland, we see Hammond General Hospital and the prisoner of war camp at Point Lookout. (See entry no. 257.)

23

5. U.S. Army, Corps of Engineers, *Report on the Defenses of Washington to the Chief of Engineers, U.S. Army, by Bvt. Maj. Gen. J. G. Barnard* (Washington: Government Printing Office, 1871), p. 33.

6. U.S. Coast Survey, *Report of the Superintendent of the Coast Survey, showing the Progress of the Survey during the Year 1861* (Washington: Government Printing Office, 1862), p. 39.

7. Ibid., p. 40.

8. Thaddeus Lowe Papers, American Institute of Aeronautics and Astronautics, Aeronautic Archives, container 82, "Sketches and Drawings" folder, Manuscript Division, Library of Congress.

9. U.S. Coast Survey, *Report of the Superintendent of the Coast Survey, Showing the Progress of the Survey During the Year 1862* (Washington: Government Printing Office, 1864), p. 15.

10. U.S. Coast Survey, *Report of the Superintendent of the Coast Survey, Showing the Progress of the Survey During the Year 1864* (Washington: Government Printing Office, 1866), p. 38.

11. U.S. War Department, *Annual Report of the Secretary of War* [1864] (Washington: Government Printing Office, 1865), p. 31, and U.S. War Department, *Annual Report of the Secretary of War* [1865] (Washington: Government Printing Office, 1866), v. 2, p. 919.

12. U.S. Coast Survey, *Report of the Superintendent of the Coast Survey, Showing the Progress of the Survey During the Year 1863* (Washington: Government Printing Office, 1864), p. 137.

13. U.S. Coast Survey, *Report of the Superintendent . . . , 1864,* p. 111.

14. Ibid.

15. Richard Taylor, *Destruction and Reconstruction: Personal Experiences of the Late War,* Richard B. Harwell, ed. (New York: Longmans, Green & Co., 1955), p. 99.

16. George B. McClellan, *Report on the Organization and Campaigns of the Army of the Potomac* (New York: Sheldon & Co., 1864), p. 157.

17. Albert H. Campbell, "The Lost War Maps of the Confederates," *Century Magazine* 35 (January 1888): 480. A copy of Campbell's map entitled "Map of the Battle-Grounds in the Vicinity of Richmond, Va. . . . 1862 and 3," is reproduced in the U.S. War Department's *Atlas to Accompany the Official Records of the Union and Confederate Armies* (Washington: Government Printing Office, 1891–1895), plate xx–1.

18. The Gilmer-Campbell maps are a valuable record of Virginia's rural landscape during the Civil War. Fortunately, many of the original manuscript maps are extant today. A few are preserved in the Library of Congress, while others are in the Virginia Historical Society and the Museum of the Confederacy at Richmond, the U.S. Military Academy at West Point, and the University of North Carolina Library, Chapel Hill.

19. Campbell, "The Lost War Maps of the Confederates," p. 480.

20. Filed with Hotchkiss's "Report of the Camps, Marches and Engagements, of the Second Corps, A.N.V. and the Army of the Valley Dist., of the Department of Northern Virginia; during the Campaign of 1864 . . ." (Hotchkiss Map Coll. no. 8).

Drawn from Nature Lith & print by E.Sachse & Cº 104 S.Charles St.Baltⁿ

FORTRESS M

Bird's-eye view of Fortress Monroe, Virginia, drawn, lithographed and printed by Edward Sachse, Baltimore, Maryland. Jefferson Davis was imprisoned here from 1865 to 1867. (See entry no. 547.1.)

, OLD POINT COMFORT AND HYGEIA HOTEL, Vᵃ.

Published by Chs Magnus 12 Frankfort St. N.Y.

21. William Tecumseh Sherman, *Memoirs of General William T. Sherman by Himself* (Bloomington: Indiana University Press, 1957), 2 vol. in 1, v. 2, p. 26.

22. Thomas B. Van Horne, *History of the Army of the Cumberland* (Cincinnati: Robert Clarke & Co., 1875), vol. 2, p. 456.

23. Ibid., pp. 456–457.

24. The base map used was James R. Butts's "Map of the State of Georgia" (1859). See R. W. Stephenson, "Mapping the Atlanta Campaign," Special Libraries Association, Geography and Map Division, *Bulletin,* 127 (March 1982): pp. 8–9.

25. Van Horne, *History of the Army of the Cumberland,* p. 457.

26. Ibid., pp. 457–458.

27. Ibid., p. 458.

28. Ibid., p. 358.

29. Jedediah Hotchkiss, *Make Me a Map of the Valley: The Civil War Journal of Stonewall Jackson's Topographer,* ed. by Archie P. McDonald, foreword by T. Harry Williams (Dallas: Southern Methodist University Press [1973], p. 10.

30. Mark Mayo Boatner III, *The Civil War Dictionary* (New York: David McKay Co., Inc., 1959), p. 739.

31. For an article about the acquisition and contents of the collection, see Clara Egli LeGear, "The Hotchkiss Map Collection," *The Library of Congress Quarterly Journal of Current Acquisitions* 6 (November 1948): 16–20.

32. The "Gazetteer of the Southern States" does not appear on the verso of the first issue of Lloyd's map copyrighted on July 12, 1861 (entry no. 14.2). He did include it, however, with issues published later in 1861 (entry no. 14.25 and 14.3) as well as in 1862 (entry no. 29) and 1863 (entry no. 41.2).

33. Advertisement on verso of "Bacon's Military Map of the United States Shewing the Forts & Fortifications" (London: 1862).

34. Ibid.

35. For a list of 1,726 bird's-eye views on file in the Geography and Map Division, Library of Congress, see John R. Hebert and Patrick E. Dempsey, *Panoramic Maps of Cities in the United States and Canada,* 2nd ed. (Washington: Library of Congress, 1984), 181 p. 4,480 views, including those in the Library of Congress, are listed in the union catalog by John W. Reps entitled *Views and Viewmakers of Urban America* (Columbia: University of Missouri Press, 1984), 570 p.

36. For a biographical sketch, see "Albert Ruger (1828–1899)" in Reps, *Views and Viewmakers of Urban America,* pp. 201–204. Ruger's personal collection of city views is in the Geography and Map Division, Library of Congress.

37. Roger Butterfield, "Pictures in the Papers," *American Heritage* 13 (June 1962): 99.

38. "Our War Map," *Harper's Weekly* 5 (November 9, 1861): 706.

39. Taylor, *Destruction and Reconstruction,* p. 99.

United States

1861

0

AP Newsfeatures (Firm).

Background map; The Civil War, 1861. [New York, 1961] Uncolored. Scale ca. 1:18,000,000. 23 × 15 cm.

Accompanies article by Charles Stafford, AP Newsfeatures writer, entitled "Divided nation of 1861 moved slowly into conflict." 2 p., ea. 36 × 22 cm.

Map of the eastern United States showing Union and Confederate states and "slave states remaining in Union." Dates of important events in 1861 appear below map.

1

Aschbach, G. A.

Pocket map showing the probable theatre of the war. Compiled by G. A. Aschbach, C.E. Allentown, Pa. Philadelphia, M. H. Traubel, ©1861. Colored. Scale ca. 1:1,700,000. 36 × 32 cm.

Map of Maryland, Delaware, and parts of Pennsylvania and Virginia, showing "camps & forts" underlined in red, "prominent places" underlined in blue, roads, railroads, drainage, towns, and boundaries.

Insets: [Street pattern of the city of Baltimore] 9 × 12 cm.—[Map of the city and county of Washington, and the county of Alexandria] 13 × 13 cm. Contains a list of 12 buildings keyed by number to the map.

Deposited for copyright on May 9, 1861, less than a month after the attack on Fort Sumter.

1.1

——————Another issue.

G3840 1861 .A8

"Camps & forts" and "prominent places" are not highlighted by the use of red and blue underlining. Handwritten note on verso reads: No. 189, filed 9 May 1861, Aschbach & Traubel Prop.

1.5

Bachmann, John.

Bird's eye view of junction of the Ohio & Mississippi Rivers, showing Cairo and part of the southern states. Drawn from nature and lith. by John Bachmann. A. Rumpf, Publisher. Agent for John Bachmann's publications, New York. ©1861. Colored view. 40 × 49 cm.

Panoramic map looking south from Vienna, Illinois, to Holly Springs, Mississippi. Waverly, Tennessee, is on the left and Poplar Bluff, Missouri, is on the right. The map shows a military encampment and fortifications at Cairo, Illinois, plus roads, railroads, rivers, towns, relief, and woodland. Distances from Cairo to Batesville, Memphis, Little Rock, Poplar Bluff, Jackson, and Paris are listed in bottom margin.

1.7

——————Birds eye view of Louisiana, Mississippi, Alabama and part of Florida. Drawn from nature and lith. by John Bachmann. [New York] ©1861. Colored view. 55 × 72 cm.

At top of map: Panorama of the seat of war.

"Entered according to act of Congress in the year 1861 by John Bachmann."

Table of distances from New Orleans in lower margin.

View of the Gulf coast centered on the Mississippi River delta, showing cities and towns, roads, railroads, rivers, and forts.

Copyright no. 197, June 8, 1961, written in ink in lower margin. Stamped: Deposited in District Clerk's Office, Southern District of New York.

2

——————Panorama of the seat of war. Birds eye view of Virginia, Maryland, Delaware, and the District of Columbia. Drawn from nature and lith. by John Bachmann. Published by J. Bachmann, N.Y. ©1861. Colored view. 46 × 72 cm.

Battle sites are noted by crossed swords. This issue lacks clouds in the sky and smoke over Manassas.

3

——————Another issue. A. Rumpf, Publisher. Agent for John Bachmann's publications. ©1861. Colored. 47 × 72 cm.

Battle sites are noted by crossed swords. This issue has clouds in the sky and smoke over the Manassas battlefield.

3.5

Barrie (George) and Sons.

Map of the United States of America showing the

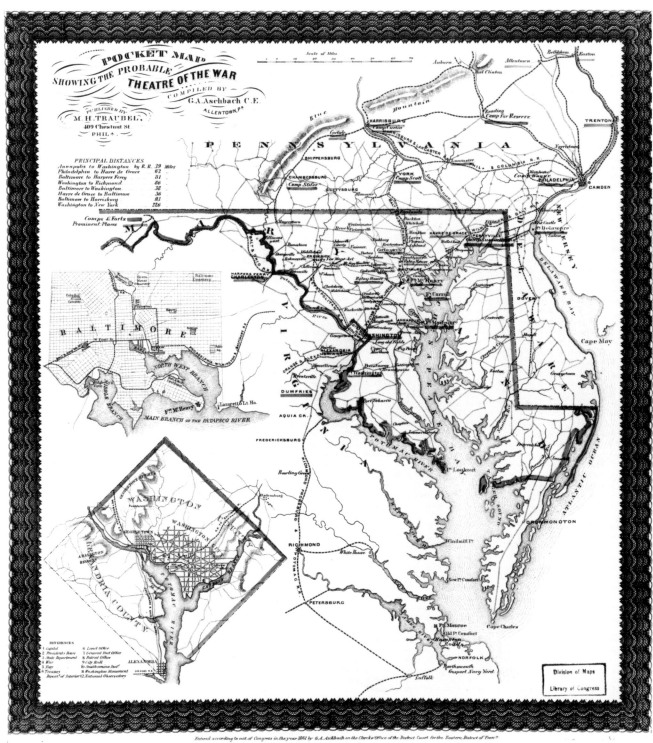

Deposited for copyright on May 9, 1861, less than a month after the attack on Fort Sumter, G. A. Aschbach's map depicts the "Prob- *able Theatre of the War" in the Middle Atlantic States. Highlighted are "camps & forts" and "prominent places." (See entry no. 1.)*

boundaries of the Union and Confederate geographical divisions and departments, June 30, 1861. Copyright 1905, by George Barrie & Sons. Colored. Scale ca. 1:15,206,400. 16 × 23 cm.

"From an original in the Map Department, Library of Congress."

4

Blair, R. Baxter.

Secession, 1860–1861. By Albert Bushnell Hart. Assisted by David Maydole Matteson. L. Philip Denoyer, geographer. Compiled and drawn by R. Baxter Blair. Chicago, Denoyer-Geppert Co., ©1917. Scale 1:4,752,000. 74 × 110 cm. (Hart American history series, no. A15)

Wall map of the United States, showing "forts held by loyal forces," and forts, arsenals, branch mints and navy yards "seized by seceding forces." Free states and territories, "loyal slave states," and "territories adhering to C.S.A." indicated by color and symbol.

Inset: Charleston harbor. Scale ca. 1:85,000. 10 × 13 cm.

5

————Edited by Edgar B. Wesley. Drawn by R. Baxter Blair. Chicago, Denoyer-Geppert Co., ©1949. Colored. Scale 1:4,752,000. 74 × 109 cm. on sheet 99 × 112 cm. (Wesley social studies: our America backgrounds and development, no. WA 22)

Based on the preceding map from the Hart American history series, no. A15.

5.5

Colton, George Woolworth.

G. Woolworth Colton's map of the country 500 miles around the city of Washington showing the seat of war in the East. Drawn, engraved & published by G. Woolworth Colton, New York, 1861. Uncolored. Scale 1:3,168,000. 78 × 53 cm.

General map centered on Washington, D.C., with five concentric circles at intervals of 100 miles.

Insets: [Map of Maryland, Delaware, and parts of Virginia, Pennsylvania, and New Jersey] Scale ca. 1:1,125,000. 31 × 48 cm.—Vicinity of Ft. Monroe & Norfolk. 10 × 6 cm.

Includes a list of the "Principle Forts and Military Stations in the Atlantic States" and a table of "Population of the United States."

A colored copy is in the James A. Garfield papers, Manuscript Division, L.C., series 8, container no. 1.

6

————Map of the southern and border states, showing the actu alpositions [sic] of the national and rebel forces, and of the blockading fletes [sic] and vessels, the positions of the various fortifications that have been erected, and the localities of all the important battles that have been fought during the present war. Drawn on wood by G. Woolworth Colton, N.Y. Uncolored. Scale ca. 1:3,220,000. 52 × 75 cm. *From* Frank Leslie's illustrated newspaper [Oct. 26, 1861]

Map includes railroads, rivers, towns, names and boundaries of states, and some relief by hachures.

Insets: The southern portion of Florida is on the same scale as the main map. 11 × 11 cm.—Vicinity of Washington City, D.C. Scale ca. 1:320,000. 13 × 16 cm.

6.2

————The Tribune war maps. [Compiled by] G. Woolworth Colton. New York, New-York Daily Tribune, 1861. Uncolored. Various scales. 17 maps on 4 p., each p. 59 × 42 cm.

From the *New-York Daily Tribune*, July 30, 1861.

Contents: Map of eastern Virginia. 24 × 19 cm.—Map from Cairo to Memphis. 22 × 13 cm.—A strategic map of the seat of war [in Virginia and Maryland] 16 × 19 cm.—Acquia Creek and its environs. 17 × 13 cm.—The seat of war in Missouri. 19 × 19 cm.—The District of Columbia. 21 × 13 cm.—A map of the seat of war in the West [Illinois, Indiana, Kentucky, and Missouri by J. H. Colton] 17 × 19 cm.—The position in western Virginia. 12 × 13 cm.—Map showing the position of the Union District in East Tennessee. 10 × 19 cm.—Fort Monroe and Norfolk. 14 × 7 cm.—Plan of Fortress Monroe. 14 × 7 cm.—Harper's Ferry and the region round about. 21 × 18 cm.—The battle field at Bull Run. 5 × 13 cm.—Map of New Orleans and Mississippi Delta. 23 × 19 cm.—Baltimore and its points of attack and defence. 24 × 19 cm.—Seat of war in Northern Virginia [with table of distances from Baltimore] 37 × 7 cm.—Great Bethel [i.e., Big Bethel, Virginia] and its batteries. 12 × 7 cm.

Includes "List of killed and wounded at the battle of Bull Run," p. 3–4.

6.5

Colton, Joseph H.

Colton's map of the southern states. Including Maryland, Delaware, Virginia, Kentucky, Tennessee, Missouri, North Carolina, South Carolina, Georgia, Alabama, Mississippi, Arkansas, Louisiana, and Texas. Showing also part of adjoining states & territories locating the forts & military stations of the U. States & showing all the rail roads, r. r. stations, & other internal improvements. New York, J. H. Colton, 1861. Colored. Scale ca. 1:1,520,640. 2 sheets, each 94 × 68 cm.

"Entered according to Act of Congress in the year 185[5?] by J. H. Colton & Co."

Inset: Southern part of Florida. 27 × 19 cm.

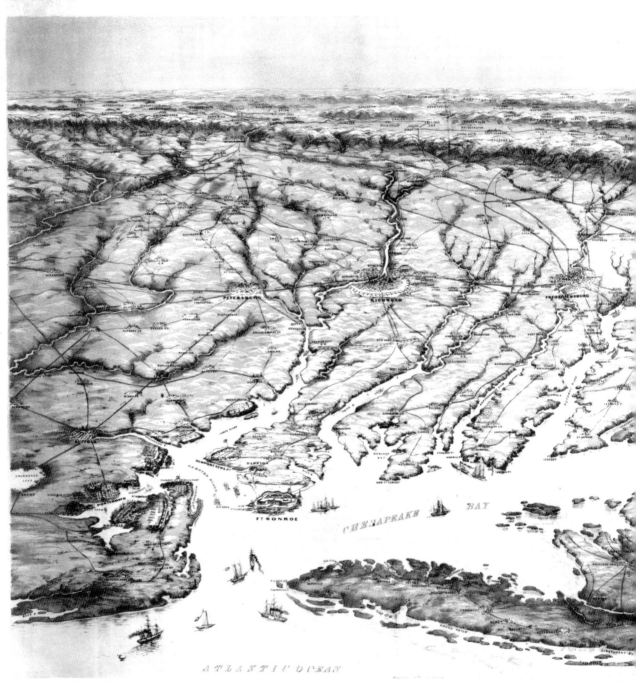

ATLANTIC OCEAN

BIRDS EYE VIEW

of VIRGINIA, MARYLAND DELAWARE AND THE D.

30

Includes tables of population based on the "United States Census for 1860."

General map.

Title printed to right of map.

"No. 6" in upper left corner.

Map is reproduced from the steel plates used to print J. Calvin Smith's "Map of the United States of America including Canada and a large portion of Texas" (New York, Sherman & Smith, 1843).

The Geography and Map Division has another copy of Colton's 1861 map which has been annotated with numbers in red and dashes in blue to indicate the limits of freshwater in the rivers as "referred to in a *Memoir on freshwater stations* along the coast of the United States, south of Cape Henlopen: compiled from the communications of the assistants and sub assistants of the U.S. Coast Survey, June 22, 1861" (G3860 1861.C6 Vault).

1862 editions listed as items 25.5–25.6; 1863 edition listed as item 37.6.

6.6

——————Colton's map of the southern states. Including Maryland, Delaware, Virginia, Kentucky, Tennessee, Missouri, North Carolina, South Carolina, Georgia, Alabama, Mississippi, Arkansas, Louisiana, Texas. Showing also part of adjoining states & territories locating the forts & military stations of the U. States & showing all the rail roads, r. r. stations, & other internal improvements. New York, J. H. Colton, 1861. Colored. Scale ca. 1:1,520,640. 96 × 137 cm.

"Entered according to Act of Congress in the year 1861 by J. H. Colton."

Printed by Lang & Laing, N.Y.

Insets: Southern part of Florida. 27 × 20 cm.—Colton's map of the United States showing the proposed railroad routes to the Pacific Ocean. 19 × 26 cm.

Includes tables of population based on the "United States Census for 1860."

"No. 6" in upper left corner.

In this edition, "and" has not been inserted before "Texas" in the map title and the entire title has been moved from the right to the upper center.

Ships are depicted along the coast denoting Union blockade of southern harbors.

7

——————Colton's United States shewing the military stations, forts &c. Entered according to Act of Congress in the year 1855, by J. H. Colton. Printed by Lang & Laing, N.Y.

John Bachmann's "Panorama of the Seat of War. Birds Eye View of Virginia, Maryland, Delaware, and the District of Columbia" is representative of the excellent panoramic maps issued by this New York artist between 1861 and 1862. (See entry no. 2.)

New York, 1861. Colored. Scale ca. 1:7,900,000. 42 × 69 cm.

"No 3" in upper left corner.

Forts are marked by red flags.

Indicates railroads, towns, names and boundaries of states and territories, rivers, and canals.

7.5

————Colton's United States shewing the military stations, forts, &c. Prepared by J. H. Colton, New York, for the "Rebellion Record." New York, G. P. Putnam, 1861. Colored. Scale ca. 1:8,000,000. 37 × 44 cm.

"Entered according to Act of Congress in the year 1855 by J. H. Colton."

General map of the United States extending from the Atlantic coast through most of Texas.

8

————J. H. Colton's topographical map of North and South Carolina. A large portion of Georgia & part of adjoining states. Entered according to Act of Congress in the year 1861, by J. H. Colton. Printed by Lang & Laing, New York. Uncolored. Scale ca. 1:1,550,000. 49 × 69 cm.

"No. 12" in upper left corner.

Copyright no. "410" and the date "Sept. 10, 1861" written in ink in lower margin.

Indicates forts, towns, roads, railroads, county names and boundaries, geographic coordinates, and rivers. Drawings of ships offshore denote naval blockade.

Insets: Beaufort and vicinity, N. Carolina. 8 × 9 cm.—Wilmington and vicinity, N. Carolina. 13 × 9 cm.—Charleston Harbor and its approaches, S. Carolina. 14 × 15 cm.—Plan of Ft. Sumter. 4 × 4 cm.—Savannah and vicinity. 10 × 15 cm.

8.2

————Reduced facsimile. Uncolored. 44 × 59 cm.

From William P. Cumming's *North Carolina in Maps* (Raleigh, State Department of Archives and History, 1966), plate XI.

G3900 1861 .C6 1966

Printed in brown ink.

This facsimile was produced from the previously described copy (entry no. 8).

9

Couzens, M. K.

Birds eye view of the Mississippi Valley from Cairo to the Gulf of Mexico. Drawn from government surveys and other authentic sources by M. K. Couzens, Civ. Eng. Printed by Lang & Laing, lith., N.Y. New York, W. Schaus, ©1861. Colored. Scale ca. 1:1,710,000. 77 × 58 cm.

At top of map: The seat of war.

This is a map and not a bird's-eye view. It covers Louisiana, Mississippi, Arkansas, Alabama, and parts of Florida, Georgia, Kentucky, Tennessee, Illinois, Missouri, Kansas, Indian Territory, and Texas, and indicates forts, towns, rivers, roads, railroads, state boundaries, and relief by shading.

Insets: Fort Pickens. 19 × 18 cm.—Camp Defiance at Cairo, the key of the West. 11 × 17 cm.

9.5

Cram (George F.) Company.

The United States in 1861. Current editor: Thomas D. Clark. Original editors: Rolla Milton Tyron, James Alton James, [and] Carl Rusell Fish. Indianapolis, The George F. Cram Company [1956] Colored. Scale ca. 1:3,420,000. 92 × 127 cm.

G3700 1861 .C7

Wall map indicating, by different colors, "free states," "states seceded before April 15, 1861," "states seceded after April 15, 1861," "slave states that did not secede," and "free" and "slave" territories.

"518" in lower right margin.

10

Duval (Peter S.) and Son.

Military map of the United States & territories showing the location of the military posts, arsenals, Navy Yards, & ports of entry. Compiled from pub-doc—1861. Published by P. S. Duval & Son, Philada. Uncolored. Scale ca. 1:6,800,000. 60 × 80 cm.

Map includes state capitals and principal towns, drainage, geographic coordinates, and names and boundaries of the states and territories.

Military posts and ports of entry are listed at bottom and sides of map.

Insets: Pensacola & Perdido Bays. 8 × 16 cm.—Key West. 5 × 11 cm.

11

Elliott, J. B.

Scott's great snake. Entered according to Act of Congress in the year 1861 by J. B. Elliott of Cincinnati. Colored. Scale not given. 35 × 44 cm.

Cartoon map illustrating Gen. Winfield Scott's plan to crush the Confederacy, economically. It is sometimes called the "Anaconda plan."

11.5

Ettling, T.

Map of the United States of North America, Upper & Lower Canada, New Brunswick, Nova Scotia & British Columbia. Mexico, Cuba, Jamaica, St. Domingo and the Bahama Islands. Paniconographie de Gillot, a Paris. 1861. Colored. Scale ca. 1:6,000,000. 69 × 95 cm.

G3700 1861 .E7

At top of map: Supplement to the Illustrated London News, June 1, 1861.

General map showing state and international boundaries, railroads, cities, rivers, and relief by hachures. Two colors are used to differentiate between Union and Confederate states.

12

Ezekiel, E.

Map of the seat of war with the lines of r. roads leading thereto, also the strategical points as laid down. Lith. by J. Manouvrier & Co., N. Orls. Published by E. Ezekiel, Exchange Bookstore, New Orleans. [1861] Uncolored. Scale ca. 1:2,080,000. 62 × 80 cm.

"To L. Pope Walker, Secty of War, this map is dedicated by his obdt. servt. W. H. Wilder, C. & T. Engineer."

Confederate imprint.

G3860 1861 .E9Vault

Map of the Southeast, showing forts, roads, railroads, distances, towns, rivers, and state boundaries. Troops are indicated at Charlottesville, Gordonsville, Manassas Junction, Harpers Ferry, Richmond, and Aquia Creek.

12.2

Gaston, Samuel N.

The campaign atlas, for 1861. New York, S. N. Gaston, 1861. 2 p. l., [1] 1, 14 col. maps. 20 × 16 cm.

G1201.S5G3 1861

General atlas containing "A Map of the United States and Territories, with the great Cantonments and strategic points indicated" and maps of Delaware and Maryland, Virginia and proposed West Virginia, North Carolina, South Carolina, Georgia, Florida, Alabama, Mississippi, Louisiana, Arkansas, Missouri, Kentucky and Tennessee, and Texas.

Listed in P. L. Phillips's *A List of Geographical Atlases in the Library of Congress* (Washington, Government Printing Office, 1909), v. 1, no. 1351.

12.5

Hall, Edward S.

Lloyd's new military map of the border & southern states. Drawn by Edward S. Hall. Published by H. H. Lloyd & Co., New York. 1861. Colored. Scale ca. 1:1,850,000. 79 × 106 cm.

At top of map: H. H. Lloyd & Co's. new military map of the southern and border states.

Inset: [Map of southern Florida] 16 × 11 cm.

Battlefields are marked by red lines and strategic places by red dots.

Indicates towns, railroads, rivers, names and boundaries of states, and relief by hachures.

1862 edition listed as item 27, 1863 edition as 38, and 1865 edition as 71.

12.6

——————Our naval and military operations at a glance. The coast and land line of the rebellious states—the Union blockade of the Atlantic and Gulf coast—the rebel batteries on the Mississippi—the forts on the southern sea line. Drawn by E. S. Hall. Engraved by Waters & Son, N.Y. New York, New York Herald, 1861. Uncolored. Scale ca. 1:6,400,000. 35 × 35 cm. on sheet 44 × 37 cm.

From the *New York Herald,* October 29, 1861, p. [1].

For a later issue of the map, see entry no. 14.8.

12.7

——————Western border states. Waters & son Eng. N.Y. New York, H. H. Lloyd & Co., ©1861. Scale ca. 1:740,000. Colored map 39 × 69 cm. on sheet 97 × 72 cm.

At top of sheet: Military portraits, map of the seat of war, uniforms, arms, & c.

Map of Missouri, Tennessee, and parts of Nebraska, Kansas, Indian Territory, Arkansas, Illinois, Indiana, Ohio, Kentucky, Virginia, North Carolina, and South Carolina, showing cities and towns, rivers, and railroads. Some important or strategic places are underlined in red or indicated by red dots.

Above map has portraits of Generals Wool, Dix, Scott, Fremont, Lyon, McClellan, Banks, Blenker, Butler, McDowell, Rosecrans (here spelled "Rosencranz"), Sprague, Burnside, and Sigel, Colonel Corcoran, and Commodore Stringham.

Stamped in margin: Copyright Library May 15, 1862.

13

Hart, Albert B.

Secession and war. [1861] By Albert Bushnell Hart. Chicago, Denoyer-Geppert Co., ©1940. Colored. Scale 1:4,752,000. 77 × 110 cm. (Denoyer-Geppert social studies: elementary American history with Old World beginnings, no. EA 11)

Wall map of the United States, showing "forts held by loyal forces," and forts, navy yards, arsenals and branch mints "seized by seceding forces." Free states and territories, "loyal slave states," and "territories adhering to C.S.A." are indicated by color and symbol.

Map is based on the Hart American history series, no. A15. (See item no. 4.)

Inset: Charleston harbor. Scale ca. 1:85,000. 12 × 13 cm.

13.2

Hergesheimer, Edwin.

Map showing the distribution of the slave population of the southern states of the United States. Compiled from the census of 1860. Drawn by E. Hergesheimer. Engr. by Th. Leonhardt. Washington, Henry S. Graham, 1861. Uncolored. Scale ca. 1:3,000,000. 69 × 86 cm.

"Entered according to Act of Congress, A.D. 1861 by Henry S. Graham."

"Sold for the benefit of the sick and wounded soldiers of the U.S. Army."

"Census Office, Department of the Interior, Washington, Sept. 9th, 1861. After a careful examination of the above very interesting map I am prepared to state that it not only furnishes the evidences of great care in its execution, but can be relied on as corresponding with the official returns of the 8th Census. [Signed in facsimile] Jos. C. G. Kennedy, Superintendent."

Map indicates by gray patterns, the percentage of slaves in each county. "It should be observed, that several counties appear comparatively light. This arises from the preponderance of whites and free blacks in the large towns in those counties. . . . The figures in each county represent the percentage of slaves . . ."

"Scale of shade" printed in lower right corner.

Includes population table based on census of 1860.

13.4

Heyne, Charles.

Map of part of Virginia, Maryland and Delaware from the best authorities. Compiled from official sources & drawn by Chas. Heyne C. E. Lith. of J. Bien, N.Y. New York, E. & G. W. Blunt, 1861. Uncolored. Scale ca. 1:400,000. 97 × 66 cm.

"Entered according to Act of Congress in the year 1861 by E. & G. W. Blunt."

Copyright deposit. Registration number "230, June 24, 1861" written in ink in lower margin.

General map of the Chesapeake Bay region showing cities and towns, state and county boundaries, railroads, roads, canals, drainage, lighthouses, forts, and soundings.

13.5

——————Another issue. Colored.

Symbol for batteries has been added to a list of "Abbreviations & references" used on the map.

Another copy is in Fillmore map collection no. 73.

13.6

——————Another issue. Colored.

Lithographer's name has been dropped. Forts Corcoran, Runyon, Albany, and Ellsworth are shown on the Virginia side of the Potomac River at Washington, D.C.

13.8

Higginson, J. H.

A new military map of the seat of war, by J. H. Higginson, New York. [1861?] Colored. Scale ca. 1:1,700,000. 34 × 38 cm.

General map of eastern and central Virginia, Maryland, Delaware, southern Pennsylvania, and northern North Carolina showing cities and towns, state boundaries, and railroads.

Includes an advertisement for the Market Fire Insurance Company, New York.

13.9

Joerg, Wolfgang L. G.

North and South in 1861. Prepared for the Chronicles of America under the direction of W. L. G. Joerg, American Geographical Society. Julius Bien lith., N.Y. Colored. Scale 1:13,000,000. 19 × 27 cm. *From* Wood, William. Captains of the Civil War; a chronicle of the blue and the gray. New Haven, Yale University Press, 1921. (The Chronicles of America series; Abraham Lincoln edition, vol. 31) facing p. 64.

Map indicates forts, barracks, camps, arsenals, navy yards, naval and military academies, navigable rivers, canals, railroads, the extent of the "Northern blockade of the South," and the "approximate line of division between North and South."

13.95

Johnson, Alvin Jewett.

Johnson's new military map of the United States showing the forts, military posts & all the military divisions with enlarged plans of southern harbors. From authentic data obtained at the War Department. Washington, Johnson and Ward, ©1861. Colored. Scale ca. 1:10,000,000. 44 × 61 cm. *In* Johnson's new illustrated (steel plate) family atlas. New York, Johnson and Browning, 1862. Map unnumbered.

G1019.J5 1862b fol.

"Entered according to Act of Congress, in the year one thousand eight hundred & sixty one, by Johnson & Browning."

Insets: New Orleans and delta of Mississippi, Louisiana. 9 × 9 cm.—Mobile Bay, Alabama. 9 × 7 cm.—Entrance to Pensacola Bay, Florida. 9 × 13 cm.—Key West, Florida. 9 × 8 cm.—Savannah River. 9 × 9 cm.—Charleston Harbor, S. Carolina. 9 × 11 cm.—Hampton Roads and Norfolk Harbor, Virginia. 12 × 8 cm.—Washington and vicinity. 11 × 8 cm.—Baltimore and vicinity. 8 × 8 cm.

Listed in P. L. Phillips's *A List of Geographical Atlases in the Library of Congress* (Washington, Government Printing Office, 1920), v. 4, no. 4343.

Map inserted between maps 19 and 20. Lacks printed

map numbers. Table of contents does not list "Johnson's new military map of the United States."

13.96

——————Johnson's new military map of the United States showing the forts, military posts &c. with enlarged plans of southern harbors. From authentic data obtained at the War Department. Washington, Johnson and Ward, ©1861. Colored. Scale ca. 1:10,000,000. 44 × 61 cm. *In* Johnson's new illustrated (steel plate) family atlas. New York, Johnson and Ward, 1862. Map 20–21.

G1019.J5 1862 fol.

"Entered according to Act of Congress, in the year one thousand eight hundred & sixty one, by Johnson & Browning."

Insets: New Orleans and delta of Mississippi, Louisiana. 9 × 9 cm.—Mobile Bay, Alabama. 9 × 7 cm.—Entrance to Pensacola Bay, Florida. 9 × 13 cm.—Key West, Florida. 9 × 8 cm.—Savannah River. 9 × 9cm.—Charleston Harbor, S. Carolina. 9 × 11 cm.—Hampton Roads and Norfolk Harbor, Virginia. 12 × 8 cm.—Washington and vicinity. 11 × 8 cm.—Baltimore and vicinity. 8 × 8 cm.

For table of contents, see P. L. Phillips's *A List of Geographical Atlases in the Library of Congress* (Washington, Government Printing Office, 1909), v. 1, no. 837.

This is a revised version of the preceding map (entry no. 13.95). Map title has been changed, and states and territories are depicted rather than military divisions. In addition, the map includes printed map numbers in the upper margin and it is listed in the table of contents.

13.97

——————*In* Johnson's new illustrated (steel plate) family atlas. New York, Johnson and Ward, 1863. Map 20–21.

G1019.J5 1863 fol.

There are no obvious differences between the 1862 (entry no. 13.96) and 1863 printings of this map.

For table of contents, see P. L. Phillips's *A List of Geographical Atlases in the Library of Congress* (Washington, Government Printing Office, 1909), v. 1, no. 840.

13.98

——————Seattle, The Shorey Book Store [1968] Facsimile. Colored. Scale ca. 1:11,500,000. 39 × 53 cm. (Reprint SJM 22/68)

G3701 .R2 1861 .J6 1968

Reduced facsimile of an unidentified edition of "Johnson's new military map of the United States." The title, publishers, and date agree with entries 13.96–13.97, but the border is different.

14

Lloyd, James T.

Lloyd's American railroad map, showing the whole seat of war. New York, London, and San Francisco [1861] Colored. Scale ca. 1:1,900,800. 4 parts, each 48 × 61 cm.

G3701 .P3 1861 .L51

On verso: Lloyd's American railroad weekly, vol. 1, no. 51, July 6, 1861.

"Entered according to Act of Congress in the year 1860 by J. T. Lloyd . . ."

Indicates "forts, batteries, and arsenals," "railroads in running order," distances, rivers, and state boundaries in the eastern United States.

Includes an advertisement in the upper right corner for "The only correct map of the southern states."

Inset: Map of Escambia & Santa Rosa Cos., F1, showing Pensacola Harbor and channel, Ft. Pickens, Ft. McRae, Bragg's batteries, and the position of the U.S. fleet now before the harbor. Surveyed and drawn by order of Congress in 1860 . . . ©1861. 28 × 31 cm.

Listed in A. M. Modelski's *Railroad Maps of the United States* (Washington, Library of Congress, 1975), no. 43.

14.1

——————New York, Louisville, London and San Francisco [1861]. Colored. Scale ca. 1:1,900,800. 94 × 120 cm.

On verso: Lloyd's American railroad weekly, vol. 2, no. 8, October 5, 1861.

Includes an advertisement in the upper right corner for "Lloyd's great military map of the fifteen southern states" and advertisements below the map title for "$100,000 topographical map of the State of Virginia" and "Official map of Missouri."

14.2

——————Lloyd's map of the southern states showing all the railroads, their stations & distances, also the counties, towns, villages, harbors, rivers, and forts. New York and London, J. T. Lloyd, 1861. Colored. Scale ca. 1: 2,000,000. 97 × 144 cm.

"Entered according to act of Congress in the year 1861 by J. T. Lloyd."

Copyright no. 290, July 12, 1861, written in right margin. Stamped: Deposited in U.S. District Clerk's Office, Southern District of New York.

General map.

1862 edition listed as item no. 29, and 1863 edition as no. 41.2.

14.25

——————Another issue.

Advertisement for the "$100,000 topographical map of the State of Virginia" printed in lower right corner.

Text printed on verso entitled "Lloyd's military map and gazetteer of the southern states" (Sept. 7, 1861).

14.3

————Another issue.

Text entitled "Sketch of the whole southern coast" printed below map.

Text printed on verso entitled "Lloyd's military map and gazetteer of the southern states" (©1861).

14.33

Magnus, Charles.

Complete map of the rail roads and water courses, in the United States & Canada. Liverpool, Eng. and New York, Charles Magnus & Co., [1861] Colored. Scale ca. 1:5,800,000. Map 37 × 48 cm. on sheet 60 × 71 cm.

Stenciled title in red, white, and blue ink in upper margin: Union military chart.

Listed in A. M. Modelski's *Railroad Maps of the United States* (Washington, Library of Congress, 1975), no. 44.

Map of the eastern half of the United States and part of Canada showing drainage, state boundaries, place names, railroads in operation, in progress, and projected, steamboat lines, and telegraph lines.

Insets: Military map of Maryland & Virginia. 11 × 20 cm.—Map of northern military movements: between New York & St. Louis. 14 × 25 cm.—[Entrance to Pensacola Bay showing forts] 8 × 13 cm.—[Map of eastern United States and Gulf of Mexico showing location of Pensacola] 8 × 7 cm.—[View of U.S. Capitol] 8 × 20 cm.

At bottom of principal map: Entered, according to Act of Congress, in the year 1859, by Charles Magnus & Co.

In bottom margin: Entered, according to Act of Congress, in the year 1861 by Charles Magnus.

14.35

————Map of northern military movements: between New York & St. Louis. Entered according to Act of Congress in the year 1861, by Charles Magnus. Colored. Scale ca. 1:5,800,000. 15 × 25 cm.

This map was originally published as an inset on Charles Magnus's *Complete Map of the Rail Roads and Water Courses, in the United States & Canada* (see entry no. 14.33). Indicated are railroads linking New York and St. Louis, but military movements are not depicted.

14.4

Mahon, Charles.

Map of the alluvial region of the Mississippi. Prepared to accompany the report of Capt. A. A. Humphreys and Lieut H. L. Abbot, Corps. of Top'l. Engrs., U.S.A. to the Bureau of Topl. Engrs., War Dept. Drawn by Chs. Mahon. 1861. Colored. Scale 1:1,500,00. 73 × 46 cm.

At head of title: U. S. Miss. Delta Survey. Plate II.

Map of the Mississippi River from Cape Girardeau to the delta showing the extent of the alluvial region.

Another copy is in Sherman map. coll. no. 185.

Another copy is in Fillmore map coll. no. 110–Q.

14.45

————Another copy.

"Errata—Plate II" pasted to map in lower left corner.

14.5

————Another edition. Bowen & Co. lith., Phil.

Completely redrawn edition, with errors corrected.

14.55

[Map of the southern states, including rail roads, county towns, state capitals, county roads, the southern coast Delaware to Texas, showing the harbors, inlets, forts and position of blockading ships. Prepared for Harper's weekly, November 1861] Uncolored. Scale ca. 1:3,000,000. 45 × 71 cm. *From* Harper's weekly, v. 5, Nov. 9, 1861. Following p. 706.

Inset: Charleston and Beaufort, South Carolina. 12 × 12 cm.

Includes portraits of Lincoln, Seward, Scott, and McClellan.

Geography and Map Division copy badly cropped. Border and map title wanting.

"Our war map. We break through our usual habits in this number, and devote four pages to the publication of a large war map of the southern states. Without intending to disparage any of the maps in existence, we think this will be found more reliable, and more useful to the student of the war, than any other we have seen." (*Harper's Weekly*, v. 5, Nov. 9, 1861. p. 706.)

Map was also published in the *Sun*, New York, Jan. 4, 1862 (entry no. 32.9) and by Bacon and Company, ca. 1863 (entry no. 37).

14.6

Mitchell, Samuel Augustus, Jr.

Map of the United States, and territories. Together with Canada &c. Mitchell's map publication office, Philadelphia, Pa. 1861. Colored. Scale ca. 1:10,500,000. 32 × 52 cm. on sheet 61 × 65 cm.

At top of map: Mitchell's military map of the United States, showing forts, &c. with separate maps of states, vicinities of cities &c. Published by S. A. Mitchell, Jr., Philada.

Insets: County map of Virginia, and North Carolina. 24 × 30 cm.—County map of Pennsylvania, New Jersey, Maryland, and Delaware. 24 × 30 cm.—[Hampton Roads] 6 × 5 cm.—[Washington, D.C.] 9 × 9 cm.—[Pensacola Bay] 6 × 7 cm.—Map of Charleston Harbor. 6 × 5 cm.—Vicinity of New Orleans, Louisiana. 11 × 9 cm.—Vicinity of Baltimore, Maryland. 11 × 9 cm.—Vicinity of Richmond, Virginia. 11 × 9 cm.

Includes population tables.

14.65

The New York Herald.

War maps and diagrams. Waters & Son, engravers, N.Y. New York, July 27, 1861. Uncolored. Various scales. 34 maps on 8 p., each p. 58 × 40 cm.

Contents: The positions of the rebel forces in Virginia. 41 × 33 cm.—A birds-eye view of the United States. Portraying at a glance those states which have seceded, those which are loyal and those which profess to be neutral. 21 × 24 cm.—Map of parts of Virginia, Maryland and Delaware. Showing the seat of war and the surrounding country. 22 × 24 cm.—The seat of war in the West. The important points of the war in Missouri, showing the object of the advance of Union and rebel troops towards the Southwest. E. S. Hall, del. 29 × 25 cm.—The Mississippi from above Cairo to Memphis showing the supposed location of the rebel camp. 17 × 6 cm.—Plan of Memphis and its approaches. 16 × 12 cm.—The proposed new arsenal at St. Louis. 13 × 6 cm.—Diagram of the camp at Cairo. 7 × 8 cm.—St. Louis and its defences. 7 × 13 cm. Cairo and Junction of Ohio and Mississippi. 10 × 6 cm.—Savannah and its defences—held by the rebels. 11 × 24 cm.—Mobile and its defences—held by the rebels. 10 × 11 cm.—New York City defences. Outline map showing the land and water approaches to New York & Brooklyn, and the localities of the existing and recently suggested defensive works. 20 × 13 cm.—Topographical sketch of Fortress Monroe. 8 × 6 cm.—Baltimore and its defences. 9 × 6 cm.—Gosport Navy Yard, previous to the fire. 12 × 6 cm.—Theatre of the Grand Army of the Potomac. The field of operations of the corps d'armee under General Irwin [sic] McDowell. The advance on Manassas Junction and the retreat. 24 × 24 cm.—The seat of war on the upper Potomac. The field of battle Tuesday, July 2, 1861, between General Patterson's Union troops and General Jackson's rebel forces. 20 × 24 cm.—View of Newport News. The intrenchments of the New York Zouaves, New York Scott Life Guard, Massachusetts and Vermont regiments, with the locations of the outposts, pickets, &c. 20 × 25 cm.—Manassas Gap Junction and surroundings. The positions of the rebel troops, their intrenchments, batteries, and encampments. 16 × 12 cm.—The upper Potomac. Showing the seat of strife at Hainesville. 16 × 12 cm.—Fort Monroe, Norfolk and Chesapeake Bay. 16 × 12 cm.—The key to the Chesapeake. 17 × 6 cm.—Point of Rocks. Place where Bollman's Rock was blown up. 14 × 6 cm.—View of Pensacola harbor and defences. The Sebastopol of the Gulf of Mexico. The probable rendezvous of the northern naval forces. 21 × 25 cm.—Charleston Bay, Fort Sumter and surroundings. 15 × 18 cm.—Topographical sketch of Fort Sumter. 16 × 12 cm.—Pensacola and its defences. The range of the guns at Fort Pickens, McCrea and Barancas. The locations of the fleet. 17 × 12 cm.—The disposition of the Federal troops near the national capital, June 5, 1861. 20

× 25 cm.—Colonel Wallace's position at Cumberland. 13 × 6 cm.—The state line between Pennsylvania and Maryland, where are located ten Pennsylvania reserve regiments to support Colonel Wallace. 11 × 6 cm.—Contemplated division of State of Virginia. 11 × 6 cm.—The positions of the Union and rebel forces in Virginia. 19 × 24 cm.

14.7

————War maps and diagrams. Waters & Son sc. [New York, after October 11, 1861] Uncolored. Various scales. 49 × 25 cm.

Incomplete copy of the map supplement issued by the *New York Herald*. Library of Congress bound copy of the newspaper for October-December 1861 does not include the map supplement.

Contents: Our brilliant nav[al] victory. Sketch of Beaufort, Port Royal and Forts Beauregard and Walker—scene of the operations of our great expedition. 41 × 24 cm.—[verso] Map of New [Orlean]s and surrounding country. The mouths of the Mississippi—[The site ?] of the naval engagement, Friday night, October 11, 1861. 22 × 24 cm.—The lower Potomac. Map of the Potomac from Washington to the Chesapeak[e] showing the rebel batteries from Cockpit Point to Mathias Point. 25 × 24 cm.

14.75

————War maps and diagrams. Waters & Son, engravers, N.Y. [New York, after Nov. 7, 1861] Uncolored. Various scales. 13 maps on 4 p., each p. 51 × 36 cm.

Incomplete copy of the map supplement issued by the *New York Herald*. Library of Congress bound copy of the newspaper for October-December 1861 does not include the map supplement.

Contents: Important operations in Kentucky and Tennessee. The battle ground of Gen. Nelson at Pikeville, Piketon—The brilliant victory over the rebels—situation of the bridges destroyed by the unionists of Tennessee—The Cumberland Gap—Positions of the contending armies, &c, &c, &c. 30 × 35 cm.—The seat of war in Kentucky. 16 × 17 cm.—The fight at Santa Rosa Island. Map of Santa Rosa Island where the reported fight between the rebels and Wilson's Zouaves took place. 17 × 12 cm.—Map of the rebel capital. Topographical sketch of the city of Richmond, Virginia, with the surrounding encampments. 26 × 34 cm.—The affair at Chicamacomico. The advance of Col. Hawkins—retreat of Col. Brown—shelling of the rebels by the Montecello [sic]. 15 × 12 cm.—Map of battles on Bull Run, near Manassas . . . made from observation by Solomon Bamberger. Richmond, West & Johnson. Photographed on wood from the original drawing & engraved by Waters & Son, N.Y. [Map is identified as a "Very curious rebel semi-official pictorial view of the battle of Bull Run."] 20 × 23 cm.—The seat of war in Missouri. The important points of the war, showing the positions of the rebels under Generals McCulloch and Price, and the advance of the Union troops under Generals Fremont, Hunter, Siegel [sic], Sturgis, &c., &c. 23 × 25 cm.—The upper Potomac. Map of the Potomac from Washington to Harper's Ferry, showing the scene of operations of Generals Banks and Stone. 25 × 24 cm.—The scene of action. Official plan of the forts at Hilton Head and Bay Point, Port Royal Harbor, S.C., showing one position of the naval vessels during the action of November 7, 1861. 14 × 12 cm.—Fort Walker. Diagram of the fort at Hilton Head, with position of guns. 14 × 12 cm.—Seat of war around Paducah and Columbus, Georgia [i.e., Kentucky] 13 × 12 cm.—The seat of war in western Virginia. The localities of the army of occupation—the positions of Generals Rosencrans, Reynolds, Cox, Schenck, Benham, & c., on the Union side, and those of the rebel Generals Lee, Floyd, Anderson &c. 25 × 24 cm.—The grea[t] naval expedition. The coast of South Carolina from Georgetown, [S.C.] and Savannah, Ga., showing Port Royal entrance and Beaufort, with their railroads and water connections with Charleston and Savannah. 25 × 24 cm.

14.8

————War maps and diagrams. Drawn by E. S. Hall. Engraved by Waters & Son, N.Y. New York, November 16, 1861. Uncolored. Various scales. 48 × 37 cm.

Incomplete copy of the map supplement issued by the *New York Herald.* Library of Congress bound copy of the newspaper for October-December 1861 does not include the map supplement.

Contents: Our naval and military operations at a glance. The coast and land line of the rebellious states—The Union blockade of the Atlantic and Gulf coast—The rebel batteries on the Mississippi—The forts on the southern sea line. 38 × 36 cm.—[verso] The seat of war in the West. Map of the scene of operations in southeastern Missouri, Illinois and Tennessee, with the positions of the rebel troops and portions of the Federal forces, and the defences at Cairo and Bird's Point. 42 × 24 cm.

For an earlier issue of the map "Our naval and military operations at a glance," see entry no. 12.6.

14.85

Philadelphia Publishing Company.

The theatre of war or the stage as set for the opening scenes of 1861. Copyright 1893 by L. H. Everts, Philadelphia, Pa. A. H. Mueller, lith., Philada. New York and Philadelphia, Philadelphia Publishing Company, ©1893. Colored. Scale ca. 1:4,500,000. 42 × 56 cm.

General map of the South and adjoining states showing state boundaries, cities and towns, projected and completed railroads, and forts.

Stamped in the lower right corner: Library of Congress, City of Washington, Copyright, Jul 8 1893. 32155 yl.

14.9

Prang (Louis) and Company.

Birds eye view of the seat of war. Arranged after the latest surveys, showing views of Washington, Baltimore, Harpers Ferry, Richmond, Manassas Junction, Ft. Monroe, Norfolk Harbor &c. their r.r. connections, & the general surface of the country in Maryland, Dist. of Columbia, & Virginia. Pubd. & lithd. by L. Prang & Co., Boston. [1861?] Colored view. 41 × 50 cm.

"J. Haven, sole agent, 31 Exchange St." printed in the lower right margin.

Panoramic map looking South from Baltimore to Cape Henry.

15

————Distance maps. Map of the Atlantic states, showing 50 mile distances from Washington. Map of the battleground [at Manassas] showing 5 mile distances from Washington. Map of the Fortress Monroe, showing 1 mile distances from the fortress. Boston, ©1861. Colored. Various scales. 3 maps on sheet 59 × 39 cm.

Imperfect. Left center portion is wanting.

Each map indicates forts, towns, railroads, and rivers.

Insets: Position of forces at Bull Run. 8 × 8 cm.—Fortress Monroe, Old Point Comfort, Virginia. 8 × 8 cm.

Population statistics given in side borders.

16

————Map of the seat of war! Containing a map of the vicinity of Washington, Baltimore, Harper's Ferry and Annapolis, with five mile distance lines from Washington. Map showing the railroad routes, coast lines and forts, between Boston and Norfolk harbor; map of Norfolk harbor, Fort Monroe and vicinity, with 1 mile distance lines from Ft. Monroe; Map of the vicinity of Richmond. Small map of the Atlantic states, showing the R.road connections; diagram of the camp at Cairo. Plan of Harper's Ferry! Portraits of Gen. B. F. Butler, the late Col. E. Ellsworth, &c. Boston ©1861. Colored. Various scales. 6 maps on sheet 70 × 54 cm.

17

————Another issue.

Includes portraits of Andrew Jackson and Gen. Winfield Scott rather than those of Gen. B. F. Butler and Col. E. Ellsworth.

17.3

Schedler, J.

Birds eye view of Virginia, Maryland, Delaware and the District of Columbia. Drawn and engr. by J. Schedler, N.Y.

Sarony, Major & Knapp liths., N.Y. New York, W. Schaus; Paris, François Delarue; London, H. Graves & Co., ©1861. Colored. Scale ca. 1:1,203,840. 47 × 52 cm.

At top of map: The seat of war.

"Entered according to Act of Congress in the year 1861 by W. Schaus."

This is a map and not a bird's-eye view. It indicates forts, towns, railroads, principal roads, and relief by shading.

Insets: [Lower Mississippi Valley] 15 × 13 cm.—[Richmond and vicinity] 7 × 8 cm.

17.35

————————Another edition. Scale ca. 1:820,000. 64 × 77 cm.

Inset: [Map of eastern United States] 21 × 18 cm.

Label pasted to the map in the lower right margin: Metropolitan Book Store, Philp & Solomons, agents, Washington, D.C.

17.4

————————Military map of the middle and southern states showing the seat of war during the great rebellion in 1861. Drawn and engr. by J. Schedler. Lith. of Sarony, Major & Knapp, N.Y. New York, W. Schaus; Paris, François Delarue; London, H. Graves & Co. [186–?] Scale ca. 1:2,370,000. Col. map 62 × 82 cm.

General map of the southeastern states showing roads, railroads, cities and towns, rivers, state boundaries, and relief by hachures.

17.45

————————Another issue. 62 × 84 cm.

Lacks names of lithographers.

17.5

Schönberg & Company.

The Mississippi, [Alton to the Gulf of Mexico] as seen from the hurricane deck. Constructed from reliable sources. New York, Schönberg & Co., 1861. Colored. Scale 1:380,160. 5 maps, each 59 × 11 cm. on sheet 77 × 60 cm.

"These five slips may be cut, and joined in one piece, forming a panorama nearly ten feet long."

Copyright no. 19, Oct. 7, 1861 written in ink in margin. Stamped "Deposited in U. S. District Clerk's Office, Southern District of New York" and "Copyright Library, May 15, 1862."

General map indicating the location of a few forts.

Another copy is mounted as a scroll. 302 × 11 cm. (See G4042 .M5 1861 .S3 Vault Shelf.)

Another copy is mounted as a scroll in a tube measuring 11 × 4 cm. The label on the tube reads "The Mississippi, Alton to the Gulf of Mexico as seen from the hurricane deck." (See G4042 .M5 1861 .S3 Vault Shelf Copy 2.)

17.55

Stanford, Edward.

Stanford's map of the seat of war in America. London, 1861. Colored. Scale ca. 1:1,800,000. 4 sheets, each 69 × 56 cm. or smaller. Each sheet cut and hinged to fold to 18 × 10 cm.

Sheet 1 is dated Aug. 21, 1861 and sheets 2, 3, and 4 are dated Oct. 1, 1861.

Map of eastern United States showing state and county boundaries, cities and towns, rivers, roads, and railroads. Although battlefields are not specifically identified, several towns in eastern Virginia and southern Pennsylvania where battles occurred have been underlined in red. Fredericksburg has been marked with an x.

17.6

Thayer, Horace.

Seat of war. Published by Horace Thayer, N. York. ©1861. Uncolored. Scale ca. 1:2,300,000. 21 × 24 cm.

General map of eastern and central Virginia, Maryland, Delaware, New Jersey, and southern Pennsylvania showing railroads and place names.

Copyright registration no. "191 June 7, 1861" written in lower margin.

Inset: Diagram of the United States, showing the political divisions and the population. 15 × 24 cm.

17.65

————————Thayer's statistical and military map of the middle and southern states. New York, H. Thayer, 1861. Uncolored. Scale ca. 1:3,800,000. 57 × 77 cm.

General map.

Stamped in the upper right corner: Nov. 15, 1861.

Includes a list of "The Principal Forts in the United States" and brief descriptions of the "Position of the Rebel and Neutral States."

Inset: Seat of war [in the Middle Atlantic States] published by Horace Thayer, N. York. 21 × 24 cm.—Diagram of the United States showing the political divisions and the population. The white and colored population being separately shown in the slave states. 16 × 24 cm.

Copyright registration no. "192 June 7, 1861" written in the right margin.

17.7

U.S. *Coast Survey.*

Preliminary chart of the Atlantic coast from Cape Hatteras to Cape Florida. Autographic transfer 1861. [Engd. by?] J. W. Maedel. [Washington, U.S. Coast Survey] 1861. Uncolored. Scale 1:1,200,000. 96 × 51 cm.

At head of title: U.S. Coast Survey, A.D. Bache, Supdt.

General chart indicating soundings, lighthouses, 10-

and 100-fathom bottom contours, and the "axis of the Gulf-stream."

Another copy in the Geography and Map Division has been annotated to show "Lights, July 1862."

17.75

——————Preliminary chart of the northeastern part of the Gulf of Mexico, including the Strait of Florida. Autographic transfer 1861. [Washington, U.S. Coast Survey, 1861] Uncolored. Scale 1:600,000. 80 × 180 cm.

At head of title: U.S. Coast Survey, A.D. Bache, Supdt.

Chart of the coast from Mobile Bay, Alabama, to St. Lucie Inlet, Florida, indicating soundings and bottom contours at 6, 12, and 18 feet.

17.8

——————Preliminary chart of the northwestern part of the Gulf of Mexico. Unfinished proof. [Washington, U.S. Coast Survey, 1861] Uncolored. Scale 1:600,000. 80 × 175 cm.

At head of title: U.S. Coast Survey, A.D. Bache, Supdt.

Chart of the Gulf coast from Pensacola Bay to the Rio Grande (Rio Bravo del Norte) showing soundings and bottom contours at 6, 12, and 18 feet.

"Note. In portions of this chart where no soundings have yet been made by the Coast Survey, they have been taken from the Admiralty chart of Gauld's survey made in 1764 to 1771, which agree well with the Coast Survey soundings in positions covered by both."

17.85

——————A reconnaissance of the Potomac River from Point Lookout to Washington City. Executed by Lieut Comd'g T. S. Phelps, U.S.N., Assist, U.S.C.S. J. W. Maedel. 1861. Uncolored. Scale 1:200,000. 67 × 60 cm.

At head of title: U. S. Coast Survey, A.D. Bache, Supdt.

Pencil note in the bottom margin reads "This is the first chart of the Potomac River issued by the Coast and Geodetic Survey. Inform. obtained from C. & G. (Mr. Ellis) Aug. 23, 1932."

Preliminary chart indicating place names and soundings.

Includes "Sailing directions for the Potomac River."

18

Viele, Egbert L., and Charles Haskins.

H. H. Lloyd & Co's. campaign military charts showing the principal strategic places of interest. Compiled from official data, by Egbert L. Viele and Charles Haskins, military and civil engineers. Published under the auspices of the American Geographical and Statistical Society. New York, H. H. Lloyd & Co., ©1861. Colored. Various scales. 16 maps on sheet 96 × 73 cm.

"H. H. Lloyd & Co's. military charts. Sixteen maps on one sheet."

Maps of Annapolis, Key West, the Mississippi River, Chesapeake Bay and vicinity, Charleston, New Orleans, Savannah, Mobile Bay, the United States, Cairo, Pensacola Bay, Galveston Bay, Norfolk, Hampton Roads, Washington, D.C., and Harpers Ferry.

In general, the maps indicate forts, towns, railroads, and rivers.

18.3

Winch, A.

Interesting bird's eye view of the seat of war. Showing parts of the states of Maryland, Delaware, Virginia, and North Carolina; and also the coast line from Cape Henry to Fort Pickens, with the United States blockading fleet. For sale by A. Winch, Philadelphia. [1861?] Uncolored view. 41 × 53 cm.

"The above bird's-eye view of the seat of war, shows the relative position of the important points embraced in all the great military operations now in progress on the Atlantic slope."

Description of early events in the war and important places appears below panoramic map.

18.5

Wyld, James.

Strategic war points of the United States. London, James Wyld [1861?] Uncolored. Scales vary. 4 maps on sheet 35 × 52 cm., cut and mounted to fold to 18 × 11 cm.

Cover title: Wyld's new map of the country round Richmond and Washington . . . London, James Wyld.

Contents: [1] The country round Washington, the Chesapeake and the Potomac. 34 × 38 cm.; [2] City of Washington and District of Columbia. 13 × 14 cm.; [3] Pensacola Bay and its fortifications, (Florida). 10 × 13 cm.; [4] Charleston and the harbour (South Carolina). 10 × 9 cm.

List of "new publications" printed on the left side of the sheet. Lists of other maps appear inside the cover and attached to the verso.

Signed "H. H. Horton" on the verso.

18.7

——————Strategic war points of the United States. [London, James Wyld 1861?] Uncolored. Scales vary. 5 maps on sheet 34 × 52 cm., cut and mounted to fold to 17 × 11 cm.

Contents: 1. Country round Washington. 18 × 25 cm.; 2. Charleston and the harbour (South Carolina). 10 × 9 cm.; 3. The country round the Chesapeake and the Potomac to Washington. 34 × 25 cm.; 4. City of Washington and District of Columbia. 13 × 14 cm.; 5. Pensacola Bay and its fortifications, (Florida). 10 × 13 cm.

List of "new publications" at the bottom of the sheet.

Advertisement for Wyld's atlases and maps of the world, London, Italy, Germany, and China is attached to the verso.

19

—————Wyld's military map of the United States, the northern states, and the southern confederate states: with the forts, harbours, arsenals, and military positions. London, May 1861. Colored. Scale ca. 1:4,600,000. 88 × 61 cm. Cut and mounted to fold to 20 × 13 cm.

"Slave states" outlined in blue.

Insets: City of Washington and District of Columbia. Scale ca. 1:190,000. 13 × 14 cm. Country round Washington. Scale ca. 1:1,020,000. 18 × 24 cm.—Pensacola bay and its fortifications. Scale ca. 1:155,000. 12 × 14 cm.—Charleston and the harbour. Scale ca. 1:132,000. 10 × 9 cm.

1862

20

Asher and Company.

The historical war map. E. R. Jewett & Co., engravers, Buffalo, N.Y. ©1862. Colored. Scale ca. 1:3,250,000. 62 × 87 cm.

Map of southeastern United States showing forts and battlefields, railroads, state boundaries, rivers, and town.

Includes brief descriptions of the principal engagements. The last battle described is the capitulation of Norfolk, May 10, 1862.

21

—————Another issue. ©1862. 62 × 62 cm.

Principal engagements are not described in this or in the following issues (entry nos. 22 and 23).

Population statistics and "Date[s] of admission and secession of the Southern States" are given in the lower left corner.

21.1

—————Another copy. *In* Russell, Benjamin B. The historical war map. Boston [1862] 24 p.

Pamphlet includes descriptions of engagements through the battle of "Culpeper or Cedar Mountain" fought August 9, 1862. Following four maps are also included in the pamphlet:

[p. 7] Map of the battle of Bull Run.

[p. 15] Fort Donelson.

[p. 17] Map of Shiloh battle ground.

[p. 21] Richmond, Va. and vicinity.

Gift of John Davis Batchelder.

22

—————Another issue. ©1862. 62 × 62 cm. *In* Russell, Benjamin B. The historical war map. Boston [186–] 72 p.

E468.3.R8

Includes inset maps entitled "South-east Virginia," "North-east Virginia," "Vicksburg and vicinity," and "Charleston and vicinity."

23

—————Another issue. ©1862. 62 × 62 cm. *From* Taylor, Hudson. The historical war map. Washington, [1863] 72 p.

Similar to the preceding issue (entry no. 22). Includes inset maps entitled "South-east Virginia," "North-east Virginia," "Vicksburg and vicinity," and "Charleston and vicinity."

23.5

Bachmann, John.

Birds eye view of Kentucky and Tennessee showing Cairo and part of the southern states. Drawn from nature and lith. by John Bachmann. New York, John Bachmann, ©1861 [i.e., 1862] Col. view 54 × 73 cm.

At top of map: Panorama of the seat of war.

Panoramic view looking south from Cairo, Illinois, showing parts of Illinois, Missouri, Kentucky, Tennessee, and Arkansas. Smoke over Fort Donelson, Tennessee, and the presence of gunboats on the Cumberland River depict the fort's fall to Union forces in February 1862.

24

Bacon and Company.

Bacon's military map of the United States shewing the forts & fortifications. Ent. Sta. Hall: Aug. 1862. London, 1862. Colored. Scale ca. 1:8,000,000. 39 × 67 cm.

At top of map: 1s. Bacon's military map of America. 1s.

Forts are named and marked by small flags. Map also includes towns, railroads, names and boundaries of states and territories, and relief by hachures.

"Free or non-slaveholding states" are colored green, "border slave states" are yellow, and "seceded or Confederate States" are pink.

25

Blunt, Edmund, *and* George W. Blunt.

Sketch of the Atlantic and Gulf Coasts of the United States showing the loyal part, and the parts of the coasts of the rebellious states in actual possession of the U.S. troops. Lith of J. Bien, N.Y. New York [1862?] Uncolored. Scale not given. 50 × 54 cm.

Lower right corner of the copy is wanting.

"This sketch was prepared to show at a glance the dif-

SKETCH

OF THE

ATLANTIC AND GULF COASTS

OF THE

UNITED STATES

Showing the Loyal part, and the parts of the coasts of the

REBELLIOUS STATES.

in actual possession of the U.S. troops.

E. & G.W. BLUNT.
179 Water Street New York.

ference in extent of the coasts of the U. States occupied by the loyal men and rebels; its circulation it is believed will have the effect of counteracting the exertions of traitors at home as well as those abroad. Persons having correspondents in Europe would do well to send copies of this sketch to them for circulation. The figures . . . show the depth of water. Geo. W. Blunt."

"Loyal part" of the coast is distinguished by a heavy line and the "rebel part" by a thin line.

Principal coastal features are named.

The well-known chartmakers Edmund and George W. Blunt produced this interesting propaganda map entitled "Sketch of the Atlantic and Gulf Coast of the United States Showing the Loyal Part, and the Parts of the Coasts of the Rebellious States in Actual Possession of the U.S. Troops." George Blunt explained that "This sketch was prepared to show at a glance the difference in extent of the coasts of the U. States occupied by the loyal men and rebels; its circulation it is believed will have the effect of counteracting the exertions of traitors at home as well as those abroad." Note how the Blunts skillfully depict the "loyal part" of the coast with a heavy (strong) line and the "rebel part" with a thin (weak) line. (See entry no. 25.)

25.3

Colton, George Woolworth.

G. Woolworth Colton's new guide map of the United States & Canada, with railroads, counties, etc. Drawn, engraved & published by G. Woolworth Colton, New York. Chicago, Rufus Blanchard, 1862. Colored. Scale 1:3,168,000. 77 × 93 cm.

"Entered according to Act of Congress in the year 1861, by G. Woolworth Colton."

General map annotated in red and blue to show military departments.

Insets: Plan of the southern portion of Florida. 16 × 13 cm.—Western portion of the United States. 18 × 20 cm.—The southern portion of Texas. 9 × 10 cm.

Includes tables of "Cities and towns with a population of 10,000 and over" and "Population of the United States."

"Drawer 47, portfolio 1, no. 28" written in the right margin.

25.5

Colton, Joseph H.

Colton's map of the southern states, including Maryland, Delaware, Virginia, Kentucky, Tennessee, Missouri, North Carolina, South Carolina, Georgia, Alabama, Mississippi, Arkansas, Louisiana, Texas, showing also part of adjoining states & territories locating the forts & military stations of the U. States & showing all the rail roads, r. r. stations, & other internal improvements. New York, J. H. Colton, 1862. Colored. Scale ca. 1: 1,520,640. 97 × 140 cut and mounted to fold to 22 × 13 cm.

"Entered according to Act of Congress in the year 1861 by J. H. Colton."

Printed by Lang & Laing, N. Y.

"No. 6" in the upper left margin.

Insets: Southern part of Florida. 27 × 20 cm.—Colton's map of the United States showing the proposed railroad routes to the Pacific Ocean. 19 × 26 cm.

Includes tables of population based on the "United States Census for 1860."

Cover title: Colton's map of the southern states of America, showing the whole seat of war on the seabord [sic] and in the interior, designating every town, railway, and stream; also showing the forts and fortifications. London, Bacon and Co.

Pasted inside the cover is a list of "Bacon's shilling series of American war maps, just published."

Advertisement for "Bacon's guide to American politics" and a list of "Colton's maps of America, and complete series of war maps" are pasted to the verso of the map.

"Explanations" (i.e., legend) is pasted over the bottom border. Map is colored to show "free, or non-slaveholding states" (pink), "border slave states" (yellow), and "seceded or confederate states" (green).

1861 editions are listed as entry nos. 6.5–6.6; 1863 edition is listed as entry no. 37.6.

25.6

——————Another issue.

"References" are printed to the right of the map off the coast of Georgia.

The Geography and Map Division has another copy of this issue which has been annotated with numbers in red and dashes in blue to indicate the limits of freshwater in the rivers as "referred to in a *Memoir on freshwater stations* along the coast of the United States, south of Cape Henolopen [sic]: compiled from the communications of assistants and sub assistants of the U.S. Coast Survey, June 22, 1861" (G3860 1862.C6 Vault).

25.7

——————Colton's new railroad & county map of the United States, the Canadas &c. New York, J. H. Colton, 1862. Colored. Scale ca. 1:3,120,000. 85 × 99 cm. mounted to fold to 22 × 13 cm.

"Entered according to Act of Congress in the year 1861 by J. H. Colton."

"Explanations" (i.e., legend) is pasted over the bottom margin. Map is colored to show "free, or non-slaveholding states" (pink), "border slave states" (yellow), and "seceded or confederate states" (green).

Inset: Colton's map of the United States showing the proposed railroad routes to the Pacific Ocean. 19 × 26 cm.

Advertisement for "Bacon's shilling war maps" is pasted onto the verso.

25.8

——————Colton's new topographical map of the states of Virginia, Maryland and Delaware, showing also eastern Tennessee & parts of other adjoining states, all the fortifications, military stations, rail roads, common roads and other internal improvements. Compiled from the latest & most authentic sources, on a scale of 12 miles to the inch. New York, J. H. Colton, 1862. Uncolored. Scale 1:760,320. 4 parts, each 40 × 57 cm.

Lang & Laing Lith, N.Y.

"Entered according to Act of Congress in the year 1862 by J. H. Colton."

"No. 9" printed in the upper left corner.

Copyright no. "150, Dec. 3, 1861" is written in ink in the left margin. Stamped "Copyright Library May 15, 1862."

General map showing state and county boundaries, roads and railroads, fortifications, and place names. Drawings of ships offshore depict the Union blockade of the coast.

Geography and Map Division also has a colored copy.

1864 edition listed as entry no. 48.2

25.9

————————Another issue.

Additional place names associated with the Civil War have been added, such as Stone Bridge on Bull Run, and Fort Darling, Fair Oaks, and Chickahominy in the environs of Richmond.

"No. 9" is dropped from the upper left corner.

26

————————Colton's plans of U.S. harbors showing the position & vicinities of the most important fortifications on the sea-board and in the interior. From U.S. surveys and other authentic sources. Printed by Lang & Laing, New York. New York, J. H. Colton, 1862. Colored. Various scales. 50 × 79 cm. Cut and mounted to fold to approximately 17 × 12 cm.

"No. 5" in upper left margin.

23 maps on one sheet as follows: The Mississippi River from Cairo to New Orleans. 49 × 14 cm.—St. Louis and vicinity. 11 × 10 cm.—Cairo and vicinity. 11 × 10 cm.—Memphis and vicinity. 11 × 8 cm.—Ft. Smith and vicinity. 8 × 10 cm—Fernandina [Florida] and vicinity. 8 × 9 cm.—Louisville and vicinity. 8 × 8 cm.—Washington, D.C. & vicinity. 19 × 13 cm.—New York and vicinity. 19 × 11 cm.—Washington, Manassas Junction, Harpers Ferry, Baltimore, Annapolis &c. &c. 16 × 20 cm—Norfolk, Fortress Monroe, James River, Richmond, Petersburgh [sic]; &c. &c. 20 × 19 cm.—Savannah and vicinity. 10 × 17 cm.—Mobile harbor, Alabama. 14 × 9 cm.—New Orleans and delta of the Mississippi, Louisiana. 17 × 16 cm.—Charleston harbor and its approaches, S. Carolina. 14 × 14 cm.—Plan of Ft. Sumter. 5 × 4 cm.—Hampton Roads and Norfolk har., Virginia. 14 × 11 cm.—Beaufort and vicinity, N. Carolina. 8 × 9 cm.—Key West and Tortugas, Florida Reefs. 6 × 17 cm.—Galveston and vicinity, Texas. 7 × 9 cm.—Vicinity of the Rio Grande. 6 × 8 cm.—Entrance to Pensacola Bay, Florida. 13 × 16 cm.—Wilmington and vicinity, N. Carolina. 13 × 10 cm.

26.3

————————Colton's rail-road and military map of the United States, Mexico, the West Indies &c, by J. H. Colton, New York, 1862. Colored. Scale ca. 1:6,500,000. 81 × 107 cm.

G3700 1862.C65

"Entered according to Act of Congress in the year 1862 by J. H. Colton."

Printed by Lang & Laing, N.Y.

General map showing state and national boundaries, place names, forts, and railroads. "Free, or non-slaveholding states" are red, "border slave states" are yellow, and "seceded or confederate states" are green. An "Explanation" (i.e., legend) has been pasted on the map in the lower margin.

Insets: Colton's map of the Americas, Africa, and a portion of Europe, showing the Atlantic and part of the Pacific Oceans. 29 × 35 cm.—New Orleans and delta of the Mississippi, Louisiana. 17 × 16 cm.—Mobile harbor, Alabama. 14 × 9 cm.—Key West and Tortugas, Florida Reefs. 7 × 17 cm.—Wilmington and vicinity, N. Carolina. 13 × 10 cm.—Beaufort and vicinity, N. Carolina. 8 × 9 cm.—Norfolk, Fortress Monroe, James River, Richmond, Petersburgh [sic] &c&c. 18 × 18 cm.—Map of Charleston, Port Royal & Savannah vicinities. 14 × 25 cm.—Washington, Manassas Junction, Harpers Ferry, Baltimore, Annapolis &c&c. 16 × 20 cm.

Includes population tables based on the 1850 and 1860 censuses.

27

Hall, Edward S.

Lloyd's new military map of the border & southern states. Drawn by Edward S. Hall. Waters & Son, engravers. Published by H. H. Lloyd & Co., New York. 1862. Colored. Scale ca. 1:1,850,000. 76 × 105 cm.

At top of Map: H. H. Lloyd & Co's. new military map of the southern and border states. Agents wanted to sell this and m[an]y other maps and charts for the times.

Inset: [Map of southern Florida] 16 × 11 cm.

Battlefields are marked by red lines and strategic places by red dots.

Indicates towns, railroads, rivers, names and boundaries of states, and relief by hachures.

Corinth, Mississippi, is incorrectly identified as Farmington in this issue.

1863 edition listed as entry no. 38 and 1865 edition as entry no. 71.

27.2

————————Another issue.

"Agents wanted to sell this and many other maps and charts for the Times" dropped from upper margin.

"Published by H. H. Lloyd & Co, 25 Howard St., New York. Agents wanted to sell this and many other new and popular works" is printed in the lower margin.

Map correctly identifies Corinth, Mississippi.

27.5

Joerg, Wolfgang L. G.

Civil War campaigns of 1862. Prepared for the Chronicles of America under the direction of W. L. G. Joerg, American Geographical Society. Julius Bien lith., N.Y. Colored. Scale 1:13,000,000. 11 × 18 cm. *From* Wood, William. Captains of the Civil War; a chronicle of the blue and the gray. New Haven, Yale University Press, 1921. (The

Chronicles of America series; Abraham Lincoln edition, vol. 31) facing p. 160.

Map depicts movements of McClellan, Grant, Buell, Farragut, Rosecrans, Lee, and Bragg, and the "Line of Federal military occupation April 15, 1862 (after Hart)."

28

Lloyd, James T.

Lloyd's map of the lower Mississippi River from St. Louis to the Gulf of Mexico. Compiled from Government surveys in the Topographical Bureau, Washington, D.C. Revised and corrected to the present time, by Captains Bart. and William Bowen, pilots of twenty years' experience on that river. New York, 1862. Colored. Scale 1:316,800. 5 sheets, each 95 × 27 cm. (Fillmore map. coll. no. 260)

Signed in ms: Millard Fillmore, March 9, 1863.

"Exhibiting the sugar and cotton plantations, cities, towns, landings, sand bars, islands, bluffs, bayous, cut-offs, the steamboat channel, mileage, fortifications, railroads, &c. along the river."

1863 edition listed as entry no. 41.

Listed in A. M. Modelski's *Railroad Maps of the United States* (Washington, Library of Congress, 1975), entry no. 139.

29

———————Lloyd's map of the southern states showing all the railroads, their stations & distances, also the counties, towns, villages, harbors, rivers, and forts. New York, 1862. Colored. Scale ca. 1:2,000,000. 97 × 145 cm. folded to 19 × 23 cm. (Fillmore map coll. no. 41)

Signed in ms: Millard Fillmore 1862.

Listed in A. M. Modelski's *Railroad Maps of the United States* (Washington, Library of Congress, 1975), entry no. 138.

1861 editions are listed as entry nos. 14.2–14.3 and the 1863 edition is listed as entry no. 41.2.

29.7

McClernand, John A.

[Map of Mississippi, Alabama and Tennessee, showing railroads, distances, rivers, and towns. September 28, 1862] Pen and ink ms. map drawn on tracing paper. Scale ca. 1:1,960,000. 38 × 44 cm.

In the Abraham Lincoln papers, Manuscript Division, L.C., vol. 88, no. 18723.

General map accompanying "Gnl. McClernand plan for putting down the rebellion, Sept. 28, 1862" (Lincoln papers, vol. 88, nos. 18709–18722).

30

McConnell, James

The Civil War, first year, 1861–1862. [Chicago, Mc-Connell Map Co., ©1919] Colored. Scale ca. 1:2,200,000. 69 × 107 cm. (McConnell's historical maps of the United States. Revised ed. Map no. 35)

Map of the Southeast, showing battles, "Confederate line" in the western theater, route of Grant and Halleck in 1862, towns, rivers, and state boundaries.

Inset: McClellan's peninsular campaign, March to September, 1862. Scale 1:950,400. 19 × 16 cm.

"Important battles [and the names of commanders], 1st year, April 1861–1862" listed in the lower left corner. Brief description of events appears in the lower right corner.

30.2

Magnus, Charles.

Magnus's county map of the United States, showing the forts, railroads, canals, and navigable waters. Published to trace the progress of operations by the government, as they occur, during the War of the Rebellion. Published by Charles Magnus, N.Y. [1862?] Colored. Scale 1:2,111,789. 79 × 103 cm.

Printed at the bottom of the map: Extra session of Congress map. Price 25 cents.

General map of the eastern United States showing finished railroads, railroads in progress, and chartered or projected railroads.

Insets: Fortress Monroe, Old Point Comfort and Hygeia Hotel, Va. [view] 10 × 19 cm.—Military map of Missouri, Kentucky & Tennessee. 12 × 19 cm.—Military map of Maryland & Virginia. 12 × 20 cm.

30.3

———————Western territory of the present war. Eastern territory of the present war. Pub. by C. Magnus, New York [1862] Colored. Scale ca. 1:1,900,000. 59 × 104 cm.

Two maps printed on sheet; the western territory map measures 59 × 43 cm. and the eastern territory map measures 59 × 48 cm.

Inset: Topographical map of the country between Fortress Monroe & Richmond. 10 × 19 cm.

Two maps have been attached to top margin: [Map of Washington, D.C., Alexandria, and Fairfax County, Virginia] 12 × 9 cm.—[Map of the Middle Atlantic and Midwestern states showing railroad lines] ©1861. 14 × 25 cm.

Includes 33 portraits of "Heroes of successful expeditions" and "Generals of the Union army and their antagonists."

31

Modern Supply School Company, *Chicago, Ill.*

The Civil War—first year, 1861–1862. Copyright by E. W. A. Rowles [Chicago, ©1919] Colored. Scale ca. 1:2,600,000. 69 × 108 cm. (Comprehensive series; historial—geographical maps of the United States, no. 31)

Wall map of the Southeast showing forts, battles, "extreme limit[s] of Federal control, April 15, 1861 [and] 1862," towns, and state boundaries. A brief description of the first year of the war appears in the upper right corner.

Inset: The Peninsular campaign, 1862. 31 × 31 cm.

31.1

Perrine, Charles O.

Perrine's new military map illustrating the seat of war. Entered according to Act of Congress, in the year 1862, by C. O. Perrine. Colored. Scale ca. 1:2,750,000. 59 × 74 cm.

G3860 1862.P4

General map of the southern states indicating place names, state boundaries, and railroads. States, coast lines, and forts are highlighted in yellow.

This issue lacks covers.

31.2

——————[Indianapolis, C.O. Perrine] 1862.

G3860 1862.P41

Publisher's name is taken from covers in which the map was originally folded.

Cover signed in pencil: Chas. Mount.

31.3

——————[New ed. Indianapolis, Asher & Co.] 1862.

G3860 1862.P42

Edition statement and name of publisher are taken from the covers in which map was originally folded.

31.5

Philadelphia Board of Trade. Committee on Inland Transportation.

Rail road map of the southern states shewing the southern & southwestern railway connections with Philadelphia. Prepared by Thomas Kimber, Jr., Chairman of the Committee on Inland Transportation of the Board of Trade of Philadelphia. From the latest accessible authorities. The coast accurately drawn from the U.S. Coast Surveys. Drawn & engraved by P. S. Duval & Son, lithrs., Philada. [Philadelphia] 1862. Colored. Scale ca. 1:1,880,000. 79 × 134 cm.

"Entered according to Act of Congress in the year 1862, by Thomas Kimber Jr."

Inset: Southern part of Florida. 25 × 18 cm.

Map depicts rail lines, roads, cities and towns, state and county boundaries, and rivers. 1863 edition published by Willis. P. Hazard is listed as entry no. 44.

Geography and Map Division also has an uncolored issue with annotations made by the Topographer, U.S. Post Office Department.

Another uncolored copy, in covers, is in the Samuel P. Heintzelman papers, Manuscript Division, L.C., container

no 11. Cover title: Map of the southern states. Map is in 29 parts, 16 × 12 cm.

31.6

Pomeroy, Samuel C.

[Proposed new railroad route from Washington, D.C. to Pittsburgh, Pa., October 15, 1862] Colored ms. map drawn on tracing linen. 27 × 56 cm.

In the Abraham Lincoln papers, Manuscript Division, L.C., vol. 90, no. 19029.

Signed on verso "S. C. Pomeroy, U.S.S."

Accompanies a three-page proposal to "lessen as much as possible the distance of travel from the Western States to the Capitol—not only in time of war, but also for the advantages of peaceful relations" (Lincoln papers, vol. 90, nos. 19027–19028).

Red ink indicates existing B&O tracks, and blue ink denotes proposed new routes.

31.7

Prang (Louis) and Company.

The model war map giving the southern & middle states, with all their water & railroad connections. Compiled from the best authorities & latest surveys by L. Prang & Co., lithographers & publishers, Boston. [1862?] Uncolored. Scale ca. 1:2,217,600. 62 × 93 cm.

General map printed in green ink.

Imperfect: pieces are missing from along the center fold and at the bottom.

Includes tables giving "routes and distances," "population of the United States from the Census of 1860," and "Number of white males in each state between the ages of 18 and 45."

"This map, in combination with our *War-Telegram Marking Map* [published in 1862] will be found a sufficient and easy guide to follow up all the various movements of the contesting armies."

32

Robertson, H. C.

First attempt to open the Mississippi. [1862. Chicago, R. O. Evans and Co. ©1898] Colored. Scale not given. 83 × 58 cm. (Robertson's geographic–historical series illustrating the history of America and the United States)

Wall map of the Western theater of war, showing location and date of engagements.

Includes an outline of events; views of "The attack on Fort Donelson," "Battle between the Monitor and Merrimac," and "New Orleans—fleet passing forts Jackson and St. Philip;" and portraits of Foote, Farragut, and Porter.

32.5

Smith, John Calvin.

The new naval and military map of the United States, by J. Calvin Smith. J. M. Atwood, map engraver, Philadelphia, Pa. 1862. Colored. Scale ca. 1:3,275,000. 2 parts, each 173 × 86 cm.

"Entered according to Act of Congress in the year 1862 by Robert P. Smith."

Stamped in right-hand corner: Copyright Library, Jan. 12, 1863.

General map of the United States, Mexico, and Central America showing national, state, and county boundaries, cities and towns, mail routes and wagon roads, railroads built and in progress, canals, and relief by hachures. The "date of organization of counties," in some instances, is noted.

Handwritten note on verso: No. 385 Deposited Oct. 27, 1862 (22245) Robert Persall [i.e. Pearsall] Smith proprietor.

Insets (maps): Map showing the fall of rain and mean annual temperature with the mountains, plains & river systems of the United States. 20 × 39 cm.—Map of the world on Mercators projection [with an inset showing prevailing religions] 22 × 37 cm.—Map showing the distribution of the slave and free colored population of the United States. 21 × 28 cm.—Map showing the distribution of staples in colors with the principle articles of export marked in the states severally also the distribution of plants, trees and animals by Thomas Meehan. 21 × 31 cm.

Insets (views, some symbolic): The rescue of the Union. 19 × 31 cm.—Washington [city] 22 × 37 cm.—Response of the army & navy. 21 × 20 cm.—The birth of the Union—battle of Bunker Hill. 19 × 31 cm.—Victory of the Monitor (2 guns) over the Merrimac (10 guns) March 9th 1862. 21 × 29 cm.—Scene of camp life. 11 × 24 cm.

Includes tables giving "the census of 1860 in advance of official publication," size, population, and date of admission of states, "ports of entry in the United States," time differences, "air-line distances," "Union loss in the present rebellion," and distances of "pony express mail and telegraph routes."

Includes profiles showing "Lieut. A. W. Whipples T.E. route for Pacific R. R. . . . ," 3 × 22 cm., "United States on latit[ud]e 42° N. from the Atlantic to the Pacific Ocean," 3 × 33 cm., and "Telegraphic plateau," Atlantic Ocean, 3 × 27 cm.

Decorative border includes the following portraits of prominent Union figures: President Lincoln, Messrs. Jos. Holt, G. G. Welles, S. P. Chase, and S. Cameron, Governor Sprague, Generals McClellan, Anderson, Sigel, Lyon, Lander, Dix, Pope, Fremont, Burnside, Banks, Scott, Wool, Halleck, Mansfield, McDowell, Blenker, Rosecrans, and Butler, Colonels Ellsworth and Corcoran, and Commodores Du Pont, Stringham, Wilkes and Foote.

32.6

————Another issue. Philadelphia, J. Baker, ©1862.

"J. M. Atwood, map engraver, Philadelphia, Pa." has been dropped from this issue.

Some views shown in insets have been repositioned. "The birth of the Union—battle of Bunker Hill" has been dropped and "Niagara Falls" has been added.

Portraits in a decorative border have been rearranged and the following changes have occurred. Dropped: Messrs. Holt and Cameron, Generals Lander, Wool, Mansfield, McDowell, and Blenker, Governor Sprague, and Commodore Stringham; Added: Messrs. Stanton, Seward, and Sumner, Generals Hooker, Hunter, Heintzelman, and Kearny, and Commodore Porter.

32.7

————Another issue.

Similar to the preceding issue except that Generals Meade's and Grant's portraits have been substituted for General Kearny's and Colonel Ellsworth's.

32.9

The Sun.

Map of the southern states, including rail roads, county towns, state capitals, county roads, the southern coast from Delaware to Texas, showing the harbors, inlets, forts and position of blockading ships. [New York] The Sun, 1862. Uncolored. Scale ca. 1:3,000,000. 51 × 77 cm.

In the Charles De Haven Jones papers, Manuscript Division, L.C.

At bottom of map: Presented to the subscribers of The Sun. Moses S. Beach, Proprietor, January 4th, 1862.

Inset: [Map of Washington, D.C. and vicinity] Scale ca. 1:380,000. 20 × 18 cm.

Includes portraits of Lincoln, Scott, Seward, and McClellan.

Map was also published in *Harper's weekly,* Nov. 9, 1861 (entry no. 14.55) and by Bacon and Company, ca. 1863 (entry no. 37).

33

Sweet, S. H.

Map shewing the several routes proposed for the passage of gun-boats to the Lakes via Erie and Oswego Canal, Champlain Canal, Illinois River and Chicago Canal, [and] Wisconsin River and Green Bay Canal. Prepared by S. H. Sweet, Dep. State Engr. and Surveyor. Lith. of C. Van Benthuysen, Albany, N.Y. 1862. Uncolored. Scale not given. 35 × 81 cm.

Map of northeast United States and part of Canada, indicating international and state boundaries, canals, and principal towns.

Annotated in red to show the "Chicago, Oswego, Rutland and Portland Rail way."

Another copy filed G3711.P5 1862. S9.

33.5

U.S. *Coast Survey.*

Chesapeake Bay from its head to Potomac River. From a trigonometrical survey under the direction of F. R. Hassler and A. D. Bache, Superintendents of the survey of the coast of the United States. [Washington, U.S. Coast Survey] 1861–1862. Uncolored. Scale 1:80,000. 3 sheets, each 76 × 96 cm. *From its* Report of the Superintendent of the Coast Survey, showing the progress of the survey during the year 1864 (Washington, Government Printing Office, 1866). Maps 17–19.

At head of title: Coast charts nos. 31, 32, 33.

Overall title cited above appears on coast chart no. 32 (map 18).

Contents: Coast chart no. 31. Chesapeake Bay from head of Bay to Magothy River . . . Triangulation by J. Ferguson, T. W. Werner, J. E. Johnstone, Capt. Topographical Engineers, U.S.A. Assistants. Topography by T. W. Werner, J. J. S. Hassler, R. D. Cutts, G. D. Wise, Assts., J. C. Neilson, Sub-Asst., J. B. Gluck & H. L. Whiting, Assts. Hydrography by the parties under the command of Lieuts. Comdg. G. M. Bache, S. P. Lee, W. P. McArthur, C. H. McBlair & R. Wainwright, U.S.N. Assts. Published in 1861. ("No. 17" in upper left corner)

No. 32. From Magothy River to Choptank River. Triangulation by J. Ferguson, F. H. Gerdes, J. E. Johnstone, Capt. Topl. Engrs., E. Blunt, J. E. Hilgard, Assts. and A. D. Bache, Supdt. Topography by H. L. Whiting, F. H. Gerdes, Assts., J. C. Neilson, Sub-Asst., J. J. S. Hassler, R. D. Cutts & G. D. Wise, Assts. Hydrography by the parties under the command of Lieut Comdg. G. M. Bache, S. P. Lee & W. P. McArthur, U.S.N. Assts. Published in 1862. ("No. 18" in upper left corner)

Coast chart no. 33. Chesapeake Bay from Choptank River to Potomac River . . . Triangulation by E. Blunt, J. E. Hilgard, J. S. Williams and R. D. Cutts, Assistants. Topography by J. J. S. Hassler, G. D. Wise, R. D. Cutts, Assts., J. Seib & S. A. Wainwright, Sub-Assts. & H. L. Whiting, Asst. Hydrography by the parties under the command of Lieuts Comdg. W. P. McArthur, S. P. Lee and J. J. Almy, U.S.N. Assistants. Published in 1862 ("No. 19" in upper left corner)

33.7

————General chart of the coast. No. IV, from Cape May to Cape Henry. From a trigonometrical survey under the direction of F. R. Hassler and A. D. Bache, Superin-

tendents of the survey of the coast of the United States. [Washington, U.S. Coast Survey] 1862. Uncolored. Scale 1:400,000. 72 × 83 cm. *From its* Report of the Superintendent of the Coast Survey, showing the progress of the survey during the year 1862 (Washington, Government Printing Office., 1864). Map 14.

"No. 14" in the upper left corner.

"The triangulation was executed by E. Blunt, J. E. Johnstone, J. Farley & J. E. Hilgard, Assistants between 1841 & 1853. The topography was executed by F. H. Gerdes, J. C. Neilson, J. J. S. Hassler, G. D. Wise, J. Seib, Assists., N. S. Finney, J. Mechan & C. Ferguson, Sub-Assists., between 1842 & 1859. The hydrography was executed by Lieuts. Comdg. T. R. Gedney, G. S. Blake, G. M. Bache, S. P. Lee, R. Bache, B. E. Sands & J. J. Almy, U.S.N. Assists., between 1841 & 1855."

34

————Historical sketch of the rebellion. Published at the Office of the Coast Survey. May 1862. Colored. Scale ca. 1:5,850,000. 47 × 45 cm.

Indicates "limits of loyal states in July, 1861," "limits occupied by United States forces March 1st 1862," "limits occupied by United States forces May 15th 1862," railroads, rivers, names and boundaries of states, and principal towns.

See also entry nos. 35, 36, 39, 40, 40.1, and 49.

35

————Another edition. July 1862.

Indicates by colored lines the "limits of loyal states in July, 1861, limits occupied by United States forces March 1st 1862 . . . May 15th 1862 . . .[and] July 15th 1862."

See also entry nos. 34, 36, 39, 40, 40.1, and 49.

35.2

————Potomac River (in four sheets). [Washington, D.C.] 1862. Uncolored. Scale 1:40,000 and 1:60,000. 4 sheets, 99 × 59 cm. or smaller.

Sheets 1 to 3 titled as above; sheet 4 titled "Preliminary chart of the Potomac River (in four sheets)."

Sheets 1 to 3 published at the scale of 1:60,000; sheet 4 is at 1:40,000.

Chart of the Potomac River from Washington, D.C., to its entrance into the Chesapeake Bay. Chart indicates soundings, lighthouses, and the shore line configuration.

Contents:

1. From entrance to Piney Point . . . Triangulation by E. Blunt, R. D. Cutts and J. Farley, Assists. Topography by R. D. Cutts, John Seib, I. Hull Adams, Assists. and S. A. Wainwright, Sub-Assist. Hydrography by the parties under the command of Lieut Comdg. S. P. Lee and Comdr. W. T. Muse, U.S.N. Assists. 59 × 74 cm. (*Its* [no. 388])

"No. 17" in the upper left corner.

1. ————Another issue. Redd. drng. by M. J. McClery & A. Lindenkohl. Engd. by A. Maedel, H. S. Barnard & A. Petersen. 59 × 74 cm. (*Its* no. 388)

"No. 388" rather than "no. 17" is printed in the upper left corner. Seal of U.S. Coast Survey is printed below the map title.

2. From Piney Point to Lower Cedar Point . . . Triangulation by John Farley, Assist., Fairman Rogers, Actg. Assist, C. Ferguson and F. P. Webber, Sub-Assists. Topography by I. Hull Adams, Assist., S. A. Wainwright, J. Mechan, Sub-Assists., and C. Hosmer, Aid. Hydrography by the parties under the command of Comdr. W. T. Muse and Lieut. Comdr. T. S. Phelps, U.S.N. Assistants. Redd. drng. by L. D. Williams and A. Lindenkohl. Engd. by A. Maedel, H. S. Barnard and A. Petersen. 59 × 78 cm. (*Its* no. 389)

3. From Lower Cedar Point to Indian Head . . . Triangulation by C. Ferguson and F. P. Webber, Sub-Assists. Topography by H. L. Whiting, A. W. Longfellow, Assists., J. Mechan, Sub-Assist., and C. Hosmer, Aid. Fairman Rogers, Acting Assistant Coast Survey in immediate charge of operations. Hydrography by the party under the command of Lt. Comdr. T. S. Phelps, U.S.N. Assistant. Redd. drng. by A. Lindenkohl, L. Karcher, and A. Balbach. Engd. by A. Maedel, A. Petersen, and F. W. Benner. 59 × 74 cm. (*Its* no. 390)

4. From Indian Head to Little Falls Bridge. 99 × 59 cm. (*Its* no. 391)

4. ————Another issue. H. Lindenkohl & Chas. G. Krebs, lith. (*Its.* no. 391)

Includes many more soundings in the Potomac River.

35.5

————Sketch H. showing the progress of the survey in section no. VIII, from 1846 to 1862. Bowen & Co. lith., Philada. [Washington, U.S. Coast Survey] 1862 Uncolored. Scale 1:600,000. 50 × 85 cm. *From its* Report of the Superintendent of the Coast Survey, showing the progress of the survey during the year 1862 (Washington, Government Printing Office, 1864). Map 35.

At head of title: U.S. Coast Survey. A. D. Bache, Superintendent.

"No. 35" in the upper left corner.

Map shows the extent of the triangulation network from Mobile Bay to the Mississippi River delta.

Insets: Plan of Fort Jackson, showing the effect of the bombardment by the U.S. mortar flotilla and gunboats, April 18th to 24th 1862. 27 × 41 cm.—Reconnoissance [sic] of the Mississippi River below Forts Jackson and St. Philip made previous to the reduction by the U.S. Fleet under the command of flag officer D. G. Farragut, U.S.N. 23 × 42 cm.

(For other copies of these maps see entry nos. 236–237.)

36

————Sketch of the eastern part of the U.S., showing territorial extent of the rebellion at different epochs during the war for its suppression; also—marching routes of the U.S. forces, localities & dates of the more important conflicts—districts of coast returned under the control of the U.S., etc. & etc.—1862. Colored ms. Scale ca. 1:6,000,000. 49 × 40 cm.

"First project of 'Rebellion Sketch,' keep, J.E.H."

Apparently this manuscript was made in late April or May 1862. The last battle indicated is that of "Pittsburg Ld," April 6–7, 1862. It appears to be the basis for the printed map entitled *Historical sketch of the rebellion,* published by the U.S. Coast Survey in May 1862 (see entry no. 34).

G3701.S5 1862 .U5 Vault

36.1

————South West pass of the Mississippi River. Reconnaissance by F. H. Gerdes, Assistant in May 1862. [Washington, U.S. Coast Survey] 1862. Uncolored. Scale 1:20,000. 47 × 38 cm. *From its* Report of the Superintendent of the Coast Survey, showing the progress of the survey during the year 1862 (Washington, Government Printing Office, 1864). Map 36.

At head of title: U.S. Coast Survey, A. D. Bache, Superintendent.

"No. 36" in the upper left corner.

36.2

————Another issue. (*Its* no. 507)

"No. 507 price 50 cents" printed in the upper margin.

36.5

Wyld, James.

Map of the southern states of North America with the forts, harbours & military positions. James Wyld, Geographer to the Queen, London [1862?] Colored. Scale ca. 1:2,090,880. 69 × 104 cm., sectioned and mounted on cloth to fold to 18 × 12 cm.

General map showing "dividing line between the free & slave-holding states."

A list of other maps and atlases by Wyld is pasted on the verso.

1863

36.8

Bacon and Company.

Bacon's steel plate map of America, political, historical & military. London, Bacon & Co. [1863] Colored. Scale 1:5,702,400. 57 × 85 cm.

"Federal free states" are outlined in red, "Federal slave

states" are yellow, "Federal territories (free)" are orange, and "Confederate states (slave)" are green.

Inset: Outline of England on the same scale. 13 × 10 cm.

Includes population tables, "Extracts from the official census report of 1860," a brief description of the Federal navy, a table listing the "Positions of the American forts, North and South," a brief "political" overview, and a "Record of important events of the war, [battle fields herein named are underlined with red on the map]." The "Record" includes information from November 6, 1860, to July 15, 1863.

37

————Map of the southern states, including rail roads, county towns, state capitals, county roads, the southern coast from Delaware to Texas, showing the harbors, inlets, forts and position of blockading ships. London [1863?] Colored. Scale ca. 1:2,970,000. 51 × 76 cm.

At top of map: Bacon's shilling series of war maps,— no. 3.

Inset: Enlarged plan of the battle fields in Virginia and Maryland. Scale ca. 1:1,040,000. 16 × 13 cm.

Includes portraits of Lincoln, Scott, Stonewall Jackson, and McClellan.

Map was also published in *Harper's Weekly,* Nov. 9, 1861 (entry no. 14.55) and in the *Sun,* New York, Jan. 4, 1862 (entry no. 32.9).

37.2

Brooks, F. W.

Lloyd's new map of the Mississippi River from Cairo to its mouth. F. W. Brooks, delr. Waters & son, engravers. New York, H. H. Lloyd & Co. [1863?] Colored. Scale 1:696,960. 2 maps, each 80 × 11 cm. on sheet 89 × 26 cm.

General map of the river indicating the location of a few forts.

37.4

Callahan, Denis.

Extract from a map entitled portions of the military departments of the Cumberland . . . of the South . . . and of the Gulf . . . Compiled in the Bureau of Engineers, War Department, 1863. Denis Callahan delt. Lith. by J. Bien, New York. Uncolored. Scale 1:350,000. 94 × 116 cm.

Map extends from Tallahassee, Florida, west to Mobile, Alabama, and the Gulf coast north to Montgomery, Ala-

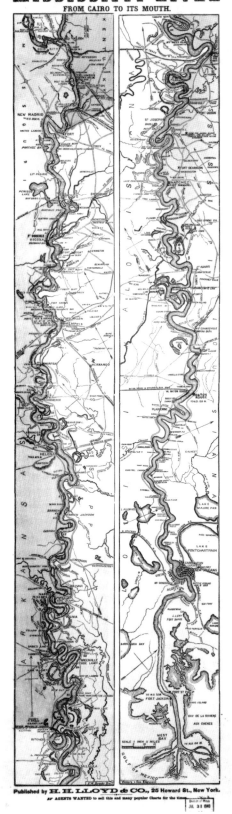

Map of the Mississippi River published about 1863 by H. H. Lloyd and Company of New York. This hand-colored map was printed from a wood engraving prepared by Waters and Company. During the war, another New York publisher, James T. Lloyd, accused H. H. Lloyd of trading on his name. (See entry no. 37.2.)

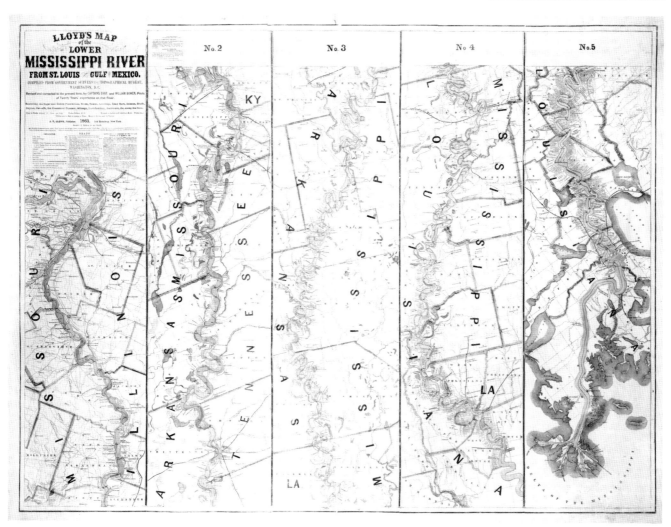

bama. Depicted are cities and towns, forts, three classes of roads, existing and contemplated railroads, swamps and prairies, river basins, mills, and a few points of historic interest.

Includes a list of authorities used in making the map.

37.6

Colton, Joseph H.

J. H. Colton's map of the southern states. Maryland, Delaware, Virginia, Kentucky, Tennessee, Missouri, North Carolina, South Carolina, Georgia, Alabama, Mississippi, Arkansas, Louisiana and Texas. Showing also part of adjoining states & territories locating the forts & military stations of the U. States & showing all the rail roads, r. r. stations, & other internal improvements. New York, J. H. Colton, 1863. Colored. Scale ca. 1:1,520,640. 2 parts, each 98 × 69 cm.

"Entered according to Act of Congress in the year 1863 by J. H. Colton."

Printed by Lang & Cooper.

Insets: Southern part of Florida. 27 × 19 cm.—Col-

James T. Lloyd's lithographed map of the Mississippi River published in 1863 is far more detailed than H. H. Lloyd's map issued about the same time. James Lloyd cautioned the public "against another 'Lloyd' by which name he hopes to deceive the public with spurious 'Lloyd Maps.' This man's maps are engraved coarsely on wood and very erroneous. He follows us with an imitation of every map we issue." (See entry no. 41.)

ton's map of the United States showing the proposed railroad routes to the Pacific Ocean. 19 × 26 cm.

General map.

1861 editions listed as entry nos. 6.5–6.6; 1862 editions listed as entry nos. 25.5–25.6.

37.8

Fisher, Richard Swainson.

A chronological history of the Civil War in America. Illustrated with A. J. Johnson's and J. H. Colton's steel plate maps and plans of the southern states and harbors. New York, Johnson and Ward, 1863. 160 p., 10 maps. 22 cm.

E468.3.F53 G&MRR

Cover title: Chronological history of the Civil War in America and hand atlas of the slave states. (Cover title is now missing from the Library of Congress copy.)

Listed in P. L. Phillips's *A List of Geographical Atlases in the Library of Congress* (Washington, Government Printing Office, 1909), v. 1, no. 1350.

Map contents:

[1] Johnson's new military map of the United States showing the forts, military posts &c. with enlarged plans of southern harbors from authentic data obtained at the War Department, Washington. [New York] Johnson and Ward, ©1861. Scale ca. 1:10,500,000. 42 × 56 cm. (between p. iv and 5)

[2] J. H. Colton's map of Virginia, Maryland, & Delaware. Scale ca. 1:3,120,000. 20 × 26 cm. (between p. 16 and 17)

[3] J. H. Colton's map of North & South Carolina. Scale ca. 1:3,120,000. 20 × 27 cm. (between p. 32 and 33)

[4] J. H. Colton's map of Georgia, Alabama and Florida. Scale ca. 1:3,120,000. 20 × 27 cm. (between p. 48 and 49)

[5] J. H. Colton's map of Mississippi and Louisiana. Scale ca. 1:3,120,000. 26 × 20 cm. (between p. 64 and 65)

[6] J. H. Colton's map of Texas. Scale ca. 1:7,800,000. 20 × 26 cm. (between p. 80 and 81)

[7] J. H. Colton's map of Arkansas and Indian Territory. Scale ca. 1:3,120,000. 20 × 26 cm. (between p. 96 and 97)

[8] J. H. Colton's map of Kentucky and Tennessee. Scale ca. 1:3,120,000. 20 × 26 cm. (between p. 112 and 113)

[9] J. H. Colton's map of Missouri and Kansas. Scale ca. 1:3,120,000. 20 × 26 cm. (between p. 128 and 129)

[10] Johnson's map of the vicinity of Richmond, and Peninsular campaign in Virginia. Showing also the interesting localities along the James, Chickahominy and York Rivers. Compiled from the official maps of the War Department. By Johnson and Ward. Entered according to Act of Congress, in the year 1862 by J. Knowles Hare. Scale ca. 1:190,000. 44 × 67 cm. (between p. 148 and 149)

38

Hall, Edward S.

Lloyd's new military map of of the border & southern states. Drawn by Edward S. Hall. Walters & Sons, engravers. Published by H. H. Lloyd & Co., New York. 1863. Colored. Scale ca. 1:1,850,000. 76 × 105 cm.

At top of map: H. H. Lloyd & Co's. new military map of the southern and border states.

Inset: [Map of southern Florida] 15 × 12 cm.

Geography and Map Division copy imperfect. Lacks portion showing northern Florida.

Battlefields are marked by red lines and strategic places by red dots.

Indicates towns, railroads, rivers, names and boundaries of states, and relief by hachures.

1862 edition listed as entry no. 27 and 1865 edition as entry no. 71.

38.5

Joerg, Wolfgang L. G.

Civil War campaigns of 1863. Prepared for the Chronicles of America under the direction of W. L. G. Joerg, American Georgaphical Society. Julius Bien lith, N.Y. Colored. Scale 1:13,000,000. 11 × 19 cm. *From* Wood, William. Captains of the Civil War; A chronicle of the blue and the gray. New Haven, Yale University Press, 1921. (The Chronicles of America series; Abraham Lincoln edition, vol. 31) facing p. 304.

Map depicts the movements of Grant, Farragut, Hooker and Meade, Lee, Morgan, and the "Line of Federal military occupation April 15, 1863 (after Hart)."

Inset: Vicksburg campaign. 2 × 3 cm.

39

Lindenkohl, Henry.

Historical sketch of the rebellion. Drawn by H. Lindenkohl. Chas. G. Krebs, lith. Published at the Office of the U.S. Coast Survey. [1863] Colored. Scale ca. 1:5,850,000. 47 × 45 cm.

Blue lines denote the "limits of the loyal states in July, 1861" and red lines indicate the "limits occupied by United States forces July 20th 1863."

See also entry nos. 34, 35, 36, 40, 40.1, and 49.

40

————Another issue. [1863]

Blue lines denote the "limits of loyal states in July, 1861," red lines denote the "limits occupied by United States forces July 1863," and small ships indicate the extent of the naval blockade.

"Population census 1860" in the lower right corner.

See also entry nos. 34, 35, 36, 39, 40.1, and 49.

Another copy is in the Sherman map coll. no. 1.

40.1

————Another issue. [1863]

G3701.S5 1863.L5

Similar to preceding issue, but legend is changed from "limits occupied by United States forces July 1863" to "limits of terr[i]tory controlled by U.S. forces July 31st 1863."

From the papers of Joseph Roswell Hawley, Manuscript Division, Library of Congress.

See also entry nos. 34, 35, 36, 39, 40, and 49.

41

Lloyd, James T.

Lloyd's map of the lower Mississippi River from St. Louis to the Gulf of Mexico. Compiled from Government surveys in the Topographical Bureau, Washington, D.C. Revised and corrected to the present time, by Captains Bart, and William Bowen, pilots of twenty years' experience on that river. New York, 1863. Colored. Scale 1:316,800. 4 parts, each 48 × 66 cm.

"Exhibiting the sugar and cotton plantations, cities, towns, landings, sand bars, islands, bluffs, bayous, cut-offs, the steamboat channel, mileage, fortifications, railroads, &c along the river."

1862 edition is listed as entry no. 28.

41.2

————Lloyd's map of the southern states showing all the railroads, their stations & distances, also the counties, towns, villages, harbors, rivers, and forts. Compiled from the latest government and other reliable sources. New York and London, J. T. Lloyd, 1863. Colored. Scale ca. 1:2,000,000. 4 parts, each 48 × 67 cm.

"Entered, according to Act of Congress, in the year 1862, by J. T. Lloyd."

Text printed on verso entitled "Lloyd's military map and gazetteer of the southern states" (©1861).

1861 editions listed as entry nos. 14.2–14.3 and 1862 edition as entry no. 29.

41.4

————Lloyd's new map of the United States, the Canadas, and New Brunswick, from the latest surveys showing every railroad & station finished to June 1862 and the Atlantic and Gulf coasts from the United States Superintendent's official reports of the Coast Survey by order of Congress. New York, J. T. Lloyd, 1863. Colored. Scale ca. 1:2,250,000. 95 × 126 cm.

"Entered according to Act of Congress, in the year 1862, by J. T. Lloyd."

General map of the eastern United States showing state and county boundaries, cities and towns, forts, roads, and railroads.

This map was in the possession of Jedediah Hotchkiss at the time of his death. Major Hotchkiss served as topographic engineer with the Army of Northern Virginia. In July 1948, the Library of Congress purchased his map collection.

Handwritten note on the verso reads "Llody's [sic] map of the United States, 1863 captured and used as part of my collection of maps, during the Civil War, 1861-5. Jed. Hotchkiss, Top. Eng., 2nd. Corps, Army N. Va."

For the 1864 edition see entry no. 50.

42

McConnell, James.

The Civil War, second year, 1862–1863. [Chicago, McConnell Map Co., © 1919] Colored. Scale ca. 1:2,200,000. 67 × 107 cm. (McConnell's historical maps of the United States. Revised ed. Map no. 36)

Map of the Southeast, showing troop movements and battles, towns, rivers, and state boundaries.

Inset: Civil War: Lee's first northern invasion, 1862. Scale 1:950,400. 16 × 18 cm.

List of "important battles, 2nd year, April 1862–1863," names of commanders, and a brief description of events appear in the lower right corner.

42.5

Magnus, Charles.

Panorama of the Mississippi valley and its fortifications. Eng. by F. W. Boell. New York, C. Magnus [1863?] Colored. Scale ca. 1:450,000–1:1,100,000. 4 maps, each 60 × 16 cm. on sheet 61 × 66 cm.

G4042 .M5 1863 .M3

Map of the Mississippi River, in four panels, from St. Louis to the Gulf of Mexico, depicting forts, islands, tributaries, cities and villages, and county names. Map includes two tables of distances and four small views of St. Louis, Memphis, Vicksburg, and New Orleans.

43

Modern School Supply Company, *Chicago, Ill.*

The Civil War—second year, 1862–1863. Copyright by E. W. A. Rowles. [Chicago, ©1919] Colored. Scale ca. 1:2,600,000. 69 × 108 cm. (Comprehensive series; historical—geographical maps of the United States, no. 32)

Wall map of the Southeast showing forts, battles, troop movements in Kentucky and Tennessee, "extreme limit[s] of Federal control, April 15, 1862 [and] 1863," towns, and state boundaries.

Brief description of the second year of war appears in the upper right corner.

Inset: Virginia campaigns of the Civil War. [1861–1865] 38 × 37 cm.

43.2

Nicholson, Dorothy A.

A year of maneuvers to topple a fortress. March, 1862 to March, 1863. Map by Dorothy A. Nicholson. Historical documentation by Edwin C. Bearss. Colored. Scale ca. 1:3,850,000. 26 × 18 cm. *From* National geographic. Washington, v. 124, July 1963. p. 43.

Map of the Mississippi River and vicinity, from Memphis to the mouth, showing cities, rivers, railroads, infantry and cavalry movements, centers of "troop concentration," and centers of "alternate troop concentrations." Confederate movements are in red and Union are in blue. Sixteen events are keyed by number to the map.

43.4

Nicholson, W. L.

Mountain region of North Carolina and Tennessee. U.S. Coast Survey, A. D. Bache Supt. Compiled by W. L. Nicholson, 1863. Drawn by A. Lindenkohl. H. Lindenkohl & Chas. G. Krebs, lith. Colored. Scale 1:633,600. 55 × 95 cm.

In top margin: Unfinished proof.
Map title printed in the lower right corner.
Unfinished proof of the following map (entry no. 43.5).

43.5

──────and Adolph Lindenkohl.

Mountain region of North Carolina and Tennessee. Compiled by W. L. Nicholson & A. Lindenkohl, 1863. Drawn by A. Lindenkohl. H. Lindenkohl & Chas. G. Krebs, lith. U.S. Coast Survey, A. D. Bache, Supt. Colored. Scale 1:633,600. 56 × 96 cm.

Map title is printed in the top margin. Map covers parts of the states of Kentucky, Tennessee, Virginia, North and South Carolina, Georgia, and Alabama, and shows relief by hachures, drainage, names and boundaries of states, roads, and railroads.

Unfinished proof for this map is described as entry no. 43.4. The 1864 edition is listed as entry no. 53 and the 1865 edition as entry no. 79a.6.

Another copy in the Geography and Map Division is from the papers of Joseph Roswell Hawley (G3900 1863.N5).

Another copy is in the James A. Garfield papers, Manuscript Division, L.C., series 8, container no. 1. In this copy, printed title in the top margin is wanting. Title has been added in ink below "authorities" in the lower right corner. "Table of distances" and "Topographical signs" cards are pasted to the verso of the map. "Gen'l Garfield Chief of Staff, most respectfully [signed] Wm. C. Margedant . . ." and "Brigadier General J. A. Garfield, Chief of Staff" is written in ink on the verso.

43.55

Owner, William.

Yazoo Pass & vicinity. [1863] Uncolored ms. Scale ca. 1:1,800,000. 2 sheets, each 19 × 15 cm. *In his* Diary, v. 4, tipped-in at front of volume.

In the William Owner papers, Manuscript Division, L.C., container no. 1.

Sheets identified as "Sketch no. 1" and "Sketch no. 2."

Map indicates place names, roads and railroads along the Mississippi River from Yazoo Pass to New Orleans. For-

tifications are indicated at Greenwood, Mississippi, and on the Yazoo River near Vicksburg.

Volume four of the diary covers from February 13 to June 27, 1863.

43.6

Perrine, Charles O.

Perrine's new topographical war map of the southern states. Taken from the latest government surveys and official reports. E. R. Jewett & Co., engravers, Buffalo, N.Y. Entered according to Act of Congress, in the year 1863, by C. O. Perrine. Colored. Scale ca. 1:2,000,000. 72 × 94 cm.

Accompanies John S. Bishop's *A Concise History of the War. Designed to Accompany Perrine's New War Map of the Southern States, with an Introduction and Statistical Appendix, Compiled from Authentic Sources* (Indianapolis, Charles O. Perrine [©1864]), 132, 9 p. 15 × 10 cm.

Map indicates state boundaries and shore lines in green and battles and engagements by small red circles.

Inset: Southern part of Florida. 17 × 13 cm.

The Geography and Map Division has two additional issues, without accompaniment, that indicate fewer battle sites.

43.8

Phelps and Watson.

Phelps & Watson's historical and military map of the border & southern states. New York, Phelps & Watson, 1863. Colored. Scale ca. 1:2,534,400. 64 × 91 cm.

"Entered according to Act of Congress; in the year 1862 by Phelps & Watson."

Includes list of "Battles of the war" in 1861 and 1862.

Accompanied by pamphlet entitled *New Historical War Map* (35 p., 17 × 12 cm.) containing a "Brief description of 10 battles and skirmishes of the war," 1861–63.

For other editions, see entry nos. 53.2, 80.2, and 80.3.

44

Philadelphia Board of Trade. Committee on Inland Transportation.

Hazard's rail road & military map of the southern states. Prepared by the Committee on Inland Transportation of the Board of Trade of Philadelphia. From the latest accessible authorities. The coast accurately drawn from the U.S. coast surveys and adopted by the War Department as the official map for government use. Drawn & engraved by P. S. Duval & Son, lithrs., Philada. Philadelphia, Willis. P. Hazard, 1863. Colored. Scale ca. 1:1,880,000. 77 × 129 cm.

G3861 .P3 1863 .P5 Vault

"Entered according to Act of Congress in the year 1862, by Thomas Kimber Jr."

Inset: Southern part of Florida. 24 × 18 cm.

Shows railroads, forts, location and dates of engagements, state and county boundaries, roads, towns, and rivers.

The Geography and Map Division has another copy which has been annotated in color to indicate "gauges of southern rail roads." The additions were "compiled under direction of Lieut. Col. J. N. Macomb, A.D.C., Chief Top. Engr." and "corrected to date Feby. 9th 1864." The map was addressed to "Mr. Nicolay," apparently John George Nicolay, President Lincoln's private secretary. The copy is partially mutilated; three of four corners are missing.

Listed in A. M. Modelski's *Railroad Maps of the United States* (Washington, Library of Congress, 1975), no. 142.

For 1862 edition, see entry no. 31.5.

44.5

Position of Union and Confederate armies on the morning of July 1, 1863. [n.p., 19–?] Colored. Scale 1:633,600 (10 miles to 1 inch). 31 × 26 cm.

No. "1" appears in the upper right margin.

Map of northeastern Virginia, Maryland, and southern Pennsylvania showing roads, railroads, cities and towns, drainage, relief by hachures, and troop positions at the beginning the Battle of Gettysburg.

45

Prang (Louis) and Company

Monitor map, showing the whole seacoast from Chesapeake Bay, down to Savannah harbor, and the whole country between Richmond & Savannah, with map on large scale of the harbor of Charleston. Boston, ©1863. Uncolored. Scale not given. 2 parts, each 48 × 61 cm.

Shows towns, roads, railroads, forts, and rivers.

Inset: Williams, W. A. Sketch of Charleston harbor. Scale ca. 1:71,000. 24 × 25 cm.

46

Preston, Noble D.

Route of the Tenth New York Cavalry from Culpeper to Gettysburg and return. Summer and fall campaigns of 1863. Uncolored ms. Scale ca. 1:440,000. 39 × 25 cm.

G3791.S5 1863 .P7 Vault

Finished pen and ink manuscript map of parts of Virginia, Maryland, and Pennsylvania, showing location and date of encampments and battles, route of the Tenth New York Cavalry, route of Capt. Pratt, roads, railroads, towns, drainage, and relief by hachures.

Printed version appears in Preston's *History of the Tenth Regiment of Cavalry, New York State Volunteers, August, 1861, to August 1865.* New York, D. Appleton, 1892. opp. p. 100.

47

Schönberg and Company.

Lloyd's new country map of the United States and Canadas showing battle fields, railroads, &c. Compiled from the latest government surveys & other reliable & official sources. Drawn and engraved by Schönberg & Co., New York. New York, H. H. Lloyd & Co., 1863. Colored. Scale ca. 1:2,500,000. 98 × 133 cm.

Indicates location and date of engagements, towns, railroads, state and county boundaries, and rivers.

Insets: Part of Florida. 19 × 14 cm.—California, Oregon, and the territories of the United States. 28 × 28 cm.

47.2

U.S. *Army. Corps of Engineers.*

Portions of the military departments of Virginia, Washington, Middle & the Susquehanna, prepared in the Engineer Department, July 1863. Denis Callahan deltr. Colored. Scale 1:200,000. 68 × 104 cm.

Roughly drawn base map covering southern Pennsylvania, Maryland, Northern Virginia, and Washington, D.C., and indicating populated places, common roads and turnpikes, contemplated and existing railroads, canals, and relief by hachures.

The Geography and Map Division has an uncolored second copy which is autographed "Gen. M. C. Meigs."

47.3

————Another edition. Uncolored. 76 × 103 cm.

Completely redrawn edition of the preceding map. Dennis Callahan's name has been dropped from this edition.

47.35

U.S. Coast Survey.

Atlantic coast of the United States (in four sheets). Sheet no. II, Nantucket to Cape Hatteras. [Washington, U.S. Coast Survey] 1863. Uncolored. Scale 1:1,200,000. 59 × 69 cm. *From its* Report of the Superintendent of the Coast Survey, showing the progress of the survey during the year 1862 (Washington, Government Printing Office, 1864). Map 24.

At head of title: U.S. Coast Survey, A. D. Bache, Supt.

"No. 24" is in the upper left corner.

47.37

————Another issue. *From its* Report of the Superintendent of the Coast Survey, showing the progress of the survey during the year 1863 (Washington, Government Printing Office, 1864). Map 19.

"No. 19" is in the upper left corner.

47.4

————Atlantic coast of the United States (in four

sheets). Sheet III, Cape Hatteras to Mosquito Inlet. [Washington, U.S. Coast Survey] 1863. Uncolored. Scale 1:1,200,000. 60 × 69 cm. *From its* Report of the Superintendent of the Coast Survey, showing the progress of the survey during the year 1863 (Washington, Government Printing Office, 1864). Map 20.

"No. 20" is in the upper left corner.

At head of title: U.S. Coast Survey, A. D. Bache, Supt.

47.42

————————Another issue.

"No. 20" has been dropped from the upper left corner.

47.44

————————Atlantic coast of the United States (in four sheets). Sheet no. IV, Mosquito Inlet to Key West. [Washington, U.S. Coast Survey] 1863. Uncolored. Scale 1:1,200,000. 60 × 69 cm. *From its* Report of the Superintendent of the Coast Survey, showing the progress of the survey during the year 1863 (Washington, Government Printing Office, 1864). Map 21.

"No. 21" is in the upper left corner.

At head of title: U.S. Coast Survey, A. D. Bache, Supt.

47.46

————————Another issue.

"No. 4" and "Electrotype copy no. 1 by G. Mathiot U.S.C.S." printed in the upper margin.

47.48

————————Another issue.

Information in the upper margin has been dropped.

47.5

————————Chesapeake Bay. Sheet no. 1, York River, Hampton Roads, Chesapeake entrance. From a trigonometrical survey under the direction of A. D. Bache, Superintendent of the survey of the coast of the United States. Triangulation by E. Blunt & J. Farley, Assistants. Topography by J. J. S. Hassler, G. D. Wise, J. Seib, Assts. & J. Mechan, Sub-Asst. Hydrography by the party under the command of Lieut. Comdg. J. J. Almy, U.S.N. Assistant. Redd. drng. by W. M. C. Fairfax, A. Strausz & L. D. Williams. Engd. by J. Knight, A. Sengteller, H. S. Barnard & J. C. Kondrup. [Washington, U.S. Coast Survey] 1863. Uncolored. Scale 1:80,000. 64 × 96 cm. (*Its* no. 131)

At head of title: Coast chart no. 31.

Printed in the upper margin: "No. 131" and "Electrotype copy no. 2 by G. Mathiot, U.S.C.S."

General chart indicating soundings, lighthouses, buoys, and coastal vegetation.

Includes sailing directions.

47.52

————————Chesapeake Bay. Sheet 6, from the mouth of York River to the entrance to bay. From a trigonometrical survey under the direction of A. D. Bache, Superintendent of the survey of the coast of the United States. Triangulation by E. Blunt & J. Farley, Assistants. Topography by J. J. S. Hassler, G. D. Wise, J. Seib, Assts. & J. Mechan, Sub-Asst. Hydrography by the party under the command of Lieut. Comdg. J. J. Almy, U.S.N. Assistant. [Washington, U.S. Coast Survey] 1863. Uncolored. Scale 1:80,000. 63 × 91 cm. (*Its* chart no. 36) *From its* Report of the Superintendent of the Coast Survey showing the progress of the survey during the year 1862 (Washington, Government Printing Office, 1864). Map 15.

"No. 15" is in the upper left corner.

At head of title: Coast chart no. 36.

Similar to the preceding chart, but with a change in the title.

47.6

————————Gulf coast of the United States; Key West to Rio Grande. [Washington, U.S. Coast Survey] 1863. Colored. Scale 1:1,200,000. 71 × 130 cm. (*Its* no. 5)

At head of title: U.S. Coast Survey, A. D. Bache, Supt.

"Electrotype copy no. 1 by G. Mathiot, U.S.G.S., no. 5" printed in upper margin.

Chart of the Gulf coast indicating soundings, lights, and bottom contours at 10 and 100 fathoms.

Stamped in the lower right corner: From collection of David Dixon Porter.

47.62

————————Gulf coast of the United States, Key West to Rio Grande. Eastern part [Key West to the Mississippi River. Washington, U.S. Coast Survey] 1863. Uncolored. Scale 1:1,200,000. 70 × 73 cm. *From its* Report of the Superintendent of the Coast Survey, showing the progress of the survey during the year 1863 (Washington, Government Printing Office, 1864). Map 22.

"No. 22" is in the upper left corner.

At head of title: U.S. Coast Survey, A. D. Bache, Supt.

47.64

————————Gulf coast of the United States, Key West to Rio Grande. Western part [Mississippi River to the Rio Grande. Washington, U.S. Coast Survey] 1863. Uncolored. Scale 1:1,200,000. 72 × 58 cm. *From its* Report of the Superintendent of the Coast Survey, showing the progress of the survey during the year 1863 (Washington, Government Printing Office, 1864). Map 23.

"No. 23" is the upper left corner.

At head of title: U.S. Coast Survey, A. D. Bache, Supt.

47.7

Wells, Jacob.

Chart of the Mississippi River from the Ohio River to Gulf of Mexico. Constructed and engraved to illustrate "The War with the South." J. Wells, del. Rae Smith, sc. [New York] Virtue, Yorston & Co., ©1863. Colored. Scale ca. 1:1,267,200. 4 maps, each 4 × 23 cm. on sheet 29 × 20 cm.

"Entered according to act of Congress A.D. 1863 by Virtue, Yorston & Co."

General map indicating the location of a few forts.

47.8

──────────Virginia, Maryland, Delaware, and part of Pennsylvania. Constructed and engraved to illustrate "The war with the South." J. Wells, del. Rae Smith Sc. ©1863. Colored. Scale ca. 1:3,300,000. 18 × 24 cm. *From* Tomes, Robert. The war with the South. New York, Virtue & Yorston, 1862–1867. v. 2, between p. 420 and 421.

"Entered according to act of Congress AD. 1863 by Virtue, Yorston & Co."

Inset: [Map of Washington, D.C. and vicinity] 7 × 7 cm.

General map indicating place names, roads, rivers, and major mountain ranges. Troop positions and movements are not depicted.

Copy of the map included in the Library of Congress copy of Tomes's *The War with the South* lacks the subtitle "Constructed and engraved to illustrate 'The war with the South.'"

1864

48

Bacon and Company.

Map of the United States, showing the territory in possession of the Federal Union, January, 1864. Lithographed by Bacon & Co., London. Colored. Scale ca. 1:7,400,000. 45 × 67 cm.

Indicates by color the territories "claimed by the Confederates in 1861," "in the military possession of the Confederates in 1861," "reclaimed from rebellion by the Federal Union," and "remaining in possession of the Rebels January, 1864." Map also includes rail lines and gauges, towns, forts, rivers, state boundaries, and distances by rail.

48.1

Bartholomew, John.

The Confederate states, with the border states & the adjoining portion of the Federal states. By J. Bartholomew

F.R.G.S. London and Liverpool, George Philip & son [1864?] Colored. Scale ca. 1:3,600,000. 52 × 62 cm., cut and mounted to fold to 17 × 11 cm. ([Philip's series of travelling maps no.] 44)

At head of title: United States of North America: (South eastern division).

General map showing state names and boundaries, countries, place names, railroads, and rivers.

Mounted on the verso is an advertisement addressed "to tourists and travellers" describing the merits of the "series of travelling maps."

48.2

Colton, Joseph H.

Colton's new topographical map of the states of Virginia, Maryland and Delaware, showing also eastern Tennessee & parts of other adjoining states, all the fortifications, military stations, rail roads, common roads and other internal improvements. Compiled from the latest & most authentic sources, on a scale of 12 miles to the inch. New York, J. H. Colton, 1864. Colored. Scale 1:760,320. 80 × 115 cm.

Printed by Lang & Laing Lith., N.Y. appears in the lower left corner.

"Entered according to Act of Congress in the year 1862 by J. H. Colton."

General map showing state and county boundaries, roads and railroads, fortifications, and place names. Drawings of ships offshore depict the Union blockade of the coast.

1862 editions are listed as entry nos. 25.8–25.9.

48.22

──────────Another issue.

Printed by H. P. Cooper, N.Y. appears in the lower right corner.

In the Samuel P. Heintzelman papers, Manuscript Division, L.C., container no. 11 (in poor condition).

48.3

General Draft Company.

Campaigns of the Civil War in the valley of history. C[opyright] General Drafting Co., Inc., Covent Station, N.J. [Hagerstown, Md., The Potomac Edison Company, ©1961] Colored. Scale ca. 1:850,000. 28 × 37 cm. on sheet 43 × 61 cm.

Title when folded: The Civil War in the valley of history. Presented by the Potomac Edison Company, Hagerstown, Maryland, a part of the Allegheny Power System.

Map centers on the Shenandoah Valley showing parts of the States of Virginia, West Virginia, Maryland, and Pennsylvania. Depicted are troop movements and battlefields during the campaigns conducted in 1862, 1863, and 1864.

Insets: Antietam, September 17, 1862. 11 × 10 cm.—Kernstown, March 23, 1862. 7 × 9 cm.—Front Royal, May 23, 1862. 7 × 9 cm.—Monocacy, July 9, 1864. 7 × 9 cm.—Opequon, September 19, 1864. 7 × 9 cm.—Cedar Creek, October 19, 1864. 11 × 10 cm.

On verso: Civil War shrines in the valley of history. Scale ca. 1:850,000. 28 × 35 cm. (Includes photographs of 18 Civil War sites, with their locations keyed by number to the map.)

Another copy is classed G3791 .E635 1961 .G4.

48.4

Gerdes, F. H.

Mississippi River, Grand Gulf, Turner's Pt., New Carthage. Reconnaissance for the use of the Mississippi Squadron, Rear Admiral D. D. Porter, U.S.N. Comdg. By F. H. Gerdes, Assistant. United States Coast Survey, A. D. Bache, Supdt. 1864. Uncolored. Scale 1:40,000. 53 × 42 cm. (U.S. Coast Survey, chart no. 3018)

At head of title: Sheet no. 2.

Joins sheet no. 1. See entry no. 48.5.

Detailed river chart indicating field patterns and vegetation along the shore lines.

"No. 30. No. 3018 price 20 cents" is printed in the upper left corner.

48.42

————Another issue. *From* Report of the Superintendent of the Coast Survey, showing the progress of the survey during the year 1864. (Washington, Government Printing Office, 1866). Map 30.

"No. 30" is in the upper left corner.

This issue lacks "No. 3018 price 20 cents" in the upper left corner.

48.5

————Mississippi River, Rodney, St. Joseph, Bruinsburg. Reconnaissance for the use of the Mississippi Squadron, Rear Admiral D. D. Porter, U.S.N. Comdg. By F. H. Gerdes, Assistant. United States Coast Survey, A. D. Bache, Supdt. 1864. Uncolored. Scale 1:40,000. 54 × 44 cm. (U.S. Coast Survey, chart no. 3017)

At head of title: Sheet no. 1.

Joins sheet no. 2. See entry no. 48.4.

Detailed river chart indicating field patterns and vegetation along the shore lines.

"No. 29 no. 3017 price 20 cents" is printed in the upper left corner.

48.52

————Another issue. *From* Report of the Superintendent of the Coast Survey, showing the progress of the survey

during the year 1864 (Washington, Government Printing Office, 1866). Map 29.

"No. 29" is in the upper left corner.

This issue lacks "No. 3017 price 20 cents" in the upper left corner.

48.55

Houston, David C.

Parts of Louisiana, Texas and Arkansas. Prepared by order of Maj. Gen. N. P. Banks. Major D. C. Houston, Chief Engineer. Del: by B. von Reizenstein. Phot: by Brown & Ogilvie. Feb. 1864. Photocopy (positive). Scale ca. 1:1,500,000. 55 × 55 cm.

In the papers of Major General Nathaniel Prentice Banks, Manuscript Division, L.C., container 76.

At head of title: Department of the Gulf Map no. 15.

"Authoritines [sic]: Colton's Southern States; Notes by: Wm. E. Young, C.E."

General map extending from the Mississippi River west to Corpus Christi Bay, Texas, and north to Fort Smith, Arkansas. Some roads have been marked in red. To the right of the map are notes describing 12 rivers in the region.

"Information on this map furnished by Wm. E. Young, C.E. and compiled under direction of Maj. D. C. Houston, Chief Engineer, Dept. of the Gulf."

48.6

Joerg, Wolfgang L. G.

Civil War campaigns of 1864. Prepared for the Chronicles of America under the direction of W. L. G. Joerg, American Geographical Society. Julius Bien lith, N.Y. Colored. Scale 1:13,000,000. 11 × 19 cm. *From* Wood, William. Captains of the Civil War; A chronicle of the blue and the gray. New Haven, Yale University Press, 1921. (The Chronicles of America series; Abraham Lincoln edition, vol. 31) facing p. 376.

Map depicts the movements of Lee, Hood, Grant, and Sherman, and the "Line of Federal military occupation April 15, 1864 (after Hart)."

Inset: Campaign in Virginia, 1864–65. 4 × 4 cm.

49

Lindenkohl, Henry.

Historical sketch of the rebellion. Drawn by H. Lindenkohl. Chas. G. Krebs, lith. Published at the Office of the U.S. Coast Survey. [1864] Colored. Scale ca. 1:5,850,000. 47 × 45 cm.

"Limit of loyal states in July, 1861, limit of territory controlled by U.S. forces July 31st 1863, [and] limit of territory gained from July 31st 1863 to Jan. 1st 1864" indicated by colored lines. Small ships denote the extent of the naval blockade.

"Population census 1860" in in the lower right corner. See also entry nos. 34, 35, 36, 39, 40, and 40.1.

Another copy is in the James A. Garfield papers, Manuscript Division, L.C., series 8, container no. 1.

49a

Lloyd (H. H.) and Company.

United States. Map showing loyal states in green, what the rebels still hold in red, and what the Union soldiers have wrested from them in yellow. New York, H. H. Lloyd & Co.; Boston, B. B. Russell; Chicago, R. R. Landon, [1864]. Colored. Scale ca. 1:13,500,000. 25 × 37 cm. on sheet 96 × 72 cm.

At top of map: Presidential campaign, 1864.

Includes portraits of Lincoln, Johnson, McClellan, Pendleton (presidential and vice-presidential candidates), as well as small portraits of 14 former presidents. Also includes short biographies of the candidates, the Union and Democratic platforms, and Lincoln's and McClellan's letters of acceptance.

50

Lloyd, James T.

Lloyd's new map of the United States, the Canadas and New Brunswick, from the latest surveys, showing every railroad & station finished to June 1863, and the Atlantic and Gulf coasts from the United States Superintendent's official reports of the Coast Survey by order of Congress. New York 1863. [Corrected to October 4, 1864] Colored. Scale ca. 1:2,250,000. 95 × 127 cm.

Map of eastern United States, showing roads, railroads, distances by rail, towns, state and country names and boundaries.

Areas shaded pink represent the "rebellious states" and the green areas represent "all the southern territory that we hold from the South, after four years' war up to October 4, 1864."

For 1863 edition see item 41.4.

51

McConnell, James.

The Civil War, third year, 1863–1864. [Chicago, McConnell Map Co., ©1919] Colored. Scale ca. 1:2,200,000. 69 × 107 cm. (McConnell's historical maps of the United States. Revised ed. Map no. 37)

Map of the Southeast, showing troop movements and battles, towns, rivers, and state boundaries.

Inset: Civil War: Lee's second northern invasion, 1863. Scale 1:950,400. 29 × 18 cm.

List of "important battles, 3rd year, April 1863–1864," names of commanders, and a brief description of events appear in the lower right corner.

51.3

Map of the rebellion, as it was in 1861 and as it is in 1864. Uncolored. Scale ca. 1:10,200,000. 24 × 35 cm. *From* Harper's weekly, v. 8, Mar. 19, 1864. p. 181.

Map indicates the "Military line of the rebellion July 1st 1861" and the eastern and western sections of the rebellion, February 1864.

51.5

Mendenhall, Edward.

Railway and county map of the southern states: embracing the states of N. Carolina, S. Carolina, Georgia, Alabama, Florida, Mississippi, Louisiana, Arkansas and Tennessee exhibiting all the towns, villages, stations, & landings; the rivers, railways, common roads, canals throughout these states. Cincinnati, E. Mendenhall, 1864. Colored. Scale ca. 1:2,000,000. 46 × 82 cm.

G3861 .P3 1864 .M4

Symbols indicate "United States battles won" and "U.S. battles lost."

Listed in A. M. Modelski's *Railroad Maps of the United States* (Washington, Library of Congress, 1975), no. 141.

52

Modern School Supply Company, *Chicago, Ill.*

The Civil War—third year, 1863–1864. Copyright by E. W. A. Rowles. [Chicago, ©1919] Colored. Scale ca. 1:2,600,000. 69 × 108 cm. (Comprehensive series; historical—geographical maps of the United States, no. 33)

Wall map of the Southeast, showing forts, battles, "extreme limit[s] of Federal control, April 15, 1863 [and] 1864," towns, and state boundaries.

Brief description of third year of war appears in lower left corner.

Insets: Gettysburg and vicinity. 18 × 13 cm. Chattanooga and vicinity. 14 × 16 cm. Vicksburg campaign. 47 × 31 cm.

52.5

Morris, Walter J.

Map of the military division of the West. (Genl. G. T. Beauregard comdg.) Hd. Qrs. Engrs. Office, Dept. Miss., Ala. &c. Selma, Ala., Walter J. Morris, Capt. and Chief Engr. in charge. Photographed at the Dept. Engineer Office, Selma, Ala. Novr. 1864 by J. F. Knight and Lee Mallory, Asst. Top Engineers. Photocopy (positive). Scale ca. 1:160,000. 49 × 61 cm., folded to 17 × 11 cm.

G3860 1864 .M6 Vault

Faded contemporary Confederate photocopy showing county names and boundaries, cities and towns, and rivers in the states of Mississippi and Alabama, and parts of Louisiana, Georgia, and Tennessee. Railroads are annotated in red ink.

Cover title: Military map. Photographed at Engineer Hd. Qrs., Selma, Ala. by J. F. Knight & Lee Mallory, Asst. Top. Engrs.

Covers annotated as follows: "Genl. G. T. Beauregard C.S.A." and "Montgomery Dec. 2d. 1864."

Endorsed in facsimile: Approved David H. Lockett, Col. & Chief Engr., Dept. Ala. &c.

53

Nicholson, W. L., *and* Adolph Lindenkohl.

Mountain region of North Carolina and Tennessee. Compiled by W. L. Nicholson & A. Lindenkohl, 1863.— With corrections to May, 1864. Drawn by A. Lindenkohl. H. Lindenkohl & Chas. G. Krebs, lith. U.S. Coast Survey, A. D. Bache, Supt. Colored. Scale 1:633,600. 56 × 96 cm.

Map of parts of the states of Kentucky, Tennessee, Virginia, North and South Carolina, Georgia, and Alabama, showing relief by hachures, drainage, names and boundaries of states, roads, and railroads. Part of the route of the "proposed military railroad from Nicholasville & Lebanon" is indicated.

Another copy in Fillmore map coll. no. 265. Signed in ms: Millard Fillmore, Dec. 6, 1864.

1863 edition listed as entry no. 43.5 and the 1865 edition as entry no. 79a.6.

53.2

Phelps and Watson.

Phelps & Watson's historical and military map of the border & southern states. New York, Phelps & Watson, 1864. Colored. Scale ca. 1:2,534,400. 64 × 91 cm.

"Entered according to Act of Congress; in the year 1862 by Phelps & Watson."

Includes list of "Battles of the war" in 1861, 1862, and 1863.

For other editions, see entry nos. 43.8, 80.2, and 80.3.

53.4

U.S. *Coast Survey.*

Potomac River (in four sheets): Sheet no. 4, from Indian Head to Georgetown. From a trigonometrical survey under the direction of A. D. Bache, Superintendent of the survey of the coast of the United States. Triangulation by A. D. Bache, Supdt., C. Ferguson, C. Hosmer and C. H. Boyd, Sub-Assts. Topography by A. M. Harrison, C. M. Bache, Assts., J. Mechan, C. Hosmer and C. H. Boyd, Sub-Assts. Hydrography by the parties under the command of Lieut. Comdr. T. S. Phelps, U.S.N. and C. P. Patterson Assts. Redd. drng. by H. Lindenkohl and L. Karcher. Engd. by A. Maedel and A. Petersen. 1864. Uncolored. Scale 1:40,000. 99 × 58 cm. (*Its* no. 391)

"Electrotype copy no. 1, by G. Mathiot, U.S.C.S." is printed in the upper margin.

Information concerning lighthouses, tides, soundings, and the geographic coordinates of the Capitol dome is given in the lower right corner.

1865

53.6

Adams, James T.

Atlas of American history; James Truslow Adams, editor in chief; R. V. Coleman, managing editor. New York, Charles Scribner's Sons, 1943. xi. [1], 360 p. incl. 147 (i.e., 131) maps. 26 × 19 cm.

 G1201 .S1A2 1943

Pages 1–296 are numbered as plates 1–147.

Listed in C. E. LeGear's *A List of Geographical Atlases in the Library of Congress* (Washington, Library of Congress, 1973), v. 7, no. 10594.

The following plates contain maps of the Civil War:

122. Randall, J. G. The United States, March 4, 1861. 17 × 24 cm. (Indicates free states, slave states, and territories.)

123. Ambler, C. H. Virginia—1861. 17 × 24 cm.

124–5. Harlow, Alvin F. Civil War, 1861–1865. 24 × 34 cm.

126. Harlow, Alvin F. Missouri region, 1861–1864. 17 × 24 cm.

127. Hay, Thomas Robson. Kentucky and Tennessee, 1862–1864. 17 × 24 cm.

128. Freeman, Douglas Southall. Virginia, Maryland and Pennsylvania, 1862–1863. 24 × 17 cm.

129. Freeman, Douglas Southall. The Peninsula, 1862. 24 × 17 cm.

130–1. Clark, Dan E., and Alvin F. Harlow. Trans–Mississippi, 1861–1865. 24 × 34 cm.

132. Hay, Thomas Robson. Chickamauga and Chattanooga, 1863. 17 × 24 cm.

133. Hay, Thomas Robson. Tullahoma to Atlanta, 1863–1864. 24 × 17 cm.

134. Hay, Thomas Robson. Memphis to the Gulf, 1862–1863. 24 × 17 cm.

135. Coulter, E. Merton. Atlanta to the Carolinas, 1864–1865. 17 × 24 cm.

136. Freeman, Douglas Southall. Virginia, 1864–1865. 24 × 17 cm.

137. Hay, Thomas Robson. Reconstruction, 1865–1877. 17 × 24 cm.

The Geography and Map Division also has separates for plates 123 to 137.

54

American Automobile Association.

Civil War historical sites. Washington, ©1960. Colored. Scale ca. 1:3,421,440. 37 × 55 cm.

Map of the Southeast showing "battle sites," "historic homes & buildings," "monuments," roads and route numbers, towns, and state boundaries.

Battle sites are keyed by number to list in the bottom margin and on the verso.

55

Artists Representatives, Incorporated.

Civil War centennial. 1861–1865. Historical consultants: Ralph G. Newman, E. B. Long. Copyright by publishers: Creative Merchandisers, Inc. [Chicago] 1960. Design direction: Artists Representatives Incorporated. Colored. Scale not given. 71 × 104 cm.

Pictorial map of the southeastern United States showing the location of 64 major battles and events keyed by numbers to a brief "Chronological history."

Includes portraits of the principal Union and Confederate leaders.

Inset: [Map of the principal battlefields in Virginia] 19 × 15 cm.

55.2

Atlas for the American Civil War. Thomas E. Griess, series editor. Wayne, N. J., Avery Publishing Group, ©1986, 4 p. 1., 58 col. maps. 28 × 36 cm. (The West Point Military History Series)

G1201 .S5A8 1986

"This atlas, designed to support the new text, *The American Civil War,* provides less detailed graphical treatment than the Esposito text-atlas, but it emphasizes the totality of the war to a greater extent. Two of the four authors of the text, Lieutenant Colonel Gerald P. Stadler and Major Arthur V. Grant, Jr., designed the maps which comprise the atlas . . . In accomplishing that task, they relied heavily but not solely upon the important Esposito work.

"The Department is also indebted to Mr. Edward J. Krasnoborski and his assistant, Mr. George W. Giddings, who drafted the maps." (Foreword)

Contents

1–2. The scene of war

3. First Bull Run campaign

4–9. War in the West: from Fort Henry to Shiloh

10. Jackson's Valley campaign

11–12. Campaigns around Richmond: Peninsular and Second Bull Run campaigns

13–14. Lee's first invasion of the North: Antietam campaign

15–23. War in the West: From Island no. 10 to the Fall of Vicksburg

16–32. Operations in Northern Virginia: Fredericksburg and Chancellorsville campaigns

33–38. Gettysburg campaign

39–44. Operations around Chattanooga: Chickamauga and Chattanooga campaigns

45. Union national military strategy, April 1864

46–47. Richmond campaign: from the Wilderness to Petersburg

48–49. Atlanta campaign

50–53. War in the West: Nashville, march to the sea

54–55. Siege of Petersburg

56–57. Operations in the Shenandoah Valley: August–September 1864

58. Appomattox campaign

55.5

Banks, Arthur.

A world atlas of military history; with an introduction by Lord Chalfont. London, Seeley Service & Co., 1973–1978.

2 vols. maps. 26 cm.

G1030 .B27 1973

"Volume one to 1500" and volume two, "1861–1945."

Maps of "The American Civil War" included in volume 2, part II, pages 10 to 31.

55.6

————Another edition. New York, Hippocrene Books, inc., [1973–1978]

2 vols. maps. 26 cm.

G1030.B27 1973b

56

Bien, Julius.

Map of United States military rail roads, showing the rail roads operated during the war from 1862–1866, as military lines, under the direction of Bvt. Brig. Gen. D. C. McCallum, Director and General Manager. Lith of J. Bien, N.Y. 1866. Colored. Scale ca. 1:1,875,000. 64 × 97 cm.

Map of the Southeast showing towns, forts, rivers, and state boundaries. Railroad gauges are printed in color.

Engraver's name appears below the map title and in the lower right margin.

56.1

————[n.p., 1976?] Facsimile edition. Uncolored. Scale ca. 1:2,100,000. 57 × 87 cm.

G3701 .P3 1866 .B5 1976

56.2

————Another issue.

Railroad gauges and the States of the Southeast are hand colored. Engraver's name appears below map title but not in margin.

Listed to A. M. Modelski's *Railroad Maps of the United States* (Washington, Library of Congress, 1975), no. 143.

57

Blair, R. Baxter.

Civil War. By Albert Bushnell Hart. Assisted by David Maydole Matteson. L. Philip Denoyer, geographer. Compiled and drawn by R. Baxter Blair. Chicago, Denoyer-Geppert Co., ©1918. Colored. Scale ca. 1:2,500,000. 76 × 109 cm. (Hart American history series, no. A16)

Wall map of the southern states, showing "lines of Federal military occupation" 1861–64, "area of Confederate military control March 1, 1865," troop movements, "raided areas," Federal blockade, railroads, canals, rivers, and towns.

Insets: Vicksburg campaign 1863. Scale 1:633,600. 12 × 18 cm.—Atlanta campaign. Scale 1:793,680. 25 × 13 cm.—Virginia campaigns. Scale 1:793,680. 43 × 38 cm.

57.2

————Another edition. [1924?]

Library of Congress copy incomplete; lacks place names and map title. Pencil note in margin reads "New A16. Black to be printed. Black plate similar to 1921 edition. [signed] R. B. Blair."

57.4

————Another edition. 1956. 78 × 110 cm. mounted to fold to 21 × 28 cm. (Denoyer-Geppert social science maps, no. A16)

58

————War between the states, 1861–1865. Edited by Edgar B. Wesley. Drawn by R. Baxter Blair. Chicago, Denoyer-Geppert Co., ©1949. Colored. Scale 1:2,534,400. 76 × 108 cm. on sheet 99 × 112 cm. (Wesley social studies: our America backgrounds and development, no. WA 23)

Based on the preceding map from the Hart American History Series, No. A16. Lacks insets showing the Virginia, Atlanta, and Vicksburg campaigns, however.

59

Case (O. D.) and Company.

Map of the seat of war. To accompany the American Conflict. Engraved by Oliver J. Stuart, New York and Brooklyn. Hartford, O. D. Case & Co., ©1865. Colored. Scale ca. 1:2,170,000. 66 × 93 cm.

Map of the southeastern United States showing battlefields, forts, infantry and calvary routes, towns, railroads, county and state boundaries, and rivers.

Insets: Map of the lower portion of Texas. 7 × 9 cm.—Map of the lower portion of Florida. 11 × 9 cm.

Prepared to accompany Greeley, Horace. *The American Conflict . . .* Hartford, 1864–66. 2v.

60

————Another edition. ©1866.

60.5

Civil Education Services, Inc.

The Civil War: visual-history wall map. Artist: Alexander Yaron. Washington, ©1966. Colored. Scale ca. 1:2,700,000. 90 × 68 cm.

G3701 .S5 1966 .C5

Inset: Civil War lineup. 13 × 17 cm. (Map of the United States showing Union states, border states, Confederate states, and "pro-Confederate territories.")

Pictorial map of the eastern United States showing important Civil War sites.

Text entitled "The cost of war to Americans" appears in the lower right corner and seven drawings showing "Weapons of the Civil War" are reproduced in the lower left corner.

61

Cockrell, Monroe F.

Flight of Confederate cabinet. Based on manuscript of Nora M. Davis, and Hanna's "Flight into Oblivion" and diaries. Prepared by Monroe F. Cockrell. Drawn by Emery L. Ring. July 18, 1942. Copyright—Monroe F. Cockrell [1942] Blue print. Scale 1:1,900,800. 60 × 43 cm.

Map extends from Virginia to Cuba and indicates the route of the cabinet and their location at various dates.

Another copy in *Notes and Articles by Monroe F. Cockrell for His Maps of the War Between the States.* ©1950. Typescript.

62

————The military campaigns of Nathan Bedford Forrest. [1861–1865] Based on Wyeth's Life of Forrest. Prepared by Monroe F. Cockrell. Drawn by Emery L. Ring. September 18, 1941. Copyright—Monroe F. Cockrell [1941] Blue print. Scale 1:887,040. 69 × 69 cm.

Map of parts of Alabama, Mississippi, Georgia, Kentucky, and Tennessee, showing lines of march, positions on various dates, towns, railroads, and state boundaries.

"Military record" appears in the upper right corner and "Major conflicts" in the lower right corner.

Another copy in *Notes and Articles by Monroe F. Cockrell for His Maps of the War Between the States.* ©1950. Typescript.

62.2

Colton, George Woolworth.

Map of the military operations during the war of 1861–1865 designed expressly to accompany "The lost cause," a standard southern history of the war. Drawn, engraved, printed & colored at Coltons Geographical Establishment, New York. New York, E. B. Treat & Co., ©1867. Uncolored. Scale 1:3,168,000. 46 × 62 cm.

"Entered according to Act of Congress in the year 1867 by G. W. & C. B. Colton."

General map of the southern states.

"Chronology of the principal events of the war" printed in the lower right corner.

From Edward A. Pollard's *The Lost Cause: A New Southern History of the War of the Confederates* (New York, E. B. Treat & Co., 1867), preceding chapter 1, p. 33.

62.4

The Comparative Synoptical Chart Company, Limited.

History of the Civil War in the United States, 1860–1865. J. Kellick Bathurst, compiler; Edward Perrin, del.; Courier Litho. Co., Buffalo, N.Y. Buffalo, N.Y.; London, England; Toronto, Canada, ©1897. Colored chart. 107 × 76 cm.

"Scaife's comparative and synoptical system of history applied to all countries."

"Entered according to Act of Congress in the year 1897, by The Comparative Synoptical Chart Co., Limited, in the Office of the Librarian of Congress at Washington. Filed in the United States, 1896. Copyright in Great Britain, 1897."

This is not a geographical map, but a historical time chart. "This history of the Civil War is drawn to a time scale of months, and the location of all events is entirely governed by this scale."

Inset: Map illustrating the Civil War in the United States shewing principal battle fields, &c, 1861 to 1865, from Colton's "Atlas" pub: N. York. 13 × 24 cm.

62.6

Cowdon, James S., *and* James D. Holman.

Statistical map of the United States of America. Prepared by James S. Cowdon and James D. Holman, Special Statisticians, under the direction of the Hon. John C. Black, Commissioner of Pensions. M. Joyce, Eng., Wash., D.C. July, 1888. Uncolored. Scale ca. 1:6,400,000. 49 × 78 cm.

The following categories of statistics are given for the United States and individual states: Population in 1860; Vote for President in 1860; Men furnished in war of 1861–'5; Volunteers; Substitutes; Personal service; Commutation; Bounty men; U.S. bounty paid in 1861–'5; Local bounty paid in 1861–'5; Proportion of white soldiers to white pop-ulation in 1860; Proportion of colored troops to colored population in 1860; [and] Pensioners, July 1, 1888.

63

Cushing, E. H.

Campaign map of Texas, Louisiana and Arkansas, showing all the battle fields and also the marches of Walker's Division. [1861–65] Entered according to Act of Congress in the year 1871 by E. H. Cushing. Engraved, printed and manufactured by G. W. & C. B. Colton & Co., New York. Published by J. P. Blessington, Houston, Texas, 16 Tex. Vol. Inf., 1871. Uncolored. Scale ca. 1:2,100,000. 70 × 94 cm.

Map includes names and boundaries of counties, existing and projected railroads, geographic coordinates, drainage, and towns.

63.5

Dodd, Mead and Company.

Seat of operations during the Civil War, 1861–1865. Copyright, 1902, by Dodd, Mead & Company. Colored. Scale ca. 1:10,500,000. 15 × 21 cm.

General map of the southern states.

63.7

Down Home Designs.

Strange incidents of the Civil War: a collection of curious & forgotten events from the years 1860–1865. Selma, Ala., Down Home Designs, ©1983. Uncolored. Scale ca. 1:3,700,000. 41 × 54 cm.

G3701 .S5 1983 .D6

Twenty-nine "strange incidents" in the Southeast are described and keyed by number to the map.

Copyright no. VA 142–095, Dec. 2, 1983.

64

Fiebeger, Gustave Joseph.

[Campaigns of the American Civil War. Atlas. West Point, N.Y., U.S. Military Academy Printing Office, 1914] 1 p. l., 7 numb. l., 48 maps on 46 l. 18 × 26 cm.

G1201 .S5F5 1914

Cover title.

Includes maps of the battles of 1st and 2d Manassas, Seven Pines, Antietam, Fredericksburg, forts Henry and Donelson, Shiloh, Stones River, Chancellorsville, Mechanicsville, Gettysburg, Chickamauga, Chattanooga, Wilderness, Spotsylvania, North Anna, Cold Harbor, Petersburg, Winchester, Fisher's Hill, Cedar Creek, Franklin, and Nashville. Some of the maps have been annotated with colored pencils.

Accompanies text with same title (432 p. 23 cm.).

Listed in C. E. Le Gear's *A List of Geographical Atlases in the Library of Congress* (Washington, Library of Congress, 1973), v. 7, no. 10656.

65

Formby, John.

The American Civil War—Maps. London, John Murray [1910] 2 p. l., 65 (i.e., 66) col. fold. maps on 59 l. 23 × 15 cm.

G1201 .S5F6 1910b

Cover title.

Issued to accompany Formby, John. *The American Civil War, a concise History of Its Causes, Progress, and Results* (London, John Murray, 1910).

Includes maps of the principal campaigns and battles of the Civil War.

66

————————Another edition. [New York, Scribners, 1910]

G1201 .S5F6 1910

Cover title.

Issued to accompany Formby, John. *The American Civil War, a Concise History of Its Causes, Progress, and Results* (New York, Scribners, 1910).

Listed in C. E. Le Gear's *A List of Geographical Atlases in the Library of Congress* (Washington, Library of Congress, 1973), v. 7, no. 10657.

66a

Fulwider, Edwin.

Battlefields and historic shrines, 1861–1865. A motorist's guide to historic sights in the South. Prepared by the Ford Times. Presented by your Ford Dealer. Artists: Edwin Fulwider. Dearborn, Michigan, Ford Motor Co., ©1961. Colored. Scale ca. 1:4,160,000. 60 × 88 cm.

Insets: Detail map of eastern Virginia. 18 × 24 cm.— [Outline map of the United States, showing limits of northern, southern and border states, and territories.] 8 × 12 cm.

Pictorial map of the southern United States, showing Civil War battlefields and historic sites.

66b

General Drafting Company.

A pictorial map showing historic shrines and battlefields of the Civil War, 1861–1865. This map prepared expressly for ESSO Standard, Division of Humble Oil & Refining Company. Convent Station, N.J., ©1961. Colored. Scale ca. 1:2,250,000. 64 × 96 cm.

Pictorial map of the Southeast showing Civil War sites, towns, railroads, rivers, and state boundaries.

Inset: The nation, 1861–1865. Scale ca. 1:34,400,000. 11 × 15 cm.

Brief descriptions of the "Strategy of the War" and "Some of the Decisive Actions and Events that Reunited our Nation," by Harnett T. Kane, appear on the verso and are illustrated by the following 13 maps.

[1] Manassas (Bull Run), July 21, 1861, August 29–30, 1862. Scale ca. 1:108,000. 15 × 17 cm.

[2] Fort Donelson, February 13–16, 1862. Scale ca. 1:21,000. 15 × 19 cm.

[3] Pea Ridge, March 6–8, 1862. Scale ca. 1:24,250. 15 × 18 cm.

[4] Shiloh, April 6–7, 1862. Scale ca. 1:65,000. 15 × 15 cm.

[5] Antietam, September 17, 1862. Scale ca. 1:45,000. 16 × 19 cm.

[6] Fredericksburg, December 13, 1862. Scale ca. 1:76,000. 14 × 19 cm.

[7] Gettysburg, July 1–3, 1863. Scale ca. 1:51,000. 18 × 19 cm.

[8] Vicksburg under siege, May 18–July 4, 1863. Scale ca. 1:62,000. 18 × 16 cm.

[9]Chickamauga, September 19–20, 1863. Scale ca. 1:44,500. 18 × 16 cm.

[10] Petersburg under siege, June 1864 to April 1865. Scale ca. 1:65,000. 18 × 20 cm.

[11] Kennesaw Mountain, June 22–27, 1864. Scale ca. 1:70,000. 13 × 14 cm.

[12] Richmond. Scale ca. 1:225,000. 16 × 14 cm.

[13] Decisive army campaigns and the naval blockade. Scale ca. 1:10,400,000. 16 × 24 cm.

Another copy is classed G3701 .S5 1961 .G4.

66b.5

General Foods Corporation.

Civil War map. Centennial edition. ©1961. Colored. Scale ca. 1:8,900,000. 41 × 60 cm.

Title when folded: Civil War centennial map.

Decorative map of the United States including 31 illustrations.

Verso includes "A Special Commemorative Report," a brief chronology of events, and portraits of Lincoln, Davis, and the principal military leaders.

67

Goff, Eugenia W., *and* Henry S. Goff.

Goff's historical map of the United States. Civil War, Spanish—Am. War, war in the Philippines, invasion of China. Philadelphia, McConnell School Supply Co., ©1907. Colored. Scale ca. 1:2,040,000. Principal map 77 × 98 cm. on sheet 136 × 102 cm.

Wall map of the South showing location and date of battles, some troop movements, towns, rivers, and state boundaries.

Following insets relate to the Civil War: The Virginia and the Monitor in Hampton Roads, 1862. 15 × 14 cm.— Grant's Vicksburg campaign, January to July 1863. 16 × 17 cm.—Lee's first northern invasion, 1862. 16 × 18 cm.—

Lee's second northern invasion, 1863. 14 × 16 cm.—[Map of the coast of Texas showing the location and date of battles] 22 × 9 cm.

Includes index to place names.

68

Goushá (H. M.) Company.

Civil War centennial map. Chicago, ©1960. Colored. Scale 1:443,520 and 1:5,575,680. 2 maps each 21 × 37 cm. on sheet 46 × 49 cm.

"Presented to the public by Cities Service in commemoration of the Civil War centennial 1961–1965."

Map of the Civil War Area (southeastern United States) and map of the *Area of the Virginia Campaigns,* showing battlegrounds, naval engagements, "dividing line between Union and Confederacy." and "towns where major events occurred."

"Major battles and events of the Civil War" are listed on verso.

68.2

————————Chicago, ©1961. Colored. Various scales. 8 maps on sheet 46 × 78 cm.

Similar in part to map prepared in 1960 for Cities Service Oil Company. See *Civil War Maps,* entry no. 68.

Contents.—**recto.** Map of the Civil War area. [S.E. United States]—Area of the Virginia campaigns.—Gettysburg National Military Park, Pennsylvania.—Fredericksburg and Spotsylvania National Military Park, Virginia.—Petersburg National Military Park, Virginia.—Richmond National Battlefield Park, Virginia.—Antietam National Battlefield Site, Maryland.—Manassas National Battlefield Park, Virginia.—**verso.** Chronological list of planned observances for 1961–1965.—[List of the] major battles and events of the Civil War.

69

Greaves, Peyton.

The Confederate States of America, 1861–1865; an historical map showing the battles in their heroic struggle for independence. Albany, Georgia, Peyton Greaves, ©1960. Uncolored. Scale ca. 1:4,000,000. 49 × 81 cm.

Indicates towns, forts, railroads, relief by hachures, rivers, land and sea battles, Confederate and Union naval blockades, and "states having both Confederate and Union governments."

70

Grosset and Dunlap, inc., *publishers, New York.*

The picture map of the Civil War showing nearly 100 places, events and campaigns of decisive importance in the Nation's epic struggle. 1861–1865. Published by Grosset & Dunlap, New York, in conjunction with The Civil War by Otto Eisenschiml, Ralph Newman and E. B. Long. ©1956. Colored. Scale ca. 1:5,000,000. 56 × 76 cm.

Map shows "Union naval blockade of Confederate ports and waters," "underground railroad," "route of Morgan's raid through Kentucky, Indiana, and Ohio, 1863," and "Sherman's march to the sea" and "through the Carolinas."

76 "places, events, and campaigns" keyed by number to map.

Includes the following eight views, each measuring 13 × 10 cm.: Stonewall Jackson; Stonewall Jackson's valley campaign, May–June, 1862.—Vicksburg; Grant's siege of Vicksburg, May 18–July 4, 1863.—The war at sea; The Alabama under Confederate Admiral Semmes sunk by Kearsarge off France, June 19, 1864.—Sheridan; Gen. Sheridan in the Shenandoah Valley, August–October, 1864.—Fort Sumter; Bombardment of Fort Sumter, April 12–13, 1861.—Bull Run.—Gettysburg.—Appomattox; Lee and Grant signing surrender at McLean House, April 9, 1865.

71

Hall, Edward S.

Lloyd's new military map of the border & southern states. [Drawn by Edward S. Hall. Waters & Son, engravers] Published by H. H. Lloyd & Co., New York. 1865. Colored. Scale ca. 1:1,850,000. 76 × 106 cm.

At top of map: The rebellion as it was and as it is.

Shows "territory held by Rebels April 1st, 1865, in red," "territory gained from Rebels since January 1st, 1862, in yellow," and "Sherman's march from Chattanooga, in blue."

Battlefields are marked by red lines and strategic places, by red dots.

Indicates towns, railroads, rivers, names and boundaries of states, and relief by hachures.

For earlier editions, see entry nos. 27 and 38.

71.5

Hammond (C. S.) and Company.

The Civil War. [1861–65] Copyright by C. S. Hammond & Co., N.Y. [©1949] 4 colored maps, each 10 × 14 cm. on sheet 14 × 32 cm. *From its* The march of civilization in maps and pictures; a graphic reference book covering man's development and conquests from 4000 B.C. to the present day. New York, ©1949. Part III, p. 23.

Same plate also appears in Hammond's *Advanced Reference Atlas; The Modern, Medieval and Ancient World* (New York, ©1949).

Scale of each map, ca. 1:16,500,000.

No. "8498" in the lower right corner of the border.

Maps show forts, battles, and Union and Confederate movements. Colors are used to differentiate areas controlled

PUBLISHED BY H. H. LLOYD & CO., 21 JOHN ST., NEW YORK.   B. B. RUSSELL & CO., 55 CORNHILL, BOSTON.   R. E. LANDON, 89 LAKE STREET, CHICAGO.

by the Union and the Confederacy and the area gained by the Union during the war.

Copyright no. F 5551, Jan. 6, 1949.

71a

———

Commemorative map, campaigns of the Civil War. Centennial edition. Published in cooperation with the Civil War Centennial Commission. Maplewood, N.J., C. S. Hammond & Co., ©1961. Colored. Scale ca. 1:2,825,000. 64 × 94 cm.

Decorative map of the Eastern United States, showing major troop movements and raids, Federal blockade, and territory under Federal control in 1861, 1862, 1863, 1864, and 1865.

Insets: The Virginia campaigns, 1861–1862. 14 × 10 cm.—The Virginia campaigns, 1863–1864–1865. 14 × 10 cm.—United States at the beginning of the Civil War, 1861. 10 × 14 cm.—The battle of Gettysburg. 16 × 12 cm.

Includes portraits of Lincoln, Grant, Sheridan, Sherman, McClellan, Meade, Davis, Lee, Bragg, Stuart, Beauregard, and Jackson.

71b

———Another issue.

"Distributed by Parade Magazine."

71c

Historical Documents Company.

Civil War battlefields, 1861–1865. ©1961, Colored. Scale ca. 1:6,000,000. 26 × 33 cm.

Map of the Southern States with principal events of the war keyed by number to "chronological history" in the bottom margin.

71c.2

Kenyon Company.

Campaigns of the Civil War in the East. The Kenyon Co., Des Moines, Iowa. Copyright, 1910, by A. B. Alderman. Uncolored. Scale ca. 1:10,000,000. 16 × 11 cm.

"Plate no. 8" in the lower right margin.

Map of the South Atlantic states showing "Shermans march."

71c.4

———Campaigns of the Civil War in the West. The

———

Battlefields are emphasized by red underlining and strategic places by red dots on this wood-engraved 1865 map entitled "Lloyd's New Military Map of the Border & Southern States." Also shown are "territory held by Rebels April 1st, 1865, in red," "territory gained from Rebels since January 1st, 1862, in yellow," and "Sherman's march from Chattanooga, in blue." (See entry no. 71.)

Kenyon Co., Des Moines, Iowa. Copyright, 1910, by A. B. Alderman. Uncolored. Scale ca. 1:10,000,000. 16 × 10 cm.

"Plate no. 7" in the lower right margin.

Map of Kentucky, Tennessee, Mississippi, Alabama, Illinois, Indiana, Ohio, and parts of adjoining states. "Shermans march" in Georgia shaded gray.

72

Kossak, William, *and* John B. Muller.

Military map showing the marches of the United States forces under command of Maj. Genl. W. T. Sherman, U.S.A., during the years 1863, 1864, 1865. Compiled by order of Maj. Genl. W. T. Sherman, U.S.A., at Head Quarters, Military Division of the Mississippi, under the direction of Bvt. Maj. W. L. B. Jenney . . . Drawn by Capt. William Kossak . . . and John B. Muller, draughtsman. Engraved at Head Qrs., Corps of Engineers, U.S.A., by H. C. Evans & F. Courtenay. Printed by Joseph F. Gedney. St. Louis, Mo., 1865. Colored. Scale 1:1,267,200 (20 miles equal 1 inch). 72 × 118 cm.

Detailed map of the southeastern United States showing fortifications, "movements of Genl. J. H. Wilson's Cavalry Corps," "pursuit of Hood," and the lines of march of the 4th, 14th, 15th, 16th, 17th, and 20th army corps and the cavalry. Map also indicates "movement on Atlanta, Ga.," roads, railroads, names and boundaries of states, towns, drainage, geographic coordinates, and relief by hachures.

Another copy of this map, from the papers of Joseph Roswell Hawley, is annotated in red ink: Compliments of Lieut. Gen. Sherman, Wm. E. Merrill, Maj. Engn. & Bvt. Col. G3866 .S5 1865 .K6

Another copy is in Sherman map coll. no. 6.

Another copy of this map, in the papers of James A. Garfield, Manuscript Division, L.C., series 8, container no. 1, is annotated in red ink: Compliments of Lieut. Gen. Sherman, Wm. E. Merrill, Maj. Engn. & Bvt. Col.

72.2

————Facsimile. [Detroit, U.S. Lake Survey, 1965] Uncolored (sepia toned). Scale 1:1,267,200. 74 × 119 cm.

72.4

————Facsimile. [Knoxville, Tennessee Valley Authority, 1975?] Blue line print. Scale ca. 1:1,700,000. (not "1:1,267,200"). 57 × 90 cm.

G3866 .S5 1865 .K6 1975

73

————Another issue (reduced). Colored. Scale 1:1,584,000 (25 miles equal to 1 inch). 59 × 94 cm.

In lower right corner: Engraved at Head Qrs., Corps of Engineers, U.S.A., by H. C. Evans & F. Courtenay.

Reduced issue of the preceding map (entry no. 72) with

the "movements of Genl. G. Stoneman's Cavalry Corps" added.

74

————Another issue (reduced). Colored. Scale 1:1,584,000 (25 miles equal 1 inch). 59 × 94 cm.

In lower right corner: Am. Photo-lithographic Co., N.Y. (Osborne's Process).

"Movements of Genl. G. Stoneman's Cavalry Corps" are not indicated on this issue.

75

————Another issue. Ferd. Mayer, gen'l. lith., N.Y. Uncolored. Scale 1:1,267,200 (20 miles equal 1 inch). 72 × 118 cm.

This issue indicates fortifications and routes of the infantry and cavalry. Individual corps, however, are not identified.

75.2

Kresse, William J.

Background map; Blockade 1861–65. [By] Bill Kresse [New York, AP Newsfeatures, 1961] Uncolored. Scale ca. 1:12,400,000. 17 × 19 cm.

Accompanies article by Tom Henshaw, AP Newsfeatures writer, entitled "Union blockade played big role in winning war for the North." 2 p., ea. 36 × 22 cm.

Map of the Southeast showing principal ports blockaded by Union ships.

75.4

Lambert, Robert D.

The American Civil War, 1861–1865. Haslett, Michigan, Historical Maps, ©1961. Uncolored. Scale ca. 1:2,000,000. 83 × 121 cm.

Map of the Southeast showing towns, forts, railroads, state boundaries, drainage, and relief by hachures. Maps of the environs of Shiloh, Vicksburg, Chickamauga, Nashville, Antietam, Fredericksburg, Gettysburg, and Petersburg are included in the insets. Neither the large map nor the inset maps include battle information.

"These maps depict areas generally as they were a century ago. Basic map data taken from the *Atlas to Accompany the Official Records of the Union and the Confederate Armies,* United States Government Printing Office."

75.6

Lathrop, H. P.

Plan of the western seat of war. J. Manouvrier & Co. lith., N. O. [New Orleans] H. P. Lathrop [1861–65?] Uncolored. Scale ca. 1:800,000. 37 × 56 cm.

Confederate imprint.

Inset: Reduced continuation of Missouri R. 4 × 7 cm.

General map of Kentucky, Tennessee, and parts of Illinois, Indiana, Ohio, Virginia, and North Carolina showing principal roads, railroads, towns, and rivers. Fortified sites and battlefields are not indicated.

75.7

Lee, Fitzhugh.

Map of the Confederate States of America. [1861–65] Des Moines, Iowa, Kenyon Co. [©1910] Colored. Scale 1:8,553,600. 20 × 28 cm. on sheet 74 × 52 cm.

General map of the South printed on a 1910 calendar entitled "Half century Confederate memorial" presented "compliments of the First National Bank, Gainesville, Georgia."

Map is surrounded by portraits of Pres. Jefferson Davis and Generals Lee, Gordon, Jackson, Beauregard, J. E. Johnston, A. S. Johnston, Stuart, Hood, and Longstreet and pictures of Confederate money and postage stamps, the capitol building, war memorials, and the flags of the Confederacy.

"Confederate poetry and song" and "important events and battles of the Civil War" are printed on the verso.

75.8

Lindenkohl, Adolph.

[Eastern Tennessee, with parts of Alabama, Georgia, South Carolina, North Carolina, Virginia, and Kentucky] Drawn by A. Lindenkohl. H. Lindenkohl & Chas. G. Krebs, lith. U.S. Coast Survey, A. D. Bache, Supdt. 1865. Colored. Scale 1:633,600. 60 × 87 cm.

General map, without title. State names and boundaries are printed in red.

"Library of the Department of State" is written in ink in the upper margin.

76

McConnell, James.

The Civil War, fourth year, 1864–1865. [Chicago, McConnell Map Co., ©1919] Colored. Scale ca. 1:2,200,000. 69 × 107 cm. (McConnell's historical maps of the United States. Revised ed. Map no. 38)

Map of the Southeast, showing troop movements and battles, towns, rivers, and state boundaries.

List of "important battles, 4th year, April 1864–1865," names of commanders, and a brief description of events appear in the lower right corner.

77

McDowell, Robert M.

Maps illustrating Gen'l. Sherman's "march to the sea" and through the Carolinas and Virginia, by Major R. M. McDowell, Chief Topographical Engineer, Left Wing, Army

of Georgia. [1864–1865] 58 l. incl. 51 col. ms. maps. 20 × 31 cm.

G1281 .S5M24 1865 Vault

Cover title.

Detailed manuscript atlas divided into five sections, each with a separate title page. Three of the title pages are manuscript and two are printed. The signature of Capt. R. M. McDowell appears on each title page and on maps 1 to 3, 41, and 42.

The line of march of the 20th Corps is shown from Chattanooga, Tenn., May 5, 1864 to Alexandria, Va., May 19, 1865, as well as part of the routes of the 14th Corps, the Michigan Engineers, and Kilpatrick's Cavalry. The atlas includes maps of the fortifications and/or battles at Atlanta, Milledgeville, Kolb's Farm, Peach Tree Creek, Resaca, New Hope Church, Pine Hill, and Savannah, Georgia; and Bentonville, Averysboro, and Raleigh, North Carolina.

Troop positions are based in part on information supplied by Lt. Col. C. W. Asmussen, Asst. Inspector General, 20th Corps.

Printed versions of 24 of the maps are reproduced in the *Atlas to Accompany the Official Records of the Union and Confederate Armies,* 1891–95, pl. 71, no. 1–11; 79, no. 4; 80, no. 1–11; and 101, no. 7, 19.

The Henry E. Huntington Library and Art Gallery, San Marino, California, has a collection of manuscript maps that are similar to some of the maps in the McDowell Atlas. Their collection contains a printed title page which reads *Maps showing the campaign of the 20th Corps from Atlanta to Savannah with the dates . . . 1864.* At the bottom of the title page is the handwritten statement "Officially issued to Surgeon H. Earnest Goodman by R. M. McDowell, Capt. and Chief Topogl. Engr., XX Corps, Savannah, Ga."

Listed in C. E. Le Gear's *A List of Geographical Atlases in the Library of Congress* (Washington, Library of Congress, 1973), v. 7, no. 10658.

77.1

——————[Maps for history of 20th Army Corps. June 1864–May 11, 1865] 28 ms. maps (mostly col.) 23 × 30 cm. or smaller.

G1281 .S5M2 1865 Vault

Maps illustrate Sherman's march from Georgia to Virginia. One of the cover sheets (now missing) contained the pencil notation "Maps for history of 20th Army Corps." Twenty of the maps are variant manuscript copies of maps in the McDowell atlas described above and eight maps either differ considerably or do not appear in the atlas at all.

77.2

Map of the seat of war. Maryland & Delaware with parts of Pennsylvania. Showing the railroads. [1861–65] Colored. Scale ca. 1:1,080,000. 52 × 51 cm.

G3791 .C5 186—.M3 Vault

U. S. Coast Survey A. D. Bache Supdt. 1865

SCALE
1 inch 10 miles

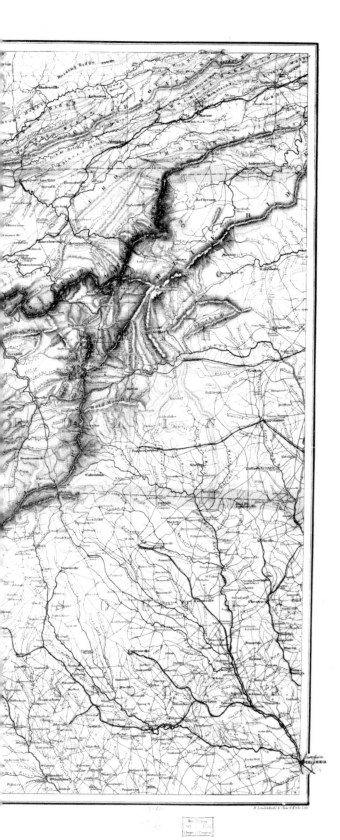

Printed map of the Middle Atlantic States with Virginia south of Gloucester and Lynchburg added in manuscript. Map has been hand-colored to show geological formations.

77.4

Melton, Harold K.

Civil War battlefields. Copyright 1970 by H. K. Melton. Colored. Scale ca. 1:3,460,000. Map and index sheet, each 43 × 55 cm.

G3701 .S5 1970 .M4

Outline map of the Southeastern United States showing the location of battles. "All locations are approximate" and are keyed by number to the accompanying list of battlefields (arranged by State) printed on a separate sheet.

77.6

Merritt, Isaac N.

Geographical history of the rail road regiment, 89th regiment of Illinois vols. infantry. [1862–1865] Platted and compiled from U.S. Coast Survey maps, by Isaac N. Merritt. Lithographed by Chas. Shober, Chicago. [18   ] Uncolored. Scale 1:633,600. 98 × 73 cm.

Map of parts of Kentucky, Tennessee, Alabama, and Georgia showing the operations of the 89th regiment of Illinois volunteers. The regiment was first attached to the 6th Brigade, 2nd Division, Right Wing, Army of the Ohio and later to the 1st Brigade, 3rd Division, 4th Army Corps, Army of the Cumberland.

Included are a "muster-in" and "muster-out" roster of officers, a "chronological record of engagements," a table of casualties and the names of officers wounded, and a brief history of the regiment.

77.8

Modern School Supply Company, *Chicago, Ill.*

The Civil War—Fourth year 1864–1865. Copyright by E. W. A. Rowles. [Chicago, ©1919] Colored. Scale ca. 1:2,600,000. 69 × 108 cm. (Comprehensive series; historical-geographical maps of the United States, no. 34)

Wall map of the Southeast showing forts, battles, "extreme limit[s] of Federal control, April 15, 1864 [and] January 1, 1865," towns, and state boundaries.

Includes brief descriptions of the closing campaigns of the war.

Inset: Sherman's march. 23 × 36 cm.

The U.S. Coast Survey produced numerous regional base maps at the scale of 10 miles to the inch for use by military commanders in the field. Some were printed without a title such as this 1865 map of eastern Tennessee and parts of Alabama, Georgia, South Carolina, North Carolina, Virginia, and Kentucky. Other maps in this series bore titles, such as the map of "North Carolina & South Carolina." (See entry no. 75.8.)

78

————The Civil War: general campaigns 1861–1865. [Edited by Olin D. Morrison and Erwin Raisz. Goshen, Ind., ©1947] Colored. Scale 1:5,068,800. 71 × 107 cm. (Comprehensive series; social studies maps of the United States, no. 23)

G1201 .S1C6 1947

Two maps of the Eastern United States on one sheet: I. Civil War 1861–1863. 71 × 54 cm.—II. Civil War 1863–1865. 71 × 54 cm.

Geography and Map Division's collections include nine editions dated 1947 to 1950, 1952, 1954, 1956, 1959, and 1960.

Editors since 1952: Franklin D. Scott [and] Erwin Raisz.

79

————General progress of the Civil War, 1861–1865. [Edited by Olin D. Morrison and Erwin Raisz. Goshen, Ind., ©1947] Colored. Various scales. 71 × 107 cm. (Comprehensive series; social studies maps of the United States, no. 24)

G1201 .S1C6 1947

Three maps on one sheet: I. General advance of Union control year by year. [Map of Eastern United States] Scale 1;5,068,800. 71 × 54 cm.—II. Virginia campaigns, 1861–1862. Scale 1:1,013,760. 34 × 54 cm.—III. Virginia campaigns 1863–1865. Scale 1:1,013,760. 34 × 54 cm.

The Geography and Map Division's collections include nine editions dated 1947 to 1950, 1952, 1954, 1956, 1959, and 1960.

Editors since 1952: Franklin D. Scott [and] Erwin Raisz.

79a

National Geographic Society.

Battlefields of the Civil War with descriptive notes. Atlas plate 14: April 1961. Compiled and drawn in the Cartographic Division of the National Geographic Society for The National Geographic Magazine. Washington, ©1961. Colored. Scale 1:2,851,200. 49 × 64 cm.

"This map portrays the country as it was charted in 1863. It is based on a map on which General Grant marked his proposed lines of operation."

Map of the Southeast showing battlefields, roads, railroads, towns, state boundaries, drainage, and relief by shading and spot heights.

"Notes printed in blue describe events that occurred before April 1, 1863; those in red took place after that date."

Inset: [Map of the Southeast showing] major offensives. Scale ca. 1:10,800,000. 13 × 18 cm.

Maps on verso: (A) War in the Southwest. Based on an 1861 map by the U.S. War Department. Scale ca.

1:7,600,000. 18 × 31 cm.—(B) Vicksburg Campaign. Scale ca. 1:700,000. 11 × 16 cm.—(C) Battles for Atlanta. Scale ca. 1:304,000. 12 × 8 cm.—(D) Memphis to Huntsville. [Map of parts of Tennessee, Mississippi and Alabama.] Scale ca. 1:1,450,000. 16 × 23 cm.—(E) Nashville to Atlanta. [Map of parts of Kentucky, Tennessee, North Carolina, Alabama and Georgia.] Scale ca. 1:1,450,000. 31 × 23 cm.—(F) Cockpit of the Civil War. [Map of Maryland and parts of Pennsylvania, West Virginia, and Virginia.] Scale ca. 1:950,000. 45 × 32 cm.—(G) Grant at Richmond. [Map of the environs of Richmond and Petersburg.] Scale ca. 1:536,000. 12 × 9 cm.—(H) Gettysburg. Scale ca. 1:100,000. 10 × 10 cm.—(J) Charleston Harbor. Scale ca 1:400,000. 6 × 8 cm.—(K) Fort Sumter, 1861. Scale ca. 1:5600. 4 × 6 cm.

79a.2

————Another ed. Washington, 1961. Colored. Scale 1:1,782,000. 79 × 103 cm.

An enlarged version of the preceding map (entry no. 79a).

Copyrighted June 18, 1962, no. F33435.

79a.4

————Another ed. Washington, ©1969. Colored. Scale 1:2,851,200. 49 × 64 cm. folded to 24 × 16 cm.

"Printed for the special publication The Civil War."

Copyrighted Nov. 25, 1969, no. F50171.

G3701 .S5 1969 .N3

79a.6

Nicholson, W. L., *and* Adolph Lindenkohl.

Mountain region of North Carolina and Tennessee. Compiled by W. L. Nicholson & A. Lindenkohl, with corrections to January 1865. Drawn by A. Lindenkohl. H. Lindenkohl & Chas. G. Krebs, lith. U.S. Coast Survey, A. D. Bache, Supt. Colored. Scale 1:633,600. 56 × 97 cm.

Map title printed in the top margin. Map covers parts of the states of Kentucky, Tennessee, Virginia, North and South Carolina, Georgia, and Alabama and shows relief by hachures, drainage, names and boundaries of states, roads, and railroads. This edition has been significantly revised in the vicinity of Chattanooga, Tennessee, and Northern Georgia.

Unfinished proof for this map is described as entry no. 43.4. The 1863 edition is listed as entry no. 43.5 and the 1864 edition as entry no. 53.

80

Paris, Louis Philippe Albert d'Orléans, *comte* de.

[Histoire de la guerre civile en Amérique] Atlas. [Paris, Michel Lévy, 1874–90] 30 col. maps. 45 × 34 cm.

G1201 .S5P3 1874 folio

Published in parts.

Incomplete: Title-pages of parts 1–2 wanting.

For table of contents see P. L. Phillips's *A List of Geographical Atlases in the Library of Congress* (Washington, Government Printing Office, 1909) v. 1, no. 1352.

The Geography and Map Division also has separates for plates 5, 11–14, 16, and 19.

80.2

Phelps and Watson.

Phelps & Watson's historical and military map of the border & southern states. New York, Gaylord Watson, successor to Phelps & Watson, 1865. Colored. Scale ca. 1:2,534,400. 64 × 92 cm.

"Entered according to Act of Congress; in the year 1862 by Phelps & Watson."

Includes list of "Battles of the war" from April 12, 1861, to May 12, 1864.

Accompanied by a pamphlet entitled *New Historical War Map* (36 p., 15 × 10 cm.) containing a "Brief description of battles and skirmishes of the war," 1861–65.

For other editions, see entry nos. 43.8, 53.2, and 80.3.

80.3

——————Another issue. 1867.

For other editions, see entry nos. 43.8, 53.2, and 80.2.

80.4

Plum, William R.

Theatre in central Kentucky and middle and eastern Tennessee, also in Missouri and Arkansas. [1861–65] Emil Heubach, designer & engraver, Chicago, Ill. Copyright, 1882, by W. R. Plum. Uncolored. Scale ca. 1:5,800,000. 2 maps on sheet 25 × 16 cm. *From his* The military telegraph during the Civil War in the United States. Chicago, Jansen, McClurg & Co., 1882. v. 1, facing p. 122.

General map indicating state names and boundaries, railroads, drainage, and place names. Troop positions are not depicted.

80.5

——————

Theatre of Pennsylvania, Maryland, Virginia and West Virginia campaigns. [1861–65] Emil Heubach [designer & engraver] Chicago. Copyright, 1882, by W. R. Plum. Uncolored. Scale ca. 1:3,600,000. 11 × 18 cm. *From his* The military telegraph during the Civil War in the United States. Chicago, Jansen, McClurg & Co., 1882. v. 1, facing p. 74.

General map indicating state names and boundaries, railroads, drainage, and place names. Troop positions are not depicted.

80.7

Quillen, I. James, *and* Eunice Johns.

The War between the States, 1861–1865. Chicago, A. J. Nystrom & Co. [©1961] Colored. Scale 1:4,118,400. 87 × 119 cm. (Quillen-Johns American history maps. Map no. Q. J. 16)

Wall map of the United States showing "free states," "loyal slave states," states which "seceded after Lincoln's election" and those which "seceded after Lincoln's call for troops," principal campaigns, and raids.

81

Rand McNally and Company.

Armed conflict and reconstruction—1861 to 1877. Chicago [©1941] Colored. Scale 1:4,000,000. 95 × 143 cm. (Earle-McKee American history series, no. EMF 101)

Wall map of the United States showing principal engagements, forts, towns, railroads, state boundaries, rivers, and principal western trails. Union states are colored green and Confederate states are yellow.

"Main map as of 1865 before the close of the war. Reconstruction inset shows the country as of 1877."

Following insets relate to the Civil War: Principal campaigns of the war. Scale 1:4,000,000. 28 × 40 cm.—Principal eastern campaigns of 1861–62–63. Scale 1:2,000,000. 20 × 22 cm.—Men and dollars of the war. (diagram) 13 × 16 cm.—Per capita national debt of the United States before and after the war. (diagram) 5 × 16 cm.

81a

——————Civil War centennial historical sites. [1861–65. Chicago, ©1961] Colored. Scale ca 1:4,000,000. 46 × 50 cm.

Title when folded: Civil War centennial events, 1861–1961.

Map of the Eastern United States showing roads, route numbers, towns, state boundaries, forts, and rivers. Union States are colored blue, Confederate States are gray, and Border States are tan. "Crossed flags with numbers locate points of historical significance to the Civil War. The corresponding number in the chronological list . . . [to the right of the map] denote the major events that occurred at these sites."

Includes portraits of Lincoln, Davis, Grant, Lee, Sherman, Jackson, McClellan, Longstreet, Farragut, Beauregard, Thomas, and Joseph E. Johnston.

On verso: Tour one [Virginia, Maryland, and southern Pennsylvania]. Scale ca. 1:3,000,000. 20 × 30 cm.—Tour two [Cairo, Ill., to Columbia, S.C., via Chattanooga, Atlanta, Savannah, and Charleston]. Scale ca. 1:3,600,000. 24 × 33 cm.—Tour three [St. Louis, Mo. to Montgomery, Ala., via Vicksburg and New Orleans]. Scale ca.

1:3,750,000. 31 × 28 cm. Each indicates suggested tours and Civil War points of interest.

81b

————Civil War centennial map; United States map featuring Civil War battlefields and sites. Designed for Sinclair Refining Company by Rand McNally & Company. [Chicago, ©1961] Colored. Various scales. 26 maps on sheet measuring 92 × 65 cm.

Contents.—**recto.** [Four maps indicating the approximate areas under Federal and Confederate control in 1861, 1862, 1863, and 1864–65.] Bombardement of Fort Sumter, South Carolina, April 12–13, 1861. Battle of First Manassas (Bull Run), Virginia, July 21, 1861. Fort Henry-Fort Donelson campaign, Tennessee, February 1862. Battle of Second Manassas (Bull Run), Virginia, August 28–31, 1862. Battle of Shiloh (Pittsburg Landing), Tenn., April 6–7, 1862. The Peninsula campaign, Virginia, March–July, 1862. Battle of Antietam (Sharpsburg), Maryland, September 17, 1862. Battle of Fredericksburg, Virginia, December 13, 1862. Battle of Stone's River (Murfreesboro), Tennessee, December 31, 1862–January 2, 1863. Battle of Fredericksburg, Virginia, December 13, 1863. Campaign for Vicksburg, Mississippi, May 1–July 4, 1863. Battle of Gettysburg, Pennsylvania, July 1–3, 1863. Battle of Chickamauga, Georgia, September 20, 1863. Battle of Chattanooga, Tennessee, November 24–25, 1863. Battles of the Wilderness & Spotsylvania, Virginia, May 5–21, 1864. Sherman's Georgia campaigns, 1864. Siege of Petersburg, Virginia, June 15, 1864–April 2, 1865. Battle of Franklin, Tennessee, November 30, 1864. Battle of Nashville, Tennessee, December 15–16, 1864. Appomattox campaign, Virginia, April 2–9, 1865.—**verso.** United States [showing by color, Union, Confederate, and Border States]. Civil War centennial. [Map of the Eastern United States showing points of interest.]

Maps indicate roads, route numbers, railroads, towns, forts, troop positions and movements, and points of interest. "Troop movements and locations have been generalized to illustrate approximate positions at the most decisive periods of the battles."

81b.2

————The country in flames, 1861–1865. Copyright by Rand McNally & Co. [Chicago, 1976] Colored. Scale ca. 1:2,350,000. 92 × 122 cm. folded in cover 30 × 27 cm. (Rand McNally Bicentennial American studies series)

G3701 .S5 1976 .R3

"Consultant: Henry F. Graff, Ph.D., Columbia University."

Wall map of the Eastern United States showing principal campaigns and battles of the war. Colors are used to denote areas controlled by the Union, the Confederacy, and the "Union penetration of Confederate area, 1862–65."

Insets: [Map of Virginia showing battles and troop movements] 1861–63. 45 × 45 cm.—[Map of Virginia, showing battles and troop movements] 1864–65. 45 × 45 cm.—Confederates charge Union lines at Gettysburg [view] 28 × 34 cm.—[Map of the United States showing] the nation divided. 28 × 29 cm.

82

Rennecamp, Charles.

Historical map of the United States indicating battlefields, names of commanders, number of troops engaged, number of killed and captured during French and Indian and Revolutionary wars, Mexican War, and the late Civil War. Buxton & Skinner litho, St. Louis. [©1890] Colored. Scale ca. 1:4,800,000. 4 parts, each 49 × 68 cm.

Principal map shows location and date of battles fought during the Civil War. The winner of each engagement is given as well as the names of the opposing commanders.

Inset: The battlefield of Virginia. Late Civil War. 21 × 24 cm.

83

Robertson, H. C.

Sherman's march to the sea. [May 15, 1864–April 26, 1865. Chicago, R. O. Evans and Co., ©1898] Colored. Scale not given. 84 × 58 cm. (Robertson's geographic-historical series illustrating the history of America and the United States)

Wall map of South Carolina and parts of Tennessee, North Carolina, and Georgia, showing Sherman's lines of march, and the location and dates of engagements.

Includes an outline of events; portraits of Generals W. T. Sherman, George H. Thomas, and J. E. Johnston; and views of "Sherman's army on its march to the sea," "Battle of Atlanta," "An incident of the march through Georgia," and "Grant writing the telegram to Sherman."

84

Ruger, Edward.

Map prepared to exhibit the campaigns in which the Army of the Cumberland took part during the War of the Rebellion. [1861–65] By order of Maj. Gen. Geo. H. Thomas, U.S.A. Compiled under the direction of Bvt. Major Genl. Z. B. Tower, Chief Eng'r., Military Div. of the Tenn., by Ed. Ruger, Sup't Top'l. Eng'r. Office at Nashville. Assistants: Capt. A. Kilp & Lieut. R. Flach, 3rd U.S.C.A. (Heavy) & Asst. Top Engrs. Julius Bien & Co., photo lith., N.Y. Colored. Scale 1:1,267,200. 68 × 82 cm.

Map of South Carolina, Kentucky, and Tennessee, and parts of Georgia, Alabama, Mississippi, North Carolina, and Virginia, showing roads, railroads, towns, rivers, names and boundaries of states, and relief by hachures. Lines of march are indicated by colors and symbols. Includes "Jeff. Davis' line of flight."

Another copy is in the Sherman Map Coll. no. 5.

84.2

————Another edition. Uncolored. Scale 1:633,600. 136 × 164 cm.

Lines of march not indicated.

Lacks name of lithographer.

84.5

Rundall, Frank M.

Sketch map of United States of North-America. [1861–65] By F. M. Rundall, Lt.-Col., Comdg. 1/4th Gurkha Rifles. [1901?] Uncolored. Scale ca. 1:4,700,000. 35 × 47 cm.

Map of the Southern States showing places where battles were fought.

85

Russia (1923– U.S.S.R) *Glavnoe upravlenie geodezii i kartografii.*

Grazhdanskaia Voina v (S SH A) 1861–1865 gg. [Civil War in the U.S.A., 1861–1865] Karta sostavelna Nauchno-redaktsionnoi kartosostavitel skoi'chast' iu GUGK v 1950 g. Redaktor Moruchkov S. A. Moskva, 1956. Colored. Scale 1:3,000,000. 2 sheets, each 55 × 95 cm. In Cyrillic.

Inset: S SH A k nachaly Grazhdanskoi Voiny. [U.S.A. at the beginning of the Civil War] Scale 1:12,000,000. 27 × 42 cm.

School wall map showing troop movements, major engagements, forts, naval blockade, Anaconda plan, towns, railroads, and state boundaries.

85.2

————Another issue. Moskva, 1963. 108 × 95 cm.

85.3

————Another issue. Moskva, 1969.

85.4

————Grazhdanskaia voina v SShA (1861–1865gg.); dlia 8–go klassa [Civil War in the U.S.A. (1861–1865); for 8th class] Moskva, Glavnoe upravlenie geodezii i kartografii pri Sovete Ministrov SSSR, 1984. Colored. Scale 1:3,000,000. 112 × 94 cm.

G3701 .S5 1984 .S6

Insets: Rasshirenie territorii SShA v pervoi polovine XIX v. [Expansion of U.S.A. territories in the 19th century] Scale 1:13,000,000. 25 × 38 cm.—SShA pered nachalom Grazhdanskoi voiny. [U.S.A. before the beginning of the Civil War] Scale 1:13,000,000. 25 × 38 cm.

School wall map.

85.7

Sabban, Elie

Major strikes of the Civil War. Produced by National Geographic Society © Geographic Art Division. Drawn by Elie Sabban, Research by Eugene M. Scheel. Based upon maps of the Civil War period. Colored. Scale ca. 1:10,200,000. 26 × 17 cm. *From* National Geographic, v. 127, April 1965. p. 441.

Map of the Southeast showing major battles, plus movements of Confederate infantry and cavalry and Union infantry, navy, and cavalry.

"Dates following the names of cities indicate when they were occupied by Union forces."

86

Sanford, Albert H., *and* **Wilbur F. Gordy.**

The Civil War, Authors: Albert H. Sanford [and] Wilbur F. Gordy. Assisted by L. P. Benezet. Chicago, A. J. Nystrom & Co. [©1925] Colored. 94 × 123 cm. (Sanford-Gordy American history series with European background and beginnings. Map S–G no. 16)

Two maps on one sheet: A. General view of the campaigns. [Map of Eastern United States]. Scale 1:4,118,400. 86 × 60 cm.—B. The Civil War in the East. [Map of eastern Virginia, Maryland, and Pennsylvania] Scale 1:633,600. 86 × 60 cm. Each indicates troop movements and engagements, towns, railroads, and rivers.

87

Sigel, Franz.

Historical sketch of the war for the Union showing the lines of demarcation, important movements and battles in each year from 1861 to the close of the war in 1865. [©1889] Colored. Scale ca. 1:8,700,000. 22 × 24 cm.

Map of Southeastern United States showing names and boundaries of states, railroads, towns, rivers, battles, troop movements, and "headquarters of southern armies surrendered or leaders captured."

Colored lines signify "natural line of defence of the North at the outbreak of the war," and "strategical line at the end of 1861 . . . 1862 . . . 1863 . . . 1864 [and] . . . 1865."

87.2

Steele, Matthew F.

American campaigns, by Matthew Forney Steele . . . Volume II—Maps. Washington, Byron S. Adams, 1909. xii p., 311 maps (part col.) 24 × 16 cm. (U.S. General Staff. Second Section. Publication no. 13)

U1.U76

Accompanies a volume of text with the same title (viii p., 1 1., 731 p. 24 cm.)

On verso of the title page: War Department. Document no. 324. Office of the Chief of Staff.

Maps 67 to 298 cover the Civil War.

The Geography and Map Division also has unbound negative photocopies of maps 94–101, 103–132, and 134–147, and positive photocopies of maps 94–101 and 103–132.

Listed in C. E. Le Gear's *A List of Geographical Atlases in the Library of Congress* (Washington, Library of Congress, 1973), vol. 7, no. 10669.

87.4

————————Another edition. Washington, United States Infantry Association, 1922. Vol 2; xii p., 311 maps (part col.) 24 × 16 cm.

E181 .S853

Accompanies a volume of text with the same title (xi p., 731 p. 24 cm.)

On verso of the title page: War Department. Document no. 324. Office of the Chief of Staff.

Maps 67 to 298 cover the Civil War.

In this edition, "plates have been reproduced from the original drawings, which fortunately had been preserved in the Army War College, while the entire text is printed from new type."

Listed in C. E. Le Gear's *A List of Geographical Atlases in the Library of Congress* (Washington, Library of Congress, 1973), vol. 7, no. 10670.

87.5

Symonds, Craig L.

A battlefield atlas of the Civil War, by Craig L. Symonds. Cartography by William J. Clipson. Annapolis, Md., Nautical and Aviation Publishing Company of America [1983] 15 p. 1., 106 p. (incl. 43 col. maps) 26 × 18 cm.

G1201.S5S9 1983

"The idea for this volume originated with my students [at the U.S. Naval Academy]. Frustrated in their efforts to follow my chalkboard maneuvers in the classroom, they asked if I could pass out sketches of the principal campaigns. This volume is the result." (Introduction, p. ix)

Contents: 1. Charleston Harbor; 2. The Anaconda plan; 3. The strategic situation in the East; 4. The first battle of Bull Run (Manassas); 5. The battle for Henry House Hill; 6. Port Royal; 7. The strategic situation in the West; 8. Shiloh; 9. New Orleans; 10. The Peninsular campaign; 11. The siege of Yorktown; 12. Fair Oaks (Seven Pines); 13. Jackson's Valley campaign; 14. The seven days I; 15. The seven days II; 16. The second battle of Bull Run (Manassas); 17. Lee's first invasion; 18. Antietam (Sharpsburg); 19. Confederate invasion in the West (Perryville); 20. Stones River (Murfreesboro); 21. Fredericksburg; 22. Chancellorsville, I; 23. Chancellorsville, II; 24. Lee's second invasion; 25. Gettysburg: The first day; 26. Gettysburg: The second day; 27.

Gettysburg: The third day; 28. Vicksburg, I; 29. Vicksburg, II; 30. Chickamauga; 31. The battles of Chattanooga; 32. Grant's strategic plan; 33. The Wilderness and Spotsylvania; 34. Butler's advance; 35. The North Anna crossing and Cold Harbor; 36. The siege of Petersburg; 37. Early's raid; 38. Sherman's advance to Atlanta; 39. The battles for Atlanta; 40. Hood's offensive; 41. Sherman's march to the sea; 42. Fort Fisher; 43. The road to Appomattox.

87.6

Tooker, M. W.

Civil War, 1861–1865. Compiled by M. W. Tooker. Copyright Apr. 12, 1912. Colored blue print. Scale ca. 1:3,920,000. 64 × 96 cm.

Map indicates military movements and principal battles. Union movements are colored yellow and Confederate movements red.

88

Tyron, Rolla M., James A. James, *and* Carl R. Fish, *eds.*

The Civil War, 1861–1865. Chicago, McConnell School Map Co. [©1928] Colored. Scale ca. 1:1,750,000. 93 × 127 cm. (McConnell's maps; American history—university series. Set no. 23. Map no 2326)

Wall map of the Southeast showing battles, "marches and raids," principal towns, railroads, "coast forts held by Federals, 1861," and "line dividing Federal and Confederate territory in 1861." "Northern States," states "held by Lincoln," states "admitted to the Union, 1863." "Southern Confederacy," and "cotton South" delineated by color and symbol.

89

————————[Indianapolis] George F. Cram Co., [©1953] Map no. 519.

Reprint of the preceding map published by McConnell School Map Co.

90

U.S. *Army. Corps of Engineers.*

Map showing route of marches of the army of Genl. W. T. Sherman, from Atlanta, Ga. to Goldsboro, N.C. [1864–65] To accompany the report of operations from Savannah, Ga. to Goldsboro, N.C. Prepared by order of the Secretary of War for the officers of the U.S. Army under the command of Maj. Gen. W. T. Sherman. Engineer Bureau, War Department. Colored. Scale ca. 1:1,900,000. 28 × 41 cm.

Map of South Carolina and parts of Georgia and North Carolina, showing roads, railroads, towns, rivers, and geographic coordinates. The routes of the 14th, 15th, 17th, and 20th corps and the cavalry are indicated by colors and symbols.

Another copy signed in ms. "Brig. Gen. Benj. Harrison, Comdg. 1st Brig. 3 Div." G3871 .S5 1865 .U5 Vault

Another copy in Sherman map coll. no. 7.

90.2

——————Another issue. Uncolored. G3871 .S5 1865 .U5

Signed in ink on verso: Brig. Gen. J. R. Hawley.

From the papers of Joseph Roswell Hawley, Manuscript Division, Library of Congress.

This edition lacks flags above the map title and the statement "Prepared by order of the Secretary of War for the officers of the U.S. Army under the command of Maj. Gen. W. T. Sherman."

91

——————Another issue.

Bowen & Co. lith., Philada. *From* 39th Cong., 1st Sess. [1866]—Report of the Chief Engineer, U.S.A. No. 3.

92

——————Military maps. U.S. Engineer Dep't. [1861–5] 25 fold. maps (chiefly col.) 78 × 52 cm.

G1201 .S5U51 1879 folio

Cover title (on mounted label).

Book plate reads "Library of Colonel Thomas Lincoln Casey, Corps of Engineers. Presented April 8, 1925 to the Engineer School Library by Mrs. Casey."

Bound collection of maps including a "Military map showing the marches of the United States forces under command of Maj. Genl. W. T. Sherman, U.S.A., during the years 1863, 1864, 1865 . . . ," "Central Virginia showing Lieut. Gen'l. U. S. Grant's campaign and marches of the armies under his command in 1864–5," and maps of the battles and/or fortifications at Atlanta, Gettysburg, Fort Sumter, Franklin, Knoxville, Chattanooga, Corinth, 1st Manassas, Cincinnati, Covington and Newport, Vicksburg, Port Hudson, Iuka, South Mountain, Harpers Ferry, Gauley Bridge, and Hagerstown, Funkstown, Williamsport, Falling Waters, Maryland.

For table of contents see C. E. Le Gear's *A List of Geographical Atlases in the Library of Congress* (Washington, Library of Congress, 1973), v. 7, no. 10672.

93

——————Military maps of the United States. [1862–5] 1 p. 1., 36 maps (part fold., part col.) 76 × 55 cm.

G1201. S5U52 1883 folio

Cover title.

Typewritten table of contents inserted.

The maps are dated 1862 to 1883.

Bound collection of maps including a "Military map showing the marches of the United States forces under com-

mand of Maj. Genl. W. T. Sherman, U.S.A., during the years 1863, 1864, 1865," and maps of the battles of Knoxville, Chattanooga, Atlanta, Blakely, Nashville, Shiloh, Fort Fisher, South Mountain, Vicksburg, Gettysburg, Franklin, Antietam, Harpers Ferry, Fredericksburg, Chancellorsville, Wilderness, Spotsylvania, North Anna, Totopotomoy, Cold Harbor, Bermuda Hundred, Richmond, Petersburg and Five Forks, Jetersville and Sailors Creek, High Bridge and Farmville, and Appomattox Court House.

For table of contents see C. E. Le Gear's *A List of Geographical Atlases in the Library of Congress* (Washington, Library of Congress, 1973), v. 7, no. 10674.

93.5

——————Part of the military department of the South, embracing portions of Georgia and South Carolina. Compiled and engraved in the Engineer Bureau, War Department. 1865. Uncolored. Scale 1:350,000. 112 × 82 cm.

Printed below bar scale in the lower right corner: Engineer Bureau, Dec. 24th 1864.

Map of western South Carolina and northern Georgia extending from the North Carolina-South Carolina border south to Jacksonville, Georgia and from Camden, South Carolina west to Athens, Georgia. Depicted are roads, railroads, rivers, place names, and some houses and names of residents.

In this issue, the Corps of Engineers insignia printed 5 cm. to the left of the map title is framed by a scroll, an eagle is on a perch looking to the left, and "Essayons" is printed on a banner below the insignia.

93.7

——————Another issue.

In this and the following issue, the Corps of Engineers insignia printed approximately 1 cm. to the left of the map title is framed by a single line, an eagle is on a perch looking to the left, and "Essayons" is printed on a banner below the insignia.

93.9

——————Another issue.

Bar scale, producing agency, and date have been dropped from the lower right corner of map.

"Library of the Department of State" is written in ink in the lower margin.

94

——————Part of the military department of the South, embracing portions of Georgia and South Carolina, and part of the military department of North Carolina. Compiled and engraved in the Engineering Bureau, War Department. 1865. Uncolored. Scale 1:350,000. 2 sheets, each 56 × 90 cm.

Printed below bar scale: Engineer Bureau, January 1865.

Map of the coast from Cape Fear, North Carolina, to Savannah, Georgia, showing coastal defenses, roads, railroads, towns, drainage, bridges, houses, and names of residents.

Insets: Sketch of vicinity of Fort Fisher . . . by Otto Julian Schultze . . . Feb. 9th, 1865. Scale 1:12,000. 37 × 25 cm. [Includes] Diagram of Fort Buchanan. 8 × 6 cm.— Plan and sections of Fort Fisher . . . Jan. 15th, 1865 . . . Scale 1:3840. 17 × 25 cm. (See entry nos. 310 and 314.)

94.2

————————Another issue (incomplete). 57 × 46 cm.

Preliminary issue of southwestern sheet of the above map. Annotated in ink as "Incomplete," "Not finished," and "From Chief Engrs. Office, Mil'y Divn. Miss., O. M. Poe, Bvt. Col: & Chf. Engr."

94.5

U.S. *Coast and Geodetic Survey.*

Selected Civil War maps: Reproduced from originals made by the U.S. Coast Survey, 1861–65. [Washington, 1961] 20 l. of maps, illus. 77 × 62 cm.

G1201 .S5U55 1961 fol.

Cover title.

At head of title: U.S. Department of Commerce, Luther H. Hodges, Secretary. Coast and Geodetic Survey, Rear Admiral H. Arnold Karo, Director.

Listed in C. E. LeGear's *A List of Geographical Atlases in the Library of Congress* (Washington, Library of Congress, 1973), v. 7, no. 10679.

Contents

1) Historical sketch of the Civil War (and index).

2) Manassas Junction and vicinity, April 1862.

3) Charleston Harbor, 1865.

4) South Carolina-Georgia coast and sketches of forts 1861–62.

5) Military map of southeast Virginia 1864.

6) City of Richmond, 1864.

7) Reconnaissance of Mississippi River 1862.

8) Fort Jackson, 1862.

9) Fort Hindman, Arkansas, 1863.

10) Approaches to Vicksburg, 1863.

11) Approach to Grand Gulf, 1864.

12) Position of gun boats at Grend Gulf, 1863.

13) Battle ground of Sabine Cross Roads and Pleasant Hill, 1864.

14) Chattanooga and its approaches.

15) Battle field of Chickamauga.

16) To Atlanta. Map showing the operations of the national forces under the command of Major General W. T.

Sherman during the campaign resulting in the capture of Atlanta, Georgia, September 1, 1864.

17) Plan of final attack on Fort Fisher and adjoining Rebel works, made January 15th 1865.

18) Sketches—(a) Position of iron clads, Fort Fisher, January 15, 1865. (b) Final attack on Fort Fisher, January 15, 1865.

19) Reconnaissance of Wilmington River and St. Augustine Creek from Wausau [i.e. Wassaw] Sound to Savannah River, Georgia.

20) Northern part of Florida (Olustee [Ocean Pond] and raids on Jacksonville).

95

U.S. *Coast Survey.*

Map of the Tennessee River for the use of the Mississippi Squadron, under command of Acting Rear Admiral S. P. Lee, U.S.N., from reconnaissance by a party of the United States Coast Survey. 1864–'65. Scale 1:40,000 and 1:500,000. Uncolored. 17 sheets and title-page, each approx. 60 × 46 cm.

Printed at top of title-page: No. 3019, in 17 sheets. Price $2.

Detailed map of the Tennessee River from Paducah, Ky., to Florence, Ala., showing soundings, distances from Paducah, fortifications, "Wilson's U.S. Cavalry Camp," vegetation, cultivated fields, houses, names of residents, and roads.

See also entry no. 519.

95.2

————————Mississippi River from Cairo Ill. to St. Marys Mo. in VI sheets. Reconnaissance for the use of the Mississippi Squadron under command of Acting Rear Admiral S. P. Lee, U.S.N. By the party of F. H. Gerdes, Assistant, assigned by A. D. Bache, Supdt. United States Coast Survey. [Washington] 1865. Uncolored. Scale 1:40,000. 6 sheets, each 58 × 40 cm. (*Its* no. 3016)

"F. H. Gerdes, Asst. Coast Survey, Chief of Party. A. T. Mosman, Sub Asst. in charge of astronomical observations. T. C. Bowie, Sub Asst. in charge of topography. F. W. Perkins, Aid. J. B. Adamson, Aid & Draughtsman."

Detailed map of part of the Mississippi showing the river channel, place names and names of land owners along the river banks, field patterns, and vegetation.

96

U.S. *Military Academy, West Point. Dept. of Military Art and Engineering.*

Atlas to accompany Steele's American campaigns. Edited by Colonel Vincent J. Esposito. West Point, N.Y., 1956. 4 p. l., 158 l. of col. maps. 28 × 37 cm.

G1201 .S1U49 1956 folio

"Since 1939 the Department [of Military Art and Engineering] has been using Steele's *American campaigns* as a text for its sub-course on the American Civil War. Feeling the need of larger-scale maps than those contained in Colonel Steele's atlas, the Department, in 1941, published a Civil War atlas . . . In the present edition additional maps have been added so as to provide a complete atlas for Colonel Steele's book."

Maps illustrating the campaigns of the Civil War are included on 138 of the 158 plates.

The maps in this work form the basis for volume 1 of the U.S. Military Academy's *The West Point Atlas of American Wars,* [1959]. (Entry no. 97)

Listed in C. E. Le Gear's *A List of Geographical Atlases in the Library of Congress* (Washington, Library of Congress, 1973), v. 7, no. 10680.

G1201 .S1U49 1956 folio

96.2

————Civil War atlas to accompany Steele's American campaigns. Prepared by the Department of Civil and Military Engineering, United States Military Academy, for its course in military history. [West Point, 1941?] 2 p. l., 137 pl. of maps (part col.) 33 × 24 cm.

G1201 .S5U57 1941?

"The following-named officers took part in the preparation of this atlas: Majors V. J. Esposito, T. M. Osborne, D. H. Tulley, J. C. B. Elliott; Captains E. I. Davis, A. F. Clark, A. D. Starbird, L. J. Lincoln, C. S. Gates. Corporal E. J. Krasnoborski did the drafting."

Listed in C. E. LeGear's *A List of Geographical Atlases in the Library of Congress* (Washington, Library of Congress, 1973), vol. 7, no. 10681.

97

————The West Point atlas of American wars. Chief editor: Colonel Vincent J. Esposito. With an introductory letter by Dwight D. Eisenhower. New York, Praeger [1959] 2 v. col. maps. 27 × 37 cm. (Books that matter)

G1201 .S1U5 1959 folio

Includes "Recommended reading list[s]."

Contents: Volume I, 1689–1900.—Volume II, 1900–1953.

Each map is accompanied by a brief narrative "specially 'tailored' to fit on the blank page opposite the map."

Volume I includes 138 maps illustrating the campaigns of the Civil War. Similar maps appear in the earlier work by the U.S. Military Academy entitled *Atlas to Accompany Steele's American Campaigns,* 1956. (Entry no. 96)

For table of contents see C. E. Le Gear's *A List of Geographical Atlases in the Library of Congress* (Washington, Library of Congress, 1973), v. 7, no. 10639.

97.2

————The West Point atlas of the Civil War. Chief editor: Vincent J. Esposito. New York, Praeger [1962] 1 v. (various pagings) 154 col. maps. 27 × 37 cm. (Books that matter)

G1201.S5U58 1962 folio

"Recommended reading list," [4] pages at the end of the volume.

"The contents of *The West Point Atlas of the Civil War* are essentially the same, with minor changes and deletions, as those of Volume 1 of *The West Point Atlas of American Wars,* published in 1959 by Frederick A. Praeger."

Listed in C. E. LeGear's *A List of Geographical Atlases in the Library of Congress* (Washington, Library of Congress, 1973), vol. 7, no. 10682.

98

U.S. *War Department.*

Atlas of the war of the Rebellion giving Union and Confederate armies by actual surveys by the Union and Confederate engineers, and approved by the officers in command, of all the maps herein published. Approved by Secretary of War, and by Major George B. Davis, U.S.A. Compiled by Captain Calvin D. Cowles . . . Revised for publication by J. A. Caldwell. New York, Atlas Publishing Co., 1892. 3 p. l., 40 col. fold. pl. (incl. illus., maps, plans) 47 × 39 cm.

G1201.S5U59 1892 folio

"This volume will contain over seven hundred maps, showing all the battle-fields from 1861–to 1865."

This atlas comprises the first 40 plates of the U.S. War Department's *Atlas to Accompany the Official Records of the Union and Confederate Armies,* 1891–5. (Entry no. 99)

Listed in C. E. Le Gear's *A List of Geographical Atlases in the Library of Congress* (Washington, Library of Congress, 1973), v. 7, no. 10683.

99

————Atlas to accompany the official records of the Union and Confederate armies. Published under the direction of the . . . Secretaries of War, by Maj. George B. Davis . . . Mr. Leslie J. Perry . . . Mr. Joseph W. Kirkley . . . Compiled by Capt. Calvin D. Cowles . . . Washington, Government Printing Office, 1891–95. 3 v. 175 (i.e. 178) col. fold. pl. (incl. illus., maps, plans) 47 × 40 cm.

G1201.S5U6 1891 folio

Issued in 37 parts. Assigned no. 261 of House Miscellaneous documents, v. 40, 52d Cong., 1st sess. (ser no. 2998). Document number does not appear in this copy; in other copies it appears in the binder's title but not on the title page.

Inserted: . . . Additions and corrections to atlas. Washington, Government Printing Office, 1902. 2 p. 23 × 14 cm.

This is the most detailed atlas yet published on the Civil

War. It consists of reproductions of maps compiled by both Union and Confederate soldiers. The atlas includes a "Table of contents," pp. 5–7; a list of the "Maps, sketches, etc., pertaining to the several volumes," pp. 9–10; a list of "Authorities—embracing the names of commanding officers and senior engineer officers responsible for the maps and sketches, with the names of assistants employed in their preparation," pp. 11–15; and an "Index—embracing the titles of all maps, plans, sketches, views, and illustrations, with the names of the states, territories, and other theaters of war represented, and the names of places mentioned in the summaries of military events in Series I and which also appear in the Atlas," pp. 17–29.

Listed in P. L. Phillips's *A List of Geographical Atlases in the Library of Congress* (Washington, Government Printing Office, 1909), v. 1, no. 1353.

99.2

————Civil war maps: a graphic index to the Atlas to Accompany the Official Records of the Union and Confederate Armies, by Noel S. O'Reilly, David C. Bosse, and Robert W. Karrow, Jr. Chicago, The Newberry Library, 1987. 68 p., paperbound. 28 × 22 cm. (Hermon Dunlap Smith Center for the History of Cartography, Occasional Publication no. 1)

G1201 .S5U6 1891 Index

"To provide an alternative to the atlas' cumbersome system of indexing, compilation of a graphic index was begun at the Newberry Library in 1981. The purpose of this index is to graphically portray the sheet lines of each map in the atlas so that geographic coverage is unambiguous . . . The maps in this index are arranged alphabetically by state, and within each state by the sequential ordering of the maps in the atlas. The number of index maps for a state is dependent on the number of maps in the atlas . . . (Introduction, p. 8).

100

————Military maps of the War of the Rebellion—Miscellaneous. [Washington, 1865–79] 27 maps (part col., part fold.) 61 × 54 cm.

G1201 .S5U53 1879 folio

Cover title (on mounted label).

The maps are dated 1865 to 1879.

Bound collection of maps presented to the Library of Congress by Col. C. M. Townsend on October 22, 1940. Collection includes a map of "Central Virginia showing Lieut. Gen'l. U. S. Grant's campaign and marches of the armies under his command in 1864–5," and maps of the battles and/or fortifications at Island no. 10 and New Madrid, Columbus, Forts Henry and Donelson, Drainsville, Blakely, Carnifex Ferry, Nashville, Spanish Fort, Logan's Cross Roads, Cumberland Gap, Perryville, Pea Ridge, Wil-

liamsburg, Shiloh, Roanoke Island, Fort Fisher, Belmont, Iuka, Knoxville, Harpers Ferry, Gauley Bridge, Corinth, Big Black River Bridge, and Hagerstown, Funkstown, Williamsport, and Falling Waters, Maryland.

For table of contents see C. E. Le Gear's *A list of geographical atlases in the Library of Congress* (Washington, Library of Congress, 1973), v. 7, no. 10675.

101

————The official atlas of the Civil War. Introduction by Henry Steel Commager. New York, Thomas Yoseloff [1958] 4 p. l., 29 p., 175 (i.e., 178) part col. pl. (incl. illus., maps, plans) 44 × 37 cm.

G1201 .S5U6 1958 folio

Slightly reduced facsimile edition of the U.S. War Department's *Atlas to Accompany the Official Records of the Union and Confederate Armies, 1891–5* (see entry no. 99).

Listed in C. E. Le Gear's *A List of Geographical Atlases in the Library of Congress* (Washington, Library of Congress, 1973), v. 7, no. 10684.

101.2

————The official military atlas of the Civil War, by Major George B. Davis, U.S. Army, Leslie J. Perry, civilian expert, Joseph W. Kirkley, civilian expert. Compiled by Capt. Calvin D. Cowles, 23d U.S. Infantry. Introduction by Richard Sommers, PhD., Archivist-Historian, U.S. Army Military History Institute. New York, Arno Press, Crown Publishers, inc. [©1978] [41] 175 [i.e., 350] p., illus. (some col.), col. maps. 42 × 34 cm.

G1201.S5U6 1978 fol.

Facsimile edition of the U.S. War Department's *Atlas to Accompany the Official Records of the Union and Confederate Armies, 1891–5* (see entry no. 99).

Scale of map is reduced 10 percent from the original edition.

101.4

————New York, Fairfax Press, 1983.

G1201 .S5U6 1983 fol.

102

Van Horne, Thomas B.

History of the Army of the Cumberland; its organization, campaigns, and battles, written at the request of Major-General George H. Thomas . . . by Thomas B. Van Horne, U.S.A. Illustrated with campaign and battle maps, compiled by Edward Ruger . . . Atlas. Cincinnati, Robert Clarke & Co., 1875. 19 l. incl. 22 col. maps. 47 × 54 cm.

G1281.S5V3 1875 folio

The format of this atlas as issued was 3 p. l., 22 col. fold. maps, 23 × 15 cm. The letter press and maps have been mounted and rebound as above.

Atlas accompanies two-volume history by Thomas B. Van Horne.

For table of contents see P. L. Phillips's *A List of Geographical Atlases in the Library of Congress* (Washington, Government Printing Office, 1920) v. 4, no. 4519.

Includes maps of the battles of Selma, Alabama; Bentonville, North Carolina; Chattanooga, Franklin, Nashville, and Stones River, Tennessee; Chickamauga and Atlanta, Georgia; and Perryville, Kentucky.

The Geography and Map Division also has separates for plates 2–5, 7–10, 17–19, and 21.

102.1

Wiser, Angelo.

Complete map of the march of the 1st Brigade, 1st Cavalry Divn., Dept. of Cumberland on the Stoneman expedition through Tenn., Va., N.C., S.C., Geo., & Ala. March to June 1865. [Signed] Sergt. Angelo Wiser, Co. H, 15th Pn. Cavly. 80 l. incl. 50 ms. maps. 20 × 13 cm.

G1281 .S5W5 1865 Vault

Title from front endpaper.

Author's name from front flyleaf. Back flyleaf is endorsed as follows: Head Quarters of Bvt. Brig. Genl. W. J. Palmer. Book—in charge of Sergt. Wiser, Co. H. 15th Penn. Cav'ly at Head Qrs.

"Signs for the use of Topographical Engineers . . ." (photocopy) pasted to the back flyleaf.

Series of pencil drawings tracing the route of march

and indicating campsites, roads, railroads, towns and villages, houses and names of residents, rivers and streams, and relief by hachures.

Maps have been drawn in a captured account book. Label on the cover reads "Treasurer of the Confederate States in Account with Wm. Thomas Hardy, Capt. & Asst. Qr. M., C.S.P.A."

102.2

Wood, Walter B., and J. E. Edmonds.

Georgia and the Carolinas. [1861–65. London] Methuen & Co. [1905] Uncolored. Scale ca. 1:2,670,000. 19 × 36 cm.

"Map XII."

Prepared to accompany W. B. Wood and J. E. Edmonds's *A History of the Civil War in the United States, 1861–5* (London, Methuen & Co. [1905]).

Map indicates battle sites.

102.4

————Lower Mississippi [River, 1861–65. London] Methuen & Co. [1905] Uncolored. Scale ca. 1:3,350,000. 20 × 25 cm.

"Map X."

Prepared to accompany W. B. Wood and J. E. Edmonds's *A History of the Civil War in the United States, 1861–5* (London, Methuen & Co. [1905]).

Map indicates battle sites.

ALABAMA

102.6

Down Home Designs.

The Civil War in Alabama. A directory of battle sites during the years 1861–1865. Selma, Ala., Down Home Designs, ©1979. Uncolored. Scale ca. 1:1,100,000. 55 × 85 cm.

G3971 .S5 1979 .D6

185 battles and skirmishes are listed and keyed by number to the map.

Copyright no. VA 34–137, Aug. 23, 1979.

102.8

Hains, Peter C.

Military map no. 54, prepared as basis for additional surveys, prepared under direction of Capt. P. C. Hains, U.S.A., Act. Chief, Engineer Dept. of the Gulf. Drawn for

stone by Helmuth Holtz. Printed by W. Pro[bert]. [1864?] Uncolored. Scale 1:380,160. 40 × 55 cm.

Map is incomplete; the bottom border is missing.

General map of southern Alabama and West Florida showing roads, railroads, towns, drainage, and a few names of residents along the Tensaw River.

102.9

————Southern Alabama. Pre[pa]red by order of Capt. McAles[t]er, Chief Engr. M.D.W.M. under direction of Capt. P. C. Hains, U.S. Engr. & Actg. [Ch]ief Engr. Dept of the Gulf. [Ma]rch 1865. Compiled & dra[wn for stone] by Helmuth Holtz & F. D'Avignon. Transferred & printed by E. Boehler. Colored. Scale 1:316,800 (5 miles to 1 inch). 93 × 71 cm.

In the Allen family papers, Manuscript Division, L.C., container no. 2.

At head of title: Engineer's Office, Department of the Gulf. Campaign map no. 56.

Imperfect. Pieces are missing and the map is in poor condition.

General map of southern Alabama and West Florida showing roads, railroads, cities and towns, forts, and state boundaries. Map belonged to Lt. Charles Julius Allen (1840–1915).

102a

Letford, William, *and* Allen W. Jones.

Federal raids in Alabama, 1861–1865; Data taken from The War of Rebellion; Official Records of the Union and Confederate Armies, by William Letford of the Department of Archives and History and Allen W. Jones of Furman University, Greenville, S.C. as a contribution of the Dept. of Archives and History to the Alabama Civil War Centennial, 1961. Phil. Neel, 1960. Colored. Scale ca. 1:950,000. 64 × 54 cm.

On verso: Official 1961 Alabama highway map. Copyright Alabama State Highway Department 1961.

Title when folded: Alabama Civil War Centennial official highway map, 1961.

Pictorial map showing raids of Col. Abel B. Streight, Maj. Gen. James H. Wilson, Brig. Gen. Thomas J. Lucas, Maj. Gen. Frederick Steele, Brig. Gen. John T. Croxton, Brig. Gen. John W. Geary, Maj. Gen. Lovell H. Rousseau, Maj. Gen. Benjamin H. Grierson, and Lt. Col. Andrew B. Spurling.

102a.5

Lindenkohl, Adolph.

Northern Alabama and Georgia. Compiled and engraved at the U.S. Coast Survey Office, from state maps, postoffice maps, local surveys, military reconnoissance and information furnished by the U.S. Engineers attached to the Military Division of the Miss. Drawn by A. Lindenkohl. H. Lindenkohl & Chas. G. Krebs, lith. [1864?] Colored. Scale 1:633,600. 66 × 55 cm.

Signed in ink in upper margin: Llewellyn F. Haskell, Lt. Col., 7 U.S.C.I. July 15, 1864.

General map of northeastern Alabama and northwestern Georgia indicating cities and towns, roads and railroads, rivers, and some relief by hachures. Map overprinted in red to highlight state boundaries and railroads.

For another copy see Sherman map coll. no. 12.

102a.6

————Another issue.

Map is overprinted in red to show state names and highlight boundaries and railroads.

102a.7

Map of North Alabama, Memphis & Charleston R.R. and part [of the] Tenn. River. [186-?] Colored ms. Scale ca. 1:228,000. 49 × 40 cm.

In the John Alexander Logan family papers, Manuscript Division, L.C., container 145, p. 94.

Title on verso

Pen and ink manuscript map drawn on tracing paper showing roads, towns, landings, ferries and railroads in northern Alabama. "Camp 46 Ohio [and] Col. Oliver's camp" are identified near Browns Cave P.O., Alabama.

103

See Sherman map collection no. 15.

103.5

Wadsworth, George.

[Map of the Alabama and Tennessee River Railroad between Blue Mountain Station and Jacksonville, Calhoun County, Alabama] Geo Wadsworth, Chf. Engr. 1863 & 4. Colored ms. Scale ca 1:9,650. 33 × 205 cm.

G3972 .A4 1864 .W3 Vault

Manuscript map signed in two places by the Confederate engineer George Wadsworth. Although military details are not indicated, the map is believed to have been made in conjunction with the Union invasion of northern Georgia in 1864. The map delineates the route of the Alabama and Tennessee River Railroad (unnamed on map), a "proposed railroad to Atlanta," roads, rivers, section lines, houses and outbuildings, names of land owners, and relief by hachures.

BALDWIN COUNTY

103.7

[Map of part of Baldwin County, Alabama, from Blakely south to Bon Secour Bay. 186-?] Uncolored ms. Scale ca. 1:130,000. 47 × 36 cm.

In the Allen family papers, Manuscript Division, L.C., container no. 2.

Map belonged to Lt. Charles Julius Allen (1840–1915).

Pen and ink manuscript map drawn on tracing linen showing roads, towns, drainage, and place names along the eastern shore of Mobile Bay.

BLAKELY

104

U.S. *Army. Corps of Engineers.*

Rebel line of works at Blakely captured by the Army of West Miss., April 9, 1865. Position & approaches by the Union forces. Engraved in the Engineer Dept. Colored. Scale 1:14,400. 26 × 38 cm.

Union positions are colored blue, and Confederate works are red. Includes roads, vegetation, drainage, and relief by hachures.

105

————Another issue. 26 × 38 cm. *From* 39th Cong., 1st Sess. [1866]—Report of the Chief Engineer U.S.A. No. 7.

In lower right corner: Bowen & Co. lith., Philada.

Union positions are colored red, and Confederate works are blue.

JACKSON COUNTY

105.3

Tuttle, Ira A.

Map of vicinity of Mud Creek &c, North Ala. [By Ira A. Tuttle. 186–?] Colored ms. Scale 1:126,720 ("½ inch to the mile"). 54 × 41 cm.

In the John Alexander Logan family papers, Manuscript Division, L.C., container 145, p. 104.

Pen and ink manuscript map of part of Jackson County showing the western shore of the Tennessee River, ferries, roads, the towns of Bridgeport, Stevenson, Bellefonte, and Larkinsville, plantations, and railroad. A "camp" is indicated on the road from Cox's Ferry to Stevenson. Although the map is unsigned, it appears to be the work of Ira A. Tuttle (see entry no. 105.5).

MADISON COUNTY

105.4

Map of country between Whitesburg and Huntsville, Ala. [186–?] Uncolored ms. Scale ca. 1:65,000. 28 × 43 cm.

In the John Alexander Logan family papers, Manuscript Division, L.C., container 145, p. 95.

Title on verso.

Pen and ink sketch map of part of Madison County, Alabama, showing Union and Confederate camps, roads, the Memphis and Charleston Railroad, rivers and streams, and the names of some land owners.

MARSHALL COUNTY

105.5

Tuttle, Ira A.

Map of northern Alabama. [By] Ira A. Tuttle. [186–?] Colored ms. Scale 1:126,720 ("½ inch to the mile"). 41 × 54 cm.

In the John Alexander Logan family papers, Manuscript Division, L.C., container 145, p. 96.

Oriented with south at top of the sheet.

Pen and ink and pencil manuscript map of the northern part of Marshall County from Woodville to the Tennessee River indicating "towns, plantations, mills, churches, Rebel pickets, Rebel camps, ferry, landing & ferry, low range of hills, [and] graveyard."

MOBILE

105.7

Bay of Mobile. Fig. 6. [1864?] Uncolored ms. Scale ca. 1:400,000. 31 × 18 cm.

In the Allen family papers, Manuscript Division, L.C., container no. 2.

Map belonged to Lt. Charles Julius Allen (1840–1915).

Pen and ink and pencil sketch map on tracing paper showing the defenses of Mobile Bay.

"From Scheliha's book" (i.e., Viktor Ernst Karl Rudolf von Scheliha's *A Treatise on Coast-defence.* London, 1868) is written in pencil below the map.

105.8

Confederate defences of the lower Bay of Mobile. [August 1864] Uncolored ms. Scale ca. 1:135,000. 25 × 43 cm.

In the Allen family papers, Manuscript Division, L.C., container no. 2.

Map belonged to Lt. Charles Julius Allen (1840–1915).

Pen and ink and pencil sketch map on tracing paper showing the "Plan of Federal attack of August 5th 1864 and following days."

"From Scheliha's book" (i.e., Viktor Ernst Karl Rudolf von Scheliha's *A Treatise on Coast-defence.* London, 1868) is written in pencil below the map.

106

See Sherman map collection no. 16.

106.1

Owner, William.

[Map of Mobile Bay showing fortifications and obstructions. 1864–1865] Uncolored ms. Scale ca. 1:250,000. 27 × 24 cm. *In his* Diary, v. 8, tipped-in at front of volume.

In the William Owner papers, Manuscript Division, L.C., container no. 2.

Volume 8 of the diary covers from August 12, 1864, to April 10, 1865.

106.2

Patterson, Jack E.

Entrance of Rear Admiral Farragut into Mobile Bay, August 5th 1864. Material supplied by Jack E. Patterson. Drawn by Marian Acker. Reproduced by Tim Wilkinson. 1962. Uncolored. Scale not given. 42 × 31 cm.

Inset: Points of collision of the different boats upon the ram [Tennessee]. 9 × 8 cm.

Indicates positions and names of ships, torpedoes, obstructions, and forts. "Explanation of diagram from the five stand points of the Mobile fight" appears in the lower left corner.

106.4

Plan of the battle of August 5, 1864. [Mobile Bay] Uncolored. Scale not given. 12 × 15 cm. *From* Harper's weekly, v. 8, Sept. 24, 1864. p. 613.

Names of ships are keyed by number and letter to the left of the map.

107

U.S. *Army. Corps of Engineers.*

Map of the defences of the city of Mobile. [1862–64] Engraved in the Engineer Bureau, War Dept. Bowen & Co. lith, Philada. Uncolored. Scale not given. 28 × 39 cm. *From* 39th Cong., 1st Sess. [1866]—Report of the Chief Engineer, U.S.A. No. 10.

Map of Mobile and environs, showing roads, "Mobile and Ohio Rail-Road," drainage, vegetation, hachures, and fortifications at Blakely and Spanish Fort and those built in 1862, 1863, and 1864 at Mobile.

108

——————Rebel defences, Mobile, Alabama, occupied by Union forces under Maj. Gen. E. R. S. Canby comdg. Engraved in the Engineer Department. S. Geismar, lith. Bowen & Co. lith., Philada. Uncolored. Scale ca. 1:18,200. 32 × 54 cm. *From* 39th Cong., 1st Sess. [1866]—Report of the Chief Engineer, U.S.A. No. 9.

Map shows the three lines of fortifications constructed in 1862, 1863, and 1864, streets, "Mobile and Ohio Rail Road," vegetation, drainage, and relief by hachures. Most of the streets are not named.

109

U.S. *Coast Survey.*

Approaches to Mobile, Ala. 1864. Colored. Scale ca. 1:205,000. 45 × 46 cm.

Map of Mobile Bay showing forts, towns, soundings, and a few roads.

110

Weir, Robert.

Chart showing the entrance of Rear Admiral Farragut into Mobile Bay. 5th of August 1864. Drawn & compiled by Robt. Weir, for Rear Admiral D. G. Farragut, Novr. 1st 1864. Lith. by Hatch & Co., N.Y. Colored. Scale ca. 1:22,500. 87 × 60 cm.

Detailed map showing five positions and the tracks of the vessels during the sea battle, obstructions, channels, banks, and shoals.

Includes small views of the "Iron-clad Tennessee," Federal ship colliding with the *Ram Tennessee,* a vessel sailing past what appears to be Mobile Point, and a general view of the battle.

Inset: [Diagram] showing points of collision of different vessels upon the *Ram* [Tennessee]. 19 × 15 cm.

SELMA

111

See Sherman map collection no. 17.

SPANISH FORT

112

McAlester, Miles D., *and others.*

Siege operations at Spanish Fort, Mobile Bay, by the U.S. forces under Maj. Gen. Canby. Captured by the Army of West Miss. on the night of April 8 & 9, 1865. Major M. D. McAlester, Senior Engr., Major J. C. Palfrey, Asst. Engr., Capt. C. J. Allen, Asst. Engr., Capt. Patten, Inspector Genl's. Dept., Vol. Asst. Engr. Engraved in the Engineer Department. Bowen & Co. lith., Philada. Colored. Scale ca. 1:16,600. 31 × 43 cm. *From* 39th Cong., 1st Sess. [1866]—Report of the Chief Engineer, U.S.A. No. 8

At head of title: Plan no. 8.

Detailed map showing entrenchments, number, type, and position of Federal guns, vegetation, drainage, roads, and relief by hachures.

STEVENSON

112.5

U.S. *Army. Department of the Cumberland. Topographical Engineers.*

[Map of Stevenson, Alabama and vicinity] Compiled from information, under the direction of Capt. Wm. E. Merrill, U.S. Engrs., Chief Engineer, Army of the Cumberland. In camp near Stevenson, Ala. Lith. August 29th 1863. Colored. Scale 1:63,360 (1 inch to the mile). 50 × 33 cm.

Military reconnaissance map lithographed at field headquarters showing roads, railroads, rivers, fords, relief by hachures, and the names of some residents.

Another copy is filed as G3964 .C3 1863 .U5 [5].

———————————————

Detailed chart of the Battle of Mobile Bay, August 5, 1864, drawn by Robert Weir for Adm. David G. Farragut. (See entry no. 110.)

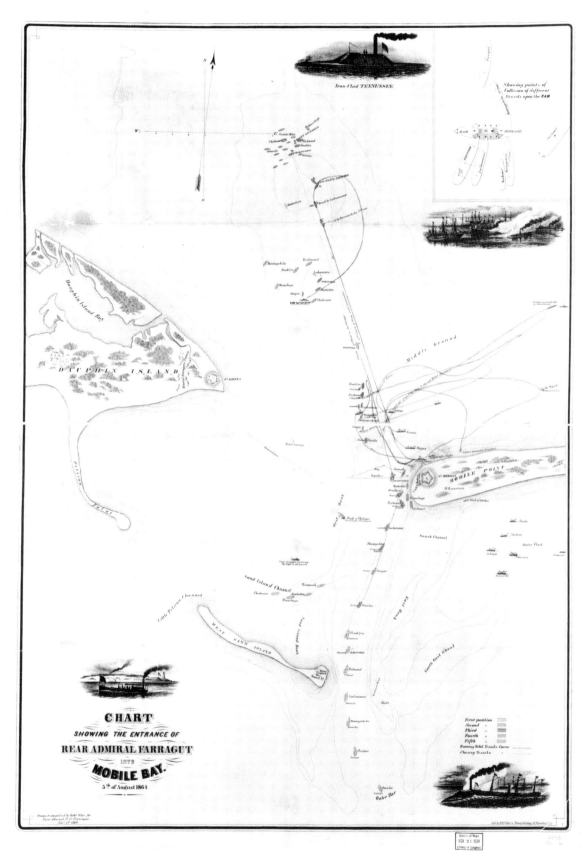

Iron-Clad TENNESSEE

Showing points of
Collision of different
Vessels upon the RAM

CHART
SHOWING THE ENTRANCE OF
REAR ADMIRAL FARRAGUT
INTO
MOBILE BAY.
5th of August 1864

ARKANSAS

ARKANSAS POST

113

See Sherman map collection no. 18.

114

See Sherman map collection no. 19.

ARKANSAS RIVER

114.2

U.S. *Navy.*

Map showing the new cut-off made by Lt. Com. T. O. Selfridge, U.S.N., 1863. Uncolored. Scale ca. 1:150,000. 20 × 11 cm. *From* Report of the Secretary of the Navy, with an appendix, containing reports from officers. December, 1863 (Washington, Government Printing Office, 1863). opp. p. 460.

Map accompanies Acting Rear Adm. David D. Porter's communication dated April 16, 1863, entitled "Selfridge's 'Cut-Off.'"

FORT HINDMAN

115

U.S. *Coast Survey.*

Approaches to Fort Hindman, Arkansas Post on the Arkansas River. Captured by the U.S. Mississippi squadron under command of Act'g. Rear Admiral David D. Porter, U.S.N., January 11th, 1863. Surveyed by C. Fendall, Sub-assistant, U.S. Coast Survey acting under orders of Rear Admiral D. D. Porter. Autographic transfer J. W. Maedel. Uncolored. Scale 1:10,000. 27 × 44 cm.

Gives fortifications, location and names of vessels,

roads, vegetation, and a view of Fort Hindman from the Arkansas River.

For another copy from the papers of Joseph R. Hawley, Manuscript Division, L.C., see G4004.A57S5 1863 .F4.

115.2

U.S. *Navy.*

View of Fort Hindman, Arkansas Post. [January 11, 1863] Uncolored. Scale ca. 1:2,450. 20 × 12 cm. *From* Report of the Secretary of the Navy, with an appendix, containing reports from officers. December, 1863 (Washington, Government Printing Office, 1863). fol. p. 414.

Inset: Appearance of IX-gun silenced by the "Cincinnati."

Small drawing of the fort showing the location and size of guns, casemates, powder magazine, and other buildings.

PEA RIDGE

116

U.S. *Army. Corps of Engineers.*

Map of the battlefield of Pea Ridge, Arkansas, showing the positions of the United States and Confederate forces on the 8th of March 1862. From a map forwarded to the Engineer Department Sept. 11th 1865 by Brevet Brig. Gen. C. B. Comstock A.D.C. [Washington] 1876. Colored. Scale not given. 29 × 32 cm.

Shows relief by hachures, drainage, vegetation, and houses.

117

————Another issue.

This issue includes the name of the lithographer, Julius Bien & Co., in the bottom margin.

CONNECTICUT

NEW HAVEN

117.1

U.S. *Coast Survey.*

New Haven Harbor. Founded upon a trigonometrical survey under the direction of F. R. Hassler, Superintendent

of the survey of the coast of the United States. Triangulation by James Ferguson and Edmund Blunt, Assistants. Topography by C. M. Eakin, W. M. Boyce & J. Farley, Assistants. Hydrography by the party under the command of G. S. Blake, Lieut. U.S. Navy. Final reduction for engraving by Jno. B. Glück, Draughtsman. Engraved by Sherman &

Smith, N.Y. Electrotype copy no. 4 by S. Siebert, U.S.C.S. [Washington, U.S. Coast Survey] 1846. Uncolored. Scale 1:30,000. 46 × 36 cm.

G3784 .N4S5 186– .U5 Vault

Harbor chart annotated in red to show the sector of fire for guns situated at Oyster Point and Fort Hale, Connecticut. Information added to chart probably reflects the situation during the Civil War.

"Transferred from Office Chf. Engr. [Defenses] of Washington, to Engr. Dept. Jan'y [1866]."

117.15

—————Another copy with annotations.

G3784 .N4S5 186– .U51 Vault

Harbor chart annotated in red to show the number and sectors of fire for guns situated at Oyster Point and Fort Hale, Connecticut. Guns at Oyster Point are numbered 1 to 5 and those at Fort Hale, 1 to 15. Information added to the chart probably reflects the situation during the Civil War.

"Transferred from Office of Chf. Engr. Defenses of Washington, to Engr. Dept. Jan'y 1866."

FLORIDA

117.2

Bachmann, John.

Birds eye view of Florida and part of Georgia and Alabama. Drawn from nature and lith. by John Bachmann. New York, John Bachmann, ©1861. Colored view. 57 × 72 cm.

At top of map: Panorama of the seat of war.

"Entered according to act of Congress in the year 1861 by John Bachmann."

Tables of distances from Key West and Tallahassee appear in the lower margin.

View of Florida and the environs showing towns, roads, railroads, forts, and rivers.

117.3

Lindenkohl, Henry.

Northern part of Florida. Drawn by H. Lindenkohl. Compiled and published at the United States Coast Survey Office, A. D. Bache, Superintendent. 1864. Colored. Scale 1:633,600. 44 × 59 cm.

General map of northern Florida and southern Georgia extending from Altamaha Sound, Georgia, to 29° North latitude.

CEDAR KEYS

117.35

U.S. *Coast Survey.*

Cedar Keys, Florida. From a trigonometrical survey under the direction of A. D. Bache, Superintendent of the survey of the coast of the United States. Triangulation by F. H. Gerdes, Asst. and B. Huger Jr., Sub-Assist. Topography by F. H. Gerdes, Asst. Hydrography by the parties under the command of Lieuts. Comdg. O. H. Berryman &

J. J. Guthrie, U.S.N. Assts. Redd. drng by A. Schoepf and A. Strauss [sic]. Engd. by W. Langran and F. Bartle. Lith. of C. Knickerbocker, Albany, N.Y. [Washington, U.S. Coast Survey] 1861. Uncolored. Scale 1:50,000. 66 × 49 cm. *From its* Report of the Superintendent of the Coast Survey showing the progress of the survey during the year 1861 (Washington, Government Printing Office, 1862). Map 17.

"No. 17" appears in the upper left corner.

CHARLOTTE HARBOR

117.37

—————Preliminary chart of main entrance to Charlotte Harbor, Florida. From a trigonometrical survey under the direction of A. D. Bache, Superintendent of the survey of the coast of the United States. Triangulation by Lieuts. J. C. Clark & W. R. Terrill, U.S.A. Assts. Topography by F. W. Dorr, C. Ferguson & C. T. Jardella, Sub-Assts. Hydrography by the party of E. Cordell, Acting Asst. [Washington, U.S. Coast Survey] 1863. Uncolored. Scale 1:40,000. 56 × 67 cm. *From its* Report of the Superintendent of the Coast Survey, showing the progress of the survey during the year 1864 (Washington, Government Printing Office, 1866). Map 28.

"No. 28" in upper left corner.

Inset: Sketch of Charlotte Harbor, Florida. Scale 1:400,000. 18 × 12 cm.

ESCAMBIA BAY

117.4

—————Preliminary chart of Escambia and Santa Maria de Galvaez [i.e., East] Bays, Florida. From a trigonometrical survey under the direction of A. D. Bache, Superintendent of the survey of the coast of the United States. Triangulation and topography by F. H. Gerdes, Asst. Hydrography by the party under the command of Lieut. Comdg. T. S. Phelps, U.S.N. Assist. [Washington, U.S. Coast Survey] 1861. Uncolored. Scale 1:30,000. 64 × 80 cm. (*Its* no. 489)

General chart showing soundings and coast vegetation. Chart is based on "long[itude] east from Public Square, Pensacola."

FERNANDINA

117.5

[Map of Fernandina region, Florida. 186–?] Uncolored ms. Scale not given. 50 × 74 cm.

G3934 .F29A1 186– .M3 Vault

From the papers of Joseph Roswell Hawley, Manuscript Division, LC.

Map of the environs of Fernandina and old Fernandina showing streets, roads, the Florida Railroad, drainage, the lighthouse, and Fort Clinch.

FLORIDA KEYS

117.52

U.S. *Coast Survey.*

Preliminary chart of western end of Florida Reefs including Tortugas Keys. [Washington, U.S. Coast Survey] 1864. Uncolored. Scale 1:200,000. 42 × 68 cm. *From its* Report of the Superintendent of the Coast Survey, showing the progress of the survey during the year 1863 (Washington Government Printing Office, 1864). Map 17.

"No. 17" is in the upper left corner.

At head of title: U.S. Coast Survey, A. D. Bache, Supdt.

117.54

————Preliminary coast chart no. 69, Florida Reefs from the Elbow to Lower Matecumbe Key. From a trigonometrical survey under the direction of A. D. Bache, Superintendent of the survey of the coast of the United States. Triangulation by J. Totten, A. H. Seward, U.S.A. and G. A. Fairfield, Assts. Topography by S. A. Wainwright, Sub-Assist., F. W. Dorr, Sub-Assist. and C. T. Jardella, Sub-Assist. Hydrography by the parties under the direction of Lieut. Comdg. T. A. Craven, U.S.N., G. Davidson, Assts. and E. Cordell, Actg. Asst. [Washington, U.S. Coast Survey] 1863. Uncolored. Scale 1:80,000. 67 × 80 cm. *From its* Report of the Superintendent of the Coast Survey showing the progress of the survey during the year 1863 (Washington, Government Printing Office, 1864). Map 15.

"No. 15" is in the upper left corner.

117.56

————Preliminary coast chart no. 70, Florida Reefs from Long Key to Newfound Harbor Key. From a trigono-

metrical survey under the direction of A. D. Bache, Superintendent of the survey of the coast of the United States. Triangulation by J. E. Hilgard, Lieuts. A. H. Seward, J. C. Clark, U.S.A. Assts., J. Rockwell and J. A. Sullivan, Sub-Assts. Topography by I. Hull Adams, Asst., C. T. Jardella and F. W. Dorr, Sub-Assistants. Hydrography by the parties under the command of Lieuts. Comdg. T. A. Craven, W. G. Temple and J. Wilkinson, U.S.N. Assists. [Washington, U.S. Coast Survey] 1863. Uncolored. Scale 1:80,000. 66 × 81 cm. *From its* Report of the Superintendent of the Coast Survey, showing the progress of the survey during the year 1863 (Washington, Government Printing Office, 1864). Map 16.

"No. 16" is in the upper left corner.

117.58

————Preliminary coast chart no. 71. Florida Reefs from Newfound Harbor Key to Boca Grande Key. From a trigonometrical survey under the direction of A. D. Bache, Superintendent of the survey of the coast of the United States. Triangulation by J. E. Hilgard, Lieut. Jas. Totten, U.S.A. Assts., J. Rockwell & J. A. Sullivan, Sub-Assts. Topography by R. M. Bache, I. Hull Adams, Assts., C. T. Jardella, S. A. Wainwright & F. W. Dorr, Sub-Assistants. Hydrography by the parties under the command of Lieuts. Comdg. John Rodgers & T. A. Craven, U.S.N. Assists. Redd. drng. by W. T. Martin and E. Hergesheimer. Engd. by A. Blondeau, H. S. Barnard and E. A. Maedel. [Washington, U.S. Coast Survey] 1862. Uncolored. Scale 1:80,000. 68 × 81 cm. *From its* Report of the Superintendent of the Coast Survey, showing the progress of the survey during the year 1862 (Washington, Government Printing Office, 1864). Map 34.

"No. 34" is in the upper left corner.

117.6

————Sketch showing the positions of the beacons on the Florida reefs erected by Lieut. James Totten, U.S. Army, Assistant, U.S.C.S. [Washington, U.S. Coast Survey] 1861. Uncolored. Scale 1:400,000. 39 × 50 cm. (*Its* no. 464)

At head of title: U.S. Coast Survey, A. D. Bache, Supdt.

"No. 464 price 15 cents" is printed in the upper margin.

Inset: Plan of beacons devised by Lieut. James Totten, U.S. Army, Assistant, U.S.C.S. 29 × 16 cm.

FLORIDA STRAITS

117.65

————Preliminary edition of general chart of the coast no. X, Straits of Florida from Key Biscayne to Marquesas Keys. From a trigonometrical survey under the direction of A. D. Bache, Superintendent of the survey of the coast of the United States. [Washington, U.S. Coast Survey] 1862.

Uncolored. Scale 1:400,000. 78 × 96 cm. *From its* Report of the Superintendent of the Coast Survey, showing the progress of the survey during the year 1863 (Washington, Government Printing Office, 1864). Map 14.

"No. 14" is in the upper left corner.

KEY WEST

117.7

—————Key West harbor and its approaches. From a trigonometrical survey under the direction of A. D. Bache, Superintendent of the survey of the coast of the United States. Triangulation by J. E. Hilgard, Assistant. Topography by L. H. Adams, Sub-Asst. Hydrography by the party under the command of Lieut. John Rodgers, U.S. Navy Assistant. Redd. drng. by E. K. Knorr. Engd. by E. Yeager, E. F. Woodward, and H. M. Knight. Published in 1855. Edition of 1864. [Washington, U.S. Coast Survey] 1864. Uncolored. Scale 1:50,000. 63 × 88 cm. (*Its* no. 469)

General chart of Key West and environs showing soundings, lights, channels, and island vegetation.

Inset: Sub-sketch of Key West harbor. Scale 1:30,000. 19 × 17 cm.

Includes sailing directions.

PENSACOLA

117.8

Dodd, Dorothy.

Battle of Santa Rosa Island. First phase, Confederate attack and Federal withdrawal.—Battle of Santa Rosa Island. Second phase, Federal attack and Confederate withdrawal. Uncolored. Scale not given. 2 maps, each 10 × 20 cm. *In her* Fort Pickens State Park. Fort Pickens and battle of Santa Rosa Island (Tallahassee, Florida Park Service [195–?] 4 p.

Each map indicates fortifications and troop movements.

118

U.S. *Army. Corps of Engineers.*

No. 2 plan of fort for Sta. Rosa Id., Pensacola Harbour, shewing the general dimensions and the relations of the several parts of the work. [186–?] Colored ms. Scale 1:600. 93 × 122 cm.

G3932.S48 186– . U5, Vault
Pen and ink manuscript drawn on tracing paper.
Four profiles in lower right corner.

119

Weiss, Jacob.

A correct map of Pensacola Bay showing topography of the coast, Fort Pickens, U.S. Navy Yard, and all other fortifications, from the latest Government surveys. J. Weiss lith. Philadelphia, Jacob Weiss [186–] Colored. Scale ca. 1:62,000. 22 × 31 cm.

120

Williams, W. A.

Sketch of Pensacola Navy Yard and Fort Pickens. From U.S. coast surveys. By W. A. Williams, Civil Engineer, Boston. Published & lith. by L. Prang & Co., Boston. [186–] Colored. Scale ca. 1:31,000. 25 × 26 cm.

Indicates fortifications, half-mile distance circles centered on Fort Pickens, beacons, roads and streets, vegetation, and a few soundings.

ST. AUGUSTINE

120.3

U.S. *Coast Survey.*

Preliminary chart of St. Augustine harbor, Florida. Triangulation by B. Huger, Jr., Sub-Assist. Topography by F. W. Dorr, Sub-Assist. Hydrography by the party under the command of Lieut. Comdg. A. Murray, U.S.N. Assist. Redd. drng. by F. Fairfax & S. B. Linton. Engd. by E. H. Sipe & J. G. Thompson. Lith. of Bowen & Co., Philada. [Washington, U.S. Coast Survey] 1862. Uncolored. Scale 1:30,000. 53 × 53 cm. *From its* Report of the Superintendent of the Coast Survey, showing the progress of the survey during the year 1862 (Washington, Government Printing Office, 1864). Map 33.

At head of title: U.S. Coast Survey, A. D. Bache, Supdt.
"No. 33" is in the upper left corner.

ST. MARYS RIVER

120.5

—————St. Mary's River and Fernandina harbor, Florida. From a trigonometrical survey under the direction of A. D. Bache, Superintendent of the survey of the coast of the United States. Triangulation by Capt. J. H. Simpson and Lieutenant A. W. Evans, U.S.A. Assistants. Topography by A. M. Harrison, Assistant. Hydrography by the party under the command of Lieut. S. D. Trenchard, U.S.N. Assist. 1857. Resurvey of bar by C. O. Boutelle, Asst. in 1862. Redd. drng. by P. Witzel. Engd. by A. Maedel and R. F. Bartle. Bowen & Co. lith., Philada. [Washington, U.S. Coast Survey 1862] Uncolored. Scale 1:20,000. 63 × 81 cm. *From its* Report of the Superintendent of the Coast Survey, showing the progress of the survey during the year 1862 (Washington, Government Printing Office, 1864). Map 31.

"No. 31" in the upper left corner.

GEORGIA

121

See Sherman map collection no. 180.

121.2

Blakeslee, G. H.

Atlanta campaign—1864. "Rossville" to "Snake Creek Gap." G.H.B. [i.e., G. H. Blakeslee] Colored ms. Scale not given 55 × 43 cm.

G3921.S5 1864 .B6 Vault

Pen and ink sketch map showing "route of Harrison's Brigade, 3rd Div.," positions of the 1st, 2nd, and 3rd Divisions of the 20th Army Corps from May 2 to May 10, 1864, roads, railroads, villages, churches, mills, drainage, and relief by hachures.

No. "9" is in the lower right corner.

Advertisement for a map of the Battle of Resaca is pasted on the verso.

121.4

—————From the Etowah to Burnt-Hickory-Ga. G.H.B. [i.e., G. H. Blakeslee, 1864] Colored ms. Scale ca. 1:27,600. 51 × 40 cm.

G3921 .S5 1864 .B61 Vault

Pen and ink sketch map showing "route of Harrison's Brigade," engagements, routes of the 20th and 23rd Army Corps, roads, railroads, drainage, relief by hachures, woods, and clearings.

122

Boutelle, Charles O.

Sketch of a part of the coast of Georgia from Savannah River to Ossabaw Sound showing the relative positions of the U.S. Iron clad steamer Montauk & the rebel Fort McAllister during the bombardment of Feb. 1st 1863. Prepared under direction of Admiral S. F. Du Pont, by C. O. Boutelle, Assistant, Coast Survey. Uncolored. Scale 1:200,000. 23 × 26 cm.

At head of title: U.S. Coast Survey. A. D. Bache, Supdt.

Shows drainage, towns, geographic coordinates, railroad from Savannah to "Way's Stat. no. 2," and the position of the vessels *Nashville, Montauk, Seneca, Wissahicon, Dawn,* and *C. P. William* in the Ogeechee River near Fort McAllister, and the *Passaic, Marblehead,* and *Conemaugh* in Wassaw Sound.

123

See Sherman map collection no. 33.

124

Bufford, John H.

Genl. Sherman's campaign war map. Boston [1864] Uncolored. Scale ca. 1:670,000. 48 × 62 cm.

Map covering most of Georgia and South Carolina, showing defenses along the sea coast and around the principal towns, Confederate prisons at Andersonville and south of Millen, Ga., roads, railroads, towns, drainage, and relief by hachures.

"The horizontal and upright lines [of the map grid] represent five miles square. By refering [sic] to the number on the left and to the letter on the base, any point may be found to show the locality of the Union armies."

125

Callahan, Dennis.

Northwestern Georgia (with portions of the adjoining States of Tennessee and Alabama) being part of the Department of the Cumberland. Engineer Bureau of the War Department, January 1863. Denis Callahan, del. Lith. of J. Bien, N.Y. [Washington, 1864] Uncolored. Scale 1:350,000 (5.524 miles to an inch) 97 × 86 cm.

"Corrections and additions from Capt. Wm. E. Merrills Map of Northern Georgia in 1864."

Troop positions and movements are not indicated.

General campaign map showing turnpike and stage roads, railroads, towns, rivers, and relief by hachures.

Another copy in the Fillmore map coll. no. 264. Signed in ms: Millard Fillmore, March 12, 1865.

125.1

—————Another issue.

Lacks the name of the lithographer in the lower margin.

125.5

Down Home Designs.

The Civil war in Georgia. Over 100 battlefield locations during the years 1861–1865. Selma, Alabama, Down Home Designs, ©1981. Uncolored. Scale not given. 54 × 85 cm.

G3921 .S5 1981 .D6

Includes a descriptive index of the battles.

126

Fleming, Brewster, and Alley.

Birds eye map of the Western and Atlantic R.R. The great Kennesaw route. Army operations, Atlanta campaign, 1864. Fleming, Brewster [and] Alley, N.Y. [July 1887] Colored. Scale not given. 81 × 43 cm.

Map of northwest Georgia from Atlanta north to Chattanooga, Tennessee, showing location and date of battles, railroads, principal roads, towns, rivers, and relief by hachures.

Title when folded: Western and Atlantic R.R. W. & A., the great Kennesaw route from Atlanta to the north and north-west. Copyright by Jos. M. Brown, 1887. Press of Fleming, Brewster & Alley, New York. July, 1887.

Listed in A. M. Modelski's *Railroad Maps of the United States* (Washington, Library of Congress, 1975), no. 614.

126.5

Georgia. *State Highway Department. Division of Highway Planning.*

The State of Georgia, Civil War Centennial, 1864, showing the major campaign areas and engagement sites of the Union and Confederate armies. Prepared by State Highway Department of Georgia, Division of Highway Planning. [Atlanta, 1964?] Colored. Scale ca. 1:860,000. 85 × 54 cm.

G3921 .S5 1964 .G4

Indicates "route of Wilson's raiders," "route of Davis' attempted escape," "route of General Sherman's main force," and "railroads existing in 1864." Points of interest are keyed by number to a list in the upper left corner.

127

See Sherman map collection no. 181.

127.5

Hansard, William Carey.

North Georgia during Civil War days. Atlanta, W. C. Hansard, ©1939. Photocopy (positive). Scale ca. 1:1,800,000. 18 × 11 cm. on sheet 21 × 26 cm.

Map shows battlefields, place names, and railroads.

Insets: [Map of Georgia] 10 × 10 cm.—[Map of the United States] 6 × 10 cm.

Copyright no. F13477, Aug. 7, 1939.

128

Hergesheimer, Edwin.

Map showing the operations of the national forces under the command of Maj. Gen. W. T. Sherman during the campaign resulting in the capture of Atlanta, Georgia, Sept.

1, 1864. Drawn by E. Hergesheimer. Chas. G. Krebs lith. Colored. Scale 1:380,160. 55 × 36 cm.

"Prepared at the Coast Survey Office, Washington, D.C., from information furnished by Capt. O. M. Poe, Chief Engr., Genl. Sherman's staff, and from Genl. Sherman's published report."

Shows entrenchments, Union troop movements, towns, roads, railroads, drainage, and relief by hachures.

Brief statement concerning "National" and "Rebel" forces is in the lower left corner.

Another copy is in Sherman map coll. no. 27.

128.2

—————[Knoxville, Tennessee, Tennessee Valley Authority, 1974] Blue line print. Scale 1:380,160. 51 × 37 cm.

G3921 .S5 1864 .H4 1974

Facsimile reproduction, with note entitled "To Atlanta" added.

"453 754 2" is stamped in the lower margin.

129

See Sherman map collection no. 28.

129.1

Lindenkohl, Adolph.

Middle Georgia & South Carolina. Drawn by A. Lindenkohl. Chas. G. Krebs, lith. U.S. Coast Survey, A. D. Bache, Supt. [1865?] Colored. Scale 1:633,600. 47 × 80 cm.

G3920 1865 .U5

Signed in ms. on verso: Brig. Gen. Jos. R. Hawley, U.S. Vols.—Fort Fisher, N.C., Feb. 17th '65.

From the papers of Joseph Roswell Hawley, Manuscript Division, L.C.

General map indicating cities and towns, roads, rivers, and forts. Map is overprinted in red to highlight railroads and state boundaries.

Another copy in Fillmore map coll. no. 263.

129.2

—————[Northern Georgia and western and central South Carolina] Drawn by A. Lindenkohl. H. Lindenkohl & Chas. G. Krebs, lith. U.S. Coast Survey, A. D. Bache, Supdt. 1865. Colored. Scale 1:633,600. 58 × 86 cm.

General map, without title, extending from Charleston west to the western boundary of Georgia. State names, boundaries, and railroads are overprinted in red.

"Library of the Department of State" is written in ink in the upper margin.

129.3

—————Another issue.

"Drawn by A. Lindenkohl" and "H. Lindenkohl & Chas. G. Krebs, lith." have been dropped from the bottom margin.

Stamped on verso: Gilbert Thompson.

"No. 5. U.S. Coast Survey. 1865. (S. Car., Ga. 1″ = 10 ms. 6 sheets)" is written in ink on the verso.

Sheet 5 of a 6-sheet series of maps used by Gilbert Thompson during the Civil War. In addition to this sheet, the Geography and Map Division has sheet 1 (see entry no. 508.5), sheet 3 (see entry no. 305a.6), sheet 4 (see entry no. 259.6), and sheet 6 (see entry no. 129.55).

129.35

——————Another issue. The Norris Peters Co., photo-litho., Washington, D.C. Uncolored.

Lacks the name of the cartographer, and the lithographers' names have been changed from H. Lindenkohl & Chas. G. Krebs to the Norris Peters Co.

"No. 3013 price 30 cents" is printed in the upper left corner.

129.4

——————Sketch of the Atlantic coast of the United States from Savannah River to St. Mary's River, embracing the coast of the State of Georgia. Drawn by A. Lindenkohl. United States Coast Survey, A. D. Bache, Superintendent, 1861. Uncolored. Scale 1:200,000. 99 × 58 cm.

Inset: [Coast of Florida from St. Johns River to St. Augustine] 32 × 24 cm.

Coastal chart showing place names, roads, railroads, rivers and streams, and swamps.

129.45

——————Southern Georgia and part of South Carolina. Drawn by A. Lindenkohl. Chas. G. Krebs, lith. U.S. Coast Survey, A. D. Bache, Supdt. 1865. Colored. Scale 1:633,600. 63 × 90 cm.

G3920 1865 .U51

General map of most of Georgia and part of South Carolina showing cities and towns, forts, rivers, and roads. Red overprint gives state names and highlights boundaries and railroads.

129.46

——————Another issue.

G3920 1865 .U52 Vault Cloth

Similar to the preceding issue, but printed on cloth. Geography and Map Division copy is imperfect; the western half is missing.

From the papers of General Orlando M. Poe, Manuscript Division, L.C.

129.5

——————Another issue.

Lacks red overprint. This copy has been hand-colored to show railroads in red and the boundaries of Georgia in blue, South Carolina and Florida in red, and Alabama in yellow.

"Library of the Department of State" is written in ink in the upper margin.

129.55

——————Another issue.

Lacks the name of the lithographer in the lower right corner and the red overprint.

Stamped on verso: Gilbert Thompson.

"No. 6. Southern Georgia and part of North Carolina. U.S. Coast Survey. 1865. 1 in. = 10 ms. 6 sheets" is written in ink on the verso.

Sheet 6 of a 6-sheet series of maps used by Gilbert Thompson during the Civil War. In addition to this sheet, the Geography and Map Division has sheet 1 (see entry no. 508.5), sheet 3 (see entry no. 305a.6), sheet 4 (see entry no. 259.6), and sheet 5 (see entry no. 129.3).

129.6

Lloyd, James T.

Lloyd's topographical map of Georgia from state surveys before the war showing railways, stations, villages, mills, &c. New York, J. T. Lloyd, 1864. Colored. Scale ca. 1:580,000. 93 × 79 cm.

"Entered according to Act of Congress in the year 1864 by J. T. Lloyd."

"Price in sheets colored in counties 50 cents. Mounted and varnished $1. Pocket edition plain $1.00. Pocket edn. with linen backs $1.50, sent free by mail."

Hand-colored general map with places where battles occurred underlined in red.

Another copy is in Fillmore map coll. no. 110-W.

The Geography and Map Division also has an uncolored copy (copyright no. 169, April 30, 1864).

129.65

——————Another issue.

". . . Pocket edn. with linen backs $200 [sic], sent free by mail." Previous issue (entry no. 129.6) was priced at $1.50

129.7

Map of the cost [sic] of Georgia & Florida. [1863?] Colored ms. Scale 1:253,440. 127 × 35 cm.

G3922 .C6 1863 .M3 Vault

Map of the coast from Savannah to St. Augustine showing forts, towns, roads, railroads, swamps, and marshes.

From the papers of Joseph Roswell Hawley, Manuscript Division, L.C.

129.74

Merrill, William E.

Part of northern Georgia. No. 2. Compiled under the direction of Capt. Wm. E. Merrill, Chief Top'l Eng'r, D.C. Lithographed Topo'l Eng'r Office, Head-Quarters, Dep't of the Cumberland. [1864] Uncolored. Scale 1:253,440. 50 × 32 cm.

G3920 1864 .M39 Vault Cloth

Printed on cloth.

Endorsed (facsim.): Official issue. Wm. C. Margedant, Capt. & Supt.

Handwritten note in the upper margin: Specimen of field maps used in Sherman's campaigns, 1864.

Sheet "no. 2" of 3 sheets printed on cloth for the use of cavalry officers during Gen. W. T. Sherman's Atlanta campaign. This sheet extends from Rome on the north to Franklin on the south and indicates towns and villages, roads, railroads, drainage, and some relief by hachures. Troop positions and movements are not indicated.

See Sherman map collection no. 22 for another copy of the second sheet and Sherman nos. 31 and 32 for copies of the first sheet. Sheet no. 3 is listed as *Civil War Maps* no. 129.75.

129.75

—————Part of northern Georgia. No. 3. Compiled under the direction of Capt. Wm. E. Merrill, Chief Top'l Eng'r, D.C. Lithographed Topo'l Eng'r Office, Headquarters Dep't of the Cumberland. [1864] Uncolored. Scale 1:253,440. 51 × 32 cm.

G3920 1864 .M4 Vault Cloth

Printed on cloth.

Endorsed (facsim.): Official issue. Wm. C. Margedant, Capt. & Supt.

Sheet "no. 3" of 3 sheets is printed on cloth for the use of cavalry officers during Gen. W. T. Sherman's Atlanta campaign. This sheet shows the environs of Atlanta and indicates towns and villages, roads, railroads, drainage, and some relief by hachures. Troop positions and movements are not indicated. See Sherman map collection nos. 31 and 32 for copies of the first sheet and Sherman map collection no. 22 for sheet 2.

129.8

Prang (Louis) and Company.

The army map of Georgia. Boston, L. Prang & Co., ©1864.

Uncolored. Scale ca. 1:800,000. 89 × 57 cm.

"Deposited [for copyright] July 27, 1864. Recorded vol. 39, page 496" and "No. 41" are written in the right margin.

"Copyright Library, 28 Jan. 1865."

"Entered according to Act of Congress in the year 1864 by L. Prang & Co."

General map printed in brown ink.

129.85

Rhodes, James F.

Sherman's campaign from Chattanooga to Atlanta. [1864] Engraved by R. D. Servoss, N.Y. Colored. Scale ca. 1:500,000. 39 × 25 cm. *From his* History of the Civil War, 1861–1865. New York, The Macmillan Co., 1917. Facing p. 314.

Map of northwest Georgia showing the "lines of works erected by the United States forces" in blue and "Confederate forces" in red.

129.87

Ruger, Edward.

Map illustrating the first epoch of the Atlanta Campaign. Commanding United States forces, Major-General W. T. Sherman, commanding rebel forces, Lieut. General J. E. Johnston. Compiled by Edward Ruger. [1864] [Knoxville, Tennessee: Tennessee Valley Authority, 1974?] Blue line print. Scale ca. 1:80,000. 85 × 51 cm.

G3961 .S5 1864 .R8 1974

In the upper right corner: 2.

In the lower left corner: Series 1, vol. XXXVIII.

Enlarged facsimile reproduction of plate LVII, map 2, in the U.S. War Department's *Atlas to Accompany the Official Records of the Union and Confederate Armies* (Washington, Government Printing Office, 1891–95).

Subtitle of map: Embracing the region from the Tennessee River to the Oostanaula River, showing the positions held and lines of works erected by the enemy; also the lines of works erected by the United States forces, the lines of march traversed by them and their relative location in line of battle when attacking the enemy.

129.9

Smith, J. Harmon.

The State of Georgia, showing the major campaign areas and engagement sites of the War between the States, 1861–1865. [Atlanta] Georgia Department of Commerce, 1961. Colored. Scale ca. 1:960,000. 73 × 61 cm.

"All place names, county lines and railroads are shown as they existed during the Civil War."

Indicates "route of Davis' attempted escape," "route of march of General Sherman's main forces," and "Confederate defense works." Engagements and other important sites are keyed by number to map.

130

See Sherman map collection no. 23.

131

U.S. *Army. Corps of Engineers.*

Map[s] illustrating the military operations of the Atlanta campaign . . . 1864. Compiled by authority of the Hon. the Secretary of War in the office of the Chief of Engineers, U.S.A. American Photo-Lithographic Co., N.Y. (Osborne's Process). [1874–1877] Colored. Scale ca. 1:87,000. 5 maps.

Detailed maps showing roads, railroads, drainage, vegetation, hachures, houses, names of residents, towns, churches, mills, fortifications, and the "lines of march pursued by the separate [Federal] armies."

The area covered by each of the following five maps is indicated by broken lines on the *Map illustrating the operations of the army under command of General W. T. Sherman in Georgia* (entry no. 127).

Map I: This map embraces the region extending from the Tennessee River to the Oostanaula River and exhibits the works of the United States and Confederate forces . . . 1875. 89 × 52 cm.

Map II: This map includes the region from Resaca on the north to Ackworth on the south, and exhibits the works of the United States and Confederate forces . . . 1877. 71 × 64 cm.

Map III: This map includes the region extending from Rome, Kingston and Cassville on the north to include Dallas and Marietta on the south and exhibits the works of the United States and Confederate forces . . . 1876. 58 × 80 cm.

Map IV: Embracing the region from Pine, Lost and Kennesaw Mountains south to include Atlanta, and its environs, exhibiting the lines of operations at Pine, Lost and Kennesaw Mts., at Smyrna camp ground, along the Chattahoochie [sic] River, and in the investment of Atlanta . . . 1874. 63 × 67 cm.

Map V: This map includes the region from the Chattahoochee River south to Jonesboro and Lovejoy's Station, and exhibits the works of the United States and Confederate forces . . . 1877. 65 × 67 cm.

Another copy is in Sherman map coll. no. 200.

132

————————Another issue.
Julius Bien & Co., photo lith., N.Y.

132.4

[U.S. *Army. Department of the Cumberland. Topographical Engineers*]

Map of Catoosa County and parts of Whitfield, Murray and Walker counties, Georgia] Chattanooga, Sept. 12 [1863?] Photocopy (negative). Scale not given. 53 × 66 cm.

Contemporary Civil War photocopy, apparently made during the Chattanooga campaign, showing roads, distances from selected places, railroads, drainage, types of vegetation, and the names of a few residents.

132.5

Western and Atlantic Railroad Company.

Map of Allatoona, New Hope Church and vicinity. [1864] Prepared for and presented with compliments of Western and Atlantic R. R. Co. Matthews, Northrup & Co., Art-Printing Works, Buffalo, N.Y. Uncolored. Scale ca. 1:280,000. 14 × 9 cm.

Shows location of battles of Allatoona, Allatoona Creek, Picketts Mill, and New Hope Church, roads, railroads, Confederate entrenchments, towns, drainage, and relief by hachures.

132.6

————————Map of army operations Atlanta campaign between Cassville and Marietta and vicinity. [1864] Prepared for and presented with compliments of Western and Atlantic R. R. Co. Matthews, Northrup & Co., Art-Printing Works, Buffalo, N.Y. Uncolored. Scale 1:285,120. 21 × 15 cm.

Map of Bartow, Cherokee, Paulding, and Cobb counties, Georgia, showing location and date of battles, entrenchments, towns, roads, railroads, drainage, and relief by hachures.

132.7

————————Map of army operations Atlanta campaign between Kingston and Atlanta. [1864] Prepared for and presented with compliments of Western and Atlantic R. R. Co. Matthews, Northrup & Co., Art-Printing Works, Buffalo, N.Y. Uncolored. Scale 1:285,120. 22 × 19 cm.

Map of Bartow, Cherokee, Paulding, Cobb, and Fulton counties, Georgia, showing location and date of battles, towns, roads, railroads, entrenchments, drainage, and relief by hachures.

132.8

————————Map of Rome, Adairsville and vicinity. [1864] Prepared for and presented with compliments of Western and Atlantic R. R. Co. Matthews, Northrup & Co., Art-Printing Works, Buffalo, N.Y. Uncolored. Scale ca. 1:350,000. 14 × 19 cm.

Shows location of battles of Lay's or Tanner's Ferry, Adairsville, and Cassville, roads, railroads, towns, drainage, and relief by hachures.

133

————————Map of the Atlanta campaign. [May–Sept. 1864] Uncolored. Scale ca. 1:830,000. 20 × 15 cm. *From Century illustrated monthly magazine, v. 34, July 1887. p. 446.*

Map of northwest Georgia showing location and date of engagements, railroads, towns, rivers, relief by hachures, and county names and boundaries.

133.2

——————Another issue. Prepared for and presented with compliments of Western and Atlantic R.R. Co. Matthews, Northrup & Co., Art-Printing Works, Buffalo, N.Y.

ALLATOONA

133.7

[Position of General George Stoneman at Allatoona and position of General Kenner Garrard on the Etowah River nearby. 1864] Uncolored ms. Scale not given. 27 × 21 cm.

In the John Alexander Logan family papers, Manuscript Division, L.C., container 145, p. 101.

Pencil sketch drawn on tracing paper.

ANDERSONVILLE

134

United States Sanitary Commission.

Prison at Andersonville, Ga. Waters & son sc., N.Y. Uncolored. Scale not given 24 × 16 cm. *From* Sanitary Commission bulletin, v. 1, no. 21, Sept. 1, 1864. opp. p. 647.

Plan of camp showing the prison, the "dead line," "Rebel camp," batteries, "Gen. Winder's headquarters," Capt. Wirtz's house, depot, cook house, dispensary, hospital, road, and drainage.

ATLANTA

135

See Sherman map collection no. 37.

135.5

Georgia. *State Highway Department. Division of Highway Planning.*

Civil War Centennial, city of Atlanta, showing the area of the three major engagements and deployment of Union and Confederate forces during the summer of 1864. Prepared by State Highway Department of Georgia, Division of Highway Planning. [Atlanta, 1964?] Colored. Scale ca. 1:24,000. 54 × 85 cm.

G3924 .A8S5 1964 .G4

Indicates troop positions and movements during the battles of Peach Tree Creek, July 20, 1864, Atlanta, July 22, 1864, and Ezra Church, July 28, 1864. Points of interest on the map are keyed by number to a list below the title.

136

See Sherman map collection no. 41.

136.5

Map showing the position [of the] 15th Army Corps, Aug. 1st 1864 in front [of] Atlanta. Uncolored ms. Scale 1:15,840 ("four inch to a mile") 37 × 75 cm.

In the John Alexander Logan family papers, Manuscript Division, L.C., container 145, p. 98.

Title on verso.

Drawn in pencil on tracing paper. Tracing paper now is brittle and broken into several pieces.

137

See Sherman map collection no. 39.

138

See Sherman map collection no. 40.

139

Poe, Orlando M.

Map illustrating the siege of Atlanta, Ga. by the U.S. forces under command of Maj. Gen. W. T. Sherman, from the passage of Peach Tree Creek, July 19th 1864, to the commencement of the movement upon the enemy's lines of communication south of Atlanta, August 26, 1864. Reduced and engraved in the Engineer Bureau, War Dept., from an original prepared under the directions of Cap. O. M. Poe, Corps of Eng's. and senr. engr. on Gen'l. Sherman's staff. E.w. Molitor, lith. Colored. Scale ca. 1:47,520. 31 × 52 cm. *From* 39th Cong., 1st Sess. [1866]—Report of the Chief Engineer U.S.A. No. 2

In lower right margin: Bowen & Co., lith., Philada.

Indicates entrenchments, relief by hachures, vegetation, drainage, roads, railroads, towns, and the names of a few residents in the environs of Atlanta.

Other issues in Sherman map coll. nos. 39–40.

140

See Sherman map collection no. 42.

141

See Sherman map collection no. 43.

142

U.S. *Army. Corps of Engineers.*

Map illustrating the military operations in front of Atlanta, Ga. From the passage of Peach Tree Creek, July 19th 1864, to the commencement of the movement upon the enemy's lines of communication, south of Atlanta, August 26th 1864. Compiled by authority of the Hon. the Secretary of War in the Office of the Chief of Engineers, U.S.A., 1875.

Julius Bien & Co., photo lith., N.Y. Colored. Scale ca. 1:32,000. 72 × 78 cm.

Insets: A portion of the Confederate defenses of Atlanta. Scale ca. 1:1300. 16 × 14 cm. A portion of the U.S. defensive works erected after the capture of Atlanta. Scale 1:1200. 21 × 25 cm. Confederate and Union defenses shown in the insets are keyed to the map by the letters A to G and the numbers 7 to 12 respectively.

Detailed map showing fortifications, headquarters, location and dates of battles, street outline of Atlanta, roads, railroads, vegetation, drainage, relief by hachures, towns, mills, churches, the location of rural houses, and the names of residents.

143

————Facsimile reproduction by the Graphic Co., N.Y.

Another copy is in Sherman map coll. no. 195.

144

Western and Atlantic Railroad Company.

Map of Atlanta and vicinity. [July 1864] Uncolored. Scale ca. 1:165,000. 9 × 9 cm. *From* Century illustrated monthly magazine, v. 34, July 1887. p. 457.

Shows fortifications, roads, railroads, rivers, and towns. The battles of Peach Tree Creek (July 20), Atlanta (July 22), and Ezra Church (July 28) are indicated.

144.2

————Another issue. Prepared for and presented with compliments of Western and Atlantic R.R. Co. Matthews, Northrup & Co., Art-Printing Works, Buffalo, N.Y.

145

Wood, Walter B., *and* J. E. Edmonds.

Atlanta. [1864. London] Methuen & Co. [1905] Uncolored. Scale ca. 1:400,000. 17 × 12 cm.

"Map XIII."

Prepared to accompany W. B. Wood and J. E. Edmonds's *A History of the Civil War in the United States, 1861–5* (London, Methuen & Co. [1905]).

Map showing the Federal and Confederate lines at Marietta, Atlanta, Jonesboro, and Lovejoy, Georgia.

AUGUSTA

146

See Sherman map collection no. 46.

147

See Sherman map collection no. 47.

BARTOW COUNTY

147.5

Blakeslee, G. H.

May 17 to 23, 1864, Adairsville to Euharlee, Ga. G.H.B. [i.e. G. H. Blakeslee] Colored ms. Scale not given. 54 × 40 cm.

G3923 .B36S5 1864 .B6 Vault

Pen and ink sketch map of part of Bartow County, Georgia, showing the route of "Harrison's Brigade," the position of the 1st, 2nd, and 3rd Divisions of the 20th Army Corps from May 19 to 22, 1864, roads, fortifications, railroads, mills, villages, churches, and drainage.

"No. 11" is in the upper right corner.

BIG SHANTY

148

See Sherman map collection no. 48.

CAMP McDONALD

149

McClellan, L. B.

Camp McDonald; a school of Instruction for the 4th Brigade Georgia Volunteers. His excellency Governor Joseph E. Brown, Commander in Chief. Souvenir edition, 1917. Atlanta, ©1917. Colored. Scale 1:2400. 33 × 54 cm.

"Lithographed and sold for the benefit of the Georgia volunteers."

Pictorial map showing parade grounds, tents, buildings, hospitals, streets, relief by hachures, and the names of principal officers.

"The Georgia Military Institute was organized at Marietta, Georgia, in 1851, by Colonel A. V. Brumby; chartered at the session of the General Assembly in the winter of 1851–1852, and modeled after the U.S. Military Academy at West Point.

"During the war between the states Camp McDonald was established, including the Georgia Military Institute grounds and extending to Big Shanty (now called Kennesaw). Here recruits for the Confederate army were drilled by the cadets and new regiments organized.

"During the campaign from Dalton to the sea in 1864 the Georgia Military Institute cadets served with great credit. Camp McDonald was destroyed by Sherman and the school was never revived.—Joseph Tyrone Derry."

CASSVILLE

149.5

Jackman, John S.

[Three positions of the 9th Kentucky Infantry Regiment, CSA, near Cassville, Georgia, on May 19, 1864] Uncolored ms. Scale ca. 1:70,000. 9 × 7 cm. *In his* Journal [1861–1908] p. 133.

In the John S. Jackman papers, Manuscript Division, L.C.

Pen and ink sketch map.

Jackman served in the 9th Kentucky Infantry Regiment, CSA.

CAUSTEN'S BLUFF

150

See Sherman map collection no. 105.

CHATTAHOOCHEE RIVER

151

See Sherman map collection no. 50.

152

See Sherman map collection no. 51.

153

See Sherman map collection no. 52.

153.2

Scupham, J. R.

Map of Rebel works near the Chattahoochee River. Compiled from information derived from a citizen who was there, June 3ed [sic] 1864. By J.R.S., Topo. Eng. 2ed [sic] Divis. 15th A. C. Colored ms. Scale 1:15,840 ("4 inches to mile"). 25 × 20 cm.

In the John Alexander Logan family papers, Manuscript Division, L.C., container 145, opp. p. 101.

Title on verso.

Pen and ink manuscript map showing "Confederate works," "hill commanding Confed. works unocupied [sic] June 3ed [sic]," and "new road bridg" [sic] near Vining's Station, Georgia.

153.3

[Sketch map showing roads near McAfee Bridge across the Chattahoochee River. 1864] Uncolored ms. Scale 1:63,360 ("one inch a mile"). 28 × 20 cm.

In the John Alexander Logan family papers, Manuscript Division, L.C., container 145, opp. p. 103.

Pen and ink map on tracing paper.

CHENEY HOUSE

153.4

Scupham, J. R.

Map of the positio[n] occupied by the Second Division, 15th A. C., July 2ed [sic] 1864. [By] J. R. Scupham, Topo. Engr 2ed [sic] Divis. 15th A. C. Colored ms. Scale 1:31,680 ("2 inches to mile"). Map 25 × 20 cm. on sheet 25 × 38 cm.

In the John Alexander Logan family papers, Manuscript Division, L.C., container 145, p. 102.

Another title, written in pencil to left of map, reads as follows: Map showing the position of 2 Div., 15 A. C. on July 2nd 1864, near the Cheney House, Georgia.

Pen and ink manuscript map showing Union positions and the "road on which Rebel baggag[e] wagons were seen."

CHICKAMAUGA

153.5

Betts, Edward E.

Relief map of the Chickamauga battlefield. Designed and constructed by Edward E. Betts, C. E. Chattanooga, Tenn., A. W. Judd, 1893. Photocopy (positive). Scale ca. 1:350,000. 13 × 22 cm.

Photograph of a relief model. Photograph is nearly illegible.

Copyright no. 13826y2.

153.9

Boyd, C. H.

Battle field of Chickamauga, Georgia, surveyed by command of Major Genl. G. H. Thomas, commanding Department of the Cumberland by Capt. C. H. Boyd, Sub-Asst. U.S. Coast Survey, April and May 1864. Assisted in levelling by Lieut Kuntze & Sergeant Wilson, Topl. Engineers, 2nd Division, 14th Army Corps. [Knoxville, Tennessee, Tennessee Valley Authority, 1975?] Blue line print. Scale 1:32,000 (not "1/20,000"). 56 × 46 cm.

G3922 .C5 1864 .B6 1975

"Register no. 934."

"Plate 15: Battle Field of Chickamauga."

Facsimile reproduction of manuscript map of the battlefield. Indicated are roads, houses, names of residents, contour lines, woodland, and field patterns. Troop positions are not shown.

154

————Battle-field of Chickamauga, surveyed by command of Maj. Gen. Thomas, comdg. Dept. of the Cumberland by Capt. C. H. Boyd, U.S. Coast Survey. April & May 1864. Autogr. & printed under direction of Col. Wm. E. Merrill, Chief Engr., D. C., Chattanooga, October, 1864. Uncolored. Scale 1:20,000. 69 × 53 cm.

Shows roads, fords, drainage, vegetation, houses, names of residents, fences, and relief by contour lines. Some fortifications are given but troop positions and movements during the Battle of Chickamauga are not indicated.

For manuscript version of this map, see entry no. 157.4.

154.5

Ferger, Edward, *and* A. J. Taylor.

Map of Chickamauga National Military Park. ©1895. Uncolored. Scale not given. 37 × 26 cm.

Copyright no. 20184aa, May 27, 1895.

98 sites are listed and keyed by number to the map.

155

McElroy, Joseph C.

Chickamauga battlefield. [Sept 19–20, 1863] Sketched by J. C. McElroy of the Ohio Commission, late Captain 18th Ohio Infantry. The Henderson-Achert-Krebs Lith. Co., Cincinnati. ©1895. Colored. Scale ca. 1:12,300. 48 × 74 cm.

Shows troop positions and movements, names of commanders, location of battlefield monuments, roads, railroads, fords, bridges, drainage, vegetation, houses, and names of residents.

156

————————Another issue. *Accompanies* The battle of Chickamauga. Historical map and guide book. By Capt. J. C. McElroy, 18th Ohio Infantry. 18p.

Pamphlet describes the battle of Chickamauga.

The map shows Gen. Robert B. Mitchell's Union cavalry on Sept. 20th deployed in the north and south of General Rosecrans's headquarters in the Lee mansion and Gen. James T. Wheeler's Confederate troops to the east and south, none of which is included in the preceding version (entry no. 155).

157

————————Another issue. The Henderson Lith. Co., Cincinnati. *Accompanies* The battle of Chickamauga. Historical map and guide book. By Capt. J. C. McElroy, 18th Ohio Infantry. Published by T. H. Payne & Co., Chattanooga, Tenn. 25 p.

Map appears to be the same as the preceding version (entry no. 156) with the exception of the change in the name of the lithographer. Pamphlet includes a list of the Union and Confederate units participating in the battle and the names of the commanding officers.

Another copy is filed as G3922.C52S5 1895 .M3.

157.4

Merrill, William E.

Battle of—"Chickamauga"—Sep. 19th & 20th 1863 under Col. W. E. Merrill. [1864] Colored ms. Scale ca. 1:20,000. 84 × 64 cm.

G3922.C5 1864.M4 Vault

Title from verso. "N.61" appears above the title.

Note in the upper left corner reads as follows: *Companion sheet to the other map marked No. 61*—The other map represents the positions of the troops at the battle of Chicamauga [sic], the roads, woods & fields, but does not represent the irregularities of the surface. This map represents the roads, rivers, and irregularities of the surface as developed by contour lines and heavy tints on the lower portions of the ground, the highest elevations being untinted. The two maps are from the *same original* and agree exactly in the roads and streams. This map was prepared as a guide to the draughtsman who might be employed to prepare the *complete* map of the Battle of Chicamauga [sic]. By carefully studying the contour lines and tints on this map an *accurate* map with hachures may be made of the ground. If then the locations of the troops are taken from the other map the battle map will be complete. W. E. M. [i.e., William E. Merrill]

"Engineer Department Dec. 5, 1865. Recd. with Col. Merrills letter of Nov. 17, 1865. (M. 5471)"

Map indicates roads, rivers and streams, and relief by shading and contour lines. Troop positions are not shown.

For a printed version of this map, see entry no. 154.

157.6

Nashville, Chattanooga, and St. Louis Railway.

Map of Chickamauga & Chattanooga National Park. The Matthews-Northrup Co., Buffalo, N.Y. Copyright, 1895, by Nashville, Chattanooga & St. Louis Ry. [Nashville, 1895] Colored. Scale ca. 1:57,000. 53 × 40 cm.

"13421" is in the lower left corner.

Title when folded: War route to Chickamauga. Dedication Chickamauga and Chattanooga National Park, September 18, 19, and 20, 1895.

Map shows roads, railroads, state boundaries, place names, and boundary of national park. "Red lines indicate government roads."

Most published maps during the Civil War employed hachures to depict relief rather than contour lines. Col. William E. Merrill's manuscript map of the battlefield of Chickamauga, Georgia, however, showed topography by contour lines at intervals of 20 feet. Explaining his use of contour lines, Merrill wrote that "This map was prepared as a guide to the draughtsman who might be employed to prepare the complete map of the battle of Chicamauga [sic]. By carefully studying the contour lines and tints on this map an accurate map with hachures may be made of the ground." (See entry no. 157.4.)

158

Norwood, Charles W.

Battle map of Chickamauga, Georgia. Saturday, 19 [and] Sunday, 20 September 1863. Chattanooga, ©1898. Colored. Scale ca. 1:32,600. 28 × 21 cm. *In his* The Chickamauga and Chattanooga battle-fields. Chattanooga, Gervis M. Connelly [1898] opp. p. 18.

Cover title of pamphlet: Book of Battles Chickamauga, Chattanooga, Lookout Mountain, and Missionary Ridge.

On verso of Chickamauga map: Map of the Chattanooga battle-fields, November, 1863. (For a full description see entry no. 401).

The Chickamauga map is divided "into quarter-mile sections, numbered 1 to 20 on the west and east margins, and lettered A to O on the north and south." Map indicates approximate troop positions, movements, commanding officers, a few houses and names of residents, roads, "Chatta., Rome & Southern R.R.," and drainage.

On pages 3 to 18 in the pamphlet, there is a description of the battle with the points under discussion keyed by letter and number to the map.

158.3

Owner, William.

Chickamauga fight. [September 1863] Uncolored ms. Scale not given. 19 × 16 cm. *In his* Diary, v. 5, tipped-in at the front of the volume.

In the William Owner papers, Manuscript Division, L.C., container no. 1.

Rough pencil sketch.

Volume 5 of diary covers from June 29 to November 16, 1863.

158.5

Ramey, B. B.

Map of Chickamauga and Chattanooga National Military Park. Drawn by B. B. Ramey. Copyrighted 1895, by W. E. Birchmore. Engraved by Buff[alo] Elec. & Eng. Co. Uncolored. Scale 1:12,000. 44 × 22 cm. *From* Lynde, Francis. Chickamauga and Chattanooga National Military Park. With narratives of the battles of Chickamauga, Lookout Mountain and Missionary Ridge. Chattanooga, W. E. Birchmore, ©1895. 40 p.

Map indicates roads, drainage, houses, and names of residents. "Key to monuments, locations, and markers" depicted on map reproduced on p. [40] of text.

Copyright no. 19605 AA. "Published June 27/95."

159

Ruger, Edward.

Map of the battlefield of Chickamauga, September 19th and 20th 1863. Compiled under the direction of Col. W. E. Merrill, Chief Eng'r., Dep't. of the Cumberland, by Edward Ruger, Sup't. Top'l. Engineer Office D.C. Redrawn by Louis Boedicker, top'l, draughtsman, 1867–1868. Corrected and positions of troops located by Captain S. C. Kellogg, 5th Cavalry, 1889. [©1892]. Julius Bien & Co., lith. Colored. Scale 1:20,000. 10 maps, each 56 × 93 cm.

Maps are loose in two folders entitled "Chickamauga, Sept. 19th and 20th 1863." The folder for the "First day" includes "Sheet no. A: Preliminary movements, Sept. 18th" and sheets 1 to 4. The "Second day" folder contains sheets 5 to 8 and "Sheet no. Z: Movements of Sept. 21st and 22nd (after the battle)."

Each map gives troop positions and movements, names of commanding officers, a legend describing the action depicted, roads, houses, names of residents, fences, relief by hachures, vegetation, drainage, and fords.

Folders are stamped "Library of Congress, City of Washington, Copyright Oct. 24, 1892.

Another copy is in Sherman map coll. no. 191.

159.5

Shutting, Rudolph J.

Aero view of Chickamauga and Chattanooga National Military Park (looking east). Painted by Rudolph J. Shutting, Chattanooga, 1913. [Knoxville, Tennessee, Tennessee Valley Authority, 1974?] Blue line print. View. 41 × 57 cm.

G3922.C5A3 1913 .S5 1974

"G-CF–435 G 501."

"Index to monuments, markers, batteries and other points of interest" is printed below the panoramic view.

160

U.S. *Chickamauga and Chattanooga National Park Commission.*

Atlas of the battlefields of Chickamauga, Chattanooga and vicinity. Published under the direction of Daniel S. Lamont and Russell A. Alger, Secretaries of War . . . Washington, Government Printing Office, 1896–7. 3 p. l., 7 fold. maps (part col.) 71 × 53 cm.

G1312.C5S5U55 1896

Cover title.

Includes a map of the theater of operations, four situation maps of the battle of Chickamauga, a map of the battles of Chattanooga and Wauhatchie, and a map of Chickamauga Park. These are preceded by a page of explanatory "legends" and a two-page list of the "Organization of Union and Confederate armies at the battles of Chickamauga, September 19 and 20, 1863, and Chattanooga, November 23–25, 1863."

Listed in C. E. Le Gear's *A List of Geographical Atlases in the Library of Congress* (Washington, Library of Congress, 1973), v. 7, no. 10677.

161

————————Atlas of the battlefields of Chickamauga, Chattanooga and vicinity. Published under the direction of Honorable Daniel S. Lamont and Honorable Russell A. Alger, Secretaries of War. Republished by order of Congress, with additional position maps, under the direction of Honorable Elihu Root, Secretary of War . . . Washington, Government Printing Office, 1901. 4 p., 14 fold maps (part col.) 71 × 53 cm.

G1312.C5S5U55 1901

Cover title.

Duplicate sheet of p. [1] and [2] inserted.

Includes a map of the theater of operations, seven maps of the battle of Chickamauga and one of Chickamauga Park, and five maps of the battlefields of Chattanooga. Maps are preceded by two pages of explanatory "legends" and a two-page list of the "Organization of Union and Confederate armies at the battles of Chickamauga . . . and Chattanooga . . ."

Listed in C. E. Le Gear's *A List of Geographical Atlases in the Library of Congress* (Washington, Library of Congress, 1973), v. 7, no. 10678.

162

————————Another issue.

Issued as House Document no. 514, 56th Cong., 2d sess., 1900–1901, serial no. 4175.

Printed title on cover label reads as follows: Atlas of Chickamauga, Chattanooga, and vicinity.

G1312.C5S5U5 1901

Listed in C. E. LeGear's *A List of Geographical Atlases in the Library of Congress* (Washington, Library of Congress, 1973), v. 7, no. 10676.

162.4

U.S. *Geological Survey.*

Chickamauga and Chattanooga National Military Park, Ga. (Chickamauga Battlefield). Albert Pike, Division Engineer. Topography by Frank Larner and R. E. Amidon. Control by U.S. Geological Survey. Surveyed in 1934. [Washington, 1934] Colored. Scale 1:9600. 86 × 80 cm.

"Advance sheet. Subject to correction."

Title at top of sheet: Georgia. Chickamauga and Chattanooga National Military Park (Chickamauga Battlefield).

Detailed topographic map indicating monuments and markers. 290 sites are listed and keyed by number to the map. Contour interval is 5 feet.

162.5

————————[Knoxville, Tennessee, Tennessee Valley Authority, 1975?] Blue line print. Scale 1:9600. 78 × 80 cm.

G3922 .C5 1934 .U5 1975

"G–CF–435 P 505."

162.6

U.S. *National Park Service.*

Chickamauga and Chattanooga National Military Park, Georgia and Tennessee. Principal roads and streets between Chattanooga and park areas. Revised Sept. 1955. Reprint 1957 [Washington] Government Printing Office, 1957. Uncolored. Scale ca. 1:164,000. 17 × 11 cm.

"NMP–CC–7004."

Illustrates descriptive leaflet by U.S. National Park Service entitled "Point Park, Lookout Mountain and Chattanooga Battlefields."

Includes text and illustrations.

162.7

————————Chickamauga and Chattanooga National Military Park [Washington, Government Printing Office] 1968. Colored. Scale ca. 1:95,000. Map 32 × 28 cm. fold. to 15 × 9 cm.

G3922 .C5 1968 .U5

Folded title: Chickamauga and Chattanooga National Military Park, Georgia-Tennessee.

"NMP–CHCH–17013."

"Reprint 1970."

Map indicates the location of 11 important sites. Text printed on verso.

162.8

————————Chickamauga Battlefield. June 1973, GJB. [Washington, U.S. National Park Service, 1973] Colored. Scale not given. Map 14 × 16 cm. on sheet 58 × 17 cm. fold. to 15 × 9 cm.

G3922 .C52 1973 .U5

Folded title: Chickamauga Battlefield, Chickamauga and Chattanooga National Military Park, Georgia and Tennessee.

Map shows "A tour of Chickamauga Battlefield."

Inset: Chattanooga and vicinity. June 1973, GJB. 18 × 17 cm.

Portrait of George H. Thomas on the verso.

Text on the verso.

162.9

————————Tour route, Chickamauga Battlefield, Chickamauga and Chattanooga National Military Park, Georgia and Tennessee. Revised Sept. 1955. Reprint 1957. [Washington] Government Printing Office, 1957. Uncolored. Scale ca. 1:55,000. 20 × 14 cm.

Illustrates descriptive brochure entitled "Chickamauga Battlefield, Chickamauga and Chattanooga National Military Park, Georgia and Tennessee."

Map indicates "Union defense line morning of Sept. 20," battlefield sites, park boundary, and tour route.

163

Wells, Jacob.

Battle-field of Chickamauga. [Sept. 18–20, 1863] Uncolored. Scale ca. 1:84,000. 14 × 22 cm. *From* Century illustrated monthly magazine, v. 33, April 1887. p. 954.

Indicates by symbols the "positions, evening of Sept. 18, 1863," "direction of lines of battle, Sept. 19th," "first lines of battle, Sept. 20th," "last lines of battle, Sept. 20th," "positions of Union troops after the battle," and positions of the cavalry. Map also includes roads, rivers, fords, bridges, relief by hachures, and houses.

164

Wood, W. A.

Map of the Chickamauga battle-field, Georgia. Drawn by W. A. Wood, expressly for Norwood's Vade-Mecum Guide. ©1895. Colored. Scale 1:14,400. 57 × 38 cm.

In upper margin: The latest and most accurate.

Indicates houses, names of residents, roads, drainage, Chattanooga, Rome, and Columbus railroad, and the boundary of the park at the time of dedication in September 1895. A description of the battle is overprinted in red with the important points of interest keyed by section, letter, and number to the map.

COBB COUNTY

164.5

Blakeslee, G. H.

[Map of the environs of Pine Mountain, Lost Mountain, Kenesaw Mountain, and Little Kenesaw Mountain] G. H. Blakeslee T. E. [June 2–22, 1864] Colored ms. Scale not given. 40 × 52 cm.

G3923 .C73S5 1864 .B6 Vault

Pen and ink sketch map of northwestern Cobb County, Georgia, showing the "route of Harrison's Brigade," Confederate and Federal works, battlefields, roads, railroads, churches, drainage, and relief by hachures. Also depicted are the locations of the "5th Ind. Bat. [that] kill[ed] Gen. Polk, June 14" and the "spot where Polk was killed."

165

See Sherman map collection no. 61.

166

See Sherman map collection no. 63.

166.5

U.S. *Army. Department of the Cumberland. Topographical Engineers.*

Map of the country between Lost Mountain & the Cha-

tohooche [sic] Traced from the Cherokee Land Map at Topl. Engs. Office, Hd. Qtrs., Army of the Cumberland. [1864] Colored ms. Scale ca. 1:63,360. 48 × 59 cm.

In the John Alexander Logan family papers, Manuscript Division, L.C., container 145, p. 106.

Title written in ink on the verso. A second title written in pencil on the verso reads: Map showing the routs [sic] from Lost Mountain to the river.

Dashed lines are "roads from Land Map," double dashed lines are "roads from information," solid lines are "roads from survey," and "Atlanta is located from Land Map of DeKalb Co." Map also indicates the location of the "Rebel line," and in a different hand and ink, the positions at Ruff's Mill and Nickajack Creek, of Logan, Blair, and another commander whose name cannot be read.

COLUMBUS

167

See Sherman map collection no. 65.

168

See Sherman map collection no. 66.

DALLAS

168.5

Jackman, John S.

[Troop positions at Dallas, Georgia, May 26–31, 1864] Uncolored ms. Scale not given. 19 × 19 cm. *In his* Journal [1861–1908] p. 136.

In the John S. Jackman papers, Manuscript Division, L.C.

Pen and ink sketch map.

"Since making this, I believe I have made too great an angle in the lines. This, though, will give a general idea of the position of our division and the federals."

Jackman served in the 9th Kentucky Infantry Regiment, CSA.

168.7

Map [of] New Hope Church, and country thereabouts. [1864] Colored ms. Scale 1:63,360 ("one inch to the mile"). 30 × 44 cm.

In the John Alexander Logan family papers, Manuscript Division, L.C., container 145, p. 97.

Title on verso.

Pencil sketch of the country east of Dallas showing roads, towns, names of land owners, and the type of topography (level or rolling).

Map is imperfect. Portion in the upper center is missing.

169

See Sherman map collection no. 67.

170

See Sherman map collection no. 71.

171

See Sherman map collection no. 68.

172

See Sherman map collection no. 69.

173

See Sherman map collection no. 70.

DALTON

174

See Sherman map collection no. 72.

175

See Sherman map collection no. 73.

175.5

Western and Atlantic Railroad Company.

Map of Dalton and vicinity. [1864] Prepared for and presented with compliments of Western and Atlantic R.R. Co. Matthews, Northrup & Co., Art-Printing Works, Buffalo, N.Y. Uncolored. Scale ca. 1:130,000. 15 × 9 cm.

Indicates the location of the battles of Dalton, Rocky Face, and Mill Creek Gap, roads, railroads, towns, drainage, and relief by hachures.

DE KALB COUNTY

176

See Sherman map collection no. 79.

177

See Sherman map collection no. 76.

178

See Sherman map collection no. 78.

EAST POINT

178.5

Map showing the march of the 15th A.C. from Jonesboro to East Point. [August ? 1864] Colored ms. Scale not given. 33 × 22 cm.

In the John Alexander Logan family papers, Manuscript Division, L.C., container 145, p. 99.

Title on verso.

Pen and ink manuscript map on tracing paper showing "route for trains and 15th Corps" and "route for 16th and 17th Corps."

ETOWAH RIVER

179

See Sherman map collection no. 81.

FLINT RIVER

180

See Sherman map collection no. 82.

FORT LEE

181

See Sherman map collection no. 106.

FORT McALLISTER

182

See Sherman map collection no. 107.

183

Ft. McAllister. Carried by assault on the 13th of Dec. [1864] by the Second Division, 15th A.C., commanded by Brig. Gen. W. B. Hazon. Colored ms. Scale not given. 31 × 39 cm.

G3924 .S3:2F5S5 1864 .F6 Vault

Pen and ink manuscript drawn on tracing cloth, showing fortifications, Union troop positions, road leading to fort, vegetation, and drainage.

Part of the defenses of Savannah, Georgia.

183.5

Owner, William.

[Map of Fort McAllister, Georgia. 1863] Uncolored ms. Scale not given. 19 × 12 cm. *In his* Diary, v. 4, tipped-in at end of volume.

In the William Owner papers, Manuscript Division, L.C., container no. 1.

Sketch shows the shape of the fort and the location of "torpedoes and obstructions" on the Big Ogeechee River.

Volume 4 of the diary covers from February 13 to June 27, 1863.

FORT TATTNALL

184

See Sherman map collection no. 108.

FORT THUNDERBOLT

185

See Sherman map collection no. 109.

FULTON COUNTY

185.5

Reese, Chauncey B,

Roads West of Atlanta. Surveyed by engineers of Army of the Tenn. under direction of Capt. C. B. Reese, Chief Engin. [1864] Colored ms. Scale 1:63,360 ("one inch to a mile"). 53 × 38 cm.

In the John Alexander Logan family papers, Manuscript Division, L.C., container 145, opp. p. 104.

Pen and ink manuscript map drawn on tracing linen showing the position of the 14th, 15th, and 16th Army Corps, roads, railroads, rivers and streams, and the names of a few residents.

185.6

————Colored ms. Scale 1:63,360 ("one inch to a mile"). 54 × 38 cm.

In the John Alexander Logan family papers, Manuscript Division, L.C., container 145, opp. p. 108.

Pen and ink manuscript map drawn on tracing paper. Tracing paper now is brittle and broken into several pieces. Map is similar in content to the preceding entry (no. 185.5). Troop positions are not noted. "Red ink marks are corrections" on this manuscript.

186

See Sherman map collection no. 83.

JONESBORO

187

See Sherman map collection no. 84.

187.3

Rout[e] from Fairburn to Jonesboro. [August ? 1864] Colored ms. Scale 1:63,360 ("One inch to the mile"). 41 × 46 cm.

In the John Alexander Logan family papers, Manuscript Division, L.C., container 145, p. 92.

Title from verso.

Pen and ink manuscript map drawn on tracing linen showing the "route of Maj. Genl. Jno. A. Logan—15 Corps" and "route of Brig. Genl. Ransom & Maj. Genl. Blair." The tracing linen is pasted over the top of another pen and ink sketch of the environs of Sandtown, Georgia.

"Roads from information."

KENNESAW MOUNTAIN

187.7

Map [of] Kennesaw Mountain and Big Shanty. [1864] Colored ms. Scale not given. 34 × 33 cm.

In the John Alexander Logan family papers, Manuscript Division, L.C., container 145, p. 103.

Pen and ink manuscript map drawn on tracing linen indicating roads, railroad, towns, houses and names of residents, and drainage in the vicinity of Kennesaw Mountain. Troop positions are not depicted.

188

See Sherman map collection no. 85.

188.5

U.S. *National Park Service.*

Kennesaw Mountain National Battlefield Park, Georgia [Washington] Government Printing Office, 1959. Uncolored. Scale ca. 1:50,000. 19 × 14 cm.

"August 1959, NBP–KM–7006."

Illustrates descriptive leaflet by U.S. National Park Service entitled "Kennesaw Mountain National Battlefield Park, Georgia."

Insets: Crest of Kennesaw Mountain. Sept. 1959. NBP–KM–7007. —Cheatham Hill area. Sept. 1959. NBP–KM–7008. Each 7 × 14 cm.

Includes text and portraits of General William T. Sherman and General Joseph E. Johnston.

MACON

189

See Sherman map collection no. 86.

190

See Sherman map collection no. 87.

MARIETTA

191

See Sherman map collection no. 94.

192

See Sherman map collection no. 91.

192.5

Position of 2nd Divn & 2nd Brigd. 4th Divn 15th A.C. north west of Marietta, June 27, 1864. Colored ms. Scale 1:7200 ("200 yards = one inch"). 25 × 37 cm.

In the John Alexander Logan family papers, Manuscript Division, L.C., container 145, p. 100.

Title is partially blurred.

Oriented with south at the top of the sheet.

Pen and ink manuscript map on tracing linen showing the Union advance and the "suposed [sic] position of rebel works."

193

See Sherman map collection no. 92.

194

See Sherman map collection no. 88.

195

See Sherman map collection no. 93.

196

See Sherman map collection no. 89.

196.5

Western and Atlantic Railroad Company.

Map of Marietta and vicinity. [June 1864] Prepared for and presented with compliments of Western and Atlantic R.R. Co. Matthews, Northrup & Co., Art-Printing Works, Buffalo, N.Y. Uncolored. Scale ca. 1:185,000. 11 × 9 cm.

Indicates location and date of battles, Confederate entrenchments, roads, towns, drainage, and relief by hachures.

NICKAJACK CREEK

196.8

Scupham, J. R.

Position 2nd Division, 15 Corps, July 10th 1864 [at Nickajack Creek, Georgia. By] J. R. Scupham, Topo. Engr. 2nd Divis. 15th A.C. July 10th [1864] Uncolored ms. Scale 1:15,840 ("4 inches to the mile"). 31 × 39 cm.

In the John Alexander Logan family papers, Manuscript Division, L.C., container 145, p. 105.

Title on the verso.

Inset: Plan & elevation of the redoubts. 6 × 8 cm.

Pen and ink manuscript map drawn on lined paper showing the redoubts, reserve works, and the positions of the 15th Corps' 1st Division and the 2nd Brigade of the 2nd Division.

OLLEY CREEK

197

See Sherman map collection no. 95.

198

See Sherman map collection no. 96.

PAULDING COUNTY

199

See Sherman map collection no. 97.

PEACH TREE CREEK

200

See Sherman map collection no. 98.

PINE HILL

201

See Sherman map collection no. 99.

PINE MOUNTAIN

201.5

Jackman, John S.

[Confederate positions on Pine Mountain, Georgia, June 6, 1864] Uncolored ms. Scale not given. 9 × 5 cm. *In his* Journal [1861–1908] p. 144.

In the John S. Jackman papers, Manuscript Division, L.C.

Pen and ink sketch map drawn with west at the top of the sheet.

Jackman served in the 9th Kentucky Infantry Regiment, CSA.

RESACA

201.7

——————[Confederate positions at Resaca, Georgia, May 11–16, 1864] Uncolored ms. Scale not given. 17 × 18 cm. *In his* Journal [1861–1908] p. 128.

In the John S. Jackman papers, Manuscript Division, L.C.

Pen and ink sketch map.

"This map is not made with a positiveness as to correctness. It is merely made to give a general idea of our position. I am not sure where Snake Creek Gap is—how far from Resaca it is. Though I have traveled out on the LaFayette road, I don't know whether it runs through this Gap or not—that is, Snak[e] Creek Gap."

Jackman served in the 9th Kentucky Infantry Regiment, CSA.

201.8

——————[Troop positions at the battle of Resaca, Georgia, May 14, 1864] Uncolored ms. Scale not given. 8 × 11 cm. *In his* Journal [1861–1908] p. 129.

In the John S. Jackman papers, Manuscript Division, L.C.

Pen and ink sketch map oriented with west at the top of the sheet.

Jackman served in the 9th Kentucky Infantry Regiment, CSA.

202

See Sherman map collection no. 101.

203

See Sherman map collection no. 102.

203.5

Western and Atlantic Railroad Company.

Map of Resaca and vicinity. [1864] Prepared for and presented with compliments of Western and Atlantic R.R. Co. Matthews, Northrup & Co., Art-Printing Works, Buffalo, N.Y. Uncolored. Scale ca. 1:165,000. 14 × 9 cm.

Map of the environs of Resaca showing entrenchments, roads, railroads, towns, drainage, and relief by hachures.

ROCKY FACE RIDGE

203.7

Jackman, John S.

[Confederate positions at Rocky Face Ridge, Buzzard Roost, and Mill Creek, Georgia, February 1–4, March 9–12, and May 7–12, 1864] Uncolored ms. Scale not given. 16 × 18 cm. *In his* Journal [1861–1908] p. 124.

In the John S. Jackman papers, Manuscript Division, L.C.

Oriented with west at the top of the sheet.

Map also indicates approximate positions of Federal troops on May 7, 8, and 9.

Jackman served in the 9th Kentucky Infantry Regiment, CSA.

ROSWELL

204

See Sherman map collection no. 103.

205

See Sherman map collection no. 104.

SAVANNAH

206

Lindenkohl, Adolph.

[Map of the environs of Savannah, Georgia. 186–]

Drawn by A. Lindenkohl. Chas. G. Krebs, lith. Uncolored. Scale not given. 57 × 44 cm.

Printed map without title. Indicates fortifications, roads, railroads, drainage, vegetation, towns, and some houses and names of residents in outlying areas.

206.5

Owner, William.

[Map of Savannah, Georgia and vicinity. 1863] Uncolored ms. Scale ca. 1:205,000. 19 × 16 cm. *In his* Diary, v. 4, tipped-in at end of volume.

In the William Owner papers, Manuscript Division, L.C., container no. 1.

Map indicates the location of Fort Jackson and fort on Cockspur Island.

Volume 4 of the diary covers from February 13 to June 27, 1863.

207

Poe, Orlando, M.

Map illustrating the defence of Savannah, Ga. and the operations resulting in its capture by the army commanded by Maj. Genl. W. T. Sherman. Dec. 21st 1864. Compiled 1880–81 under the direction of Bvt. Brig. Genl. O. M. Poe, Maj. Corps of Engs., Col. & A.D.C., late Chief Engineer, Military Division of the Mississippi. Julius Bien & Co. photo lith, N.Y. Colored. Scale ca. 1:85,000. 75 × 64 cm.

The following inscription in the author's handwriting is reproduced above the title: Washington, D.C., Sept 17th 1881. Transmitted to the office of the Chief of Engineers, U.S. Army, with my letter of this date. [Signed] O. M. Poe, Major of Engrs., B. Brig. Gen., U.S.A., Col. A.DC

Detailed map of Savannah and vicinity, showing "Union works in blue," "Confederate works in red," roads, railroads, vegetation, drainage, houses, names of a few residents in outlying areas, fences, and geographic coordinates.

Includes plans of the following fortifications: Works at eastern point of Whitmarsh Island; Fort Thunderbolt; Bastion on the line of defence across Whitmarsh Island; Fort Tattnall; Battery on Turner's Rocks; Fort McAllister; Causten's Bluff; and Fort Lee.

208

See Sherman map collection no. 189.

208.2

U.S. *Navy.*

"Causten's Bluff" fort. [Defenses of Savannah, Georgia. 1865] W.A.S. Lith. of Bowen & Co., Philada. Uncolored. Scale 1:2000. 28 × 40 cm. *From* Message of the President of the United States, and accompanying documents, to the two houses of Congress, at the commencement of the first session of the thirty-ninth Congress. —Report of the Secretary of the Navy (Washington, Government Printing Office, 1865). fol. p. 324.

Printed in the upper left margin: 39th Cong. 1st sess. —Annual Report of the Secretary of the Navy.

Map accompanies report of Rear Admiral John A. Dahlgren entitled "Defences and works of Savannah, Georgia," p. 323–325.

208.3

Map showing the defences of Savannah, on the approaches of Wilmington and Savannah Rivers, Georgia. Flag St[eame]r "Harvest Moon" Feb. 8th 1865. W.A.S. Bowen & Co., lith., Philada. Uncolored. Scale 1:40,000. 33 × 45 cm. *From* Message of the President of the United States, and accompanying documents, to the two houses of Congress, at the commencement of the first session of the thirty-ninth Congress. —Report of the Secretary of the Navy (Washington, Government Printing Office, 1865). fol. p. 324.

Printed in the upper left margin: 39th Cong. 1st sess.— Annual Report of the Secretary of the Navy.

Map accompanies the report of Rear Admiral John A. Dahlgren entitled "Defences and works of Savannah, Georgia," p. 323–325.

Insets: Turner's Rocks Battery. Scale 1:2000. 11 × 16 cm.—Ft. Thunderbolt. Scale 1:2000. 6 × 10 cm.

SAVANNAH RIVER

208.5

Hillhouse, David F., *and* John R. McKinnon.

Map of Savannah River from Augusta to Savannah surveyed & drawn by David F. Hillhouse Esqr., from Savannah to Tybee Lighthouse surveyed & drawn by John R. McKinnon Esqr. copied 1853 under the direction of Lieut. J. F. Gilmer, C. of Engr. [186–] Uncolored ms. Scale not given. 250 × 24 cm.

G3922 .S3 1853 .H5 Vault Shelf

Signed in ms.: N. S. Finney, 1st Lieut. CSA, Asst. Engr.

Endorsed: From Chief Engr's. Office, Mily. Divn. Miss.

From the papers of Gen. Orlando M. Poe, Manuscript Division, L.C.

Handwritten title on the verso: Hillhouse's map of Savannah river from Savannah to Augusta.

Contains "Table of Distances."

Pen and ink and pencil manuscript map drawn on tracing linen indicating the creeks flowing into the Savannah River, islands, and place names. Soundings are not given.

209

Smith, J. C.

Charts of Savannah River, Pensacola Bay, and Key West. Showing the positions of the several fortifications. From the United States Coast Survey. New York, ©1861. Colored. 3 charts on sheet 41 × 50 cm.

[1] Savannah River from U.S. Coast Survey. Scale ca. 1:63,360. 18 × 26 cm.

[2] [Pensacola Bay] Scale ca. 1:80,000. 18 × 23 cm.

[3] Chart of Key West, Florida. Scale ca. 1:125,000. 22 × 20 cm.

Each chart indicates fortifications, place names, "line of 18 feet depth of water," and a few soundings.

TRENTON

209.5

U.S. *Army. Department of the Cumberland. Topographical Engineers.*

[Map of Trenton, Georgia, and vicinity] Compiled under the direction of Capt. W. E. Merrill, U.S. Engrs., Chief Engineer, Army of the Cumberland. Lithograp[hed at Head Quarters, Stevenson, August 28th 1863] Colored. Scale 1:63,360 (1 inch to the mile). 52 × 34 cm.

Imperfect. Lower right corner missing.

Military reconnaissance map lithographed at field headquarters showing roads, railroads, streams, relief by hachures, and the names of a few residents. The incomplete nature of the survey is revealed by the use of such terms as "indefinite," "not definite," and "information wanted."

Another copy is filed as G3964 .C3 1863 .U5 [6].

TURNER'S FERRY

210

See Sherman map collection no. 112.

TURNER'S ROCKS

211

See Sherman map collection no. 110.

WALKER COUNTY

211.3

U.S. *Army. Department of the Cumberland. Topographical Engineers.*

[Map of part of Walker and Dade counties, Georgia, showing Lookout Mountain, Missionary Ridge, McLamore's Cove, and Pigeon Mountains] Compiled under the direction of Capt. Wm. E. Merrill, U.S. Engineers. Chief Engineer, Army of the Cumberland. Lith. at head qs.—Stevenson, Ala. August 28, 1863. Colored. Scale 1:63,360 (1 inch to the mile). 50 × 33 cm.

G3964 .C3 1863 .U5 [7]

Military reconnaissance map lithographed at field headquarters showing roads, railroads, rivers, fords, relief by hachures, and the names of some residents.

WASSAW SOUND

211.5

U.S. *Coast Survey*

Preliminary chart of Wassaw Sound, Wilmington and Tybee Rivers, Georgia. From a trigonometrical survey under the direction of A. D. Bache, Superintendent of the survey of the coast of the United States. Triangulation by C. O. Boutelle, C. P. Bolles, A. W. Longfellow and Lieut. A. W. Evans, U.S.A. Assists. Topography by W. H. Dennis and C. Fendall, Sub-Assists. Hydrography by the parties under the direction of C. O. Boutelle, W. S. Edwards, Assists. and C. Fendall, Sub-Assist. [Washington, U.S. Coast Survey] 1864. Uncolored. Scale 1:40,000. 52 × 83 cm. *From its* Report of the Superintendent of the Coast Survey, showing the progress of the survey during the year 1864 (Washington, Government Printing Office, 1866). Map 27.

"No. 27" is in the upper left corner.

WHITMARSH ISLAND

212

See Sherman map collection no. 111.

ILLINOIS

CAIRO

213

Gerdes, F. H.

Ohio River between Mound City and Cairo. Surveyed by the party of F. H. Gerdes, Asst., assigned by A. D. Bache, Supdt., U.S. Coast Survey, to act under orders of Rear Admiral D.D. Porter, U.S.N., commanding Mississippi Squadron. 1864. Uncolored. Scale ca. 1:23,500. 38 × 56 cm.

Indicates Fort Cairo, naval depot, and "harbor for powder barges" at Mound City, soundings in feet, roads and streets, and vegetation.

213.5

————Another issue. *From its* Report of the Superintendent of the Coast Survey, showing the progress of the survey during the year 1864 (Washington, Government Printing Office, 1866). Map 31.

"No. 31" is in the upper left margin.

214

————Another issue.

In the upper left margin: No. 31. No. 3020. Price 20 cents.

ROCK ISLAND

215

Speidel, C.

Rock Island Barracks, Ill. Lith. C. Vogt. H. Lambach sct., Davenport Io. Rock Island, Ill., C. Speidel, 1864. Colored view. 36 × 48 cm.

"Print, by J. McKittrick & Co., St. Louis Mo."

Perspective drawing of the prison for Confederate soldiers at Rock Island. Principal buildings and features are listed and keyed by number to the appropriate position in the view.

KENTUCKY

215.5

Blakeslee, G. H.

Across Kentucky, 1862. Drawn by G.H.B. [i.e., G. H. Blakeslee] Colored ms. Scale ca. 1:1,020,000. 53 × 43 cm.

G3951 .S5 1862 .B6 Vault

Pen and ink sketch map showing "route of regiment" of the "38th Brigade, Gilbert's Division, of Buel's [sic] Army" from Louisville to "Mitchelsville" (i.e., Mitchell-ville), Tennessee.

215.7

Campbell and Barlow.

New map of Kentucky and Tennessee from authentic reports of county surveyors throughout the states of Kentucky and Tennessee with a new key for measuring distances and specifying localities (which key is secured by copyright.) Louisville, Ky., Campbell & Barlow, ©1861. Uncolored. Scale ca. 1:600,000. Map 96 × 133 cm. in 4 parts, each 48 × 67 cm.

"Entered according to Act of Congress in the year 1861 by Campbell & Barlow."

Index to cities and counties is printed below the map.

General map indicating roads and railroads, county names and boundaries, cities and towns, rivers, and relief by hachures. Some roads and railroads in Kentucky have been colored red and black respectively. A nearly illegible pencil note in the lower right corner states that this map was "Turned into Bureau of Tpl. Eng. by Lieut. O. M. Poe, Top. Engr., August 1861, referred [to] in his letter of Aug. 17, 1861."

Insets: The city of Memphis, Tennessee. 20 × 29 cm.—The city of Louisville, Kentucky. 19 × 32 cm.

Map stamped "U.S.C. & G. Survey Library and Archives no. 1567."

215.8

—————Another edition. Cincinnati, Middleton Strobridge & Co., ©1861. Colored. Scale ca. 1:690,000. 82 × 129 cm.

"Entered according to Act of Congress in the year 1861 by Campbell & Barlow."

In this edition, the index to place names has been dropped.

Map is annotated in blue to show the "Great national military rail road" and in red to show the "Great national military road."

Map stamped "U.S.C. & G. Survey Library and Archives no. 1567."

216

Clark, W. P.

Map of the surveys made for the U.S.M.R.R., 1863 & 4, from Kentucky to East Tenn. By order of Maj. Gen. A. E. Burnside. Under the direction of Lt. Col. J. H. Simpson, Corps Engr's., Chief Eng'r., Dep't. of the Ohio. W. A. Gunn, Ch. Eng. M.R.R. Drawn by W. P. Clark, Ast. Engr. Nov. 15th 1864. Colored ms. Scale 1:12,000. 17 parts; 16 measure 68 × 56 cm. and 1 measures 68 × 81 cm.

G3951 .P3 1864 .C6 Vault

"Office U.S. Engineers, Cincinnati, O. Official: [signed] J. H. Simpson, Lt. Col. Eng'rs., U.S. Army."

"Annual report of Lt. Col. J. H. Simpson, Nov. 15th 1864"

"S.9371"

Pen and ink manuscript map of parts of Lincoln, Boyle, and Pulaski counties, Kentucky, showing the proposed route of the military railroad. Roads, towns, houses, names of residents, fences, relief, vegetation, and drainage are indicated along the proposed route.

216.1

[A correct sketch of the Cumberland and Tennessee rivers country. February 17, 1862] Colored ms. on tracing linen. Scale not given. 30 × 39 cm.

In the Edwin M. Stanton papers, Manuscript Division, L.C., vol. 3, no. 50804.

Map accompanies Thomas A. Scott's report dated February 17, 1862 to Edwin M. Stanton concerning General Henry W. Halleck's plans for "united action in the armies of the West." (Stanton papers, vol. 3, nos. 50795–50802)

Scott describes the map as follows: I enclose [for] you a correct sketch of the Cumberland and Tennessee Rivers country—showing strong-points of the enemy from Nashville southwest to Memphis—with railroads leading to New Orleans & Mobile. The places marked with red circles will be destroyed, & if necessary be occupied by General Halleck. All this being effected, their armies at Nashville and Columbus being destroyed or obliged to surrender, they will be without facilities to concentrate. What shall prevent a successful movement South?

216.2

Kentucky. *Tourist and Travel Division.*

The Civil War in Kentucky. [Signed] Sandman. Produced by the Kentucky Tourist and Travel Division, Department of Public Information, Frankfort, Kentucky, in cooperation with Kentucky Civil War Commission, Lexington, Kentucky. Text by Joe Creason, Courier-Journal staff writer, Louisville, Kentucky. Frankfort [1961] Colored. Scale ca. 1:760,000. 44 × 90 cm.

"An account of the Civil War in Kentucky appears on the reverse side of this map. The red numerals on the map refer to that section of the account which describes the illustrated battle or event."

Title when folded: Kentucky Civil War map.

Pictorial map.

216.3
Lloyd, James T.

Lloyd's official map of the State of Kentucky. Compiled from actual surveys and official documents, showing every rail road & rail road station with the distances between each station. Also the counties and county seats, cities, towns, villages, post offices, wagon roads, canals, forts, fortifications, &c. New York and Cincinnati, J. T. Lloyd, 1862. Colored. Scale ca. 1:506,880. 79 × 109 cm.

"Entered according to Act of Congress in the year 1862, by J. T. Lloyd."

Stamped in the upper left corner: Copyright Library, Nov. 19, 1862.

General map showing forts and fortifications and the "military rail road propos[ed] by the President in his last message to connect Danville, Ky. with Knoxville, Ten[n]."

216.4

—————Another issue. New York and Louisville, J. T. Lloyd, 1862. Colored. Scale ca. 1:506,880. 80 × 110 cm., cut and mounted to fold to 13 × 22 cm. (Fillmore map coll. no. 111–A)

G3950 1862 .L6 Fi11 111–A Vault

Signed on recto: Millard Fillmore Fby. 13, 1862; signed on verso: Millard Fillmore March 4, 1862.

216.5

—————Another edition. New York, J. T. Lloyd, 1863. Colored. Scale ca. 1:506,880. 78 × 111 cm., cut and mounted to fold to 20 × 14 cm.

Listed in A. M. Modelski's *Railroad Maps of the United States* (Washington, Library of Congress, 1975), no. 225.

216.6

Map of Kentucky and Tennessee. [1864] Uncolored. Scale ca. 1:6,200,000. 9 × 14 cm. *From* Century illustrated monthly magazine, v. 34, Aug. 1887. p. 596.

Title in the lower margin: Map of Hood's invasion of Tennessee.

General map.

216.7
Swann, Charles E.

Military map of the States of Kentucky and Tennessee, within eleven miles of the 35th parallel of latitude or southern boundary of Tennessee; compiled from the best authentic original maps, various documents, and miscellaneous latest sources of information; commenced under the authority of Major General Don Carlos Buell, commanding the Department of the Ohio, by Capt. N. Michler, Corps Topogl. Engrs. U.S.A., continued under Major General H. G. Wright by Maj. L. Sitgreaves Corps Topogl. Engrs. U.S.A., and completed under Major General Ambrose E. Burnside, commanding the Department, by Lieut. Col. J. H. Simpson, Corps Engrs. U.S.A., Chief Engr. in the Department. Drawn by Charles E. Swann, Ass't. Engr. Ehrgott, Forbriger & Co., Lithographers, Engraphers [sic] and Printers, Cincinnati, O. Cincinnati, Ohio, Office of Chief Engineer, Department of the Ohio, November 1863. Colored. Scale 1:350,000 (5.524 miles to one inch). 4 parts, each 64 × 107 cm., sectioned and mounted to fold to 34 × 19 cm.

Signed in facsimile: Official: J. H. Simpson, Lieut. Col. Engrs. U.S. Army, Chief Engr., Dpt. of the Ohio.

Detailed map of Kentucky and most of Tennessee showing towns and villages, county seats, iron works and forges, salt works, mills, post offices, existing and proposed railroads, roads, rivers, and limits of coal fields.

Map has been annotated in red ink to show the location of "Camp Burnside" on the Cumberland River south of Somerset, Kentucky.

Handwritten note on the verso reads "Full of errors— worthless so far as the 5 northern counties are concerned. F. Walley Perkins AC&GS."

216.8

—————Another issue. Ehrgott, Forbriger & Co., Lithographers, Engravers & Printers, Cincinnati, O. 128 × 215 cm. mounted to fold to 33 × 19 cm.

In this issue Camp Burnside on the Cumberland River is named, the lithographer's name has been revised, and a dotted line representing the "out line of coal field" has been added in the southeastern quadrant.

216.9
Wood, Walter B., *and* J. E. Edmonds.

Kentucky and Tennessee. [London] Methuen & Co. [1905] Uncolored. Scale ca. 1:2,820,000. 20 × 32 cm.

"Map VI."

Prepared to accompany W. B. Wood and J. E. Edmonds's *A History of the Civil War in the United States, 1861–5* (London, Methuen & Co. [1905]).

Map indicates battle sites.

BOWLING GREEN

216.92

Michler, Nathaniel.

Topographical sketch of Bowling Green, Ky. and environs. Compiled from actual surveys and from other sources of informations [sic] under the direction of Capt. N. Michler, Capt. of Engineers, U.S.A. G. A. Bauer, 1st Lieut. Del. Photocopy (positive). Scale ca. 1:88,000. 25 × 24 cm.

In the John M. Schofield papers, Manuscript Division, L.C., container no. 74.

Photocopy has been hand-colored to show railroads in red, turnpikes in brown, and rivers in blue.

Number 3 is written in red ink on the verso.

216.93

U.S. *Army. Department of the Ohio.*

[Map of Bowling Green, Kentucky, and vicinity showing field works and entrenched sites] Louisville, Ky., Headquarters, Department of the Ohio, February 1, 1862. Colored ms. on tracing paper. Scale ca. 1:29,400. 67 × 55 cm.

In the Edwin M. Stanton papers, Manuscript Division, L.C., vol. 2, no. 50557.

Detailed map showing streets and roads, railroad, and a few houses and names of residents. Eight houses in Bowling Green are keyed by number to the list. Red crosses "denote fieldworks" and black crosses are sites "reported to be intrenched."

COLUMBUS

216.95

Cullum, George W.

Map of the rebel fortifications at Columbus, Ky. Surveyed under the direction of Brig. Genl. Geo. W. Cullum, Chief of Staff & Engineers, Dept. of the Mississippi. [1862] Uncolored ms. Scale 1:7200 ("600 feet to one inch"). 46 × 47 cm.

G3954.C515S5 1862 .C8 Vault

Finished manuscript map displaying six "cross sections of the different intrenchments," roads, city streets without names, buildings, drainage, some vegetation, "Mobile and Ohio R.R.," relief by hachures, and the location of "abattis or felled trees" which obstructed the approaches to the fortifications.

In the lower right corner: Engr. Dept. July 18/64. Recd. with Gen. Cullum's letter of the 16th inst. (C.5621)

217

————Lith of J. Bien, N.Y. 45 × 47 cm.

Published version of the preceding manuscript map.

218

Muller, John B., *and* J. Clough.

Map of the fortifications of Columbus, Ky. Surveyed & drawn by J. B. Muller [and] J. Clough. [1862] Colored ms. Scale 1:3600. 96 × 94 cm.

G3954.C515S5 1862 .M8 Vault

In the lower right corner: Engineer Dept., July 18/64. Recd. with Gen. Cullum's letter of the 16th inst. (C.5621).

"Cross sections of the different intrenchments" and a list of "references" are given in the upper left corner.

Detailed map of Columbus and environs, showing Confederate fortifications, rifle pits and gun emplacements, roads, railroad, drainage, and relief by hachures.

FORT ANDERSON

219

Rziha, John.

Fort Anderson, Paducah, Ky. [1861] John Rziha, Captain, 19th Infantry, U.S. Army. Colored ms. Scale 1:240. 88 × 65 cm.

G3954.P2:2F6 1861.R9 Vault

"Hd. Qr., U.S. Forces, Paducah, Keny., Jany. 4, 1861. Respectfully forwarded to the Hd. Qr. of the Dept. of the Missi., [signed] C. F. Smith, Brigr. Genl., comdg."

"Engr. Dept., July 18/64. Recd. with Gen. Cullum's letter of the 16th inst. (C.5621)."

Includes a profile of the main building.

FORT HOLT

220

Sketch plan of Columbiad Battery, Fort Holt, Ky. [opposite Cairo, Ill.] Colored ms. Scale 1:240. 39 × 51.

G3954 .F579 186– .U5 Vault

"Engr. Dept., July 18/64. Recd. with Gen. Cullum's letter of the 16th inst. (C5621)."

FRANKFORT

220.5

Brooks, J. H.

Military map of the vicinity of Frankfort, Kentucky. Made by order of Brig. Gen. Q. A. Gillmore, Comd'g District of Central Kentucky under direction of T. B. Brooks, Capt. Vol. Engr's. A.D.C., by J. H. Brooks, civil assistant to U.S. Topog. Engr's. February 1863. Colored ms. Scale 1:4800 ("133-⅓ yds. to 1 inch or 13-²/₁₀ inches to 1 mile"). 70 × 98 cm.

G3954.F7S5 1863 .B7 Vault

Map is endorsed: A correct copy, [signed] T. B. Brooks, Capt. N.Y. Vol. Engrs. A.D.C. Engineers Office, District of Central Kentucky, Lexington, Ky. Feb. 18, 1863.

"Notes. The heights of hills (in red) are estimated by eye above medium high water in the river, which fluctuates 53 feet. The river was fordable last year for the first time at Frankfort since the erection of the dams for slack water navigation."

"Positions for defensive works proferred [sic] by Col. Gilbert with force and armament marked blue."

Endorsed on the verso: Vicinity of Frankfort. T. B. Brooks, 1862. No. 26.

Pen and ink manuscript map drawn on tracing linen showing streets, rivers and creeks, location of the arsenal and "U.S. Hd. Qrs.," and recommended defensive positions.

From the papers of Gen. Orlando M. Poe, Manuscript Division. L.C.

LOGAN'S CROSS ROADS

221

Michler, Nathaniel.

Sketch of the battlefield of Logan's Cross Roads . . . Jan. 19th 1862. From a survey by Lt. Col. Hunten, 1st Mich. Engrs. Drawn under the direction of Capt. N. Michler, Topl. Engrs., U.S.A. Photocopy (positive). Scale 1:12,672. 28 × 23 cm.

Hand-colored sun print showing four positions of Union and Confederate soldiers, troop camps, location of graves, roads, drainage, vegetation, houses, and fences.

222

Michler, Nathaniel, *and* **Edward Ruger.**

Sketch of the battlefield of Logan's Cross Roads and of the enemys fortified position at and opposite Mill Spring, Ky. to which he retreated after his defeat, Major General George H. Thomas comdg. the U.S. forces, General G. B. Crittenden comdg. the Confed. forces, Jan. 19th 1862. Drawn under the direction of Capt. N. Michler, Topl. Engrs, U.S.A. and Edward Ruger. From a survey by Lt. Col. Hunten 1st Mich. Engrs. Published by authority of the Hon. the Secretary of War in the office of the Chief of Engineers, U.S.A. 1877. Colored. Scale 1:15,840. 34 × 29 cm.

Map of Logan's Cross Roads indicates four positions of Union and Confederate soldiers, troop camps, location of graves, roads, drainage, vegetation, houses, fences, and a few hachures.

Map of Mill Spring shows Confederate entrenchments, roads, drainage, vegetation, hachures, houses and the names of residents. Eight-mile stretch of road between Logan's Cross Roads and Mill Spring is not shown.

223

————————Another issue. Julius Bien & Co., photo lith.

LOUISVILLE

223.2

Nicholson, George B.

Louisville and its environs. Drawn by Rob.[?] G. Phillips, from original [map com]piled by G. B. Nicholson. Cincinnati, Office U.S. Engineers, June 1865. Photocopy (positive). Scale 1:12,000. 79 × 116 cm.

Signed (facsim.): Official J. H. Simpson, Lt. Col. Engrs., U.S. Army.

Stamped in red beside the map title and in the lower right corner: General Staff map collection, file copy.

Bar scales, sources, and references are faded or slightly blurred.

Oriented with south at the top, the map indicates fortifications, government buildings, houses, roads, churches, fences, and the names of residents in the environs of the city.

A manuscript copy of this map, oriented with north at the top, is in the Records of the Office of the Chief of Engineers, RG 77:T 124–3, Cartographic and Architectural Branch, National Archives, Washington, D.C.

PADUCAH

224

Plan of a fort opposite Paducah, Ky. [1864] Colored ms. Scale 1:384. 57 × 83 cm.

G4103.M55S5 1864 .U5 Vault

In the lower right corner: Engr. Dept., July 18/64. Recd. with Gen. Cullum's letter of the 16th inst. (C. 5621).

Map of the environs of the proposed fort in Massac County, Illinois, appears below plan, part of which, however, is wanting.

225

Sketch and plan for a fortification opposite Paducah, Ky. [1864] Uncolored ms. Various scales. 53 × 82 cm.

G4103 .M55S5 1864 .U51 Vault

In the lower right corner: Engr. Dept., July 18/64. Recd. with Gen. Cullum's letter of the 16th inst. (C5621).

Includes a sketch of the environs of the proposed fort in Massac County, Illinois (scale not given, 11 × 31 cm.), a plan of the fort (scale 1:180, 27 × 25 cm.), and a profile (scale 1:120, 6 × 24 cm.). Part of the profile is wanting.

PERRYVILLE

226

Michler, Nathaniel, *and* **John E. Weyss**

Topographical sketch of the battlefield of Chaplin Hills, near Perryville, Kentucky. October 9th 1862. Surveyed by Capt. N. Michler, Topl. Engr., U.S.A., and Maj.

J. E. Weyss, Principal Asst. Photocopy (positive). Scale ca. 1:23,250. 25 × 27 cm.

Sun print of Perryville and vicinity annotated in blue and red crayon to show what may be the position of the Union and Confederate troops on October 9, the day after the battle of Perryville. Opposite four of the five positions marked in blue are written the names "Gilbert," "Buell," "McCook," and what appears to be "MacCon."

227

Ruger, Edward, *and* Anton Kilp.

Map of the battlefield of Perryville, Ky. Major General Don Carlos Buell commanding the U.S. forces, General Braxton Bragg commanding the Confederate forces. October 8th 1862. Surveyed and compiled by order of Major General George H. Thomas U.S.A., by Edward Ruger and Anton Kilp. Published by authority of the Hon. the Secretary of War in the office of the Chief of Engineers, U.S. Army. 1877. Colored. Scale ca. 1:48,000. 29 × 32 cm.

"Authorities: surveys by Edward Ruger and Anton Kilp [and] official reports of officers of both armies."

Map gives "position of General Gilbert's corps on the evening of October 7th" and the positions of both the Union and Confederate troops "on the 8th before being brought into action," "while engaged," and "after dark on the evening of the 8th." Roads, the railroad from Lebanon to Stanford, drainage, vegetation, relief by hachures, houses, and the names of residents are also represented.

227.2

————Colored facsimile. (Historic maps of Kentucky no. 10)

G3954 .P45S5 1862 .R8 1979

Accompanied by Thomas D. Clark's *Historic Maps of Kentucky* (Lexington, University Press of Kentucky, ©1979), 89 p. (filed G3950 1794 .B3 1979).

228

————Another issue. Julius Bien & Co., photo lith.

229

Work, J. B.

Map of the battle-field of Perryville, Ky., October 8th 1862. Compiled from the records and other sources by J. B. Work, 52d Ohio Vol. Inf., Chicago, Ill. [©Aug. 27, 1900] Uncolored. Scale ca. 1:38,000. 29 × 23 cm.

Indicates roads, drainage, vegetation, houses, names of residents, relief by hachures, names of commanders; and by symbols, the positions of the Union and Confederate troops on the "evening Oct. 7th," "Oct. 8th before being brought into action," "Oct. 8th while engaged," "Oct. 8th after dark," "in reserve during the battle," and "batteries while engaged."

SNOW'S POND

229.3

Sketch of vicinity of head qtrs. U.S. forces Snows Pond, Kentuckey [sic. Sept. 25, 1862] Uncolored ms. Scale 1:63,360. 40 × 25 cm.

G3952 .S6S5 1862 .S4 Vault

Title is from verso.

Pen and ink sketch map, drawn on ruled note paper, indicating road names, houses, and names of residents.

From the papers of Gen. Orlando M. Poe, Manuscript Division, L.C.

LOUISIANA

229.5

Abbot, Henry L.

New Orleans to Vicksburg. Prepared by order of Maj. Gen. N. P. Banks. Henry L. Abbot, Capt. & Chief Top. Eng'rs. C. D. Elliot—Del. Photographed by Brown & Ogilvie. Jan. 14th, 1863. Photocopy (positive). Scale ca. 1:310,000. 39 × 55 cm. folded to 20 × 10 cm.

G4014 .N5A1 1863 .A2

At the head of the title: Department of the Gulf. Map no. 2.

From the papers of Maj. Gen. Nathaniel Prentice Banks, Manuscript Division, L.C.

"Authorities: Township surveys—La Tourett's [sic] maps—Manuscript maps by Swamp Land Commissioners & State Engineer of Louisiana—Notes by Lt. Wrotnowski, Lt. Hollingsworth, Mr. Gorlinski, Mr. Myer, & other authorities."

Map appears to have been carried in the field during the war. It is worn and soiled and the photocopy is indistinct in numerous places. Troop positions and movements are not noted. The map shows the Mississippi River and environs from Vicksburg to Lake Pontchartrain and indicates towns, roads, railroads, drainage, mills, and the names of some land owners. Map has been annotated in ink and pencil.

229.6

Broome, David W.

Louisiana Civil War battlefields. C[opyright by] David W. Broome. [Baton Route?] ©1972. Colored. Scale ca. 1:850,000. 72 × 59 cm.

    G4011 .S5 1972 .B7

    Copyright no. F 53930 Feb. 28, 1972.

"The battlefields shown on this map were mostly skirmishes and they represent only a small number of almost six hundred fought on Louisiana soil."

230

Holtz, Helmuth.

Map of Louisiana & Arkansas. Prepared under direction of 1st Lieut. Wm. Hoelcke, 39 U.S. Infty, acting Chief Engineer at hd. qts. Dept. of La., by Helmuth Holtz. [1864?] Colored. Scale ca. 1:650,000. 3 parts, each approx. 48 × 89 cm.

At head of title: Department of Louisiana.

General map showing roads, railroads, drainage, names and boundaries of counties, towns, forts, "military road to Memphis," and camp sites in St. Francis County, Ark. on August 2, 3, and 6, 1864.

231

Lindenkohl, Henry.

Map of a part of Louisiana and Mississippi, illustrating the operations of the U.S. forces, in the Department of the Gulf. Drawn by H. Lindenkohl. E. Molitor lith. 1863. Colored. Scale ca. 1:380,160. 65 × 71 cm.

In margin at bottom: Line of marsh [sic] of Gen. Banks corps d'armée April & Mai 1863.

Map extends from Natchez, Mississippi, in the north to Marsh Island, Louisiana, in the south, and Columbia, Mississippi, in the east to Alexandria, Louisiana, in the west. Roads, railroads, drainage, and towns are shown.

231.5

————————Another issue.

This issue lacks the name of the lithographer in the lower left corner. In addition, an American flag has been added at Port Hudson.

For another copy from the papers of Joseph R. Hawley, Manuscript Division, L.C., see G4011 .S5 1863 .U51.

232

————————Another issue.

This issue lacks the statement "Line of marsh . . ." It also differs from the preceding map in that it does not show the route of the army between Semmesport and Baton Rouge, and from Alexandria south by railroad to Bayou Boeuf.

Another copy is in the papers of Maj. Gen. Nathaniel Prentice Banks, Manuscript Division, L.C. (G4011 .S5 1863 .U5).

232.5

————————Military map of part of Louisiana. Compiled at the U.S. Coast Survey Office, A. D. Bache, Supt. 1863. Drawn by H. Lindenkohl. E. Molitor, lith. Colored. Scale ca. 1:390,000. 40 × 66 cm.

General map of southern Louisiana from St. Francisville south to Atchafalaya Bay and Lake Borgne west to Vermilion Bay.

232.7

[Map of western Louisiana and eastern Texas. 186–?] Colored ms. Scale ca. 1:2,205,000, 25 × 30 cm.

In the papers of Maj. Gen. Nathaniel Prentice Banks, Manuscript Division, L.C., container 76.

Pen and ink manuscript map drawn on tracing linen showing roads, railroads, rivers, and towns.

ALEXANDRIA

232.8

Arnold, Richard.

Country south of Alexandria. From a sketch furnished by Brig. Gen. Arnold—May 1st 1864. Colored ms. Scale ca. 1:32,000. 47 × 71 cm.

In the papers of Maj. Gen. Nathaniel Prentice Banks, Manuscript Division, L.C., container 76.

Map oriented with south at the top of the sheet.

Detailed pen and ink manuscript map drawn on tracing linen showing rifle pits, roads, drainage, open country, cultivated fields, tilled fields, woodland, swamps, houses, and names of residents.

232.84

Defences of Alexandria. [1864] Uncolored ms. Scale not given. 25 × 40 cm.

In the papers of Maj. Gen. Nathaniel Prentice Banks, Manuscript Division, L.C., container 76.

Map oriented with south at the top of the sheet.

Title is on the verso.

Pencil sketch drawn on lined paper with letterhead "Headquarters, Department of the Gulf, 1864" printed on verso.

Map indicates "line of defence," rifle pit, and headquarters.

232.86

Long, Walter S.

Vicinity of Alexandria, La. Prepared by order of Maj. Gen. N. P. Banks. Engineer's Office, Dept. of the Gulf, Alexandria, La. Apr. 30, 1864. [Signed] W. S. Long, Major 96th U.S. Infy. (Cold.) Actg. Chf. Engr., in the field. Colored ms. Scale ca. 1:6,000, 47 × 63 cm.

In the papers of Maj. Gen. Nathaniel Prentice Banks, Manuscript Division, L.C., container 76.

Pen and ink manuscript map drawn on tracing linen showing streets and roads, rivers, some buildings, headquarters, and the line of entrenchments.

ATCHAFALAYA BASIN

232.88

Abbot, Henry L.

Atchafalaya Basin. Prepared by order of Maj. Gen. N. P. Banks. Henry L. Abbot, Capt. & Chief Top. Engrs. C. D. Elliot [and] B. von Reizenstein, dels. Feb. 8th 1863. Photocopy (positive). Scale ca. 1:290,000. 70 × 55 cm.

At head of title: Department of the Gulf. Map no. 8.

In the papers of Maj. Gen. Nathaniel Prentice Banks, Manuscript Division, L.C., container 76.

Annotated and hand-colored photocopy depicting Louisiana from the Red River south to Atchafalaya Bay. Colors show "land below high water mark" (green), "roads—passable" (red), and "streams—navigable" (blue).

AVOYELLES PARISH

232.9

Sketch of the country from Opelousas to Marksville, La. [186–?] Uncolored ms. Scale not given. 25 × 20 cm.

In the papers of Maj. Gen. Nathaniel Prentice Banks, Manuscript Division, L.C., container 76.

Title is on the verso.

Pencil sketch of parts of Avoyelles and St. Landry Parishes, Louisiana, showing roads, bayous, and towns.

BRASHIER CITY

232.92

Defenses of Bresher [i.e., Brashier City] N. P. Banks. [186–?] Uncolored ms. Scale not given. 25 × 20 cm.

In the papers of Maj. Gen. Nathaniel Prentice Banks, Manuscript Division, L.C., container 76.

Title and Banks's signature are on the verso.

Rough pen and ink sketch of the location of Fort Brashier on Bayou Boeuf and Berwicks Bay, Louisiana.

233

U.S. *Coast Survey.*

Approaches to Fort Butte La Rose, Louisiana, captured by the U.S. fleet, co-operating with the forces under the command of Major Gen. N. P. Banks. April 20th 1863. Surveyed by J. G. Oltmanns, Sub-asst., U.S. Coast Survey, acting under orders of Major Gen. N. P. Banks. J. W. Maedel. Uncolored. Scale 1:31,680. 34 × 41 cm.

Gives vegetation, drainage, houses, fences, road leading from fort, and the position of the U.S. steamers *Clifton, Arizona, Calhoun* and *Estrella,* and the Confederate transport *Anna* and gunboat *Marytie.*

Insets: [Plan of] Fort Butte La Rose. 1:600. 22 × 20 cm.—[Two] cross sections. 1:300. 7 × 15 cm.

FORT DE RUSSY

233.5

Map of Fort De Russy. [1864] Uncolored. Scale not given. 12 × 9 cm. *From* Harper's weekly, v. 8, April 30, 1864. p. 277.

234

U.S. *Coast Survey.*

Sketch of Fort De Russy, Louisiana. Surveyed by C. Fendall, Sub Assist. 1864. Uncolored. Scale 1:10,000. 34 × 28 cm.

Shows rifle pits, breastworks, location and number of guns, roads, houses, fences, woods, and drainage.

234.2

U.S. *Navy.*

Plan showing the defences of the fort on Red River, built by Gen. De Russey [sic], rebel army, destroyed May 9, 1863, by the flagship *Benton.* Uncolored. Scale ca. 1:9,600. 20 × 12 cm. *From* Report of the Secretary of the Navy, with an appendix, containing reports from officers. December, 1863 (Washington, Government Printing Office, 1863). opp. p. 482.

Map of Confederate Fort De Russy, Louisiana, and vicinity. Original sketch from which this was reproduced was sent to the Secretary of the Navy by Acting Rear Adm. David D. Porter on May 16, 1863.

FORT JACKSON

235

Gerdes, F. H.

Reconnaissance of the Mississippi River, by the party under the command of F. H. Gerdes, Asst., U.S. Coast Survey, April 13, 14, 15, 1862. Uncolored ms. Scale 1:10,000. 107 × 47 cm.

> G4014 .F6S5 1862 .G4 Vault

At head of title: U.S. Coast Survey. Prof. A. D. Bache, Supt.

Stamped in lower right corner: From collection of David Dixon Porter.

Pen and ink manuscript drawn on tracing cloth, covering the environs of forts St. Philip and Jackson, Louisiana.

"Note: The forts and their immediate vicinity were taken from data furnished by Major Barnard, U.S.E., excepting the trigonometrical determinations of the forts and the hulks. This chart to be returned to Capt. D. D. Porter, U.S.N., after its use in the river ceases."

236

————Reconnoissance [sic] of the Mississippi River below forts Jackson and St. Philip made previous to the reduction by the U.S. Fleet under the command of flag officer D. G. Farragut, U.S.N. By the party under the direction of F. H. Gerdes, Asst., U.S. Coast Survey; A. D. Bache, Supdt. Bowen & Co., lith., Philada. [1862] Uncolored. Scale ca. 1:40,000. 24 × 43 cm.

Map of the environs of Fort Jackson and Fort St. Philip, showing "hulks & chain" in the river, "upper limit of casemate fire," "sector without casemate fire," "lower limit of casemate fire," triangulation points, shoreline vegetation, houses, and fences.

"The forts from data furnished by the Chief Engineer, U.S. Army."

Note below the map title describes the positions of the Union "mortar flotilla" on April 18–21, 1862.

For another copy from the papers of Joseph R. Hawley, Manuscript Division, L.C., see G4014.F6S5 1862 .U5.

237

Hergesheimer, Edwin.

Plan of Fort Jackson, showing the effect of the bombardment by the U.S. mortar flotilla and gunboats, April 18th to 24th 1862. Flag officer D. G. Farragut commanding fleet; Com. D. D. Porter commanding flotilla. Surveyed by J. S. Harris under the direction of F. H. Gerdes, Asst., U.S. Coast Survey; A. D. Bache, Supdt. Drawn by E. Hergesheimer, Coast Survey Office. Bowen & Co., lith., Philada. Uncolored. Scale ca. 1:1700. 27 × 43 cm.

Detailed plan showing "holes made by bombs," "holes made by shot," "parts that were burned," and "injuries on the ramparts repaired with sandbags." A description of the condition of the fort after the bombardment is contained in a brief note below the map title.

For another copy from the papers of Joseph R. Hawley, Manuscript Division, L.C., see G4014.F6S5 1862 .H4.

NEW ORLEANS

237.5

Abbot, Henry L.

Approaches to New Orleans. Prepared by order of Maj. Gen. N. P. Banks. Henry L. Abbot, Capt. & Chief Top. Engrs. Feb. 11th [?] 1863. Photocopy (positive). Scale ca. 1:150,000. 33 × 31 cm.

In the papers of Maj. Gen. Nathaniel Prentice Banks, Manuscript Division, L.C., container 76.

Badly faded sun print annotated in red to show fortifications.

At head of title: Department of the Gulf. Map no. 5.

237.7

Loper, J. H.

[Sketch maps of the defenses of New Orleans, April 4, 1862] 2 uncolored ms. maps on recto and verso of lined note paper. Scales not given. 12 × 5 19 cm.

In the Ethan Allen Hitchcock papers, Manuscript Division, L.C., container no. 3, general correspondence folder, April 1–April 20, 1862.

Maps were drawn by J. H. Loper who served aboard the Confederate steamer *Bienville* on Lake Pontchartrain. The maps, and an accompanying letter written by Loper to his father on April 4, 1862, were captured by Federal troops at Tuscumbia, Alabama, and forwarded to the War Department on April 20.

The first sketch shows the approximate location of "8 miles of breastworks" defending New Orleans and the location of the "Mobile & N. O. steamer packet wharf" on Lake Pontchartrain. Also depicted on Bayou St. John are the shipyards where the steamers *Bienville* and *Carondelet* were built.

The second sketch shows Fort Pike on Lake Pontchartrain and the positions of the Confederate ships *Oregon, Pamlico, Carondelet,* and *Bienville.* Also depicted are pilings placed in the Lake to defend the fort. Loper notes in the accompanying letter that "the Safty [sic] Committee has ordered piles to be drove down 4 in a row and about 3 ft apart commencing from the shore opposite the fort and stoping within 50 yard[s] of the shore, on which is the fort, leaving that vacancy for our own convenience, and rather too close for the enemy ship to attempt to pass."

PORT HUDSON

238

Houston, David C., *and* Peter C. Hains.

Map of Port Hudson and vicinity. Prepared by order of Major General N. P. Banks under the direction of Major D. C. Houston, Chief Engineer, Department of the Gulf and Captain Peter C. Hains, Corps of Engr's. 1864. Published by authority of the Hon. the Secretary of War., office of the Chief of Engineers, U.S. Army. 1875. Colored. Scale ca. 1:7950. 86 × 63 cm.

Map indicates fortifications, drainage, hachures, vegetation, roads, railroad, and houses. Positions of Confederate batteries are shown with the number of guns in each. Inset contains a keyed list of the Union batteries giving the number and type of guns in each position, and the names of the battery commanders.

239

McGregor, Charles.

Port Hudson. Compiled from government surveys and other sources and drawn by Charles McGregor, Historian of the 15th N.H. Volunteers. [Lith. by] Geo. H. Walker & Co., Boston. Nashua, N.H., ©1900. Uncolored. Scale ca. 1:8250. 74 × 51 cm.

Shows fortifications, relief by hachures, vegetation, drainage, roads, railroad, houses, and contains an index to artillery batteries and principal points of action. The index includes the number and type of Confederate and Union guns, and the names of the Union battery commanders.

239.2

Owner, William.

[Map of Port Hudson and vicinity showing fortifications. 1863] Uncolored ms. Scale ca. 1:135,000. 20 × 15 cm. *In his* Diary, v. 4, tipped-in at front of volume.

In the William Owner papers, Manuscript Division, L.C., container no. 1.

Volume 4 of the diary covers from February 13 to June 27, 1863.

239.3

————[Map of the fortifications at Port Hudson, Louisiana. 1863] Uncolored ms. Scale ca. 1:47,500. 30 × 24 cm. *In his* Diary, v. 5, tipped-in at front of volume.

In the William Owner papers, Manuscript Division, L.C., container no. 1.

Volume 5 of the diary covers from June 29 to November 16, 1863.

239.5

Sholl, Charles.

Port Hudson and its defences. Constructed and engraved to illustrate "The war with the South." [Compiled by Charles Sholl] Engd. by W. Kemble. c1863. Colored. Scale ca. 1:72,500. 23 × 17 cm. *From* Tomes, Robert. The war with the South. New York, Virtue & Yorston, 1862–1867. v. 3, between p. 16 and 17.

Signed (facsim.): Charles: Sholl, Topl. Engineer.

"Entered according to act of Congress AD. 1863 by Virtue, Yorston & Co."

Caption in lower margin: A topographical map of Port Hudson and its vicinity, shewing earthworks, &c. that were in existence at the time of its fall.

239.6

————Another issue.

"Constructed and engraved to illustrate 'The war with the South'" has been dropped from the map title.

240

Tomlinson, George W.

Tomlinson's map of Port Hudson. Showing all of the batteries, strongholds, principal plantations, &c. Lith. by J. Mayer & Co., Boston. ©1863. Uncolored. Scale ca. 1:65,000. 57 × 40 cm.

Printed in green ink.

At top of map: New map of Port Hudson. Showing the scene of Gen. Banks operations, together with all of the fortifications, batteries, &c.

Text to right of map: Sketch of Port Hudson and the surrounding batteries.

Map extends from Port Hudson in the north to Baton Rouge in the south and shows fortifications surrounding Port Hudson, roads, railroads, towns, drainage, relief by hachures, a few names of plantations, property lines, and the names of residents.

Another copy from the papers of Maj. Gen. Nathaniel Prentice Banks, Manuscript Division, L.C. See G4014 .P75S5 1863 .T6

RED RIVER

240.5

De Russy, Lewis G.

Falls in Red River, surveyed by L. G. De Russy. [1864?] Colored ms. Scale ca. 1:2,200, 48 × 105 cm.

G4012 .R4S5 1864 .D4 Vault

Pen and ink manuscript map drawn on tracing linen showing soundings and obstructions in the Red River. A red line delineates the river channel.

Stamped at bottom: From collection of David Dixon Porter.

241

Gerdes, F. H.

Sketch of the two breakwaters above Alexandria in the Red River, constructed by Lieut. Col. Bailey, U.S.A., to extricate the heavy ironclads and transports of the Mississippi Squadron, under command of Rear Admiral D. D. Porter. Drawn from Col. De Russy's map and from information re-

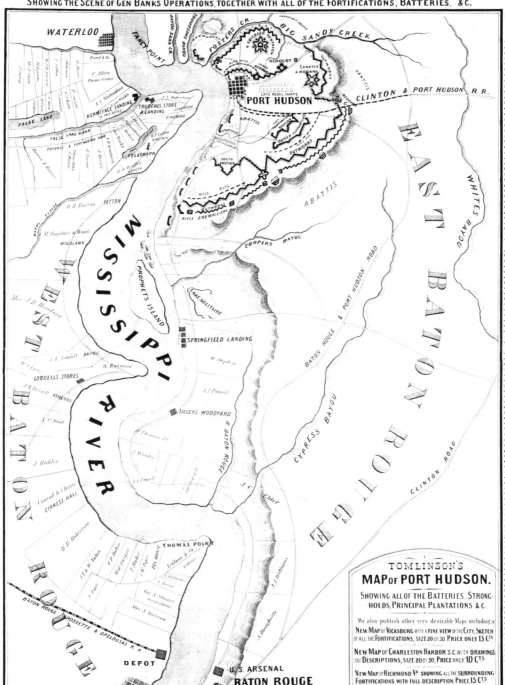

NEW MAP OF PORT HUDSON.

SHOWING THE SCENE OF GEN BANKS OPERATIONS, TOGETHER WITH ALL OF THE FORTIFICATIONS, BATTERIES, &C.

Published by G. W. Tomlinson, Boston, Mass.

ceived from the Admiral, by F. H. Gerdes, Asst., U.S. Coast Survey. [1864] Colored ms. Scale ca. 1:2000. 60 × 122 cm.

G4012 .R4S5 1864 .G4 Vault

"M. Section VIII.66."

Detailed map showing upper and lower dams, falls, "Tennyson's channel," "De Russy's Channel," and some relief by hachures.

241.1

[U.S. *Army. Department of the Gulf*]

Red River. [1864?] Photocopy (positive) Scale ca. 1:360,000. 28 × 31 cm.

In the papers of Maj. Gen. Nathaniel Prentice Banks, Manuscript Division, L.C., container 76.

Incomplete; the bottom portion of the map and part of the cartouche are missing. Reconnaissance map of parts of Caddo, Bossier, Webster, and Bienville Parishes, Louisiana, showing township and section lines, rivers and lakes, place names, and the names of a few land owners. The map has been annotated in red to indicate roads.

241.2

Venable, Richard M.

[Map of the Red River campaign, March 10–May 22, 1864.] Colored ms. on tracing linen. Scale 1:253,440 (4 miles per inch). 94 × 58 cm.

G3992 .R4 1864 .V4 Vault

Endorsed in lower left corner: No. 210. Respectfully forwd. Richd. M. Venable Capt. & Chf. Topol. Bur. West La. & Ark.

Map of the Red River valley in Arkansas and Louisiana showing rivers and streams, roads, and towns. The map in-

dicates the location of Camp Worth near Logansport, Louisiana, and the battle sites of April 8 and 9, 1864, between Mansfield and Pleasant Hill, Louisiana.

Printed version published in the *Atlas to Accompany the Official Records of the Union and Confederate Armies,* 1891-95, plate 53, no. 1. The copy reproduced in the atlas originally accompanied "the report of Gen. E. Kirby Smith, C. S. Army, Series I, vol. XXXIV, part 1, page 481."

ST. MARY PARISH

241.3

[Map of part of St. Mary Parish, Louisiana showing troop positions. 186–?] Colored ms. Scale not given. 30 × 31 cm.

In the papers of Maj. Gen. Nathaniel Prentice Banks, Manuscript Division, L.C., container 76.

Anonymous pen and ink manuscript map drawn on tracing linen showing location of Simms, Pelican, and Fournette's batteries, rifle pits, fort, and the positions of the "Texas Cavalry [sic] about 150 men" and "18 La. about 400 men" along Bayou Teche near Paterson.

SHREVEPORT

241.4

[Shreveport, Louisiana, and vicinity. 186–?] Photocopy (positive). Scale ca. 1:60,000. 32 × 32 cm.

G4014 .S5A1 186– .S5

From the papers of Maj. Gen. Nathaniel Prentice Banks, Manuscript Division, L.C.

General map of the environs of Shreveport showing roads, railroad, rivers, lakes, and woodland.

MARYLAND

241.5

Hopkins, Griffith M.

War map, showing the vicinities of Baltimore & Washington. Compiled from the latest surveys by G. M. Hopkins,

This map of Port Hudson, Louisiana, and vicinity, copyrighted on July 23, 1863, only 14 days after the fall of the stronghold to Union forces, is typical of commercially produced battlefield maps made during the war. Produced by Boston publisher George W. Tomlinson, the map is supplemented by a column of text printed beside the map describing Port Hudson's geographical setting and its defenses. (See entry no. 240.)

C. E. Philadelphia, Jacob Weiss, ©1861. Colored. Scale ca. 1:450,000. 35 × 45 cm.

G3840 1861 .H6

"Entered according to act of Congress in the year 1861 by G. M. Hopkins."

General map of eastern and central Maryland, Washington, D.C., and northern Virginia.

241.7

Knauff, Milton.

Civil War events in Maryland, 1861–1865. Prepared by Maryland Civil War Centennial Commission, Committee on History, Theme and Memorials. [Drawn by] Milton Knauff.

©1962. Colored. Scale ca. 1:450,000. 59 × 99 cm.

Appears on the verso of the Maryland State Roads Commission's "Map of Maryland" ([Annapolis] ©1962). (G3841 .P2 1962 .M3)

Pictorial map indicating historic Civil War sites. "Calendar of Events" in the upper right corner.

242

Mattern, H. W.

Theatre of operations, Maryland campaign, September 1862. Drawn by H. W. Mattern. Photocopy (positive). Scale ca. 1:410,000. 8 maps, each 28 × 36 cm.

Base map extends from Washington, D.C., north to Gettysburg, Pennsylvania, and from Winchester, Virginia east to Baltimore, Maryland. Roads, railroads, towns, fords, drainage, and relief by hachures are indicated.

Position of troops on the nights of September 6, 8, 9, 10, 11, 12, 13, and 14 have been added in red and blue ink. The annotations are probably the work of General Ezra A. Carman. Carman's unpublished history of the Civil War is in the Manuscript Division, L.C. Accompanying this work are numerous small maps, many of which are from the *Atlas to Accompany the Official Records of the Union and Confederate Armies* (entry no. 99).

242.5

Russell, Benjamin B.

The new war map of Maryland, part of Virginia & Pennsylvania. Mayer & Co.'s. lith., Boston. Boston, B. B. Russell [1863] Uncolored. Scale ca. 1:520,000. 53 × 67 cm.

General map printed in blue ink. Gettysburg is labeled "Victory is ours. Battlefield of July 2d. & 3d."

243

Russell, Robert E. L.

Thirty pen and ink maps of the Maryland Campaign, 1862. Drawn from descriptive readings and map fragments. By Robert E. Lee Russell. Baltimore, 1932. 1 p. l., 30 maps. Photocopy (positive). 47 × 62 cm.

G1271.S5R8 1932

Confederate troop positions are colored red.

Geography and Map Division also has an unbound negative photocopy.

Listed in C. E. Le Gear's *A List of Geographical Atlases in the Library of Congress* (Washington, Library of Congress, 1973), v. 7, no. 10668.

244

Sheppard, Eric W.

Map of the Maryland campaign, Sept. 3rd to 29th 1862. London, George Allen & Co., Ltd., [1911] Photocopy (positive). Scale ca. 1:193,000. 43 × 39 cm.

Positive photostat of map in E. W. Sheppard's *The Campaign in Virginia and Maryland, June 26th to Sept. 20th 1862* (London, Geo. Allen & Co., ltd., 1911) annotated in different colors to show the routes between Sept. 4th and 14th of the "9th Corps, Reno," "1st Corps, Hooker," "12th Corps, Williams," "2nd Corps, Sumner," "6th Corps, Franklin," "Couch's Division," and "Sykes' Division."

245

U.S. *Army. Corps of Engineers.*

Map of the vicinity of Hagerstown, Funkstown, Williamsport, and Falling Waters, Maryland. Accompanying the report of Major General G. G. Meade, on the battle of Gettysburg, dated October 1st 1863. Published by authority of the Hon. the Secretary of War. Office of the Chief of Engineers, U.S. Army. 1879. Colored. Scale ca. 1:21,500. 87 × 92 cm.

"United States forces are shown in blue [and] Confederate forces are shown in red."

Indicates houses, names of residents, stone fences, roads, vegetation, drainage, and relief by hachures.

245.1

————Portion of the military department of Washington embracing lower counties of Maryland. [Washington, D.C.] Engineer Bureau, War Dep., 1865. Uncolored. Scale 1:200,000. 63 × 56 cm.

G3840 1865 .U5

General map extending from Washington, D.C., south to Point Lookout, Maryland.

245.15

————Upper Potomac from McCoy's Ferry to Conrad's Ferry and adjacent portions of Maryland and Virginia compiled from county maps and maps prepared by Col. J. N. Macomb, A.D.C. Lt. Col. Engrs. with additions and corrections by Lt. Col. D. H. Strother, A.D.C. Engineer Department, 1863. Uncolored. Scale ca. 1:130,000. 78 × 83 cm.

G3840 1863 .U5

Map, without border, extends from Frederick, Maryland, west to Winchester, Virginia, and Hagerstown, Maryland, south to Front Royal, Virginia. Depicted are roads, railroads, canals, drainage, houses, cities and towns, and relief by hachures. In some areas, countryside is described by terms such as "hilly & wooded country," "open country," etc.

Stamped in lower left corner: Gilbert Thompson, 9—759.

245.17

————Another edition. Lith. by J. F. Gedney, Washn., D.C. 78 × 89 cm.

G3840 1863 .U51

Includes border.

Inset: Strasburg to Manassas Gap from recent survey. 15 × 24 cm.

This map was acquired by the Library of Congress in 1948 with the purchase of the papers and maps of Maj. Jedediah Hotchkiss.

Hand-colored to show major rivers in blue and some roads and railroads in red. A few place names have been added in red ink.

245.2

————————Another edition. Corrections S.W. of Winchester by Capt. Meigs, Sept. 1864. 79 × 91 cm.

G3840 1864 .U5

245.25

U.S. *Army. Corps of Topographical Engineers.*

Part of "Map of portions of the militry. dep'ts of Washington, Pennsylvania, Annapolis, and north eastern Virginia. Compiled in the Bureau of Topographical Engrs., War Department &c, July 1861, scale 1:200,000". Washington, D.C., Bureau of Topogl. Engineers, Sept. 15, 1862. Photocopy (positive). Scale 1:200,000. 58 × 85 cm.

G3840 1861 .U5

Endorsed in ink "For Hon. W. H. Seward, Sec. of State" and "With additions and emendations by John S. Clark, Col. A.D.C. to Gen. Banks."

General map of Maryland, Washington, D.C., and northern Virginia hand-colored to show major rivers in blue, railroads in red, and canals and roads in yellow.

245.3

————————Another issue. Sept. 17, 1862. 56 × 87 cm.

Endorsed in ink "For Head Quarters, Maj. Genl. McClellan."

A grid at intervals of one mile has been added in black and red ink, and drainage has been emphasized by blue ink.

This map was acquired by the Library of Congress in 1948 with the purchase of the papers and maps of Maj. Jedediah Hotchkiss.

ANNAPOLIS

234.35

Magnus, Charles.

Bird's eye view of the city of Annapolis, Md. New York, Chas. Magnus, ©1864. Ithaca, N.Y., Historic Urban Plans, 1967. Colored view. 34 × 44 cm.

G3844.A6A3 1864 .M3 1967

"Entered according to Act of Congress A.D. 1864 by Chas. Magnus."

"Reproduced in 1967 by Historic Urban Plans, Ithaca,

New York from the original in the Hambleton Collection of The Peale Museum. This is number 14 of an edition limited to 500 copies."

Panoramic map showing streets, public buildings, and houses. Legend in the bottom margin identifies three Civil War sites: 1 Camp Parole, 2. U.S. Genl. Hospital, Div. no. 1, [and] 3. U.S. General Hospital, Div. no. 2.

Includes portrait of Maj. Gen. Ambrose E. Burnside, to whom the panoramic map is dedicated.

245.37

Rees, Edwin.

Birds' eye view of the camp of the 67th regt. P.V. Annapolis, Md. on the ground occupied by the troops of Washington & Lafayette. Pubd. & designed by Edwin Rees. Lithd. by L. Rosenthal, Philada. [Philadelphia] 1863. Colored view. 37 × 50 cm.

G3844 .A6S5 1863 .R4 Vault

Panoramic map of Federal camp with full dress parade depicted in foreground led by a military band.

"Entered according to act of Congress in the year 1863, by Edwin Rees."

245.39

Sachse (Edward) and Company.

Parole camp Annapolis, Md. Lith. by E. Sachse & Co., Balto. [Baltimore] 1864. Colored view. 23 × 45 cm.

G3844.P34S5 1864 .E2 Vault

"Entered according to Act of Congress in the year 1864 by E. Sachse & Co."

Imperfect copy; the top of map and the lower left corner are missing. The map was once torn in half, but has since been repaired.

Bird's-eye view of the camp on the outskirts of Annapolis which was occupied by men of the Union Army that had been captured and paroled by the Confederacy. Buildings are keyed by number to the legend in the bottom margin.

ANTIETAM

245.4

Antietam Battlefield Commission of Pennsylvania.

Map of the battlefield of Antietam with the locations of monuments erected by the Commonwealth of Pennsylvania to the 3rd, 4th, 7th, 8th regiments of infantry, Pennsylvania Reserve Corps. Prepared for Antietam Battlefield Commission of Pennsylvania. Reduced and drawn by S. A. Hammond, Ass't. Eng. [1908?] Blue print. Scale 1:18,000. 48 × 38 cm.

"Reduced by permission of the Antietam Commission, Brig. Gen. E. A. Carman, Commissioner, from their map of the battlefield that was surveyed and drawn by the engineers of the Gettysburg National Park Commission, Lt. Col. John P. Nicholson, Chairman, Bvt. Lt. Col. E. B. Cope, Engineer, H. W. Mattern, Ass't. Engineer, [and] E. M. Hewitt, Ass't. Engineer."

Detailed map indicating roads, drainage, fence lines, houses, names of residents, woodland, and relief by contour lines.

Inset: Mansfield Avenue enlarged to show positions of Pennsylvania Reserve monuments. 7 × 25 cm.

245.45

Antietam Battlefield Memorial Commission.

Map of the battlefield of Antietam with the locations of monuments erected by the Commonwealth of Pennsylvania. Prepared for the Antietam Battlefield Memorial Commission. Reduced and drawn by S. A. Hammond, Asst. Eng. Julius Bien & Co., lith., N.Y. [1908?] Colored. Scale 1:18,000. 46 × 38 cm.

"Reduced by permission of the Antietam Commission, Brig. Gen. E. A. Carman, Commissioner, from their map of the battlefield that was surveyed and drawn by the engineers of the Gettysburg National Park Commission, Lt. Col. John P. Nicholson, Chairman, Bvt. Lt. Col. E. B. Cope, Engineer."

Detailed map indicating roads, drainage, fence lines, houses, names of residents, woodland, and relief by contour lines. Battlefield monuments are located by red squares.

245.5

Bowlby, James D.

Site of the battle of Antietam Creek or Sharpsburg, Maryland, 17 September 1862. Alexandria, Va., James D. Bowlby, 1863. Reprinted by Kirby Lithographic Co., Inc., Wash., D.C. for the Parks and History Association, Inc., 1972. Uncolored. Scale ca. 1:8000. 96 × 65 cm.

G3842 .A6 1963 .B6

"This map is based on the topographic survey data and original drawings of the Antietam Battlefield Board and reflects their accuracy of detail."

Map indicates four classes of roads, five classes of fences, houses and names of residents, orchards, woods, "open, grassy or pasture" lands, and fields that were in corn, stubble, or plowed. Troop positions are not given.

245.55

Gould, Oliver C.

Antietam. Enlarged and corrected from map of Gen. Michler, U.S. Eng., by Oliver C. Gould, Portland, Maine. [189–?] Uncolored. Scale not given. 31 × 24 cm.

"No. 1 = Confeds. opposing 10 Me. & 128 P.V., 7:30 to 8:00 A.M. No. 2 & 3 = Confeds. marching behind no. 1."

This map was in the possession of Jedediah Hotchkiss at the time of his death. Major Hotchkiss served as topographic engineer with the Army of Northern Virginia. In July 1948, the Library of Congress purchased his map collection.

245.6

Hotchkiss, Jedediah.

Antietam battlefield. Preliminary map no. 3. Jed. Hotchkiss, The Norris Peters Co., photo-litho., Washington, D.C. July 1895. Uncolored. Scale ca. 1:5,040. 88 × 52 cm.

Detailed map of the battlefield showing roads and lanes, fences, houses, names of residents, crops, woodland, and relief by hachures. Troop positions are not noted.

This map was acquired by the Library of Congress in 1948 with the purchase of the papers and maps of Maj. Jedediah Hotchkiss.

245.65

Kahler, Charles P.

Map of Antietam National Cemetery at Sharpsburg, Maryland. Designed by A. A. Biggs, M. D., President & Genl. Supt., Sharpsburg, 1866. Surveyed and drawn by Chas. P. Kahler, C. E., Baltimore. Lith. by A. Hoen & Co., Balto. 1867. Uncolored. Scale 1:600. 43 × 56 cm.

"Entered according to Act of Congress in the year 1867 by the Board of Trustees of the 'Antietam National Cemetery' in the Clerks Office of the U.S. District Court for Maryland."

29 "references" are keyed by number to the map.

245.7

Klep, Rolf.

The battlefield of Antietam. [Drawn by] Rolf Klep '37. Uncolored. Scale ca. 1:25,000. 2 sheets, each 36 × 26 cm. *From* Life Magazine, September 1937. p. 84–85.

Insets: 1. The Dunker Church.—2. "The Bloody Lane."—3. Burnside's Bridge. Each inset 7 × 7 cm.

245.75

Map of the battlefield of Antietam. [19–?] Uncolored. Scale ca. 1:5280 (about 12 inches equals 1 mile, not "10 in. = 1 mile") 153 × 122 cm., in 6 parts, each 77 × 46 cm. or smaller.

Very detailed anonymous and undated map of the battlefield indicating roads and lanes, drainage, houses, names of residents, grass fields, stubble, corn fields, plowed fields, rock outcrops, rail, post and rail, stone, and pailing fences, "fence[s], kind unknown," hay stacks, and woodland. Relief is depicted by contour lines at intervals of 10 feet. Troop positions are not noted.

245.8

Michler, Nathaniel.

Antietam. Prepared by Bvt. Brig. Genl. N. Michler, Major of Engineers, from surveys under his direction, by order of Brig. Genl. & Bvt. Maj. Genl. A. A. Humphreys, Chief of Engineers, and under the authority of the hon. Secretary of War. Surveyed & drawn by Maj: J. E. Weyss, assisted by F. Theilkuhl, J. Strasser & G. Thompson. Photolith. by the N.Y. Lithographing, Engraving & Printing Co., Julius Bien, Supt. 1867. Colored. Scale 1:21,120. 58 × 66 cm.

"General direction of Confederate line of battle, Sept. 16th 1862" and "(General direction of) Confederate line of battle, Sept. 17th 1862 (evening)" are hand-colored in red. Union troop positions are not indicated.

Detailed map of the environs of Sharpsburg showing roads, the "Washington Co. R.R.," fences, houses, names of residents, vegetation, drainage, villages, the "Burnside Bridge," "Bloody Lane," "Dunker's Chapel," "National Cemetery," and relief by hachures.

In this issue, the map is printed on a yellow background with the Potomac River colored green.

245.85

————————Another issue. Uncolored.

Confederate lines of battle are hand-colored in red.

245.9

————————Another copy.

Stamped at top of map: 320 Union.

Handwritten note on verso: War Records Office. Washington, D.C. Feb. 8, 1892. Respectfully referred to the Postmaster, Sharpsburg, Md. with request that he will please examine this map, correct the spelling of the names and return it to me as early as practicable. [Signed] C. D. Cowles, Capt. U.S.A.

Confederate positions and the corrections apparently made by the Sharpsburg Postmaster are in red ink.

This map was in the possession of Jedediah Hotchkiss at the time of his death. Major Hotchkiss served as topographic engineer with the Army of Northern Virginia. In July 1948, the Library of Congress purchased his map collection.

245.95

————————Another copy.

Map is annotated by hand to show the Confederate positions in red, additional hachures in pencil and blue ink, and a ¾-inch grid.

This map was in the possession of Jedediah Hotchkiss at the time of his death. Major Hotchkiss served as topographic engineer with the Army of Northern Virginia. In July 1948, the Library of Congress purchased his map collection.

246

Roebling, Washington A., *and* **W. S. Long.**

Battle of the Antietam fought September 16 & 17, 1862. Reconnoissance of the ground occupied by the 1st Army Corps commanded by Maj. Gen. Hooker. Made under the direction of Maj. D. C. Houston, Chf. Engr., by Lieut. W. A. Roebling and W. S. Long, C. E. Uncolored ms. Scale 1:10,560. 59 × 57 cm.

G3844 .A68S5 1862 .H6 Vault

Pen and ink manuscript drawn on tracing cloth, showing "line of Hooker's advance," roads, houses and names of occupants, fences, vegetation, drainage, and relief by hachures. Troop positions are not given.

246.2

Sholl, Charles.

Antietam Sharpsburg and vicinity. Constructed and engraved to illustrate "The war with the South." [Compiled by Charles Sholl] Engd. by Rae Smith. ©1864. Colored. Scale ca. 1:26,700. 23 × 18 cm. *From* Tomes, Robert. The war with the South. New York, Virtue & Yorston, 1862–1867, v. 2, between p. 426 and 427.

Signed (facsim.): Charles: Sholl, Topl. Engineer.

"Entered according to act of Congress AD. 1864 by Virtue, Yorston & Co."

Caption in lower margin: A topographical map of the battle field at Antietam from an actual survey by an engineer officer on General Doubleday's staff.

246.3

————————Another issue.

This issue lacks the copyright notice in the lower margin.

247

U.S. *Antietam Battlefield Board.*

Atlas of the battlefield of Antietam, prepared under the direction of the Antietam Battlefield Board . . . Surveyed by Lieut. Col. E. B. Cope, Engineer, H. W. Mattern, Assistant Engineer, of the Gettysburg National Park. Drawn by Charles H. Ourand, 1899. Position of troops by Gen. E. A. Carman. Published by authority of the Secretary of War, under the direction of the Chief Engineers, U.S. Army, 1904. Washington, Government Printing Office, 1904. 2 p. l., 14 col. maps. 69 × 45 cm.

G1272 .A6S5 .U45 1904 folio

Cover title.

Detailed series of 14 situation maps showing Union positions in blue and Confederate positions in red. Each map

measures about 78 × 63 cm. and indicates roads and
streets, houses, names of residents, fences, vegetation, drainage, bridges, fords, and relief by contour lines. Maps are
preceded by a three-page list of the "Organization of the
Union and Confederate armies at the battle of Antietam
(Sharpsburg), September 17, 1862," which gives the names
of commanders down to the regimental level.

Listed in P. L. Phillips's *A List of Geographical Atlases
in the Library of Congress* (Washington, Government Printing Office, 1909), v. 1, no. 1354.

248

————————Another edition. [Washington, Government
Printing Office, 1908] 4 p. l., 14 col. maps. 71 × 45 cm.

G1272.A6S5.U5 1908 folio

Listed in C. E. Le Gear's *A List of Geographical Atlases
in the Library of Congress* (Washington, Library of Congress,
1973), v. 7, no. 10685.

249

————————Map of the battlefield of Antietam. No. 1. This
map shows the position of the Union and Confederate
forces on the morning of Sept. 17th, 1862, prior to the battle
of Antietam which opened at daybreak. Drawn under the
direction of Antietam Board, Col. John C. Stearns, Gen. H.
Heth. Theo. Friebus, Jr. Norris Peters Co., photo-litho.,
Washington, D.C. 1893. Colored. Scale 1:14,080. 79 × 71
cm.

Confederate forces are shown in red and Union forces
in blue. Headquarters of McClellan and Lee are clearly indicated. Legend lists the names of the corps, division, and
brigade commanders. Brigades are keyed by number to positions on the map.

Shows roads, railroad, houses, fences, names of residents, "Burnside Bridge," "Bloody Lane," "Dunker's
Chapel," "National Cemetery," towns, vegetation, drainage,
fords, and relief by hachures.

249.5

————————Map of the battlefield of Antietam. Published
under the direction of Daniel S. Lamont and Russell A. Alger, Secretaries of War, by the Antietam Battlefield Board,
Major Geo. W. Davis, U.S.A. President, General E. A. Carman, late Union army, [and] General H. Heth, late Confederate army. Surveyed and drawn by Col. E. B. Cope, Engineer [and] H. W. Mattern, Ass't Engineer, Gettysburg
National Park. 1898. Blue print. Scale ca. 1:10,560. 79 × 65
cm.

"Drawn by H. W. Mattern" in the lower right corner.

"Note: Figures in black and crosses, thus (+) marked
along roadsides indicate numbers of tablets. For legends on
tablets showing positions of troops and their movements,
see final report of the Antietam Battlefield Board to the Secretary of War, dated 1898."

Detailed map of the battlefield showing roads, lanes,
fences, houses, names of residents, woodland, and relief by
contour lines at intervals of 10 feet. Troop positions are not
noted.

249.6

————————Another issue.

Similar to the preceding map but it lacks the title and
place names.

250

————————Map of the battlefield of Antietam. This map
shows the position of each of the forty-two different com-
mands of the regular army engaged in the battle of Antie-
tam, September 17, 1862. Battery "G", 2d U.S. Artillery, Lt.
J. H. Butler, commanding, was not engaged in the battle,
being attached to Gen'l. Couch's Division, near Harper's
Ferry. Drawn under the direction of Antietam Board, Col.
John C. Stearns, Gen. H. Heth. Theo. Friebus, Jr. Norris
Peters Co., photo-litho., Washington, D.C. 1893. Colored.
Scale 1:14,080. 79 × 72 cm.

Legend lists Union commands and the names of the
commanders. Each unit is keyed by number to a position on
the map. Confederate positions are not indicated.

Shows roads, railroad, houses, fences, names of residents, "Burnside Bridge," "Bloody Lane," "Dunker's
Chapel," "National Cemetery," towns, vegetation, drainage,
fords, and relief by hachures.

250.1

————————(No. 2) Map of the battlefield of Antietam.
Drawn under the direction of Antietam Board, Col. John C.
Stearns [and] Gen. H. Heth. The Norris Peters Co., photo-
litho., Washington, D.C. 1894. Uncolored. Scale 1:14,908.
79 × 72 cm.

Map of the battlefield showing roads and lanes, houses
and names of residents, fences, drainage, woodland, and relief by hachures. Troop positions are not indicated.

This map was acquired by the Library of Congress in
1948 with the purchase of the papers and maps of Maj.
Jedediah Hotchkiss.

250.2

————————Northwest, or no. 1, sheet of preliminary map
of Antietam (Sharpsburg) battlefield. Enlarged from the
"Michler" map of the war records atlas with corrections and
additions. Antietam Battlefield Comission [sic] Maj. Geo. B.
Davis. U.S.A., President, H. Heth, E. A. Carman, Expert
Historian, [and] Jed. Hotchkiss, Expert Topographer. The
Norris Peters Co., photo-litho., Washington, D.C. Nov.
1894. Uncolored. Scale ca. 1:10,400. 65 × 78 cm.

The Geography and Map Division has sheets 1 and 2
of 4 sheets. For a description of sheet 2, see entry no. 250.3.

Map extends from Sharpsburg north to Bakersville and shows roads and lanes, houses and names of residents, fences, drainage, and woodland. Troop positions are not noted.

This map was acquired by the Library of Congress in 1948 with the purchase of the papers and maps of Maj. Jedediah Hotchkiss.

250.3

————Southwest, or no. 2, sheet of preliminary map of Antietam (Sharpsburg) battlefield. Enlarged from "Michler" map of the war records atlas with corrections and additions. Antietam Battlefield Comission [sic] Maj. Geo. B. Davis, U.S.A., President, H. Heth, E. A. Carman, Expert Historian, [and] Jed. Hotchkiss, Expert Topographer. The Norris Peters Co., photo-litho., Washington, D.C. Jan. 1895. Uncolored. Scale ca. 1:10,400. 57 × 78 cm.

The Geography and Map Division has sheets 1 and 2 of 4 sheets. For a description of sheet 1, see entry no. 250.2.

Map extends from Sharpsburg south to Antietam Iron Works and shows roads and lanes, houses and names of residents, fences, and drainage. Troop positions are not noted.

This map was acquired by the Library of Congress in 1948 with the purchase of the papers and maps of Maj. Jedediah Hotchkiss.

250.4

U.S. *National Park Service.*

Antietam ([Washington] Government Printing Office, 1980. Colored. Scale ca. 1:31,680. 40 × 21 cm.

G3842 .A6 1980 .U5

Map illustrates a descriptive leaflet entitled "Antietam National Battlefield, Maryland" and shows nine tour stops and the tour route.

Inset: [Map of the environs of Antietam National Battlefield] 5 × 6 cm.

250.5

————Antietam national battlefield site, Maryland. Drawn by John J. Black, November 1948. Reprint 1959. Uncolored. Scale ca. 1:54,000. 18 × 13 cm.

Map indicates the main battle lines and the tour route.

Inset: Vicinity map. 5 × 6 cm.

Illustrates a descriptive leaflet by the U.S. National Park Service entitled "Antietam national battlefield site, Maryland."

250.6

————The battle of Antietam, September 17, 1862 Washington, Government Printing Office, 1968. Colored. Scale not given. Map 44 × 20 cm. on sheet 47 × 41 cm.

G3842 .A6S5 1968 .U5

Map illustrates a descriptive leaflet entitled "Antietam"

and indicates the placement and movement of troops during the three phases of the battle.

Map showing "A tour of the battlefield" is printed on the verso.

250.7

————Antietam battlefield. New 1972 [Washington] Government Printing Office, 1972. Colored. Scale ca. 1:24,000. 29 × 25 cm.

G3842 .A6 1972 .U5

Map illustrates a descriptive leaflet entitled "Antietam National Battlefield Site, Maryland" and shows nine points of interest and the tour route.

250.8

————Another issue. Reprint 1973.

G3842 .A6 1972 .U51

250.9

————Another edition. Rev. Nov. 1977. Reprint 1978.

G3842 .A6 1978 .U5

251

Wells, Jacob.

The field of Antietam. [September 16–17, 1862] Uncolored. Scale ca. 1:48,500. 19 × 14 cm. *From* Century illustrated monthly magazine, v. 32, June 1886. p. 290.

Shows batteries, troop positions and movements, names of commanders, roads, street pattern of Sharpsburg, drainage, vegetation, relief by hachures, houses, names of residents, and fences.

Chronology of events appears below the map.

252

Willcox, William H.

Map of the battlefield of Antietam, prepared by Lieut. Wm. H. Willcox, Top. Off. & A.A.D.C. on Brig. Genl. Doubleday's staff. [Sept. 17, 1862] Lith. of P. S. Duval & Son, Philada. Colored. Scale ca. 1:13,300. 49 × 43 cm.

Handwritten inscription in the upper right-hand corner reads "Lieut Crawford with compts of Lt. Wm. H. Willcox."

Shows roads and streets, houses, fences, vegetation, drainage, hachures, and troop positions.

Inset: [Map of the environs of Sharpsburg] 12 × 10 cm.

253

————3d edition.

Inscribed in longhand as follows: Obtained from Washington & presented to Gen. R. E. Lee by J. E. B. Stuart.

This map was in the possession of Jedediah Hotchkiss at the time of his death. Major Hotchkiss served as topographic engineer with the Army of Northern Virginia. In July 1948, the Library of Congress purchased his map collection.

254

————[4th?] edition.

BALTIMORE COUNTY

254.5

Kaiser, George.

Military map, Baltimore Co., Md. Compiled from the best authorities and corrected by actual survey under the direction of Col. W. F. Raynolds A.D.C., Chief Eng. 8th Army Corps. Drawn and lithographed in the office of the Chief Eng., 8th Army Corps, by Geo. Kaiser, Pvt. 10th N.Y. Vols. 1863. Colored. Scale 1:63,360. 101 × 78 cm.

G3843 .B3 1863 .R3

At head of title: Middle Department and 8th Army Corps, Major Genl. R. C. Schenck Comdg.

Stamped in right corner: Topographer, Post Office Department.

"Library of Congress, Maps & Charts no. 4748."

Detailed map indicating forts, camps, military hospitals, roads, toll gates, railroads, towns, mills, houses and names of residents. The names of a few towns are underscored in red or blue.

Listed in R. W. Stephenson's *Land Ownership Maps* (Washington, Library of Congress, 1967), no. 285.

254.7

[Rough pencil and pen and ink sketch of Baltimore, Maryland and vicinity. 1861] Uncolored ms. Scale not given. 29 × 26 cm.

In the papers of Maj. Gen. Nathaniel Prentice Banks, Manuscript Division, L.C., container 76.

Map indicates the names of several forts and a few place names.

"G.10.1 Hd Qrs Dept Penna May 7, 1861" is written in ink on the verso.

BUDD'S FERRY

255

Williamson, Robert S.

Surveys & reconnaissances in the vicinity of Budd's Ferry, Charles Co., Md., by R. S. Williamson, Capt. Topl. Engrs. [1861–2] Colored ms. Scale 1:31,680. 93 × 101 cm.

G3843 .C6S5 1862 .W5 Vault

"211, L. Sheet 5."

"Transferred from Office of Chf. Engr., Defenses of Washington, to Engr. Dept., Jan'y 1866."

Shows roads, drainage, houses, names of residents, a few hachures along the Potomac River, "Hd. Qrs. Genl. Hooker's Dvn.," "Hd. Qrs. Sickles Brgd.," breastwork and battery at Budd's Ferry, and the location of batteries in Prince William County, Virginia, with the number of guns indicated in pencil.

CAMP PATTERSON PARK

256

Butler, J. B.

Map and directory of Camp Patterson Park [Baltimore, Maryland] One Hundred and Tenth Regiment of New York Volunteers. Col. D. C. Littlejohn, commanding. By J. B. Butler, engineer and surveyor. Printed by F. Bourquin & Co., Philadelphia. September 27, 1862. Colored. Scale 1:360. Map 33 × 36 cm. on sheet 63 × 51 cm.

Detailed map indicating position of tents, principal buildings, wagon roads, and "earthwork intrenchments of the War of 1812."

Tents are keyed by number to a list of occupants printed at the sides and bottom of the map.

Includes portraits of nine officers of the regiment.

CARROLL COUNTY

256.3

Macomb, John N.

Part of Carroll County, Maryland. Prepared under the direction of Col. J. N. Macomb, A.D.C., Maj. Top. Engrs. Drawn from S. J. Martenet's map by John de la Camp [and from] photographs by G. Mathiot & D. Hinkle by permission of Prof. A. D. Bache, Supt. U.S. Coast Survey. 1862. Uncolored ms. Scale ca. 1:44,500. 105 × 92 cm.

G3843 .C4 1862 .M31 Vault

Pen and ink manuscript map drawn on tracing linen of the western two-thirds of the county showing roads, railroads, towns, shops and factories, taverns, mills, stores, post offices, schools, and churches. The map does not include military information.

Former ownership stamp in lower right corner: U.S.C. & G. Survey Library and Archives [no.] 624.

256.4

Shearer, W. O.

Map of Carroll County, Md. Entered according to act of Congress in the year 1863 by W. O. Shearer in the clerk's office of the district court of the eastern district of Pennsylvania. [Philadelphia?] ©1863. Colored. Scale 1:31,600. 139 × 141 cm. in 2 parts, each 70 × 141 cm.

G3843.C4 1863 .S5

"Made for military purposes only."

Relatively crude hand-colored lithographic map showing roads and railroads, towns and villages, houses and names of residents, rivers, and district boundaries. The map includes fewer personal names than shown on "Martenet's map of Carroll County, Maryland" (Baltimore, Simon J. Martenet, 1862). Military information is not depicted.

Listed in R. W. Stephenson's *Land Ownership Maps* (Washington, Library of Congress, 1967), no. 288.

FREDERICK COUNTY

256.5

Frederick, Md. Chamber of Commerce.

Civil War tour map, Frederick County, Maryland. Prepared by the Frederick Chamber of Commerce. [Frederick, 195–?] Uncolored. Scale not given. 28 × 22 cm.

G3843 .F7 195–.F72

Sketch map showing a few roads and towns.

Battles and skirmishes are listed on the verso and keyed by number to the map.

256.6

Hergesheimer, Edwin.

Frederick County, Maryland. Prepared under the direction of Lieut. Col. J. N. Macomb, Chf. Topl. Engr. for the use of Maj. Gen. G. B. McClellan, Commanding U.S. Army. Drawn from I. Bond's map by E. Hergesheimer. Photographs by G. Malliot & D. Hinkle, by permission of Prof. A. D. Bache, Sup't., U.S. Coast Survey. 1861. Photocopy (positive). Scale ca. 1:125,000. 54 × 42 cm.

G3843 .F7 1861 .H4

Signed in ink: Copy no. 7, J. N. Macomb, Lt. Col. A.D.C.

Based on Isaac Bond's map of Frederick County, Maryland, published in 1858, this map indicates towns and villages, rivers and canals, roads and turnpikes, houses, and relief by hachures. Major rivers have been colored blue, and two place names have been added in pencil.

LAUREL

256.8

Munther, Frederick R.

Sketch of defences at Laurel Station—R.Rd. from Washington to Baltimore over Big Pautuxent [sic]. Laurel, Septbr. 20th 1862. [Signed] F. R. Munther, Capt. a A.D.C. [i.e., Additional Aide-de-Camp] Uncolored ms. Scale ca. 1:31,000. 25 × 20 cm.

In the papers of Maj. Gen. Nathaniel Prentice Banks, Manuscript Division, L.C., container 76.

Title is on the verso.

Pencil and ink sketch map drawn on lined paper showing the camps of the 131st New York City regiment and the 141st New York State regiment, the position of the blockhouse and palisade tambour on the road from Washington, D.C., to Baltimore at the Patuxent River, and rifle pits between the village of Laurel and Laurel Station.

POINT LOOKOUT

257

Everett, George.

Point Lookout, Md. View of Hammond Genl. Hospital & U.S. genl. depot for prisoners of war. Lith. by E. Sachse & Co., Baltimore. Point Lookout, 1864. Colored view. 49 × 78 cm.

Sixty-three sites are listed in the margin and keyed by number to the appropriate position in the view.

Inset: Headquarters of the general commanding St. Mary's District. View. 17 × 13 cm.

SOUTH MOUNTAIN

258

U.S. *Army. Corps of Topographical Engineers.*

South Mountain showing the positions of the forces of the United States and the enemy during the battle fought by the Army of the Potomac under the command of Major General G. B. McClellan, Sept. 14th 1862. Prepared in the Bureau of Topographical Engineers. 1872. Colored. Scale ca. 1:17,600. 84 × 54 cm.

Detailed map giving the morning and evening positions of the Union troops and the morning position of the Confederate troops, roads, contour lines, drainage, vegetation, houses, names of residents, and fences.

259

————Another edition. Am. Photolitographic Co., N.Y. (Osborne's process). Uncolored. Scale ca. 1:18,500. 80 × 51 cm.

MISSISSIPPI

259.2

Grierson's route from La Grange to Baton Rouge. [April 17–May 2, 1863] Uncolored. Scale ca. 1:3,625,000. 16 × 12 cm. *From* "Monthly record of current events," Harper's new monthly magazine, v. 27, June–Nov., 1863. p. 271.

Map of "The seat of war on the Mississippi" is on the verso. 18 × 13 cm.

259.4

Lindenkohl, Adolph.

Northern Mississippi and Alabama. Compiled and engraved at the U.S. Coast Survey Office, from state maps, post office maps, local surveys, etc., with additions from campaign maps and information furnished by Capt. O. M. Poe, Chief Engineer, Military Division of the Mississippi and by Capt. W. E. Merrill, Chief Engineer, Department of the Cumberland. Drawn by A. Lindenkohl. H. Lindenkohl & Chas. G. Krebs, lith. 1864. Colored. Scale 1:633,600. 62 × 82 cm.

General map indicating cities and towns, roads and railroads, rivers, and some relief by hachures. The map is overprinted in red to show state names and highlight state boundaries and railroads.

Another copy is in the James A. Garfield papers, Manuscript Division, L.C., series 8, container no. 1.

259.5

————[Northern Mississippi and Alabama] Drawn by A. Lindenkohl. H. Lindenkohl & Chas. G. Krebs, lith. U.S. Coast Survey, A. D. Bache, Supdt. 1865. Colored. Scale 1:633,600. 58 × 86 cm.

General map, without title. State names, boundaries, and railroads are colored red.

259.6

————Another issue. Uncolored.

Lacks the names of the cartographer and lithographers. Stamped on verso: Gilbert Thompson.

"Portions Alabama, Mississippi, etc. U.S. Coast Survey. 1865. 1 in = 10 ms. No. 4. 1865 sett [sic] 6 sheets" is written in ink on the verso.

Sheet 4 of a 6-sheet series of maps used by Gilbert Thompson during the Civil War. In addition to this sheet, the Geography and Map Division has sheet 1 (see entry no. 508.5), sheet 3 (see entry no. 305a.6), sheet 5 (see entry no. 129.3) and sheet 6 (see entry no. 129.55).

259.7

————Another issue. Uncolored.

Lacks the names of the cartographer and lithographers. "No. 3014 price 30 cents" is printed in the upper left corner.

260

U.S. *Coast Survey.*

Southern Mississippi and Alabama showing the approaches to Mobile. Edw. Molitor lith. Coast Survey Office, A. D. Bache, Supt., 1863. Colored. Scale ca. 1:650,000. 60 × 63 cm.

Indicates forts, towns, roads, railroads, and drainage. Railroads are colored red, and water is blue. Another copy, without railroads highlighted in red, is in the Geography and Map Division's Fillmore map collection no. 261.

Another copy is in the Allen family papers, Manuscript Division, L.C., container no. 2. This copy belonged to Lt. Charles Julius Allen (1840–1915) and has been annotated to show "Itinerary, march to Montgomery April 12 (or 13) to April 25, 1865, 16th A.C."

260.1

————Another issue.

Author's statement in the lower right corner reads "U.S. Coast Survey Office, A. D. Bache, Supt., 1863" rather than "Coast Survey Office . . ."

Listed in A. M. Modelski's *Railroad Maps of the United States* (Washington, Library of Congress, 1975), no. 140.

261

Wilson, James H.

Map of the country between Millikens Bend, La. and Jackson, Miss. shewing the routes followed by the Army of the Tennessee under the command of Maj. Genl. U. S. Grant, U.S. Vols. in its march from Millikens Bend to the rear of Vicksburg in April and May 1863; compiled, surveyed and drawn under the direction of Lt. Col. Js. H. Wilson, A.I. Gnl. & 1st Lt. Engrs. Published by authority of the Hon. the Secretary of War. Office of the Chief of Engineers, U.S. Army. 1876. Julius Bien & Co., photo lith., N.Y. Colored. Scale 1:126,720. 69 × 89 cm.

Drawn by: Maj. O. H. Matz, Asst. Eng. & 1st Lt. L. Helmle, 3d Mo. Vols. Inft. Surveys by: 1st Lt. P. C. Hains, U.S. Eng. & Asst. Engrs. Ulffers, Wrigley, Tunica, McComas & Mason. Geographl. authorities: La Tourette's sectl. map, U.S. land surveys, official county and city maps."

Map of Hinds and Warren counties, Mississippi and parts of Claiborne County, Mississippi, and Madison County, Louisiana, showing Union positions in blue and Confederate positions in red, fortifications, "routes followed by the Army of the Tenn.," roads, railroads, drainage, some vegetation along the Mississippi River, towns, relief by hachures, and a few houses and names of residents.

Legend contains a brief description of the "face of country," "soil," "productions," "roads," "streams," "fords," and "bayous."

262

————Another edition. Drawn on stone by John D. Hoffmann. Lith. of J. F. Gedney, Washington, D.C. Uncolored. Scale 1:126,720. 69 × 89 cm.

Similar to the preceding map but drawn on stone by Hoffmann and lithographed by Gedney instead of Bien. This edition denotes the positions of the Union and Confederate troops by symbols rather than by colors, and the legend lacks the statement "Published by authority of the Hon. the Secretary of War. Office of the Chief of Engineers, U.S. Army. 1876."

BIG BLACK RIVER

263

See Sherman map collection no. 114.

BIG BLACK RIVER BRIDGE

264

Mason, F.

Map of battlefield of Big Black River Bridge, Mississippi, showing the positions of the U.S. troops, May 17th 1863. Prepared under the direction of Lieut. P. C. Hains, U.S. Engrs., by F. Mason, Act. Asst. Engineer. Published by authority of the Hon. the Secretary of War. Office of the Chief of Engineers, U.S. Army. 1876. Colored. Scale ca. 1:7200. 49 × 45 cm.

Inset: [Cross] section of parapet A. 6 × 16 cm.

Detailed map indicating "confederate works," Union troop positions and names of commanders, artillery positions, roads, "Vicksburg and Jackson Rail Road," houses, fences, vegetation, drainage, and relief by hachures.

265

————Another issue. Julius Bien & Co., photo. lith.

CHICKASAW BLUFFS

265.5

Munn, Edward A.

No. 1. First Vicksburg campaign or Chickasw [sic] Bayou. Dec. 27th 1862—Jan. 3rd 1863.—No. 2. Map of battle ground of Chickasaw Bayou, Dec. 28th and 29th 1862. Enlarged and drawn by E. A. Munn from Gen. Morgan's map. Uncolored. Scale of map 1, ca. 1:150,000; scale of map 2 not given. 2 maps, each 12 × 18 cm. *From* Illinois infantry. 13th regt., 1861–1864. Military history and reminiscences of the Thirteenth regiment of Illinois volunteer infantry in the Civil War in the United States, 1861–65. Prepared by a committee of the regiment, 1891. Chicago, Woman's Temperance Publishing Association, 1892. Between p. 244 and 245.

Maps indicate troop movements and positions.

COLDWATER RIVER

265.7

[Camp of the Third Division commanded by General John A. Logan situated on the Coldwater River and Holly Springs road, Mississippi. January 6, 1862] Uncolored ms. Scale not given. 20 × 22 cm.

In the John Alexander Logan family papers, Manuscript Division, L.C., container 145, p. 108.

Rough pencil sketch similar in content to map entitled "Sketch, Camp 3d Division, Jany 6th 1862" (entry no. 265.8).

265.8

Sketch, Camp 3d Division, Jany 6th 1862. Uncolored ms. Scale not given. 2 maps, each 20 × 25 cm.

In the John Alexander Logan family papers, Manuscript Division, L.C., container 145, p. 107.

Rough pencil sketches of the 3rd Division's camp along Coldwater River, Mississippi. One of the drawings seems to be the preliminary sketch for the other. Situated where the road to Holly Springs crossed the river, the sketches show the positions of the 1st, 2nd, and 4th brigades, batteries, the division train, and Gen. John A. Logan's headquarters.

CORINTH

266

Cockrell, Monroe F.

Battle of Corinth, Miss., Fri–Sat. Oct. 3–4, 1862. Prepared by Monroe F. Cockrell. Outline in part from "OR" plates 13–25. Drawn by Russell E. Trauth, April 30, 1946. Blue print. Scale 1:31,680 and 1:95,040. 54 × 67 cm. (Series 5)

"Scale: 2″ = 1 mi. From rd. & RR X to Chewalla scale: 1″ = 1½ mi."

Gives troop positions and movements, names of field commanders, and brief notes describing the "Federal occupation of Corinth, May 30, 1862," "fight at Iuka, Sept.

19, 1862," and the "Confederate retreat—battle at the Hatchie." Roads, railroads, distances, drainage, and towns are also included.

Another copy is in *Notes and Articles by Monroe F. Cockrell for His Maps of the War Between the States.* ©1950. Typescript.

267

Matz, Otto H.

Map of the country between Monterey, Tenn: & Corinth, Miss: showing the lines of entrenchments made & the routes followed by the U.S. forces under the command of Maj. Genl. Halleck, U.S. Army, in their advance upon Corinth in May 1862: Surveyed under the direction of Col. Geo. Thom, A.D.C. & Chief of Topl. Engrs., Department of the Mississippi, by Lieuts. Fred. Schraag and C. L. Spangenberg, Asst. Topl. Engrs. and drawn by Lieut. Otto H. Matz, Asst. Topl. Engr. Lith. of J. Bien, N.Y. Colored. Scale 1:31,680. 77 × 61 cm.

Includes houses, names of residents, fences, roads, railroads, vegetation, fields, drainage, and relief by hachures.

Another copy is in the Sherman map coll. no. 115.

267.1

—————Another issue. Lith. of J. Bien.

Address of the lithographer is deleted from this issue.

268

Michler, Nathaniel, *and* John E. Weyss.

Topographical sketch of Corinth, Mississippi, and its environs. Showing the enemy's entrenchments, and the approach of the U.S. forces. [Center:] Maj: Genl. Buell: com'dg. Surveyed from May 17th to June 6th 1862, by Capt: N. Michler, Topog'l Eng'rs., U.S.A. and Maj: J. E. Weyss, U.S. Vol's. Photocopy (positive). Scale ca. 1:29,000. 24 × 30 cm.

Hand-colored sunprint giving Confederate entrenchments in red and Union entrenchments in blue. "Head Qs. of Genl. Buell," roads, railroads, vegetation, drainage, relief by hachures, houses, fences, and the names of a few residents in the outlying areas are also included.

269

Shraag, F., *and* F. Theinert.

General plan of the field-fortifications around Corinth, Miss. Also exhibiting the rebel entrenchments and the approaches of the U.S. forces during May 1862 under Major Genl. H. W. Halleck, U.S.A. Surveyed and drawn under the direction of Captain Fred. E. Prime, Corps of Engineers, Chief Engineer, Department of Tennessee. Surveyed and drawn by F. Shraag and F. Theinert. [1862] Colored ms. Scale 1:6000. 9 parts measuring 73 × 56 cm. each, and 3 parts measuring 74 × 45 cm. each. Over-all size 209 × 211 cm.

G3984 .C8S5 1862 .S5 Vault

"Engineer Department, March 3, 1863. Received from Capt. Prime. See his letter of 19 January 1863 (P. 1266)."

Detailed topographic map showing Union and Confederate fortifications by the colors blue and red respectively, powder magazines, city streets and buildings (both unnamed), rural houses and names of a few residents, fences, roads, railroads, vegetation, drainage, artesian wells, and relief by hachures.

FORT PEMBERTON

269.5

U.S. *Navy.*

Map of operations of the Yazoo Pass expedition under command of Lt. Com. Watson Smith, U.S.N., 1863. Uncolored. Scale ca. 1:225,000. 20 × 12 cm. *From* Report of the Secretary of the Navy, with an appendix, containing reports from officers. December, 1863 (Washington, Government Printing Office, 1863). fol. p. 454.

Map of the attack of the Yazoo Pass Expedition on Confederate Fort Pemberton, near Greenwood, Mississippi, March–April, 1863.

Map illustrates "Additional report of Lieutenant Commander [James P.] Foster" dated April 13, 1863.

GRAND GULF

270

Gerdes, F. H.

Approaches to Grand Gulf, Miss. From a topographical & hydrographical survey by F. H. Gerdes, Assistant, assigned by A. D. Bache, Supdt, U.S. Coast Survey, to act under orders of Rear Admiral D. D. Porter, U.S. Navy, commanding Mississippi Squadron. 1864. Uncolored. Scale 1:10,000. 57 × 39 cm.

Shows "Ft. Cobun," "Ft. Wade," streets of Grand Gulf, "R.R. to Port Gibson," plantation of "Col. Coffee," vegetation, soundings, and relief by hachures. "The fortifications facing the river are those erected by the rebels, and captured by the Mississippi Squadron, under the command of Admiral Porter, on May 3d 1863."

271

—————Photocopy (positive). Scale ca. 1:10,000.

Stamped at bottom: U.S.C. & G. Survey Library and Archives, no. 567.

Sunprint with annotations in pencil and ink. It appears to be a preliminary work copy of the preceding map (entry no. 270) by F. H. Gerdes. The photocopy differs from the published version in that relief is indicated by contour lines rather than hachures, and the fortifications at Fort Wade are considerably more extensive.

271.2

U.S. *Navy.*

Batteries at Grand Gulf captured by the United States Mississippi Squadron, May 3, 1863. Uncolored. Scale ca. 1:8,700. 15 × 24 cm. *From* Report of the Secretary of the Navy, with an appendix, containing reports from officers. December, 1863 (Washington, Government Printing Office, 1863). opp. p. 480.

Map indicates batteries, rifle pits, streets, relief by hachures, and the position of the Mississippi Squadron during the attack.

HAINES'S BLUFF

271.5

U.S. *Navy.*

Sketch of rebel fortifications at Hayne's Bluff. [May 1863] Uncolored. Scale ca. 1:23,000. 19 × 26 cm. *From* Report of the Secretary of the Navy, with an appendix, containing reports from officers. December, 1863 (Washington, Government Printing Office, 1863). opp. p. 492.

Map accompanies Acting Rear Adm. David D. Porter's report dated May 20, 1863, entitled "Destruction of the fortifications at Haines's Bluff."

HARRISBURG

272

Allman, Eugene H.

Map showing the battle field at Harrisburg, Miss. July 13–15, 1864. Mobile, Alabama, Aynsley Litho. & Eng. Co. Inc., ©1912. Uncolored. Scale not given. Map 30 × 17 cm. on sheet 41 × 63 cm.

"Legend: This map shows the position of the Confederate and the Federal forces during the three days encounter, showing in detail the position of the several commands.

"The tables show the record of casualties, in offices [sic] and men, killed, wounded and captured during the three days, as compiled from the official records of the Union and Confederate armies, and is authentic.

"This compilation is made by E. H. Allman, late private of Company "H"—6th Miss. Cavalry, Gen. H. P. Mabry's command, Confederate forces, and is tendered to the veterans of the Blue and Gray."

Indicates entrenchments, batteries, roads, towns, vegetation, drainage, and some relief by hachures. There are colored portraits of "Maj. Gen. Nathan B. Forrest, C.S. Army"

and "Maj. Gen. Andrew J. Smith, U.S. Army" in the top margin, as well as a drawing of an eagle perched on the crossed flags of the Confederate States and United States with "at peace" printed below the flags.

IUKA

273

U.S. *Army. Corps of Engineers.*

Map of the battle of Iuka, Mississippi, showing the positions of the United States and Confederate troops on the 19th of September 1862. Accompanying the report of Maj. Gen. W. S. Rosecrans. Published by authority of the Hon. the Secretary of War, office of the Chief of Engineers, U.S. Army. 1876. Colored. Scale 1:6336. 61 × 72 cm.

"The United States forces are shown in blue [and] the Confederate forces are shown in red."

Detailed map indicating roads, the "route to heights commanding Fulton Road," street pattern and buildings in Iuka, houses and names of residents in outlying areas, fences, "Memphis & Charleston R.R.," vegetation, drainage, and relief by hachures.

JACKSON

274

Duff, William H.

Map of Jackson, Miss: and surroundings during the siege July 10th–16th, 1863, and location of the Cooper home whence a piano was carried by a company of pioneers, commanded by a Capt: McPheely, to the position of 5th Company, Washington (Louisiana) Battery, and there remained during the siege, and played upon while the battle, July 12th, 1863, was in progress. [Copyrighted May 16, 1908, by William H. Duff] Uncolored. Scale not given. 20 × 48 cm.

Sketch map showing the "Confederate's line of works," positions of "Slocomb's Louisiana Battery" and "Cobb's Kentucky Battery," "Federal's line," "Mrs. Cooper's home," railroads, roads, and drainage.

VICKSBURG

275

Badeau, Adam.

Map of the siege of Vicksburg. [1864] Uncolored. Scale not given. 21 × 14 cm. *From* Century illustrated monthly magazine, v. 30, Sept. 1885. p. 756.

Shows fortifications, "Maj. Gen. Grant's Hd. Qrs. during the siege," street pattern of Vicksburg, houses, roads, railroads, drainage, vegetation, and relief by hachures.

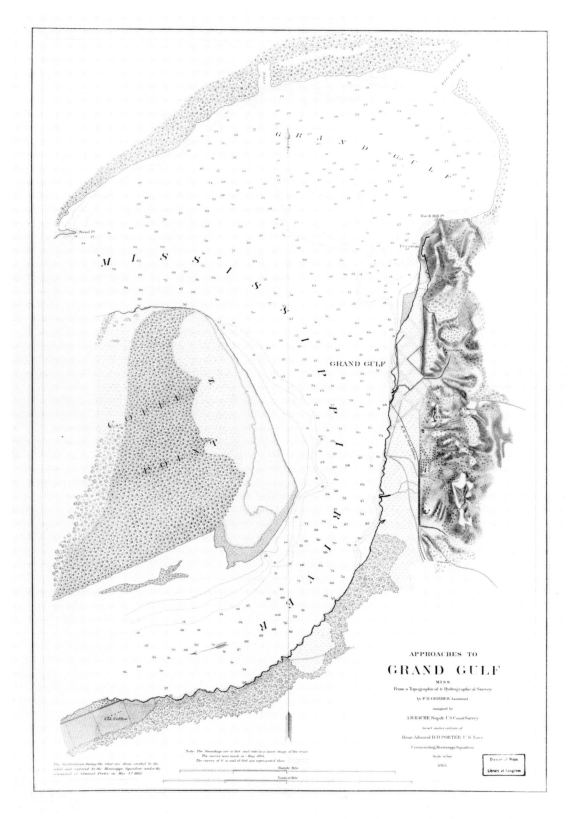

F. H. Gerdes's published chart of the "Approaches to Grand Gulf" reveals that the U.S. Coast Survey preferred hachures over con-

tours to depict the topography of the area. The annotated photocopy of a preliminary version of the Grand Gulf chart, probably used by

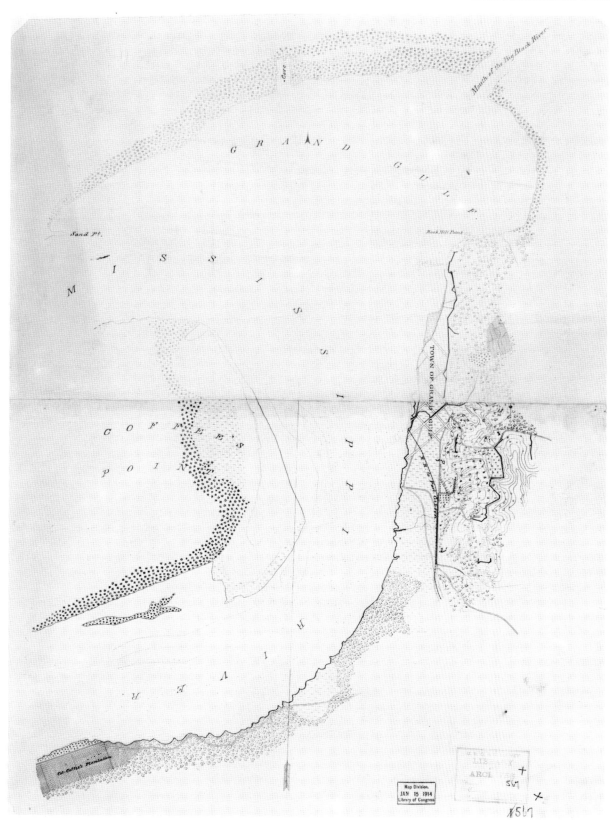

Gerdes in the field, however, shows that he elected to indicate relief by contour lines rather than by hachures. After the war, contour lines became the standard method employed to accurately record topographic details. (See entry nos. 270–271.)

276

Cockrell, Monroe F.

The siege of Vicksburg, May 18, 1862 to July 4, 1863. Prepared by Monroe F. Cockrell. Drawn by Emery L. Ring, January 19, 1949. Blue line print. Scale 1:633,600. 78 × 55 cm.

    G3984 .V8S5 1949 .C6

    "Outline from O.R. plates 154–5."

Map of the Mississippi River and vicinity from Memphis, Tennessee to Fort Adams, Mississippi, showing towns, dates of engagements, drainage, roads, and railroads.

Insets: Vicksburg, Miss. [and vicinity]. 1863. Scale 1:48,274. 22 × 17 cm.—Fort De Russy [La.]. 10 × 16 cm.—[View of the] Confederate States ram "Arkansas". 11 × 19 cm.

Contains a list of ten sieges of Vicksburg giving the names of the commanders, the approach or method used, and the inclusive dates of each. Another list gives the distances between strategic towns by river, railroad, and road.

Another copy is in *Notes and Articles by Monroe F. Cockrell for His Maps of the War Between the States.* ©1950. Typescript.

277

Davis, Z. M.

Map of the Vicksburg National Military Park and vicinity. Compiled from topographical map prepared under the direction of the Secretary of War for the Vicksburg National Park Commission. [©1927] Uncolored. Scale ca. 1:40,000 (not "1:10,000"). 28 × 20 cm. *From* History of the siege of Vicksburg and map of the Vicksburg National Military Park. Vicksburg, Z. M. Davis [©Mar 14, 1927] 32 p. 19 × 11 cm.

Indicates headquarters, camps, hospitals, earthworks, batteries, names of commanders, roads, street pattern of Vicksburg, railroads, and drainage.

278

Fendall, C.

Approaches to Vicksburg and Rebel defences. From a reconnaissance by C. Fendall, Sub. Assist., under the direction of F. H. Gerdes, Assist., assigned by A. D. Bache, Supdt., U.S. Coast Survey, to act under orders of Rear Admiral D. D. Porter, U.S. Navy, commanding Mississippi Squadron. 1863. Uncolored. Scale 1:20,000. 58 × 39 cm.

Indicates fortifications, names and positions of boats, roads, streets, railroads, canal across De Soto Point, houses, vegetation, drainage, and relief by hachures.

279

Fendall, C., *and* A. Strausz.

[Environs of Vicksburg, Mississippi. 1863.] Uncolored. Various scales. 4 maps on sheet 84 × 54 cm.

[a] Haines' Bluff, Miss., showing the positions of the attacking gunboats, April 30th–May 1st 1863. Sketched by C. Fendall, Sub. Asst., U.S.C.S., under direction of Rear Admiral D. D. Porter, U.S.N. Autogr. by A. Hausmann. Scale 1:40,000. 27 × 15 cm.

[b] Yazoo River defences at Walnut Hills near Vicksburg, Miss. Occupied by the U.S. Naval forces, May 20, 1863. Surveyed for Rear Admiral D. D. Porter, commanding Mississippi flotilla, by Sub Asst. C. Fendall, U.S. Coast Survey. Autogr. by A. Hausmann. Scale ca. 1:20,500. 30 × 27 cm.

[c] Vicksburg and vicinity. Surveyed by C. Fendall & A. Strausz under the direction of Rear Admiral D. D. Porter, U.S. Navy. 1863. Scale ca. 1:41,000. 34 × 15 cm.

[d] Survey of a canal connecting Walnut Bayou with the Mississippi River. Dug by the U.S. forces under Genl. Grant in April 1863. Surveyed by C. Fendall & A. Strausz. Scale ca. 1:10,100. 25 × 45 cm.

For another copy from the papers of Joseph R. Hawley, Manuscript Division, L.C., see G3984 .V8S5 1863 .U5.

280

Hardee, T. S.

The siege of Vicksburg, its approaches by Yazoo Pass and other routes. T. S. Hardee, del. W. R. Robertson, Mobile, Ala., lith. Mobile, S. H. Goetzel & Co., May 1st, 1863. Uncolored. Scale not given. 46 × 31 cm.

"Entered according to the Act of Congress, in the year 1863, by S. H. Goetzel & Co., in the Clerk's Office of the District Court of Alabama, for the Confederate States of America."

Gives towns, Fort Pemberton, railroads, drainage, and the location of "Gen. Grant's Army 75000" opposite Vicksburg. Brief notes describe the "land lying between the Mississippi and Yazoo rivers" and the first and second "inland expedition[s] of the enemy."

281

Logan, James H.

Approaches to Vicksburg, Miss. & Rebel defences. Traced by James H. Logan, Oct. 14, 1863. Colored ms. Scale not given. 128 × 92 cm.

    G3984 .V8S5 1863 .L6 Vault

    "No: 103. Recd. & regd. Nov. 6, 1863."

Detailed pen and ink drawing on tracing cloth, showing fortifications, roads, street names, railroads, houses, fences, drainage, vegetation, and contour lines.

Map title is written in each corner on the verso.

281.5

McClernand, John A.

[Pen and ink sketch of the environs of Vicksburg, Mississippi. February 14, 1863] Uncolored ms. Scale not given. 32 × 20 cm.

In the Abraham Lincoln papers, Manuscript Division, L.C., vol. 102, no. 21731.

General map accompanying McClernand's report dated February 14, 1863, "On the Situation before Vicksburg" (Lincoln papers, vol. 102, no. 21727–21730). In the final paragraph of his report McClernand notes that "Herewith you will find a hasty sketch which will, in some degree, illustrate the foregoing views."

282

See Sherman map collection no. 119.

282.2

Nicholson, Dorothy A.

Grant's campaign for Vicksburg, March 29, 1863–May 19, 1863. Cartography by Dorothy A. Nicholson, N.G.S. Staff. Historical documentation by Edwin C. Bearss, National Park Service Regional Research Historian at Vicksburg. [Signed by] Dick Loomis. Colored view. Not drawn to scale. 26 × 35 cm. *From* National geographic. Washington, v. 124, July 1963. p. 44–45.

Perspective drawing of the environs of Vicksburg showing movements of the Union and Confederate armies.

282.3

—————[Vicksburg and vicinity] May 19 to July 4, 1863. Map by Dorothy A. Nicholson. Historical documentation by Edwin C. Bearss. Colored. Scale ca. 1:48,000. 26 × 17 cm. *From* National geographic. Washington, v. 124, July 1963. p. 47.

Map of Vicksburg and vicinity showing streets and roads, railroads, Union and Confederate entrenchments, and direction of "Union attack of May 22."

"Confederate officers are named in italic type; Union leaders in roman."

282.35

Owner, William.

[Map of Vicksburg and vicinity. 1863] Uncolored ms. Scale not given. 19 × 14 cm. *In his* Diary, v. 4, tipped-in at end of volume.

In the William Owner papers, Manuscript Division, L.C., container no. 1.

General map centered on Vicksburg showing towns, roads, and railroads.

Volume 4 of the diary covers from February 13 to June 27, 1863.

282.42

—————[Map of Vicksburg showing fortifications.

1863] Uncolored ms. Scale ca. 1:160,000. 19 × 15 cm. *In his* Diary, v. 4, tipped-in at end of volume.

In the William Owner papers, Manuscript Division, L.C., container no. 1.

Volume 4 of the diary covers from February 13 to June 27, 1863.

282.44

—————Vicksburg & vicinity. [1863] Uncolored ms. Scale ca. 1:103,000. 30 × 19 cm. *In his* Diary, v. 5, pasted inside rear cover.

In the William Owner papers, Manuscript Division, L.C., container no. 1.

Map shows fortifications, place names, roads, railroad, and rivers.

Volume 5 of the diary covers from June 29 to November 16, 1863.

282.5

Poole Brothers.

The Vicksburg National Military Park and vicinity showing lines of siege and defense of the city. National cemetery in background. Chicago, Poole Bros., ©1925. Colored view. 20 × 42 cm.

Map accompanies pamphlet entitled *Vicksburg for the Tourist,* rev. ed. ([Chicago] Passenger Department, Illinois Central System, 1925) 32 p.

Copyright no. class F 49617, Apr. 11, 1925.

Panoramic map in which "black lines indicate the Union trenches," "red lines indicate the Confederate line of defense," "white lines show the park roads," and "the stars mark general headquarters."

283

Robertson, H. C.

Fall of Vicksburg. [May 1–July 4, 1863. Chicago, R. O. Evans and Co. ©1898] Colored. Scale not given. 84 × 59 cm. (Robertson's geographic-historical series illustrating the history of America and the United States)

Wall map of the environs of Vicksburg showing the location and dates of engagements. Includes an outline of events; portrait of General Grant; and views of "The surrender at Appomatox," "Grant's army crossing the James River," "Winter camp at headquarters, City Point," "Grant's headquarters in the Wilderness," "Capture of Lookout Mountain near Chattanooga," "Farragut entering Mobile Bay," "Turn, boys, turn, we're going back," and "Lee leaving Appomattox."

283.2

Sholl, Charles.

Vicksburg and its defences. Constructed and engraved

to illustrate "The war with the South." [Compiled by Charles Sholl] Engd. by W. Kemble. ©1863. Colored. Scale ca. 1:72,500. 25 × 17 cm. *From* Tomes, Robert. The war with the South. New York, Virtue & Yorston, 1862–1867. v. 2, between p. 566 and 567.

Signed (facsim.): Charles Sholl, Topl. Engineer.

"Entered according to act of Congress AD. 1863 by Virtue, Yorston & Co."

Caption in lower margin: A topographical map of Vicksburg & its vicinity showing all batteries that were in existence at the time of its fall, with the names of the owners of plantations, &c.

283.3

————————Another edition. ©1877.

"Constructed and engraved to illustrate 'The war with the South'" has been dropped from from the map's title, and the facsimile of Charles Sholl's signature has been eliminated.

284

See Sherman map coll. no. 120.

285

Spangenberg, Charles.

Map of the siege of Vicksburg, Miss. by the U.S. forces under the command of Maj. Genl. U.S. Grant, U.S. Vls. Maj. F. E. Prime, Chief Engr. Surveyed and constructed under direction of Capt. C. B. Comstock, U.S. Engrs. and Lt. Col. Js. H. Wilson, A. I. Genl., 1st Lt. Engrs., by Major Otto H. Matz, Ills. Vols., Chs. Spangenberg, Asst. Engr., Lts. Patton, Karnasch & Helmle, Mo. Vols., L. Zwanziger, S. R. Tresilian, B. Barth, S. Hartwell, Asst. Engs. Drawn by Chs. Spangenberg, Asst. Engr. Engr. on stone by J. Schedler, N.Y. Vicksburg, Miss., Head Qrs. of the Dept. of the Tenn., Aug. 20th, 1863. Colored. Scale ca. 1:17,000 (not "1:15,840"). 74 × 70 cm.

Signed (facsim.): C. B. Comstock, Capt. of Engrs.

Detailed map showing entrenchments, roads, streets, railroads, hachures, vegetation, houses, and drainage.

Contains five topographic profiles, six cross sections of artillery batteries, and one cross section of a "rebel rifle pit."

For another issue, see Sherman map coll. no. 120.

285.1

————————Map of the siege of Vicksburg, Miss. Vicksburg, Miss., Aug. 20th 1863. C. B. Comstock, Capt. of Engrs. [Jackson, Mississippi State Geological Survey, 1935] Uncolored. Scale ca. 1:29,250. Map 42 × 29 cm. on sheet 43 × 45 cm.

Accompanies William Clifford Morse's *The Geologic History of the Vicksburg National Military Park Area* ([Jackson] Mississippi State Geological Survey, 1935), frontispiece.

"Reproduced with only minor changes from a 'Map of the siege of Vicksburg, Miss.' bearing the date of August 20, 1863, and the signature of C. B. Comstock, Captain of Engineers."

Printed in brown ink.

Title page of text inscribed: with the compliments of W. C. Morse.

286

Tomlinson, George W.

Tomlinson's map of Vicksburg, showing all of the surrounding fortifications, batteries, principal plantations, &c. J. Mayer & Co., lith., Boston. ©1863. Uncolored. Scale ca. 1:65,000. 56 × 40 cm.

At top of map: New map of Vicksburg, showing the scene of Gen. Grants operations, together with all of the fortifications, batteries, rifle pits &c.

Text to right of map: Sketch of Vicksburg and the surrounding batteries.

Map is printed in green ink and extends from Haines Bluff south to Port Gibson.

287

U.S. *Coast Survey.*

Map illustrating the operations of the U.S. forces against Vicksburg. J. W. Maedel. [1863] Colored. Scale ca. 1:390,000. 44 × 41 cm.

"Indicates "Genl. Grant's track," "Union forces surrounding Vicksburg," and "track of Genl. Blair." Roads, railroads, drainage, and towns are shown. "Union victories" are noted by colored U.S. flags.

288

————————Another issue.

Later issue of the preceding map with the addition of "Adml. Porters track" and Union victories at Yazoo City, Milliken's Bend, Haines Bluff, Warrenton and Grand Gulf.

289

————————Another issue.

Later issue of the preceding map (entry no. 288) with the addition of a U.S. flag at Vicksburg denoting a Union victory.

289.5

————————Another issue.

G3984 .V8S5 1863 .U51

Later issue of the preceding map (entry no. 289). The name "Hard Times" opposite Grand Gulf has been substituted for "Coffee Point" which appears on earlier editions. Also "Genl. Grant's track" from Grand Gulf has been re-

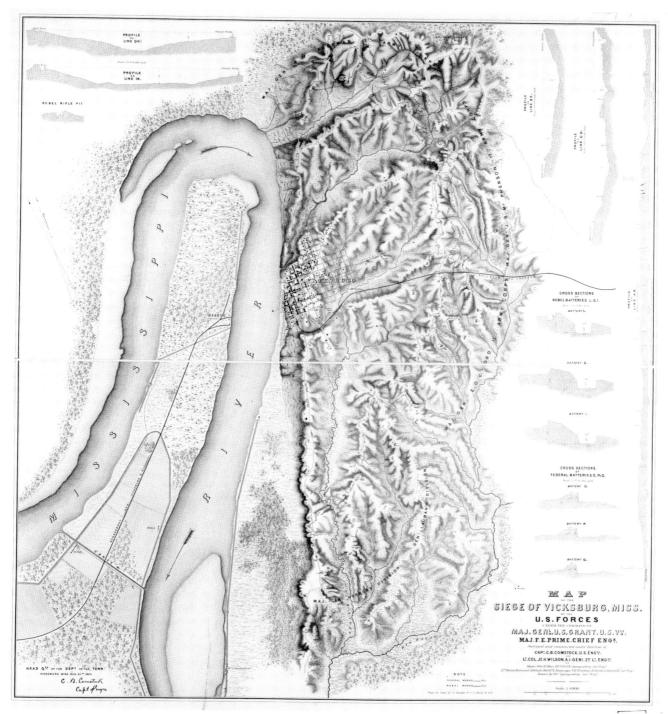

Detailed map of the siege of Vicksburg, Mississippi, published at Headquarters, Department of the Tennessee, Vicksburg, on August 20, 1863. After a siege of 47 days, Confederate Gen. John C. Pemberton surrendered on July 4, 1863, to Union forces under command of Gen. Ulysses S. Grant. (See entry no. 285.)

positioned to follow "L. St. Joseph," "Princess L.," "Bayou Vidal," "Roundaway B.," "Brushy B.," "Canal B.," "Cypress L." to Milliken's Bend.

From the papers of Joseph R. Hawley, Manuscript Division, L.C.

290

————Another edition. Chas. G. Krebs, lith.

Similar in content to the preceding map (entry no. 289.5) but redrawn and lithographed by Chas. G. Krebs. Krebs's name appears in the lower left corner in place of J. W. Maedel.

290.5

U.S. *Geological Survey.*

Vicksburg National Military Park, Miss. Albert Pike, Division Engineer. Topography by Frank Larner, H. G. Warner, and J. G. Harrison. Control by U.S. Geological Survey. Surveyed in 1935. [Washington] U.S. Geological Survey [1935] Colored. Scale 1:9600. 116 × 84 cm.

Detailed topographic map. Contour interval 10 feet. "Advance sheet. Subject to correction."

Includes a detailed list of monuments, markers, batteries, and approaches keyed by number to the map.

291

U.S. *National Park Service.*

Vicksburg National Military Park and Vicksburg National Cemetery. Reprint 1952. Uncolored. Scale ca. 1:62,000. 20 × 14 cm.

Illustrates a descriptive leaflet by the U.S. National Park Service entitled "Vicksburg National Military Park, Mississippi."

Map indicates Union and Confederate lines, "significant structures" in the park, a park tour, roads, and railroads.

291.1

—————Reprint 1958.

291.2

—————Another issue [196–] Uncolored. Scale ca. 1:45,000. 26 × 18 cm.

Enlarged issue of the map only.

291.4

—————Vicksburg National Military Park, Mississippi, [Washington] Government Printing Office, 1963.

Descriptive leaflet illustrated with the following two maps:

[a] Vicksburg National Military Park, Mississippi. Colored. Scale ca. 1:14,400. 11 × 22 cm. (Shows names of commanders roads, railroad, and tour route.)

[b] The Vicksburg campaign. Aug. 1962. Colored. Scale ca. 1:2,350,000. 40 × 23 cm. (Map of the Mississippi River from Memphis to the Gulf of Mexico showing drainage, railroads, and towns.)

291.6

—————Vicksburg National Military Park, Mississippi.

Revised April 1969. [Washington, Government Printing Office, 1969.] Colored. Scale ca. 1:34,000. Map 27 × 14 cm. on sheet 29 × 33 cm.

G3984 .V8:2V5 1969 .U5

Map illustrates descriptive leaflet. Depicted are 15 tour sites and a tour route.

291.7

—————Another issue. Revised 1973. Colored. Scale ca. 1:28,000. Map 29 × 17 cm. on sheet 29 × 41 cm.

G3984 .V8:2V5 1973 .U5

291.8

—————Another issue. Reprint 1978.

G3984 .V8:2V5 1978 .U5

291.9

U.S. *Navy.*

Vicksburg and vicinity. [1863] Uncolored. Scale ca. 1:58,000. 21 × 12 cm. *From* Report of the Secretary of the Navy, with an appendix, containing reports from officers. December, 1863. (Washington, Government Printing Office, 1863). opp. p. 430.

Map shows forts, railroads, levees, roads, and the positions of the "Ram Queen of the West" and the "Steamer Vicksburg."

292

Vicksburg National Park Commission.

Vicksburg National Military Park. Topographical survey. 1902. Blue print. Scale 1:2500. 76 × 104 cm.

"Sheet 4"

Large-scale topographic map showing contour lines, drainage, and fortifications in the vicinity of the Alabama and Vicksburg R.R. at Two Mile Bridge.

293

Wood, Walter B., *and* J. E. Edmonds.

Vicksburg. [1863. London] Methuen & Co. [1905] Uncolored. Scale ca. 1:950,000. 12 × 15 cm.

"Map XI."

Prepared to accompany W. B. Wood and J. E. Edmonds. *A History of the Civil War in the United States, 1861–5.* (London, Methuen & Co. [1905]).

Map of the environs of Vicksburg showing Union and Confederate lines and the location of engagements.

294

Wrotnowski, L. A.

View of Vicksburg and plan of the canal, fortifications & vicinity. Surveyed by Lieut. L. A. Wrotnowski, Top: Engr.

Drawn & lithogd. by A. F. Wrotnowski C.E. 1863. Colored. Scale 1:63,360. 40 × 54 cm.

Indicates fortifications, location, type and names of boats, roads, railroads, levees, drainage, vegetation, and the names of a few residents.

Inset: [View of Vicksburg] 17 × 54 cm.

Inscribed in the lower right hand corner "Major David C. Houston, Chief Engineer, 19th Army Corps, with the compliments from the author."

YAZOO RIVER

295

Strausz, A.

Route of the late expedtion [sic] commanded by Act'g. Rear Admiral D. D. Porter U.S.N. attempting to get into the Yazoo River by the way of Steels Bayou and Deer Creek. Compiled & drawn by A. Strausz, U.S. Coast Survey. [Washington] U.S. Coast Survey, April 1863. Uncolored. Scale ca. 1:215,000. 42 × 44 cm.

"The shaded bayou shows the route actually travelled by the gun boats. The dotted line shows the remaining proposed route."

Indicates the location of bridges, Indian mounds, and names of residents along Deer Creek.

295.2

U.S. *Navy*

Map showing the route of the late expedition, commanded by Rear Admiral Porter, U.S.N., in attempting to get into the Yazoo River by the way of Steel's Bluff [i.e., Bayou] and Deer Creek. [April 1863] Uncolored. Scale ca. 1:500,000. 17 × 25 cm. *From* Report of the Secretary of the Navy, with an appendix, containing reports from officers. December, 1863 (Washington, Government Printing Office, 1863). opp. p. 455.

Inset: Plan showing the place from which Gunboats first commenced to fall back, to open communications behind them, which had been obstructed. Scale ca. 1:36,000. 10 × 7 cm.

Map is similar in content to the map drawn by A. Strausz, U.S. Coast Survey (entry no. 295).

MISSOURI

296

Konig, A.

Battle grounds in Missouri during Price's raid in the fall 1864. Surveyed & published by A. Konig, 2d Colorado Cavy. J. C. Wood, St. Louis. Entered according to Act of Congress in the year 1865 by A. Konig. Uncolored. Scales not given. 4 maps on one sheet, each measuring approximately 13 × 10 cm. Over-all size 30 × 26 cm.

Maps of the battlefields at "Mine Creek, Oct. 22d 64," "Westport, Oct. 23d 64," "Charlot, Oct. 25th 64," and "Newtonia, Nov. 4th 64," showing the positions of troops, roads, drainage, a few houses, and relief by hachures.

296.2

Lloyd, James T.

Lloyd's official map of Missouri. Drawn and engraved from actual surveys for the Land Office Department. New York, Louisville, [and] London, J. T. Lloyd, 1861. Colored. Scale 1:760,320. 60 × 68 cm.

"Entered, according to Act of Congress, in the year 1861 by J. T. Lloyd."

General map of the state indicating county names and boundaries, cities and towns, railroads in operation and projected, roads, and rivers.

Includes advertisements for "$100,000 topographical map of the State of Virginia" and "Lloyd's great military map of the fifteen southern states."

296.3

————Another issue.

Advertisements have been reset and "Agents wanted in every county" has been added below an advertisement for a Virginia map.

296.5

Manouvrier, J.

Map of the present seat of war in Missouri. Published by J. Manouvrier 30, Camp St. N.O. [1862] Uncolored. Scale 1:316,800. Map 26 × 21 cm. on sheet 29 × 48 cm.

Confederate imprint.

Map of parts of Illinois, Missouri, and Kentucky in the environs of Cairo and New Madrid, showing roads, railroads, towns, troop positions at New Madrid, drainage, and fortifications at Cairo, Illinois, and Birds Point, Missouri.

The following handwritten note appears to the left of the map: Dear Mr. Phillips: I send you some interesting maps. Two of local origins and probably scarce. This one must I suppose have been intended for correspondence. Yours truly William Beer.

296.7
Wood, Walter B., *and* **J. E. Edmonds.**

Missouri. [London] Methuen & Co. [1905] Uncolored Scale ca. 1:3,880,000, 12 × 15 cm.

"Map IX."

Prepared to accompany W. B. Wood and J. E. Edmonds's *A History of the Civil War in the United States, 1861–5* (London, Methuen & Co. [1905]).

Map indicates battle sites.

BELMONT

297
U.S. *Army. Corps of Engineers.*

Map of the battlefield near Belmont, Missouri. United States forces commanded by Brig. Gen. U. S. Grant. Nov. 7th 1861. Published by authority of the Hon. the Secretary of War. Office of the Chief of Engineers, U.S. Army, 1876. Colored. Scale not given. 42 × 52 cm.

Detailed map showing Confederate camp and batteries near Columbus, Kentucky, "Camp and battery of secessionists" near Belmont, Missouri, Union troop positions and movements during battle, location and names of Union gunboats, roads, vegetation, fences, and relief by hachures.

ISLAND NO. 10

298
Bissell, J. W.

Map of the Mississippi at Island no. 10. Showing (corrected) line of the channel cut by the Engineer Regiment. [1862] Uncolored. Scale ca. 1:325,000. 7 × 7 cm. *From* Century illustrated monthly magazine, v. 30, June 1885. p. 324.

Fortifications, Confederate batteries, mortar and gun boats, and vegetation are shown.

299
Cullum, George W.

Map showing the Rebel batteries at Island no. 10 & vicinity for the defence of the Mississippi River, captured by U.S. forces, April 7th 1862. Surveyed under the direction of Brig. Genl. Geo. W. Cullum, Chief of Staff & Engineers, Dept. of the Mississippi. Lith. of J. Bien, N.Y. Uncolored. Scale 1:12,000. 32 × 46 cm.

The number and type of guns in the "batteries on Kentucky shore" and in the "batteries on Island no. 10" are included in the legend.

299.8
Hoelcke, William.

Map showing the system of rebel fortifications on the Mississippi River at Island no. 10 and New Madrid, also the operations of the U.S. forces under General John Pope against these positions. [1862. Compiled by] Captn. Wm. Hoelcke, Addl. A. de C., U.S.A. Bowen & Co. lith. Phila. Uncolored. Scale 1:84,480 ("¾ of an inch = one mile"). 51 × 44 cm. *From* U.S. Congress. Joint Committee on the Conduct of the War. Supplemental report of the Joint Committee on the Conduct of the War, in two volumes. Supplemental to Senate report no. 142, 38th Congress, 2d session (Washington, Government Printing Office, 1866). v. 2, fol. p. 56.

Accompanies "Report of Major General John Pope, to the hon. Committee on the Conduct of the War." 217 p.

"No. 1" is in the upper right margin.

Shows Union troop positions, Confederate camp, batteries, location and type of Union boats, houses and names of residents, roads, towns, drainage, and vegetation.

300
————Map showing the system of Confederate fortifications on the Mississippi River at Island no. 10 and New Madrid, also the operations of the United States forces under General John Pope against these positions. [1862] Published by authority of the Hon. the Secretary of War. Office of the chief of Engineers, U.S. Army. [Compiled by] Captn. Wm. Hoelcke, Addl. A. de C., U.S.A. Colored. Scale 1:84,480. 51 × 44 cm.

In lower left margin: Report of Maj. Gen. John Pope to the Committee on the Conduct of War.

"No. 1" is in the upper right margin.

Similar to the preceding map, but the title has been revised.

301
————Another issue. Bowen & Co. lith., Phila.

Lacks "No. 1" in the upper right margin.

LEXINGTON

302
Wilson, J. A.

Battle field of Lexington, Mo., showing plan of earthwork defended by Federal and State troops under command of Col. James A. Mulligan, U.S.A. during the 18th, 19th and 20th Sept. 1861. Surrendered to Genl. Sterling Price,

C.S.A., Sept. 20th 1861. Drawn by Capt. J. A. Wilson for the Court of Inquiry, held by Gen. McNulta in 187–. Copied by Cadet J. B. Raymond, W.M.A. for the Lexington Historical Society. Uncolored. Scale 1:2400. 24 × 18 cm.

"Compliments of Henry C. Chiles."

Shows fortifications, troop positions, vegetation, drainage, streets, and relief by hachures and spot heights. Important sites are listed in the legend and keyed to the map by letters.

303

This entry was found not to be a Civil War map, and therefore it has been removed from this edition.

ST. LOUIS

304

U.S. *Army. Corps of Engineers.*

[Original plattings of forts at St. Louis, Mo. 186–] 29 ms. maps (mostly colored). Various scales and sizes.

G4164.S4S5 186– .U5 Vault

"145.D"

"Engr. Dept., July 18/64. Recd. with Gen. Cullum's letter of the 16th inst. (C. 5621)."

Some of the maps are signed "Franz Kappner, Major, Engr. Corps" and "F. Hassendeubel, Col. com. Engineer Corps."

Detailed series of pen and ink drawings of the forts defending St. Louis.

[1] Original plattings of forts at St. Louis, Mo. Scale not given. 32 × 57 cm. (Sketch map drawn on tracing cloth, showing location of forts and some streets. Forts are drawn in red ink and numbered 1 to 10.)

[2] Plan of Fort no. 1. Scale 1:192. 64 × 53 cm.

[3] Plan of fort no. 1. Scale 1:192. 60 × 56 cm.

[4] Plan of Fort no. I, St. Louis, Mo. Scale 1:120. 105 × 122 cm.

[5] Plan of Fort no. 2. Scale 1:192. 53 × 94 cm.

[6] [Plan of Fort no. 2] Scale ca. 1:192. 53 × 78 cm.

[7] Plan of Fort no. 2, St. Louis, Mo. [Drawn by] Otto H. Matz. Scale 1:120. 100 × 90 cm.

[8] Plan of the fort no. 2. Scale 1:192. 64 × 59 cm.

[9] Plan of Fort no. III, St. Louis, Mo. [Drawn by] Chs. Lambecker. Scale 1:120. 85 × 128 cm.

[10] Plan of Fort no. 3 & 4. Scale ca. 1:232. 39 × 72 cm.

[11] Plan of the forts no. 3 and 4. Scale ca. 1:232. 57 × 78 cm.

[12] Plan of Fort no. 4, St. Louis, Mo. Scale 1:120. 83 × 127 cm.

[13] Plan of Fort no. 5. Scale 1:192. 53 × 72 cm.

[14] Plan of Fort no. 5. Scale 1:192. 53 × 72 cm.

[15] Plan of Fort no. 5, St. Louis, Mo. [Drawn by] Bruno Drohuck. Scale 1:120. 132 × 89 cm.

[16] Plan of Fort no. 6. Scale 1:240. 40 × 62 cm.

[17] Plan of Fort no. VI, St. Louis, Mo. [Drawn by] Chas. Lambecker. Scale 1:120. 78 × 114 cm.

[18] Plan of Fort no. 6 & 7. Scale 1:240. 56 × 75 cm.

[19] Plan of Fort no. 6 & 7. Scale ca. 1:240. 56 × 60 cm.

[20] Plan of Fort no. 6 & 7. Scale 1:240. 39 × 67 cm.

[21] Plan of Fort no. 8. Scale 1:240. 39 × 53 cm.

[22] Plan of Fort no. VIII, St. Louis, Mo. [Drawn by] Chs. Lambecker. Scale 1:120. 82 × 104 cm.

[23] Plan of Fort no. 8 & 9. Scale ca. 1:240. 57 × 64 cm.

[24] Plan of Fort no. 9. Scale 1:240. 57 × 81 cm.

[25] Plan of Fort no. 9. Scale 1:240. 58 × 53 cm.

[26] Plan of Fort no. IX, St. Louis, Mo. Scale 1:120. 89 × 132 cm.

[27] Plan of Fort no. 10. Scale 1:192. 58 × 63 cm.

[28] Plan of Fort no. 10. Scale 1:192. 54 × 68 cm.

[29] [Plan of unidentified fort]. Scale not given. 79 × 91 cm.

WILSON'S CREEK

304.1

Boardman, N.

Map of the battle field of Wilsons Creek. [Aug. 10, 1861] Surveyed and drawn by (sgd:) N. Boardman, Capt. Batty "M", 2nd Mo. Lt. Arty. Office Chief Engineer, Division of the Missouri. Tracing made Feb'y 6th 1885. Colored ms. on tracing linen. Scale not given. 66 × 42 cm.

In the John M. Schofield papers, Manuscript Division, L.C., container no. 96.

Detailed map of the battlefield showing Union positions in blue, Confederate positions in red, camps, roads, woodland, field patterns, drainage, and relief by hachures.

NEW MEXICO

304.2

Stedman, Wilfred.

Historic battlefields in New Mexico. [Santa Fe, New Mexico] Tourist Division, Department of Development

[1961] Colored. Scale ca. 1:2,150,000. 43 × 30 cm.

Pictorial map showing "the location of Civil War battles and skirmishes, and also other historic battle sites dating back to the first conquest by white men."

NORTH CAROLINA

304.5

Bachmann, John.

Birds eye view of North and South Carolina and part of Georgia. [New York, John Bachmann, ©1861] Colored view. 56 × 71 cm.

At top of map: Panorama of the seat of war.

View of the coast from Currituck Sound, North Carolina, to Savannah, Georgia, indicating towns, roads, railroads, and rivers. The shelling of Fort Hatteras is shown.

Includes a table of distances from Cape Hatteras.

304.55

——————Reduced facsimile. Uncolored. 47 × 58 cm.

From William P. Cumming's *North Carolina in Maps* (Raleigh, State Department of Archives and History, 1966), plate XII.

Printed in brown ink.

This facsimile was produced from the previously described copy (entry no. 304.5).

304.6

——————Another issue.

G3901 .A35 1861 .B3

"Drawn from nature and lith. by John Bachmann" appears in the bottom left margin and the publisher's address, "John Bachmann, Publisher, 115 & 117 Nassau St., New York" is printed below the map title.

304.66

Campbell, Albert H.

Map of a part of eastern North Carolina from a map in progress. Compiled from surveys & reconnaissances made under the direction of Capt. A. H. Campbell in chg., Top. Dep., D.N.V. 1864. Photocopy (positive). Scale 1:160,000. 94 × 77 cm. mounted on cloth to fold to 16 × 13 cm.

G3900 1864 .C3 Vault

At head of title: Chief Engineers Office D.N.V., Maj. Gen. J. F. Gilmer, Chief Engineer.

Endorsed (facsim.): Approved Aug. 11th 1864, Albert H. Campbell, Capt. P. Engrs in chg. Top. Dep., D.N.[V.]

Detailed Confederate map extending from the Virginia border south to the Neuse River and the Chowan River west to Wilson and Goldsboro and showing roads, railroads, towns and villages, woodland, rivers and streams, and houses and names of residents. Principal rivers are colored blue, and major roads are red.

Inscribed in ink on verso: Map of the vicinity of Weldon, Goldsboro &c North Carolina. Wm. A. Obenchain, Capt., C. S. Engineers, 1864.

304.7

Colton, Joseph H.

Colton's new topographical map of the eastern portion of the State of North Carolina with part of Virginia & South Carolina from the latest & best authorities. New York, J. H. Colton, 1861. Uncolored. Scale ca. 1:506,880. 102 × 72 cm.

Printed by Lang & Laing, N.Y.

"Entered according to Act of Congress in the year 1855 by J. H. Colton & Co." printed inside bottom neat line.

Copyright no. 411, Sept. 10, 1861, is written in ink in the lower margin.

"No. 11" is printed in the upper left corner.

General map. Coastal forts and naval blockade are depicted.

Inset: Plan of the sea coast from Virginia to Florida. 13 × 65 cm.

Newspaper clipping describing coastal fortifications is pasted to the map in the left margin.

304.75

——————Another issue. Colored.

Copyright statement inside the bottom neat line has been changed to read "Entered according to Act of Congress in the year 1861 by J. H. Colton [& Co.]"

Bar scale has been added to this and subsequent issues.

304.8

——————Another issue. Colored.

Pasted to the right of the map is a notice that the map was "Sold by J. Disturnell, Washington, D.C and 240 Broadway, New York." Otherwise, the map is similar to the preceding issue.

304.85

——————Another issue. 1863. Uncolored.

Copyright statement inside the bottom neat line has been changed to read "Entered according to Act of Congress in the year 1860 by J. H. Colton."

A second copy of this map is classed G3900 1863 .C6.

For an 1864 edition, see Sherman map coll. no. 122.

305

See Sherman map collection no. 122.

305a

Johnson, Betsy.

Map of North Carolina, 1861–1865. September, 1960. Uncolored. Scale ca. 1:1,400,000. 23 × 60 cm.

"This map locates the principal forts, towns, railroads, and engagements fought in the State during the Civil War."

305a.1

——————Another issue. [Oct. 1962]

In the lower left corner: 5M–10–62.

305a.2

Lindenkohl, Adolph.

Coast of North Carolina & Virginia, compiled at the Coast Survey Office, Febr. 1862. Drawn by A. Lindenkohl. Lith. by H. Lindenkohl. [Washington, D.C., U.S. Coast Survey, 1862] Uncolored. Scale 1:200,000. 124 × 84 cm.

At head of title: U.S. Coast Survey, A. D. Bache, Supt.

Map is printed in two sheets which have been joined together to form a continuous map. The northern sheet measures 57 × 84 cm., and the southern sheet measures 68 × 84 cm.

Map of the coast from Hampton, Virginia, to Old Cedar Inlet, North Carolina, showing roads, railroads, rivers and streams, and place names. Soundings are not given.

Northwestern corner of the northern sheet is blank.

305a.3

——————Another edition.

Northern sheet has been thoroughly revised. Many place names, roads, and railroads have been added or repositioned. The northwestern corner of the northern sheet has been completed.

305a.4

——————North Carolina & South Carolina. Drawn by A. Lindenkohl. Chas. G. Krebs, lith. U.S. Coast Survey, A. D. Bache, Supdt. 1865. Colored. Scale 1:633,600. 64 × 90 cm.

General map.

"Authorities" used in making the map are listed below the title.

State names, boundaries, and railroads are overprinted in red.

Another copy is in the Fillmore map coll. no. 258.

305a.5

——————[North Carolina. Drawn by A. Lindenkohl] H. Lindenkohl & Chas. G. Krebs, lith. U.S. Coast Survey, A. D. Bache, Supdt. 1865. [Raleigh, State Department of Archives and History, 1966] Uncolored. Scale ca. 1:950,000 (not "1 inch = 10 miles") 41 × 92 cm.

G3900 1865 .U5 1966

Reduced facsimile from William P. Cumming's *North Carolina in Maps* (Raleigh, State Department of Archives and History, 1966), plate XIII.

Printed in brown ink.

This facsimile was produced from a composite map in the State Department of Archives and History, Raleigh, N.C. The composite was made up from Lindenkohl's map of "[Eastern Tennessee, with parts of Alabama, Georgia, South Carolina, North Carolina, Virginia, and Kentucky]" (entry no. 75.8) and his "[North Carolina, with adjacent parts of Virginia and South Carolina]" (entry no. 305a.6).

305a.6

——————[North Carolina, with adjacent parts of Virginia and South Carolina] Drawn by A. Lindenkohl. U.S. Coast Survey, A. D. Bache, Supdt. 1865. Uncolored. Scale 1:633,600. 59 × 85 cm., cut and mounted to fold to 31 × 25 cm.

General map, without a title.

Inset: [Charleston, S.C., and environs] 18 × 23 cm.

Stamped on verso: Gilbert Thompson.

"No. 3 Parts of Virginia, N. Carolina, S. Car. 1865. U.S. Coast Survey. 1″ = 10 ms. 6 sheets" is written in ink on the verso.

Sheet 3 of a 6-sheet series of maps used by Gilbert Thompson during the Civil War. In addition to this sheet, the Geography and Map Division has sheet 1 (see entry no. 508.5), sheet 4 (see entry no. 259.6), sheet 5 (see entry no. 129.3), and sheet 6 (entry no. 129.55).

305a.7

—————Another issue. Colored.

State names and boundaries are printed in red.

305a.75

[Map of central North Carolina covering parts of the counties of Wake, Harnett, Johnston, Wilson, Wayne, Cumberland, Sampson, and Duplin. 1865?] Colored ms. Scale not given 25 × 24 cm.

In the John Alexander Logan family papers, Manuscript Division, L.C., container 145, opp. p. 105.

Pen and ink manuscript map drawn on tracing linen indicating place names, county boundaries, roads, railroads, streams, and mills. Troop positions are not indicated.

305a.8

Prang (Louis) and Company.

North Carolina coast line. Showing every inlet, sound, & bay of special interest, from Fortress Monroe to South Carolina. Boston [1862] Colored. Scale not given. 27 × 16 cm.

At top of map: Burnside's expedition map.

Portrait of "Genl. Burnside" is in the lower right corner.

Map identifies coastal forts.

305a.9

U.S. *Army. Army of the James.*

[Map of eastern North Carolina] Army of the James, Chief Engineer Office in the field. Dec. 4th 1864. Official [signed] Peter S. Michie, 1st Lt. U.S. Engrs., Bvt. Maj. U.S.A. & Act. Chief Engr., Dept. Va. & N.C. Photocopy (positive). Scale ca. 1:750,000. 53 × 50 cm.

In the Benjamin F. Butler papers, Manuscript Division, L.C., container no. 188.

General map showing roads annotated in red, railroads, cities and towns, rivers, and swamps.

306

U.S. *Army. Corps of Engineers.*

Eastern portion of the military department of North Carolina compiled from the best and latest authorities in the Engineer Bureau, War Department, May 1862. Uncolored.

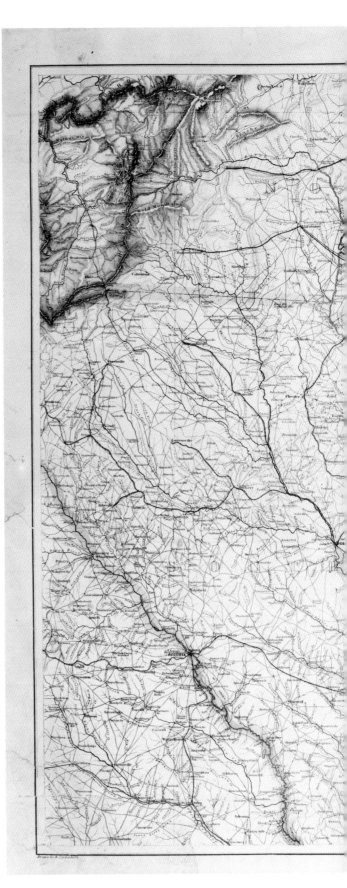

The U.S. Coast Survey's map of North and South Carolina published in 1865. This is one of numerous regional base maps published by the Coast Survey at the scale of 10 miles to an inch. (See entry no. 305a.4.)

NORTH CAROLINA
&
SOUTH CAROLINA.

U.S. Coast Survey A.D. Bache Supdt

1865.

SCALE
1 inch = 10 miles

AUTHORITIES
U.S. Coast Survey Topographical Sheets
Botts Map of Georgia
Mills Atlas of South Carolina
Map of South Carolina, by W.B. Walker & J.Johnson
Map of Charleston & Savannah Rail Road (1860)
The mountains and interior valleys of North Carolina are
provisionally drawn, some furnished by Prof. Arnold Guyot

145

Scale 1:350,000. 2 parts 51 × 74 cm. and 53 × 74 cm. (Fillmore map coll. no. 259)

Signed in ms: Millard Fillmore, March 12, 1865.

"Engraved in the Engineer Bureau, War Dept."

Indicates coastal fortifications, roads, railroads, drainage, canals, swamps, and towns.

Insets: Entrances to Cape Fear River, North Carolina. 29 × 20 cm.—[View of] Rebel works for the defense of the New Inlet entrance to Cape Fear River. 6 × 36 cm.

In this issue, the Corps of Engineers's insignia printed to the left of the map title is framed by a single line, an eagle is on a perch looking to the left, and a banner below the insignia is labeled "Essayons."

306.1

——————Another issue.

In this issue, the Corps of Engineers's insignia printed to the left of the map title is framed by a scroll, an eagle is on a perch looking to the left, and "Essayons" is printed on a banner below the insignia.

306.2

——————Another issue.

In this issue, the Corps of Engineers's insignia printed to the left of the map is framed by a single line and an eagle clutching two arrows in its talons is standing on a banner above the insignia labeled "Essayons."

Endorsed in ms.: Engineer Department, Decr. 24th 1864—For Major Genl. Sherman. Richd. Delafield, Genl. & Chief Engineer, U.S. Army.

306.5

U.S. *Coast Survey.*

Sketch of the coast of North Carolina from Oregon Inlet to Ocracoke Inlet. [Washington, U.S. Coast Survey] 1861. Uncolored. Scale 1:200,000. 51 × 38 cm.

At head of title: U.S. Coast Survey, A. D. Bache. Supdt.

Chart of Cape Hatteras and environs showing soundings, lighthouses, and bottom contours at 6, 12, and 18 feet.

ALBEMARLE SOUND

306.7

U.S. *Navy.*

Diagram showing the position of the Sassacus and ram Albemarle at the time of collision. [May 5, 1864] Uncolored. Scale not given. 12 × 20 cm. *From* Report on the Secretary of the Navy, with an appendix, containing reports from officers. December, 1864 (Washington, Government Printing Office, 1864). opp. p. 121.

Map of part of Albemarle Sound showing the first and second positions of the U.S. Steamer *Sassacus* after its collision with the Confederate ironclad *Albemarle.*

BEAUFORT HARBOR

307

Colton, George Woolworth.

The war in North Carolina. Map of the entrance to Beaufort harbor, N.C. showing the position of Fort Macon, etc. [1861] Uncolored. Scale ca. 1:48,000. 19 × 23 cm.

Shows fortifications, "camp Parke's div.," shoals, islands, and ship channel.

308

U.S. *Coast Survey.*

Beaufort harbor, North Carolina. Re-survey in June and July 1862. Corrected up to April 20th 1864. Chas. G. Krebs, lith. Preliminary edition. [Washington, U.S. Coast Survey, 1864] Uncolored. Scale 1:20,000. 48 × 47 cm. *From its* Report of the Superintendent of the Coast Survey, showing the progress of the survey during the year 1863 (Washington, Government Printing Office, 1864). Map 11.

"No. 11" is in the upper left corner.

At head of title, U.S. Coast Survey, A. D. Bache, Supdt.

BENTONVILLE

309

Battle of Bentonville, March 19, 1865. Colored ms. Scale ca. 1:4410. 3 maps, each 87 × 87 cm.

G3904 .B56S5 1865 .B3 Vault

Maps of the first, second, and third positions of the Union and Confederate forces. Each indicates roads, vegetation, drainage, and hachures. Maps are accompanied by two organization charts which give the names of the commanding officers down to the brigade level. The charts measure 116 × 93 cm. and 141 × 92 cm.

CAPE FEAR

309.2

Nicholson, Somerville.

[Map of the position of the Confederate steamer Antonica when she ran aground on Frying Pan Shoals, December 20, 1863] Uncolored ms. Scale ca. 1:730,000. 27 × 21 cm.

In the Samuel Phillips Lee papers, Manuscript Division, L.C., container no. 35, December 17–26, 1863 folder.

Map is accompanied by a letter of transmittal dated December 26, 1863, from Cdr. Somerville Nicholson to Rear Adm. Samuel P. Lee, commanding the North Atlantic Blockading Squadron.

CAPE LOOKOUT

309.5

U.S. *Coast Survey.*

Reconnoissance [sic] of Cape Lookout shoals by the party under command of Lieut. Comdr. T. S. Phelps, U.S.N. Assist. Coast Survey. Engd. by W. H. Davis. [Washington, U.S. Coast Survey] 1864. Uncolored. Scale 1:80,000. 52 × 44 cm. *From its* Report of the Superintendent of the Coast Survey, showing the progress of the survey during the year 1864 (Washington, Government Printing Office, 1866). Map 25.

"No. 25" is in the upper left corner.

At head of title: U.S. Coast Survey, A. D. Bache, Supdt.

CORE SOUND

309.7

————Core Sound and Straits, North Carolina. [Washington, U.S. Coast Survey] 1864. Uncolored. Scale 1:40,000. 51 × 85 cm. *From its* Report of the Superintendent of the Coast Survey, showing the progress of the survey during the year 1864 (Washington, Government Printing Office, 1866). Map 24.

At head of title: U.S. Coast Survey, A. D. Bache, Supdt.

"No. 24" is in the upper left corner.

FORT ANDERSON

309.9

U.S. *Navy.*

Plan of Fort Anderson, Cape Fear River, N.C. showing the line of attack by the gun-boats February 18th 1865, under Rear Admiral D. D. Porter, when the rebels evacuated under a heavy fire. Three hundred and eighty shells an hour, thirteen hours bombardment. Bowen & Co., lith., Philada. Uncolored. Scale ca. 1:5500. 34 × 33 cm. *From* Message of the President of the United States, and accompanying documents, to the two houses of Congress, at the commencement of the first session of the thirty-ninth Congress.—Report of the Secretary of the Navy (Washington, Government Printing Office, 1865). fol. p. 184.

Printed in the upper left margin: 39th Cong. 1st Sess.—Annual Report of the Secretary of the Navy.

FORT FISHER

310

Comstock, Cyrus B.

Plan and sections of Fort Fisher carried by assault by the U.S. forces, Maj. Gen. A. H. Terry commanding, Jan.

15th, 1865. Engraved in the Engineer Bureau, War Dept. E. Molitor, lith. Uncolored. Scale 1:3840. 28 × 39 cm.

"Head Qurtrs., U.S. forces, Fort Fisher, Jan. 27th 1865. Forwarded to Engineer Dept. with letter of this date. C. B. Comstock, Lt. Col., A.D.C. & Brvt. Brig. Gen. &&."

Detailed plan of the fort showing the position, type, and size of guns, rifle pits, and electric wires leading to a "line of torpedoes."

Three cross sections of ramparts are given in the inset.

Another copy is in the Sherman map coll. no. 124.

Another copy is from the Orlando M. Poe papers, Manuscript Division, L.C. (G3904 .F62S5 1865 .C6)

311

————Another issue. *From* 39th Cong., 1st Sess. [1866] —Report of the Chief Engineer U.S.A. No. 6.

In lower right corner: Bowen & Co., lith., Philada.

312

————Sketch of Fort Fisher surveyed under the direction of Bvt. Brig. Gen. C. B. Comstock, Chief Engineer. [1865] Colored ms. Scale ca. 1:1500. 20 parts, each approximately 91 × 53 cm. Over-all size about 360 × 262 cm.

G3904 .F62S5 1865 .U5 Vault

Large-scale plan of the fort showing the position, type and size of guns, and the location of "torpedoes," roads, buildings, rifle pits, telegraph station, vegetation, drainage, and hachures. Four cross sections of ramparts are given in the inset.

This plan is similar in content to two printed maps entitled *Plan and sections of Fort Fisher carried by assault by the U.S. forces . . .* and *Sketch of vicinity of Fort Fisher . . .* For complete descriptions of printed maps see entry nos. 310 and 314.

313

[Fort Fisher, defensive work protecting the entrance to the port of Wilmington, North Carolina, captured by the Federals, Jan. 15, 1865] Colored ms. Scale ca. 1:5050. 74 × 112 cm.

G3904 .F62S5 1865 .F6 Vault

Lacks title.

Stamped in the lower right corner "From Collection of David Dixon Porter."

Similar to pl. 67, no. 1, in the *Atlas to Accompany the Official Records of the Union and Confederate Armies* (Washington, Government Printing Office, 1891–95).

Indicates the location and names of vessels, and soundings.

313.7

Schultze, Otto Julian.

Line of defence of Federal Point. Sketched by Otto Jul.

Schultze, Privat. of the 15th Regt.N.Y.V. Eng. [1865?] Uncolored ms. on tracing linen. Scale 1:10,000. 69 × 29 cm.

In the Cyrus B. Comstock papers, Manuscript Division, L.C., container no. 3, General Correspondence folder—undated.

Inset: Fort Buchanan. Scale ca. 1:2,000. 7 × 12 cm.

Neatly drawn pen and ink map of the defenses at Fort Fisher and Fort Buchanan.

314

————Sketch of vicinity of Fort Fisher surveyed under the direction of Brvt. Brig. Gen. C. B. Comstock, Chief Engineer, by Otto Julian Schultze, Private, 15th N.Y.V. Eng. Engraved at the Engineer Bureau, War Dept. [1865] Uncolored. Scale 1:12,000. 37 × 25 cm.

"Ft. Fisher, Feb. 9th 1865. Forwarded to Engineer Department with letter of this date. C. B. Comstock, Lt. Col. A.D.C. & Brvt. B. Gen."

Map of Federal Point showing forts Buchanan, Fisher, and Lookout, roads, commissary, hospital, headquarters, vegetation, drainage, and relief by hachures.

Inset: Fort Buchanan. Scale ca. 1:2400. 6 × 8 cm.

Another copy is in the Sherman map coll. no. 125.

Another copy is from the Orlando M. Poe papers, Manuscript Division, L.C. (G3904.F62S5 1865 .S3).

315

————Another issue. *From* 39th Cong., 1st Sess. [1866]—Report of the Chief Engineer U.S.A. No. 5.

In lower right corner: Bowen & Co., lith., Philada.

316

U.S. *Coast Survey.*

Order of attack on Fort Fisher by the Squadron under command of Rear Admiral D. D. Porter, U.S.N. in the combined naval and military operations which resulted in the capture of the Rebel defences at New Inlet, N.C. January 14th & 15th 1865. Chas G. Krebs, lith. Uncolored. Scale ca. 1:10,100. 52 × 46 cm.

Detailed map showing the location and names of vessels, fortifications, telegraph wires leading to torpedoes and a few soundings.

316.2

U.S. *Navy*

First attack upon Fort Fisher, by the U.S. Navy under Rear Admiral D. D. Porter, Dec. 24 and 25, 1864. Showing the position of vessels and line of fire. Bowen & Co., lith., Philada. Uncolored. Scale not given. 49 × 45 cm. *From* Message of the President of the United States, and accompanying documents, to the two houses of Congress, at the commencement of the first session of the thirty-ninth Con-

gress.—Report of the Secretary of the Navy (Washington, Government Printing Office, 1865). fol. p. 10.

Printed in upper left margin: 39th Cong. 1st sess.—Annual Report of the Secretary of the Navy.

316.3

————Part of Federal Point entrance to Cape Fear River. Sketch showing line of rebel fortifications captured by the combined naval and military forces under command of Rear Admiral D. D. Porter, U.S.N. and Major General Terry, U.S.A. January 15th, 1865. Bowen & Co., lith., Phila. Uncolored. Scale 1:2500, 33 × 57 cm. *From* Message of the President of the United States, and accompanying documents, to the two houses of Congress, at the commencement of the first session of the thirty-ninth Congress.—Report of the Secretary of the Navy (Washington, Government Printing Office, 1865). fol. p. 178.

Printed in upper left margin: 39th Cong. 1st Sess.—Annual Report of the Secretary of the Navy.

316.4

————Second attack upon Fort Fisher by the U.S. Navy under Rear Admiral D. D. Porter, Jan. 13, 14, 15, 1865. Showing the position of vessels and line of fire. Bowen & Co., lith., Philada. Uncolored. Scale ca. 1:9800. 47 × 44 cm. *From* Message of the President of the United States, and accompanying documents, to the two houses of Congress, at the commencement of the first session of the thirty-ninth Congress.—Report of the Secretary of the Navy (Washington, Government Printing Office, 1865). fol. p. 178.

Printed in upper left margin: 39th Cong. 1st sess.—Annual Report of the Secretary of the Navy.

FORT JOHNSTON

316.42

Bradford, J. S.

Fort Johnston, Smithville, N.C. Evacuated Jan. 16, 1865. Taken possession of by naval and military forces Jan. 17, 1865. Surveyed by J. S. Bradford, U.S. Coast Survey, A.D.C. to Admiral Porter. Bowen & Co., lith., Philada. Uncolored. Scale 1:2500. 26 × 21 cm. *From* Message of the President of the United States, and accompanying documents, to the two houses of Congress, at the commencement of the first session of the thirty-ninth Congress.—Report of the Secretary of the Navy (Washington, Government Printing Office, 1865). fol. p. 180.

At head of title: North Atlantic Squadron. Rear Admiral D. D. Porter, Comdg.

Printed in upper left margin: 39th Cong. 1st Sess.—Annual Report of the Secretary of the Navy.

FORT STRONG

316.44

U.S. *Navy.*

Plan of the attack by gun-boats on Forts Strong and Lee, Cape Fear River, N.C. February 20th and 21st 1865, under Rear Admiral D. D. Porter. Showing their position and the line of fire. Bowen & Co., lith., Philada. Uncolored. Scale ca. 1:9250. 33 × 41 cm. *From* Message of the President of the United States, and accompanying documents, to the two houses of Congress, at the commencement of the first session of the thirty-ninth Congress.—Report of the Secretary of the Navy (Washington, Government Printing Office, 1865). fol. p. 188.

Printed in upper left margin: 39th Cong. 2d [sic] Sess.—Annual Report of the Secretary of the Navy.

GOLDSBORO

316.5

Foster, John G.

Sketch showing route pursued in the advance to Goldsboro, N.C., in Dec. 1862. Bowen & Co., lith., Phila. Uncolored. Scale not given. 25 × 18 cm. *From* U.S. Congress. Joint Committee on the Conduct of the War. Supplemental report of the Joint Committee on the Conduct of the War, in two volumes. Supplemental to Senate report no. 142, 38th Congress, 2d session (Washington, Government Printing Office, 1866). v. 2, fol. p. 23.

Accompanies "Report of Major General J. G. Foster, to the Committee on the Conduct of the War." 23 p.

At head of map title: D.

Crossed swords delineate where there were "Engagement[s] fought."

HATTERAS INLET

316.7

U.S. *Coast Survey.*

Preliminary chart of Hatteras Inlet, North Carolina. From a trigonometrical survey under the direction of A. D. Bache, Superintendent of the survey of the coast of the United States. Triangulation by A. S. Wadsworth, Asst. Coast Survey. Hydrography by the party under the command of Lieut. Comdg. T. S. Phelps, U.S.N., Asst. Coast Survey, Bowen & Co. lith. Phila. Uncolored. Scale 1:20,000. 41 × 38 cm. [Washington, U.S. Coast Survey] 1862. *From its* Report of the Superintendent of the Coast Survey, showing the progress of the survey during the year 1862 (Washington, Government Printing Office, 1864). Map 23.

"No. 23" is in the upper left corner.

LOCKWOOD'S FOLLY INLET

316.72

Devens, Edward F.

Diagram of the position of "Aries" on the night of the capture of the "Pet." [February 15, 1864] Uncolored ms. on tracing paper. Scale ca. 1:87,000. 20 × 23 cm.

In the Samuel Phillips Lee papers, Manuscript Division, L.C., container no. 36, February 16–19, 1864, folder.

Map is accompanied by a letter of transmittal dated February 19, 1864, from Edward F. Devens, Acting Volunteer Lieutenant, forwarded by James Madison Frailey, Commander and Senior Officer present, to Rear Adm. S. P. Lee, Commanding North Atlantic Blockading Squadron.

316.74

Harris, John H., *and* William H. Bryant.

Diagram of positions U.S. Stmrs. "Montgomery" & "Vicksburg" at capture of English Str. "Pet." [Signed] John H. Harris, Act. Ensign [and] Wm. H. Bryant, Act. Ensign. [February 15, 1864] Colored ms. on tracing linen. Scale ca. 1:729,620. 23 × 28 cm.

In the Samuel Phillips Lee papers, Manuscript Division, L.C., container no. 36, February 16–19, 1864, folder.

Map is accompanied by a letter of transmittal dated February 19, 1864, from D. L. Braine, Lt. Cdr. to Rear Adm. S. P. Lee, Commanding North Atlantic Blockading Squadron.

NEW INLET

316.76

Sands, Benjamin F.

[Map of the positions of the North Atlantic Blockading Squadron off New Inlet and Cape Fear, N.C. May 5, 1864] Uncolored ms. on tracing linen. Scale not given. 40 × 65 cm.

In the Samuel Phillips Lee papers, Manuscript Division, L.C., container no. 36, May 1–9, 1864, folder.

Map accompanies a letter from Capt. Benjamin F. Sands to Rear Adm. Samuel P. Lee dated May 5, 1864, explaining the reason for repositioning the blockading ships.

NEWBERN

316.8

Foster, John G.

Sketch showing the route to Newbern, pursued by the Burnside expedition, March 13 & 14, 1862. Bowen & Co., lith., Philada. Uncolored. Scale 1:350,000. 22 × 18 cm. *From* U.S. Congress. Joint Committee on the Conduct of the

War. Supplemental report of the Joint Committee on the Conduct of the War, in two volumes. Supplemental to Senate report no. 142, 38th Congress, 2d session (Washington, Government Printing Office, 1866). v. 2, fol. p. 16.

Accompanies "Report of Major General J. G. Foster, to the Committee on the Conduct of the War." 23 p.

At head of map title: C.

Map shows "anchorage on night of March 12, 1862," "landing place of the troops, March 13, 1862," "deserted entrenchments," "battlefield March 14, 1862," "line of obstructions," and "line of Yankee catchers" on the Neuse River.

OREGON INLET

316.9

U.S. *Coast Survey.*

Oregon Inlet, N. Carolina. Triangulation by W. M. Boyce, Assist. Topography by John Mechan, Sub-Assist. Hydrography by Henry Mitchell, Assist. Bowen & Co. lith. Philada. [Washington, U.S. Coast Survey] 1862. Uncolored. Scale 1:20,000. 40 × 44 cm. *From its* Report of the Superintendent of the Coast Survey, showing the progress of the survey during the year 1862 (Washington, Government Printing Office, 1864). Map 22.

At head of title: U.S. Coast Survey, A. D. Bache, Supdt.

"No. 22" is in the upper left corner.

ROANOKE ISLAND

317

Andrews, William S.

Map of the battlefield of Roanoke Id. Feb. 8th 1862. Drawn by Lt. Andrews, 9th N.Y. Regt. Published by authority of the Hon. the Secretary of War, office of the Chief of Engineers, U.S. Army. Colored. Scale ca. 1:1650 and 1:82,000. 40 × 62 cm.

Detailed map of Roanoke Island battlefield and a map of Roanoke Island and vicinity. The former indicates Union and Confederate troop positions, the location of a Confederate battery, a road bisecting the battlefield, and vegetation, while the latter shows forts and the number of guns at each, positions of Union and Confederate vessels, drainage, and names of principal features.

317.1

Foster, John G.

Sketch of Roanoke Island, N.C. [February 8, 1862] Bowen & Co., lith., Phila. [1866] Scale not given. 19 × 17 cm. *From* U.S. Congress. Joint Committee on the Conduct of the War. Supplemental report of the Joint Committee on the Conduct of the War, in two volumes. Supplemental to

Senate report no. 142, 38th Congress, 2d session (Washington, Government Printing Office, 1866). v. 2, fol. p. 16.

Accompanies "Report of Major General J. G. Foster, to the Committee on the Conduct of the War." 23 p.

At head of map title: A.

Map indicates the location of forts Huger, Blanchard, and Bartow, Federal and Union gunboats, the "landing place," and the place where the "battle was fought," and the site where the "Rebels surrendered."

317.12

——————Sketch showing route of the Burnside expedition [to Roanoke Island, N.C., February 6, 1862] Bowen & Co., lith., Phila. Uncolored. Scale not given. 32 × 16 cm. *From* U.S. Congress. Joint Committee on the Conduct of the War. Supplemental report of the Joint Committee on the Conduct of the War, in two volumes. Supplemental to Senate report no. 142, 38th Congress, 2d session (Washington, Government Printing Office, 1866). v. 2, fol. p. 16.

Accompanies "Report of Major General J. G. Foster, to the Committee on the Conduct of the War." 23 p.

At head of map title: B.

Map shows the route of the expedition and anchorages.

317.2

Map of Roanoke Island. [February 8, 1862] Uncolored. Scale ca. 1:155,000. 16 × 12 cm. *From* Abbott, John S. C. "The Navy in the North Carolina Sounds," Harper's new monthly magazine, v. 32, Dec. 1865 to May 1866. p. 575.

Map indicates the positions of the fleet in the sound and forts and troop positions on the island.

ROANOKE RIVER

317.3

U.S. *Coast Survey.*

Mouths of Roanoke River, North Carolina. Triangulation and topography by R. E. Halter, Sub-Assist. Hydrography by J. S. Bradford, Sub-Assist. acting under orders of Actg. Rear Admiral S. P. Lee, U.S. Navy, Comdg. North Atlantic Blockading Squadron. (Date of first publication 1864). [Washington, U.S. Coast Survey] 1864. Uncolored. Scale 1:30,000. 55 × 48 cm. (*Its* no. 409)

"No. 409 price 10 cents" and "Plate no. 983" are printed in the upper margin.

"(Roanoke River) U.S.C. & G.S. 409" is in the bottom margin.

General chart indicating soundings and bottom contour at 12 feet.

SALISBURY

317.35

Kraus, C. A.

Bird's eye view of Confederate prison pen, at Salisbury, N.C., taken in 1864. J. H. Bufford's Sons Lith., Boston, New York & Chicago. ©1886. Colored view. 58 × 87 cm.

G3904 .S2:2S3A35 1864 .K7 Vault

Perspective drawing with 12 points of interest keyed by number to a list in the bottom margin. One of the places identified is the "hole from which prisoners tunnelled and escaped."

SMITH'S ISLAND

317.37

Bradford, J. S.

Line of rebel works, Smith's Island, N.C. Evacuated January 16th, 1865. Taken possession of by naval and military forces January 17th, 1865. Surveyed by J. S. Bradford, U.S. Coast Survey, A.D.C. to Admiral D. D. Porter. Bowen & Co., lith., Philada. Uncolored. Scale 1:5000. 26 × 21 cm. *From* Message of the President of the United States, and accompanying documents, to the two houses of Congress, at the commencement of the first session of the thirty-ninth Congress.—Report of the Secretary of the Navy (Washington, Government Printing Office, 1865). fol. p. 178.

At head of title: N. Atlantic Squadron. Rear Admiral D. D. Porter, Com'g.

Printed in upper left margin: 39th Cong. 1st Sess.— Annual Report of the Secretary of the Navy.

317.38

Stothard, Thomas.

Diagram showing the relative positions of the vessels of the fleet approximately when the "Ceres" was boarded and abandoned on the 6th of December 1863 by the U.S.S. "Aries" and "Violet." To Actg. Rear Admiral S. P. Lee, Comdg. N.A. Blockading Squadron. Actg. Ensign Thos. Stothard, Comdg. Uncolored ms. Scale ca. 1:72,000. 40 × 32 cm.

In the Samuel Phillips Lee papers, Manuscript Division, L.C., container no. 35, December 1–7, 1863, folder.

Pen and ink manuscript map drawn on lined note paper.

Map accompanied by letter of transmittal dated December 7, 1863, from Thomas Stothard to Rear Adm. S. P. Lee.

The "blockade runner 'Ceres' [went] aground and on fire, on Western Bar or Shoal near Smith's Island, N.C."

317.39

————————Diagram showing the relative positions of the

vessels of the fleet approximately when the "Ceres" was boarded on the 7th of December 1863 by the U.S.S. "Violet" and towed to anchorage. To Actg. Rear Admiral S. P. Lee, Comdg. N.A. Blockading Squadron. Actg. Ensign Thos. Stothard, Comdg. Uncolored ms. Scale ca. 1:69,000. 40 × 32 cm.

In the Samuel Phillips Lee papers, Manuscript Division, L.C., container no. 35, December 1–7, 1863, folder.

Pen and ink manuscript map drawn on lined paper.

Map is accompanied by a letter of transmittal dated December 7, 1863, from Thomas Stothard to Rear Adm. S. P. Lee.

The "blockade runner 'Ceres' [went] aground and on fire, on Western Bar or Shoal near Smith's Island, N.C."

WASHINGTON

317.4

Foster, John G.

Sketch showing the position of the attacking and defending forces at the siege of Washington, N.C., March 29 to April 16, 1863. Bowen & Co., lith., Phil. [1866] Uncolored. Scale ca. 1:207,000. 31 × 21 cm. *From* U.S. Congress. Joint Committee on the Conduct of the War. Supplemental report of the Joint Committee on the Conduct of the War, in two volumes. Supplemental to Senate report no. 142, 38th Congress, 2d session (Washington Government Printing Office, 1866). v. 2, fol. p. 23.

Accompanies "Report of Major General J. G. Foster, to the Committee on the Conduct of the War." 23 p.

At head of map title: E.

"Notes" listing Federal batteries and garrisons and Confederate batteries are reproduced in the lower right corner.

WILMINGTON

317.45

Fennel, James.

[Plan of the entrance by New Inlet to Wilmington, N.C. with the defenses then in progress of erection April 22, 1863] Uncolored ms. Scale not given. 33 × 56 cm.

In the Samuel Phillips Lee papers, Manuscript Division, L.C., container no. 34, June 1–17, 1863, folder.

Pencil sketch and the environs of Wilmington showing Fort Fisher, Fort Caswell, Fort St. Philip, Green Hill Battery, and Railroad Battery. A note in ink in the lower right corner reads "A true & correct copy of the original draught made by James Fennel, Master of the Schooner St. George of Bermuda captured as a prize by U.S. Steamer Mount Vernon off New Inlet, N.C., April 22nd 1863 at 2.30 a.m. in 3-1/2 fathoms water and given to Acting Ensign E. Harry Walkys,

Prize Master of said schooner on her voyage to New York."

Sketch is accompanied by the following letter of transmittal:

U.S. Steamer Mount Vernon
Off New Inlet N.C. June 17th [i.e., 29th] 1863.
To Rear Admiral Lee, Commd. North Atlantic Blockading Squadron.
Sir

I have the honour to present & forward for your inspection a plan of the entrance by New Inlet to Wilmington [sic] N.C. with the defences then in progress of erection April 22, 1863 furnished me by one James Fennel, Captain of the Schooner St. George, captured by the U.S. Steamer Mount Vernon . . .

E. Harry Walkys   [Signed]
Acting Ensign, U.S.
Steamer Mt. Vernon
Prize Master Schooner St.
George

Forwarded without any confidence in the accuracy of the accompanying plan.

James Trathen   [Signed]
A. V. Lieut. U. S. N.
Comdg.

317.5

Foard, Charles H.

A chart of wrecks of vessels sunk or captured near Wilmington, N.C., circa 1861–65. Compiled, Mar.–Sept. 1962. Wilmington, N.C., ©1962. Colored. Scale ca. 1:183,333. 58 × 37 cm.

G3904.W6S5 1962.F6

"Sources, U.S. Coast surveys, official records of the Union and Confederate navies, CSA engineers surveys, map by L. Hatch for Col. W. J. Woodard CSA, and the author's recollections and knowledge of local waters."

Map of the coast of North Carolina from New River Inlet to Tubbs Inlet, showing the names, locations, and dates of sinking of lost vessels, and fortifications in the vicinity of Wilmington.

317.6

————Revised. Compiled and drawn by Charles H. Foard, June 1968. Copyright applied for 1968 by Charles H. Foard. Carolina Beach, N.C., Blockade Runner Museum, 1968. Colored. Scale ca. 1:250,000. 43 × 52 cm.

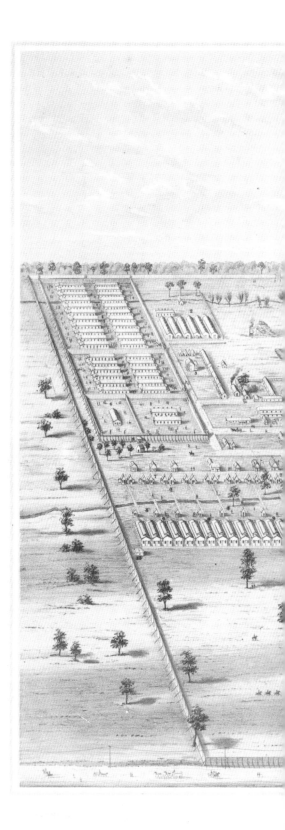

"Bird's Eye View of Camp Chase, near Columbus, Ohio," drawn by Albert Ruger, Company H., 88th Regiment, Ohio Volunteer Infantry. After the war Ruger became a successful artist and publisher of panoramic maps of American cities and towns. This map is no. 155 in his personal collection of 213 bird's-eye views purchased by the Library of Congress in 1941. (See entry no. 318.)

BIRD'S EYE VIEW OF
CAMP CHASE
NEAR COLUMBUS, OHIO

G3904 .W6S5 1968 .F6 Tr 41

Includes a list of "Captures and destruction of vessels, salt works, etc., in the vicinity of Wilmington, N.C., 1861–1865."

Listed in Donald A. Wise's *A Descriptive List of Treasure Maps and Charts in the Library of Congress* (Washington, Library of Congress, 1973), no. 41.

317.63

Owner, William.

[Map of Wilmington, N.C. and vicinity. January 1865] Uncolored ms. Scale ca. 1:410,000. 17 × 12 cm. *In his* Diary, v. 8, tipped-in opposite entries for January 18 and 19, 1865.

In the William Owner papers, Manuscript Division, L.C., container no. 2.

Volume 8 of the diary covers from August 12, 1864, to April 10, 1865.

General location map.

317.65

Sketch showing the positions of roads &c. around Wilmington, N.C. [186–?] Uncolored ms. on tracing linen. Scale not given. 27 × 33 cm.

In the Samuel Phillips Lee papers, Manuscript Division, L.C., container no. 62.

"39" is in the lower left corner.

Map shows defenses of Wilmington.

317.7

Turner, L. C.

Map showing the entrenchments around Wilmington. Surveyed & mapped under the direction of Capt. W. H. James, Prov. Engrs., by L. C. Turner C.E. 1863. Colored ms. Scale 1:7920 (8 inches to 1 mile). 71 × 97 cm.

G3904 .W6S5 1863 .T8 Vault

From the papers of Joseph Roswell Hawley, Manuscript Division, L.C.

Pen and ink, watercolor, and pencil map drawn on tracing linen showing fortifications surrounding the city of Wilmington, N.C. Copy is ink stained.

Map is oriented with east at the top.

317.8

U.S. *Coast Survey.*

Part of North Carolina showing approaches to Wilmington. Compiled at the U.S. Coast Survey Office, March 1864. Uncolored. Scale 1:253, 440. 67 × 70 cm.

"Coast line from U.S. Coast Survey topographical sheets. Interior, from State map of North Carolina."

Map of the coast of North Carolina from Cape Lookout to Cape Fear.

"Transferred from Office of Chf. Engr., Defenses of Washington to Engr. Dept. Jany. 1866."

OHIO

CAMP CHASE

318

Ruger, Albert.

Bird's eye view of Camp Chase, near Columbus, Ohio. Drawn by A. Ruger, Comp. H., 88 Rgt. O.V.I. Ehrgott, Forbriger & Co., lith, Cin. [186–] Uncolored. Not drawn to scale. 47 × 63 cm. (Ruger map coll. no. 155)

G4084 .C372A3 186–.R8 Rug 155

Principal buildings are keyed by number to a list in the bottom margin.

CAMP DENNISON

318.2

Johnson.

Camp Dennison, taken from Old Aunt Roady's Hill.

Drawn by Johnson in the Zouave Lt. Guard, Company A. Gibson & Co. Lith., Cincinnati. [186–] Uncolored view. 36 × 68 cm.

G4084 .C225A3 186– .J6

Perspective map not drawn to scale.

Map of Camp Dennison, Hamilton County, Ohio, showing tents, houses, men in marching formations, and the Little Miami Railroad.

CINCINNATI

318.5

Geaslen, Chester F.

Official placement of Union batteries that defended greater Cincinnati. Sketch from original map by Mr. Geaslen [i.e., Geaslen]. Uncolored. Scale not given. 21 × 26 cm. *From* The Cincinnati Enquirer, Saturday, Feb., 11, 1967. p. 21.

Map adapted from the U.S. Army, Corps of Engineers's "Map showing the military defences of Cincinnati, Covington and Newport" (see entry no. 319).

319

U.S. *Army. Corps of Engineers.*

Map showing the military defences of Cincinnati, Covington and Newport. Constructed under the direction of Brig. O. M. Mitchell, by Col. Charles Whittlesey in 1861: repaired and extended under the direction of Major Genl. H. G. Wright commanding Department of the Ohio, by Maj. J. H. Simpson, Chief Topogl. Engr. of the Dept. Bvt. Capt. W. E. Merrill, & Lieut. J. A. Tardy, Corps of Engs., and Col. Chas. Whittlesey, in 1862. Compiled by order of Maj. Genl. H. G. Wright commanding Department of the Ohio, chiefly from surveys made under the direction of Maj. J. H. Simpson by W. H. Searles, G. A. Aschbach, O. P. Ransom, and J. R. Gilliss, in Septr. & Octr. 1862. Published by authority of the Hon. the Sec. of War, in the office of the Chief of Engineers, U.S. Army. 1877. Colored. Scale ca. 1:16,000. 64 × 94 cm.

Detailed map showing batteries and rifle pits, common and military roads, turnpikes, city streets and names, bridges, ferries, rural houses and names of some residents, drainage, vegetation, towns, and relief by hachures.

CUYAHOGA FALLS

319.5

Ruger, Albert.

[Army camp at Gaylord's Grove, Cuyahoga Falls, Ohio] Drawn by A. Ruger . . . Ohio. Beck & Pauli Lith., Milwaukee, Wis. Madison, Wis., J. J. Stoner, [188–?] Uncolored view. 36 × 63 cm.

G4084.C9R4 186– .R8

Perspective map not drawn to scale.

L.C. copy annotated in pencil: Gaylords Grove, Carihoga [sic] Falls, O. Old army camp.

L.C. copy is imperfect; pieces are missing along the edge.

This map was probably drawn by the author while he was serving in the Ohio Volunteers during the Civil War. Ruger also made a map of the "Camp of the 196th Regt., O.V.I. . . . Stevensons Station [i.e., Stephenson's Depot] near Winchester, Va." (See Civil War Maps entry no. 660.)

JOHNSON'S ISLAND

320

Gould, Edward.

View of Johnson's Island, near Sandusky City, O. Sketched by Edward Gould. Middleton, Strobridge & Co., lithographers, Cincinnati, O. ©1865. Uncolored view. Not drawn to scale. 52 × 86 cm.

Perspective drawing showing fortifications, prison, buildings, and vegetation. Principal buildings are keyed by number to a list in the lower left corner.

OKLAHOMA

320.4

Oklahoma. *Department of Transportation. Planning Division.*

Civil War in Indian Territory, 1861–1865. Prepared by: Oklahoma Department of Transportation, Planning Division. Reviewed by: Oklahoma Historical Society. [Oklahoma City, 1979?] Colored. Scale ca. 1:1,375,000. 44 × 62 cm.

G4021 .S5 1979 .O4

Map of the area that now comprises the state of Oklahoma, showing county names and boundaries, forts, towns, rivers, the north and south "California road," the "Texas road," the "Butterfield overland mail" route, "Col. Emory's withdrawl [sic] route" and the location of 27 battle sites.

Text below the map describes the "Civil War in Indian Territory."

Reproduced on verso are photographs of Jefferson Davis, Generals James G. Blunt, Stand Watie, William H. Emory, Douglas H. Cooper, and Albert Pike, Colonel Daniel N. McIntosh (Creek Indian), Captain George Washington (Caddo Indian), and Chief Opothle Yoholo (Creek Indian). Also reproduced is a view of the "Battle of Honey Springs July 17, 1863," a map entitled "Today's Transportation Moves on Historic Trails," and "a letter from a group of leading citizens of Arkansas admonishing Stand Watie to use his influence as a prominent leader of the Cherokees and the other civilized tribes to arm themselves and join with Arkansas in the Confederate cause."

Title when folded: Oklahoma. Oklahoma Department

of Transportation—Historical Map Series. Civil War in Indian Territory.

"This publication, issued by the Oklahoma Department of Transportation as a part of its Transportation-Historical series, was prepared as authorized by R. A. Ward, Director. Approximately 25,000 copies have been printed at a cost to the taxpayer of the State of Oklahoma of $0.10 per copy."

320.5

Wright, Muriel H., *and* **LeRoy H. Fischer.**

Civil War centennial map; Oklahoma—1963. Prepared . . . for the Oklahoma Civil War Centennial Commission. Colored. Scale ca. 1:925,000. 56 × 87 cm.

Printed on the verso of an official highway map entitled "Oklahoma 1963."

Indicates six "Civil War routes," rivers, and county names and boundaries. "Approximate locations of related [Civil War] sites are indicated by numbers; approximate locations of combat sites are indicated by crossed swords."

PENNSYLVANIA

320.55

Owner, William.

Seat of war in Pa. [1863] Uncolored ms. Scale not given. 19 × 16 cm. *In his* Diary, v. 5, tipped-in at front of volume.

In the William Owner papers, Manuscript Division, L.C., container no. 1.

Map is centered on Gettysburg showing parts of Pennsylvania, Maryland, and Virginia. Indicated are cities and towns, roads and railroads, rivers, and relief by hachures.

Volume 5 of the diary covers from June 29 to November 16, 1863.

BRANDYWINE CREEK

320.6

Whiting, Henry L.

Map of reconnaissance of the valley of Brandywine Creek including the section from Smiths Bridge to the State road. Made under the direction of A. D. Bache, engr. in charge of the defenses of Philadelphia. By Henry L. Whiting, Assist. U.S. Coast Survey. Dec. 1863. Colored ms. Scale ca. 1:9600. 173 × 74 cm.

G3822.B7S5 1863 .W4 Vault

Pen and ink manuscript on tracing linen showing roads, railroad, bridges, relief by form lines and spot elevations, and fortifications and batteries along Brandywine Creek, Chester County, Pennsylvania. The map also includes numerous references to the American Revolution, such as "Gen. Washington's Hd. Qrs." and "House where Lafayette was taken after being wounded."

Former ownership stamp in lower right corner: U.S.C.

& G. Survey. Library and Archives. Jan. 28, 1902. Acc. no. 53678.

Includes signature of Henry L. Whiting.

GETTYSBURG

320.7

American Automobile Association.

Gettysburg National Military Park, Gettysburg—Pennsylvania. Area of three day battle July 1, 2 & 3, 1863. ©1946. Uncolored. Scale 1:36,000. 28 × 22 cm.

Title on verso: Map of Gettysburg National Military Park with points of interest.

Copyright no. F783, July 19, 1946.

Map indicates battle sites, Heth's and Pickett's advances, and principal roads.

320.8

American Heritage Publishing Company.

The American Heritage battle map of Gettysburg. [Drawn by] David Greenspan. [New York] ©1961. Colored view. Not drawn to scale. 40 × 59 cm.

Bird's-eye view showing principal sites and events of the battle.

321

Bachelder, John B.

Gettysburg battle-field. Battle fought at Gettysburg, Pa., July 1st, 2d & 3d, 1863 by the Federal and Confederate armies, commanded respectively by Genl. G. G. Meade and Genl. Robert E. Lee. Jno. B. Bachelder, del. Endicott & Co., lith, N.Y. Boston and New York, Jno. B. Bachelder, ©1863. Colored view. 53 × 92 cm.

Inset: Plan of the Soldiers National Cemetery. Uncolored. 6 × 13 cm.

Bears a "Proof" mark in the lower left corner.

Endorsed (facsim.): I am perfectly satisfied with the accuracy with which the topography is delineated and the position of the troops laid down. [Signed] Geo. G. Meade, Maj. Gen. of Vols. comd. A. P.

The reproduced signatures of A. Doubleday, John Newton, Winf. St. Hancock, D. B. Birney, Geo. Sykes, John Sedgwick, O. O. Howard, A. S. Williams, and H. W. Slocum appear below the following statement: The positions of the troops of our respective commands represented upon this picture have been arranged under our immediate direction and may be relied upon as substantially correct.

Colored bird's-eye view showing the topography of the battlefield by the perspective of the drawing, shading, and coloring. Drainage, vegetation, roads and streets, railroads, bridges, houses and names of residents, fences, points of interest on the battlefield, including designations of places where officers were killed or wounded, are indicated.

The locations of the corps, divisions, brigades, etc. of both armies, with the names of commanding officers, are given in detail. Badge symbols are used to identify the Federal corps.

The Library has 1864, 1865, and 1866 editions of the *Key to Bachelder's Isometrical Drawing of the Gettysburg Battle-field, with a Brief Description of the Battle.* This 10- or 12-page work, published in New York by C. A. Alvord, apparently was intended to accompany the print.

321.1

——————Facsimile. Gettysburg, American Print Gallery [1979]

G3824 .G3S5 1863 .B3 1979

Accompanied by *Key to Bachelder's Isometrical Drawing of the Gettysburg Battle-field, with a Brief Description of the Battle* (New York, C. A. Alvord, 1865; Gettysburg, American Print Gallery, 1979) 12 p. 20 cm.

322

——————Another issue. Colored. 53 × 92 cm

Bears a "Proof" mark in the lower left corner.

General Meade's statement is enclosed in quotation marks, and the signature of H. W. Slocum does not appear below the endorsement in this issue.

323

——————Another issue. Colored. 37 × 92 cm.

This issue is printed in one tint, lacks a portion of the sky, and bears no proof mark.

324

——————Another issue. Uncolored. 39 × 88 cm.

Endorsed (facsim.): I have examined Col. Bachelder's isometrical drawing of the battle field of Gettysburg and am perfectly satisfied with the accuracy with which the topography is delineated and the position of the troops laid down. [Signed] Geo. G. Meade, Maj. Gen. of Vols. comd. A. P.

This issue is overprinted with a grid. It accompanies Bachelder's *Gettysburg: What to See, and How to See It.* The detailed index of this work lists the various units of the armies and gives the grid coordinates for each. It was issued in many editions of which the library has the 1873 edition and the tenth edition, 1890.

324.2

——————Another issue. Boston, Geo. H. Walker & Co., ©1863 Uncolored. 46 × 81 cm.

G3822 .G4S5 1863 .B3

This edition is overprinted with a grid and reduced in size. It accompanies Bachelder's *Gettysburg Battlefield Directory, with Index.* This is an "index to military organizations showing the positions of troops on the isometrical drawing."

On the previous editions Bachelder's addresses are given as 125 Washington St., Boston, and 59 Beekman St., N.Y. On this edition his addresses are Hyde Park, Massachusetts and 361 Washington St., Boston.

General Meade's endorsement appears in the margin in the shortened form and without quotation marks (see entry no. 321).

325

——————Map of the battle field of Gettysburg. July 1st, 2nd, 3rd, 1863. Published by authority of the Hon. the Secretary of War, office of the Chief of Engineers, U.S. Army. 1876. Positions of troops compiled and added for the Government by John B. Bachelder . . . Boston, John B. Bachelder, 1876. Colored. Scale 1:12,000. 3 maps, each 74 × 71 cm.

"Topography engraved by Julia Bien . . . N.Y. Positions & lettering by Louis E. Neuman . . . N.Y."

"Printed by Endicott & Co. . . . N.Y."

The maps are entitled: First day's battle. Second day's battle. Third day's battle.

"The map is reduced from one on a scale of 200 feet to the inch, deposited in the Archives of the office of the Chief of Engineers. The survey was ordered by Brevet Major General A. A. Humphreys, Chief of Engineers, and conducted under Brevet Major General G. K. Warren, Major of Engineers."

An extremely detailed topographic map with spot elevations and contours "given for every change of 4 feet in elevation." Drainage, vegetation, roads, railroads, fences, houses with names of residents, and a detailed plan of the town of Gettysburg are shown. "Every object is represented here as near as possible as it was at the time of the battle."

A very minute analysis of the deployment of the various

units of both armies, with the names of commanding officers, period of time spent in a particular position, and other pertinent information is given. Dotted lines and arrows indicate the movements of the troops, and the positions at various times of the day are shown by symbols explained in the legend.

326

—————————New edition 1883. Positions of troops compiled by John B. Bachelder, 1876. Colored. Scale 1:12,000. 3 maps, each 74 × 71 cm.

This edition lacks any statement of publication, printing, or engraving.

327

—————————Map of the field of operations of Gregg's (Union) & Stuart's (Confederate) cavalry at the battle of Gettysburg, July 3, 1863. Surveyed by Frank O. Maxson, C.E. under the direction of John B. Bachelder, authorized by Act of Congress, approved June 9th, 1880. Julius Bien & Co. lith. Colored. Scale 1:12,000. 4 maps, each 86 × 31 cm.

The maps are entitled "No. 4a. 6–8 P.M., July 2," "No. 10. 4–11 A.M., July 3," "No. 11. 11 A.M.–2 P.M., July 3" and "No. 12. 2–5 P.M., July 3."

Detailed topographic map with spot elevations and contours "given for every change of four feet in elevation . . . Every object is represented, as nearly as possible, as it was at the time of the battle." Shows drainage, vegetation, roads, railroads, fences, and houses with names of residents.

Minute analysis of the movement of the cavalry units of both armies, with names of commanding officers and the period of time spent in a particular position. Dotted lines and arrows indicate the movements of the troops.

The Geography and Map Division has second copies of sheets 4a, 10, and 11, each of which is marked in manuscript in the lower right corner, "Note. Subject to change as regards the location of troops."

327.5

Battle of Gettysburg, July 1, 1863. First day. General position of troops, 2 to 3.30 p.m. [n.p., 19–?] Colored. Scale 1:23,400 (1950 feet to the inch). 41 × 36 cm.

No. "II" in the upper right margin.

Map of the environs of Gettysburg showing troop and artillery positions, roads, houses and names of residents, relief by contour lines at intervals of 20 feet and spot heights, woodland, the Gettysburg & Hanover R.R., and drainage.

328

Bien (Julius) and Company.

Field of cavalry operations east of Gettysburg, July 2nd & 3rd 1863. Julius Bien & Co., lith., N.Y. [18–?]Colored. Scale ca. 1:56,000. 18 × 15 cm.

Map of the country east of Gettysburg, showing the location of cavalry engagements by crossed swords, positions of the 3rd and 16th Pennsylvania cavalry, roads, houses and names of residents, vegetation, and relief by hachures.

329

Burk and McFetridge Company.

Gettysburg and vicinity, showing the lines of battle, July, 1863. Burk & McFetridge Co., lith., Phila. [18–?]Colored. Scale 1:15,840. 41 × 31 cm.

Inset: Site of Gen. Gregg's cavalry operations. Three miles east of Gettysburg. Uncolored. Scale. 1:63,360. 13 × 7 cm.

Lower right corner: Compliments of Holtzworth Bros., propr's of the Ziegler and Holtzworth Livery, in rear of Eagle Hotel, Gettysburg, Pa.

Shows drainage, vegetation, roads, railroads, fences, dwellings with names of inhabitants, and land owned by the United States. Union and Confederate positions are shown, with names of corps and divisions, sometimes including names of commanding officers, and location of artillery.

See entry no. 334 for an earlier version of this map.

329.5

Cope, Emmor B.

Perspective view of Gettysburg National Military Park. Drawn under the direction of the Gettysburg National Park Commission, Colonel John P. Nicholson, Chairman, Major Charles A. Richardson, Commissioner. Drawing made February, 1916, by Lieut.-Colonel E. B. Cope, Engineer. Colored view. 46 × 54 cm.

Panoramic map, with Round Top in the foreground, showing roads, railroads, field patterns, woodland, observation towers, monuments, and houses.

329.6

—————————Another edition. 1919.

Park commissioner Maj. Charles A. Richardson's name has been dropped from this edition.

330

Cope, Emmor B., and E. M. Hewitt.

Gettysburg battlefield. Surveyed 1863 by E. B. Cope, U.S.T.E. Drawn under direction U.S. Commission, Col. John P. Nicholson, Chairman, by E. B. Cope, Eng. [and] E. M. Hewitt, Asst. Eng. Blue print, with Confederate positions hand colored in red. Scale ca. 1:26,000. 44 × 26 cm.

Upper right corner: No. 825.

Shows troops and artillery points, drainage, roads, railroads, dwellings with names of occupants, several points of interest on the battlefield, and a few of the highest points by hachures.

331

Ditterline, Theodore.

Field of Gettysburg, July 1st, 2nd & 3rd, 1863. Prepared by T. Ditterline. P. S. Duval & Son lith., Philada. Colored. Scale ca. 1:25,500. 49 × 40 cm. *From his* Sketch of the battles of Gettysburg . . . New York, C. A. Alvord, 1863. 24 p.

Oval-shaped map depicting troop and artillery positions, relief by hachures, drainage, roads, railroads, and houses with names of residents.

332

Elliott, S. G.

Elliott's map of the battlefield of Gettysburg, Pennsylvania. Made from an accurate survey of the ground by transit and chain. F. Bourquin & Co., liths., Philada. [Philadelphia] S. G. Elliott & Co., ©1864. Uncolored. Scale 1:9051. 81 × 58 cm.

Shows breastworks and rifle pits, graves of Union and Confederate soldiers, "dead horses" reads and streets, relief by hachures, vegetation, drainage, houses and names of residents.

333

————Map of the battlefield of Gettysburg. Made from an accurate survey of the ground by transit and chain by S. G. Elliott, C.E. Published by H. H. Lloyd & Co., New York. ©1864. Colored. Scale 1:9051. 80 × 58 cm.

Inset: Plan of the National Cemetery.

Lower right corner: Sketch of the battle of Gettysburg. [Text]

333.5

Gettysburg. [19–?] Photocopy (negative). Scale not given. 13 × 23 cm.

Anonymous, undated map of Gettysburg and vicinity showing troop positions.

334

Gettysburg Battlefield Memorial Association.

Gettysburg and vicinity, showing the lines of battle July, 1863, and the land purchased and dedicated to the public by General S. Wylie Crawford and the Gettysburg Battlefield Memorial Association. Published by the Gettysburg Battlefield Memorial Association, 1886. Burk & McFetridge lith., Phila. Colored. Scale 1:15,840. 41 × 31 cm.

Inset: Site of General Gregg's operations. Three miles east of Gettysburg. Uncolored. Scale 1:63,360. 13 × 7 cm.

Accompanies a folded leaflet entitled: Gettysburg Battlefield Memorial Association; Its Organization, Plans and Purposes.

Shows drainage, vegetation, roads, railroads, property lines, fences, dwellings with names of inhabitants, points of interest on the battlefield, and in addition to the land owned by the association, that which is proposed to be purchased.

Union and Confederate positions are shown, with names of corps and divisions, sometimes including the name of the commanding officer, and the location of artillery.

See entry no. 329 for a similar map showing more extensive land holdings.

335

————Gettysburg and vicinity, showing the position of the troops July 1st and 3rd, 1863, and the land purchased and dedicated to the public by General S. Wylie Crawford and the Gettysburg Battlefield Memorial Association. Published by the Gettysburg Battlefield Memorial Association, 1885. Uncolored. Scale ca. 1:15,840. 41 × 31 cm.

Indicates Union troop positions and movements, points of interest on the battlefield, dwellings with names of inhabitants, drainage, fences, roads, and railroads.

336

————Gettysburg and vicinity, showing the position of the troops July 3, 1863 (third day's fight), and the land purchased and dedicated to the public by General S. Wylie Crawford and the Gettysburg Battlefield Memorial Association. Thos. Hunter, lith., Phila. Published by the Gettysburg Battlefield Memorial Association, March, 1883. Colored. Scale ca. 1:15,840. 41 × 31 cm.

"Land of battlefield Memorial Association tinted pink" and "land of General Crawford tinted blue."

Indicates troop positions and movements, roads, "Gettysburg and Hanover Railroad," houses, names of residents, fences, and drainage.

Another copy is in the Charles W. Reed papers, Manuscript Division, L.C., container no. 5 (oversize cabinet 5, drawer 5).

336.5

Gettysburg Monuments Commissioners. New York Board.

Map of the battlefield of Gettysburg. Office of the New York Board of Gettysburg Monuments Commissioners, A. J. Zabriskie, Engineer. Feby. 20, 1894. Blue print. Scale ca. 1:12,000. 2 parts, each 41 × 70 cm.

Map indicates lands owned by the Gettysburg Battlefield Memorial Association and the U.S. government and the "proposed purchases of lands."

336.7

Gettysburg Travel Council.

Gettysburg National Military Park, Pennsylvania. Design by R. Morris. [Gettysburg, Gettysburg Travel Council, 1965?] Colored. Scale ca. 1:20,000. 54 × 40 cm.

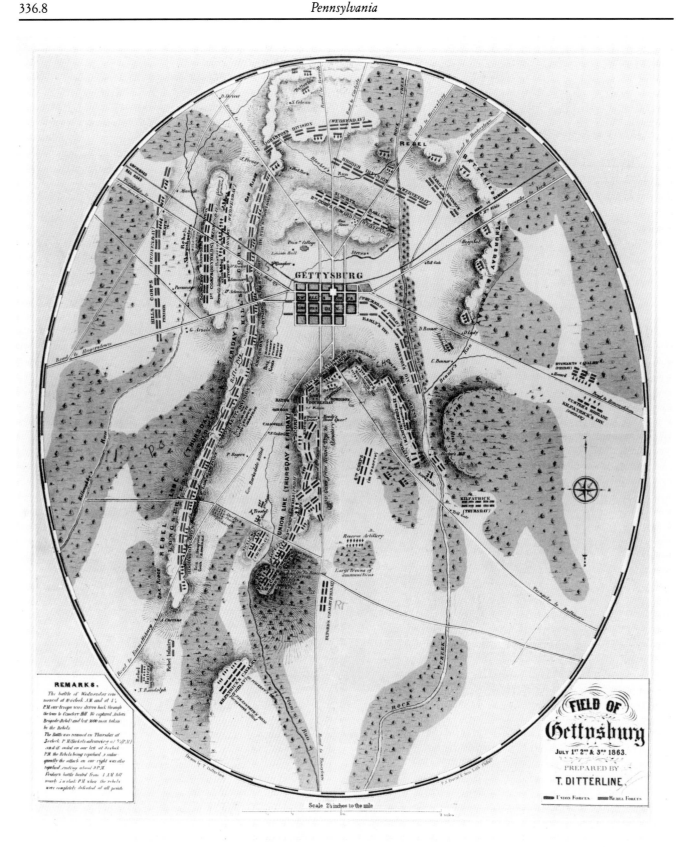

Attractive oval-shaped map of the battle of Gettysburg, Pennsylvania, July 1–3, 1863. The map was prepared by Theodore Ditterline *to illustrate his 24-page pamphlet entitled* Sketch of the Battles of Gettysburg *(New York, C. A. Alvord, 1863). (See entry no. 331.)*

Title on verso: Historic Gettysburg, Adams County, Pennsylvania.

Includes color photographs of park sites.

336.8

—————Another edition. [1975?]
G3822 .G4 1975 .G4
Includes list of "1975 annual events."

337

Gilbert, J. Warren.

Gettysburg and vicinity, showing the lines of battle, July, 1863. Copyrighted April 1922, by Prof. J. Warren Gilbert. Colored. Scale ca. 1:22,500 (not "4 inches = 1 mile") 32 × 24 cm. *From his* The Blue and Grey . . . ©1922.

Inset: Site of Gen. Greggs cavalry operations. Three miles east of Gettysburg. July 3rd 1863. Colored. Scale not given. 10 × 5 cm.

Shows Union positions in black and Confederate positions in red, roads, railroad, houses and names of residents, fences, vegetation, and drainage.

338

Goodhue, W. F.

The battlefield of Gettysburg, July 1st, 2d, 3d, 1863, showing the movements of the 12th Army Corps. Uncolored. Scale ca. 1:21,250. 37 × 28 cm.

Shows drainage, vegetation, roads, railroads, houses and names of inhabitants, and points of interest on the battlefield. In addition to the movements of the 12th Army Corps, the Union and Confederate positions are shown, with names of the commanding officers of some units.

338.2

Hammond, Schuyler A., *and* Edgar M. Hewitt.

Monumental guide to the Gettysburg battlefield. A map showing the location of every monument, marker and tablet with approaching roads and avenues. Copyright 1899 by Schuyler A. Hammond & Edgar M. Hewitt. Uncolored. Scale ca. 1:12,800. 79 × 55 cm.

"Library of Congress, Maps & Charts, no. 2502" is stamped in the lower right corner.

338.5

Lehman, Ambrose E.

Relief map of the battle field of Gettysburg. Looking south. Showing the town, fields, farm buildings, forests, streams, roads and lanes as they were at the time of the battle. [©1886] Uncolored. Scale ca. 1:27,000. 20 × 38 cm.

Signed in ink in the lower right corner "Ambrose E. Lehman."

Copyright no. 20433, Oct. 4, 1886.

Oblique view of a relief model.

Stamped on verso: A. E. Lehman, civil engineer and topographical geologist, 711 Walnut St., Phila., Pa.

338.7

Lenz, Russell H.

The battle of Gettysburg, July 1,2,3, 1863. Copyright 1965 by Russell H. Lenz, Cartographer, W. Newbury, Mass. Uncolored. Scale ca. 1:19,000. 55 × 61 cm.

Printed in brown ink on buff-colored paper.

Map indicates troop and cavalry positions, troop movements, names of Union and Confederate generals, roads, houses, and relief by hachures and spot elevations.

"Numbers 1–24 on map are chronological events told in accompanying story" appearing in the lower right corner.

Copyright no. F39248, March 1, 1965.

339

Lippincott (J.B.) and Company.

Map of the battle field of Gettysburg. [July 1st, 2nd, and 3rd 1863] T. Sinclair's lith. Entered according to an Act of Congress in the year 1863 by J. B. Lippincott & Co. . . . Colored. Scale 1:15,840. 42 × 28 cm. *From* Jacobs, Michael. Notes on the rebel invasion of Maryland and Pennsylvania . . . Philadelphia, J. B. Lippincott, 1864.

Indicates Union positions in red and Confederate positions in blue, Union artillery positions, roads, railroads, houses and names of residents, drainage, and vegetation.

340

—————Another edition *From* Jacobs, Michael. Notes on the invasion of Maryland and Pennsylvania . . . Philadelphia, [1888?]

Revised edition of the preceding map including Confederate artillery positions, location of the Federal "11th Corps 3 P.M.," and additional houses. Union positions are colored blue and Confederate positions are red.

Lacks the name of the lithographer in the lower right corner.

Geography and Map Division's copy bears annotations in pencil.

This map was formerly in the possession of the Confederate topographic engineer, Maj. Jedediah Hotchkiss. In July 1948, the Library of Congress purchased his map collection.

341

Long, Harry W.

Gettysburg and vicinity, showing the lines of battle of both armies, July 1, 2, 3, 1863. (Copyrighted by Harry W. Long, 1926). Colored. Scale ca. 1:18,500 (not "4 inches = 1 mile") 36 × 27 cm.

Inset: Site of Gen. Gregg's cavalry operations. Three miles east of Gettysburg. Uncolored. Scale ca. 1:75,000 (not "1 inch = 1 mile") 11 × 6 cm.

Shows Union positions in blue and Confederate positions in red, roads, railroad, houses and names of residents, fences, vegetation, and drainage.

342

Long, James T.

Gettysburg and vicinity, showing the lines of battle, July, 1863, and the land purchased and dedicated to the public by General S. Wylie Crawford and the Gettysburg Battlefield Memorial Association. Eng'd. by American Bank Note Co., New York. Colored. Scale 1:15,840. 41 × 32 cm. *From his* Gettysburg: How the battle was fought. ©1891.

Inset: Site of Gen. Gregg's calvary [sic] operations. Three miles east of Gettysburg. Uncolored. Scale 1:63,360. 13 × 7 cm.

Shows Union positions in blue and Confederate positions in red, roads, houses and names of residents, fences, railroad, vegetation, and drainage.

342.1

——————Another issue.

"Presented with the compliments of the Baltimore & Ohio Railroad" is printed in red in the lower right corner.

343

Meisel, Augustus.

Plan of Gettysburg with the battlefield of July 2nd & 3rd, 1863 and the National Cemetery. A. Meisel, lith. [18–?]Uncolored. Scale 1:7920. 66 × 45 cm.

Inset: [Plan of the] National Cemetery. Uncolored. 26 × 16 cm.

Shows troop positions, roads, railroads, streams, and a few houses.

344

Minnigh, L. W.

The battlefield of Gettysburg, July 1st, 2nd and 3rd, 1863. Gatchel & Manning. Phila. Gettysburg, L. W. Minnigh, 1905. Colored. Scale 1:15,840. 41 × 28 cm.

Shows Union positions in black and Confederate positions in red, names of field commanders, relief by hachures, drainage, vegetation, roads, railroad, and a few houses and names of residents.

For a later edition copyrighted in 1912 by Tipton & Blocher, see entry no. 350.

344.5

Nicholson, Robert W.

The battle of Gettysburg, July 1, 1863; July 2, 1863;

July 3, 1863. Paintings by Robert W. Nicholson, assisted by J. E. Barrett, with Lisa Biganzoli and Snejinka Stefanoff, National Geographic Society staff. Historical documentation by Dr. Frederick H. Tilberg, Historian, Gettysburg National Military Park. 3 colored views. Not drawn to scale. 1 measures 26 × 49 cm. and 2 measure 26 × 35 cm. *From* National geographic. Washington, v. 124, July 1963. p. 15–21.

Three bird's-eye views, one for each day of battle, showing fields, streams, roads, and troop positions and movements. "Confederate officers are named in italic type; Union leaders in roman."

345

Pennsylvania cavalry. *3d. regt.,* **1861–1865.**

Map showing the positions occupied by the Third Pennsylvania Cavalry in the engagements on the right flank at Gettysburg, Pa., between the Union cavalry under Gen. D. McM. Gregg and the "Stonewall" Brigade of Confederate infantry on July 2d, 1863, and the Confederate cavalry under Gen. J. E. B. Stuart on July 3d, 1863. [1905] Colored. Scale ca. 1:24,200. 22 × 31 cm. *From* History of the Third Pennsylvania Cavalry ... Philadelphia, Franklin Printing Company, 1905. opp. p. 261.

Indicates troop, cavalry, and artillery positions, roads and streets, railroad, houses and names of residents, vegetation, and drainage.

Base map was drawn by Noble D. Preston.

345.5

Pennsylvania Railroad.

Gettysburg battlefield today. Pennsylvania Railroad. ©1913. Colored view. 40 × 53 cm.

Copyright no. 59616R June 3, 1913.

Panoramic map of the Gettysburg battlefield. Round Top is in the foreground.

345.7

Plan of the battle of Gettysburg, fought, July 1st, 2d & 3d, 1863. Showing the positions, on July 2, 1863. Drawn by reporter of Pittsburg [sic] Gazette. Pencil and pen and ink ms. Scale 1:50,688 ("1-1/4 in. to the mile"). 27 × 21 cm.

In the George Hay Stuart collection, Manuscript Division, L.C., container no. 1.

Sketch map showing "Rebel right wing," "Rebel line," "Rebel left wing," Union line, and "Gen. Meade's Hd. Qrs."

346

Presto, Noble D.

Map showing the positions occupied by the Tenth New York Cavalry, in the cavalry engagements on the right flank at Gettysburg, Penn., on July 2 & 3, 1863, between the Union cavalry under Gen. D. McM. Gregg and the Confederate cavalry under Gen. J. E. B. Stuart. [1891?] Uncolored ms. Scale 1:12,000. 42 × 60 cm.

    G3822 .G4S5 1863 .P7 Vault

Finished pen and ink manuscript showing Federal cavalry positions and movements, camp and barracks of the 10th N.Y. Cavalry in 1861–62, drainage, vegetation, roads and streets, railroad, houses and names of occupants.

Printed version appears in Preston's *History of the Tenth Regiment of Cavalry, New York State Volunteers, August, 1861, to August, 1865.* New York, D. Appleton, 1892. opp. p. 116.

The Library of Congress also has two incomplete manuscript maps, presumably done as preliminary studies, on which the Union cavalry action has been sketched partly in ink and partly in pencil. In addition, the Library has four incomplete manuscript studies of the movements of "Stuart's cavalry, July 3, 2 to 5 P.M." Apparently these were preliminary studies for the Confederate troop information which appears in red on the printed map.

346.1

————————Colored. Scale ca. 1:22,700. 22 × 32 cm.

Printed version of the preceding manuscript map submitted for copyright on Dec. 14, 1891, copyright no. 45482w. Union positions are indicated in black and Confederate positions in red.

346.8

Reed, Charles W.

[Gettysburg campaign—Map of the environs of Black Horse Tavern on Marsh Creek, Pa. showing site where General Andrew A. Humphreys, 3rd Corps, Army of the Potomac, was nearly captured on July 1, 1863] Pencil sketch. Scale not given. 22 × 14 cm. *In his* Sketch book number 1. 9th Massachusetts Battery, 1863. Verso of sketch no. 64.

In the Charles W. Reed papers, Manuscript Division, L.C., container no. 1.

Map indicates Confederate camp and location of "2-1/2 mile lane to Emmittsburg [sic] road down which Humphrey came mistaking his road."

The following note appears in the lower right corner: Gen. Humphrey saved from capture with his entire command by a native after he had marched clear into Lee's army encamped for the n[ight].

"44" is in the upper right corner.

347

————————Plan of the Gettysburg battle ground. Chas. W. Reed, 9th Mass. Battery. ©1864. Colored. Scale ca. 1:36,500. 38 × 31 cm.

Map gives Union positions in black and Confederate positions in red, batteries and lines of fire, roads and streets, vegetation, drainage, and relief by hachures.

Two additional copies are in the Charles W. Reed papers, Manuscript Division, L.C., container no. 5 (oversize cabinet 5, drawer 5).

347.5

Roberts, Charles S.

Gettysburg, by Charles S. Roberts. Baltimore, The Avalon Hill Company, ©1958. Colored. Scale 1:15,840. 71 × 56 cm.

Map of the battlefield showing roads, railroad, woodland, and ridges and hills. Troop positions are not given.

348

Robertson, H. C.

Battle of Gettysburg. [July 1–3, 1863. Chicago, R. O. Evans and Co., ©1898] Colored. Scale not given. 82 × 58 cm. (Robertson's geographic-historical series illustrating the history of America and the United States)

Wall map indicating troop positions and names of commanders, roads, woods, drainage, and relief by hachures.

Includes an outline of events; views of "Battle of Gettysburg" and the "High-water mark monument;" and portraits of Generals Lee and Meade.

348.2

Rubincam, Barclay L.

The battlefield of Gettysburg. Drawn by Barclay Rubincam. Copyright 1953. Gettysburg, Bookmart, [1953] Colored. Scale not given. 40 × 52 cm.

Copyright no. F15146.

"Lithographed by William N. Cann, inc., Wilmington, Del."

"Sold and distributed by Bookmart, Gettysburg, Pa."

"Dedicated to the spirit of Gettysburg by N. A. Meligakes.

Map includes drawings of some of the principal battle sites, portraits of Lee and Meade, and "President Lincoln's address at Gettysburg, dedicating the National Cemetery, Nov. 19, 1863."

348.5

Schmidt, Ernst Reinhold.

Plan der Schlacht von Gettysburg am 1,2 &3 Juli, 1863.—Plan zur Erläuterung von Gen. Grant's Vicksburg Campagne Mai–Juli, 1863. Gez v. E. R. Schmidt. Th. Leonhardt, lith., Philada. [Philadelphia, 1867–69] Uncolored. Scales vary. 2 maps, each 11 × 14 cm. on sheet 24 × 18 cm. *From his* Der Amerikanische Bürgerkreig; Geschichte des Volks der Vereinigten Staaten vor, während und nach der Rebellion. Philadelphia and Leipzig, Schäfer und Koradi, 1867–69. facing p. 255.

Gettysburg map shows the location of Union and Confederate corps. The Vicksburg campaign map indicates the route followed by General Grant.

349

Sholl, Charles.

Gettysburg and vicinity. Constructed and engraved to illustrate "The war with the South." A topographical map of the battles of Gettysburg, July 1st, 2nd & 3rd, 1863, from an actual survey by an engineer officer on General Doubleday's staff. Entered according to Act of Congress A.D. 1864 by Virtue & Yorston . . . Colored. Scale ca. 1:53,000. 21 × 17 cm. *From* Tomes, Robert. The War with the South. New York, Virtue & Yorston, 1862–1867. v. 3, between p. 156 and 157.

Signed (facsim.): Charles: Sholl, Topl. Engineer.

Indicates Union positions in red, Confederate positions in blue, artillery positions, roads, railroad, vegetation, and streams.

349.5

Smith, Leroy E.

Gettysburg, Pennsylvania. Illustrated Gettysburg battlefield map and story. Gettysburg, Leroy E. Smith, ©1957 [i.e., 1958] Colored. Scale not given. 65 × 56 cm.

Title from verso.

Map indicates tour route, other roads, monuments and points of interest, battle lines, streams, and wooded areas. "Key to the Gettysburg battlefield map" is printed below the map.

"History of the battle of Gettysburg" is printed on the verso.

Copyright no. F25267, Sept. 8, 1958.

350

Tipton and Blocher.

The battlefield of Gettysburg, July 1st, 2nd and 3rd 1863. Gatchel & Manning, Phila. Gettysburg, Tipton & Blocher, ©1912. Colored. Scale 1:15,840. 42 × 28 cm.

For a complete description see the earlier edition published in 1905 by L. W. Minnigh (entry no. 344).

350.5

U.S. *Army. Corps of Engineers.*

Extract from the original (large scale) map of Gettysburg battle field in 4 sheets, being portions of sheets 2 and 3 lying S. & S.W. of the town of Gettysburg. Washington, Office of the Chief of Engineers, U.S.A, 1886. Colored ms. Scale 1:2400 ("1″ = 200 feet"). 121 × 72 cm.

G3822 .G4S5 1886 .U5 Vault

Manuscript map drawn on tracing linen of the intersection of the Emmitsburg and Taneytown roads. Depicted are roads, buildings, names of residents, fence lines, vegetation,

and fortifications, and relief by contour lines at intervals of 4 feet.

351

U.S. *Army War College.*

Gettysburg. [Washington, 1906?] 3 p. l., 10 maps on 6 l. Colored. Various scales. 14 × 25 cm.

Cover title.

"Memoranda for Gettysburg campaign, 1863. Army War College, Session of 1906–7."

The three preliminary leaves give a chronological summary of the battle. Maps are numbered 9 to 18. They show the troop positions in color from June 29th through July 3rd. Corps and divisions are identified, sometimes with numbers, more frequently by names of commanding officers. Cavalry and artillery are located by symbol, and arrows show movements of battle. The larger scale maps give topography by hachures, drainage, vegetation, roads, railroads, and a few place names.

These maps bear the same numbering and are almost identical with those in Abner Doubleday's *Gettysburg Made plain* (New York, Century Co., 1909).

351.1

U.S. *Gettysburg National Military Park Commission.*

Birds-eye view of the battlefield of Gettysburg. Copyright June 18, 1901. Photocopy (positive). 11 × 24 cm.

Photograph of a relief model entitled "Relief map of the battlefield of Gettysburg as it was in 1863."

351.2

————Map of a part of the east cavalry field showing positions of division and brigade markers and batteries. Prepared under the direction of the Gettysburg National Park Commission, Col. John P. Nicholson, Chairman, Maj. C. A. Richardson, Commissioner, Maj. Gen. L. L. Lomax, Commissioner [and] E. B. Cope, Engineer. August 12th, 1910. Blue print. Scale 1:7200. 64 × 46 cm.

"No. 692" is in the upper left corner.

Map of the area between York Pike and Hanover Road showing battlefield markers, fence lines, roads, woodland, and contour lines at intervals of 12 feet. "Residents 1863 in Egyptian letters" and "Residents 1906 in italics."

351.3

————Map of Gettysburg battlefield showing routes that must be taken by all wheeled conveyances during the anniversary celebration, from June 28 to June 30, July 1 to 5, 1913. Prepared by direction of the Gettysburg National Park Commission, Col. John P. Nicholson, Chairman, Lt. Col. E. B. Cope, Engineer. [1913] Colored. Scale ca. 1:21,250. 39 × 28 cm.

Routes to be followed are shown by red dashed lines. A description of the routes is printed on the verso.

351.4

————Map of one square mile or ¹⁄₂₅ of the battlefield of Gettysburg. Surveyeyd and drawn under the direction of Gettysburg National Military Park Commission, Col. John P. Nicholson, Ch'm., Maj. W. M. Robbins, Maj. C. A. Richardson, Lt. Col. E. B. Cope, Engineer, [and] S. A. Hammond, Ass't. Engineer. Feb. 1st 1898. Blue print. Scale ca. 1:2400. 75 × 72 cm.

At top of map: No. 3; Culp's Hill.

Map title, legend, and a brief account of the "Work completed on United States property on this square by the Gettysburg National Park Commission," signed by E. B. Cope, Engineer, is attached to the map in the lower left corner.

Detailed map of Culp's Hill, with manuscript annotations and hand coloring, showing the extent of U.S. property, telford roads, stone walls, rebuilt stone walls, mounted guns, monuments and markers, lines of earth works, and lunettes for artillery.

351.45

————Map of the battlefield of Gettysburg from original surveys by the engineers of the Commission. By authority of the Secretary of War under the direction of the Gettysburg National Park Commission, Lt. Col. John P. Nicholson, Chairman, Major General L. L. Lomax, Major Charles A. Richardson, Lt. Col. E. B. Cope, Engineer, S. A. Hammond and H. W. Mattern, Asst. Engineers. Drawn by S. A. Hammond, 1903. Washington, Norris Peters Co. [1903] Colored. Scale ca. 1:8350. 130 × 85 cm.

Detailed map of the battlefield indicating monuments and markers, roads, railroads, stone walls, four types of fences, woodland, and relief by contour lines at intervals of 12 feet. "Property owners name 1903 italics" and "Property owners name 1863 Gothic." Lands owned by the United States are tinted green.

351.5

————Another edition. By authority of the Secretary of War, Hon. Lindley M. Garrison, under the direction of the Gettysburg National Park Commission, Lt. Col. John P. Nicholson, Chairman, Major Charles A. Richardson, Lt. Col. E. B. Cope, Engineer. Drawn by S. A. Hammond, Asst. Engineers [sic], 1914. Washington, Norris Peters Co. [1914]

G3822 .G4S5 1914 .U5

351.55

————Another edition. By authority of the Hon. Newton D. Baker, Secretary of War, July 1st, 1916, under the direction of the Gettysburg National Park Commission, Lt. Col. John P. Nicholson, Chairman, Major Charles A. Richardson, Lt. Col. E. B. Cope, Engineer. Drawn by S. A. Hammond, Asst. Engineer, 1916. Philadelphia, John T. Palmer Co. [1916] Colored. Scale ca. 1:8450. 128 × 84 cm.

The map was redrawn for this edition.

351.6

————Map of the battlefield of Gettysburg. Prepared under the direction of the Gettysburg National Park Commission, Colonel John P. Nicholson, Chairman, Major Wm. M. Robbins, Major C. A. Richardson, L't. Col. E. B. Cope, Engineer [and] S. A. Hammond, Ass't Engineer. February 1st., 1898. Colored. Scale ca. 1:12,000. 2 parts, each 39 × 70 cm.

"No. 1" is in the upper margin.

Title and "Explanatory notes" are attached to the map in the lower left corner and a list of "Work on the field accomplished by this Commission to date" is attached to the map in the lower right corner.

Map of the battlefield, with manuscript annotations and hand coloring, showing lands belonging to the United States tinted yellow, additional land "needed for the work in hand" tinted green, completed telford roads in red, roads in "need of piking" in black and "public roads ceded to the United States" in blue.

351.7

————Map of the Gettysburg battlefield. Prepared by authority of the Hon. Daniel S. Lamont, Russell A. Alger, Elihu Root, Secretaries of War, under the direction of the Gettysburg National Military Park Commission, Lt. Col. John P. Nicholson, Chairman, John B. Bachelder Esq., Brig. General William H. Forney, Major William M. Robbins, Major Charles A Richardson. Original survey by Lt. Col. E. B. Cope, Engineer, S. A. Hammond and H. W. Mattern, Ass't Engineers. Reduced from the original by H. W. Mattern. [ca. 1900] Photocopy (positive). Scale ca. 1:7000. 118 × 78 cm.

"Number 436" is in the upper left corner.

Hand-colored photocopy showing four classes of roads, stone walls, Union and Confederate defenses, relief by coutour lines and shading, "property owners name 1863 small italics," and "property owners name 1900 large italics."

351.8

————Map of the Gettysburg battlefield. Prepared by direction of the Gettysburg National Park Commission, Col. John P. Nicholson, Chairman, Col. E. B. Cope, Engineer. May, 1921. Uncolored. Scale ca. 1:21,250. 39 × 28 cm.

Map indicates roads, park towers, and the location of the cyclorama. Troop positions are not indicated.

351.9

————United States property on the Gettysburg battlefield. Gettysburg National Park Commission, Col. John P. Nicholson, Chairman, Major W. M. Robbins, Major C. A. Richardson, [and] Col. E. B. Cope, C. E. [Drawn by] H. W. Mattern, Ass't. Feb. 1st., 1898. Blue print. Scale 1:12,000. 81 × 71 cm.

"Number 256" is in the upper left corner.

Hand-colored and annotated blueprint showing lands "Conveyed by the Gettysburg Battlefield Memorial Association," lands "purchased by the U.S.G.B. Commission and the G.N.P. Commission," and the land devoted to the National Cemetery.

352

U.S. *National Park Service.*

The battle of Gettysburg. February 1948, revised 1951. Uncolored. Scale ca. 1:60,000. 19 × 13 cm. *In its* Gettysburg National Military Park, Pennsylvania. [Washington, Government Printing Office, 1957]

Insert: Cavalry battlefield. Sclae ca. 1:60,000. 4 × 3 cm.

Indicates troop positions and movements, roads, railroad, drainage, relief by hachures, principal points of interest, and a suggested tour route.

352.1

————Reprint 1959.

352.2

————Gettysburg. National Park Service, U.S. Department of the Interior [Washington] Government Printing Office, 1978. Colored. Scale ca. 1:27,500. 36 × 42 cm.

G3822 .G4 1978 .U5
Title from verso.
Map illustrates a descriptive leaflet.
Inset: Gettysburg vicinity map. 7 × 7 cm.
Maps showing troop positions on July 1, 2, and 3, 1863, appear on the verso.
Map indicates auto and bike tours, bridle trail, foot trails, and paved roads.

352.3

————Another issue. 1979.
G3822 .G4 1979 .U5

352.4

————Another edition. 1982. Colored. Scale ca. 1:27,000. 36 × 43 cm. on sheet 40 × 43 cm.

G3822 .G4 1982 .U5
"GPO: 1982–361–578/129 Reprint 1982."
Includes text and a descriptive index to points of interest.

Text, illustrations, and a map of the vicinity of the park headquarters are on the verso.

352.5

————Another issue. 1983.
G3822 .G4 1983 .U5
"GPO: 1983–381–578/266 Reprint 1983."

352.7

————Gettysburg National Military Park, Pennsylvania. Rev. Jan. 1973, GJB [Washington] Government Printing Office, 1973. Colored. Scale ca. 1:28,000. Map 32 × 18 on sheet 33 × 29 cm.

G3822 .G4 1973 .U5
Title from the verso.
Map illustrates a descriptive leaflet.
Inset: Gettysburg vicinity. 7 × 7 cm.
Map indicates 17 tour sites and a tour route.

352.8

Wade (Jennie) Museum.

Map of the battlefield of Gettysburg. [Gettysburg, 19–?] Uncolored. Scale ca. 1:23,700. 40 × 29 cm. *In its* Gettysburg in paragraph with map. Gettysburg, Jennie Wade Museum [19–?]

Map indicates avenues, public roads, turnpikes, railroad, drainage, woodland, houses, and names of residents. Troop positions are not depicted.

"Description of map of battlefield" is printed below the map.

353

Wallace, George W.

Ideal map of Gettysburg battlefield. Designed and drawn by George W. Wallace of the 116th Regt., Ohio Volunteer Infantry. ©1907. Scale ca. 1:18,500. 60 × 54 cm.

Map of the battlefield over which has been drawn a series of squares and circles, the lines of which bear numbers, letters, and the names of military leaders. The "explanatory" text states that "the double-numbered crossings of lines are the main strategic points. The double or parallel lines are military railroads. The straight lines and curves mark the course of shots and charges."

353.5

Warren, Gouverneur K.

Battle field of Gettysburg. [Washington, U.S. Army, Office of the Chief of Engineers, 187–?] Uncolored. Scale 1:12,000 (1 inch equals 1000 feet). 81 × 70 cm.

From the Jubal Early Collection in the Manuscript Division, L.C.

Detailed topographic map subsequently used as the

base for John B. Bachelder's "Map of the Battle Field of Gettysburg" (see entry nos. 325 and 326).

"Positions of troops are not given."

"The map is reduced from one on a scale of 200 feet to the inch, deposited in the Archives of the office of the Chief of Engineers. The survey was ordered by Brevet Major General A. A. Humphreys, Chief of Engineers, and conducted under Brevet Major General G. K. Warren, Major of Engineers." The survey was made in 1868 and 1869 and revised on the ground by P. M. Blake, Civil Engineer in 1873. The original is in the National Archives, Cartographic and Architectural Branch, Record Group 77: E 81.

353.8

——————Map of the battle-field of Gettysburg, Pa. July 1, 2 and 3, 1863. An authentic copy of General G. K. Warren's map from the Atlas to accompany the official records of the Union and Confederate armies 1861–65. Philadelphia, Aero Service Corporation, 1963. Colored. Scale ca. 1:35,000. 46 × 28 cm.

G3824 .G4S5 1863 .W3 1963

In upper right corner: Note on copy filed in the Office of Engineers: "This is a photograph from a map mainly made by Major (then Sergeant) E. B. Cope of my force (while the Chief Engineer of the Army of the Potomac) and under my direction. It is valuable as showing how a good topographer can represent a field after a personal reconnaissance. It was mostly made from horseback sketches based upon the map of Adams County, Pa. G. K. Warren."

Map indicates roads, railroads, houses, names of residents, drainage, relief, and woodland. Union lines and defenses are in blue and Confederate lines and defenses are in red.

A description of the battle is printed in the lower margin.

354

——————Map of the battle-field of Gettysburg, Pa. July 1, 2 and 3, 1863. An authentic copy of General G. K. Warren's map from the "Atlas to accompany the official records of the Union and Confederate armies, 1861–1865." Republished in 3-dimensional form. 1st ed. Philadelphia, Aero Service Corporation [1959] Relief model. Colored. Scale ca. 1:35,000. 47 × 30 cm.

G3822 .G4C18 1863. W35 Model

Printed on vinyl plastic.

The topography, shown by the raised relief, is further augmented by the original hachures. Shows drainage, vegetation, roads, railroads, fences, dwellings with names of inhabitants, and some points of interest on the battlefield. Union and Confederate lines, with defenses, are shown as they were at the conclusion of the battle on July 3, 1863.

A brief resumé of the battle appears below the map.

354.5

The Washington Daily News.

The battle of Gettysburg [July 1, 2, and 3, 1963.] Washington, 1963. Colored. Various scales. 5 maps on sheet 38 × 29 cm. *From* The Washington daily news, Friday, June 28, 1963. p. 18.

Includes maps of the first, second, and third days of battle; a map entitled "Lee invades the North"; and a map of Gettysburg and vicinity showing troop positions, headquarters of Meade and Lee, and other battlefield sites.

Maps are accompanied by descriptive text.

355

Weeks, Gaylord.

Map of Gettysburg and vicinity. Drawn by Gaylord Weeks, Denison, Iowa. Colored ms. Scale 1:3,520. 8 parts, each approx. 46 × 78 cm. Over-all size 164 × 141 cm.

G3822 .G4S5 1863.W4 Vault

Inset: Site of Gen. Gregg's cavalry operations, three miles east of Gettysburg. Scale ca. 1:13,900. 56 × 29 cm.

Typewritten label in the lower right corner reads "Under direction of Mrs. Georgia Wade McClellan, 1898 for her personal use."

Union lines are shown by blue dashes and Confederate lines by red dashes. Shows location of artillery, significant features of the battlefield, some dwellings with names of residents, vegetation, drainage, roads, and railroads.

356

Wells, Jacob.

[Maps illustrating the Gettysburg campaign. June 3–July 3, 1863] Uncolored. Various scales. 20 small maps mounted on 9 sheets measuring 22 × 14 cm. or smaller. *From* Century illustrated monthly magazine, v. 33, Nov. 1886.

Maps indicate troop and cavalry positions and lines of march from Fredericksburg (June 3) to Gettysburg (July 3, 3:15–4:30 P.M.) Maps 19 and 20 illustrate the cavalry engagement on July 3rd.

356.5

Western Maryland Railway Company.

Map of Gettysburg battlefield. Copyright by the Western Maryland Railway Co., 1910. Uncolored. Scale not given. 16 × 21 cm.

Map indicates roads, observation towers, and a few monuments. Troop positions are not depicted.

357

Willcox, William H.

Map of the battle of Gettysburg, Pa., July 1st, 2nd &

3rd, 1863, showing line of battle on P.M. of 2nd. Prepared by Wm. H. Willcox, Captn. & A.D.C. on Maj. Genl. Reynold's staff. 3d ed. Lith of P. S. Duval & Son, Philada. J. G. Shoemaker, engr. Colored. Scale ca. 1:13,100. 49 × 43 cm.

Shows topography by hachures, vegetation, drainage, roads, railroads, houses, stonewalls, cultivated areas, churches, and cemeteries. Union and Confederate positions are shown, including the location of the artillery. Confederate corps are named; Union forces are given in more detail, including names of some division commanders. Shows the Union breast works and cavalry positions.

357.2

Woeltje and Cutting.

Map of the battle field of Gettysburg. July 1st, 2nd, 3rd, 1863. Copyrighted, June 1888, by Woeltje & Cutting, N.Y. Colored. Scale 1:12,000. 77 × 69 cm.

"For sale by Woeltje & Cutting, 115 Pearl Street, New York."

Copyright no. 18291, Aug. 3, 1888.

This map is based on Gouverneur K. Warren's map of the Gettysburg battlefield (see entry no. 353.5), but with the addition of hachures. Names of land owners are overprinted in red. Troop positions are not noted.

357.3

——————Map of the field of operations of Gregg's (Union) & Stuart's (Confederate) cavalry at the battle of Gettysburg, July 3, 1863. Copyrighted, June 1888, by Woeltje & Cutting, N.Y. The American Graphic Co., N.Y. Colored. Scale 1:12,000. 79 × 29 cm.

"For sale by Woeltje & Cutting, 115 Pearl Street, New York."

Copyright no. 18292, Aug. 4, 1888.

This map is based on the map surveyed by Frank O. Maxson under the direction of John B. Bachelder (entry no. 327), but with the addition of hachures. Names of land owners are overprinted in red. Cavalry positions are not noted.

HANOVER

358

Russell, Robert E. L.

Battle of Hanover, Pa., Tuesday, June 30, 1863. Drawn by R. E. L. Russell, Baltimore, 1945, after map by Robert R. Spangler, 1936. Photocopy (positive). Scale ca. 1:19,500. 8 maps, each 20 × 24 cm.

"Environs of Hanover, Pa., 1863."

Hand-colored photocopies showing Confederate positions in red, roads in brown, and vegetation in green.

Geography and Map Division's collections also include a negative photocopy of each map.

PHILADELPHIA

358.1

Taylor, Frank H.

Military map of Philadelphia 1861–1865. Drawn by Frank H. Taylor [1914?] Uncolored. Scale not given. 37 × 25 cm.

Important buildings and sites are keyed by number to the map. Hospitals are identified by letters.

358.2

U.S. *Coast Survey.*

General diagram. [Map showing lines of defenses in Philadelphia west of the Schuylkill River and in part of Delaware County, Pennsylvania. 1863] Colored ms. Scale ca. 1:9600. 2 sheets, 143 × 273 cm. and 129 × 189 cm.

G3824 .P5S5 1863 .U51 Vault

Partial tracing of the following manuscript map (entry no. 358.22) showing 1st- and 2nd-class fortifications and batteries, roads, railroads, towns, rivers and streams, and relief by form lines.

Northern sheet is numbered in the corner "2866X" and "854W 1863" and the southern sheet, "2867X" and "854W 1863."

Accompanied by the following seven maps showing additional details for selected areas:

[1. Fairmont Park area, Philadelphia] Scale not given. 31 × 41 cm.

[2. Paschall subdivision, Philadelphia] Scale 1:2400. 36 × 44 cm.

——————Another copy. 38 × 41 cm.

[3. Haddington subdivision, Philadelphia. Haverford Road, 66th Street, Darby Road and Oregon Ave.] Scale 1:2400. 37 × 53 cm.

[4. Haddington subdivision, Philadelphia, Hunter's Lane, Haverford Road, Merion Road, and Lancaster Turnpike] Scale 1:4800. 46 × 38 cm.

——————Another copy. 45 × 37 cm.

[5. West Philadelphia area, Philadelphia] Scale not given. 31 × 52 cm. Signed "R. M. Bache" in lower left corner.

[6. Darby, Delaware County, Pa.] Scale 1:4800. 38 × 36 cm.

——————Another copy. 38 × 35 cm.

[7. Upper Darby, Delaware County, Pa.] Scale 1:2400. 28 × 38 cm.

——————Another copy. 30 × 37 cm.

358.22

U.S. *Coast Survey.*

——————————Map of a reconnoissance [sic] of the approaches to Philadelphia showing the positions and lines of defence [sic] on the west front of the city. Made under the direction of A. D. Bache, Supt. U.S. Coast Survey, Engineer in charge of defences [sic] General field reconnoissances [sic] by H. L. Whiting, Assist. U.S. Coast Survey. Detailed portions by R. M. Bache, R. E. Halter, C. Rockwill [i.e. Rockwell] & E. Hergesheimer, U.S. Coast Survey. Outlines from local published maps enlarged & drawn by W. B. McMurtrie. 1863. Colored ms. Scale 1:9600 ("800 feet to an inch"). 13 parts, 85 × 68 cm. or smaller. Overall size 242 × 275 cm.

G3824 .P5S5 1863 .U52 Vault

Former ownership stamp is to the left of the map title: U.S.C. & G. Survey, Library and Archives, no. 1.

"U.S. C. and G. Survey, Library and Archives, Acc. no. 54399" and "854ST 1863" are in the corner of each sheet.

Detailed pen and ink manuscript map of western Philadelphia showing 1st- and 2nd-class fortifications and batteries, roads, railroads, towns, rivers and streams, and relief by form lines.

358.25

————Map of a reconnaissance of the approaches to Philadelphia showing the positions and lines of defence [sic] on the north front of the city. Made under the direction of A. D. Bache, Supt. U.S. Coast Survey, Engineer in charge of the Defences [sic]. General field reconnaissance by George Davidson, Assistant U.S. Coast Survey. Details by George Davidson, assisted by C. M. Bache, P. C. F. West, and A. R. FauntLeRoy, U.S. Coast Survey, John B. Atkinson, Joseph Lesley and Thomas R. Stockett, Esqrs. Map plotted and drawn by George Davidson, assisted by A. R. FauntLeRoy and W. E. Weber. 1863. Colored ms. Scale 1:9600 ("800 feet to one inch"). 10 parts; 8 are 78 × 72 cm. or smaller and 2 are 39 × 85 cm. each. Overall size 153 × 296 cm.

G3824 .P5S5 1863 .U53 Vault

Signed in manuscript: George Davidson, Asst. Engr. Fortifications.

Former ownership stamp below map title: U.S.C. & G. Survey, Library and Archives, no. 127.

"No. 2865X" and "854W 1863" (former U.S. Coast Survey numbers) are in the corner of each part.

Pen and ink manuscript map showing northern Philadelphia from Chestnut Hill to Frankford and showing proposed 1st-, 2nd- and 3rd-order batteries. This finely drawn map also depicts turnpikes and common roads, single- and double-track railroads, telegraph lines, rivers and streams, bridges, houses and barns, and relief by contour lines at intervals of 10 feet.

358.3

————Tracing by A. R. FauntLeRoy and W. E. Weber.

1863. Colored ms. Scale 1:9600 ("800 feet to one inch"). 10 parts, each 78 × 61 cm. or smaller. Overall size 154 × 299 cm.

G3824 .P5S5 1863 .U5 Vault

Signed in manuscript: George Davidson, Assistant Engineer Fortifications.

Former ownership stamp below map title: U.S.C. & G. Survey, Library and Archives, no. 126.

"No. 2868X" and "854W 1863" (former U.S. Coast Survey numbers) are in the corner of each part.

Pen and ink tracing of the preceding manuscript map (entry no. 358.25).

358.4

Whiting, Henry L.

Map of supplementary reconnaissannce of the approaches to Philadelphia by the Lancaster Turnpike including the section between Villa Nova and Paoli. Made under the direction of A. D. Bache, engr. in charge of the defenses of Philadelphia, by Henry L. Whiting, Asst. U.S. Coast Survey. [1863] Colored ms. Scale ca. 1:9600. 47 × 196 cm.

G3824 .P5S5 1863 .W41 Vault

Pen and ink manuscript map on tracing linen showing fortifications and batteries at Villanova ("Villa Nova") and Radnor ("Radnorville") in Delaware County and Paoli in Chester County, Pennsylvania.

Former ownership stamp in lower right corner: U.S.C. & G. Survey. Library and Archives, Jan. 28, 1902. Acc. no. 53677.

Includes the signature of Henry L. Whiting.

358.5

————Map of supplementary reconnaissance of the approaches to Philadelphia by the West-Chester road including the section from Newtown Square to the East Branch of Brandywine Creek. Made under the direction of A. D. Bache, engr. in charge of the defenses of Philadelphia, by Henry L. Whiting, Asst. U.S. Coast Survey. [1863] Colored ms. Scale ca. 1:9600. 47 × 268 cm.

G3824 .P5S5 1863 .W4 Vault

Pen and ink manuscript map on tracing linen indicating suggested picket stations and fortifications and batteries in the vicinity of the East Branch of Brandywine Creek and Crum Creek, Chester County, Pennsylvania. Relief is depicted by form lines and spot heights. The map also identifies the "Road taken by the British in flanking the American army (battle of Brandywine, 1777)."

"No. 2863" and "854W" (former U.S. Coast Survey numbers) appear in the lower right corner.

Includes the signature of Henry L. Whiting.

SOUTH CAROLINA

358.6

Coast line from Charleston to Savannah. [1862?] Uncolored ms. Scale ca. 1:430,000. 27 × 33 cm.

G3912 .C6 1862 .C6 Vault

Manuscript map drawn in pencil and ink showing cities and towns, place names, railroads, and coastal fortifications.

From the papers of Joseph Roswell Hawley, Manuscript Division, L.C.

358.7

Colton, Joseph H.

Colton's South Carolina. New York, J. H. Colton, 1865. Colored. Scale ca. 1:1,300,000. 33 × 41 cm.

"Entered according to Act of Congress in the year 1855 by J. H. Colton."

General map showing county and state boundaries, cities and towns, roads and railroads, rivers, and forts.

Insets: Colton's plan of Charleston, vicinity & harbor. 12 × 10 cm.—Fort Sumter. 3 × 3 cm.

359

Evans and Cogswell.

Map of the seat of war, in South Carolina, and Georgia. Published and lithographed by Evans & Cogswell, Charleston, S.C. [1861] Uncolored. Scale ca. 1:450,000. 53 × 66 cm.

Inset: Portion of Georgia [around Savannah]. Uncolored. Scale not given. 11 × 17 cm.

Confederate imprint.

Shows coastal area from Georgetown, South Carolina, to Savannah, Georgia, and territory inland as far north as Kingstree, South Carolina, to Orangeburgh, South Carolina. Gives the location of forts and shows coastal shoals, drainage, roads, railroads, ferries, bridges, dwellings with names of inhabitants, churches, and post offices.

359.5

Foster, John G.

Sketch showing position of Boyd's Neck, Honey Hill, and Devaux' Neck, in Decr. 1864. Bowen & Co., lith., Philada. Uncolored. Scale ca. 1:670,000 (not "1 inch = 10 miles"). 19 × 21 cm. *From* U.S. Congress. Joint Committee on the Conduct of the War. Supplemental report of the Joint Committee on the Conduct of the War, in two volumes. Supplemental to Senate report no. 142, 38th Congress, 2d session (Washington, Government Printing Office, 1866). v. 2, fol. p. 16.

Accompanies "Report of Major General J. G. Foster, to the Committee on the Conduct of the War." 23 p.

Map indicates "lines of investment of Gen. Sherman" at Savannah, Georgia, Boyd's Neck, Honey Hill and Devaux' Neck, South Carolina, and "position of rebel ironclads" on the Savannah River.

360

Lindenkohl, Adolph.

Sketch of portions of seacoast of South Carolina & Georgia. Drawn by A. Lindenkohl. Autogr. copy by H. Lindenkohl. 1862. Uncolored. Scale 1:200,000. 41 × 95 cm.

Autographed in ink: Gen. M.C. Meigs USA.

Map of the coast from Bull's Bay, South Carolina, to Ossabaw Sound, Georgia, showing forts, drainage, roads, railroads, and towns.

"References" at the bottom center of the map give dates on which forts were captured by the Federal forces.

361

——————Another issue.

"Bombardment and surrender of Fort Pulaski (Savannah River) to the National forces April 11, 1862" is added to the list of "References" at the bottom center.

362

——————Another edition. 1863. 40 × 96 cm.

"References" is printed in the lower left corner.

The names of the cartographer and lithographer are not indicated on this edition.

363

——————Sketch of sea coast of South Carolina and Georgia, from Bull's Bay to Ossabaw Sound. Drawn by A. Lindenkohl. E. Molitor, lith. 1863. Uncolored. Scale 1:200,000. 41 × 96 cm.

Another edition of the preceding maps (entry nos. 360–362).

"References" appears in the lower left corner.

Another copy in the Geography and Map Division is from the papers of Joseph Roswell Hawley. It is lightly colored, varnished, and mounted on cloth to fold to 22 × 13 cm. The cover in which the map was folded is annotated as follows: "For the Senior Officer of the Boat Infantry" Dept. of the South. Procured from the U.S.C.S. Office Nov. 18th 1863 by T.B. Brooks, Maj. & A.D.C. (G3912 .C6 1863 .L5)

364

————————Another issue. 41 × 98 cm.
Lacks list of "References."
Another copy is in the Sherman map coll. no. 127.

364.1

————————Another issue. 39 × 87 cm. (Fillmore map coll. no. 257)
G3912 .C6 1863 .L5 Fill 257 Vault
Signed on recto and verso: Millard Fillmore Dec. 6, 1864.

Includes a list of references in the lower left corner. Map extends from Bull's Island to Great Wassaw Island rather than Bull's Bay to Ossabaw Sound as shown on previous editions (entry nos. 360 to 364).

365

Manigault, Gabriel.

Sea coast defences. [1861?] Uncolored. Scale not given. Map 16 × 13 cm. on sheet with text 39 × 22 cm.
Confederate imprint.
Suggested "system of defence for smaller ports and inlets" in South Carolina, signed "G. M." and illustrated by a plan of a fort.
Gabriel Manigault (1809–1888) was the author of a "Letter Addressed to Governor M. L. Bonham, of South Carolina, on the Defences of Charleston" (1863).

365.2

Owner, William.

Map of the Sea Islands.[1863] Uncolored ms. Scale ca. 1:380,000. 19 × 31 cm. *In his* Diary, v. 4, tipped-in at front of volume.
In the William Owner papers, Manuscript Division, L.C., container no. 1.
General map of the coast from Charleston to Savannah showing islands, cities and towns, railroad, and roads.
Volume 4 of the diary covers from February 13 to June 27, 1863.

365.5

U.S. *Army. Corps of Engineers.*

[Part of South Carolina and Georgia] Engineer Bureau, Dec. 24th 1864. Uncolored. Scale 1:350,00. 59 × 81 cm.
Southern half of an unidentified printed map. Sheet extends from Augusta south to Jacksonville, Georgia, and Beaufort, South Carolina, west to Eatonton, Georgia. Indicated are roads and railroads, cities and towns, houses and names of residents, rivers, and forts.
Handwritten title on verso: War map of Georgia.
Map is endorsed "From Chief Engrs. Office, Mil'y Divn. Miss., Bvt. Col: & Chf. Engr."

365.7

U.S. *Coast Survey.*

Coast of South Carolina from Charleston to Hilton Head. [Washington, U.S. Coast Survey] 1862. Uncolored. Scale 1:200,000. 51 × 89 cm. *From its* Report of the Superintendent of the Coast Survey, showing the progress of the survey during the year 1862 (Washington, Government Printing Office, 1864). Map 25.
At head of title: U.S. Coast Survey, A. D. Bache, Supdt.
Insets: Plan and view of Fort "Beauregard"—Bay Point, S.C. Scale 1:2000. 16 × 17 cm.—Fort on Fenwick's Island, S.C. Scale 1:1000. 13 × 15 cm.—Ground plan and view of fort on Bay Point—South Edisto R., S.C. Scale 1:1000. 14 × 15 cm.—Plan and view of fort on Otter Isld. Point—St. Helena Sound, S.C. Scale 1:1000. 12 × 15 cm.—Fort on Sam's Point, Coosaw River, S.C. Scale 1:1000. 13 × 15 cm.—Ground plan and view of fort on Botany-Bay Isld., North Edisto R. Scale 1:2000. 12 × 15 cm.—Fort "Walker"—Hilton Head Isld., S.C. Scale 1:2000. 13 × 15 cm.—Sketch E showing the progress of the survey in section no. V from 1847 to 1862. [Triangulation network from Winyah Bay, South Carolina, to Amelia Island, Florida] Scale 1:600,000. 24 × 74 cm.
"No. 25" is in the upper right corner.

366

Wallace, D. D.

War of Secession, 1861–1865. Edited by D. D. Wallace. L. Philip Denoyer, geographer. Chicago, Denoyer-Geppert Co., [©Dec. 28, 1936] Colored. Scale 1:760,320. 77 × 107 cm (South Carolina history series. SC6. War of Secession and Reconstruction)
School wall map of South Carolina and western and central North Carolina, showing troop movements, engagements, fortifications, "Jeff. Davis' line of flight" and route of "Palmer in pursuit of Davis," towns, rivers, and railroads. Dates of Confederate victories are colored red, and dates of Union victories are printed in black.
Insets: Charleston Harbor during the War of Secession. 34 × 25 cm.—Period of Reconstruction [in South Carolina] 1865–77. 37 × 45 cm.

367

Willenbucher, E.

Plans & views of Rebel defences, coast of South Carolina. Drawn by E. Willenbucher, under the direction of C. O. Boutelle, Assist., U.S. Coast Survey. Bowen & Co., lith., Philada. 1862. Uncolored. 7 plans on sheet 65 × 45 cm.
Contents: Fort "Walker," Hilton Head Isld., S.C. Scale 1:2000. 17 × 15 cm.—Ground plan and view of fort on Botany-Bay Isld. North Edisto R. Scale 1:2000. 12 × 15

cm.—Fort on Sam's Point, Coosaw River, S.C. Scale 1:1000. 13 × 15 cm.—Ground plan and view of fort on Bay Point South Edisto R., S.C. Scale 1:1000. 14 × 15 cm.—Plan and view of Fort "Beauregard," Bay Point, S.C. Scale 1:2000. 17 × 17 cm.—Plan and view of fort on Otter Isld. Point, St. Helena Sound, S.C. Scale 1:1600. 12 × 17 cm.—Fort on Fenwick's Island, S.C. Scale 1:1000. 13 × 17 cm.

At the bottom of each map is a view of the fort.

368

William (A.) and Company.

Map of St. Helena Sound, and the coast between Charleston and Savannah. Compiled from the U.S. Coast Survey. Lith by C. D. Andrews & Co., Boston. Boston, A. Williams & Co., 1861. Uncolored. Scale ca. 1:385,000. 24 × 31 cm.

Shows forts, towns, roads, railroads, rivers, and islands. Insets: Fort Walker. 4 × 3 cm.—Fort Beauregard. 4 × 3 cm.

368.1

————Another issue.

Lacks insets.

BEAUFORT

368a

Prang (Louis) and Company.

Beaufort Harbor and coast line between Charleston, S.C. and Savanna [sic] Ga., with 5 mile distance lines in circles round Beaufort, and R.R. connections, roads, &c, &c. Boston [1861?] Colored. Scale not given. 23 × 30 cm.

Indicates ships in Beaufort Harbor and a few of the coastal forts. "The naval force in the great expedition" appears above the map, followed by the names of commanding officers. Below the neat line at the bottom of the map appear the names of the ships, the captains, and the number of guns aboard each ship.

368a.2

Schelten, B.

Copy of the plot of the city of Beaufort, South Carolina. Drawn by B. Schelten, 103, N.Y. expressily [sic] for Dr. Clymer, Surg. U. S. [186–?] Colored ms. Scale not given. 46 × 70 cm.

G3914 .B4E58 186- .S3 Vault

Map shows the locations of 15 hospitals, the Chief Medical Office, and the homes of "Gen. Saxton" and "Dr. Clymer, Chief. Med. Officer." A list of hospitals appears in the upper left corner.

Inset: [View of] Chief Office. 12 × 15 cm.

BEAUFORT RIVER

368a.3

U.S. *Coast Survey.*

Preliminary chart of Beaufort River, Station Creek, Story and Harbor Rivers forming inside passage between Port Royal and St. Helena Sounds, South Carolina. From a trigonometrical survey under the direction of A. D. Bache, Superintendent of the survey of the coast of the United States. Triangulation by C. O. Boutelle, Assist. Topography by John Seib, Asst. & C. Rockwell, Sub-Asst. Hydrography by the parties under the command of Lieuts. Comdg. J. N. Maffitt, J. P. Bankhead, U.S.N., C. O. Boutelle & W. S. Edwards, Assts. Coast Survey. [Washington, U.S. Coast Survey] 1864. Uncolored. Scale 1:40,000. 61 × 71 cm. *From its* Report of the Superintendent of the Coast Survey, showing the progress of the survey during the year 1864 (Washington, Government Printing Office, 1866). Map 26.

"No. 26" is in the upper left corner.

BROAD RIVER

368a.35

Platt, R., *and* Eugene Willenbücher.

Broad River and its tributaries, S.C. From a reconnaissance made, under direction of Rear Admiral J. A. Dahlgren, Commd'g S.A.B. Squadron, by R. Platt, Act. Master, U.S.N. und[sic] E. Willenbücher, U.S.C.S. 1864. Drawn by Eugene Willenbücher. Bowen & Co., lith., Philada. Uncolored. Scale ca. 1:230,000. 32 × 18 cm. *From* Message of the President of the United States, and accompanying documents, to the two houses of Congress, at the commencement of the first session of the thirty-ninth Congress.—Report of the Secretary of the Navy (Washington, Government Printing Office, 1865). fol. p. 216.

At head of title: U.S.C.S., A. D. Bache, Supt.

Printed in upper left margin: 39th. Cong. 1st Sess.— Annual Report of the Secretary of the Navy.

CALIBOGUE SOUND

368a.4

U.S. *Coast Survey.*

Preliminary chart of Calibogue Sound and Skull Creek forming inside passage from Tybee Roads to Port Royal Sound, South Carolina. From a trigonometrical survey under the direction of A. D. Bache, Superintendent of the survey of the coast of the United States. Triangulation by C. O. Boutelle, C. P Bolles, Capt. E.O.C. Ord, and Lieut. D. T. Van Buren, U.S.A. Assts. Typography by C. Rockwell, Sub Asst. Hydrography by the parties under the command

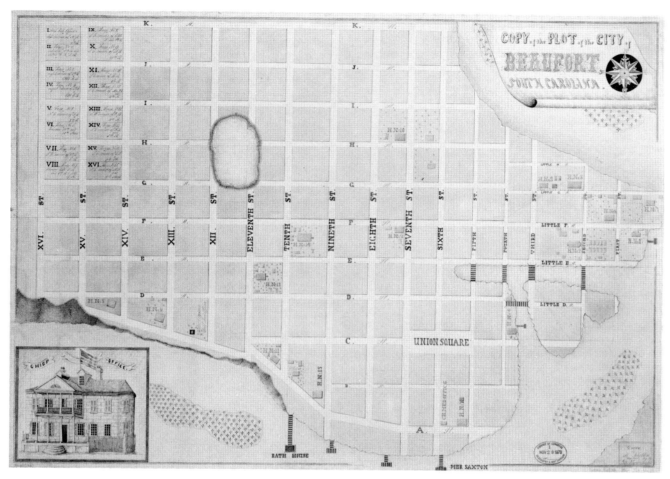

Manuscript map of Beaufort, South Carolina, drawn by B. Schelten for Dr. Meredith Clymer, Chief Medical Officer. Beaufort was held by Federal forces from November 1861 until the end of the war. Depicted here are the locations of 15 Union hospitals, as well as the homes of Dr. Clymer and Gen. Rufus Saxton. (See entry no. 368a.2.)

of Lieut. Comdg. J. N. Maffitt, U.S.N. Asst. and W. S. Edwards, Sub-Asst. [Washington, U.S. Coast Survey] 1862. Uncolored. Scale 1:40,000. 54 × 70 cm. *From its* Report of the Superintendent of the Coast Survey, showing the progress of the survey during the year 1862 (Washington, Government Printing Office, 1864). Map 27.

"No. 27" is in the upper left corner.

CHARLESTON

368a.5

Adams (Peter) Company.

[Map of Charleston Harbor showing defenses. 186–.] Section from Atlas accompanying war records U.S.A. by

courtesy of Julius Bien & Co. [18–?] Colored. Scale not given. 16 × 24 cm.

Printed in upper margin: Peter Adams Co.'s.—vellum map.

368a.7

AP Newsfeatures.

Background map; [Map of Charleston Harbor showing position of Fort Sumter and surrounding batteries. New York, 1961] Uncolored. Scale not given. 11 × 20 cm.

Accompanies an article by Sid Moody, AP Newsfeatures writer, entitled "It All Began at Ft. Sumter." 3 p., ea. 36 × 22 cm.

369

Blunt, Edmund, *and* George W. Blunt.

E. & G. W. Blunt's map of Charleston and vicinity. [New York] 1862. Uncolored. Scale ca. 1:151,000. 46 × 52 cm.

Indicates fortifications, roads, railroads, towns, street pattern of Charleston, drainage, vegetation, and ship channels.

370

Boutelle, Charles O.

General map of Charleston Harbor, South Carolina, showing Rebel defences and obstructions. Prepared by direction of Rear Admiral J. A. Dahlgren, U.S.N., commanding South Atlantic Blockading Squadron, by C. O. Boutelle, Asst., U.S. Coast Survey. Drawn by E. Willenbücher, U.S. Coast Survey. Chas G. Krebs, lith. 1865. Colored. Scale 1:30,000. 56 × 63 cm.

G3914.C3 1865 .W5 TR133

"Shore line, channels, fortifications & armaments are from surveys and data of U.S. Coast Survey. Positions of obstructions & torpedoes from information furnished by persons who removed them." Water is shaded to show depth at 6, 12, and 18 feet; Union batteries are in black, Rebel batteries are in red. Shows wrecks, as well as torpedoes and obstructions, roads, railroads, and a plan of the city. A chart gives "Armament of Rebel forts."

Listed in D. A. Wise's *A Descriptive List of Treasure Maps and Charts,* 2nd ed. (Washington, Library of Congress, 1973), no. 133.

370.1

————————Another issue. Lith. at U.S. Coast Survey by C. G. Krebs. Bowen & Co. lith. Philada. *From* Message of the President of the United States, and accompanying documents to the two houses of Congress, at the commencement of the first session of the thirty-ninth Congress.—Report of the Secretary of the Navy (Washington, Government Printing Office, 1865). fol. p. 256.

Printed in upper left margin: 39th Cong. 1st Sess.—Annual Report of the Secretary of the Navy.

A second copy of this map in the Geography and Map Division is from the papers of Henry R. Schoolcraft.

371

Bowen and Company.

Map of Charleston Harbor, S.C. Bowen & Co's lith., Philada. [18—?] Colored. Scale ca. 1:15,800. 45 × 58 cm.

Upper right corner: Mil. aff., vol. v., no. 591b.

Red curves are marked 6, 12, 18, and 24 feet to show depths at mean low water. The area always covered with water is blue, the surface between high and low water marks is indicated by wavy lines and colored with bistre. Shows drainage, vegetation, cultivated areas, roads, and houses. The forts are circumscribed by 9-inch circles, which show the range of their guns, with the exception of Fort Sumter, where the range is different and is indicated by three radii.

372

Dobelmann, D.N. and G. Huck

Charleston Harbor and city defences. Entered according to Act of Congress in the year 1864 by D. N. Dobelmann & G. Huck . . . Published by T. B. Usser. Colored. Scale ca. 1:170,000. 40 × 59 cm.

"Key to the map of Charleston Harbor and defences" is pasted to the right of the map.

"Green represents the Confederates' land [and] pink the Federal possessions."

Indicates "torpedoes in the channels," obstructions, bridges, roads and streets, railroads, and rivers. Letters A to K represent fortifications, headquarters, depots, and "place where Clarck of Brooklin was executed." Forts and batteries are numbered 1 to 40. The number of guns and mortars for each is shown opposite the name given in the "Key."

373

Elliot and Ames.

Plan of Charleston Harbor, and its fortifications, compiled by Elliot & Ames from government surveys. C. D. Andrews' lith. Boston, 1861. Uncolored. Scale 1:31,680. 37 × 52 cm.

Shows channel, low water mark and soundings, drainage, roads, railroads, some dwellings, a plan of the city, and forts.

373.5

Map of Charleston and vicinity. 1862. Colored ms. Scale ca. 1:173,000. 44 × 51 cm.

G3914 .C3A1 1862 .M3 Vault

Pen and ink manuscript map drawn on tracing linen showing roads, railroads, towns, and forts in the vicinity of Charleston.

From the papers of Joseph Roswell Hawley, Manuscript Division, L.C.

373.8

Owner, William.

Charleston Harbour. [1862–1863] Uncolored ms. Scale ca. 1:155,000. 19 × 15 cm. *In his* Diary, v. 3, tipped-in at front of volume.

In the William Owner papers, Manuscript Division, L.C., container no. 1.

Map shows "Swash" and "Ship" channels, forts, railroads, and soundings.

Volume 3 of the diary covers from Sept. 11, 1862, to Feb. 13, 1863.

374

Perry, George T.

Part of Charleston Harbor, embracing forts Moultrie, Sumter, Johnson, and Castle Pinckney, also Sullivan, James & Morris islands; and showing the position of the Star of the West, when fired into from Morris Island. Lith. P. S.

Duval & Son, Philadela. ©1861. Uncolored. Scale ca. 1:31,000. 35 × 48 cm.

Shows the channel, drainage, vegetation, roads, plan of the city, and forts. A portrait of Major Anderson, commander of Fort Sumter, is in the upper right corner. Below the neat line is a view of the harbor and city from Fort Johnson to Mt. Pleasant.

374.5

The Philadelphia Inquirer.

Charleston and its defences. Philadelphia, 1863. Uncolored. Scale ca. 1:52,000. 30 × 24 cm. *From* The Philadelphia Inquirer, Saturday, April 11, 1863, p. 1.

Map indicates forts, batteries, obstructions, and torpedoes (i.e., mines).

375

Schwerin, J. A., Jr.

The Confederate defense of Charleston Harbor and vicinity. Aiken, S.C., ©1958. Uncolored. Scale not given. 26 × 23 cm.

Shows channel, drainage, plan of part of the city, location of forts and batteries, and the spot where the "stone fleet" was sunk, Dec. 20, 1861.

375.5

Spence, Edward Lee.

Shipwrecks of the Civil War, Charleston, South Carolina, 1861–1865, researched and drawn by E. Lee Spence, M.H.D., underwater archeologist, Sea Research Society. Sullivan's Island, S.C., E.L. Spence, ©1984. Colored. Scale ca. 1:39,000. 39 × 56 cm.

G3914 .C3P57 1865 .S6

Annotated in black ink in lower margin: E. Lee Spence, hand-signed and colored, April 30, 1984, Charleston, South Carolina, copy #41 of 4500.

Map of Charleston Harbor and vicinity indicating the location of shipwrecks and the names of the vessels. A list of the ships and the dates of sinking appears in the lower left corner.

Stamped on verso: Library of Congress, Copyright Office, June 21, 1984, VA 157–808.

376

Tomlinson, George W.

New map of Charleston Harbor, showing the scene of the great naval contest between the iron clad monitors and the Rebel batteries, also the lines of fire, forts, obstructions, inlets, princl. plantations, & e.t.c. Lith. by J. Mayer & Co. Boston, ©1863. Uncolored. Scale not given. 56 × 39 cm.

Shows the coast from Long Island to the North Edisto River. Indicates drainage, roads, railroads, and dwellings with names of inhabitants. Channels, water depths, forts and batteries, with lines of fire, are given.

The following title appears in the lower right corner: Tomlinson's map of Charleston Harbor, S.C., and vicinity, showing the fortifications and batteries, together with a full description of the harbor, forts, obstructions, bombardment & et.c.

Drawings of the Ericsson "Devil" and the iron clad "Keokuk," and plans of Fort Sumter, Fort Moultrie, and Castle Pinckney are in the lower right corner. A column of text entitled "Description of the harbor, forts, &c." is in the right margin.

377

U.S. *Army. Corps of Engineers.*

Map of the defences of Charleston city and harbor, showing also the works erected by the U.S. forces in 1863 and 1864. To accompany the report of Major Genl. Q. A. Gillmore, U.S. Vols. [186–] Uncolored. Scale 1:60,000. 52 × 68 cm.

At bottom of map: View off North Channel, Fort Sumter 3½ miles distant, bearing W. ¾ N., Febry. 18th 1865.

This map without the Corps of Engineers' insignia appears as Plate II of the *Supplementary Report* published with Q.A. Gillmore's *Engineer and Artillery Operations Against the Defenses of Charleston Harbor in 1863; with a Supplement.* (New York, D. Van Nostrand, 1868). 314, 172 p. (U.S. Army. Corps of Engineers. Professional papers, no. 16)

Shows drainage, vegetation, roads, railroads, soundings, shoals, channels, forts, batteries, picket line of the U.S. forces, plan of the city with the "effective, annoying [and] extreme range" of guns from Cumming's Point.

The obstructions in the channel are marked A to R and are explained in a letter of William H. Dennis, dated March 17, 1865, to Gillmore, which appears in the *Supplement,* p. 31–32.

378

U.S. *Coast Survey.*

Charleston Harbor and its approaches showing the positions of the Rebel batteries. 1863. Uncolored. Scale 1:30,000. 61 × 50 cm.

Shows roads, railroads, houses, vegetation, a street plan of Charleston, drainage, soundings, and shoals.

379

————Another copy.

Includes manuscript annotations in red and blue showing the "defences still held by the Rebels [and] Rebel batteries in possession of Union forces [on] July 14, 1863," "position of Union besieging army," and "position of attacking fleet, during action."

379.5

————Another issue. Colored.

In the James A. Garfield papers, Manuscript Division, L.C., series 8, container no. 1.

Overprinted to show positions occupied by the Union Army and Navy, and "Rebel batteries in possession [of] National forces [and] batteries still held by the Rebels [on] July 17, 1863."

380

————Another issue. Colored.

Overprinted to show positions occupied by the Union Army and Navy, and "Rebel batteries in possession [of] National forces [and] batteries still held by the Rebels [on] Sept. 7, 1863."

381

————Another issue. Lith. of J. Bien, N.Y. Colored.

Overprinted to show ¼-mile concentric circles centered on St. Michaels, Charleston; positions occupied by the Union Army and Navy; "Rebel batteries in possession of National forces [and] batteries still held by the Rebels [on] Sept. 7th 1863." Union positions are based "on the authority of Maj. T. B. Brooks . . ."

382

————Another issue. J. Bien, lith., N.Y. Colored. Scale ca. 1:30,000. 68 × 68 cm.

Enlarged issue covering all of James Island and indicating ½-mile concentric circles centered on St. Michaels, Charleston, "first [and] second line[s] of Rebel defences," positions occupied by the Union Army and Navy, and "Rebel batteries in possession [of] National forces [and] batteries still held by the Rebels [on] Sept. 7th 1863."

383

————Preliminary chart of Charleston Harbor and its approaches. Published in 1858. Additions in 1862. Uncolored. Scale ca. 1:30,000. 82 × 93 cm.

"Transferred from Office of Chf. Engr., Defenses of Washington, to Engr. Dept., Jany. 1866."

Shows fortifications, towns, soundings, roads and streets, vegetation, and drainage.

Includes "view of main ship channel" and "view off north channel."

384

————Resurvey of Charleston Bar by W. S. Edwards, Asst. and F. P. Webber, Sub-Asst., under the direction of C. O. Boutelle, Assistant, 1864. Redd. Drng. by J. J. Ricketts & A. Boschke. Engd. by F. Dankworth, J. Knight, E. Yeager & G. McCoy. Colored. Scale 1:30,000. 79 × 81 cm.

"No. 15" is in the upper left corner.

Revised and redrawn edition of the preceding chart published in 1862.

384.5

Walker, William A.

Map of Charleston and its defences. Compiled from surveys of portions of St. Andrews and Christ Ch. parishes by Lieut. John Johnson, C.S. Engrs., the harbor, James Id., Folly Id., Morris Id., Sullivans Id., & Long Id., from U.S. Coast Survey, Johns Id., from Mills Atlas. Under the direction of Maj; Wm. H. Echols, C.S. Engr. Corps, by Wm. A. Walker, Draughtsman, C.S. Engr. Corps. Drawn by John R. Key, 2nd. Lieut., C.S. Engrs. Charleston, S.C., Nov: 28th, 1863. [1885] Uncolored. Scale 1:63,360 (not "2 inches to 1 mile"). 51 × 65 cm.

In upper left corner: Copied for his excellency M. L. Bonham Governor of the State of South Carolina.

In lower margin: Reproduced for Mayor Courtenay's city year book, from the original map in the possession of the Chamber of Commerce, Charleston, S.C.

Endorsed (in facsimile): Approved G. T. Beauregard, Genl. Comdg.; Approved D. B. Harris, Col. & Chef. Engr.

Detailed map showing forts and batteries, roads, railroads, towns, houses and names of residents, vegetation, drainage, and soundings in Charleston Harbor and offshore.

384.6

Willenbücher, Eugene.

Defences of Charleston Harbor. Fortifications on James Island. From a reconaissance made under direction of C. O. Boutelle, Assistant U.S.C.S., by Eugene Willenbücher. 1865. Lith. Bowen & Co., Philada. Uncolored. Scale 1:2000 and 1:4000. 33 × 46 cm. *From* Message of the President of the United States, and accompanying documents, to the two houses of Congress, at the commencement of the first session of the thirty-ninth Congress.—Report of the Secretary of the Navy (Washington, Government Printing Office, 1865). fol. p. 256.

At head of title: No. 2, U.S. Coast Survey.

Printed in upper left margin: 39th Cong. 1st sess.— Annual Report of the Secretary of the Navy.

Includes plans of batteries Glover, Haskall and Wampler, and Fort Johnson. Also included are 18 profiles of the defensive works.

384.7

————Defences of Charleston, S.C. Fortifications on Sullivan's Island. From a reconnaissance made under direction of C. O. Boutelle, Assistant U.S.C.S., by Eugene Willenbücher. 1865. Bowen & Co., lith., Philada. Uncolored. Scale ca. 1:4000. 29 × 63 cm. *From* Message of the President of the United States, and accompanying documents, to the two houses of Congress, at the commencement of the

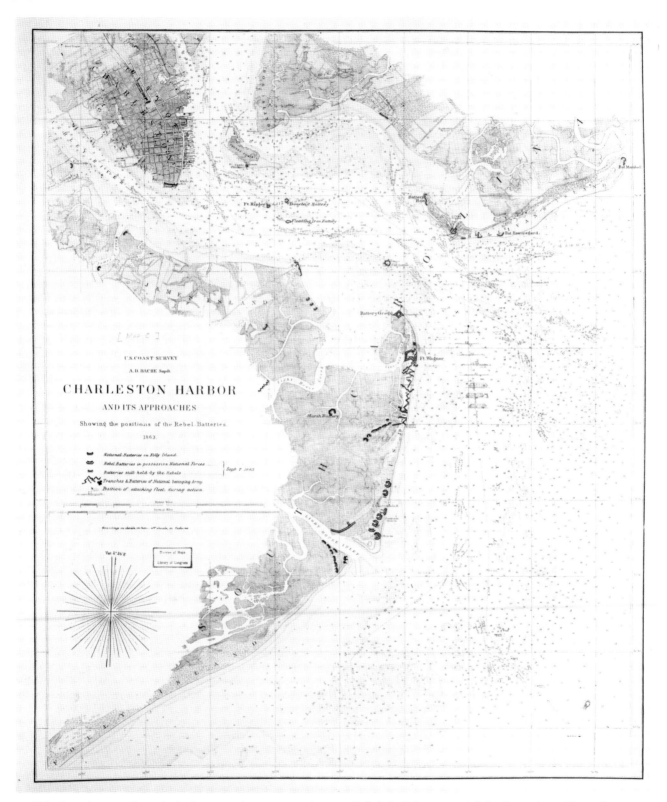

U.S. Coast Survey's chart of Charleston Harbor overprinted to show positions occupied by Union army and navy, and "Rebel batteries in possession [of] National forces [and] batteries still held by the Rebels [on] Sept. 7, 1863." On September 8, Union forces were repulsed in their attempt to capture Fort Sumter. (See entry no. 380.)

first session of the thirty-ninth Congress.—Report of the Secretary of the Navy (Washington, Government Printing Office, 1865). fol. p. 256.

At head of title: U.S. Coast Survey.

"No. 3" is printed below the map title and bar scales.

Printed in upper left margin: 39th Cong. 1st. sess.—Annual Report of the Secretary of the Navy.

Map shows Battery Bee and forts Moultrie, Beauregard, and Marshall. Included are 21 profiles of the defensive works. A "List of guns" appears in the lower left corner.

384.8

————Defences of Charleston, South Carolina. From a reconnaissance made by direction of C. O. Boutelle, Asst. U.S.C.S., by E. Willenbücher. 1865. Bowen & Co., lith., Philada. Uncolored. Scales 1:2000 and 1:4000. 38 × 59 cm. *From* Message of the President of the United States, and accompanying documents, to the two houses of Congress, at the commencement of the first session of the thirty-ninth Congress.—Report of the Secretary of the Navy (Washington, Government Printing Office, 1865). fol. p. 256.

At head of title: U.S. Coast Survey.

"No. 4" is printed to the left of the map title.

Printed in upper left margin: 39th Cong. 1st sess.—Annual Report of the Secretary of the Navy.

Includes 14 ground plans and 32 profiles.

385

Williams, W. A.

Sketch of Charleston Harbor. By W. A. Williams, Civil Engineer. Boston, L. Prang & Co., [186–?] Colored. Scale ca. 1:70,000. 24 × 25 cm.

Shows fortifications, street pattern of Charleston, vegetation, and a few soundings.

Insets: Castle Pinckney. 7 × 5 cm—Fort Sumpter [sic]. 7 × 6 cm—Fort Moultrie. 5 × 6 cm.

FORT JOHNSON

386

U.S. *Army. Corps of Engineers.*

Fort Johnson, section of map of the defences of Charleston Harbor, South Carolina, surveyed between March 7th & May 20th, 1865, under the direction of Brevet Major General R. Delafield, Chief Engineer, U.S. Army. Surveyed April 20th, 1865, by J. E. Weyss, Maj., U.S.V.; assisted by Mr. F. Theilkuhl & E. Schumann. Am Photo. Litho. Co., N.Y. Uncolored. Scale 1:1200. 32 × 42 cm.

Below neat line of map: Furnished by the War Department to the City Council of Charleston, S. C.

Shows topography by hachures, drainage, vegetation, batteries, and a detailed plan of the fortifications.

FORT SUMTER

386.5

Foster, John G.

Sketch showing position of besieging batteries. [Fort Sumter] April 12–13, 1861. Bowen & Co., lith., Phila. Uncolored. Scale ca. 1:30,800. 24 × 19 cm. *From* U.S. Congress. Joint Committee on the Conduct of the War. Supplemental report of the Joint Committee on the Conduct of the War, in two volumes. Supplemental to Senate report no. 142, 38th Congress, 2d session (Washington, Government Printing Office, 1866). v. 2, fol. p. 8.

Accompanies "Report of Major General J. G. Foster, to the Committee on the Conduct of the War." 23 p.

387

[Plan of Fort Sumter, South Carolina] Surveyed: March 20th, 22, 27: 1865. Colored ms. Scale not given. 56 × 62 cm.

G3914 .C3:2S92 1865 .P6 Vault

Lacks title and authority.

"Red lines [denote] remainder of walls of old Ft. Sumter; Red dotted [lines indicate] souterains of walls of old Ft. Sumter; blue dotted [lines signify] souterains built out of the rubbish; [and] black [lines indicate] interior and exterior limits of Sumter at date."

388

U.S. *Army. Corps of Engineers.*

Fort Sumter, South Carolina at the time of its capture February 18th, 1865. Showing the effects of the bombardment from Morris Island. To accompany the report of Maj. Genl. Q. A. Gillmore, U.S. Vols., comdg. Dept. of the South. Julius Bien & Co., photo-lith., N.Y. [186–] Uncolored. Scale 1:240 and 1:600. 59 × 79 cm.

Sheet contains a plan of the fort, a horizontal section, 3 elevations, and 13 sections.

This map appears also as Plate III of the *Supplementary Report* published with Q. A. Gillmore's *Engineer and Artillery Operations Against the Defenses of Charleston Harbor in 1863; with a Supplement.* (New York, D. Van Nostrand, 1868). 314, 172 p. (U.S. Army. Corps of Engineers. Professional papers, no. 16)

FORT WAGNER

389

Brooks, T. B.

Map showing siege operations against forts Sumter and Wagner, between July 13th & Sept. 7th, 1863, by Maj. T. B. Brooks, A.D.C. & Assist. Engrs. Published by permission of

Genl. Gillmore at the U.S. Coast Survey Office. Uncolored. Scale ca. 1:6,750. 33 × 24 cm.

Shows drainage, roads, high and low water line, 6-ft. and 12-ft. depth curve, batteries, trenches, stockades, and a plan of Fort Wagner. Fort Sumter does not appear on this map, only the line of fire to the fort from the breaching batteries south of Fort Wagner.

ISLE OF PALMS

389.1

Spence, Edward Lee.

Wreck chart: [showing the shipwreck location of the Confederate ships Georgiana and Mary Bowers off the coast of Isle of Palms, South Carolina] prepared by E. Lee Spence. Sullivan's Island, S.C., E. L. Spence, ©1978 (i.e., © 1983). Colored. Scale ca. 1:18,000. 36 × 56 cm.

G3914 .I78P57 1978 .S6

LC copy annotated in pencil in lower margin: E. Lee Spence, Isles of Palms, South Carolina, April 17, 1983, hand colored limited edition, #320 of 500.

Inset: Cross section of the "Georgiana" starboard side, forward cargo hold. 19 × 14 cm.

Text to the right of the map describes the sinking of the *Georgiana* on March 19, 1863, and the *Mary Bowers* on August 31, 1864.

Stamped on verso: Library of Congress, Copyright Office, Apr 18, 1983, VA 124–632.

MORRILL'S INLET

389.12

Organization of an expedition against Morrill's Inlet, S.C. [December 1863–January 1864] Uncolored ms. Scale ca. 1:15,840. 34 × 56 cm.

In the Joseph F. Green papers, Manuscript Division, L.C., folder labeled "Instructions for attack on Morrill's Inlet, S.C. 1863–64."

Pencil drawing showing buildings, Confederate building, sand hills, woodland, soundings, and position of the ship *I. A. Ward* off-shore.

Title from the verso of the map.

"11" appears at the top of the map.

389.13

[Sketch of Morrill's Inlet, S.C. December 1863–January 1864] Uncolored ms. Scale not given. 32 × 21 cm.

In the Joseph F. Green papers, Manuscript Division, L.C., folder labeled "Instructions for attack on Morrill's Inlet, S.C. 1863–64."

Rough pencil and pen and ink sketch drawn on lined note paper. Map indicates the location of houses, marshes, and an inlet.

"5" appears in the upper right corner.

PORT ROYAL SOUND

389.14

Colton, George Woolworth.

Carte de Port Royal et des environs, avec un plan de la côte du sud, depuis Bull's Bay (Caroline du Sud), jusqu'a Brunswick (Georgia), indiquant les moyens de communication entre Beaufort, Savanah [sic] Ft. Charleston. Drawn by G. Woolworth Colton, N.Y. [New York] Le courrier des États-Unis [186–?] Uncolored. Scale ca. 1:160,000. 38 × 51 cm.

G3912 .P62 186– .C6

At top of map: Publié par Le courrier des États-Unis.

Map of part of the coast of South Carolina showing the Union blockage of Port Royal Sound.

Inset: Part of the coast of S. Carolina showing the relative positions of Charleston, Beaufort I. & Savannah. 18 × 21 cm.

389.15

Owner, William.

[Map of Port Royal Sound. 1863] Uncolored ms. Scale not given. 19 × 15 cm. *In his* Diary, v. 4, tipped-in at end of volume.

In the William Owner papers, Manuscript Division, L.C., container no. 1.

Map indicates the location of forts on Phillps Island and Hilton Head Island.

Volume 4 of the diary covers from February 13 to June 27, 1863.

389.16

U.S. *Coast Survey.*

Preliminary chart of Port Royal entrance, Beaufort, Broad and Chechessee Rivers, South Carolina. From a trigonometrical survey under the direction of A. D. Bache, Superintendent of the survey of the coast of the United States. Triangulation by C. O. Boutelle, Assist. Hydrography by the parties under the command of Lieuts. Comdg. J. N. Maffitt, C. M. Fauntleroy, and J. P. Bankhead, U.S.N., Assists. and of C. O. Boutelle, Asst. and W. S. Edwards, Sub-Asst. [Washington, U.S. Coast Survey] 1862. Uncolored. Scale 1:60,000. 83 × 56 cm. *From its* Report of the Superintendent of the Coast Survey, showing the progress of the survey during the year 1862 (Washington, Government Printing Office, 1864). Map 26.

"No. 26" is in the upper left corner.

389.17

————1863. **Another issue.** *From its* Report of the Superintendent of the Coast Survey, showing the progress of the survey during the year 1863 (Washington, Government Printing Office, 1864). Map 12.

"No. 12" is in the upper left corner.

Identified in the report of the Superintendent as the "resurvey of 1863."

389.2

U.S. *Coast Survey.*

Preliminary chart of Port Royal entrance. Beaufort, Chechessee, and Colleton Rivers, South Carolina. From a trigonometrical survey under the direction of A. D. Bache, Superintendent of the survey of the coast of the United States. Triangulation by C. O. Boutelle, Assist. Hydrography by the parties under the command of Lieuts. Commdg. J. N. Maffitt and C. M. Fauntleroy, U.S.N., Assists. [Washington, U.S. Coast Survey] 1862. Uncolored. Scale 1:60,000. 74 × 57 cm.

"No. 18" is in the upper left corner.

Detailed nautical chart showing Hilton Head Island and vicinity. Indicated are soundings, bottom contours, and vegetation.

Includes sailing directions.

ST. HELENA SOUND

389.3

U.S. *Coast Survey.*

Preliminary chart of St. Helena Sound, South Carolina. From a trigonometrical survey under the direction of A. D. Bache, Superintendent of the survey of the coast of the

United States. Triangulation by C. O. Boutelle and C. P. Bolles, Assistants. Topography by John Seib, Assistant. Hydrography by the parties under the command of Lieut. Comdg. J. N. Maffitt, U.S.N. and C. O. Boutelle, Assists. [Washington, U.S. Coast Survey] 1864. Uncolored. Scale 1:40,000. 62 × 71 cm. (*Its* no. 436)

Triangulation, topography, and hydrography executed in 1851, 1856, and 1857.

General chart indicating soundings and bottom contours.

Includes sailing directions.

STONO INLET

389.4

Willenbücher, Eugene.

Stono Inlet, South Carolina. From a trigonometrical survey under the direction of A. D. Bache, Superintendent of the survey of the coast of the United States. Triangulation, topography and hydrography by the parties under the direction of C. O. Boutelle, Assist., Coast Survey. Drawn by E. Willenbücher. Chas. G. Krebs, lith. Preliminary edition. [Washington, U.S. Coast Survey] 1862. Uncolored. Scale 1:20,000. 50 × 54 cm.

"The triangulation was executed in 1852; the topography and hydrography were executed in 1862."

General chart showing soundings and bottom contours.

Includes sailing directions.

Listed as no. 118 in the *Catalogue of Hydrographic Maps, Charts, and Sketches, Published by the United States Coast Survey* (Washington, Government Printing Office, 1866).

TENNESSEE

389.7

Blakeslee, G. H.

Middle Tennessee. G. H. Blakeslee—1863. Colored ms. Scale not given. 53 × 41 cm.

G3961 .S5 1863 .B6 Vault

Pen and ink sketch map showing Federal troop movements, engagements, railroads, villages, drainage, and relief by hachures.

Note at the bottom of the map reads "Fourteen trips across Tennessee. 1862–1864."

389.75

Brooks, Alfred F.

[Civil War sketch book—Tennessee and Kentucky. By Alfred F. Brooks, Acting Topographical Engineer, 2nd Brigade, 5th Division, 14th Army Corps. 1862–1863] 13 maps and 2 views (uncolored), 13 × 19 cm. or smaller.

G1326 .S5B7 1863 Vault

Maps 1 through 12, covering parts of the counties of Cannon, De Kalb, Smith, Wilson, and Rutherford, Tennessee, depict Union and Confederate campsites in February

1863. The two views (numbers 13 and 14) are drawn on different paper than that which was used for the maps.

Sketchbook is accompanied by a piece of tracing paper, measuring 9 × 10 cm., containing autographs of "O. O. Howard Maj. Gen." and "P. H. Sheridan Maj. Genl."

Contents

1. [Map of the environs of Readyville, Tennessee, showing location of Federal camp] 13 × 10 cm.

2. [Map of the environs of Middleton, Liberty, and Carthage, Tennessee, showing locations of Federal camps on February 3 and 4, 1863, and the position of a "Rebel camp still smoking"] 13 × 19 cm.

3. [Map of the environs of Lebanon, Shop Springs, and Cherry Valley, Tennessee, showing Federal camps on February 5 and 6, 1863] 13 × 10 cm.

4. [Road from Lebanon to Fall Creek showing the place where Federal forces were "attacked by the Rebels"] 13 × 10 cm.

5. [Continuation of the road from Fall Creek showing "old Rebel camp," cotton gin, and grist mill on an unnamed river, probably the East Fork, Stones River] 13 × 10 cm.

6. [Unfinished sketch of Murfreesboro, Tennessee, and vicinity] 13 × 10 cm.

7. [Roads in the vicinity of Lascasses, Tennessee, showing "camp on Feb. 19th 1863] 13 × 10 cm.

8. [Roads in the vicinity of Fall Creek Church, Tennessee, showing "Morgan's old camp" and Federal campsites on February 20 and 21, 1863] 13 × 10 cm.

9. [Roads in the vicinity of Milton, Tennessee] 13 × 10 cm.

10. [Road from Readyville to Murfreesboro, Tennessee, showing Fort Transit] 13 × 10 cm.

11. [Road from Readyville to Breadyville, Tennessee, showing the location of two Confederate camps] 13 × 10 cm.

12. [Roads in the environs of Woodbury and Readyville, Tennessee, showing the location of the Confederate camp] 13 × 10 cm.

13. Battle of Mumfordsville [i.e., Munfordsville, Kentucky, Sept. 1862] View. 6 × 13 cm. (Title on verso)

14. [View of an unidentified river encampment] 6 × 11 cm.

15. Map of the battl[e] ft. near Milto[n] Tenness[ee] Engagement the 20th Mar[ch] 1863. By A. F. Brooks, Act. Topl. Engr. 2nd Brig. 5th Div., 14 A.C. Map 11 × 9 cm. (This is sometimes called the engagement at Vaught's Mill.)

389.77

Finegan, N.

Map of a part of Tennessee. Reduced under direction of Capt: Merrill, U.S. Engineers. From Capt: Michler's military map of Tennessee. June 1st, 1863. N. Finegan draughts-man. G. A. Bauer 1st Lieut. del. Photocopy (positive). Scale not given. 34 × 56 cm. Cut and mounted to fold to 17 × 11 cm.

In the James A. Garfield papers, Manuscript Division, L.C., series 8, container no. 1.

Title on the cover is pasted on the verso. Cover signed in ink: J. A. Garfield, Brig. Gen. Chief of Staff.

Reconnaissance map of central Tennessee from Nashville south to Chattanooga showing roads, railroads, cities and towns, rivers and streams, and fords.

389.8

Lloyd, James T.

Lloyd's official map of the State of Tennessee. Compiled from actual surveys and official documents, showing every rail road & rail road station with the distances between each station. Also the counties and county seats, cities, towns, villages, post offices, wagon roads, canals, forts, fortifications, &c. New York, J. T. Lloyd, 1863. Colored. Scale ca. 1:506,880. 78 × 120 cm.

"Entered according to Act of Congress in the year 1862 by J. T. Lloyd."

Battle sites are not underlined in this edition.

389.9

————————Lloyd's official map of the State of Tennessee. Drawn & engraved from actual surveys and used by our commanders. New York, J. T. Lloyd, 1862. Colored. Scale ca. 1:506,880. 80 × 121 cm., cut and mounted to fold to 22 × 13 cm.

"Entered according to Act of Congress in the year 1862 by J. T. Lloyd."

Cover title (in ms.): Map of Tennessee. Brig. Genl. J. C. Brown, Army of Tennessee, 1863. Cover signed in inside, "G. T. Beauregard, Genl. Comdg. 1864–5."

Map indicates county names and boundaries, cities and towns, roads and railroads, rivers, and fortifications. Battle sites are underlined in red.

Another copy is in the Fillmore map coll. no. 112-A

390

See Sherman map collection no. 159.

391

See Sherman map collection no. 160.

392

See Sherman map collection no. 161.

392.2

[Map of part of the counties of McNairy and Hardin, Tennessee, and Alcorn and Tishomingo, Mississippi. April

1862] Colored ms. on tracing linen. Scale 1:126,720 ("1/2 inch to the mile"). 31 × 38 cm.

In the Edwin M. Stanton papers, Manuscript Division, L.C., vol. 5, no. 51222.

Sketch map annotated in red ink to show approximate locations of Pope, Buell, and Grant's armies and the picket line in advance of Beauregard's lines during the Shiloh Campaign.

393

Mergell, C. S.

Military map of middle Tennessee and parts of East Tennessee and the adjoining states, being part of the Department of the Cumberland, commanded by Maj. Gen. Geo. H. Thomas, U.S.A. Compiled and drawn under the direction of Col. Wm. E. Merrill, 1st U.S.V.V. Eng'rs, Capt. Corps of Eng's, & Chief Engr. Dept. of the Cumberland, with the assistance of Prof. J. M. Safford, late State Geologist of Tennessee, by C. S. Mergell, Asst. Engr., 1865. Published by authority of the Hon. Secretary of War, and the office of the Chief of Engineers, U.S. Army, 1874. Am. Photo-Lithographic Co., N.Y. (Osborne's process). Uncolored. Scale ca. 1:350,000. 88 × 140 cm.

Shows topography by hachures, drainage, roads, railroads, dwellings with names of inhabitants, and battlefields, giving dates of engagements and names of opposing commanding officers. The authorities from which the map is compiled are listed in detail, followed by a key to the topographical signs.

393.5

Michler, Nathaniel.

Map of middle and east Tennessee and parts of Alabama and Georgia. Compiled from various authorities for the use of the Armies of the Ohio and Cumberland, by Capt. N. Michler, Corps of Topographical Engineers, U.S.A., assisted by Major John E. Weyss, U. S. Volunteers, Principal Assistant, and C. S. Mergell, Draughtsman, from March 1862 to December 1862. Photocopy (positive). Scale not given. 115 × 179 cm. Cut and mounted to fold to 29 × 22 cm.

Railroads are colored red, drainage is blue, and some roads are brown.

For another copy see Sherman map coll. no. 162.

394

See Sherman map collection no. 158.

395

Michler, Nathaniel.

Topographical sketch of the line of operations of the Army of the Ohio, under the command of Major General

D. C. Buell, U.S. Volunteers. Evacuation of Corinth by the enemy: May 30th, 1862. Surveyed from the 8th of April to the 6th of June 1862, by N. Michler, Capt., Topogl. Engrs. U.S.A. Assisted by John E. Weyss, Maj., Ky. Vols. Photocopy (positive). Scale not given. 45 × 32 cm.

Hand-colored sun print showing drainage, roads, railroads, dwellings with names of inhabitants, churches, "Buell's landing," "battleground, 6th and 7th of Apr., 1862," and the location of Buell's various headquarters, numbered I through VII, as he moved south from Shiloh Church to north of Farmington, Mississippi. Red lines show the Confederate retreat after the battle. A cavalry symbol in red appears a few miles south of Shiloh, close to headquarters III.

395.5

Owner, William.

[Map of central Tennessee from Chattanooga north to Nashville. 1862–1863] Uncolored ms. Scale ca. 1: 490,000. 31 × 37 cm. *In his* Diary, v. 3, tipped-in at end of volume.

In the William Owner papers, Manuscript Division, L.C., container no. 1.

General map showing cities and towns, roads and railroads, rivers, and relief by hachures.

Volume 3 of the diary covers from Sept. 11, 1862, to Feb. 13, 1863.

396

U.S. *Army. Corps of Engineers.*

The middle Tennessee and Chattanooga campaigns of June, July, August and September 1863. [New York, J. Bien, lith., 1891] 1 p.l., 7 l. incl. 8 col. maps. 63 × 52 cm.

G1336 .S5U5 1891

"Enlarged from a map compiled in 1865, by C. S. Mergell, under the direction of Col. W. E. Merrill . . . and published by the Chief of Engineers of the Army in 1874." (See entry no. 393).

"Positions of troops located in 1891 by Captain S. C. Kellogg, 5th Cavalry."

Maps 1–6 drawn by J. von Glümer; maps 7–8 drawn by Ward P. Winchell.

Includes three maps of the "Middle-Tennessee Campaign of June and July 1863," four maps of the "Chattanooga Campaign of August and September 1863," and a map of the "movements and positions preceding battle of Chickamauga." Each is at the scale of about 1:170,000, measures 59 × 92 cm. and indicates troop positions and movements, towns, roads, railroads, drainage, and relief by hachures.

"General orders, no. 101 . . . Adjutant General's Office . . . Sept. 12, 1890 . . . An act to establish a national military park at the battlefield of Chickamauga" (5 p.) inserted preceding the title page.

Listed in C. E. Le Gear's *A List of Geographical Atlases*

in the Library of Congress (Washington, Library of Congress, 1973), v. 7, no. 10671.

396.2

Von Reizenstein, B., *and* **F. D'Avignon.**

Western Tennessee, and part of Kentucky. Prepared by order of Capt. McAlester, Chief Engr. M.D.W.M. under direction of Capt. P. C. Hains, U. S. Engr. & Actg. Chief Engr. Dept. of the Gulf. Compiled & drawn for stone by B. von Reizenstein, & F. D'Avignon. Printed by E. Boehler. Feb. 1865. Uncolored. Scale 1:633,600. 41 × 65 cm.

At head of title: Engineer's Office, Department of the Gulf. Map no. 55.

"Authorities: U. S. Coast Surveys, & Lloyd's military map."

Indicates cities and towns, forts, roads, railroads, rivers, and some relief by hachures.

396.25

Weyss, John E., John Earhart, *and* **William H. Greenwood.**

Topographical sketch of the country adjacent to the turnpike between Nolensville and Chapel Hill, Tenn. Compiled from original reconnoissances [sic] under the direction of Capt. N. Michler, Topographical Engrs. U.S.A. By Major J. E. Weyss, Capt. John Earhart, Lieut. W. Greenwood. [1863?] Photocopy (positive). Scale ca. 1:72,500 (not "1 mile to the inch"). 59 × 33 cm.

Hand-colored photocopy of parts of Williamson, Marshall, Rutherford, and Bedford counties, Tennessee, indicating roads, towns, distances, rivers, houses and names of residents, and relief by hachures.

BLUE SPRINGS

396.3

Blue Springs [Tennessee. October 10, 1863] Colored ms. Scale ca. 1:15,840 ("about 4 in. to 1 mile"). 48 × 29 cm.

G3964.B57S5 1863.B4 Vault

Rough pencil sketch showing the position of "Willcox Reserve" (i.e., Gen. Orlando B. Willcox). Map has been partially traced in ink on the verso.

From the papers of Gen. Orlando M. Poe, Manuscript Division, L.C.

CAMP BRENTWOOD

396.35

Smith, Anson S.

[Sketch map of Camp Brentwood, Tennessee, while serving as quarters for the 86th and 104th regiments of the

Illinois volunteers] Ans. Smith, Brentwood, Tenn., June: 1863. Colored ms. Scale not given. 25 × 40 cm.

G3964.B76:2C3S5 1863 .S4 Vault

This pen and ink sketch map, drawn by Anson S. Smith, Co. D, 104th regiment, Illinois volunteers, shows earthworks, ditches, abatis, gun emplacements, rifle pits, campgrounds, the Louisville and Nashville Railroad, and the nearby Harpeth River. Smith describes the colors used and how to interpret the map as follows: "Red for all dirt thrown up for redoubts & breast work, black for ditches & rifle pits, 2 rows of brush & limbs from trees for the abattus [sic] of which there are 2 rows around or nearly around the fort. Guess at what you dont know as that is the way that I do." The map is drawn on the verso of a letter from Smith dated June 3, 1863, to John J. Taylor, La Salle Co., Illinois. Smith notes in his letter that "I have just come in from picket & the fort that I have started to draw for you is all torn to hell, the banks & breast works are all all [sic] leveled to the ground. Convalescents are ordered to report to the Doctor at 2 oclock. I suppose we will march for Franklin or Columbia [sic] or some place toward the front tonight & skedaddle from here."

CANEY FORK

396.4

Weyss, John E.

Sketch of the vicinity of the falls of Caney Fork of Cumberland River, Ten. Constructed from information received of W. Bosson Esq. under the direction of Capt. N. Michler, Topl. Engrs. U.S.A., by John E. Weyss, Maj. Ky. Vols. April 1863. Photocopy (positive). Scale ca. 1:31,680. 9 × 22 cm.

Hand-colored photocopy of parts of Warren and Van Buren counties, Tennessee, indicating rivers, falls, roads, houses and names of residents, woodland, and relief by hachures.

CHATTANOOGA

396.6

American Heritage Publishing Company.

The American Heritage battle map of Chattanooga. [Drawn by] David Greenspan. [New York] ©1961. Colored view. Not drawn to scale. 39 × 59 cm.

Bird's-eye view showing principal sites and events of the battles of Orchard Knob, Lookout Mountain, and Missionary Ridge.

397

Badeau, Adam.

Battle of Chattanooga, Nov. 23, 24, 25, 1863. Uncolored. Scale ca. 1:108,000. 17 × 13 cm. *From* Century illustrated monthly magazine, v. 31, Nov. 1885. p. 132.

Shows troop positions, "National works," "Confederate works," roads, rivers, railroads, houses, and relief by hachures.

398

Bien (Julius) and Company.

Map of a portion of Missionary Ridge, illustrating the positions of Baird's & Wood's div's., Nov. 23, 24 and 25, 1863. Julius Bien & Co., photo. lith. [18–?] Colored. Scale ca. 1:11,800. 39 × 54 cm.

Shows topography by contours, drainage, roads, railroads, and dwellings with names of inhabitants. Names of corps and commanding officers are given. Arrows indicate battle movements.

398.2

Blakeslee, G. H.

Chattanooga, Tenn., 1863. Colored ms. Scale ca. 1:24,000. 54 × 42 cm.

G3964.C3S5 1863.B6 Vault

Pen and ink sketch map showing fortifications, Union and Confederate picket lines, rifle pits, "rebel camps," roads, drainage, and relief by hachures.

No. "8" is in the lower right corner.

Pasted on the verso is a printed map of Chickamauga by G. E. Dolton, dated Oct. 12, 1893 (size 19 × 28 cm.).

399

[Circular panorama of Chattanooga and vicinity showing troop positions in 1863] Uncolored. Not drawn to scale. 43 × 39 cm.

399.5

Dorr, F. W.

Chattanooga and its approaches, showing the Union and Rebel works, before and during the battles of 23d, 24th and 25th November, 1863. Surveyed under the direction of Brigr. Genl. Wm. F. Smith, Chief Engineer of the Military Division of the Mississippi, during parts of November and December 1863, by F. W. Dorr, U.S. Coast Survey. [1863. Knoxville, Tenn., Tennessee Valley Authority, 1974?] Blue line print. Scale ca. 1:17,:000 (not "1/10,000."). 67 × 50 cm.

G3964 .C3S5 1863 .D6 1974

Map indicates roads, railroads, houses, drainage, woodland, relief by contour lines, and fortifications.

"Before, during, and after this battle, Coast Survey Sub-Assistant F. W. Dorr, under the direction of the Union's Engineering Brigadier General William F. Smith, made a detailed field survey of the area and produced this accurate

tactical map. The accuracy of the terrain representation and the correctness of the location of the cultured features are excellent attributes of this map, which was useful to the Union forces; but the clarity and correctness of the location of both Union and Confederate fortifications, entrenchments, and troop deployment gives it a unique place among military maps of the period."

400

See Sherman map collection no. 169.

400.2

Illinois infantry. *13th regt., 1861–1864.*

Battlefield of Chattanooga. [October–November 1863] Uncolored. Scale ca. 1:73,000. 19 × 11 cm. *From its* Military history and reminiscences of the Thirteenth regiment of Illinois volunteer infantry in the Civil War in the United States, 1861–65. Prepared by a committee of the regiment, 1891. Chicago, Woman's Temperance Publishing Association, 1892. Facing p. 366.

Map indicates troop positions "when Gen. Grant took command, Oct. 23, 1863," and on November 23, 24, and 25.

400.4

Lindenkohl, Henry.

Sketch of the battles of Chattanooga, Nov. 23–26, 1863. U.S. Coast Survey Office, A. D. Bache Supdt. From a sketch by Capt. Preston C. F. West, U.S. Coast Survey. Drawn by H. Lindenkohl. H. Lindenkohl & Chas. G. Krebs, Lith. Colored. Scale 1:63,360. 48 × 54 cm.

Map of the environs of Chattanooga showing troop positions and movements, roads, railroads, towns, drainage, and relief by shading.

400.6

Lynde, Francis.

Map of Chattanooga and environs. Copyright 1895 by W. E. Birchmore. Engraved by Buff[alo] Elec. & Eng. Co. Uncolored. Scale 1:30,000. 54 × 36 cm. *From his* Chickamauga and Chattanooga National Military Park. With narratives of the battles of Chickamauga, Lookout Mountain and Missionary Ridge. Chattanooga, W. E. Birchmore, ©1895. 40 p.

Map indicates the location of monuments and tablets. Copyright no. 19606 AA. "Published June 27/95."

Pen-and-ink sketch map of the environs of Chattanooga, Tennessee, by G. H. Blakeslee, showing fortifications, rifle pits, picket lines, Grant and Bragg's headquarters, and Confederate camps. This is one of 11 manuscript maps by Blakeslee acquired by gift by the Library of Congress in February 1966. (See entry no. 398.2.)

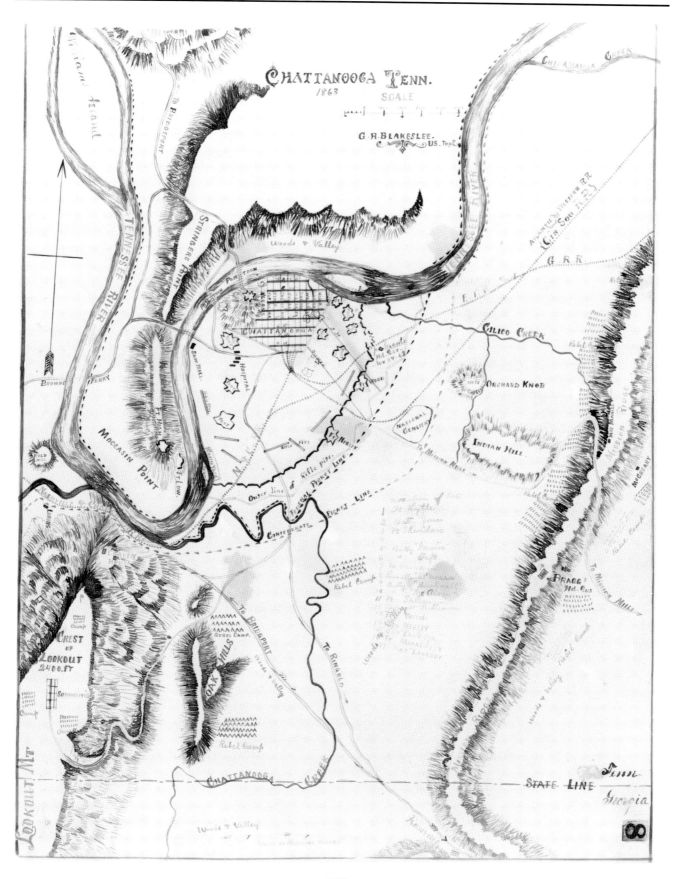

CHATTANOOGA TENN.
1863
SCALE

G. H. BLAKESLEE.
US. Top E.

401

Norwood, Charles W.

Map of the Chattanooga battle-fields, November, 1863. Orchard Knob, 23d, Lookout Mountain, 24th, Missionary Ridge, 25th. Chattanooga, ©1898. Uncolored. Scale ca. 1:63,360. 28 × 19 cm. _In his_ The Chickamauga and Chattanooga battle-fields. Chattanooga, Gervis M. Connelly [1898] opp. p. 19.

Cover title of pamphlet: Book of Battles Chicamauga, Chattanooga, Lookout Mountain and Missionary Ridge.

On verso of Chattanooga map: Battle map of Chickamauga, Georgia. (For a full description see entry no. 158.)

The Chattanooga map is divided "into half-mile sections, numbered 1 to 19 on the west and east sides, and lettered A to L on the north and south." The map includes positions of "troops only in their critical situations," relief by hachures, drainage, railroads, and the outline of the streets of Chattanooga.

On pages 19 to 31 in the pamphlet, there is a description of the battles with the points under discussion keyed by letter and number to the map.

401.2

Purse, Reginald.

Chattanooga and surrounding battlefields. [By Reginald] Purse. Chattanooga, [Purse Printing Co.] ©1913. Colored view. 22 × 50 cm.

Copyright no. F23876, Sept. 8, 1913.

Eighty-three points of interest are listed in the lower margin and keyed by number to the panoramic map.

401.3

Riemann, H.

Map showing the army—movements around Chattanooga, made to accompany the Report of Maj. Genl. Geo. H. Thomas, by direction of Brig. Genl. Wm. F. Smith, Chief Engr. Mil: Div: Miss: Compiled and drawn by H. Riemann, 44th Ills. Vols. Topogl. Engr. Office, Hd. Qrs., Army of the Cumbd., Chattanooga, Jan. 4th 1864. Photocopy (positive). Scale ca. 1:130,000. 68 × 103 cm. Cut and mounted to fold to 23 × 26 cm.

In the James A. Garfield papers, Manuscript Division, L.C., series 8, container no. 1.

Railroads are colored red, and some rivers are blue.

Map of the environs of Chattanooga showing cities and towns, roads, railroads, rivers, fords and ferries, and relief by hachures. The "Battlefield of Chicamauga" is identified, but troop positions are not noted.

Signed in ink in lower margin: J. A. Garfield.

A reduced version measuring 32 × 48 cm. is in the Sherman map coll. no. 4.

401.4

Sholl, Charles.

Chattanooga and its defences. Constructed and engraved to illustrate "The war with the South." [Compiled by Charles Sholl] Engd. by Rae Smith. ©1865. Colored. Scale ca. 1:157,500. 24 × 17 cm. _From_ Tomes, Robert. The war with the South. New York, Virtue & Yorston, 1862–1867. v. 3, between p. 222 and 223.

Signed (facsim.): Charles Sholl, Topl. Engineers.

"Entered according to act of Congress AD. 1865 by Virtue & Yorston."

Caption in lower margin: A topographical map of the ground on which the battles of Chickamauga and Ringgold were fought for the possession of the great railroad triangle of Tennessee and Georgia.

402

Smith, William F.

Battlefield of Chattanooga with the operations of the national forces under the command of Maj. Gen. U. S. Grant during the battles of Nov. 23, 24, & 25, 1863. Published at the U.S. Coast Survey Office, from surveys made under the direction of Br. Genl. W. F. Smith, Chief Engr., Mil. Div. Miss. . . . Chas. G. Krebs, lith. Colored. Scale ca. 1:42,500. 46 × 41 cm.

Signed in ms: Gen. M. C. Meigs.

Indicates troop positions, Union and Confederate headquarters, roads, railroads, drainage, vegetation, relief by shading, and the names of a few residents in the outlying areas.

Another copy is in the Fillmore map coll. no. 113–A.

See Sherman map coll. no. 164 for another edition with different blue overprinting indicating Union positions and headquarters.

403

————Another issue.

"Printed for the benefit of the Sanitary Commission by the Lithographers' Association of (New York)."

404

See Sherman map collection no. 166.

405

Smith, William F.

Map of the battlefield of Chattanooga. Prepared to accompany report of Maj. Genl. U. S. Grant. By direction of Brigd. Genl. W. F. Smith, Chief Engr., Milty. Div. Miss. 1864. Published by authority of the Secretary of War in the office of the Chief of Engrs., U.S.A. 1875. Julius Bien & Co., photo lith., N.Y. Colored. Scale ca. 1:26,600 (not "1:20,000") 74 × 69 cm.

Gives troop positions, "route of Hooker's command, Nov. 20th," "route of pontoons," "line of retreat of enemy," relief by hachures, vegetation, drainage, roads, railroads, houses, and the names of a few residents.

406

————————Another issue.
Graphic Co. photo-lith. Colored. Scale ca. 1:27,500. 73 × 66 cm.

406.1

U. S. *Army. Department of the Cumberland. Topographical Engineers.*

Chattanooga and its approaches. Compiled in Topl. Engr. Office, Hd. Qrs. Army Cumbd. . . . Drawn and printed at Topl Engr. Office, Army of the Cumbd., Febr. 1864. Colored. Scale ca. 1:126,720. 68 × 102 cm. Cut and mounted to fold to 26 × 23 cm.
In the papers of James A. Garfield, Manuscript Division, L.C., series 8, container no. 1.
Printed title pasted on verso with signature in manuscript of "J. A. Garfield, Ohio."
Map of parts of Tennessee, Georgia, and Alabama in the vicinity of Chattanooga showing roads, railroads, cities and towns, rivers, and relief by hachures.
In the lower right corner is an extensive list of "Authorities" consulted in the making of this map.

406.15

————————[Map of Chattanooga, Tennessee, and vicinity] Compiled under the direction of Capt. W. E. Merrill, Corps of Engineers, U.S.A. Lith. Stevenson, Ala. August 12, 1863. Colored. Scale 1:63,360 (1 inch to the mile). 49 × 34 cm.
G3964 .C3 1863 .U5 [2]
Military reconnaissance map lithographed at field headquarters showing roads, railroads, rivers, ferries, relief by hachures, and the names of some residents.

406.2

U.S. *Chickamauga and Chattanooga National Park Commission.*

Map of the battlefields of Chattanooga, movement against Orchard Knob. Prepared under the direction of the Honorable Daniel S. Lamont, Secretary of War, by the Chickamauga and Chattanooga National Park Commission. Republished by order of Congress, with additional position maps under the direction of Honorable Elihu Root, Secretary of War, from official reports and maps of both contending armies. Compiled and drawn by Edward K. Betts, C.E., Park Engineer. [Washington?] 1901. [Knoxville, Tenn., Tennessee Valley Authority, 1974?] Blue line print. Scale ca. 1:48,000. 42 × 56 cm.
G3964 .C3S5 1901.U5 1974

Map indicates roads, railroads, place names, fortifications, troop positions, and relief by contour lines and spot heights.
"Property of A. W. Atwater" appears below the map title and in the border.

406.4

Western and Atlantic Railroad Company.

Map of Chattanooga and vicinity. [1863–1864] Prepared for and presented with compliments of Western and Atlantic R. R. Co. Matthews, Northrup & Co., Art-Printing Works, Buffalo, N.Y. Uncolored. Scale ca. 1:310,000. 12 × 9 cm.
Indicates the battles of Missionary Ridge, Chickamauga Station, Graysville, Chickamauga, Ringgold, and the "battle among the Clouds," roads, railroads, towns, drainage, and relief by hachures.

CLEVELAND

406.5

Merrill, William E.

[Map of Cleveland, Tennessee, and environs] Compiled under the direction of Capt. Wm. E. Merrill, U.S. Engrs., Chief Engineer, Army of the Cumberland. Lithographed at Head Quarters, Winchester, Ten., August 14th 1863. Colored. Scale 1:63,360. 52 × 33 cm.
Field reconnaissance map showing towns, roads, railroad, drainage, houses, and names of residents. The general appearance of the land is identified by such expressions as "poor country," "swampy," "broken country," "good farms," and "plenty of roads across this country."
Another copy is filed G3964 .C3 1863 .U5 [4].

COLLIERVILLE

406.6

Colliersville [i.e., Collierville] shewing camp of 1st Brig. Jany 12 & 13 [1862 and Moscow showing head quarters of General John A. Logan and Colonel Mortimer D. Leggett, January 9, 1862] Uncolored ms. Scale not given. 2 maps on sheet measuring 25 × 39 cm.
In the John Alexander Logan family papers, Manuscript Division, L.C., container 145, p. 111.
Rough pencil sketches.

COLLINS RIVER

406.7

Weyss, John E.

Sketch of crossings on Collins' and Calf-Killer Rivers,

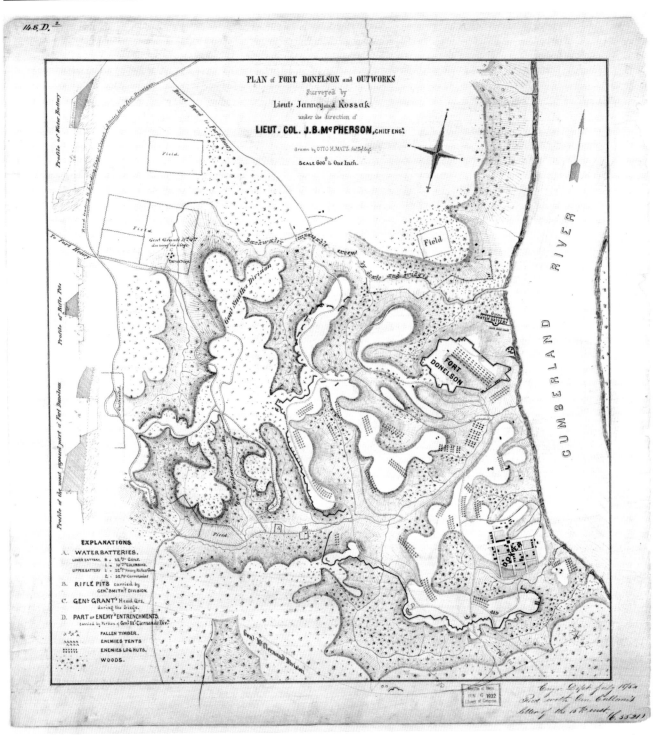

Tenn., constructed from information received of W. Bosson Esqr. under the direction of Capt. N. Michler, Topl. Engrs., U.S.A., by J. E. Weyss, Maj. Ky. Vols. April 1863. Photocopy (positive). Scale ca. 1:63,360. 32 × 18 cm.

Three maps on one sheet: Bridge and ford at Genl. Simpson's, White Co: Tenn. 8 × 18 cm.—Ferry and ford crossing at Sligo, De Kalb Co: Tenn. 9 × 18 cm.—Ferry

Detailed manuscript plan of Fort Donelson, Tennessee, drawn by topographical engineer Otto H. Matz from surveys conducted by Lt. Col. (later General) James B. McPherson. Fort Donelson fell to forces under Gen. Ulysses S. Grant on February 16, 1862. The loss of this fort and Fort Henry nearby were an immense blow to Confederate forces in Tennessee. (See entry no. 411.)

and fords crossing Collins' River, at and below Black's Ferry. 14 × 18 cm.

Hand-colored.

COLUMBIA

406.9

Michler, Nathaniel, *and* John E. Weyss.

Columbia, Tenn: and vicinity. Compiled from various information, by Capt. N. Michler, U.S. Corps of Engineers, assisted by Maj. John E. Weyss, Ky: Vols. [1863?] Photocopy (positive). Scale ca. 1:20,000. 33 × 41 cm.

Twenty-three sites are listed in the legend and keyed by letter to the map. Rivers are colored blue, and railroads are red.

CUMBERLAND GAP

407

Ruger, Edward.

Map illustrating the operations of the Seventh Division under Brig. General G. W. Morgan at Cumberland Gap, Tennessee, during a portion of the year 1862. Compiled by Edward Ruger at Headqr's., Dept. of the Cumberland. Published by authority of the Hon. the Secretary of War in the office of the Chief of Engineers, U.S. Army, 1877. Colored. Scale 1:253,440. 36 × 31 cm.

Shows troop movements and fortifications, roads, towns, drainage, and hachures.

DECHERD

408

Michler, Nathaniel, *and* John E. Weyss.

Topographical sketch of Decherd, Tennessee. Surveyed August 26th and 27th, 1862, by Capt. N. Michler, Corps of Topogl. Engrs., U.S.A., assisted by J. E. Weyss, Maj. Ky. Vols. Photocopy (positive). Scale ca. 1:4800. 30 × 23 cm.

Hand-colored sun print giving railroads in red and rivers in blue. Indicates what appears to be a fort with artillery, relief by hachures, vegetation, roads, and houses and names of a few residents.

FORT DONELSON

409

McPherson, James B.

Plan of Fort Donelson and its outworks. [Feb. 1862] Surveyed under the direction of Lieut. Col. J. B. McPherson, A.D.C. & Capt. of Engineers, by Lieuts. Janney and Kossak. Published by authority of the Hon. the Secretary of War, office of the Chief of Engineers, U.S. Army, 1875. Lith. by T. Schrader, St. Louis. Colored. Scale 1:7200. 52 × 44 cm.

Shows topography by hachures, drainage, vegetation, roads, houses, fences, a plan of Dover, fallen timber, "enemy's" tents and log huts, water batteries, entrenchments, Grant's headquarters, and the location of the divisions of General Smith, General Wallace, and General McClernand. A profile of the fort, another profile of the rifle pits, and one of the water battery appear on the left side of the map.

See also entry no. 411.

409.1

——————Another issue.

Lacks the name of the lithographer in the lower left corner.

410

[Map of the environs of Fort Donelson, Tennessee. Feb. 1862?] Colored ms. Scale ca. 1:22,400. 26 × 40 cm.

G3964 .F62S5 1862 .U5 Vault

In upper left corner: 148.D.[5]

In lower right corner: Engr. Dept. July 18/64. Recd. with Gen. Cullum's letter of the 16th inst. (C.5621).

Pen and ink manuscript lacking the title and authority. Indicates Fort Donelson, the town of Dover, "reported battery on Jackson's Hill," "reported position of obstructions" on the Cumberland River, and the position of mortar boats below the obstructions.

411

Matz, Otto H.

Plan of Fort Donelson and outworks. [Feb. 1862] Surveyed by Lieuts. Janney and Kossak under the direction of Lieut. Col. J. B. McPherson, Chief Engr. Drawn by Otto H. Matz, Asst. Topl. Engr. Colored ms. Scale 1:7200. 59 × 44 cm.

G3964 .F62S5 1862 .U51 Vault

In upper left corner: 148D.[5]

In lower right corner: Engr. Dept., July 18/64. Recd. with Gen. Cullum's letter of the 16th inst. (C.5621).

Similar to printed versions published first in 1875 (see entry no. 409) and later in the *Atlas to Accompany the Official Records of the Union and Confederate Armies*, 1891–95, pl. 11, no. 5.

411.5

U.S. *National Park Service.*

Fort Donelson National Military Park, Tennessee. Drawn by R. M. Montesano, January 1947. Reprint 1959 [Washington] Government Printing Office, 1959. Uncolored. Scale ca. 1:22,500. 14 × 19 cm.

Illustrates the descriptive leaflet. The map indicates the park boundary, earthworks, roads, and "tactical disposition of troops on the night of Feb. 15, 1862."

FORT HENRY

412

Lambecker, Charles.

Sketch showing the relative positions of Fort Henry and Fort Donelson with the roads connecting the two places. [Feb. 1862] Drawn under the direction of Lt. Col. J. B. McPherson, Chief Engineer, by Chas Lambecker. Colored ms. Scale 1:95,040. 40 × 55 cm.

G3964.F67S5 1862.U51 Vault

In upper left corner: 148. D.[1]

In lower right corner: Engr. Dept., July 18/64. Recd. with Gen. Cullum's letter of the 16th inst. (C. 5621).

Similar to printed versions published first in 1875 (see entry no. 415) and later in the *Atlas to Accompany the Official Records of the Union and Confederate Armies,* 1891–95, pl. 11, no. 2.

413

McPherson, James B.

Plan of Fort Henry and its outworks. [Feb. 1862] Drawn under the direction of Lieut. Col. J. B. McPherson, A.D.C. and Capt. of Engineers. Published by authority of the Hon. the Secretary of War, office of the Chief of Engineers, U.S. Army, 1875. Colored. Scale ca. 1:6488. 39 × 44 cm.

Shows topography by hachures, drainage, vegetation, roads, fallen timber, and a plan of the fort, with guns and quarters lettered and explained by a key. A profile of the fort and one of the rifle pits appears at the right.

See also entry no. 414.

413.1

————————Facsimile edition. [Knoxville, Tennessee, Tennessee Valley Authority, 1974?] Blue line print. Scale not given. 39 × 44 cm.

G3964 .F67S5 1862 .M3 1974

413.2

————————Another issue.

Lith. by T. Schrader, St. Louis.

414

————————[Plan of Fort Henry and its outworks. Feb. 1862. Drawn under the direction of Lieut. Col. J. B. McPherson, A.D.C. and Capt. of Engineers] Colored ms. Scale ca 1:6638. 38 × 50 cm.

G3964 .F67S5 1862 .U5 Vault

Lacks title.

In upper left corner: 148. D.[8]

In lower right corner: Engr. Dept., July 18/64. Recd. with Gen. Cullum's letter of the 16th inst. (C. 5621).

Similar to printed versions published first in 1875 (see entry no. 413) and later in the *Atlas to Accompany the Official Records of the Union and Confederate Armies,* 1891–95, pl. 11, no. 1.

414.1

————————Facsimile edition. [Knoxville, Tenn., Tennessee Valley Authority, 1974?] Blue line print. Scale not given. 38 × 50 cm.

G3964 .F67S5 1862 .U5 1974

415

————————Sketch showing the relative positions of Fort Henry and Fort Donelson, also the roads connecting the two positions. [Feb. 1862] Drawn under the direction of Lieut. Col. J. B. McPherson, A.D.C. & Capt. of Engineers. Published by authority of the Hon. the Secretary of War, office of the Chief of Engineers, U.S. Army, 1875. Colored. Scale 1:95,040. 40 × 55 cm.

Shows topography by hachures, drainage, vegetation, roads, and the landing place of the troops.

See also entry no. 412.

415.1

————————Facsimile edition. [Knoxville, Tennessee, Tennessee Valley Authority, 1974?] Blue line print. Scale 1:95,040. 41 × 55 cm.

G3964 .F67S5 1862 .M31 1974

415.2

————————Another edition.

Uncolored. Scale ca. 1:96,000. 20 × 28 cm.

Reduced and redrawn.

416

Original maps of forts Henry & Donelson and vicinity. [Feb. 1862] Uncolored ms. Not drawn to scale. 50 × 65 cm.

G3964 .F67S5 1862 .07 Vault

Title on verso.

In upper left corner: 148.D.[4]

In lower right corner: Engr. Dept., July 18/64. Recd. with Gen. Cullum's letter of the 16th inst. (C. 5621).

Indicates the location and size of guns.

416.1

————————Facsimile edition. [Knoxville, Tenn., Tennessee Valley Authority, 1974?] Blue line print. Scale not given. 49 × 62 cm.

G3964 .F67S5 1862 .07 1974

417

Pitzman, Julius.

Scetch [sic] a. [Map of Fort Henry, Tennessee, and environs. Feb. 1862] J. Pitzman. Colored ms. Scale ca. 1:42,750. 29 × 19 cm.

G3964 .F67S5 1862 .P5 Vault

In upper left corner: 148.D.³

In lower right corner: Engineer Department, July 18/64. Recd. with Gen. Cullum's letter of the 16th inst. (C.5621).

Printed version appears in the Atlas to Accompany the Official Records of the Union and Confederate Armies, 1891–95, pl. 11, no. 4.

Shows fortifications, roads, "landing place of the troops," "routes taken at the reconnaissance," houses, relief by hachures, vegetation, and drainage.

417.1

—————Facsimile edition. [Knoxville, Tennessee, Tennessee Valley Authority, 1974?] Photocopy (positive). Scale ca. 1:42,000. 29 × 19 cm.

G3964 .F67S5 1862 .P5 1974

417.2

—————Lith. by T. Schrader, St. Louis. [1863?] Uncolored. 29 × 11 cm.

Printed version of a map by Julius Pitzman. See entry no. 417 for the manuscript version.

FRANKLIN

417.5

Blakeslee, G. H.

Franklin—Tenn. Profield [i.e., profiled] June 1863, by G. H. Blakeslee. Colored ms. Scale not given. 40 × 53 cm.

G3964 .F7S5 1863 .B6 Vault

Pen and ink sketch map showing troop positions around Franklin, roads, railroads, drainage, and relief by hachures. Indicates the location of the "Cherry tree, where was hung the rebel spies Col. Williams and Lieut. W. G. Peter—June 10, 1863."

"Positions of troops at the battle here, added since close of the war—G. H. B."

Includes small views of "Carter House west of Columbia pike," "Gin house east of Columbia pike," and "Bridge over the Harpeth."

Two maps, one manuscript and one printed, of the environs of Lookout Mountain, Tennessee, are pasted onto the verso. The manuscript is without title or author, while the printed map notes that it is a "Copy by G. H. Blakeslee, Feb. 1893, from a map made by him in 1864."

418

Cockrell, Monroe F.

Battle of Franklin, Tenn., Nov. 30, 1864. Prepared by Monroe F. Cockrell. Outline in part from "O.R." plate 135-C. Drawn by Gordon Johnson, May 7, 1945. Copyright [May 20, 1945] by Monroe F. Cockrell. Blue line print. Scale ca. 1:10,500. 51 × 47 cm.

Indicates entrenchments, troop positions, movements and names of commanders, street pattern of Franklin, roads, "Tenn. & Ala. R.R.," and a few houses.

Includes drawings of the "Carter House," "Carnton Gallery—Confederate Mortuary," and the entrance to an unidentified house.

Another copy is in *Notes and Articles by Monroe F. Cockrell for His Maps of the War Between the States.* ©1950. Typescript.

419

—————Uncolored. Scale ca. 1:17,500. 33 × 30 cm.

Reduced black and white issue of the preceding map.

420

Cowen, J.

Battlefield of Franklin, Tenn. Nov. 3rd 1864. Compiled from the official map. Uncolored. Scale ca. 1:50,000. 12 × 11 cm. *From* Century illustrated monthly magazine, v. 34, Aug. 1887. p. 602.

Indicates troop and cavalry positions, the street pattern of Franklin, rivers, relief by hachures, houses, names of occupants, fences, and vegetation.

421

Field works at Franklin, Tenn., occupied by the 23d and 4th corps during engagement of Nov. 30th 1864, Maj. Gen. J. M. Schofield, comdg. Uncolored. Scale ca. 1:28,000. 23 × 17 cm.

Indicates troop positions and names of commanders, roads, "Nashville and Decatur R.R.," drainage, relief by hachures, and a few houses and names of occupants.

The scale of the map is cited as "275 feet = 1 inch." This does not agree with the bar scale.

422

Merrill, William E.

[Battlefield in front of Franklin, Tenn., November 30th 1864] Colored ms. Scale ca. 1:10,650. 99 × 66 cm.

G3964 .F7S5 1864 .M4 Vault

Unfinished pen and ink manuscript lacking title and authority. It appears to be a preliminary drawing for the printed map "compiled under the direction of Col. W. E. Merrill" and "published by authority of the Hon. Secretary of War" in 1874. (See entry no. 423.)

Indicates troop positions, roads and streets, railroad, houses and names of residents, fences, vegetation, drainage, and relief by hachures.

423

————Battlefield in front of Franklin, Tenn. where the United States forces, consisting of the 4th & 23rd Corps and the Cavalry Corps M.D.M., all under the command of Maj. Gen'l. J. M. Schofield, severely repulsed the Confederate army, commanded by Lt. Gen'l. Hood, November 30th 1864. Published by authority of the Hon. Secretary of War in the office of the Chief of Engineers, U.S. Army, 1874. Colored. Scale ca. 1:10,650. 71 × 45 cm.

"Compiled under the direction of Col. W. E. Merrill, Chief Eng., D.C., from surveys made by Maj. James R. Willett . . . & Maj. T. J. L. Remington . . ."

Indicates troop positions, roads, railroad, houses, names of residents, fences, drainage, vegetation, and relief by hachures.

The name of the lithographer is not indicated on this issue.

Preliminary manuscript map is listed at entry no. 422.

424

————Another issue.

Julius Bien & Co. photo lith., N.Y. Colored. Scale ca. 1:10,550. 71 × 45 cm.

425

————Another issue.

Am. Photo-Lithographic Co., N.Y. (Osborne's process). Uncolored. Scale ca. 1:10,350. 70 × 46 cm.

HARRISON'S FERRY

426

————[Map of the area surrounding Harrison's Ferry, Tennessee, northeast of Chattanooga] Compiled from best information under the direction of Capt. Wm. E. Merrill, Corps of Engineers, U.S.A. Lith at Head Qs., Stevenson, Ala., August 27, 1863. Colored. Scale 1:63,360. 49 × 34 cm.

Shows topography by hachures, drainage, roads, distances, railroads, ferries, fords, dwellings with names of inhabitants, and miscellaneous reconnaissance information.

An unidentified fort is indicated ½-mile southwest of the town of Harrison.

Another copy is filed G3964 .C3 1863 .U5 [3].

JASPER

426.1

U.S. *Army. Department of the Cumberland. Topograhical Engineers.*

[Map of Jasper, Tennessee, and vicinity] Compiled from best information, under direction of Capt. Wm. E. Merrill,—Corps of Engineers, U.S.A. Lith: in camp near Stevenson, Ala. August 1863. Colored. Scale 1:63,360 (1 inch to the mile). 50 × 34 cm.

G3964 .C3 1863 .U5 [1]

Military reconnaissance map lithographed at field headquarters showing roads, railroads, rivers, ferries, relief by hachures, and the names of some residents.

KINGSTON

426.2

Michler, Nathaniel.

Topographical sketch of the vicinity of Kingston, Tennessee. Drawn from information furnished by order of Col. Shelby, by Mr. Charles Ruff. [Compiled by] Capt. N. Michler, T. Engrs., U.S.A. April 3d 1863. Photographed by Carpenter. [1863] Photocopy (positive). Scale ca. 1:65,000. 24 × 21 cm.

Map shows roads, houses, rivers, fords, ferries, and relief by hachures. Elevations given for three hills. Rivers have been hand-colored with a blue tint.

KNOXVILLE

426.4

Orth, John G.

[Map of Fort Sanders, Tennessee, showing the Confederate assault of November 29, 1863] Colored ms. Scale not given. 36 × 25 cm.

G3964 .K7:2F6S5 1863 .O7 Vault

Manuscript map drawn in black and red ink and lead pencil on paper. Important sites are keyed by number to a list on the verso.

Map was drawn by John G. Orth, Arcadia, Ohio, who served with the Federal Army from August 22, 1862, to June 24, 1865.

Fort Sanders was part of the defenses of Knoxville, Tennessee.

427

Poe, Orlando M.

Topographical map of the approaches and defences of Knoxville, E. Tennessee, shewing the positions occupied by the United States & Confederate forces during the siege. Surveyed by direction of Capt. O. M. Poe, Chf. Engr., Dept. of the Ohio, during Dec., Jan. and Feb. 1863–4. Published by authority of the Hon. Secretary of War in the office of the Chief of Engineers, U.S. Army. The Graphic Co., photo.-lith., N.Y. Colored. Scale ca. 1:9900. 67 × 76 cm.

Union and Confederate positions shown by the colors

blue and red respectively. Indicates roads, railroads, contour lines, spot elevations, vegetation, drainage, and houses.

427.1

Rockwell, Cleveland, *and* R. H. Talcott.

Topographical map of the approaches and defences of Knoxvile, E. Tennessee, shewing the positions occupied by the United States & Rebel forces during the siege. Surveyed by direction of Capt. O. M. Poe, Chf. Engr. Dept. of the Ohio during Dec., Jan. and Feb. 1863–4, by Cleveland Rockwell, Subasst. U.S. Coast Survey [and] R. H. Talcott, Aid. Photocopy (positive). Scale ca. 1:20,000. 33 × 38 cm.

G3964 .K7S5 1864 .R6 Vault

"No. 22" is written in ink at the head of the title.

Photocopy annotated to show hachures in black, "Union lines in blue," "Rebel lines in red," and "lines of Union forces captured by the Rebels" in blue and red. The photocopy is similar to one in the Sherman map coll. no. 167, but it is annotated differently.

From the papers of Gen. Orlando M. Poe, Manuscript Division, L.C.

428

See Sherman map collection no. 167.

428.2

Rockwell, Cleveland, *and* R. H. Talcott.

Map of the approaches and defences of Knoxville, Tenn. showing the positions occupied by the United States & Confederate forces during the siege. Surveyed by direction of Capt. O. M. Poe, Chief Engr., Dept. of the Ohio, during Dec., Jan. & Feb. 1863–4. By Cleveland Rockwell & R. H. Talcott, U.S. Coast Survey. [1864. Knoxville, Tennessee Valley Authority, 1974?] Blue line print. Scale ca. 1:9600. 59 × 77 cm.

G3964 .K7S5 1864 .R6 1974

Map indicates "Union positions," "Confederate positions," and "Union picket lines captured by the Confederates."

LOOKOUT MOUNTAIN

428.4

Blakeslee, G. H.

Winter quarters 1864. Profile by G. H. Blakeslee T.E. March 10, 1864. Colored ms. Scale ca. 1:11,700. 39 × 51 cm.

G3962 .L6S5 1864 .B6 Vault

Pen and ink ms. map of the environs of Lookout Mountain, Tennessee, showing Union troop positions, "Confederate Picket Post" on Lookout Mountain, roads, railroads, drainage, and relief by hachures and spot elevations.

Map is signed "G. H. Blakeslee 129th Ill. Inft." in the lower left corner.

The following printed map is pasted on the verso: Chattanooga, Tenn., Nov. 2, 1863. Photo-engraved copy of original, one fourth size. Sketched on the spot by Geo. E. Dolton. 15 × 22 cm.

MEMPHIS

429

See Sherman map collection no. 168.

MOSCOW

429.1

Map of position of 2nd Brig. & 4th, 3d Div. Jany 9th 1862. Uncolored ms. Scale not given. 20 × 32 cm.

In the John Alexander Logan family papers, Manuscript Division, L.C., container 145, p. 110.

Rough pencil and pen and ink sketch map of the 3rd Division's camp at Moscow, Tennessee. A note in a different hand reads "Position of Brigade at Jackson, Tenn."

MURFREESBORO

429.2

Michler, Nathaniel.

Plat of Murfreesboro. Taken from a top'l. sketch of Murfreesboro and its environs. Surveyed under the direction of Capt. N. Michler, Top'l. Engs., U.S.A. [1863?] Photocopy (positive). Scale not given. 28 × 35 cm.

Map indicates streets and buildings. Sites occupied by the 14th and 21st Corps of the Army of the Cumberland, Department Headquarters, and the Quarter Master are identified.

Bar scale appears in the lower right corner, but units of measure are not given.

Another copy is in the James A. Garfield papers, Manuscript Division, L.C., series 8, container no. 1. This copy has been signed in ink below the map title: Brig. Gen. J. A. Garfield 1863. Garfield has annotated the map to show "My old quarters," "My present Hd. Qrs.," "Disciple Church," and the Department Headquarters have been labeled "Rosy" (i.e., Maj. Gen. William S. Rosecrans).

NASHVILLE

429.4

Blakeslee, G. H.

Nashville—Tenn. and vicinity, 1863—G. H. Blakeslee Topo. Eng. Colored ms. Scale ca. 1:21,000. 41 × 51 cm.

G3964 .N2S5 1863 .B6 Vault

Pen and ink sketch map showing fortifications, picket line, camps of the 105th and 129th Illinois regiments, roads and streets, railroads, drainage, and relief by hachures.

No. "4" is in the upper right corner.

430

Cowen, J.

Map of the battle of Nashville, Dec. 15th & 16th 1864. Based on the Government map surveyed and drawn under the direction of Gen. Tower by M. Peseux. Uncolored. Scale ca. 1:110,000. 14 × 17 cm. *From* Century illustrated monthly magazine, v. 34, Aug. 1887. p. 611.

Indicates troop and cavalry positions, roads, railroads, drainage, vegetation, and relief by hachures.

431

Peseux, M.

Battlefields in front of Nashville where the United States forces commanded by Major General Geo. H. Thomas defeated and routed the Rebel army under General Hood, December 15th & 16th, 1864. Surveyed and drawn under the direction of: Gen. Tower, by M. Peseux. C. S. Mergell, auth. Printed at Topl. Engr. Office, Dept. Cumbd., Chattanooga. [186–] Colored. Scale 1:21,120. 78 × 66 cm.

Detailed map indicating troop positions, names of commanders, fortifications, roads, railroads, houses, vegetation, and relief by hachures. Map includes a brief resumé of the battle. Streets and houses of Nashville are not depicted.

432

——————Reduced and engraved in the Engineer Bureau. Bowen & Co. lith., Philada. Colored. Scale 1:42,240. 33 × 40 cm. *From* 39th Cong., 1st Sess. [1866]—Report of the Chief Engineer, U.S.A. No. 4.

Reduced version of the preceding map.

433

——————Another issue. Reduced and engraved in the Engineer Bureau.

This issue lacks the name of the lithographic establishment in the lower right corner and "No. 4" in the upper right corner.

Another copy is in the Sherman map coll. no. 170.

433.2

U.S. *Army. Military Division of the Mississippi. Engineer's Office.*

Map of Nashville, Tennessee. [186–?] Uncolored ms. Scale ca. 1:10,000. 58 × 101 cm.

G 3964 .N2 186– .U5 Vault

Signed in ms: From Chief Engrs. Office, Hd. Qurs.

Mily. Divn. of the Mis. O. M. Poe Capt. & Actg. Chf. Engr.

Detailed map showing streets, railroads, houses and important buildings, and relief by form lines. It appears to have been compiled on a reduced scale from the lithographed map entitled "City of Nashville and Edgefield, Davidson County, Tennessee" [Nashville] Haydon and Booth, 1860. A copy of this map is in the general map collection of the Geography and Map Division, L.C.

433.4

Weyss, John E., *and others.*

Topographical sketch of the environs of Nashville, Tennessee surveyed in the months of March, September and December 1862. For the information of the Armies of the Ohio and Cumberland under the direction of Capt. N. Michler, Corps of Topographical Engrs. U.S.A., by Major John E. Weyss, Capt. J. Earhart and Lieut Greenrood (i.e., Greenwood), U.S. Volunteers. Photocopy (positive). Scale ca. 1:69,000. 42 × 34 cm.

Map indicates railroads, turnpikes, and common roads merging on Nashville from the south. Villages, churches, and the names of some residents are depicted along these routes.

434

Willett, James R.

Topographical map of Nashville, Tenn., from a survey made by Lieut. Jas. R. Willett, 38th Ill. Vol. Infantry. Commd'g. Eng. Department. Nashville, Tenn. [186–] Photocopy (positive). Scale 1:20,000. 18 × 27 cm.

G3964 .N2C2 186– .W5 Vault

"Copy for the Head Quarters of the post."

Signed in ms: From Office Chief Engrs., Hd. Qrs. Mily. Divn. of the Miss., O. M. Poe, Capt. Engrs, Actg. Chf. Engr.

Indicates fortifications, railroads, relief by hachures, and some streets and buildings.

SHELBYVILLE

434.5

Weyss, John E.

Sketch of the environs of Shelbyville, Wartrace & Normandy, Tennessee. Compiled from the best information under the direction of Capt. N. Michler, Corps of Topographical Engrs. U.S.A., by John E. Weyss, Maj. Ky. Vols., Chief Asst. Drawn by C. S. Mergell. Photographed by M. Carpenter. April 1863. Photocopy (positive). Scale ca. 1:105,000. 30 × 47 cm.

Hand-colored photocopy showing roads, railroads, houses and names of residents, towns, rivers, and mills. Descriptions of six "Crossings (i.e., fords) of Duck River" appear below the map title.

Listed in R. W. Stephenson's *Land Ownership Maps* (Washington, Library of Congress, 1967), no. 868.

434.6

───────Another issue.
Scale ca. 1:150,000. 21 × 33 cm.

SHILOH

435

Buell, Don Carlos.

General Buell's map of the battle-field of Shiloh. [April 6–7, 1862] Copyright, 1886, by the Century Co. Uncolored. Scale ca. 1:14,500. 42 × 54 cm.

"This map is an enlarged copy of the one accompanying General D. C. Buell's article, 'Shiloh Reviewed,' in *The Century* for March, 1886."

"This edition includes a few corrections which do not appear in the map as printed in *The Century* for March, 1886."

Detailed map showing the positions of the armies of the Ohio and Tennessee, Confederate lines, headquarters, "regimental camps at the date of the battle," roads, houses, drainage, vegetation, fields, and relief by hachures. The letters A–W identify Union divisions and batteries. "Numbers indicate hours of the day, or periods of the battles . . ."

435.2

Coppée, Henry.

Battle of Pittsburgh Landing [i.e., Shiloh]. Engraved for "Grant and his campaigns." [April 6–7, 1862] Uncolored. Scale not given. 24 × 14 cm. *From his* Grant and his campaigns: a military biography. New York, C. B. Richardson; Cincinnati, C. F. Vent & Co., 1866. facing p. 85.

Map indicates morning and evening positions of Union forces on April 6 and 7, 1862. Legend notes that "The positions of Rebel forces were generally parallel to those thereon indicated."

435.3

Frémaux, Léon J.

Map of the battle field of Shiloh, April 6 & 7, 1862. Léon J. Frémaux, Capt. of Engrs. P.A.C.S. [1862] Colored ms. Scale 1:101,376 ("5/8 of an inch per mile") 15 × 21 cm.

G3962 .S5S5 1862 .F7 Vault

Endorsed in ink: Approved G. T. Beauregard Genl. Comdg.

Finely drawn map indicating "Hd. Qrs. C.S.A.," the location of the "Hornet nest," Confederate and Federal positions, locations of the "U.S. Camps," and the positions of gunboats on the Tennessee River.

435.4

Manska, J. M.

Birdseye view of Tennessee River, Pittsburgh Landing, and the battlefield of Shiloh, April 6, 1862. Painted by J. M. Manska, 1917. Photocopy (positive). Scale not given. 19 × 29 cm.

Copyright no. (on verso), J223085, Apr. 24, 1917.

Shows roads, rivers, fields, and woodland. Division headquarters are numbered 1, McClernand, 2, W. H. L. Wallace, 4, Hurlbut, 5, Sherman, and 6, Prentiss.

This is a photocopy of a map, not a view.

435.6

Map of the battlefield of Shiloh. [1920?] Colored. Scale 1:10,560. 83 × 55 cm.

Stamped in red below title: Reproduced in Photographic Section, Military Information Division, General Staff.

Anonymous map indicating roads, drainage, fields, woodland, contour lines, and the "boundary line of park." Troop positions and fortifications are not delineated.

436

Matz, Otto H.

Map of the field of Shiloh, near Pittsburgh Landing, Tenn., shewing the positions of the U.S. forces under the command of Maj. Genl. U. S. Grant, U.S. Vol. and Maj. Genl. D. C. Buell, U.S. Vol. on the 6th and 7th of April 1862. Surveyed under the direction of Col. Geo. Thom, Chief of Topl. Engrs. Drawn by Otto H. Matz, Asst. Topl. Engr. Lith. by Chas. Robyn & Co., St. Louis, Mo. Colored. Scale 1:14,400. 45 × 63 cm.

"Transferred from Office of Chf. Engr., Defenses of Washington, to Eng'r. Dep't., Jan'y. 1866."

"Dep't. of the Mississippi" added in ink to the map title.

Shows relief by hachures, vegetation, drainage, houses, fields, fences, mills, and roads.

437

───────Another edition. Lith. of J. Bien, N.Y.

Similar in content to the preceding map but lithographed by Bien rather than Robyn & Co. Fences are not shown on this edition.

Another copy is in the Sherman map coll. no. 172.

438

Michler, Nathaniel.

Sketch of the battlefield of Shiloh showing the disposition of the troops under the command of Major General D. C. Buell on the 6th and 7th of April 1862. Surveyed from the 8th to the 15th of April by Capt. N. Michler, Topl.

MAP

OF THE

FIELD OF SHILOH,

NEAR PITTSBURGH LANDING, TENN.

SHEWING THE POSITIONS of the U.S.Forces
under the Command
OF
MAJ.GEN: U.S.GRANT U.S.VOL.
AND
MAJ.GEN: D.C.BUELL U.S.VOL.
ON THE 6TH AND 7TH OF APRIL 1862.
SURVEYED UNDER THE DIRECTION
OF
COL.GEO.THOM.CHIEF of TOPL ENG.RS
DEP'T OF THE MISSISSIPPI.

SCALE = ONE INCH TO 1200 FEET

Engrs., U.S.A. Assisted by John E. Weiss [i.e., Weyss], principal assistent [sic]. Head quarters, Army of the Ohio, in camp, May 19th, 1862. Photocopy (positive). Scale ca. 1:12,200. 46 × 58 cm.

"Official—[signed in facsimile] N. Michler, Capt. Topl. Engrs., U.S.A."

Rivers and Union positions are colored blue, and Confederate positions are colored red. Shows location of batteries, roads, railroads, houses, fences, vegetation, and relief by hachures.

438.5

Plan of the field of Shiloh showing the positions of the Union troops under Gen. Grant at 7 a.m. of April 6th 1862. Also the positions of Mc[C]lernands and Shermans divisions at noon and the attack of the 46th Ohio on a Rebel force in ambush marked A. Drawn from recollection and evidence adduced during Col. Worthingtons trial at Memphis, Tennessee. April 1862. Colored ms. on tracing linen. Scale 1:15,840 ("4 inches to the mile"). 31 × 39 cm.

In the Edwin M. Stanton papers, Manuscript Division, L.C., vol. 5, no. 51220.

Union positions are colored green, and Confederate positions are colored red.

"Note: For the convenience of the plan A (i.e., attack of the 46th Ohio), Shiloh Church is placed near 700 yards west of its proper position."

438.6

Plan of the field of Shiloh traced from a map by Col. Geo. Thom. Position of divisions in black ink, corrected in green from recollection & by Worthington late of the Army of Tennessee. [April 6, 1862] Colored ms. on tracing linen. Scale ca. 1:14,600. 39 × 31 cm.

In the Edwin M. Stanton papers, Manuscript Division, L.C., vol. 5, no. 51224.

Confederate positions are depicted in red ink.

439

Thompson, Atwell.

Map of the territory between Corinth, Miss. and Pittsburg Landing, Tenn. showing positions and route of the Confederate army in its advance to Shiloh, April 3, 4, 5 & 6, 1862. From official maps and actual surveys. Atwell Thompson, B.E., engineer in charge. June 27, 1901. Uncolored. Scale ca. 1:82,000. 49 × 61 cm.

Map of the battle of Shiloh or Pittsburg Landing, Tennessee, drawn by Otto H. Matz from Surveys made under the direction of Chief Topographical Engineer Colonel George Thom. After initial success against the Union forces on April 6, 1862, the Confederate army under Gen. Pierre Gustave T. Beauregard was forced to withdraw to Corinth. (See entry no. 436.)

At head of title: Shiloh National Military Park.

Includes fortifications, roads, railroads, rivers, towns, and the names of a few residents. Some roads have been hand-colored.

439.2

U.S. *Geological Survey.*

Shiloh National Military Park, Tenn. Albert Pike, Division Engineer. Topography by J. K. Bailey and F. H. Sargent. Control by U.S. Geological Survey. Surveyed in 1934. [Washington, 1934] Colored. Scale 1:9600. 75 × 53 cm.

"Advance sheet. Subject to correction."

Title at top of sheet: Tennessee (Hardin County) Shiloh National Military Park.

Detailed topographic map indicating monuments, plaques, markers, and burial grounds. One hundred forty-five monuments are listed and keyed by number to the map. The contour interval is 5 feet.

439.4

U.S. *National Park Service.*

Shiloh National Military Park. Reprint 1957. [Washington] U.S. Government Printing Office, 1957. Uncolored. Scale ca. 1:40,500. 21 × 13 cm.

Illustrates a descriptive leaflet entitled "Shiloh National Military Park, Tennessee."

Map indicates the park boundary, tour route, and points of interest.

439.5

——————Shiloh National Military Park [Washington] Government Printing Office, 1969. Colored. Scale ca. 1:28,000. Map 24 × 18 cm. fold. to 15 × 9 cm.

G3962 .S5 1969 .U5

Folded title: Shiloh National Military Park, Tennessee.

Map depicts a self-guided auto tour of the battlefield. Main points of interest are listed to the right of the map.

439.6

——————Shiloh National Military Park, Tennessee. National Park Service, U.S. Department of the Interior. [Washington] 1978. Colored. Scale ca. 1:28,000. Map 28 × 21 cm. fold. to 10 × 21 cm.

G3962 .S5 1978 .U5

Title from verso.

"GPO:1978 - 261-212/50."

Map depicts a self-guided auto tour of the battlefield. Fourteen points of interest are highlighted.

Includes portraits of Albert Sidney Johnston, P.G.T. Beauregard, Ulysses S. Grant, Don Carlos Buell, and William T. Sherman.

Insets: First day of action, Sunday, April 6, 1862.—Second day of action, Monday, April 7, 1862. Each 5 × 6 cm.

Text is on the verso.

440

See Sherman map collection no. 171.

SPARTA

440.5

Weyss, John E.

Sparta and its vicinity. Constructed from information received of W. Bosson, Esq: Under the direction of Capt: N. Michler, U.S. Corps of Engineers, by J. E. Weyss, Maj: Ky. Vol's. May 1863. Photocopy (positive). Scale 1:71,000 (not "one inch to the mile"). 46 × 29 cm.

Map of the environs of Sparta showing towns, sawmills, roads, houses and names of residents, rivers, and relief by hachures.

Inset: Plan of the town of Sparta. 9 × 9 cm.

440.6

——————Another issue. Scale ca. 1:89,000 (not "one inch to the mile"). 38 × 24 cm.

Includes additional physical and cultural features, especially below the inset and above the map title.

Another copy is in the John M. Schofield papers, Manuscript Division, L.C., container no. 74. Number 2 is written in red ink on the verso.

STONES RIVER

441

See Sherman map collection no. 173.

442

Dahl, O. R.

Topographical sketch of the battle field of Stone River. [Dec. 31, 1862] Drawn by Lt. O. R. Dahl, Topographical Engineer, 2nd Brigade, 1st Div. Chas. Shober's lith., Chicago. Colored. Scale ca. 1:25,100. 34 × 45 cm.

Stamped "Copyright Library, 17 Aug. 1864" in the upper right corner.

"The history of the battle of Stone River" appears to the right of the map.

Detailed map showing the Union forces' first and second positions and the Confederate forces' position "on the morning the 31st of Dec. 1862." The red line denotes "direction of retreat of Col. Carlin's Brigade on the 31st of December 1862 [and the letters a, b, and c mark] the places where the Brigade made a stand during the retreat."

Map also includes fortifications, location of graves, roads, "Nashville & Chattanooga Rail Road," houses and names of occupants, fences, fields, woods, drainage, and relief by hachures.

Includes portraits of Lt. O. R. Dahl and Maj. Gen. W. M. S. Rosecrans.

442.3

Mergell, C.S., *and* **Paul Kuntze.**

Topographical sketch of the battlefield of Stone River, near Murfreesboro, Tenn. From December 30th 1862, to January 3d 1863, Major General W. S. Rosecrans, commanding the U.S. forces, General Braxton Bragg, commanding forces of the enemy. From surveys of Capt. Michler, U. S. Engrs. and published official reports of the commanding generals. Compiled and drawn by C. S. Mergell and Paul Kuntze. Hart & Mapother lith., Louisville, Ky. [1865?] Uncolored. Scale ca. 1:33,000. 30 × 30 cm.

In the Abraham Lincoln papers, Manuscript Division, L.C., vol. 97, no. 20614.

Detailed battle map showing troop positions on December 31st (first, intermediate, and last) and on January 2nd (first and final).

442.5

U.S. *National Park Service.*

Stones River National Military Park, Tennessee. Reprint 1957 [Washington] Government Printing Office, 1957. Uncolored. Scale ca. 1:58,000. 9 × 14 cm.

Illustrates a descriptive leaflet. The map indicates Union and Confederate lines, the direction of the Confederate attack, roads and streets, and the park boundary.

443

Weyss, John E., *and others.*

Topographical sketch of the battle field of Stones River near Murfreesboro, Tennessee, December 30th 1862 to January 3d 1863 . . . Position of the U.S. troops on the 31st of December 1862. Surveyed under the direction of Capt. N. Michler, Corps of Topographical Engrs., U.S.A., by Major J. E. Weyss, assisted by Captains W. Starling, D. P. Thruston, J. W. Stinchcomb, and Lieut. M. Allen—U.S. Vols. Photocopy (positive). Scale 1:15,840. 51 × 68 cm.

Hand-colored photocopy showing the first and last positions of the U.S. 14th Army Corps.

Indicates "line of works of the enemy," roads, "Nashville and Chattanooga R.R.," houses, names of residents, drainage, and vegetation.

443.5

————Topographical sketch of the battle field of Stone River near Murfreesboro, Tennessee, December 30th 1862 to January 3d 1863 . . . Positions of the U. S. troops on the 31st of Dec. and the first position of the enemy. Surveyed

under the direction of N. Michler, Capt. Topogl Engineers U. S. A. by Major John E. Weyss, assisted by Captains W. Starling, D. P. Thruston, J. W. Stinchcomb, and Lt. M. Allen, U. S. Vols. Drawn by C. S. Mergell. Photocopy (positive). Scale ca. 1:22,500. 33 × 44 cm.

In the James A. Garfield papers, Manuscript Division, L.C., series 8, container no. 1.

"Sheet no. I."

Photocopy is very faint in places.

Detailed map showing troop positions, roads, railroad, houses and names of residents, drainage and vegetation.

444

————Topographical sketch of the battle field of Stone River near Murfreesboro, Tennessee, December 30th 1862 to January 3d 1863 . . . Position of the U.S. troops on the 2d of Jan. 1863. Surveyed under the direction of Capt. N. Michler, Corps of Topogl. Engrs., U.S.A., by Major J. E. Weyss, assisted by Captains W. Starling, D. P. Thruston, J. W. Stinchcomb, and Lieut. M. Allen, U.S. Vols. Photocopy (positive). Scale ca. 1:23,000. 32 × 45 cm.

"Sheet no. III."

Gives positions of the U.S. 14th Army Corps, "line of works of the enemy," roads, "Nashville and Chattanooga R.R.," houses, names of residents, drainage, and vegetation.

445

————Topographical sketch of the environs of Murfreesboro, Tennessee. Surveyed Jan. 1863 under the direction of: Capt. N. Michler, U.S.A., Chief Topl. Engr., Army of the Cumberland, by Maj. J. E. Weyss, Capt. W. Starling, Capt. D. Thruston, Capt. J. W. Stinchcomb, Lieut. M. Allen, Lieut. Mackelfatrick, U.S. Vols. Photocopy (positive). Scale ca. 1:41,500. 51 × 50 cm.

Roads, railroads, drainage, and troop positions are indicated in color. There is no explanation for the numbers or colors used to denote troop positions. The base has faded leaving only the information that was added in color and the map title. For a legible copy of virtually the same base map, see entry no. 446.

446

————Topographical sketch of the environs of Murfreesboro, Tennessee. Surveyed Jan. 1863 under the direction of Capt. N. Michler, U.S.A., Chief Topogl. Engr., Army of the Cumberland, by Major John E. Weyss, assisted by Captains: W. Starling, D. Thruston, J. W. Stinchcomb, R. Rose and Lts. M. Allen and H. Greenwood, U.S. Volunteers. Photocopy (positive). Scale ca. 1:43,000. 48 × 49 cm.

Shows "line of battle of the United States forces," "line of battle of the Confederate forces," roads, distances, houses, names of residents, fields, and vegetation. Drainage is colored blue and the "Nashville and Chattanooga R.R." is colored red.

SUMNER COUNTY

446.2

Blakeslee, G. H.

From Mitchelsville, [i.e., Mitchellville] to Gallatin—Sumner Co., Tenn. 1862. G.H.B. Colored ms. Scale not given. 39 × 51 cm.

G3963 .S9S5 1862 .B6 Vault

Pen and ink sketch map showing engagements, forts, roads, railroads, drainage, and relief by hachures.

View of "Picket Post," "Buck Lodge," "Stockade at Kings Bridge," "McClouds" farm, "Hd-Qrs," "Rodamore" farm, "South Tunnel," "Court House—Mill—Gallatin," and a plan of "Ft. Smith" are included in the insets. Each measures 7 × 11 cm.

No. "3" is in the upper right corner.

WAUHATCHIE

446.4

Tyndale, Hector.

Rough plan of part of battle of Wauhatchie, Tenn., night of Oct. 28–29, 1863. Drawn from memory by H. T. [i.e., Hector Tyndale. 188–] Uncolored. Scale not given. 21 × 31 cm. *From* McLaughlin, John. A memoir of Hector Tyndale, brigadier-general and brevet major general, U.S. Volunteers. Philadelphia [Collins, printer] 1882. Follows p. 118.

Accompanied by: Index to map. p. 118. (Photocopy, 36 × 28 cm.)

Map indicates troop positions and lines of march.

WILLIAMSON COUNTY

446.5

Weyss, John E.

Topographical sketch of the country adjacent to the turnpike between Franklin and Columbia, Tenn: Compiled from various authorities under the direction of Capt: N. Michler, U.S. Corps of Engineers. By Maj: J. E. Weyss, Ky. Vols. [1863?] Photocopy (positive). Scale ca. 1:75,000. 58 × 25 cm.

In the John M. Schofield papers, Manuscript Division, L.C., container no. 74.

Photocopy has been hand-colored to show rivers in blue, turnpikes in brown, and railroads in red. Settlements and houses and names of residents are indicated along the railroad and the road between Franklin and Columbia in Williamson and Maury counties, Tennessee.

Number 1 is written in red ink on the verso.

TEXAS

446.8

Bachmann, John.

Birds eye view of Texas and part of Mexico. Drawn from nature and lith. by John Bachmann. New York, John Bachmann ©1861. Colored view. 57 × 72 cm.

G4031 .A35 1861 .B3 Vault

At top of map: Panorama of the seat of war.

"Entered according to act of Congress in the year 1861 by John Bachmann."

View of the coast from "Littel [i.e., Little] Constance Bay," Louisiana to the Rio Grande, indicating towns, roads, railroads, and rivers.

446.82

Proposed line of operations from Sabine Pass to Galveston Sept: 1863, proposed line of supply from Velasco to Houston, [and] proposed line of march from coast landing. [1863] Colored ms. Scale not given. 20 × 23 cm.

In the papers of Maj. Gen. Nathaniel Prentice Banks, Manuscript Division, L.C., container 76.

Pen and ink manuscript map drawn on tracing linen.

446.83

——————Another ms. copy.

In the Abraham Lincoln papers, Manuscript Division, L.C., vol. 129, no. 27392.

Map accompanies General Banks's report to Lincoln dated October 22, 1863 (Lincoln papers, vol. 129, no. 27388–27391).

446.85

[U.S. *Army. Department of the Gulf.*]

Texas coast. [186–?] Photocopy (positive). Scale 1:1,013,760 ("16 miles to an inch"). 52 × 49 cm.

In the papers of Maj. Gen. Nathaniel Prentice Banks, Manuscript Division, L.C., container 76.

At head of title (in ink): Map no. 19.

Heavily annotated sun print showing place names, roads, railroads, and a table of distances.

447

Texas coast showing points of occupation of expedition under Maj. Gen. N. P. Banks. Novr. 1863. Colored ms. Scale ca. 1:1,540,000. 42 × 49 cm.

  G4031 .S5 1863 .B3 Vault

Pen and ink manuscript drawn on tracing cloth, showing towns, rivers, roads, and a few shipwrecks. "Points of occupation" are marked by U.S. flags.

Reduced printed copy appears in the *Atlas to Accompany the Official Records of the Union and Confederate Armies,* 1891–95, pl. 43, no. 8.

BOCA CHICA INLET

447.1

Bocca [sic] Chica Inlet. Octr. 10th [1864] Uncolored ms. Scale not given. 25 × 20 cm.

In the papers of Maj. Gen. Nathaniel Prentice Banks, Manuscript Division, L.C., container 76.

Pencil sketch showing the location of the cavalry outpost, bridge, house, shipwreck, sand hills, and breakers at the mouth of the inlet. The map indicates the depth of water on the bar as of October 10, the depth of water at 30, 60, 120, 300, and 500 yards outside of the bar, and the position of the "Stm. Tennessee" 1 ¾ miles offshore.

447.15

Sketch of fortifications on South end of Brazos Island [1864] Uncolored ms. Scale 1:3600 ("300 feet to an inch"). 19 × 25 cm.

In the Allen family papers, Manuscript Division, L.C., container no. 2.

Map belonged to Lt. Charles Julius Allen (1840–1915).

Pen and ink and pencil map of the defenses at Boca Chica Inlet.

GALVESTON

447.2

Abbott, Henry L.

Galveston, Texas, showing the fortifications &c. Prepared by order of Maj. Gen. N. P. Banks. Henry L. Abbot, Capt. & Chief Topl. Engs. Photographed by Brown & Ogilvie. [December 1862] Photocopy (positive). Scale ca. 1:41,000. 35 × 49 cm.

  G4034 .G3S5 1862 .A2

From the papers of Maj. Gen. Nathaniel Prentice Banks, Manuscript Division, L.C. 2 copies.

At head of title: Department of the Gulf. Map no. 3.

"Authorities: Coast Survey charts—Reconnoissances [sic] made by W. S. Long, Asst. Engr. in Decr. 1862."

Legend identifies eight fortified locations in the environs of Galveston.

447.3

————Another photocopy, with annotations.

In the papers of Maj. Gen. Nathaniel Prentice Banks, Manuscript Division, L.C., container 76.

Map has been annotated to show "position of vessels during the attack on the morning of Jan. 1st 1863." Red indicates U.S. gunboats, and blue other U.S. vessels. The "route of Rebel gunboats" is depicted by a dashed blue line, and that of the U.S. vessels by a dashed red line.

447.4

[Map of Galveston, Texas, showing forts Point, Magruder, Bankhead and Scurry. 186–?] Uncolored. Scale not given. 18 × 30 cm.

In the papers of Maj. Gen. Nathaniel Prentice Banks, Manuscript Division, L.C., container 76.

Accompanied by "Description of forts on sketch." 2 p., each 31 × 20 cm.

The map indicates the location of the forts and the yardage in between.

447.5

U.S. *Navy.*

Attack on Federal fleet at Galveston, January 1, 1863, Uncolored. Scale ca. 1:91,202. 20 × 12 cm. *From* Report of the Secretary of the Navy, with an appendix, containing reports from officers. December, 1863 (Washington, Government Printing Office, 1863). opp. p. 314.

Eighteen positions of ships are listed in "References" and are keyed by number to the map.

PASS CAVALLO

447.7

Plan of—Pass Cavallo—Nov. 28, 1863. Colored ms. Scale not given. 25 × 20 cm.

In the papers of Maj. Gen. Nathaniel Prentice Banks, Manuscript Division, L.C., container 76.

Title on verso.

Rough sketch of the siege of Fort Esperanza at Pass Cavallo. Map indicates the location of "rebel troops," fort and barracks, tents, and "earthwork & rifle pit."

447.8

[Sketch map of Pass Cavallo, Texas, and vicinity showing the location of Fort Esperanza. 1863?] Uncolored ms. Scale not given. 24 × 20 cm.

In the papers of Maj. Gen. Nathaniel Prentice Banks, Manuscript Division, L.C., container 76.

Rough pencil sketch drawn on lined paper.

VIRGINIA

1861

448

Bruff, Joseph G.

Army map of the seat of war in Virginia, showing the battle fields, fortifications, etc. on & near the Potomac River. Drawn by J. G. Bruff. Lith. of P. S. Duval & Son, Philada. Published by J. Disturnell, New York, and Hudson Taylor, Washn., D.C. ©1861. Colored. Scale ca. 1:183,000. 70 × 64 cm.

Map of the Potomac River and vicinity from Harpers Ferry to Swan Point showing towns, roads, railroads, names and boundaries of counties, drainage, and relief by hachures. Principal Union and Confederate positions are marked by small flags or underlined in blue and red respectively.

List of 33 forts defending Washington is in the right corner.

1862 edition is listed as entry no. 455.

449

Bufford, John H.

Map showing the war operations, in Virginia & Maryland. Boston, J. H. Bufford, ©1861. Colored. Scale not given. 64 × 93 cm.

Indicates railroads, principal towns, and a few batteries.

449.2

————Pocket war map of Virginia, with portraits of Scott & his generals. Also views and plans of the principal places of note connected with the war. Lith. & published by J. H. Bufford, Boston. ©1861. Colored. Scale not given. 28 × 36 cm.

"Entered according to Act of Congress in the year 1861 by J. H. Bufford."

"No. 76, Deposited [for copyright] Sept. 27, 1861. Recorded vol. 36, page 503."

General map.

Decorative border includes portraits of Scott, Harney, McClellan, Sprague, Fremont, Butler, Banks, Dix, Lyon, McDowell, Mansfield, and Wool.

Insets: Cairo. 4 × 6 cm.—Charleston. 4 × 6 cm.—Washington. 5 × 6 cm.—The Vermont regiment at Newport News. [view] 3 × 4 cm.—Fortress Monroe. [view] 2 × 9 cm.—Baltimore. 4 × 6 cm.—New Orleans. 4 × 6 cm.—Richmond. 6 × 6 cm.—Savannah. 3 × 6 cm.—[Fortress] Monroe. 6 × 6 cm.

449.4

Duval (Peter S.) and Son.

Map of the seat of war. Supplement to P. S. Duval & Son's military map, showing the locations of the present military operations expressly compiled from the latest surveys. Philadelphia, P. S. Duval & Son, ©1861. Colored. Scale ca. 1:1,950,000. 38 × 33 cm.

"Entered according to Act of Congress in the year 1861 by P. S. Duval & Son."

General map of Virginia, Maryland, and Delaware.

Insets: [Washington, D.C.] 8 × 7 cm.—[Baltimore and vicinity] 8 × 7 cm. —[Parts of the Ohio and Mississippi rivers above Memphis] 9 × 9 cm.—Pensacola Bay. 8 × 10 cm.

449.5

Gaston (S. N.) and Company.

Birds eye view of Maryland and Virginia. Published by S. N. Gaston & Co., ©1861. Colored view. Not drawn to scale. 36 × 41 cm.

G3881 .A3 1861 .G3

Panoramic map looking south from southern Pennsylvania showing relief, rivers, place names, and railroads.

449.6

Grant, M. B.

Map of the seat of war [in Virginia and Maryland] Compiled & drawn by M. B. Grant C.E. Lithographed by R. H. Howell, Savannah. Published by T. A. Burke, Morning News Office, Savannah, Ga. [1861?] Colored. Scale ca. 1:800,000. 43 × 55 cm.

G3880 1861 .G5 Vault

Confederate imprint.

General map showing cities and towns, roads, railroads, and rivers and streams. Place names in Maryland north of Baltimore and Frederick, and south of Washington, D.C. (with the exception of Fort Washington), are not indicated.

449.7

————Another issue.

G3880 1861 .G51 Vault

Includes place names in Maryland north of Baltimore and Frederick, and south of Washington, D.C.

449.8

Higginson, J. H.

A new bird's eye view of the seat of war by J. H. Higginson, New York. ©1861. Uncolored. Scale ca. 1:1,700,000. 33 × 38 cm.

"Entered according to Act of Congress in the year 1861 by J. H. Higginson."

Map copyrighted June 26, 1861, no. 295.

General map of Virginia, Maryland, and Delaware. It is not a bird's-eye view.

450

Lloyd, James T.

Lloyd's official map of the state of Virginia from actual surveys by order of the Executive 1828 & 1859. Corrected and revised by J. T. Lloyd to 1861. New York, 1861. Colored. Scale ca. 1:640,000. 78 × 122 cm. folded to 22 × 12 cm. (Fillmore map coll. no. 77)

Signed in ms. on verso: No. 77, Millard Fillmore, Nov. 7, 1861.

Indicates forts, "places remarkable for military incidents," roads, distances, railroads, towns, mills, factories, state and county boundaries, drainage, and relief by hachures.

"N.B. This is the only map used to plan campaigns in Virginia by Gen. Scott."

Text printed to the left of the map includes "Deviation of the magnetic needle from the true meridian, as ascertained from observations made during the years 1823 and 1824, by H. Boye," "Memoranda" describing the sources and projection used to make the map, "Geological remarks," "Situation, extent, &c," and "Table of the population."

Listed in A. M. Modelski's *Railroad Maps of the United States* (Washington, Library of Congress, 1975), no. 310.

1862 edition listed as entry no. 465–465.1, and the 1863 printing as entry no. 481.2.

450.1

——————Another issue.

G3880 1861 .L4

Includes advertisements in the lower margin for Lloyd's "Great steel plate military map of the 15 southern states," "Military map of the southern states of North America," "Military map of the southern states," "Official steel plate map of Missouri," and "United States railroad map."

450.3

The London American.

Map of the seat of war, positions of the rebel forces, batteries, entrenchments, and encampments in Virginia—

the fortifications for the protection of Richmond. Waters & Son, engravers, N.Y. [London, The London American, 1861] Uncolored. Scale ca. 1:800,000. 52 × 35 cm.

Includes a mileage table.

Reference is made in the lower margin to the "battle of Bull's [sic] Run, fought on Sunday, the 21st July [1861], about 22,000 unionists and about 60,000 rebels were in the engagement."

An earlier version of this map was published in the morning edition of the *New York Herald,* June 17, 1861. See entry no. 451.3.

450.8

Magnus, Charles.

[Theatre of war in Virginia. 1861] Colored. Various scales. 3 maps and 1 view on sheet 27 × 22 cm.

Contents: Fortress Monroe, Old Point Comfort and Hygeia Hotel, Va. [view]. Entered according to Act of Congress in the year 1861 by E. Sachse & Co. 8 × 19 cm.— Richmond & Alexandria. 13 × 13 cm.—Military map of Maryland & Virginia. 12 × 7 cm.—Country between Fortress Monroe & Richmond. 6 × 19 cm.

Maps are printed on the verso of lined note paper.

451

——————Topographical map of Virginia between Washington and Manassas Junction. New York, Chs. Magnus, [1861?] Uncolored. Scale ca. 1:270,000. 12 × 20 cm. on sheet 28 × 22 cm.

Indicates Union and Confederate positions at "battle of Bull Run, July 21st 1861," Union encampments, towns, roads, the street pattern of Washington, railroads, rivers, and relief by hachures.

Inset: Leesburg to Harpers Ferry. 4 × 5 cm.

"Panoramic view of the fortifications around Washington" (12 × 20 cm.) appears above the map.

451.1

Manouvrier (J.) and Company.

Plan of the seat of war. [New Orleans] Lith by J. Manouvrier & Co. [1861?] Uncolored. Scale ca. 1:750,000. 38 × 24 cm.

Confederate imprint.

General map of eastern Virginia showing place names, roads, railroads, and rivers.

Inset: Harpers Ferry and vicinity. 9 × 7 cm.

451.2

Monk, Jacob.

Map of the seat of war exhibiting the surrounding country, the approaches by sea & land to the capitol of the United States, and the military posts, forts, &c. T. Sinclair's lith., Phila. Philadelphia, Jacob Monk, 1861. Colored. Scale 1:633,600. 78 × 59 cm.

"Entered according to Act of Congress in the year 1861 by Jacob Monk."

General map of eastern Virginia, Maryland, and Delaware.

Includes "Table of distances from Washington by rail road."

451.3

The New York Herald.

The seat of war in Virginia. Positions of the rebel forces, batteries, intrenchments and encampments in Virginia—the fortifications for the protection of Richmond. Waters & Son, engravers, N.Y. [New York] 1861. Uncolored. Scale ca. 1:800,000. 51 × 33 cm.

From the *New York Herald,* morning edition, June 17, 1861. p. 1.

Later version of this map was published in the *London American.* See entry no. 450.3.

451.4

Paterson, J. T.

Map of Virginia, Maryland &c., seat of war, compiled from the latest maps, 1861. Published by J. T. Paterson, sold by George L. Bidgood, Richmond, Va. and Tucker & Perkins, Augusta, Ga. Hoyer & Ludwig, lithographic establisht., Richmond, Va. [1861] Colored. Scale ca. 1:760,000. 44 × 56 cm.

General map.

Confederate imprint.

Pencil note in the lower margin reads "This map was advertised in the Augusta, Ga. Daily Chronicle, Oct. 27, 1861."

Includes "Table of distances."

451.5

Perris, William.

Map of the seat of war in Virginia. Drawn by Wm. Perris C. E. & Surveyor, N. York. Lithographed by C. W. Corss. Printed by Lang & Laing, N.Y. ©1861. Uncolored. Scale ca. 1:1,090,000. 53 × 63 cm.

"Entered according to Act of Congress in the year 1861 by William Perris."

Copyright no. "355, Aug. 14, 1861" is written in the lower margin.

General map of Virginia, Maryland, Delaware, and parts of Pennsylvania and North Carolina.

451.6

U.S. *Army. Corps of Topographical Engineers.*

Copy of an unfinished map of a portion of the military

department of north eastern Virginia and Fort Monroe compiled in the Bureau of Topographical Engineers, War Department, from the best and latest authorities. August, 1861. Photocopy (positive). Scale 1:200,000. 112 × 132 cm. mounted to fold to 28 × 33 cm.

G3880 1861 .U5

"Gen. Meigs 21 June 1862" is written in pencil on the verso.

General map of southeastern Virginia extending from Fredericksburg south to the Virginia-North Carolina border, showing cities and towns, railroads, canals, a turnpike, stage, common and plank roads, mills, manufactories, iron works, academies and colleges, churches, and rivers. The map has been annotated to show crossed swords and flags at Fredericksburg and the Spotsylvania Court House.

1862

451.7

Abert, James W.

[Map of northern Virginia and part of Maryland. 1862?] Photocopy (positive). Scale ca. 1:205,000. 45 × 53 cm.

G3882 .N6 186– .A3 Vault

Signed in ms.: Capt. James W. Abert, Capt. U.S. Army Topog. Engrs. Note on verso reads "From Capt. James W. Abert, U.S. Army Topog. Engrs."

Map extends from Frederick, Maryland, south to Colchester, Virginia, and Baltimore, Maryland, west to Harpers Ferry, West Virginia. Indicated are roads, railroads, cities and towns, drainage, and relief by shading. A few place names have been added in ink as well as fortifications at "Munsons" Hill near Baileys Cross Roads, Fairfax County, Virginia. The map was endorsed by Abert before he was promoted to Major of Engineers on March 3, 1863.

452

Bacon and Company.

Bacon's new army map of the seat of war in Virginia, showing the battle fields, fortifications, etc., on & near the Potomac River. Compiled from the army map of the Federal Government, and other authentic sources. London, 1862. Colored. Scale ca. 1:180,000. 75 × 55 cm.

Map of northeast Virginia, Washington, D.C., and part of Maryland showing the location and date of engagements, battles in which cannons were used, country names and

Wood-engraved map of "The Seat of War in Virginia" published in the New York Herald, *June 17, 1861. Executed by Waters and Son, Engravers, New York, it is typical of the maps that appeared throughout the war in newspapers and weekly journals. (See entry no. 451.3.)*

THE NEW YORK HERALD.

WHOLE NO. 9047.   MORNING EDITION—MONDAY, JUNE 17, 1861.   PRICE TWO CENTS.

THE SEAT OF WAR IN VIRGINIA.

Positions of the Rebel Forces, Batteries, Intrenchments and Encampments in Virginia---The Fortifications for the Protection of Richmond.

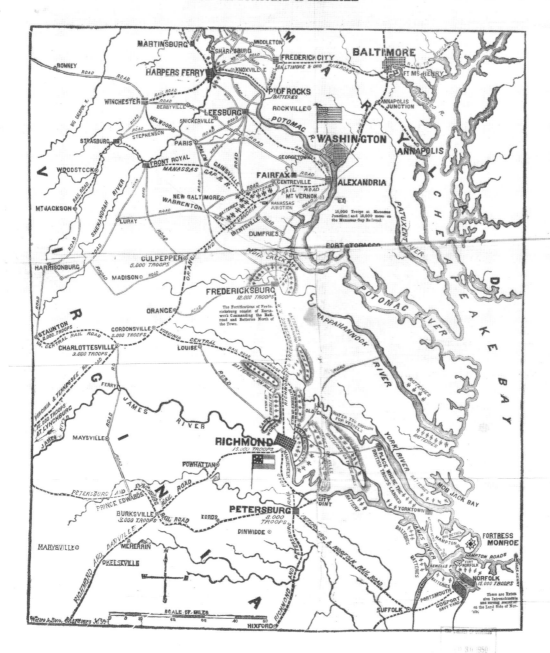

boundaries, roads, railroads, towns, drainage, hachures, and a few soundings in the Potomac River. Positions held by Union and Confederate forces are marked by flags.

453

————Seat of war in America, 6d. Waters & Son, engravers, N.Y. London, July 1862. Colored. Scale ca. 1:820,000. 40 × 32 on sheet 56 × 32 cm.

Map of eastern Virginia and part of Maryland showing batteries, towns, roads, railroads, and rivers. McClellan's position on the Peninsula is shaded red.

Names of Union and Confederate generals, "Exports in 1860," and "Colton's seetl [i.e., steel]—plate maps of the United States of America" are listed at the top of the map.

See entry no. 476.5 for the 1863 edition.

454

Bohn, Casimir.

Map of the seat of war in Virginia. Lith. by E. Sachse & Co., Baltimore. Published by C. Bohn, Washington, D.C. & Old Point Comfort, Va. ©1862. Colored. Scale ca. 1.440,000. 30 × 41 cm.

Map of southeast Virginia showing fortifications and camps underlined in brown, roads, railroads, towns, and drainage.

"Table of distances from Norfolk" is in the lower left corner.

Another copy is in the Ezra A. Carman papers, Manuscript Division, L.C., container no. 14.

454.5

Bowen, Nicolas.

Map of a portion of Virginia, compiled from Böye's State map under the direction of Nicolas Bowen, 1st. Lieut. Top'l Eng'rs—in charge. With additions & corrections by D. H. Strother, Lt. Col. 3'd. Va. Cavalry, A.A.D.C. Nov. 1862. Capt. Jas. C. Duane, Chief Eng'r Army of the Potomac. Photocopy (positive). Scale ca. 1:570,240 (9 miles to 1 inch). 48 × 44 cm.

G3880 1862.B6

Signed in ink on verso: Orlando M. Poe, Col. 2d Michn. Vols., Comdg. 1st Brig., 1st Div., 9th A.C.

From the papers of Gen. Orlando M. Poe, Manuscript Division, L.C.

Map extends from Richmond west to Lexington and from the Staunton River north to Winchester. Depicted are roads, railroads, towns, and rivers.

Another copy of this map is in the Hotchkiss map coll. no. 14.

455

Bruff, Joseph G.

Army map of the seat of war in Virginia, showing the

battle fields, fortifications, etc. on & near the Potomac River. Drawn by J. G. Bruff. Lith. of P. S. Duval & Son, Philada. Published by J. Disturnell, New-York, and Hudson Taylor, Washn., D.C. 1862. Colored. Scale ca. 1:183,000. 70 × 63 cm.

Map of the Potomac River and vicinity from Harpers Ferry to Swan Point showing towns, roads, railroads, names and boundaries of counties, drainage, and relief by hachures. Principal Union and Confederate positions are marked by small flags or underlined in blue and red respectively.

List of 34 forts defending Washington is in the lower right corner.

1861 edition is listed as entry no. 448.

456

Colton, Joseph H.

Colton's map of the seat of war in Virginia showing minutely the interesting localities in the vicinity of Richmond. Printed by Lang & Laing. N.Y. New York, 1862. Colored. Scale 1:760,320. 50 × 48 cm. (Fillmore map. coll. no. 267)

Signed in ms: Millard Fillmore, Augt. 4, 1862.

Map of eastern Virginia showing roads, railroads, towns, names and boundaries of counties, drainage, relief by hachures, and a few forts.

457

Duncan, Blanton.

Map of the seat of war in Virginia. Columbia, S.C., Dec. 1, 1862. Uncolored. Scale ca. 1:240,000. 37 × 24 cm.

Confederate imprint.

Map of northeast Virginia showing the location and date of engagements, roads, railroads, towns, drainage, and some relief by hachures.

Two copies. The second copy is from the Orlando M. Poe papers, Manuscript Division, L.C. (G3881 .S5 1862 .D8)

458

Hausmann, A.

[Western Virginia from Petersburg to Warm Springs, showing the movement of the Union army, 1862] Drawen

---

Relatively few maps were published in the South for sale to the general public. Those that were issued were simple in construction, small in size and generally lacking in coloring. Blanton Duncan's "Map of the Seat of War in Virginia" published in Columbia, South Carolina, on December 1, 1862, is representative of Confederate imprints. This particular copy was owned by Confederate topographical engineer Jedediah Hotchkiss. (See entry no. 457.)

[sic] by A. Hausmann. Colored ms. Scale ca. 1:320,000. 45 × 30 cm.

    G3891 .S5 1862 .H3 Vault.

    "Sheet no. 1."

    "Most of the roads are from the description of the inhabitants. Those travelled by the main body are from memory assisted by notes. The other sheet is most trustworthy with regard to the roads between Gibsons' Store, Huntersville and Warm Springs. The whole country is thickly wooded with the exception of the bottom lands."

    Map covers parts of the present-day counties of Grant, Randolph, Pendleton, and Pocahontas, West Virginia, and Highland and Bath, Virginia.

459

Heald, D. A.

    The battle fields and military positions in the Virginian Peninsula, from surveys supplied by officers of the army. Entered according to Act of Congress in the year 1862 by D. A. Heald . . . Colored. Scale ca. 1:375,000. 34 × 48 cm.

    "Presented by the Home Insurance Compy. of New York."

    A few battle sites are marked by crossed swords. Shows roads, railroads, towns, county names and boundaries, and drainage.

460

Hove, B., Jr.

    [Southeastern part of Virginia, from York River, and west to Black Water River] Traced from the tracing of the original by B. Hove, Jr., January 8th 1862. Colored ms. Scale ca. 1:200,000. 67 × 58 cm.

    G3882 .H3S5 1862 .H6 Vault

    Pen and ink manuscript drawn on tracing cloth, showing location of "collison [sic] between U.S. forces 10 June/ 61" and "battle ld 11 June 1861," principal fortifications, roads, existing and proposed railroads, canals, mills and factories, churches, towns, rivers, bridges, and lighthouses.

460.5

Joerg, Wolfgang L. G.

    Civil War Virginia campaigns, 1862. Prepared for the Chronicles of America under the direction of W. L. G. Joerg, American Geographical Society. Julius Bien lith., N.Y. Colored. Scale 1:3,750,000. 11 × 11 cm. *From* Wood, William. Captains of the Civil War; A chronicle of the blue and the gray. (New Haven, Yale University Press, 1921.) (The Chronicles of America series; Abraham Lincoln edition, vol. 31) facing p. 208.

    Black lines indicate the routes of McClellan and Burnside, and red lines the routes of Lee and Jackson.

461

Kappner, Franz.

    Map of route and positions, First Corps, Army of Va., Maj. Gen. Sigel comg., from July 7th to Septr. 10th 1862. Compiled from maps, and actual surveys. Septr. 1862. Franz Kappner, Maj. and Chef [sic] Engr. Uncolored. Scale not given. 58 × 90 cm.

    In upper right corner: Ho. Reps. Ex. Doc. no. 81–37th Cong. 3rd Sess.

    The route of the First Corps is shown from Middletown, Virginia, to the defenses of Washington. Roads, towns, vegetation, drainage, houses, and names of residents are indicated along the line of march.

462

Lindenkohl, Adolph

    Map of part of south eastern Virginia. Compiled at the U.S. Coast Survey Office . . . Drawn by A. Lindenkohl. H. Lindenkohl & Chs. G. Krebs, lith. [1862?] Uncolored. Scale 1:200,000. 54 × 69 cm.

    Shows fortifications used during the Seven Days battles, roads, railroads, towns, drainage, and vegetation.

463

    ————Military map of south-eastern Virginia. A. Lindenkohl, del. H. Lindenkohl & Chas. G. Krebs, lith. [1862?] Colored. Scale ca. 1:220,000. 43 × 74 cm.

    "Transferred from Office of Chf. Engr., Defenses of Washington, to Engr. Dept., Jany. 1866."

    Indicates 5-mile concentric circles centered on Richmond, fortifications, roads, railroads, towns, houses, drainage, and vegetation.

464

Lloyd (H. H.) and Company.

    Lloyd's new war map of Virginia. New York, ©1862. Colored. Scale ca. 1:980,000. 36 × 68 cm.

    Shows battlefields underlined in red, towns, roads, railroads, drainage, and relief by hachures.

465

Lloyd, James T.

    Lloyd's official map of the State of Virginia from actual surveys by order of the Executive, 1828 & 1859. Corrected and revised by J. T. Lloyd to 1862, from surveys made by Capt. W. Angelo Powell, of the U.S. Topographical Engineers. Colored. Scale ca. 1:650,000. 76 × 120 cm.

    "Entered according to Act of Congress in the year 1861 by J. T. Lloyd . . ."

    Indicates forts, towns, mills, factories, iron works,

drainage, relief by hachures, county names and boundaries, roads, and railroads.

"N.B. This is the only map used to plan campaigns in Virginia by Gen. McClellan."

The text printed to the left of the map includes "Deviation of the magnetic needle from the true meridian, as ascertained from observations made during the years 1823 and 1824, by H. Boye," "Memoranda" describing the sources and projection used to make the map, "Geological remarks," "Situation, extent, &c," and "Table of the population."

List of new maps that are "Ready" is printed to the right of the map title.

1861 edition listed as entry nos. 450–450.1, and the 1863 printing as entry no. 481.2.

465.1

————Another issue.

G3880 1862 .L41

Includes a warning to the right of the map title which begins, "The traveling public are cautioned against stopping at the Burnett House, Cincinnati, O., as no respect or attention is shown to guests, excepting when their bills are presented . . ."

List of new maps that are "Ready" printed to the left of the map. "Deviation of the magnetic needle . . ." and "Memoranda" describing the sources and projection used to make the map have been dropped from this issue.

Another copy is in the Sherman map coll. no. 175.

465.15

Macomb, John N.

Map of Loudon [sic], Jefferson, Berkeley, Frederick Counties, Va., compiled under the direction of Lieut. Col. J. N. Macomb A.D.C., Chf. Topl. Engr., for the use of Maj. Gen. Geo. B. McClellan, commanding Army of the Potomac. 1862. Photographed by D. R. Holmes. Photocopy (positive). Scale ca. 1:125,000. 2 sheets, each 38 × 86 cm.

General map showing towns and villages, roads, railroads, rivers and streams, relief by hachures, and the names of new residents.

Imperfect; pieces missing.

465.2

————Another issue. Photographed by L. E. Walker, Treasy. Extn. and D. B. Woodbury, Ast. Phor. 81 × 91 cm.

G3880 1862 .M3

Later issue containing additional place names.

465.22

Map of locality & roads Sperryville to Amissville, 18 miles by pike S. to A., 14 miles by cross [?] rd. S. to A. [1862?] Colored ms. Scale not given. 16 × 11 cm.

In the papers of Maj. Gen. Nathaniel Prentice Banks, Manuscript Division, L.C., container 76.

Title from the verso.

Pen and ink sketch of principal roads between Fairfax, Woodville, Sperryville, Washington, Gaines X Roads, and Amissville, Virginia.

465.25

The New York Herald.

The important strategic movements in Virginia. Scene of operations in front of Richmond, in the Valley and on the line of the upper Potomac—the threatened offensive movements of the rebels. Waters & Son, sc. New York, 1862. Uncolored. Scale not given. 50 × 35 cm.

From the *New York Herald*, May 27, 1862, p. 1.

General map of eastern Virginia.

465.26

Nicholson, W. L.

Map of eastern Virginia, compiled from the best authorities, and printed at the Coast Survey Office, A. D. Bache, Supdt. 1862. Compiled by W. L. Nicholson. Lith. by Chas. G. Krebs. Colored. Scale ca. 1:887,040. 62 × 48 cm.

G3880 1862 .N54

General map of eastern Virginia showing cities and towns, roads, rivers, and relief by hachures. The map is overprinted in red to indicate railroads and concentric circles centered on Richmond. Circles are at intervals of ten miles.

In his report to the Superintendent of the Coast Survey dated November 1, 1862, Nicholson notes that "In addition to the printing of our charts proper, a map representing the seat of war in Virginia was, at the suggestion of the Superintendent, compiled by myself during the past year, and printed in colors, partly as an experiment in that class of work, and partly to meet the popular demand for information on the movements of our armies. This map has met with unexpected success, and has been much called for, and copies quite freely distributed; but, in order to cover the expenses of its getting up and printing, a number of copies have been placed in the hands of our sale agents, the proceeds of which have more than covered expenses; in all, some five thousand five hundred copies have been printed, over twenty-five hundred sold, and nearly three thousand copies gratuitously distributed." (*Report of the Superintendent of the Coast Survey, showing the Progress of the Survey during the Year 1862* (Washington: Government Printing Office, 1864). p. 151.)

This is the first of seven issues in the Library of Congress published in 1862. Distinguishing characteristics include the depiction of the "Blairsville Branch" railroad, the "Manassas Gap R. R." extending to Harrisonburg, Virginia, and the "Delaware R.R." on the Eastern Shore extending to Seaford.

465.27

————————Another issue.

G3880 1862 .N55

Shows the "Blairsville Branch" railroad, the "Delaware R.R." extending to Princess Ann, and the "Manassas Gap R.R." extending to Mt. Jackson.

465.28

————————Another issue.

G3880 1862 .N56

Similar to the preceding issue except that "Blairsville Branch" railroad has been dropped.

Handwritten note in the lower right corner reads "Transferred from Office of Chf. Engr., Defenses of Washington to Engr. Dept. Jan'y 1866."

465.29

————————Another issue.

G3880 1862 .N57

Similar to the preceding issue except that "Mechanicsville" has been substituted for "Cold Harbor."

465.3

————————Another issue.

G3880 1862 .N58

Similar to the preceding issue except that the lettering for Fair Oaks and Manchester has been changed, and the lettering for some railroads has been repositioned. The "Newc. & F. R.R." in Delaware has been relabeled to read "Newcastle & Frenchtown R.R."

465.35

————————Another issue.

G3880 1862 .N59 Vault Shelf

Similar to the preceding issue but issued folded in covers. Cover title: Map of eastern Virginia. Compiled in the office of the United States Coast Survey. W. H. & O. H. Morrison, Washington, D.C.

Inscribed inside front cover: Geo. W. Lay to Genl. Beauregard.

465.4

————————Another issue.

G3880 1862 .N591

Similar to the preceding two issues but displays blue concentric circles centered on Washington, D.C.

Another copy is in the Fillmore map coll. no. 253.

465.45

————————Map of the State of Virginia, compiled from the best authorities, and printed at the Coast Survey Office. A. D. Bache, Supdt. 1862. Compiled by W. L. Nicholson. Lith. by Chas. G. Krebs. Colored. Scale ca. 1:887,040. 58 × 88 cm.

G3880 1862 .N53

General map of Virginia, West Virginia, Maryland, Delaware, and southern Pennsylvania showing cities and towns, roads, rivers, and relief by hachures. The map is overprinted in red to indicate railroads, the proposed state name "West Virginia,' and concentric circles centered on Richmond. Circles are at intervals of ten miles. A table of "Distances by Rail Roads" appears below the map title.

465.5

————————Map of western Virginia, compiled from the best authorities, and printed at the Coast Survey Office, A. D. Bache, Supdt. 1862. Compiled by W. L. Nicholson, Civ. Engr. Lith. by Chas. G. Krebs. Colored. Scale ca. 1:887,040. 58 × 50 cm.

G3880 1862 .N5

General map of western Virginia extending from Staunton to Cumberland Gap and showing roads, railroads, cities and towns, rivers, and relief by hachures. This is the first of three issues in the Library of Congress published in 1862. This issue is characterized by the appearance of "Civ. Engr." after the compiler's name and a break in the border at the bottom of the map.

465.55

————————Another issue.

G3880 1862 .N51

Similar to the preceding issue except that "Civ. Engr." after the compiler's name has been dropped.

465.6

————————Another issue.

G3880 1862 .N52

Similar to the preceding issue except that there is no break in the bottom border. In addition, the "Nolechucky R." (i.e., Nolichucky) and the town of "Greenville" (i.e., Greeneville), Tennessee, are not depicted or named in the portion of the map that extends through the bottom border into the margin.

465.65

The Philadelphia Inquirer.

Scene of the present terrible conflict in front of Richmond. Positions formerly held by our right wing—Mechanicsville, White House, Meadows Bridge, Gaines' House, Dispatch and Tunstall's Station's—The Pamunkey River still commanded by our gunboats—Fort Darling menaced by the Union fleet—James River our present base of operations, and forming our means of communication for supplies. Philadelphia, 1862. Uncolored. Scale not given. 29 × 35 cm.

From the *Philadelphia Inquirer,* Tuesday, July 1, 1862. p. 1.

Map of the area east of Richmond showing Union headquarters on the Chickahominy near Bottoms Bridge, the skirmish at Barhamsville (Eltham's Landing), May 8, 1862, and the battleground at West Point, May 2, 1862.

465.67

Pope, John.

Map of the field operations of the Army of Virginia during the months of July and August 1862. Bowen & Co., lith., Phila. Uncolored. Scale ca. 1:350,000. 39 × 42 cm. *From* U.S. Congress. Joint Committee on the Conduct of the War. Supplemental report of the Joint Committee on the Conduct of the War, in two volumes. Supplemental to Senate report no. 142, 38th Congress, 2d session (Washington, Government Printing Office, 1866). v. 2, fol. p. 108.

Accompanies "Report of Major General John Pope to the hon. Committee on the Conduct of the War." 217 p.

General map showing roads, railroads, place names, drainage, and relief by hachures. Troop positions and movements are not indicated.

465.7

Prang (Louis) and Company.

War telegram marking map. Boston, L. Prang & Co., ©1862. Uncolored. Scale ca. 1:490,000. 88 × 57 cm.

Base map depicting eastern Virginia printed in brown ink.

"Entered according to Act of Congress in the year 1862 by L. Prang & Co.

"Explanations. The extraordinary large scale on which this map is drawn has been adopted to make it just what we designed it to be, namely 1st. The most distinct map ever published of the whole Virginia territory, where the decisive battles for the Union will be fought. 2nd. A marking map, that is a map to mark the change of positions of the Union forces in red pencil and the rebel forces in blue, on the receipt of every telegram from the seat of war . . ."

465.75

————————Another issue.

In this issue, Hixford, Virginia, south of Petersburg, has been changed to Hicksford.

465.8

————————6th improved edition.

Edition statement is printed at the top of the map. Includes additional place names.

465.85

Ridgeway, Thomas S.

[Geological map of Virginia] Made under the direction of Maj: A. A. Humphreys by Tho. S. Ridgeway, Geologist &c, formerly of the Geological Survey of Va. March 1862. Colored ms. Scale ca. 1:650,000. 2 parts, 78 × 58 and 78 × 62 cm.

G3881 .C5 1862 .R5 Vault

Photocopy of Herman Böÿe's "A Map of the State of Virginia Reduced from the Nine Sheet Map of the State" (1859) annotated to show geological information. A legend, entitled "Geological Explanations," is pasted to the base map below the map title.

Military information is not shown.

465.9

U.S. *Army. Corps of Topographical Engineers.*

Central Virginia, compiled in the Bureau of Topographl. Engrs. of the War Department for military purposes. July 1862. Print. by J. F. Gedney, Washn. Uncolored. Scale 1:350,000. 66 × 79 cm.

G3880 1862 .U5

General map extending from Washington, D.C., south to Petersburg, Virginia.

1864 edition is listed as entry no. 501.5.

466

————————Map of n. eastern Virginia and vicinity of Washington compiled in Topographical Engineers Office at Division Head Quarters of General Irvin McDowell. Arlington, January 1th [sic] 1862, from published and manuscript maps corrected by recent surveys and reconnaissances. Engraved on stone by J. Schedler, N.Y. Uncolored. Scale 1:63,360. 2 parts, each 84 × 125 cm.

At head of title: "Surveys for military defences."

"Presented to Brig. Genl. S. Williams, A. A. Genl. Hd. Qrs. Army, by order of Maj. Genl. McClellan, Comd. in Chf. U.S.A. [signed] A. W. Whipple, Maj. T. E."

Detailed map extending from Waterford south to Fredericksburg, and Washington west to Warrenton, and indicating the defenses of Washington, street pattern of Washington, Alexandria, and Georgetown, county names and boundaries, roads, railroads, houses, names of residents, vegetation, drainage, and relief by hachures. Map is based on a plane table survey conducted by field parties under the direction of H. L. Whiting, U.S. Coast Survey.

467

————————Another issue. 4 sheets, each approximately 83 × 63 cm.

G3882 .N6S5 1862 .U5 Vault

Dedicated in ms. on verso: Major General Sigel to Colonel L. P. di Cesnola, Chantilly, Novbr. 1862.

Bookplate of "Palma di Cesnola" is also on the verso.

More vegetation is indicated on this issue, particularly in the west. Geography and Map Division's copy has been annotated with colored inks to show troop positions and engagements.

A second copy of this issue has been annotated in ink to show the following forts in the vicinity of Washington, D.C.: De Russy, Slemmer, Thayer, Davis, Baker, Wagner, Riketts [i.e., Ricketts], and Snyder. In addition, the name "Ft. Towson" printed on the map has been corrected in ink to read "Ft. Totten." "211, L. Sheet 1" and "Transf'd from Office of Chf. Engr. Defenses of Washington, to Engr. Dept. [Ja]ny 1866" have been written in ink above and below the map title, respectively.

468

—————Another issue. 2 parts, each 166 × 63 cm.

This issue has added to the "Data used in compilation," the statement "Additions & corrections for Rappahannock and Rapid Ann Rivers and their vicinity furnished from the records in the office of Lt. Coll. J. N. Macomb, A. D. Camp and Chf. Topl. Engr., Army of Potomac."

Another copy of this issue, cut into six parts, is stamped "Gilbert Thompson" on verso. The Library acquired the Thompson map collection in 1910.

469

—————Another issue. 4 sheets. 2 sheets 83 × 64 cm. and 2 sheets 65 × 62 cm. The N.E. and N.W. sheets are cut and mounted to fold to about 17 × 11 cm.

This issue identifies the "Battle field at Bull Run fought July 21st 1861."

470

—————Another edition. Corrected from recent surveys and reconnaissances under direction of the Bureau of Topographical Engineers, August 1st 1862. Drawn by J. J. Young [and] W. Hesselbach. Engr. on stone by J. Schedler, N.Y. Uncolored. Scale 1:63,360. 2 sheets measuring 69 × 132 cm. and 67 × 122 cm. Each cut in 3 parts and mounted to fold.

G3880 1862 .U51

471

—————Part of the map of the military department of S.E. Virginia & Fort Monroe compiled in the Bureau of Topogl. Engrs. of the War Department, August 1861. Engr. on stone by J. Schedler, N.Y. [1862?] Uncolored. Scale 1:200,000. 2 sheets, each 67 × 53 cm.

Indicates fortifications on the Peninsula, roads, railroads, towns, and drainage.

Map has been annotated to include county names and boundaries, additional villages, and a few houses and the names of residents in the area south and southwest of Fredericksburg.

472

U.S. *Coast Survey.*

Military map of south-eastern Virginia. H. Lindenkohl & Chs. G. Krebs, lith. [1862?] Uncolored. Scale 1:200,000. 81 × 74 cm.

Gives fortifications, towns, roads, railroads, drainage, and some vegetation.

List of authorities is in the lower right corner.

473

—————Another issue.

This and the following two maps have "drawn by A. Lindenkohl" in the lower left corner.

List of authorities differs slightly from other issues.

474

—————Another issue. Colored.

Chesapeake Bay and principal rivers are colored green. List of authorities differs slightly from other issues. Another copy is filed G3880 1862 .U52.

475

—————Another issue.

G3882 .T5S5 1865 .U5 Vault

List of authorities differs slightly from other issues.

In lower right corner in purple ink: Camps and routes of march of the U.S. Engineer Battln. during the Peninsuela [sic] Campaign—1862. [Signed] Gilbert Thompson, U.S. Eng'r. Battln.—1862.

Map is also annotated in blue ink to show the lines of march in 1864 and in green ink to show the routes of 1865.

475.5

West and Johnston.

Map of the State of Virginia containing the counties, principal towns, railroads, rivers, canals & all other internal

---

A great variety of maps were published in the North for sale to an eagerly awaiting public in need of up-to-date geographical information. Few families were without someone in the armed forces serving in a little-known place in the American South. Louis Prang and Company of Boston, for example, published a "War Telegram Marking Map" of eastern Virginia on which one could follow the events of the war. The publishers noted that the map had been designed to permit the user "to mark the change of positions of the Union forces in red pencil and the rebel forces in blue, on the receipt of every telegram from the seat of war." (See entry no. 465.75.)

WAR TELEGRAM MARKING MAP.

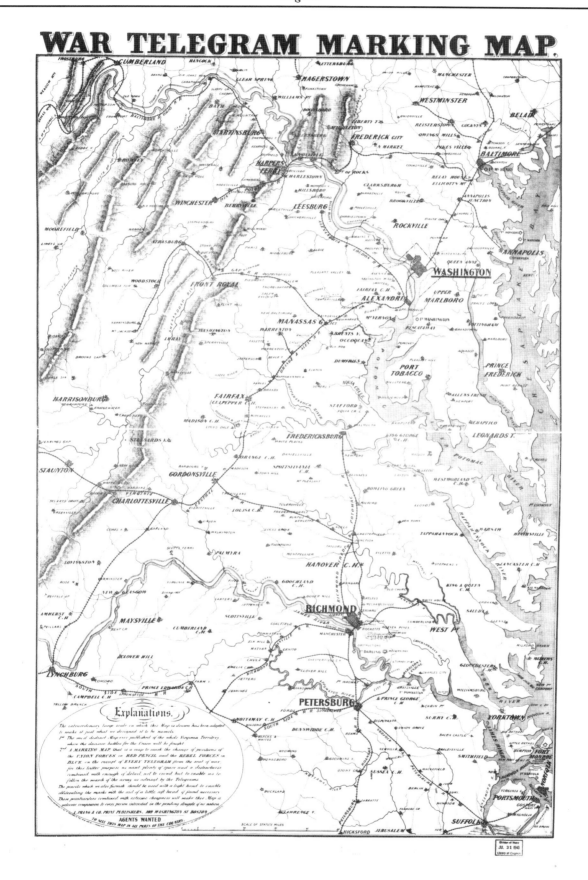

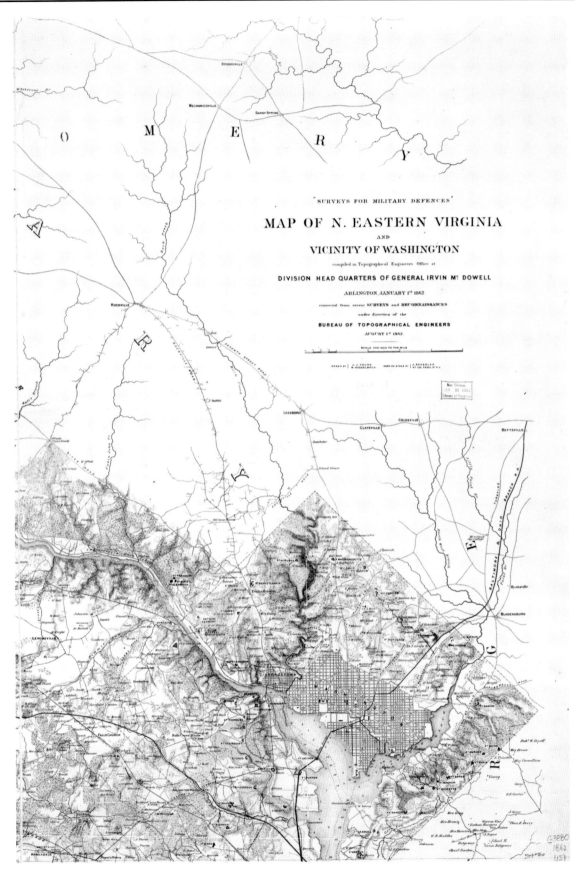

improvements. Richmond, Va., West & Johnston, 1862. Scale ca. 1:820,000. 65 × 95 cm.

> G3880 1862 .W41 Vault
> "Copyright secured by W. & J. May 1, 1862."
> Confederate imprint.
> Military information is not indicated.

476

Worret, Ch.

S.E. portion of Virginia and N.E. portion of Nth. Carolina, drawn b. Sergt. Ch. Worret & compiled under the direction of Col. T. J. Cram, Chief Topl. Engr. Dept. Va [1862] Colored ms. Scale ca. 1:430,000 (not "1:400,000") 66 × 56 cm.

> G3882 .T5 186- .C5 Vault
> Finished manuscript map showing fortifications, roads, railroads, canals, drainage, vegetation, towns, and distances.
> "Military considerations" for reducing Norfolk, Virginia, are given below the map.

1863

476.5

Bacon and Company.

Seat of war in America, 6d. London, [1863] Colored. Scale ca. 1:820,000. 54 × 32 cm.

> G3881 .S5 1863 .B3
> Map of eastern Virginia and parts of Maryland and Pennsylvania showing batteries, towns, roads, railroads, and rivers.
> An advertisement for "Bacon's Shilling War Maps" is printed in the lower left corner.
> See entry no. 453 for the 1862 edition.

477

Bruff, Joseph G.

New map of the seat of war in Virginia and Maryland. Drawn by J. G. Bruff. Lith of Lang & Cooper, New York. Published by J. Disturnell, New York, and W. H. and O. H.

On January 1, 1862, a map of northern Virginia at the scale of one inch to the mile was published at the headquarters of Gen. Irvin McDowell in Arlington, Virginia. Based on a plane table survey conducted by field parties under the direction of H. L. Whiting, U.S. Coast Survey, it was the first detailed map of Northern Virginia to be compiled and published. Another edition, incorporating corrections "from recent surveys and reconnaissances under direction of the Bureau of Topographical Engineers" was issued on August 1, 1862, only 28 days before the second Battle of Manassas, Virginia. Displayed here is the portion of the map showing the title and the environs of Washington, D.C. (See entry no. 470.)

Morrison, Washington, D.C. 1863. Colored. Scale ca. 1:360,000. 68 × 72 cm.

> Map of eastern Virginia and Maryland showing the location and date of battles, forts, roads, railroads, towns, drainage, and relief by hachures.

478

—————Another issue.

This issue contains the following additions:

a) Washington is described as being "Surrounded by forts, batteries, and redoubts."

b) Fredericksburg is labeled "H. 2 Rebel forces, Dec. 1862."

c) "Explanation" contains the statement that "Washington City is the centre of the circles of measurement, 10 miles apart."

d) Town and county names have been added.

479

Cockrell, Monroe F.

The military campaigns of Stonewall Jackson. Based on [George F. R.] Henderson's life of Jackson. Prepared by Monroe F. Cockrell. Drawn by Emery L. Ring, June 1, 1940. Copyright—Monroe F. Cockrell [Jan. 18, 1941] Blue print. Scale 1:696,960. 42 × 40 cm.

Indicates the routes of Stonewall Jackson, his position on selected days, and the names and dates of battles in which he participated.

Another copy is in *Notes and Articles by Monroe F. Cockrell for His Maps of the War Between the States.* ©1950. Typescript.

479.2

Colton, Joseph H.

J. H. Colton's topographical map of the seat of war in Virginia, Maryland &c. New York, J. H. Colton's Geographical Establishment, [1863?] Colored. Scale ca. 1:750,000. 68 × 49 cm.

> G3880 186- .C6
> "Entered according to Act of Congress in the year 1852 by J. H. Colton."
> Printed by Lang & Cooper, N.Y.
> General map of eastern Virginia, Maryland, Delaware, southern Pennsylvania, and nothern North Carolina.

479.3

—————Another issue. Colored. Scale 1:760,320. 66 × 48 cm.

> G3880 186-.C61
> "Entered according to Act of Congress in the year 1855, by J. H. Colton & Co."
> Includes the bar scale below the publisher's statement.

479.5

Forbes (W. H.) and Company.

Theatre of the war! A complete map of the battle ground of Hooker's army!! Showing all the approaches from Richmond and the scene of Stoneman's successful foray, and truthfully depicted in a bold, clear, and comprehensive manner. Boston, W. H. Forbes & Co., ©1863. Uncolored. Scale not given. 56 × 46 cm.

"Entered according to Act of Congress in the year 1863 by Forbes & Co."

"Deposited [for copyright] May 11, 1863, vol. 38, page 179, no. 124" is written on the verso.

General map of central Virginia extending from Richmond north to Stafford Court House.

480

Heald, D. A.

The battle fields and military positions in eastern Virginia, from surveys supplied by officers of the army. Entered according to Act of Congress in the year 1862, by D. A. Heald. [New York, 1863] Colored. Scale ca. 1:450,000. 50 × 64 cm.

"Presented by the Home Insurance Compy of New York."

Inset: [Map of northern Virginia, Maryland, Delaware, and southern Pennsylvania] 16 × 32 cm.

Gives names and boundaries of Virginia counties, roads, railroads, towns, and drainage. Battles are indicated by crossed swords.

481

Hotchkiss, Jedediah.

Map of a portion of the Rappahannock River and vicinity, Virginia. To illustrate the operations of the Army of Northern Virginia, C.S., and the Army of the Potomac, U.S., from the close of the battle of Fredericksburg, Decemr. 15th 1862, to the battle of Chancellorsville, Saturday, May 2nd 1863. Compiled from surveys by C. S. Engineers, by Jed. Hotchkiss, Top. Eng., Staunton, Va. Drawn by S. B. Robinson. W. S. Barnard Sc., N. York. Entered according to Act of Congress in the year 1866, by D. Van Nostrand. Uncolored. Scale 1:158,400. 31 × 53 cm.

G3882 .R38S5 1863 .H6 Vault

At head of title: No. 2. "The battle fields of Virginia."

Proof copy with manuscript annotations by Hotchkiss. An uncorrected version appears in Hotchkiss, Jedediah, and Allan, William. *The Battle-fields of Virginia: Chancellorsville.* (New York, D. Van Nostrand, 1867).

Map of parts of Orange, Spotsylvania, Caroline, Culpeper, Fauquier, Stafford, and King George counties, Virginia, showing troop positions, towns, county names, roads, railroads, drainage, fords, vegetation, and houses.

481.2

Lloyd, James T.

Lloyd's official map of the State of Virginia from actual surveys by order of the Executive, 1828 & 1859. Corrected and revised by J. T. Lloyd to 1862, from surveys made by Capt. W. Angelo Powell, of the U. S. Topographical Engineers. New York, J. T. Lloyd [1863] Colored. Scale ca. 1:650,000. 76 × 120 cm.

G3880 1863 .L4

Includes a testimonial from William A. Bryan, Chief Clerk, Post Office Department, dated February 10, 1863. 1861 editions are listed as entry nos. 450 and 450.1 and the 1862 editions as 465 and 465.1.

481.4

Map of a part of eastern Virginia. 1863. Blue print. Scale 1:240,000. 68 × 77 cm.

G3880 1863 .M3

Anonymous map of the counties of Berkeley, Jefferson, Loudoun, Fairfax, Prince William, and Fauquier showing cities and towns, roads and railroads, rivers and streams, and names of residents.

481.5

Nicholson, W. L.

Map of eastern Virginia, compiled from the best authorities and printed at the Coast Survey Office. A. D. Bache, Supdt. 1863. Compiled by W. L. Nicholson. Lith. by Chas. G. Krebs. Colored. Scale ca. 1:887,040. 62 × 48 cm.

G3880 1863 .N5

"August" is printed in blue in the lower right corner.

General map of eastern Virginia showing cities and towns, roads, rivers, and relief by hachures. The map is overprinted in red to indicate railroads and concentric circles centered on Richmond, and in blue to show water and concentric circles centered on Washington, D.C. Circles are at intervals of ten miles.

From the papers of Joseph Roswell Hawley, Manuscript Division, L.C.

481.6

————Map of the State of Virginia, compiled from the best authorities at the Coast Survey Office. A. D. Bache, Supdt. July 1863. Compiled by W. L. Nicholson. Lith by Chas. G. Krebs. Colored. Scale ca. 1:887,040. 58 × 89 cm.

G3880 1863 .N51

General map of Virginia, West Virginia, Maryland,

W. H. Forbes and Company of Boston depended on the bold title, "Theatre of the War! A complete Map of the Battle Ground of Hooker's Army!!," to sell his unimaginative map of central Virginia. (See entry no. 479.5.)

THEATRE OF THE WAR!

A Complete Map of the Battle Ground of

HOOKER'S ARMY!!

Showing all the Approaches from Richmond and the scene of STONEMAN'S successful foray,

And truthfully depicted in a bold, clear, and comprehensive manner.

W. H. FORBES & CO., Publishers,

265 Washington Street, Boston.

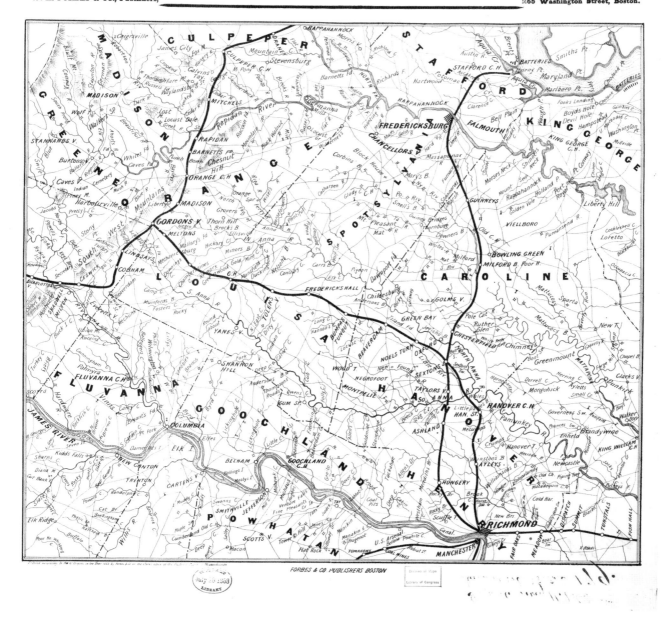

FORBES & CO. PUBLISHERS BOSTON

Delaware, and southern Pennsylvania showing cities and towns, roads, rivers, and relief by hachures. The map is overprinted in red to indicate railroads, the state name "West Virginia," and concentric circles centered on Richmond. Circles are at intervals of ten miles. A table of "Distances by Rail Roads" appears below the map title.

481.7

——————Another issue. August 1863.
    G3880 1863 .N52

481.9

Owner, William.

[Sketch map of eastern Virginia. 1862–1863] Uncolored ms. Scale ca. 1:210,000. 19 × 15 cm. *In his* Diary, v. 3, tipped-in at end of volume.

In the William Owner papers, Manuscript Division, L. C., container no. 1.

Map shows railroads leading to Richmond, the road linking Fredericksburg to Richmond and Petersburg, and the road connecting Norfolk and Suffolk.

Volume 3 of the diary covers from Sept. 11, 1862, to Feb. 13, 1863.

"On to Richmond" and "W.O." are written above the map.

482

Schwerin, J. A., Jr.

The war between the states campaigns of Stonewall Jackson, July 1861–May 1863. Aiken, S.C., ©1958. Uncolored. Scale ca. 1:1,550,000. 27 × 20 cm.

Map of eastern Virginia and Maryland showing the marches of Jackson, engagements in which he participated, towns, rivers, and relief by hachures.

483

Stenberg, T. R.

Map of the marches and battles of T. J. "Stonewall" Jackson, Lieut. Gen.—C.S.A. [1861–1863]. Printed by Florida Photo & Printing, Inc. [©1956] Uncolored. Scale not given. 40 × 49 cm.

"Chronology" is to the right of the map. A list of battles is in the upper left corner.

483.5

U.S. *Army. Army of the Potomac. Engineer Department.*

[Miscellaneous lithographed proof sheets of areas in Virginia. 1863?] Uncolored. Scale not given. 13 sheets, 48 × 95 cm. or smaller.

Field surveys compiled and printed by the Engineer Department, Army of the Potomac. Each sheet indicates

roads, railroads, names of residents, towns and villages, and rivers and streams. The sheets are without titles and, for the most part, without dates. The sheet covering the environs of Dumfries, Acquia, and Stafford is marked "Proof sheet issued June 12th 1863 Hd. Qr. Army of the Potomac, Engineers Department" and the sheet covering the Warrenton and Bristoe Station area is marked "Office of Surveys and Maps for the Army of the Potomac, 78 Winder's Building, Sept. 15th 1863."

1864

484

Bacon and Company.

Bacon's large print war map showing 50 miles round Washington and Richmond. London [1864] Colored. Scale ca. 1:480,000. 85 × 55 cm.

Map of eastern Virginia and part of Maryland, showing engagements by crossed swords, fortifications surrounding Richmond, routes of the opposing armies to Petersburg, roads, railroads, towns, drainage, and relief by hachures. A few important Civil War sites are underlined in red.

484.2

Bacon and Company.

Bacon's new map of the seat of war in Virginia and Maryland. Showing the interesting localities around Richmond, Washington, Baltimore &c. London, Bacon & Co., 1864. Colored. Scale ca. 1:804,000. 60 × 46 cm.

At top of map: Bacon's new shilling war map.

"No. 4" is printed in the lower margin.

General map

Cover title: Shilling series—no. 4. Bacon's seat of war in Virginia designating minutely over 3,000 names of towns, streams, &c., around Richmond and Washington. The most elaborate ever issued. London, Bacon & Co.

Covers include advertisements for "Bacon's shilling war maps" and "Colton's [i.e., J. H. Colton] maps of America, and complete series of war maps."

485

Bechler, Gustavus R.

Atlas showing battles, engagements, and important localities connected with the campaigns in Virginia, completing the campaign map. Philadelphia [©1864] 4 p. l., 16 col. maps. 19 × 22 cm.

    G1291 .S5B4 1864

For table of contents see P. L. Phillips's *A List of Geographical Atlases in the Library of Congress* (Washington, Government Printing Office, 1909), v. 1, no. 1348 or 2606.

486

——————Military map refering [sic] to the campaigns of the Army of the Potomac in Virginia, including the adjoining parts of Maryland & Pennsylvania, expressly compiled from the latest & most reliable sources on record for military & private use, by Gustavus R. Bechler, Philadelphia. ©1864. Colored. Scale ca. 1:332,000. 125 × 96 cm.

Indicates location and date of battles, county names and boundaries, roads, railroads, drainage, towns, and relief by hachures.

1865 edition is listed as entry no. 502.

486.3

Confederate States of America. *Army. Department of Northern Virginia. Chief Engineer's Office.*

[Map of a portion of eastern Virginia. 1864?] Photocopy (positive). Scale ca. 1:160,000. 84 × 66 cm.

G3880 1864 .G4 Vault

Badly worn, nearly illegible photocopy indicating towns and villages, roads, railroads, drainage, and the names of residents in the counties of Rappahannock, Culpeper, Madison, Fluvanna, Spotsylvania, Goochland, Orange, Greene, and Louisa counties, Virginia. The photocopy has been annotated to show some roads and rivers in red, black, and blue, as well as a few additional place names.

The Geography and Map Division has a second copy of the northern half of the map (41 × 66 cm.).

486.5

——————[Map of parts of Hanover, Goochland, Fluvanna, Albemarle, Louisa, Spotsylvania, and Orange counties, and the city of Richmond, Virginia. 1864] Photocopy (positive). Scale ca. 1:160,000. 4 sheets, each 31 × 33 cm.

Sheets lack title or author statements. Sheets are numbered "Plate B, no. 2," "Plate C, no. 1," "Range C, no. 2," and "Range C, no. 3."

Sheet "Range C, no. 3" is dated in the bottom margin Mar. 31st 1864 (date is nearly illegible).

Detailed maps showing cities and towns, county boundaries, roads, railroads, rivers and streams, houses and names of residents, fortifications around Richmond, woodland, and hachures.

486.7

——————[Northern Virginia with adjacent parts of Maryland and West Virginia] Copied by J. Paul Hoffmann, Topl. Office, A. N. Va. [1864] Photocopy (positive). Scale 1:126,720. 43 × 48 cm.

G3880 1864 .C6

Endorsed (facsim.): Approved S. Howell Brown, 1st Lt. Engs: troops, in chg: Topl. Dept., A. N. Va., March 23rd 1864.

"No. 22" is in the upper left corner.

Map of Loudoun County, Virginia, and parts of the counties of Clark, Virginia, Berkeley and Jefferson, West Virginia, and Frederick and Washington, Maryland, showing towns and villages, drainage, roads, railroads, houses and names of residents, and relief by hachures.

Signed on verso: W. T. Griswold.

487

Gatchel, Theodore D.

Early's raid on Washington, June–July, 1864. Photocopy (positive). Scale ca. 1:1,700,000. 20 × 21 cm.

Outline map showing General Early's route to Washington and the towns through which he passed.

488

Heald, D. A.

The approaches from Washington, to Richmond. From surveys supplied by officers of the army. Entered according to Act of Congress in the year 1862 by D. A. Heald . . .[New York, 1864] Colored. Scale ca. 1:445,000. 50 × 64 cm.

"Presented by the Home Insurance Compy. of New York."

Map of eastern Virginia showing roads, railroads, towns, drainage, and some relief by hachures. Battlefields are identified by crossed swords.

Inset: The strategic points of east Tennessee, northern Alabama, and Georgia, from the U.S. official military map, 1864. Entered according to Act of Congress in the year 1864, by D. A. Heald . . . Scale ca. 1:1,300,000. 23 × 31 cm.

Another copy is in the Fillmore map coll. no. 252.

488.2

Index sheet of battlefield maps for Fredericksburg, Spottsylvania C.H., Wilderness, Chancellorsville, Virginia. [1862–64] To accompany report of the Battlefield Commission created by Act of Congress public no. 261, 68th Congress dated 1925. 26 × 34 cm. Colored. Scale ca. 1: 135,000. 26 × 34 cm.

Map indicates troop positions, trenches, public roads, "roads, special, to be built," "property to be acquired," and "some of the important points to be marked."

Inset: Locality sketch. 9 × 7 cm.

Another issue with the imprint "Engineer Reproduction Plant, U.S. Army, Washington Barracks, D.C., 1926" accompanies the report "To establish a national military park at and near Fredericksburg, Va.," 1926. (69th Cong., 1st sess., Report no. 814). 3 p.

488.4

Isometric view of General Grant's Virginia campaign.

[1864] Uncolored view. Not drawn to scale. 24 × 36 cm. *From* Harper's weekly, v. 8, Sept. 10, 1864. p. 580.

Panoramic view of the environs of the James and Appomattox rivers showing Union and Confederate lines at Petersburg, and Butler's lines at Bermuda Hundred.

Points of interest are keyed by number to a legend printed in the lower margin.

489

Lindenkohl, Adolph.

Military map of south-eastern Virginia. Drawn by A. Lindenkohl. H. Lindenkohl & Chs. G. Krebs, lith. [1864] Colored. Scale 1:200,000. 47 × 83 cm.

Map title appears inside the border in the upper right corner.

Indicates 5-mile concentric circles centered on Richmond, roads, bridges, railroads, towns, houses, drainage, vegetation, and some fortifications in the Richmond-Petersburg area.

490

—————Another issue. A Lindenkohl, del. H. Lindenkohl & Chas. G. Krebs, lith. [1864] Colored. Scale 1:200,000. 47 × 82 cm.

Map title on this and the following two issues appears outside of the top border.

Fortifications and vegetation in the Richmond-Petersburg area are more extensive here than on the preceding issue.

Another copy is in the Fillmore map coll. no. 256.

Another copy is in the James A. Garfield papers, Manuscript Division, L.C., series 8, container no. 1.

491

—————Another issue. Drawn by A. Lindenkohl. H. Lindenkohl & Chs. G. Krebs, lith. [1864] Colored. Scale 1:200,000. 48 × 83 cm.

This is rather similar to the preceding issue but contains more detail to the southwest of Petersburg.

492

—————Another issue.

Same as the preceding issue but with the statement "No. 3010 price 30 cents" outside of the border in the upper left corner.

492.5

Map illustrating General Grant's campaign in Virginia. [1864] Uncolored. Scale ca. 1:900,000. 24 × 24 cm. on sheet 41 × 28 cm. *From* Harper's weekly, v. 8, July 9, 1864. p. 438.

This map was acquired by the Library of Congress in

1948 with the purchase of the papers and maps of Maj. Jedediah Hotchkiss.

Map of central Virginia showing place names, roads, railroads, and rivers. Troop positions are not depicted.

493

Michler, Nathaniel.

[Map of Fairfax and Alexandria counties, Virginia, and parts of adjoining counties. 1864] Photocopy (positive). Scale not given. 69 × 87 cm.

"Recd. Engineer Bureau, April 25th 1864, with letter April 23d '64, fm. Capt. Michler, [signed] J. C. Woodruff, Maj. of Engineers."

Lacks title.

Map showing the defenses of Washington situated in Virginia, roads, railroads, towns, drainage, vegetation, houses, and names of residents.

493.2

The New York Herald.

Important operations in Virginia. The Army of the Potomac across the Rapidan—Scene of the impending conflict between Generals Grant and Lee. New York, 1864. Uncolored. Scale not given. 22 × 25 cm. *From* The New York Herald, Friday, May 6, 1864. p. 1.

General map of central Virginia from Fredericksburg south to Richmond. The Battle of the Wilderness began the day before this map was published.

493.4

Nicholson, W. L.

Map of eastern Virginia, compiled from the best authorities and printed at the Coast Survey Office, A. D. Bache, Supdt. 1864. Compiled by W. L. Nicholson. Lith. by Chas. G. Krebs. Colored. Scale ca. 1:887,040. 61 × 48 cm.

G3880 1864 .N5

General map of eastern Virginia showing cities and towns, roads, rivers, and relief by hachures. The map is overprinted in red to indicate railroads and concentric circles centered on Richmond and in blue to show concentric circles centered on Washington, D.C.

Another copy is in the Fillmore map coll. no. 253.

493.6

—————Map of the State of Virginia, compiled from the best authorities, and printed at the Coast Survey Office. A. D. Bache, Supdt. May 1864. Compiled by W. L. Nicholson. Lith. by Chas. G. Krebs. Colored. Scale ca. 1:887,040. 58 × 88 cm.

G3880 1864 .N51

General map of Virginia, West Virginia, Maryland,

Delaware, and southern Pennsylvania showing cities and towns, roads, rivers, and relief by hachures. The map is overprinted in red to indicate railroads, the state name "West Virginia," and concentric circles centered on Richmond. Printed in blue are concentric circles centered on Washington, D.C. A table of "Distances by Railroads" appears below the map title.

493.7

──────Another issue. October 1864.
G3880 1864 .N52
Concentric circles centered on Washington, D.C., have been dropped from this issue.

494

Operations of the Army of the Potomac, May & June 1864. Uncolored. Scale not given. 27 × 27 cm.
"Map no. 3" is in the upper left corner.
Map of Virginia from Culpeper south to Malvern Hill and Gordonsville east to White House, showing fortifications around Richmond, roads, railroads, towns, and rivers.

495

Preston, Noble D.

Map of a part of the eastern portion of Virginia showing the route of the Cavalry Corps of the Army of the Potomac under Major General P. H. Sheridan on the raid to Richmond in May, 1864. Together with the route followed by the Confederate Cavalry under Major General J. E. B Stuart. Drawn by Capt. N. D. Preston . . . 1903. Uncolored ms. Scale ca. 1:126,000. 87 × 46 cm.
G3882.T5S5 1864 .P7 Vault
"Drawn by Capt. N. D. Preston, to accompany the paper, 'The Cavalry Raid to Richmond, in May, 1864,' read by him before the Commandery of the State of Pennsylvania, Military Order of the Loyal Legion of the U.S., Wednesday evening, May 6, 1903."
Finished pen and ink manuscript, showing troop movements, engagements, encampments, roads, railroads, towns, drainage, and the fortifications surrounding Richmond.

496

──────From pen and ink drawing by N. D. Preston. Copyrighted Mar. 18, 1907. Uncolored. Scale ca. 1:235,000. 46 × 25 cm.
Printed version of the preceding manuscript map.

497

──────Map [of] central Virginia showing the movements of the Tenth New York Cavalry in the campaigs [sic] of 1864. Uncolored ms. Scale ca. 1:350,000. 46 × 30 cm.
G3882 .T5S5 1864 .P71 Vault
Finished pen and ink manuscript map extending from Rappahannock Station south to Dinwiddie C.H. and from Trevillian Station east to King & Queen C.H. Encampments, battles, troop movements, roads, railroads, drainage, and towns are indicated.
Printed version appears in Preston's *History of the Tenth Regiment of Cavalry, New York State Volunteers, August, 1861, to August, 1865*. New York, D. Appleton, 1892. opp. p. 168.

497.5

Russell, Benjamin B.

The Potomac army war map. Designed to show the present fighting ground in Virginia to meet the demand of the times. Forbes & Co., lith., Boston. Boston, B. B. Russell, [1864] Uncolored. Scale ca. 1:520,000. 55 × 45 cm.
General map of eastern Virginia printed in blue ink. The map indicates the site of the "Battleground of May 11 & 12, 1864" at Spotsylvania Court House.

498

Schönberg and Company.

Schönberg's Virginia campaign map, 1864. New York, 1864. Colored. Scale ca. 1:425,000. 52 × 35 cm.
Map extends from Ashby's Gap south to Winfield and Charlottesville east to Tappahannock and shows the location and date of engagements, towns, roads, railroads, county names and boundaries, drainage, and some relief by hachures. A few place names are underlined in red.

498.5

Sheridan's last raid. The line of Sheridan's march, from Newcastle, on the Pamunkey, to Gordonsville. [June 7–June 11, 1864] W. Waters [&] Son sc., N.Y. Uncolored. Scale ca. 1:385,000. 36 × 13 cm.
Anonymous, undated newspaper map showing the location and dates of encampments and the "rout of rebels, June 11th" at Trevilians Station.

499

Sholl, Charles.

Military topographical map of eastern Virginia showing the routes taken by the several army corps & the battles fought in the present campaign of 1864 under Lt. Gen. U. S. Grant. Compiled and drawn by Charles Sholl, Civil & Topographical Engineer. Published by Capt. R. Chauncy, H.M.B.N.I., N. York. Entered according to Act of Congress A.D. 1864 by R. Chauncy . . . J. Bien, lith., N.Y. Colored. Scale ca. 1:135,000. 91 × 56 cm.
Includes fortifications surrounding Richmond and Petersburg, roads, railroads, drainage, vegetation, towns, and houses.

499.5

Sifton, Praed & Company, Ltd.

Sifton, Praed's new map of Virginia and Maryland to illustrate the campaigns of 1861 to 1864. London, Sifton, Praed & Co., Ltd., "The Map House", 1912. Uncolored. Scale 1:633,600. 52 × 47 cm.

General map with place names associated with the war indicated. Troop positions are not indicated.

500

U.S. *Army. Army of the Potomac. Engineer Department.*

[Map of the lines of march of the Army of the Potomac from Culpeper to Petersburg, Virginia] Engineer Dept., Hd. Qrs. Army of the Potomac, 1864. Scale 1:63,360. Photocopy (positive). 6 sheets, each 33 × 48 cm. or smaller.

Each sheet is hand-colored to show the lines of march of the Federal II, V, VI, IX, and XVIII corps and the cavalry.

Sheets 2, 3, and 5 are signed by Maj. N. Michler and are dated July 28, August 2, and November 7, 1864, respectively.

Base map indicates roads, railroads, towns, drainage, houses, and names of residents.

501

—————Another copy.

Lines of march differ very slightly. Sheet 6 is signed in manuscript "N. Michler, Major of Engineers, U.S.A."

501.2

U.S. *Army. Corps of Engineers.*

Portions of Virginia and North Carolina, embracing Richmond & Lynchburg, Va. and Goldsboro & Salisbury, N.C., compiled in the Engineer Bureau, War Department, for military purposes. 1864. J. Schedler, N.Y. Uncolored. Scale 1:350,000. 84 × 102 cm.

G3880 1864 .U52

General map extending from Richmond, Virginia, south to Fayetteville, North Carolina.

Map title is printed with an oval border.

Another copy is in the Fillmore map coll. no. 254.

Another copy, with annotations in red and blue pencil, is in the Montgomery C. Meigs papers, Manuscript Division, L.C., 10, oversize cabinet 4, drawer 3.

501.3

—————Another issue.

G3880 1864 .U53

This issue lacks the border around the map title.

501.4

[U.S Army. Corps of Engineers.

South central Virginia showing lines of transportation.

1864] Colored ms. Scale ca. 1:350,000, 40 × 43 cm.

G3881.P1 1864 .S6 Vault

Map extends from Richmond, Virginia, south to Weldon, North Carolina, and shows railroads, roads, rivers, and towns. It appears to be a tracing of the lithographed map entitled "Portions of Virginia and North Carolina, embracing Richmond & Lynchburg, Va. and Goldsboro & Salisbury, N.C." (1864). See entry nos. 501.2 and 501.3.

501.5

U.S. *Army. Corps of Topographical Engineers.*

Central Virginia, compiled in the Bureau of Topographl. Engrs. of the War Department for military purposes. July 1862. Corrections and additions Oct. 27, 1864. Print. by J. F. Gedney, Washn. Uncolored. Scale 1:350,000. 66 × 81 cm.

G3880 1864 .U5

Signed in ms.: From Chf. Engrs. Office, Mily. Divn. Miss., O. M. Poe, Bvt. Col. & Chf. Engr.

General map extending from Washington, D.C., south to Petersburg, Virginia.

Another copy in the Geography and Map Division is from the Orlando M. Poe papers, Manuscript Division, L.C. (G3880 1864 .U55). It is signed in ink: From Chief Engrs. Office, Mily. Divn. Miss: O. M. Poe, Bvt. Col: & Chf: Engr.

501.6

—————Another issue.

G3880 1864 .U51

"Print. by J. F. Gedney, Washn." has been dropped from the lower right corner.

Another copy is in the James A. Garfield papers, Manuscript Division, L.C., series 8, container no. 1.

501.7

—————[Central Virginia. Lith. by J. F. Gedney, Washington, 1864] Colored. Scale 1:63,360. 29 sheets, each approx. 68 × 99 cm.

G3880 s63 .U5

Geography and Map Division has the map index and sheets 8, 10–13, 16–17, 21, and 24. The index consists of a copy of a printed map entitled "Central Virginia, compiled in the Bureau of Topographl. Engrs. of the War Department for Military purposes. July 1862" (entry no. 465.9) which has been annotated in red ink to show sheet lines and numbers. These are rough field surveys lithographed in Washington, D.C., by Gedney for the army. The sheets, consisting of two parts joined in the middle, indicate towns and villages, roads and railroads, rivers and streams, and houses and names of residents.

Contents

8. [Occoquan, Dumfries, Stafford C.H., and vicinity] April 13, 1864 (western half), April 18, 1864 (eastern half).

8. ——Another issue. April 28, 1864 (western half), April 18, 1864 (eastern half).

10. [Madison, C.H., Blue Ridge Mountains, Shenandoah River, and vicinity] April 13, 1864 (western half), April 19, 1864 (eastern half). 2 copies.

11. [Fredericksburg, Port Royal, Rappahannock River, and vicinity] April 6, 1864 (western half), April 9, 1864 (eastern half)

11. ——Another issue. April 28, 1864 (both halves).

12. [Orange C.H., Gordonsville, Louisa C.H., Spotsylvania C.H., and vicinity] April 23, 1864 (both halves). 2 copies, one of which is annotated in ink.

13. [Charlottesville, Port Republic, Gordonsville, and vicinity] April 11, 1864 (western half), April 9, 1864 (eastern half).

16. [Hanover C.H., King William C.H., and vicinity] April 6, 1864 (both halves). 2 copies, both of which are annotated in pencil. One copy is marked to show the location of "Hd. Qrs, 1st Div., 5 Corps May 29 64."

16. ——Western half only. May 2, 1864.

17. [Palmyra C.H., Goochland C.H., and vicinity] April 2, 1864 (Western half), March 26, 1864 (eastern half). 2 copies.

21. [Richmond, Charles City C.H., and vicinity] May 19, 1864 (western half), May 27, 1864 (eastern half). 2 copies, one of which is annotated in pencil and red ink.

24. [Lynchburg and vicinity. 1864] Hand-colored photocopy. Endorsed "April 8th 1864. Forwarded by letter of same date ch. [?] Michler, Capt. of Engineers U.S.A."

24. ——Eastern half only. May 2, 1864.

501.8

West and Johnston.

Map of the State of Virginia containing the counties, principal towns, railroads, rivers, canals & all other internal improvements. Richmond, Va., West & Johnston, 1862 [i.e., 1864]. Uncolored. Scale ca. 1:820,000. 65 × 95 cm. folded to 17 × 11 cm.

G3880 1864 .W41 Vault Shelf

"Copyright secured by W. & J. May 1, 1862."

Cover title: New map of Virginia. 1864. Richmond, West & Johnston, 145 Main Street.

Confederate imprint.

Military information not indicated.

1865

502

Bechler, Gustavus R.

Military map refering [sic] to the campaigns of the Army of the Potomac in Virginia, Maryland and Pennsylvania. Entered according to Act of Congress in the year 1864 by Gustavus R. Bechler. Published by H. H. Lloyd & Co., New York. 1865. Colored. Scale ca. 1:332,000. 125 × 95 cm.

Indicates location and date of battles, county names and boundaries, roads, railroads, drainage, towns, and relief by hachures.

1864 edition is listed as entry no. 486.

502.5

Biganzoli, Lisa.

The Appomattox campaign. [March 31–April 9, 1865] Produced by the National Geographic Society, Geographic Art Division. Drawn by Lisa Biganzoli, Research by Eugene M. Scheel. Colored. Scale ca. 1:445,000. 26 × 35 cm. *From National geographic*, v. 127, April 1965. p. 452–453.

Map of south central Virginia showing troop movements, fortifications, battlefields, roads, railroads, towns, and drainage. Union victories are marked with blue stars, and Confederate victories with red stars. "Route numbers show how closely 1965 highways follow Civil War road network."

503

Bliley (Joseph W.) Company.

Major battlefields in Virginia in the war between the states. Richmond, Virginia, Joseph W. Bliley Co. [©1960] Colored. Scale not given. 41 × 51 cm.

Decorative map indicating principal engagements and 14 pictures depicting Confederate troops in action.

504

Chesapeake and Ohio Railway Company.

Map showing the location of battle fields of Virginia. Compiled from official war records and maps for the Chesapeake & Ohio Railway Co., 1891. ©1892. Poole Bros., Engr's., Chicago. Colored. Scale ca. 1:680,000. 51 × 62 cm.

Map includes "Chesapeake & Ohio R.R. after the war," "other railroads after the war," "railroads during the war," "plank roads and turnpikes," "other roads," rivers, towns, and relief by hachures.

Title when folded: 26th annual encampment, G.A.R. Sept. 20th 1892. Washington, D.C., via Chesapeake & Ohio Ry. Poole Bros., Chicago.

505

——————Another edition.

Title when folded: 29th annual encampment, G.A.R. Sept. 10th 1895. Louisville, Ky., via Chesapeake & Ohio Ry. Poole Bros., Chicago.

Similar to preceding item published for the 26th encampment, G.A.R.

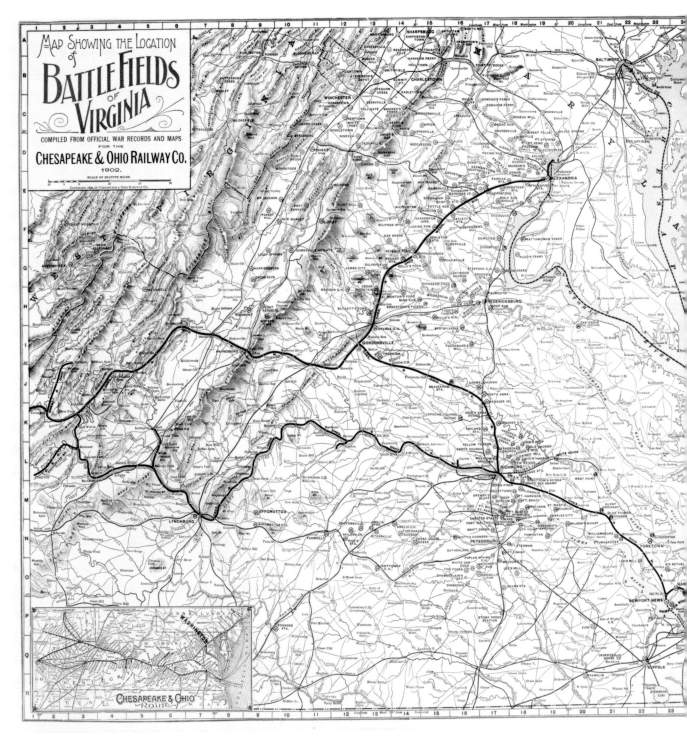

The Chesapeake and Ohio Railway Company's "Map Showing the Location of Battle Fields of Virginia." It was published for the 36th annual encampment of the Grand Army of the Republic held in Washington, D.C., on October 6, 1902. (See entry no. 507.)

506

————Another edition. ©1898. 51 × 62 cm. on sheet 53 × 85 cm.

Title when folded: 32nd annual encampment, G.A.R. Sept. 5th 1898. Cincinnati, Ohio, via Chesapeake & Ohio Ry. Poole Bros., Chicago.

To right of map: Principal battles and engagements oc-

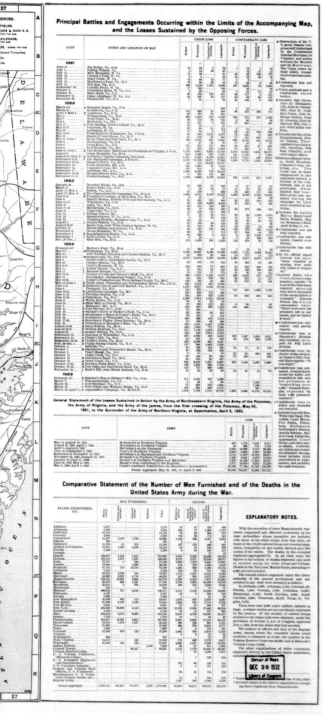

Title when folded: 36th annual encampment, G.A.R. Oct. 6th 1902. Washington, D.C., via Chesapeake & Ohio Ry.

Similar to the preceding entry published for the 32d encampment, G.A.R.

507.5

[Country between Washington, D.C. and Richmond, Virginia. 186–?] Colored ms. Scale not given. 47 × 29 cm.

In the John Alexander Logan family papers, Manuscript Division, L.C., container 145, opp. p. 107.

Pen and ink manuscript map drawn on tracing linen showing roads, railroads, cities and towns, rivers and streams, taverns, and mills. Troop positions are not indicated.

508

Grant's and Sheridan's campaigns, 1864–[1865] Scale ca. 1:670,000. Photocopy (negative). 2 parts, each approximately 26 × 30 cm.

Map of eastern Virginia showing troop movements, engagements, roads, railroads, towns, drainage, and relief by hachures.

508.2

Lang and Laing.

Country between Washington & Manassas Junction [and] Topographical map of the country between Fortress Monroe & Richmond. New York, Lang & Laing, [1861–65?] Colored. Scales ca. 1:200,000 and 1:400,000. 2 maps, 17 × 30 cm. and 17 × 34 cm. on sheet 20 × 64 cm.

G3880 186– .L3

General maps showing roads, railroads, rivers, and place names.

508.4

Lindenkohl, Adolph.

[Southern Virginia and northern North Carolina] Drawn by A. Lindenkohl. H. Lindenkohl & Chas. G. Krebs, lith. U.S. Coast Survey, A. D. Bache, Supdt. 1865. Colored. Scale 1:633,600. 59 × 85 cm.

General map, without a title. State names, boundaries, and railroads are colored red.

508.5

————Another issue. Uncolored. 60 × 86 cm., cut and mounted to fold to 31 × 25 cm.

Lacks cartographer's and lithographers' names as well as the red overprint.

"Gilbert Thompson" is stamped on the verso.

"No. 1. Parts of Virginia and N. Carolina. 6 sheets . . . U.S.C.S. 1865. 1″ = 10 ms." is written in ink on the verso.

Sheet 1 of a 6-sheet series of maps used by Gilbert

curring within the limits of the accompanying map, and the losses sustained by the opposing forces—Comparative statement of the number of men furnished and of the deaths in the United States Army during the war.

Inset: Chesapeake & Ohio route. 8 × 18 cm.

507

————Another edition. ©1898. Published 1902.

Thompson during the Civil War. An index which is pasted on the verso shows the areas covered by the sheets. In addition to this sheet, the Geography and Map Division has sheet 3 (see entry no. 305a.6), sheet 4 (see entry no. 259.6), sheet 5 (see entry no. 129.3), and sheet 6 (see entry no. 129.55).

508.54

[Map of eastern and central Virginia and Maryland. 186–?] Uncolored ms. Scale ca. 1:1,850,000. 21 × 23 cm.

In the John Alexander Logan family papers, Manuscript Division, L.C., container 145, opp. p. 109.

Pen and ink manuscript map on tracing linen indicating county names and boundaries, railroads, and cities and towns. Troop positions are not indicated.

508.55

[Map of eastern Virginia and parts of Maryland and northern North Carolina showing railroads and principal cities and towns. 1861–1865?] Uncolored ms. Scale ca. 1:750,000. 52 × 41 cm.

G3880 186– .M32 Vault

Anonymous map drawn in pencil. With the exception of Fort Monroe, no military information is given.

508.56

[Map of the country between Fredericksburg and Richmond, Virginia, showing roads, railroads, and some place names. 1861–1865?] Uncolored ms. Scale ca. 1:290,000. Map 40 × 22 cm. on sheet 59 × 45 cm.

G3880 186– .M31 Vault

Anonymous pen and ink manuscript map drawn on tracing linen.

508.6

Map of the seat of war in Virginia. 1865. Colored ms. Scale ca. 1:800,000. 28 × 42 cm.

G3881.S5 1865 .M3 Vault

At head of title: I.

Anonymous pen and ink manuscript map of southern Virginia and northern North Carolina extending from Richmond, Virginia south to Raleigh, North Carolina and showing state and county boundaries, roads, railroads, rivers, and towns. The "line of march" from Richmond and Petersburg to Appomattox Court House has been sketched in, along with the locations of the "first fight at Genito Bridge," "second [fight] at Amelia C.H.," "third [fight] at High Bridge," and "fourth fight & surrender at New Hope Church."

508.8

Michler, Nathaniel.

Map of the region between Gettysburg, Pa. and Appomattox Court House, Va. including all the battle-fields of the Army of Northern Virginia. Expressly prepared for this work from the United States government map based on surveys made by Bvt. Brig. Gen. N. Michler, Major of Eng'rs. and others, under the authority of the Hon. Secretary of War. Reproduced in Photographic Rooms, War College Division, General Staff. [Washington, 1915?] Photocopy (positive). Scale 1:500,000. 67 × 40 cm.

G3882 .N6S5 186– .M5

Reduced and redrawn version of the index map in the U.S. Army, Corps of Engineers' *Military Maps Illustrating the Operations of the Armies of the Potomac & James . . .* ([Washington] War Dept., Office of the Chief of Engineers, 1869). For a complete description of the atlas see entry no. 518.

Map indicates cities and towns, roads, railroads, drainage, relief by hachures, and defensive works in the vicinity of Richmond and Petersburg.

509

National Engraving Company, *Washington, D.C.*

Battlefields in vicinity of Washington, D.C., reached via Southern Railway. [1902] Colored. Scale not given. 20 × 19 cm. on sheet 23 × 65 cm.

Title when folded: G.A.R. Reunion, Washington, D.C. Battle field folder. Southern Railway.

Map of eastern Virginia showing the Southern Railway line in red, other railroads in blue, towns, and rivers. Battlefields are located by crossed swords.

Folder contains brief descriptions of "some Virginia battlefields along the line of the Southern Railway," "list of National Cemeteries near Washington, D.C." cost of railroad tickets "to battlefields and other historic points," and a list of 52 "scenes of the strife between the Blue and Gray" each of which is keyed by number to the map.

509.2

Nicholson, W. L.

Map of the State of Virginia, compiled from the best authorities, and printed at the Coast Survey Office. A. D. Bache, Supdt. 1865. Compiled by W. L. Nicholson. Lith. by Chas. G. Krebs. Colored. Scale ca. 1:887,040. 58 × 89 cm.

G3880 1865 .N51

General map of Virginia, West Virginia, Maryland, Delaware, and southern Pennsylvania showing cities and towns, roads, rivers, and relief by hachures. The map is overprinted in red to indicate railroads, the state name "West Virginia," and concentric circles centered on Richmond. Printed in blue are concentric circles centered on Washington, D.C. A table of "Distances by Railroads" appears below the map title.

509.4

Northrup, William P.

Map of Virginia and neighboring states showing the location of battles in the Civil War 1861–1865. The Matthews-Northrup Works, Buffalo, N.Y. Buffalo, ©1912. Colored. Scale ca. 1:366,000. 25 × 17 cm.

Map of eastern Virginia and parts of North Carolina, Maryland, West Virginia, and Pennsylvania, showing "battles in which New York regiments were engaged," "railroads at time of war," and "turnpikes and plank roads." Union states are colored yellow, and Confederate states are green.

Copyright no. "C1. F 22761."

510

Preston, Noble D.

From Dinwiddie C. H. to Appomattox C. H.—Route and operations of the 10th New York Cavalry. [1865] Uncolored ms. Scale ca. 1:980,000. 13 × 20 cm.

G3881 .S5 1865 .P7 Vault

Finished pen and ink manuscript map of central Virginia, showing the location and date of engagements, roads, railroads, towns, and rivers.

Printed version appears in Preston's *History of the Tenth Regiment of Cavalry, New York State Volunteers, August, 1861, to August, 1865* (New York, D. Appleton, 1892). opp. p. 252.

510.2

————————Map covering the field of operations of the Army of the Potomac. Prepared to accompany the History of the Third Pennsylvania Cavalry. Compiled from official maps of the War Department. Drawn by N. D. Preston, Phil'a. [1905] Uncolored. Scale ca. 1:650,000. 55 × 42 cm. *From* History of the Third Pennsylvania Cavalry . . . Philadelphia, Franklin Printing Company, 1905.

General map of eastern and central Virginia and part of Maryland showing roads, railroads, and place names. Troop movements are not depicted.

510.4

Rhodes, James F.

Grant's and Sheridan's campaigns, 1864 [and 1865] Colored. Scale ca. 1:880,000. 37 × 23 cm. *From his* History of the Civil War, 1861–1865. New York, The Macmillan Co., 1917. Facing p. 430.

Map of central Virginia and the Shenandoah Valley indicating the operations of Union forces in blue and "Gen. Lee's line of retreat" in red.

511

Russell, Robert E. L.

The retreat from Petersburg, April 2–9, 1865. A series of 32 pen and ink maps picturing the progress of Lee's retreat and Grant's pursuit from Petersburg to Appomattox

Courthouse . . . Drawn entirely from descriptions in the Official War Records and other sources by R. E. L. Russell. Baltimore, 1934. 1 p. 1., 32 maps. Photocopy (positive). 35 × 50 cm.

G1294 .P4S5 R8 1934

Bound set of maps hand-colored to show infantry and cavalry positions. Geography and Map Division also has an unbound negative photocopy.

Listed in C. E. Le Gear's *A List of Geographical Atlases in the Library of Congress* (Washington, Library of Congress, 1973), v. 7, no. 10665.

511.5

Seat of war in Virginia [1861–65] Uncolored. Scale ca. 1:2,600,000. 13 × 11 cm.

General map. Troop positions are not indicated.

512

Smith, Joshua.

Map of the main battlefields, routes, camps and head qrs., in the Gettysburg, Wilderness and Appomattox campaigns of the Civil War in U.S. Compiled and published by Joshua Smith, 1st Lieut., Co. K, 20th Pa.' Cav., 2nd Brig., 1st Div., Sheridan's command. Chicago, ©1899. Colored. Scale 1:506,880. 82 × 81 cm. *From his* Map and description of the main battlefields, routes, camps and headquarters in the Gettysburg, Wilderness and Appomattox campaigns of the Civil War in the United States. Chicago, 1900. 24 p. 23 cm.

Shows "places and dates of battles," "blue lines—Union routes," "red lines—Confederate routes," railroads, canals, towns, rivers, and relief by hachures.

"Losses in some of the battles," "Union Army campaign organizations," "Confed.' Army campaign organizations," and a number of engagements in the states of Pennsylvania, Maryland, Washington, D.C., West Virginia, and Virginia are indicated beneath the map title.

List of the "authorities used" is in the lower left corner.

512.2

Smith, Karl.

[Map of Virginia and parts of West Virginia, Maryland, and Pennsylvania showing events and operations with which General Robert E. Lee was concerned, 1861 to 1865. Charlotte, N.C.] Karl Smith, c1949. Colored. Scale not given. 41 × 56 cm.

Attractive map containing portrait of Robert E. Lee and 11 drawings illustrating events or places associated with his life. Also included are a "Genealogical chart of the family of Robert E. Lee," "A brief outline of the life of Robert E. Lee," and list of "Important events and operations of the Civil War with which General Robert E. Lee was chiefly concerned."

512.5

Tidwell, William A.

Confederate spy country, 1861–1865. Compiled and drawn by Brigadier General William A. Tidwell, Fairfax, Virginia, 1979. Uncolored. Scale ca. 1:118,000. 92 × 61 cm.

G3883 .K5S5 1979 .T5

Copyright no. VA 38–134, Nov. 13, 1979.

Accompanied by text: Confederate spy country. 1 leaf, 28 × 22 cm.

Map of King George County, Virginia, and parts of Caroline and Essex counties, Virginia, and Prince Georges, Charles, and St. Marys counties, Maryland, showing roads, trails, drainage, and place names. "This map was compiled by tracing rivers and streams from the U.S. Geological Survey map series at a scale of 1/24,000. The general location of roads, houses, and towns was taken from maps made during the Civil War or as near to that time as possible."

"This is the area in which several Confederate spy networks operated successfully throughout the Civil War."

512a

Turner, W. R.

Map showing roads used by General Lee in his retreat from Richmond and Petersburg and General Grant's advance on Appomattox. [April 2–9, 1865] Blackstone, Va., 1953. Blue line print. Scale ca. 1:126,720. 61 × 124 cm.

"DR. NO. TT–2–E."

Map shows troop movements, roads, route numbers, railroads, and rivers.

512a.5

U.S. *Army. Army of the Potomac. Engineer Department.*

Map showing the operations of the Army of the Potomac under command of Mag.[sic] Gen. George G. Meade, from March 29th to April 9th, 1865. Engineer Department, Headquarters, Army of the Potomac. [1865] Photocopy (positive). Scale ca. 1:160,000. 36 × 88 cm.

Endorsed (facsim.): Official. J. C. Duane, Major of Engineers, Bvt. Col. U.S.A., Chief Engineer, Army of the Potomac.

Map of the country between Petersburg and Appomattox Court House showing roads, railroads, cities and towns, and some houses and names of residents. Troop positions and movements are not depicted.

513

U.S. *Army. Corps of Engineers.*

Central Virginia showing Lieut. Gen'l. U. S. Grant's campaign and marches of the armies under his command in 1864–65. Engineer Bureau, War Dept. Prepared by order of the Secretary of War for the officers of the U.S. Army under the command of Lieut. Gen. U. S. Grant. [186–]Colored. Scale 1:350,000. 66 × 81 cm.

Map extends from Dinwiddie C. H. to about four miles north of the District of Columbia and from Lexington east to Heathsville. The routes of the II, V, VI, IX, X, XVIII, XIX, XXIV, and XXV corps, the regular cavalry, and Sheridan's cavalry are identified by colored lines. The badges of the corps are given in the legend. Fortifications and battlefields are marked in blue. The map also indicates roads, railroads, towns, drainage, and relief by hachures.

Another copy is in the Fillmore map coll. no. 160.

514

——————Another issue. 31 × 32 in.

Map extends from Martinsburg south to Dinwiddie C.H. and from Lexington east to Heathsville.

515

——————Another issue.

Same as the preceding issue but with the cavalry badge (crossed swords in an oval) added to the legend.

Another copy is in the Fillmore map coll. no. 160-A.

516

——————Another edition. Colored. Scale 1:350,000. 79 × 59 cm. *From* 39th Cong., 1st Sess. [1866]—Report of the Chief Engineer U.S.A. No. 11.

In lower right corner: Bowen & Co. lith., Philada.

Map extends from Martinsburg south to Dinwiddie C.H. and from Staunton east to Port Tobacco. In this edition, the map title and legend have been moved from the right hand side of the sheet to the upper left corner.

Another copy is in the Samuel P. Heintzelman papers, Manuscript Division, L.C., container no. 11 (in poor condition).

517

——————Military maps. Illustrating the operations of the armies of the Potomac and James against Richmond, May 4th 1864, to April 9th 1865. Including battlefields of the Wilderness, Totopotomoy, North Anna, Spottsylvania, Cold Harbor, the movements north of the James River, siege of Petersburg, battlefields of Five Forks, Sailor's Creek, Farmville & Appomattox Court House, as also the routes of march of the opposing armies. [1867] Photocopy (positive). Title-page, 18 maps on 17 sheets (part fold.) 61 × 42 cm. (Thompson coll.)

G1291 .S5U5 1867 Vault

Unbound series of detailed maps, somewhat similar to those in the atlas published in 1869 entitled *Military Maps Illustrating the Operations of the Armies of the Potomac & James* . . . (see entry no. 518). Some of the sheets have the map title, border, and the names of the responsible surveyors and draftsmen added in black ink. Fortifications are sometimes colored red and blue.

518

————Military maps illustrating the operations of the armies of the Potomac & James, May 4th, 1864 to April 9th 1865, including battlefields of the Wilderness, Spottsylvania, Northanna [sic], Totopotomoy, Cold Harbor, the siege of Petersburg and Richmond, battle-fields of Five Forks, Jetersville & Sailor's Creek, Highbridge, Farmville & Appomattox Court-house. [Washington] War Dept., Office of the Chief of Engineers, 1869. 1 p. 1., 16 maps (part fold., part col.) 61 × 47 cm.

G1201 .S5U515 1869 folio

"These surveys and maps were executed under the direction of Bvt. Brig. Genl. N. Michler, Major of Engineers, and Bvt. Lieut. Col. P. S. Michie, Capt. of Engrs."

Detailed series of maps indicating fortifications, roads, railroads, houses, names of residents, fences, drainage, vegetation, and relief by hachures.

For the table of contents see P. L. Phillips's *A List of Geographical Atlases in the Library of Congress* (Washington, Government Printing Office, 1914) v. 3, no. 3688.

519

————Another copy.

G1201 .S5U515 1869b folio

Bound with *Map of the Tennessee River for the Use of the Mississippi Squadron, under Command of Acting Rear Admiral S. P. Lee, U.S.N., from Reconnaissance by a Party of the United States Coast Survey. 1864–'65.* 1 p. 1., 17 maps. 61 × 49 cm. (See also entry no. 95.)

Printed label on front cover reads as follows: Military maps showing the operations of the armies of the Potomac & James. Map of the Tennessee River for the use of the Mississippi Squadron.

Title page of Tennessee River map signed in ms. "J. N. Macomb, Col., Corps of Engrs. 1867."

520

————Another issue. 1869 [i.e., 1872]

G1201 .S5U515 1872 Folio

Includes map of "South Mountain showing the positions of the forces of the United States and of the enemy . . . Sept. 14th 1862. Prepared in the Bureau of Topographical Engineers. 1872."

Printed label on front cover reads as follows: Military maps—Armies Potomac & James.

520.5

Van Hook, J. C., *and* C. G. Van Hook.

Battle-field map showing field of operations of the Armies of the Potomac and James. Compiled from latest gov-

ernment surveys and published by J. C. & C. G. Van Hook. A. B. Graham, photo-lith., Washington, D.C. Washington, 1892. Colored. Scale ca. 1:508,500. 74 × 60 cm.

Title when folded: 26th annual encampment, G.A.R., Washington, D.C., September 20th, 1892. Battlefield map, Maryland & Virginia. Location of battle fields of 1861 to 1865, furnished by Gilbert Thompson, Topographical Engineer, Headquarters, Army of the Potomac.

Map of Virginia and Maryland showing engagements, railroads, rivers and streams, place names, and relief by hachures. "Dates and locations of principal engagements as shown on this map" are listed in the lower left corner.

Another copy is in the Jeremiah T. Lockwood papers, Manuscript Division, L.C.

520a

Virginia. *Department of Highways.*

Commonwealth of Virginia: Official Civil War centennial map. [Richmond, Virginia, 1961] Colored. Scale not given. 50 × 75 cm. on sheet 65 × 96 cm.

Printed on verso of map entitled *Commonwealth of Virginia: State Highway System and Connections* (Richmond, Virginia, Department of Highways, ©1961).

"Pictured in red are principal points of interest connected with the Civil War. Crossed flags indicate major battles of the more than 1,000 engagements fought in Virginia." The map includes roads, towns, rivers, and relief by shading. Views of 10 Civil War sites appear in the insets.

520a.5

von Reizenstein, B.

Central [Virginia] showing Maj. Gen'l P. H. Sherida[n's campaigns] and marches of the cavalry under his [command] in 1864–65, drawn and lithographed under direction of Brvt. Maj. G. L. Gillespie, U.S.A. Chief Eng. Mil. Div. of the Gulf, Oct. 1865. Drawn for stone by B. von Reizenstein. Printed by A. Forger. Colored. Scale 1:350,000. 95 × 68 cm.

At head of title: Engineers Office Mi[lit. Div. of the Gulf] map n[o. 6]

Imperfect. Part of the title and the extreme eastern portion of the map are wanting.

Map is annotated, in different colors, to show seven cavalry raids by General Sheridan.

Map extends from Martinsburg south to Danville, and Lexington east to Washington, D.C., and indicates towns, railroads, drainage, bridges, and battlefields.

Pasted in the upper left hand corner of the map is a printed description of the "Routes of the Raids Made by the Cavalry under Major General P. H. Sheridan, U.S.A."

Another copy is described as item 2.217 in *A Guide to Civil War Maps in the National Archives* (Washington, 1986).

520a.6

Wood, Walter B. *and* **J. E. Edmonds.**

Southern Virginia. [London] Methuen & Co. [1905]
Uncolored. Scale ca. 1:1,000,000. 16 × 33 cm.

"Map VII."

Prepared to accompany W. B. Wood and J. E. Edmonds's *A History of the Civil War in the United States, 1861–5* (London, Methuen & Co. [1905]).

Map indicates battle sites.

Battlefields and Other Locations

ALBEMARLE COUNTY

520a.8

Dwight, C. S.

Map of Albemarle County from surveys and reconnaissances made under the direction of Albert H. Campbell Capt. P. Eng. & Chief of Topographical Dept. D.N.V. by Lieutt. C. S. Dwight. [1864] Scale 1:80,000. Col. ms. 80 × 68 cm.

G3883 .A3G46 1864 .C3 Vault

At head of title: Chief Engrs. Office, Maj. Genl. G. [i.e., J.] F. Gilmer Chief Engr.

Endorsed in ms.: Approved June 15, 1864 Albert H. Campbell Capt. P. Engrs in chge. Top. Dep. D.N. Va.

Detailed manuscript map on tracing linen showing roads, railroads, villages, houses, names of residents, woodland, and relief by hachures.

ALEXANDRIA CITY AND COUNTY

520a.9

Bache, C. M.

Topography of the north side of Hunting Creek near Alexandria, Va. Surveyed for the Engineer Dept. May 1863 by C. M. Bache, Sub-Asst. Washington, D.C., Coast Survey Office, May 26, 1863. Colored ms. Scale 1:1000. 95 × 126 cm.

G3884 .A3 1863 .B3 Vault

"211, L. Sheet 6."

"Copied from the Archives of the U.S. Coast Survey for Gen. J. G. Barnard. [Signed] J. E. Hilgard, Asst. Coast Survey in ch. of office."

At head of title: U. S. Coast Survey, A. D. Bache, Supdt.

Pen and ink manuscript map on tracing linen showing contour lines at intervals of 2 feet, shoreline configuration by hachures, tree stumps and cedar trees, and the location of the smallpox hospital.

"Transferred from Office of Chf. Engr., Defenses of Washington to Engr. Dept., Jan'y 1866."

Stamped on verso: By Transfer, Chief Engineers Office, War Department.

521

Church, B. S.

Reconnaissance in advance of Camp Mansfield by 12th Regiment Engr. Capt. B. S. Church. [186–] Uncolored ms. Scale not given. 61 × 63 cm.

G3883 .A8S5 186– .C5 Vault

At head of title: 211, L. Sheet 12.

In lower right corner: Transferred from Office of Chf. Engr., Defenses of Washington, to Engr. Dept.—1866.

Pen and ink manuscript map of Alexandria County, showing military camps, roads, railroad, drainage, and relief by hachures.

522

Corbett, V. P.

Sketch of the seat of war in Alexandria & Fairfax Cos., by V. P. Corbett. Washington City, May 31st 1861. Uncolored. Scale not given. 28 × 38 cm.

Gives the location and names of Union regiments, entrenchments, houses, names of residents, railroads, roads, and drainage. "Arlington Heights," Alexandria Heights" and "Shooter's Hill" are indicated by hachures.

522.3

Magnus, Charles.

Birds eye view of Alexandria, Va. New York & Washington, D.C., Chas. Magnus, ©1863. Colored view. 39 × 59 cm.

Pen and ink manuscript map of Albemarle County, Virginia, drawn on tracing linen in 1864 by Confederate topographical engineer Lt. C. S. Dwight. It is representative of the series of maps of counties in eastern and central Virginia prepared under the direction of Maj. Gen. Jeremy F. Gilmer, Chief of Engineers and Maj. Albert H. Campbell, head of the Topographical Department, Department of Northern Virginia. As copies of the county maps were requested by army commanders, sunprints were made and forwarded to the field for their use. (See entry no. 520a.8.)

G3884 .A3A3 1863 .M32

"Entered according to act of Congress A.D. 1863 by Chas. Magnus."

Panoramic map depicting the city during its occupation by Federal forces. Indicated are streets, public buildings, houses, the railroad depot, and important military sites. The legend in the bottom margin identifies 12 points of interest.

522.4

—————Reduced facsimile. Alexandria, Alexandria Drafting Company [1974] Colored. 34 × 46 cm.

G3884 .A3A3 1863 .M32 1974

"Original map courtesy Geography and Map Division, Library of Congress."

Charles Magnus's name has been dropped from this facsimile edition.

522.5

—————Reduced facsimile. Alexandria, The Picture Place, 1974. Colored. 24 × 33 cm.

G3884 .A3A3 1863 .M31 1974

"Reproduced in 1974 from an original lithograph courtesy of the Library of Congress, Washington, D.C."

522.6

—————Reduced facsimile. Ithaca, N.Y., Historic Urban Plans, 1974. Colored. 33 × 48 cm.

G3884 .A3A3 1863 .M3 1974

"Reproduced in 1974 by Historic Urban Plans, Ithaca, New York from a lithograph in the Mariners Musuem, Newport News, Virginia. This is number 23 of an edition limited to 500 copies."

523

U.S. *Army. Corps of Engineers.*

[Detailed map of part of Virginia from Alexandria to the Potomac River above Washington, D.C. 186–] Uncolored ms. Scale not given. 92 × 170 cm.

G3883 .A8 186– .U5 Vault

"211, L. Sheet 2"

Pen and ink manuscript map drawn on tracing cloth, showing part of the defenses of Washington, roads, railroads, towns, vegetation, contour lines, houses, fences, names of residents, and drainage.

523.2

—————Plan e. [Map showing two blockhouses between "Turn Pike Road" and "Bridge," Alexandria, Virginia. 186–] Uncolored ms. Scale not given. 48 × 58 cm.

G3884 .A3S5 186– .U5 Vault

"211, L. Sheet 13."

Pen and ink and pencil map and cross section of part of the defenses of Washington situated between Little River

Turnpike (Duke Street) and the Telegraph Road bridge crossing Cameron Run.

"Transferred from Office of Chf. Engr., Defenses of Washington, to Engr. Dept.—1866."

Stamped on verso: By Transfer, Chief Engineers Office, War Department.

523.5

U.S. *Coast Survey.*

Jones Point, Potomac River near Alexandria, Virginia, surveyed for the Engineer Department, April 1863. By A. M. Harrison, Assistant. Washington, Coast Survey Office, April 29th 1863. Colored ms. Scale 1:1000. 114 × 94 cm.

G3884 .A3 1863 .U5 Vault

"211, L. Sheet 7."

"Copied from the Archives of the U.S. Coast Survey for the Engineer Department. [Signed] J. E. Hilgard, Asst., U. S. Coast Survey in charge of office."

At head of title: U.S. Coast Survey, A. D. Bache, Supdt.

Detailed map on tracing linen showing trees and tree stumps, marsh land and "quagmire impassable," lighthouse and other buildings, contour lines at intervals of two feet, and "the low water line April 21st [1863] wind fresh, North."

Stamped on verso: By Transfer, Chief Engineers Office, War Department.

523.6

—————Plan of Alexandria. [Washington, U.S. Coast Survey, 1862] Uncolored. Scale 1:5400. 41 × 55 cm.

G3884 .A3 1862 .U5

Annotated in margin: Printed at the Coast Survey Office, October 25, 1862. Autographic transfer from an old map of Alexandria furnished by the U.S. Sanitary Commission.

"U.S.C. and G. Survey, Library and Archives, acc. no. 1350."

"U.S.C. and G. Survey, Libra[ry] and Archiv[es] no. 354, shelf 509, case 4."

Label in lower right corner: 863C 1862.

Street plan depicting some public and commercial buildings. No military sites are indicated.

APPOMATTOX

524

Henderson and Company

Map of Appomattox Court House and vicinity. Showing the relative positions of the Confederate and Federal armies at the time of General R. E. Lee's surrender, April 9th

1865. Lith. by A. Hoen & Co., Baltimore. ©1866. Colored. Scale 1:31,680. 23 × 29 cm. on sheet 41 × 50 cm.

Shows positions of Union and Confederate troops by the colors blue and red respectively, houses, names of residents, roads, relief by hachures, drainage, and vegetation. Bordering the map, there are "historical notes" concerning the surrender, "Gen. Lee's farewell to his army," and views of "Lee's Head-Quarters," "McLane's [i.e., McLean's] House," "Appomattox Court House," "place where the arms were stacked," and "Grant's Head-Quarters."

525

Memoranda. April 9, 1865. 10 o'clock A.M. Clover Hill (Appomattox Court House), Virginia. Uncolored ms. Scale not given. 25 × 20 cm.

G3884 .A6S5 1865 .M4 Vault

Pen and ink sketch map indicating "house at which Gen'l. Lee received Gen'l. Sheridan afterwards Grant,—when agreement was signed," "Appomatox C.H.," "Custar's [sic] (3rd) Cav. Div.," "reserve cavalry brigade in advance on extreme right," "Lee's army massed," and "wagon's retiring."

This map was received in the Library in an envelope marked in ink, "Map of Lee's surrender. Found in one of the back closets of one of the old Scrimshaw Pavement Co's desks, 16 Court St. Fged."

525.2

Michler, Nathaniel.

Appomattox Court House. [1865] From surveys under the direction of Bvt. Brig. Gen. N. Michler, Maj. of Engineers, by command of Bvt. Maj. Genl. A. A. Humphreys, Brig. Genl. & Chief of Engineers. Surveyed & drawn by Maj: J. E. Weyss, assisted by F. Theilkuhl, J. Strasser & G. Thompson. Photolith. by the N. Y. Lithographing, Engraving & Printing Co., Julius Bien, Supt. 1867. Uncolored. Scale 1:21,120. 78 × 57 cm.

Stamped in red beside title: U.S. Geological Survey Library 1894, [no.] 4637.

Detailed map of the environs of Appomattox Court House showing roads, railroads, houses and names of residents, drainage, and woodland. Troop positions are not depicted.

A second copy of this map in the Geography and Map Division has been annotated by an unknown hand to indicate a few positions, including "Grant Hd Qrs."

525.3

——————Another issue.

G3884 .A6 1867 .W4

In this issue, the map is printed on a yellow background with the North Branch of the Appomatox River colored blue.

ARLINGTON COUNTY

525a

Sims, Benjamin L., 3d.

Civil War fortifications in Arlington County [Virginia]. Drafted by B. L. Sims, III. [Arlington, Va., 1960] Blue line print. Scale ca. 1:14,400. 93 × 62 cm.

Shows boundary stones, streams, Civil War fortifications, and present-day roads and bridges.

525b

——————Civil War fortifications, Indian villages and quarry sites in Arlington County [Virginia]. Drafted by B. Sims. [Arlington, Virginia, 1960] Blue line print. Scale ca. 1:14,400. 93 × 62 cm.

Similar to the preceding map but including railroads, Indian quarries and villages, and relief by hachures.

BALL'S BLUFF

525b.1

Holien, Kim Bernard.

Map of Ball's Bluff—21 Oct. 1861. Prepared by Kim Bernard Holien for camp tour of 11 Oct. 1980. [Alexandria, Virginia] ©1980. 12 maps. Photocopy (some colored). 28 × 22 cm.

G1292 .B3S5 .H6 1980

Atlas submitted for copyright September 12, 1984, class no. VA 170–440.

Roughly drawn sketch maps of the battle showing troop positions and movements.

BERMUDA HUNDRED

525b.2

Michler, Nathaniel, *and* Peter S. Michie.

Bermuda Hundred. [1864–1865] From surveys under the direction of Bvt. Brig. Gen. N. Michler, Maj. of Engineers and Bvt. Lieut. Col. P. S. Michie, Capt. of Engineers, by command of Bvt. Maj. Genl. A. A. Humphreys, Brig. Genl. & Chief of Engineers. Surveyed & drawn by Maj: J. E. Weyss, assisted by F. Theilkuhl, J. Strasser & G. Thompson. Photolith. by the N. Y. Lithographing, Engraving & Printing Co., Julius Bien, Supt. 1867. Colored. Scale 1:42,240. 49 × 73 cm.

In this issue, the map is printed on a yellow background with the James and Appomattox rivers colored blue.

Map indicates roads, railroads, towns, drainage, vegetation, relief by hachures, houses, and names of residents. Union and Confederate entrenchments are colored blue and red respectively.

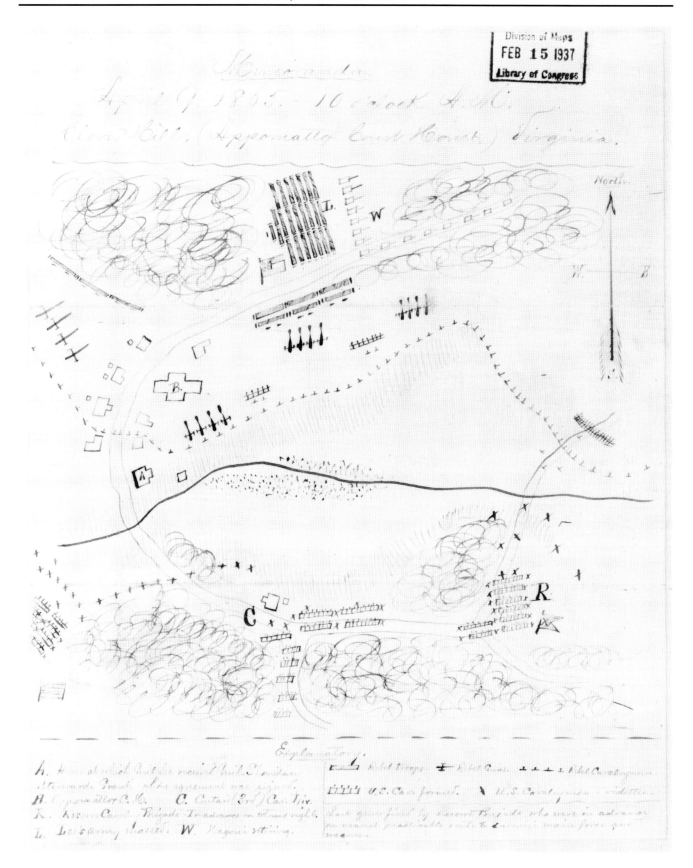

525b.3

——————Another issue.
Background and water are not colored.

525b.4

——————Another issue.
Lacks names of the surveyors and lithographer.

CEDAR CREEK

526

Russell, Robert E. L.

Battlefield of Cedar Creek, Va., Oct. 19, 1864. Sketch map showing Early's flank move at Cedar Creek. Baltimore, 1932. Photocopy (positive). Scale not given. 19 × 11 cm.

Hand-colored. Geography and Map Division also has a negative photocopy.

CEDAR MOUNTAIN

526.5

Pope, John.

Battlefield of Cedar Mountain, August 9th, 1862. Bowen & Co., lith., Uncolored. Scale 1:31,680. 24 × 16 cm. *From* U.S. Congress. Joint Committee on the Conduct of the War. Supplemental report of the Joint Committee on the conduct of the War, in two volumes. Supplemental to Senate report no. 142, 38th Congress, 2d session (Washington, Government Printing Office, 1866). v. 2, fol. p. 190.

Accompanies "Report of Major General John Pope to the hon. Committee on the Conduct of the War." 217 p.

"No. 2" is in the upper right margin.

Map indicates Union and Confederate positions, roads, houses and names of residents, drainage, railroad, and relief by hachures.

Another copy is in the Ezra A. Carman papers, Manuscript Division, L.C., container no. 14.

CHANCELLORSVILLE

527

[Battle of Chancellorsville] Colored. Scale ca. 1:190,000. 3 maps, each 23 × 46 cm.

Map 1: Dispositions of the Union and Confederate armies prior to the battle of Chancellorsville.

Map 2: Dispositions of Union and Confederate forces about 11:30 P.M., 30 April, 1863.

Anonymous pen-and-ink sketch map of Appomattox Court House, Virginia, dated April 9, 1865, indicating the "house at which Gen'l. Lee received Gen'l. Sheridan afterwards Grant,—when agreement was signed." (See entry no. 525.)

Map 3: Dispositions of Union and Confederate forces at 4:00 P.M., 2nd May, 1863.

Each map indicates troop positions, roads, railroads, towns, drainage, fords, and a few houses and names of inhabitants.

527.5

Haupt, Herman.

[Pen and ink sketch of Chancellorsville and vicinity, by Herman Haupt. May 1, 1863] Col. ms. on tracing linen. Scale 1:63,360. 28 × 45 cm.

In the Abraham Lincoln papers, Manuscript Division, L.C., vol. 109, no. 23244.

Map indicates roads, rivers, fords, towns, houses, and names of residents. Dashed red lines show approximate positions of Reynolds, Meade, Sickles, Couch, and Sedgwick.

"Not much—Haupt's map" written in pencil in an unknown hand on an accompanying envelope (Lincoln papers, vol. 109, no. 23245).

527.7

Hotchkiss, Jedediah.

Sketch of the battles of Chancellorsville, Salem Church and Fredericksburg, May 2, 3 and 4, 1863. Prepared by order of General R. E. Lee, by Jed. Hotchkiss, Topogl. Engr. 2d Corps, A.N.V. [Philadelphia, Eastern National Park and Monument Association, 1984?] Colored. Scale ca. 1:92,000. 38 × 62 cm.

G3884 .C36S5 1891 .H6 1984

Reproduced from the U.S. War Department's *Atlas to Accompany the Official Records of the Union and Confederate Armies* (Washington, Government Printing Office, 1891–95), plate XLI, map 1.

Confederate positions are colored red and Union positions are purple.

Inset: Map of the action at Dranesville, Va. December 20th, 1861 . . . Drawn by H. H. Strickler, Co. A, 9th Pa. Reserves . . . 1875. Scale not given. 14 × 22 cm. [Map no.] 2.

528

Map of the battlefield of Chancellorsville, Va., 1863. Colored ms. Scale 1:63,360. 31 × 56 cm.

G3884 .C36S5 1863 .M3 Vault

Shows troop positions and movements, roads, railroad, drainage, fords, and vegetation.

528.2

Michler, Nathaniel.

Chancellorville [sic] [May 1–3, 1863] Prepared by Bvt. Brig. Genl. N. Michler, Major of Engineers, from surveys under his direction, by order of Brig. Genl. & Bvt. Maj.

Genl. A. A. Humphreys, Chief of Engineers, and under the authority of the hon. Secretary of War. Surveyed & drawn by Maj: J. E. Weyss, assisted by F. Theilkuhl, J. Strasser & G. Thompson. Lettering by J. de la Camp. Photolith. by the N.Y. Lithographing, Engraving & Printing Co., Julius Bien, Supt. 1867. Colored. Scale 1:21,120. 57 × 62 cm.

In this issue, the map is printed on a yellow background with the Rappahannock and Rapidan rivers colored green.

Detailed map showing entrenchments, houses, fences, names of residents, roads, "unfinished railroad," vegetation, drainage, fords, and relief by hachures.

528.3

——————Another issue. Uncolored.

529

Russell, Robert E. L.

Fifteen pen and ink maps of the battle of Chancellorsville. Drawn from descriptive readings and map fragments to form an easily understandable picture of the battle. By Robert E. Lee Russell. Baltimore, 1931. 1 p. l., 15 maps. Photocopy (positive). 47 × 62 cm.

G1294 .C5S5 R8 1931 folio

Bound set of maps with Confederate troop positions colored red by hand.

Duplicate of Map 1 is inserted.

Geography and Map Division also has an unbound negative photocopy of each sheet.

Listed in C. E. Le Gear's *A List of Geographical Atlases in the Library of Congress* (Washington, Library of Congress, 1973), v. 7, no. 10661.

530

U.S. *Geological Survey.*

Topographic maps of Chancellorsville and Salem Church battlefields, Spotsylvania County, Virginia. Surveyed in cooperation with the Fredericksburg and Spotsylvania County Battlefields Commission. Topography by Shirley Waggener, J. G. Groninger and G. A. Mock. Control by U.S. Geological Survey. Surveyed in 1932. Colored. Scale 1:24,000. 33 × 54 cm.

"Advance sheet. Subject to correction."

Two maps on one sheet. Map of Chancellorsville measures 21 × 32 cm., and that of Salem Church, 13 × 17 cm. Each indicates "trenches and gun positions," roads, houses, monuments, drainage, and relief by contour lines and spot elevations. "Contour interval 10 feet."

CHARLES CITY COUNTY

530.5

U.S. *Army. Corps of Topographical Engineers.*

Sketch of country between Haxall's Landing and Charles City Court House. Reconnoissances [sic] under the direction of Brig. Genl. A. A. Humphreys, Comdg. Topl. Engr's., by 1st. Lieut. N. Bowen, Topl. Engr's., 2d. Lieut. C. McClellan, 32d. N.Y. Vols., Mr. F. W. Dorr, Assist., U.S.C.S., Mr. Joseph McMakin, Drftsmn., Mr. H. H. Humphreys, [and] Mr. Walter Taylor. [186–] Photocopy (positive). Scale 1:30,000. 2 sheets, each 40 × 54 cm.

Incomplete; Geography and Map Division has 2 of 4 sheets.

Sketch map showing roads and trails, houses and names of residents, rivers and streams, relief by hachures, and woodland and swamps.

CHICKAHOMINY RIVER

530.6

Humphreys, Andrew A.

The Chickahominy from Mechanicsville to Bottoms Bridge, from reconnaissance and survey made by order of Maj. Gen. George B. McClellan U.S.A. commanding the Army of the Potomac in May and June 1862. A. A. Humphreys, Brig. Gen. and Chief of Top. Engrs. Photographed June 3rd 1862. Photocopy (positive). Scale ca. 1:31,000. 41 × 47 cm.

G3883 .H4 1862 .H9

Hand-colored photocopy indicating the river in blue, woodland in green, and roads in red.

"Surveys by Capt. P. C. F. West, S. of Gen. Smith, Mr. F. W. Dorr, Asst. C. Sur., [and] Mr. J. W. Donn, Asst C. Sur. Reconnoissances [sic] by Lt. C. B. Comstock, Corps Engrs., Lt. N. Bowen, Corps Top. Engrs., [and] Mr. F. A. Churchill, C.E."

COLD HARBOR

531

Michler, Nathaniel, *and* Peter S. Michie.

Cold Harbor. [June 1–3, 1864] From surveys under the direction of B'v't. Brig.-Gen. N. Michler, Maj. of Engineers, and B'v't. Lieut.-Col. P. S. Michie, Capt. of Engineers. 1867. Uncolored. Scale ca. 1:55,000. 19 × 14 cm. *From* Century illustrated monthly magazine, v. 34, June 1887. p. 296.

"Union works are marked . . . U" and "Confederate works are marked . . . C."

Shows roads, houses, names of residents, drainage, vegetation, and relief by hachures.

531.2

——————Cold Harbor. [June 1–3, 1864] From surveys under the direction of Bvt. Brig. Gen. N. Michler, Maj. of Engineers, and Bvt. Lieut. Col. P. S. Michie, Capt. of Engineers, by command of Bvt. Maj. Genl. A. A. Humphreys, Brig. Genl. & Chief of Engineers. Surveyed & drawn by Maj: J. E. Weyss, assisted by F. Theilkuhl, J. Strasser & G. Thompson. Photolith. by the N. Y. Lithographing, Engraving & Printing Co., Julius Bien, Supt. 1867. Colored. Scale 1:21,120. 51 × 83 cm.

In this issue, the map is printed on a yellow background with the Chickahominy River colored green.

Shows roads, "Virginia Central R. R.," houses, fences, names of inhabitants, vegetation, drainage, and relief by hachures. Entrenchments are colored red and blue.

531.3

————Another issue.
Background and water are not colored.

531.5

Richmond. *Civil War Centennial Committee.*

Troop movements at the battle of Cold Harbor, 1984. [Richmond, 1964] 16 1. of maps. 32 × 47 cm. (*Its* Official publication 21)

G1292 .C6S5 R5 1964 fol.
Cover title.
Scale of each map, ca. 1:36,000.
"These maps show troop movements from 31 May to 13 June, when Grant successfully withdrew his whole army from the front lines and crossed the James River."

"The Richmond Civil War Centennial Committee has based these contemporary interpretive maps on an original set prepared by the National Park Service . . ."

The maps in the atlas were delineated by the staff of the Division of Preliminary Engineering, Department of Public Works, City of Richmond.

CULPEPER COUNTY

531.7

U.S. *Army. Army of the Potomac.*

[Map of Culpeper County and parts of the counties of Warren, Rappahannock, Madison, Orange, and Fauquier] Office of Surveys and Maps for the Army of the Potomac. Sept. 21st 1863. Uncolored. Scale not given. 151 × 84 cm.

G3883 .C8 1863 .U5
Reconnaissance map showing villages and towns, houses and names of residents, relief, and woodland principally alongside roads and rail lines.

532

U.S. *Army. Corps of Engineers.*

[Culpeper County, with parts of Madison, Rappahannock, and Fauquier counties, Virginia] Engr. by J. Schedler,

N. York. [186–] Uncolored. Scale 1:63,360. 71 × 100 cm.
G3883 .C8 186– .U5 Vault
Printed map without title or border, showing fortifications, roads, railroads, towns, drainage, fords, vegetation, and relief by form lines.

533

————Another issue.
G3883 .C8 186– .U51 Vault
Lacks the name of the engraver and the scale.

DINWIDDIE COUNTY

533.5

U.S. *Army. Army of the Potomac.*

[Map of Dinwiddie and parts of Prince George and Sussex counties, Virginia] Engineer Dept., Hd. Qrs., Army of the Potomac. Sept. 21st 1864. Photocopy (negative). Scale 1:63,360. 80 × 136 cm.

G3883 .D6 1864 .U5
Endorsed (facsim.): Official: N. Michler, Major of Engineers, U. S. A.

Badly faded photocopy of the region south of Petersburg. The map indicates roads, railroads, towns and villages, drainage, houses, and names of residents.

DRAINSVILLE

534

Strickler, H. H.

Map of the action at Drainsville, Va., December 20th 1861. U.S. forces commanded by Brig. Gen. E. O. C. Ord. Drawn by H. H. Strickler, Co. A, 9th Pa. Reserve. Published by authority of the Hon. the Secretary of War, office of the Chief of Engineers, U.S. Army, 1875. Colored. Scale not given. 40 × 26 cm.

Shows troop positions and unit numbers, houses, roads, vegetation, and drainage.

DREWRYS BLUFF

535

Griffin, Tristram.

Battle-field of Drewry's Bluffs, Va., showing position of troops at 4.45 a.m. and 6.30 a.m., May 16–1864. Boston, Tristram Griffin [1932]. Blue print. Scale not given. 40 × 75 cm.

Indicates entrenchments, troop positions and movements, unit numbers and names of commanders, roads, "Richmond & Petersburg R.R.," drainage, houses, and names of residents.

536

U.S. *Army. Tenth Corps. Engineer Office.*

Sketch no. 4 of roads between H.-Q. 10 Army Corps, and Swift Creek on the south, with enemy's 2nd line of intrenchements [sic] around Drury's [sic] Bluff on the north. [May 1864] Colored ms. Scale 1:40,000. 37 × 51 cm.

G3883 .C5S5 186– .U5 Vault

At head of title: Engineer Office, 10th Army Corps.

Pen and ink manuscript map of the area north of Petersburg, Virginia, in eastern Chesterfield County, showing fortifications, batteries, headquarters, roads, railroads, vegetation, drainage, relief by hachures, and houses and names of residents.

FAIR OAKS

536.1

Battle field of Fair Oaks, Va. May 31st 1862. Blue line print. Scale not given. 31 × 31 cm.

In the Charles W. Reed papers, Manuscript Division, L.C., container no. 5 (oversize cabinet 5, drawer 5).

Map indicates Union and Confederate positions during battle.

Map on verso: Region of the Upper Chickahominy, Virginia. Scale not given. 27 × 42 cm. (Map shows troop positions at Fair Oaks and vicinity).

FAIRFAX COUNTY

536.2

[Frost?] Edward

Topographical sketch of ground 1½ miles south west from Alexandria. Nov. 28, 1862, Edward [Frost?] Engineer. Colored ms. Scale ca. 1:2360. 50 × 63 cm.

G3883 .F2 1862 .F7 Vault

"211, L. Sheet 8."

Pen and ink manuscript drawn on tracing linen showing relief by contour lines and drainage along an unidentified section of the "Accotink Road." North is to the right of the map.

"Transferred from Office of Chf. Engr., Defenses of Washington, to Engr. Dept. Jany 1866."

Stamped on verso: By Transfer: Chief Engineers Office, War Department.

536.3

[Map of part of Fairfax and Prince William Counties, Virginia. 186–?] Colored ms. Scale 1:63,360. 48 × 60 cm.

G3882 .N6 186– .F5 Vault

From the Jubal Early Collection in the Manuscript Division, Library of Congress.

Manuscript map drawn on tracing linen showing roads, railroad, drainage, towns, and mills, Map extends from Fairfax Station to the north to Dumfries on the south and the Potomac River on the east to Manassas Station on the west. The landscape near Manassas Station is labeled "generally rough & broken country with pine, ivy & oak." Troop positions and other military information are not depicted.

536.4

Mead, F. F.

Map of part of Fairfax County, Virginia, south of the city of Alexandria and the Orange and Alexandria Railroad] F. F. Mead, Lt. Co. I, 16th N.Y.V. Del., Aug. 30th 1861. Colored ms. Scale 1:28,160. 95 × 92 cm.

G3883 .F2 1861 .M4 Vault

Manuscript map on tracing cloth, showing roads in red, rivers in blue, and railroads, villages, churches, houses, and names of residents in black. Beside the names of some of the residents appears an "S" or "U." The map does not define these abbreviations but it is possible that they signify the sympathies of the occupant (i.e., Unionist or Secessionist).

Oriented with north at the bottom of the sheet.

536.5

Sketch of eastern portion of Fairfax County, Va. June 1861. Colored ms. Scale ca. 1:63,360. 76 × 61 cm.

G3883 .F2 1861 .E3 Vault

From the Jubal Early Collection in the Manuscript Division, L.C.

Pen and ink manuscript map on tracing linen showing roads and railroads in red, place names in black, and the Potomac River in blue.

536.6

Young, J. J.

Military reconnaissance of Virginia. Made under the orders of Brigr. Genl Irvin McDowell U.S.A. by Capt. A. W. Whipple, Chief Topl. Engrs. of Dept. [and] H. S. Putnam, Topl. Engrs. Drawn by [J. J. Young, Civil Engineer. 186–?] Photocopy (positive). Scale 1:63,360. 109 × 86 cm.

G3883 .F2 186– .U5 Vault

At head of title: Head Qrs. Dept. N. E. Virginia. Map no. 1.

"211, L. Sheet 19."

"Transferred from Office of Chf. Engr., Defenses of Washington to Engr. Dep't. Jany 1866."

Stamped on verso: By transfer, Chief Engineers Office, War Department.

Map of Fairfax County and parts of Loudoun and Prince William counties, Virginia, showing towns and villages, rivers, and fortifications in the environs of Washington. Photocopy has been annotated to depict roads in red and railroads in blue, and a few additional place names in black. The photocopy is very faded.

FARMVILLE

536.7

Michler, Nathaniel.

High Bridge and Farmville. [1865] From surveys under the direction of Bvt. Brig. Gen. N. Michler, Maj. of Engineers, by command of Bvt. Maj. Genl. A. A. Humphreys, Brig. Genl. & Chief of Engineers. Surveyed & drawn by Maj: J. E. Weyss, assisted by F. Theilkuhl, J. Strasser & G. Thompson. Photolith. by the N. Y. Lithographing, Engraving & Printing Co., Julius Bien, Supt. 1867. Colored. Scale 1:21,120. 55 × 77 cm.

In this issue, the map is printed on a yellow background with the Appomattox River colored green.

Shows entrenchments, roads, "South Side R. R.," street plan of Farmville, houses, fences, names of residents in rural areas, drainage, vegetation, towns, and relief by hachures. Troop positions are not depicted.

536.8

—————Another issue. Uncolored.

FISHERS HILL

537

Gillespie, G. L.

Battle fields of Fisher's Hill [22 Sept. 1864] and Cedar Creek, Virginia [19 Oct. 1864]. Prepared by Bvt. Lt. Col. G. L. Gillespie, Major of Engineers, U.S.A., from surveys made under his directions, by order of Lt. Gen. P. H. Sheridan, and under the authority of the Hon. Secretary of War, and, of the Chief of Engineers, U.S.A. George B. Strauch and E. Siegesmund, assistants. 1873. Uncolored. Scale 1:12,000. 2 sheets, each 121 × 69 cm. Overall size 121 × 138 cm.

Detailed map indicating earth and wood entrenchments, troop positions and movements, names of commanders and some unit numbers, roads, "Manassas Gap Railroad," houses, names of inhabitants, fences, vegetation, drainage, fords, street pattern of Middletown and Strasburg, and relief by contour lines, hachures, and spot elevations. Union and Confederate troop positions are hand-colored blue and red respectively.

538

—————Another issue. J. Bien, N.Y., photo lith.

539

Russell, Robert E. L.

Battle of Fisher's Hill, Va., Sept. 23 [i.e., 22] 1864. Sketch map. Baltimore, 1932. Photocopy (positive). Scale not given. 12 × 18 cm.

Hand-colored photocopy showing the Confederate position in red, roads in brown, and vegetation in green. Geography and Map Division also has a negative photocopy.

FIVE FORKS

540

Michler, Nathaniel.

Map of the battlefield of Five-Forks. [March 30–April 1, 1865] Compiled from surveys made under the direction of N. Michler, Major of Engineers, Brv't. Brig. Gen'l U.S.A. Surveyed by Maj. J. E. Weyss, Theilkuhl, Burchard, Schumann, Thompson. Drawn by F. Theilkuhl, Thompson, Schumann. [1865?] Uncolored. Scale 1:15,840. 112 × 72 cm.

Shows entrenchments, villages, roads, "South Side Rail Road," drainage, vegetation, relief by hachures, houses, and names of residents.

540.1

—————Another issue. 2 sheets, each 62 × 73 cm.
Map extends north to the Appomattox River.

541

Perham, A. S.

[Map showing portions of the Federal and Confederate forces at the battle of Five Forks fought April 1, 1865. It also shows the country over which was fought the Battle of Quaker Road and the Battle of Dinwiddie Court House, fought March 31, 1865] Colored ms. Scale not given. 9 parts, each approx. 92 × 51 cm. Over-all size 270 × 156 cm.

G3883 .D6S5 1865 .P5 Vault
Presented to the Library of Congress in 1920 by Mr. A. S. Perham.

Pen and ink manuscript wall map showing roads, towns, houses and names of some residents, drainage, and the "South Side R.R."

Troop positions and movements are not given for the battles of Quaker Road and Dinwiddie Court House.

FORT DARLING

541.2

[B]alloon view of the attack on Fort Darling in the James River, by Commander Rogers's [i.e., Rodgers's] gun-boat flotilla, "Galena," "Monitor," etc. [May 16, 1862] Uncolored view. Not drawn to scale. 28 × 24 cm. on sheet 42 × 28 cm. *From* Harper's weekly, v. 6, May 31, 1862. p. [337]

This view was acquired by the Library of Congress in 1948 with the purchase of the papers and maps of Maj. Jedediah Hotchkiss.

FORT ETHAN ALLEN

541.4

Dimmick, B.

Section from Mary Hall to flags-staff Ethan Allen. Maping [sic] by B. Dimmick, Private, 2nd Art P. V. Batt. M. 26/4/64. [Signed] R. A. Chodasiewicz. [1864] Uncolored ms. Scale 1:2500. 20 × 76 cm.

     G3882 .F63 1864 .D4 Vault

     "211, L. Sheet 17."

     Cross section.

     "Transferred from Office of Chf. Engr., Defenses of Washington, to Engr. Dept. Jan'y 1866."

     Stamped on verso: By Transfer, Chief Engineers Office, War Department.

FORT SEDGWICK

542

Duane, James C., *and* Nathaniel Michler.

Fort Sedgwick. Constructed under the direction of Major J. C. Duane and Major N. Michler, Corps of Engrs., by Capts. G. H. Mendall, F. Harwood, G. L. Gillespie & Lieut W. H. H. Benyaurd, U.S. Engineers, & Capt. D. F. Schenck, 50th N.Y. Volunteer Engrs. Head quarters, Army of the Potomac, Engineer Department, July, September & October, 1864. Photocopy (positive). Scale 1:480. 47 × 64 cm.

     At head of title: Siege of Petersburg.

     Detailed plan of Fort with four cross sections.

543

Hopkins, William P.

Plan of Fort Sedgwick generally known as Fort Hell. W. P. Hopkins, Oct. 20th 1902. ©1903. Uncolored. Scale ca. 1:3880. 13 × 19 cm.

     Shows "front [and] rear line of works," artillery positions, magazines, bomb proofs, covered ways, stockade, and sutler's tent.

FORTRESS MONROE

544

Bohn, Casimir.

Map of Fortress Monroe and surroundings. Washington [1861] Uncolored. Scale not given. 15 × 19 cm. on sheet 28 × 21 cm.

     Sketch map showing the location of batteries on the James River and Hampton Roads, and a few place names.

     Inset: [View of] Fortress Monroe, Old Point Comfort and Hygeia Hotel, Va. Entered according to Act of Congress in the Year 1861 by E. Sachse & Co. 9 × 19 cm. See entry no. 547 for a description of the view on which this is based.

545

Couzens, M. K.

The key to East Virginia showing the exact relative positions of Fortress Monroe, Rip Raps, Newport News, Sewalls [sic] Point, Norfolk, Gosport Navy Yard and expressing the soundings of every part of Hampton Roads & Elizabeth River. Compiled from government surveys & drawn by M. K. Couzens, Civ. Eng. Litho. Lang & Laing, N.Y. New York, W. Schaus, ©1861. Colored. Scale ca. 1:40,000. 63 × 47 cm.

     "Description of Fortress Monroe" appears in the lower left corner of the map. The important features at Fortress Monroe are keyed by letters to a list.

     Inset: [Map of eastern Virginia and Maryland] Scale ca. 1:4,000,000. 13 × 14 cm.

545.5

Dix, John A.

[Map showing position of U.S. Navy gunboat and proposed position for same. March 7, 1863] Colored ms. on tracing linen. Scale not given. 43 × 39 cm.

     In the Abraham Lincoln papers, Manuscript Division, L.C., vol. 105, no. 22275.

     Map accompanies Maj. Gen. John A. Dix's appeal to Lincoln to reposition the navy's gunboat off Fortress Monroe (Lincoln papers, vol. 105, no. 22268–22271). "I enclose a map," Dix writes, "showing the position of the gun-boat at 'A' and I request that she may be required to be removed and placed as far west as 'B,' and that this Fort be left open to the access of vessels as it was under Admirals Goldsborough and Wilkes, not only to such as have army supplies, but such as come here for shelter, subject to the usual revenue and military inspection which is never omitted."

546

Dutton, E. P.

Fort Monroe and vicinity showing entrance to Chesapeake Bay, Norfolk, Portsmouth, Gosport Navy Yard &c. [Boston, 186–] Colored. Scale ca. 1:375,000. 15 × 18 cm.

     Shows forts Monroe, Calhoun, Nelson, and Norfolk, Confederate batteries on Sewell's Point, towns, names of features, drainage, roads, and railroads. "View of Fort Monroe" is in the lower left corner.

547

Sachse, Edward.

Fort Monroe, Old Point Comfort and Hygeia Hotel, Va. Drawn from nature, lith. & print. by E. Sachse & Co., Balto. Pub. & sold by C. Bohn, Washington, D.C. ©1861. Colored view. 46 × 71 cm.

     Bird's-eye view.

547.1

—————————Another issue. New York, Chs. Magnus, ©1861.

G3884 .H2:2F6A35 1861 .E2 Vault

In this issue, Magnus has replaced Bohn as the publisher.

547.2

—————————Fortress Monroe, Old Point Comfort, & Hygeia Hotel, Va. in 1861 & 1862. The key to the South. Entered according to Act of Congress in the year 1862 by E. Sachse & Co. Published by C. Bohn Washington, D.C. Colored view. 28 × 44 cm.

Bird's-eye view.

548

Wells, Jacob.

Fortress Monroe, Va. and its vicinity. J. Wells, del. R. Hinshelwood, sc. [New York] Virtue & Co., ©1862. Uncolored view. 16 × 23 cm.

Perspective drawing with 20 important places keyed by number to a list below the map.

FRAYSER'S FARM

549

—————————Map of the battle of Frayser's Farm (Charles City cross roads or Glendale), June 30, 1862, showing approximate positions of Union and Confederate troops. Also disposition of troops during the artillery engagement at White Oak Bridge. Uncolored. Scale ca. 1:73,000. 7 × 8 cm. *From* Century illustrated monthly magazine, v. 30, July 1885. p. 470.

Brigades and batteries are identified and keyed by numbers and letters to the map. Gives roads, streams, fords, "White Oak Swamp," and relief by hachures.

FREDERICK COUNTY

549.5

Brown, William H.

Cap: Browns report of reconnaissance of country between Middletown road & river [?] [1862?] Uncolored ms. Scale not given. Map 9 × 19 cm. on lined note paper measuring 25 × 20 cm.

In the papers of Major General Nathaniel Prentice Banks, Manuscript Division, L.C., container 76.

Title is on the verso.

Pen and ink sketch map of parts of Frederick and Shenandoah counties, Virginia, showing roads between Winchester, Middletown, Strasburg, and "Genl. Crawfords Head Quarters now Hospital" on the Shenandoah River.

Captain Brown's brief report written above the map reads as follows: Many of the cross roads are hard clay fit for cavalry and artillery trains except after heavy rains. At present stage of river very good ford at mouth of "Passage Creek." Two fords very near together, both good. One road leads up to pass at mouth of Little Fort Valley. Pass can be defended by one Co. of infantry against largely superior force.

FREDERICKSBURG

550

Brown, Samuel Howell.

Sketch of the battle field of Fredericksburg. Drawn by S. H. Brown, Topl: Engr: P.A.C.S. Decr: 13th 1862. Colored ms. Scale ca. 1:44,000. 30 × 22 cm.

G3884 .F7S5 1862 .B7 Vault

Presented to the Library of Congress in 1960 by Mrs. Percy J. Edmunds, Pittsburgh, Pa., daughter of Samuel Howell Brown.

It shows Confederate infantry in white, "Yankee infantry" in blue, cavalry in yellow, and woodland in green. Roads, "Richmond & Fredericksburg rail road," streams, houses and names of residents, headquarters of Generals Lee, Pendleton, Jackson, and Longstreet, and the names of Confederate field commanders and the Union corps commanders are indicated in black ink.

550.8

Hotchkiss, Jedediah.

[Map of the Fredericksburg and Chancellorsville battlefields. 1862–1863] Colored ms. Scale not given. 372 × 500 cm.

Number "49" is on the verso.

Wall map is drawn on muslin indicating roads, railroads, cities and towns, rivers, fords, woodland, and relief by hachures. Troop positions are not delineated. Sometimes referred to as the "bed sheet map," it was used by Hotchkiss after the war for lecture purposes. It was acquired in July 1948 when the Library of Congress purchased his map collection.

551

—————————Sketch of the battle of Fredericksburg, Saturday, Dec. 13th 1862, Right Wing, C.S.A., Lt. Gl. Jackson's corps, by Jed. Hotchkiss, T.E., 2nd Corps, A.N. Va. Uncolored. Scale ca. 1:47,000. 32 × 23 cm.

G3884 .F7S5 1862 .H6 Vault

Signed (facsim): Maj. Genl. Franklin, compliments, Danl. Butterfield, Chief of Staff.

This map was compiled by the Confederate engineer Jedediah Hotchkiss and was apparently printed by the

Union Army since the inscription contains the names of the Union generals Franklin and Butterfield.

Shows Union and Confederate positions, names of the field commanders in Jackson's Corps, headquarters of Lee, Jackson, and Longstreet, roads, railroad, hachures, drainage, some vegetation, houses, and names of residents.

551.5

Jeck, Michael C.

Historical overlay: [Fredericksburg and Spotsylvania National Military Park, Virginia] Historical features compiled by Michael Jeck. [Washington, 1981] Photocopy (negative). Scale 1:7920. 3 sheets each approximately 121 × 101 cm. and 1 sheet 141 × 91 cm.

G3882 .F7S5 s7 .J4

Map in four sheets covering the battlefields of Chancellorsville, the Wilderness, Spotsylvania Court House, and Fredericksburg and indicating roads, buildings, orchards or gardens, fences, woodland, drainage, and entrenchments.

Accompanied by text: Fredericksburg and Spotsylvania National Military Park. Vegetation community structure and historical features survey. Final report, June 1981. [By] Richard R. Anderson, Dennis M. McFaden, Michael C. Jeck, and Susan J. Murray [and] Greg England. (NPS contract no. CX–2000–0–0017) 62 leaves (L.C. copy incomplete; leaves 7–17 wanting).

Accompanied by an index map entitled "Locater Key."

552

Kishpaugh, Robert A.

Battlefield map of the Fredericksburg-Spotsylvania Battlefield Park. Fredericksburg [19–?] Uncolored. Scale not given. 24 × 30 cm.

Map of the battlefields of the Wilderness, Chancellorsville, Fredericksburg, and Spotsylvania, showing troop positions, names of commanders, roads, railroads, towns, and drainage.

Inset: Locality sketch. Scale ca. 1:5,750,000. 8 × 6 cm. (Map of the environs of the Chesapeake Bay showing the location of the four battlefields.)

"Losses on the battlefields" are given in the lower right corner.

553

————Map showing the locations of the battlefields of Fredericksburg, Hamilton's Crossing, Chancellorsville, Salem Church, Wilderness [and] Spotsylvania, and also showing the boundaries of the battlefield park surveys of 6556 acres. Fredericksburg, ©1906. Uncolored. Scale ca. 1:90,000. 29 × 42 cm.

Accompanied by a pamphlet entitled *Map of the Six Battlefields: Fredericksburg, Hamilton's Crossing, Chancellorsville, Salem Church, Spotsylvania, Wilderness, and Illus-* *trated Sketch of Fredericksburg* (Fredericksburg, Virginia, R. A. Kishpaugh, ©1906).

Map indicates Union and Confederate works, roads, railroads, towns, and drainage.

553.5

Mallory, C. A.

Part of the north bank of the Rappahannock River showing the approaches to Fredericksburg, prepared under the direction of Capt. R. S. Williamson & 1st. Lt. Nicolas Bowen, Corps Topogl. Engrs., U.S.A. for the use of the Army of the Potomac. Compiled by Fred. Churchill, vol. A.D.C. Decr. 1862. Drawn by C. A. Mallory. Reduced and photographed by L. E. Walker, Treasy. Dept. Photocopy (positive). Scale 1:20,000. 44 × 87 cm.

"Authorities: U.S. Coast Survey chart of the Rappahannock River [and] surveys and reconnoissances [sic] by C. A. Mallory, Chas. Shoemacker, L. C. Oswell, H. H. Marvin [and] Geo. F. Lathrop, assistants."

General map showing roads, houses, names of residents, woodland, and relief by hachures.

553.6

Michler, Nathaniel.

Fredericksburg. [Dec. 1862] Prepared by Bvt. Brig. Genl. N. Michler, Major of Engineers, from surveys under his direction, by order of Brig. Genl. & Bvt. Maj. Genl. A. A. Humphreys, Chief of Engineers, and under the authority of the hon. Secretary of War. Surveyed & drawn by Maj: J. E. Weyss, assisted by F. Theilkuhl, J. Strasser & G. Thompson. Photolith. by the N.Y. Lithographing, Engraving & Printing Co., Julius Bien, Supt. 1867. Colored. Scale 1:21,120. 82 × 57 cm.

In this issue, the map is printed on a yellow background with the Rappahannock River colored green.

Detailed map of the environs of Fredericksburg giving Union entrenchments in blue and Confederate entrenchments in red, roads, "Richmond, Fredericksburg and Potomac Rail Road," street plan of Fredericksburg and Falmouth, houses, fences, names of residents in rural areas, vegetation, drainage, and relief by hachures.

553.7

————Another issue.
Background and water are not colored.

553.8

————Another issue.
Lacks names of the surveyors and lithographer.

553.9

Owner, William.

[Map of the environs of Fredericksburg, Virginia, December 1862] Uncolored ms. Scale ca. 1:180,000. 19 × 16 cm. *In his* Diary, v. 3, tipped-in at front of volume.

In the William Owner papers, Manuscript Division, L.C., container no. 1.

Neatly drawn manuscript showing Federal and Confederate batteries, General Burnside's headquarters, roads, river, railroad, and some indication of relief by hachures. The road to the rear of the Confederate works is identified as "New cut road to facilitate Rebel operations."

"On to Richmond" appears at the top of the map.

Volume 3 of the diary covers from Sept. 11, 1862, to Feb. 13, 1863.

553.95

Paine, William H.

Map of a part of eastern Virginia including portions of Spotsylvania Co. and adjoining counties. Compiled under the direction of Col. J. N. Macomb, A.D.C., Maj. Topl. Engrs. by Capt. W. H. Paine, A.D.C. November 1862. Autographic transfer printed at the Coast Survey Office. Colored. Scale 1:63,360 ("1 inch to the mile") 93 × 77 cm. cut and mounted to fold to 24 × 27 cm.

In the Abraham Lincoln papers, Manuscript Division, L.C., vol. 93, no. 19843.

"No. 53bis" is written in ink beside the map title.

Signed in green pencil "G. K. Warren, Brig. Genl. Vols., A.P."

Printed reconnaissance map annotated by Warren to show "Bank's Ford," "Franklin's Crossing" on December 11–12, 1862, and "Lower Crossing" of the Rappahannock River in green pencil and Confederate positions in red pencil.

554

Sachse, Edward.

View of Fredericksburg, Va. Nov. 1862. Lith. & print. by E. Sachse & Co., Balto. ©1863. Colored view. 23 × 43 cm.

G3884 .F7A3 1862 .S3

Perspective drawing showing fortifications in the background and troops and destroyed bridges in the foreground.

Listed in John R. Hébert and Patrick E. Dempsey's *Panoramic Maps of Cities in the United States and Canada.* 2nd ed. (Washington, Library of Congress, 1984), no. 956.

555

U.S. *Army. Army of the Potomac.*

Approaches of A. of P. to Fredericksburg. [Dec. 1862] Colored ms. Scale 1:21,120. 36 × 44 cm.

G3884 .F7S5 1862 .U5 Vault

Title from verso of map.

Indicates "Genl. Hd Qrs.," routes of approach of the

2nd, 3rd, 5th and 6th Corps, roads, railroad, towns, drainage, and houses and names of residents.

555.5

U.S. *Army. Corps of Topographical Engineers.*

Map of field of occupation of Army of the Potomac. Prepared by order of Gen. Hooker from reconnaisances [sic] made under Capt. R. S. Williamson, Lt. N. Bowen, Gen. D. P. Woodbury and others. [1863] Colored ms. Scale 1:63,360 (one inch per mile). 64 × 95 cm.

G3884 .F7 1863 .U5 Vault

Endorsed below title: Sent from Top'l Eng'rs office, February 25, 1863. [signed] G. K. Warren Brig. Genl. Vols, Capt. Topl. Engrs.

Title on verso: Field of occupation of the Army of the Potomac, March 1863.

Pen and ink manuscript map drawn on tracing linen showing roads, railroads, towns, houses, and names of residents in the environs of Fredericksburg, Virginia. Troop positions are not shown.

555.8

U.S. *Geological Survey.*

Fredericksburg-Spotsylvania Battlefield National Monument, Virginia. Surveyed in part in cooperation with the War Department and the Fredericksburg and Spotsylvania County Battlefields Memorial Commission. Surveyed in 1931–1934. Topography by H. A. Bean, G. E. Sisson, Paul Blake, Benjamin Munroe, Jr., J. G. Groninger, Shirley Waggener, G. A. Mock, J. H. Lycett, Severin Sabas, F. E. Doane, R. V. Ford, and J. G. Harrison. Control by U.S. Geological Survey. [Washington, 1934] Colored. Scale 1:24,000. Map 76 × 145 cm., in 2 parts, each 76 × 73 cm.

G3882 .F7 1934 .U5

"Advance sheet. Subject to correction."

Detailed topographic map. Contour interval 10 feet. The base map is printed in brown, and place names are in black. Troop positions and movements are not indicated.

556

————Topographic map of Fredericksburg and vicinity, Virginia, showing battlefields. Surveyed in cooperation with the War Department and the Fredericksburg and Spotsylvania County Battlefields Memorial Commission. Topography by G. E. Sisson, Paul Blake, and Benjamin Munroe. Control by U.S. Geological Survey and U.S. Coast and Geodetic Survey. Surveyed in 1931. Colored. Scale 1:24,000. 60 × 35 cm.

"Advance sheet subject to correction."

Detailed topographic map indicating relief by contour lines and spot heights, fortifications, roads and streets, houses, and drainage.

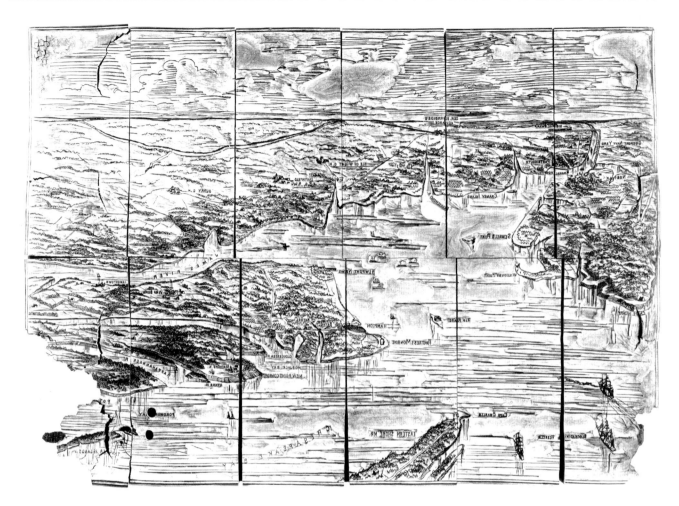

556.4

U.S. *National Park Service.*

Fredericksburg [Washington] Government Printing Office, 1979. Colored. Scale ca. 1:92,000. 39 × 42 cm.

G3882 .F7 1979 .U5

Map illustrates a descriptive leaflet entitled "Fredericksburg. Fredericksburg/Spotsylvania National Military Park.

Inset: [Map of Fredericksburg showing] routes to/from Chatham. 5 × 7 cm.

Map indicates battlefield sites, parkland, and roads connecting park areas.

556.5

—————Fredericksburg and Spotsylvania National Military Park. Rev. 1972 [Washington, Government Printing Office, 1972]. Colored. Scale ca. 1:95,000. Map 22 × 31 cm. on sheet 29 × 33 cm.

G3882 .F7 1972 .U5

Map illustrates a descriptive leaflet entitled "Fredericksburg & Spotsylvania National Military Park, Virginia."

Woodblock, in 12 parts, used to print the panoramic map entitled "Scene of the Late Naval Fight and Environs of Fortress Monroe, and Norfolk and Suffolk, now Threatened by General Burnside," published in the March 22, 1862, edition of the New York Illustrated News. *Most newspaper and journal illustrations were printed from woodcuts such as this. This form of reproduction, albeit crude, was inexpensive, reasonably quick to execute, and the woodblocks could be inserted into pages of text and printed on newspaper presses without difficulty. (See entry no. 558.7.)*

556.6

—————Reprint 1974. 28 × 31 cm.

G3882 .F7 1974 .U5

557

Wells, Jacob.

Battle of Fredericksburg. Dec. 13, 1862. Uncolored. Scale ca. 1:50,000. 21 × 14 cm. *From* Century illustrated monthly magazine, v. 32, Aug. 1886. p. 622.

"In indicating the Union artillery, we have followed an

Proof copy pulled from a woodblock showing the "Scene of the Late Naval Fight and the Environs of Fortress Monroe, and Norfolk and Suffolk, now Threatened by General Burnside." (See entry no. 558.7.)

official map made under the direction of General Henry J. Hunt, chief of artillery."

Gives troop positions, batteries, names of commanders, roads, R. F. & P Railroad and the unfinished railroad, houses and names of residents, street pattern of Fredericksburg, drainage, vegetation, and relief by hachures.

GAINES MILL

558

————Map of the battle-field of Gaines's Mill, showing approximately the positions of infantry and artillery en-

gaged. (The topography from the official map.) [June 27, 1862] Uncolored. Scale ca. 1:33,000. 14 × 14 cm. *From Century illustrated monthly magazine, v. 30, June 1885. p. 317.*

Indicates names of commanders, roads, relief by hachures, houses, names of a few residents, drainage, and vegetation.

558.1

————Another issue.

This issue is without title and contains less information.

GREENE COUNTY

558.5

Confederate States of America. *Army of Northern Virginia. 2nd Corps. Engineer Office.*

Greene Co., Virginia. Engr. Office, 2nd Corps. November 1863. Colored ms. Scale ca. 1:160,000. 31 × 22 cm.

G3883 .G8 1863 .C6 Vault

Map indicates towns, roads, drainage, relief by hachures, and the names of residents. Map is drawn on a 1-centimeter grid. Military information is not depicted.

Transferred to the Library of Congress in September 1964 by the U.S. Geological Survey, this map is thought to be the work of Confederate engineer Jedediah Hotchkiss. It is one of several county maps that Hotchkiss lent to the Survey in the mid-1880s to assist in the preparation of topographic maps of Virginia. Due to an apparent oversight, this manuscript was not returned to Hotchkiss with the rest of his maps.

Listed in R. W. Stephenson's *Land Ownership Maps* (Washington: Library of Congress, 1967), no. 1267.

HAMPTON ROADS

558.7

[Scene of the late naval fight and the environs of Fortress Monroe, and Norfolk and Suffolk, now threatened by General Burnside] View on wood, 25 × 36 cm. *From* New York illustrated news, v. 5, no. 124, Saturday, March 22, 1862. Text, p. 314; map, p. 317.

G3882 .H3S5 1862 .S3 Vault Shelf

Wood block composed of 12 separate parts joined together; each part is 13 × 6 cm. Wood block is imperfect; lower left and right corners are damaged.

Accompanied by proof copy pulled from the wood block.

Bird's-eye view of Hampton Roads, the James River, and the lower Chesapeake Bay showing fortifications, camps, the *Monitor* lying off Fortress Monroe, and "Gen. Burnside's advance" on Suffolk, Virginia. The accompanying newspaper article notes that "the possession of Suffolk will not only give the Union army the means of effectually reducing Norfolk, and capturing all the rebels there congregated, with the naval and military stores there collected, but it will be an alarming menace to Richmond. To this point public attention is now turned with excited interest."

559

Worret, Ch.

Copy of a map military reconnaissance Dept. Va: drawn and compiled under the direction of Col. T. J. Cram, Chief Topl. Enger., Dep. Va., by Sergt. Ch. Worret. [1862] Colored ms. Scale 1:60,000. 55 × 93 cm.

G3882 .H3S5 1862 .W6 Vault

"For/Maj. Gen'l Hitchcock, U.S. Vol., with the regards of T. J. Cram."

"Note—This map shows the positions of the rebel forces and their batteries as they were some six weeks since.

At the present time no doubt many of these forces say to the number of 10,000 have gone to reinforce the Rebel ranks on the Peninsula."

Map of Hampton Roads and vicinity showing Confederate fortifications and camps, towns, street pattern of Norfolk and Portsmouth, roads, railroads, canals, drainage, vegetation, relief by hachures, and soundings. Locates "Minnesota 8 & 9 March 1862 on ground" and "Monitor & Merrimac engagement on the 9th of March 1862."

HARRISON'S LANDING

559.12

Briscoe, James C.

Map of roads from Hd. Qrs. 3rd Corps to Harrison's Landing. Surveyed & drawn by J. C. Briscoe, Lt. & Actg. Engr. Kearney's [sic] Divn. July 29th 1862. Uncolored ms. Scale 1:15,000. 24 × 19 cm.

In the Samuel P. Heintzelman papers, Manuscript Division, L.C., container no. 11.

Title on verso: Sketch of camp of 3rd. Corps, Harrison's Landing, Va. July 29, 1862.

Map indicates the location of the headquarters of the 3rd Corps, as well as the headquarters of Hooker, Kearny, Robinson, Berry, and Sumner.

559.14

Map of the front of Kearney's [sic] command, July 5th [1862] Uncolored ms. Scale not given. 37 × 30 cm.

In the Samuel P. Heintzelman papers, Manuscript Division, L.C., container no. 11.

Pen and ink sketch drawn on lined note paper, depicting "swamp," "timber," "felled trees," "roads," "pickets," "Pickets reserve," "rifle pits," and "camps." Although the site is unnamed, it is probably near Harrison's Landing, Virginia.

559.16

Winsor, H., Jr.

[Map of Federal positions at Harrison's Landing, Virginia, on July 11, 1862] Uncolored ms. Scale not given. 25 × 40 cm.

In the Samuel P. Heintzelman papers, Manuscript Division, L.C., container no. 11.

The following note appears on the verso: Camp 6th Penna. Cavalry, July 11th 1862. General, In accordance with an order from your H'd Qrs, I have the honor to submit the following diagram of the positions of the different Corps d'Armée of the Army of the Potomac, as the result of my labors. Yrs respectfully [Signed] H. Winsor Jr. 1st Lieut 6th Penna. Cavalry. Also written in ink on the verso is "Camp 6th Penna. Cavalry July 11, 1862, Harrison's Lan." and in pencil, in a different hand, "Harrison's Landing, Va."

Map indicates the approximate location of corps and divisions and the "enclosure where the army encamped on night of its arrival."

HENRICO COUNTY

559.18

Henrico County, Virginia. 1862. Photocopy (positive). Scale ca. 1:100,000. 29 × 36 cm.

G3883 .H4 1862 .H4

Map of the portion of Henrico County southeast of Richmond showing roads, railroads, rivers, houses, names of residents, and woodland. The map is based on James Keily's "Smith's map of Henrico County, Virginia" (Richmond, Robert P. Smith & C. Carpenter, 1853).

Listed in R. W. Stephenson's *Land Ownership Maps* (Washington, Library of Congress, 1967), no. 1279.

559.2

Hergesheimer, Edwin.

Henrico County, Virginia. Prepared under the direction of Lieut. Col. J. N. Macomb A.D.C. Chf. Topl. Engr. for the use of Maj. Gen. Geo. B. McClellan commanding Army of Potomac. Drawn from Smith's map in collection of U. S. Coast Survey by permission of Prof. A. D. Bache Supdt. Drawn by E. Hergesheimer. Photographs by G. Mathiot & D. Hinkle, C. S. Office. 1862. Photocopy (positive). Scale ca. 1:126,720. 49 × 29 cm.

G3883 .H4 1862 .H41

Pen and ink inscription reads "Presented to P.O. Dep't. by W. L. Nicholson, Topographer, P. O. Dep't. 1863."

General map showing roads, railroads, drainage, houses, churches, mills, and woodland. Map is based on James Keily's "Smith's map of Henrico County, Virginia" (Richmond, Robert P. Smith & C. Carpenter, 1853).

Inset: [Map of the City of Richmond] 14 × 16 cm.

559.22

————Another issue. Photocopy (positive). Scale ca. 1:76,000. 81 × 46 cm.

In the Samuel P. Heintzelman papers, Manuscript Division, L.C., container no. 11.

"Copy no. 1. For Maj. Genl. McClellan, Comd. Genl. U.S. Army."

Signed in ink: Bri. Gen. S. P. Heintzelman, Baltimore Store, May 21, 1862."

Photocopy has been hand-colored and extensively annotated. "Genl Head Qrs." is indicated near "New Tavern."

559.3

U.S. *Coast Survey.*

Henrico County, Virginia. Photographed from Smith's

map at the office of the U.S. Coast Survey, 1864. Photocopy (positive). Scale ca. 1:60,000. 88 × 42 cm.

G3883 .H4 1853 .K4

Title is added in manuscript.

Photocopy of James Keily's "Smith's map of Henrico County, Virginia" (Richmond, Robert P. Smith & C. Carpenter, 1853).

Listed in R. W. Stephenson's *Land Ownership Maps* (Washington, Library of Congress, 1967), no. 1278.

JAMES RIVER

559.4

U.S. *Coast Survey.*

Hydrographic reconnaissance of James River, Virginia, from entrance to City Point, by Comr. W. T. Muse & Lieuts. R. Wainwright & J. N. Maffitt, U.S.N., Assts. Coast Survey from 1854 to '59. Autographic transfer, July 1862. [Washington, U. S. Coast Survey, 1862] Uncolored. Scale 1:80,000. 70 × 103 cm. (*Its* no. 401).

G3882. J3P5 1862 .U5 Vault

At head of title: U.S. Coast Survey, A. D. Bache, Supt.

General chart indicating soundings, bottom contours, and lighthouses.

Another copy of this chart in the Library of Congress has been annotated in red and black ink to show the location of buoys.

Includes sailing directions.

JETERSVILLE

559.5

Michler, Nathaniel.

Jetersville and Sailors Creek. [1865] From surveys under the direction of Bvt. Brig. Gen. N. Michler, Maj. of Engineers, by command of Bvt. Maj. Genl. A. A. Humphreys, Brig. Genl. & Chief of Engineers. Surveyed & drawn by Maj: J. E. Weyss, assisted by F. Theilkuhl, J. Strasser & G. Thompson. Photolith. by the N.Y. Lithographing, Engraving & Printing Co., Julius Bien, Supt. 1867. Colored. Scale 1:21,120. 51 × 87 cm.

In this issue, the map is printed on a yellow background with the Appomattox River colored green.

Shows entrenchments, roads, "Richmond and Danville R. R.," drainage, vegetation, hachures, houses, fences, and names of residents.

559.55

————Another issue. Uncolored.

559.6

————Another issue. Uncolored.

G3884 .J55 1867 .M5
Lacks names of the surveyors and lithographer.

LOUDOUN COUNTY

559.7

Hergesheimer, Edwin.

Loudon [sic] County, Virginia. Compiled under the direction of Lieut Col. J. N. Macomb A.D.C. Chf. Topl. Engr. for the use of Maj. Gen. Geo. B. McClellan commanding Army of the Potomac. Drawn from R. P. Smith's map by E. Hergesheimer. Photographs by G. Mathiot & D. Hinkle by permission of Prof. A. D. Bache Supt. U.S. Coast Survey. 1861. Photocopy (positive). Scale ca. 1:126,720. 46 × 45 cm.

G3883 .L5 1861 .H4
At head of title (in manuscript): No. 25.

Hand-colored photocopy showing roads, towns, houses, the Loudoun & Hampshire Railroad, and county districts. The map is based on Yardley Taylor's "Map of Loudoun County, Virginia from Actual Surveys" (Philadelphia, Thomas Reynolds and Robert Pearsall Smith, 1853).

This map was acquired by the Library of Congress in 1948 with the purchase of the papers and maps of Maj. Jedediah Hotchkiss.

559.8

Loudoun County, Virginia. [186–?] Photocopy (positive). Scale ca. 1:90,000. 48 × 55 cm.

G3883 .L5 186– .L6
General map indicating roads, railroads, drainage, and the names of a few villages.

"Gilbert Thompson" is stamped on the verso.

LYNCHBURG

559.9

Craighill, Edley.

Lynchburg campaign "War between the States." June 17–18, 1864. Copyright 1960 [by] Edley Craighill C.E., Colonel infantry (ret.) Colored. Scale ca. 1:44,000. 28 × 21 cm.

Map of the environs of Lynchburg showing positions of troops and artillery, rifle pit, "light works," roads, railroads, drainage, and relief by contour lines and spot elevations.

Eleven points of interest are listed and keyed by number to the map.

MALVERN HILL

560

Wells, Jacob.

Map of the battle of Malvern Hill, showing, approximately, positions of brigades and batteries. [July 1, 1862] Uncolored. Scale ca. 1:23,500. 18 × 12 cm. *From* Century illustrated monthly magazine, v. 30, Aug. 1885. p. 617.

Gives names of commanders, roads, drainage, vegetation, relief by hachures, houses, and names of residents.

Brief description of the battle appears below the map.

MANASSAS (FIRST)

561

Abbot, Henry L.

Reconnaissance of the battle field at Bull Run, Va., fought July 21, 1861. Made on March 14, 1862, by Henry L. Abbot, 1st Lieut., Top. Engineers. Photocopy (positive). Scale 1:12,000. 45 × 36 cm.

G3884 .M25S5 1861 .A2 Vault
Signed in ms: With respects of Genl. J. G. Barnard.

Base map indicates roads, houses, names of residents, relief by hachures and spot elevations, drainage, vegetation, and "the remains of battery horses." Troop positions and movements have been added in red ink.

561.5

American Heritage Publishing Company.

The American Heritage battle map of First Bull Run. [Drawn by] David Greenspan. [New York] ©1961. Colored view. Not drawn to scale. 39 × 59 cm.

Bird's-eye view showing principal sites and events of the battle.

561a

Atkinson, W. G.

Map of the battle fields of Manassas and the surrounding region showing the various actions of the 21st July 1861 between the armies of the Confederate States and the United States. Surveyed and drawn by W. G. Atkinson, acting 1st lieut., Engineers. Headquarters 1st Corps, Army of Potomac, Manassas Junction, August 1862. Photographed by Brown & Ogilvie. Photographed for the use of the U.S. Army by order of Maj. Gen. N. P. Banks comdg. Dept. of the Gulf. Henry L. Abbot, Capt. & Chief Topl. Engrs. N. Orleans, Dec. 1862. Photocopy (positive). Scale ca. 1:28,000. 35 × 34 cm.

Dedicated (facsim.): Presented to the city of New-Orleans by General G. T. [i.e., P. G. T.] Beauregard, gen. comdg.

Dedicated in ms: Prof. A. D. Bache with respects of Capt. Abbot.

Detailed map showing troop positions and movements, roads, houses and names of residents, fences, vegetation, relief by hachures, drainage, and fords.

562

Battle field of Bull Run, Va. July 21st 1861. Showing the positions of both armies at 4 o'clock, P.M. Uncolored. Scale ca. 1:30,000. 16 × 21 cm.

Indicates troop positions and names of commanders, roads, drainage, vegetation, houses, names of residents, and relief by hachures.

562.3

Bowen, James L.

Battle field of Young's Branch or Manassa [i.e., Manassas] Plains. Battle fought July 21, 1861. Relief survey and map by James L. Bowen, topographical engineer. Linear survey by Warder & Catlett, surveyors and publishers. Lith. of Hoyer & Ludwig, Richmond, Va. [Richmond, Enquirer Book and Job Press, 1862] Uncolored. Scale 1:11,880 (15 chains to the inch) 52 × 47 cm.

G3884 .M25S5 1861 .B6 Vault

Confederate imprint.

From T. B. Warder and James M. Catlett's *Battle of Young's Branch, or, Manassas Plain, fought July 21, 1861.* Richmond, Enquirer Book and Job Press, 1862. 156 p. [1] p.

Detailed map of the first battle of Manassas showing troop positions, roads, houses and names of residents, rivers, relief by hachures, oak and pine forests, "cemetery [of the] 8th Geo. Regt.," and places where "distinguished men fell." Confederate units are listed in upper right and left corners and keyed by number to map.

562.5

Britton, Richard H.

Map of the battle-fields of Manassas, Sunday, July 21st, 1861. Drawn by R. H. Britton. [Charlottesville, Virginia, Iron Crown Enterprises] ©1980 [i.e., 1981]. Colored. Scale ca. 1:5500. 92 × 116 cm., in 2 sheets, each 96 × 62 cm.

G3884 .M25S5 1981 .B7

Game board designed to be used with game entitled "Manassas, Sunday, July 21st, 1861: a Wargame of the 1st Battle of Bull Run, ©1981."

Printed on a hexagonal grid, map indicates roads, railroads, houses and names of residents, rivers, woodland, and relief. Troop positions are not depicted.

562.7

—————Another issue.

G3884 .M25 1983 .B7 Vault Shelf

Accompanies game entitled "Manassas, Sunday, July 21st, 1861: a Wargame of the 1st Battle of Bull Run, ©1981." Game contains rules booklet (2nd ed., ©1983, errata sheet, tables, 320 die-cut counters, and 2 die.

563

Corbett, V. P.

Map of the seat of war showing the battles of July 18th & 21st 1861. Lith. by A. Hoen & Co., Baltimore. Washington, ©1861. Colored. Scale ca. 1:115,000. 45 × 51 cm.

"Entered according to act of Congress in the Clerks office of the U.S. District Court by V. P. Corbett in the year 1861 for the Dist. of Columa."

Map of northern Virginia showing troop camps, entrenchments, forts, batteries, roads, railroads, street pattern of Washington and Alexandria, towns, drainage, vegetation and some indication of relief by hachures.

Geography and Map Division's copy has the imprint covered by a label which reads "Metropolitan Book [Store], Philp & Solomo[ns, Agents], 332 Pennsylvania A[ve.], Washington, D.[C.]"

563.1

—————Another issue.

Additional details added such as "Camp Sprague," "U.S. Hospital," "Soldier's Home," and other place names in the northern part of Washington, D.C.

563.2

—————Another issue.

Houses of Vanderweckins, Cary, and Hall in northern Virginia are identified as having been "burnt by rebels Sept. 13th."

563.3

—————Another issue.

Includes flags, drawings of four ships in the Potomac River, additional place names, and camp sites (such as "rebel camp" at Annandale).

563.4

—————Another issue.

Similar to the preceding issue but with the addition of compass directions.

564

—————Map of the seat of war showing the battles of July 18th, 21st, & Oct. 21st 1861. Lith. by A. Hoen & Co., Balto. Washington, ©1861. Uncolored. Scale ca. 1:115,000. 66 × 56 cm.

Map of the battles of first Manassas and Ball's Bluff, showing troop camps, entrenchments, forts, batteries, positions during engagements, roads, railroads, street pattern of Washington and Alexandria, towns, drainage, vegetation, and some indication of relief by hachures.

Insets: Leesburg to Harpers Ferry. Scale ca. 1:400,000. 9 × 9 cm.—Map from the mouth of Occoquan River to

Richmond showing rebel batteries on the Potomac River. Scale ca. 1:810,000. 16 × 18 cm.

Another copy is in the Fillmore map coll. no. 251.

Another copy is in the Benjamin F. Wade papers, Manuscript Division, L.C., container no. 18.

564.2

First Bull Run battle field, July 21st 1861. Uncolored. Scale ca. 1:180,000. 13 × 10 cm.

General map. Troop positions are not noted.

564.4

Harris, D. B., *and* **John Grant.**

Topographical map of the Bull Run battle-field. [1861] Uncolored. Scale ca. 1:27,000. 22 × 13 cm. *From* Century illustrated monthly magazine, v. 29, Nov. 1884. p. 82.

"The original of this map was made for General Beauregard, soon after the battle, from actual surveys by Captain D. B. Harris, assisted by Mr. John Grant. It is here reproduced by the courtesy of General H. L. Abbot, U.S.A., from a photograph in his possession."

General map of the battlefield showing roads, drainage, vegetation, houses, and names of residents. Troop positions are not noted.

564.5

Hotchkiss, Jedediah.

[Map of the Manassas battlefield area in Northern Virginia. 186–?] Colored ms. Scale ca. 1:7000. Map 220 × 282 cm. cut into 6 parts, each 110 × 94 cm.

G3882 .N6S5 186– .H6 Vault

Signed in ms. on verso: Major Jed. Hotc[hk]iss, Staunton, Va.

Wall map apparently used by Hotchkiss after the war for lecture purposes. The map indicates roads, railroads, houses and names of residents, place names, fortifications near Little Rocky Run and Bull Run, rivers, woodland, and relief by form lines.

564.6

————Another ms. copy.

G3882 .N6S5 186– .H61 Vault

Unfinished copy of the preceding map. Lacks woodland, relief, place names, and names of residents.

564.7

Jeck, Michael C.

Quadrangle overlay, historic vegetation. [Prepared by Michael C. Jeck for the National Capital Parks. Washington, Department of Biology, American University, 1976] Photocopy (negative). Scale ca. 1:4800. 4 sheets, each 91 × 101 cm.

G3882 .M3D2 s4 .J4

At head of sheet titles: NE; NW; SE; SW.

Map of Manassas National Battlefield Park showing vegetation, fence rows, roads, drainage, and man-made structures that existed at the time of the Civil War.

Accompanied by "Historic Vegetation Section, Manassas National Battlefield Park, Resources Basic Inventory, Final Report." 36 leaves. L.C. copy imperfect: leaves 3–18 wanting.

564.8

King, Porter.

Map of the positions of the fourth Alabama Regt. during the battle of Stone Bridge. [Drawn by Capt. Porter King, C.S.A. July 20–21, 1861] Colored ms. Scale not given. 21 × 16 cm.

G3884 .M25S5 1861 .K5 Vault

This manuscript map was acquired in March 1982 from the estate of Thomas Cobb King, grandson of Capt. Porter King. The latter served in the 4th Alabama Regiment during the battle of Manassas. The map indicates the position of the "4th Ala. Reg.," its route of advance, the "enemies position," and "Sherman's battery." The position of the N.Y. regiment on the left flank of the Alabama regiment is identified as "Enemies whom we took for friends." Also depicted is the position of "Capt. King's Comp.," "Road to Alexandria," Young's Branch of Bull Run, old fields, corn fields, fences, woods, and the place where "21 Georgin's [sic] buried."

564.9

————Plan of Bull Run. [Drawn by Capt. Porter King, 4th Alabama Regiment, C.S.A. July 18–21, 1861] Colored ms. Scale ca. 1:168,000. 47 × 66 cm. on matte board 59 × 76 cm.

G3884 .M25S5 1861 .K51 Vault

Title written in pencil on matte board.

This manuscript map was acquired in March 1982 from the estate of Thomas Cobb King, grandson of Captain Porter King. The latter served in the 4th Alabama Regiment during the battle of Manassas. The map extends from Washington, D.C., to Warrenton, Virginia, and shows "enemy's [i.e., Union] camp night of July 20, 1861," "battle field July 18th, 1861," "battle field July 21, 1861," troop positions, batteries, rivers, roads, and railroads. The positions of several Confederate brigades are identified.

564.95

McClelem, A. L.

A deserter sketch of field works at Manassas Oct. 16– 1861. Drawn from recollection by A. L. McClelem. Deserted from Co. A, 5 Infy Octo 16/61. Uncolored ms. Not drawn to scale. 32 × 40 cm.

In the papers of Maj. Gen. Nathaniel Prentice Banks, Manuscript Division, L.C., container 76.

Title is from the verso.

Rough pencil sketch drawn on lined paper showing "Beauregards Army" and "Johnsons Army on the 16° inst."

Map contains the following notes: "From Manassas to Centreville 9.m. From Centreville to Fairfax 6.m. From Fairfax to Anandale [sic] 6.m. The combined forces of Johnson & Beauregard does not exceed 140 thousand, 20 thousand of which are sick, 20 thousand more on detached service furlough etc.

"The signal of the pickests [sic] are as follows—When you approach their pickets, they will halt you by throwing up their hand, upon which you describe a cross upon your breast—(Night Signal) Upon the command halt—you strike your body with the open hand, 2 or 3 times—you will then be told to advance by a low whistle."

565

Meeker, E. J.

Plan of the Bull Run battle-field. [July 21, 1861] Uncolored. Scale ca. 1:37,000. 8 × 10 cm. *From* Century illustrated monthly magazine, v. 30, May 1885. p. 95.

Shows "Griffin's battery," "Ricketts' battery," "Griffin and Ricketts last position," "Imboden's first position," and "Imboden's second position."

566

Mitchell, Samuel P.

Sketch of the country occupied by the Federal & Confederate Armies on the 18th & 21st July 1861. Taken by Capt. Saml. P. Mitchell, of 1st Virginia Regiment. Lithographed by F. W. Bornemann, Charleston, S.C. Richmond, W. Hargrave White, [1861?]. Uncolored. Scale not given. 30 × 39 cm.

Confederate imprint.

Shows troop positions, notes concerning battle, roads, "Orange & Alexandria R.R.," vegetation, houses, names of residents, and drainage.

Inset: [Sketch of the environs of Bull Run from Washington to Fredericksburg.] 12 × 9 cm.

566.2

————Colored ms. Scale not given. 31 × 41 cm.

In the papers of Samuel P. Heintzelman, Manuscript Division, L.C., container no. 11.

Attractive manuscript copy on tracing linen of the lithographed map described in entry no. 566.

567

National Tribune.

The first battle of Bull Run. July 21, 1861. Washington,

Dec. 26, 1895. Colored. Scale not given. 32 × 39 cm. on sheet 58 × 42 cm. (National Tribune War Maps. No. 1. Supplement to the National Tribune, Washington, D.C., Dec. 26, 1895.)

Union position colored blue and "1st position of enemy" colored red.

Indicates hachures along the Bull Run and its tributaries, roads, railroads, towns, and drainage. Includes portraits of Generals McDowell, Slocum, Ricketts, and Griffin.

"The story of the battle, by John McElroy" appears below the map. This includes a description of the battle, the organization of the Union army, and a table giving the number of Union casualties by regiment and division.

567.5

Frémaux, Léon J.

Sketch showing the position of Cap: F. B. Schaeffer's Comd. on July the 21st 1861. Camp Pickens, Manassas, Augt. 24th 1861. L. Fremaux, Cap. Co. A, 8th La. Vols. Colored ms. Scale not given. 40 × 29 cm.

G3884 .M25S5 1861 .F7 Vault

Inset: Profile [of terrain] 8 × 28 cm.

Pen and ink manuscript map with watercolor wash showing the position of "Cap: F. B. Schaeffer's Command" along Bull Run some 600 yards from the Lewis house.

568

Richmond Enquirer.

Seat of war, Manassas and its vicinity. Engraved by J. Baumgarten. Printed and for sale at the office of the Richmond Enquirer. [1861] Uncolored. Scale ca. 1:322,000. 27 × 25 cm. on sheet 41 × 33 cm.

Confederate imprint.

Shows "battle ground, July 18th," "battle ground July 21st," roads, railroads, towns, and drainage. "Blue Ridge," "Thorough Fare Mountains," and two unnamed mountains are indicated by hachures. Troop positions are not given.

Roads, railroads, bridges, and distances are described in a brief text below the map.

569

Robertson, H. C.

Battle of Bull Run. [Chicago, R. O. Evans and Co., ©1898] Colored. Scale ca. 1:176,000. 82 × 58 cm. (Robertson's geographic-historical series illustrating the history of America and the United States)

Wall map showing the location of 1st Manassas and Balls Bluff battlefields, railroads, principal towns, roads, and rivers.

Includes an outline of events; views of Fort Sumter, Harper's Ferry and "Stonewall Jackson at Bull Run"; and a portrait of Jackson.

570

Russell, Robert E. L.

Small sketch, first Manassas, July 21, 1861. Situation on Henry Hill at 3 P.M. Baltimore, 1934. Photocopy (positive). Scale not given. 19 × 25 cm.

Hand-colored positive photocopy. Geography and Map Division also has a negative photocopy.

571

Struthers, Servoss and Company.

General map of the battle-field of Manassas. [July 16–21, 1861] Struthers, Servoss & Co., Engr's., N.Y. Uncolored. Scale ca. 1:105,000. 14 × 14 cm. *From* Century illustrated monthly magazine, v. 30, May 1885. p. 103.

Indicates troop positions, rivers, roads, railroads, towns, houses, and names of residents.

572

U.S. *Army. Corps of Engineers.*

Map of the battlefield of Bull Run, Virginia. Brig. Gen. Irvin McDowell commanding the U.S. forces, Gen. [P.] G. T. Beauregard commanding the Confederate forces, July 21st 1861. Compiled from a map accompanying the report of Brig. Genl McDowell and a map made under the direction of Genl. Beauregard. Published by authority of the Hon. the Secretary of War in the office of the Chief of Engineers, U.S. Army. 1877. Colored. Scale 1:21,120. 61 × 92 cm.

Gives roads, railroads, hachures, vegetation, drainage, villages, houses, fences, and names of residents. "Dotted lines near Centreville indicate sites of [Union] bivouacs on the night of July 20th. Full lines denote the position of the forces on the next day at the commencement of the engagement at Sudley's Springs; blue marking the United States Forces, and red the Confederates."

Another copy is in the Ezra A. Carman papers, Manuscript Division, L.C., container no. 14.

572.2

U.S. *National Park Service.*

Manassas National Battlefield Park, Virginia [Washington] Government Printing Office, 1971. Colored. Scale ca. 1:48,000 2 maps, each 10 × 16 cm. on sheet 43 × 25 cm.

G3882 .M3 1971 .U5

Descriptive leaflet illustrated with two maps: First Manassas—[verso] Second Manassas.

Map of the first Battle of Manassas (Bull Run), Virginia, fought July 21, 1861. This is one of several battlefield maps published in the 1870s by the U.S. Army's Office of the Chief of Engineers. (See entry no. 572.)

MAP

OF THE

BATTLEFIELD OF BULL RUN VIRGINIA

Brig. Gen. IRVIN McDOWELL Commanding the U.S Forces,

Gen. G.T.BEAUREGARD Commanding the Confederate Forces.

JULY 21ST 1861.

Compiled from a map accompanying the report of Brig.Genl McDowell and a map made under the direction of Genl Beauregard.

Published by authority of the HON. THE SECRETARY OF WAR in the Office of the CHIEF OF ENGINEERS U.S.Army.

1877.

572.3

————Manassas National Battlefield Park, Virginia. Showing action of first battle, July 21, 1861. [Washington] Polygraphic Company of America, April, 1942. Uncolored. Scale ca. 1:126,720. 13 × 17 cm.

Map illustrates National Park Service's descriptive leaflet entitled "Manassas National Battlefield Park, Virginia."

Inset: Second battle, August 1862. 5 × 5 cm.

572.4

————Another issue ([Washington] Government Printing Office [1943?]). Uncolored. Scale ca. 1:90,000. 17 × 23 cm.

Accompanies National Park Service pamphlet entitled "Manassas National Battlefield Park, Virginia." 15 p.

MANASSAS (SECOND)

572.45

Crawford, L.

[Map of the second battle of Manassas, Virginia, showing the positions and movements of the 1st Division, 3rd Army Corps, Army of Virginia, under command of General Rufus King, on August 28, 1862. Signed] Lt. L. Crawford, Sept. 5th, 1878. Colored ms. on tracing paper. Scale not given. 47 × 55 cm.

In the Fitz-John Porter papers, Manuscript Division, L.C., container no. 55.

Pencil drawing with troop positions in red and black ink.

572.5

The field of Bull Run [August 1862] Philadelphia, Thos. Hunter, lith. [18–?] Colored. Scale 1:125,000. 29 × 22 cm.

In the Fitz-John Porter papers, Manuscript Division, L.C., container no. 55.

Map of Manassas battlefield showing "Confederate works," towns, roads, railroads, houses, woodland, rivers, and some relief by hachures.

572.55

General position of the contending armies at 2. p.m. Aug. 30th 1862, when Gen. Fitz John Porter, with his own corps (less Griffin & Piatt) and King's division under Hatch of McDowell's corps attacked Jackson and was turned and attacked by Longstreet. Colored ms. annotations on printed base map. Scale ca. 1:63,360. 24 × 44 cm.

In the Fitz-John Porter papers, Manuscript Division, L.C., container no. 55.

Pen and ink annotations in red, blue, and black ink on a portion of the base map by the U.S. Army Corps of Engineers entitled "Map of N. Eastern Virginia and Vicinity of Washington . . ." published after the first battle of Manassas (entry nos. 469 and 470).

For another copy, with a slightly different title, see entry no. 572.56.

572.56

General position of the contending armies at 2. p.m. Aug. 30th 1862, when Genl Fitz John Porter, with his own corps (5th) and Kings Division under Hatch, of McDowell's Corps, attacked Jackson, and while fighting, was turned and attacked by Longstreet. Colored ms. annotations on printed base map. Scale ca. 1:63,360. 25 × 40 cm.

In the Fitz-John Porter papers, Manuscript Division, L.C., container no. 55.

Pen and ink annotations in red, blue, and black ink on a portion of the base map by the U.S. Army Corps of Engineers entitled "Map of N. Eastern Virginia and Vicinity of Washington . . ." published after the first battle of Manassas (entry nos. 469 and 470).

For another copy, with a slightly different title, see entry no. 572.55.

572.6

Illustrative map of the battle-field of Manassas, Va. showing positions and movements of troops August 29th, 1862. To accompany closing argument of counsel for the government. Positions laid down by him, time of day 6 P.M. H. L. Ripley, del. [Washington, Government Printing Office, 1879] Colored. Scale ca. 1:36,500. 38 × 76 cm. *From* Gardner, Asa Bird. Argument of Asa Bird Gardner, counsel for government, after conclusion of the evidence in the case of Fitz-John Porter, before the board of army officers at West Point, January 1879 (Washington, Government Printing Office, 1879), 233 p.

    G3884 .M25S5 1862 .I42

At head of title: No. 2.

Detailed map of the second battle of Manassas showing Union positions in blue and Confederate positions in red.

572.7

Illustrative map of battle-grounds of August 28th, 29th & 30th, 1862 in the vicinity of Groveton, Prince William Co., Va., of counsel for the government. Chiefly from the survey made under the authority of the Hon. G. W. McCrary, Secretary of War [Washington, Government Printing Office, 1879]. Colored. Scale ca. 1:22,500. 57 × 68 cm. *From* Gardner, Asa Bird. Argument of Asa Bird Gardner, counsel for government, after conclusion of the evidence in the case of Fitz-John Porter, before the board of army officers at West Point, January 1879 (Washington, Govt. Print. Off., 1879) 233 p.

    G3884 .M25S5 1862 .I41

At head of title: No. 1

Accompanied by: Letter-press descriptive of illustrative map no. 1 of counsel for the government. 1 leaf, 31 × 35 cm.

Detailed map of the second battle of Manassas "showing the relative positions of the Confederate and United States armies in the battle of the 29th of August 1862, at 2 p.m., as given in the evidence of witnesses on the trial, in 1862, before the Army Board, in the official reports, and laid down on the map by the counsel."

Base map chiefly from the survey of the battlefield made in June 1878 by Bvt. Maj. Gen. G. K Warren, assisted by Capt. J. A. Judson and H. D. Garden. (See entry no. 577.5.)

572.8

————Another issue. W. Boell, photo-lin. [sic] Phila. G3884 .M25S5 1862 .I4

From the papers of Joseph Roswell Hawley.

Map is annotated in ink on verso: Maj. Gardner's map adopted by Gen. Logan & Gen. Cox.

Accompanied by: Letter-press descriptive of illustrative map no. 1 of counsel for the government. 1 leaf (photocopy), 31 × 35 cm.

Two additional copies, both in poor condition, are in the Fitz-John Porter papers, Manuscript Division, L.C., container no. 55. One copy is marked in ink "Gen. Logan's map" and "Map used by Senator Logan March 5 188[0?]"

573

Judson, J. A.

Map of battle-field of Manassas, Va., giving positions and movements of troops August 30th 1862. From surveys made in June, 1878, by authority of the Hon. Secretary of War, by Bvt. Maj. Gen. G. K. Warren, Major of Engineers, U.S.A., assisted by Capt. J. A. Judson, C.E. (A.A. Gen. "King's Division") and H. D. Gorden, C.E., of Warrenton, Va. J. A. Judson, del. Julius Bien, photo lith, N.Y. Colored. Scale 1:63,360. 22 × 57 cm.

"Positions of troops were given in testimony before the Army Board at West Point, and laid down on maps by the witnesses and officers present on the field."

Indicates four positions of the Union and Confederate troops, roads, railroads, towns, vegetation, drainage, houses, and names of residents.

The names of the principal field commanders are listed below the map title.

573.1

[Map of the second battle of Manassas, Virginia, showing the positions and movements of troops under the command of Gen. Philip Kearny on August 29 and the route of Col. Orlando M. Poe's Brigade in retreat, 6 p.m., August 30, 1862] Uncolored pencil sketch drawn on irregular shaped piece of tracing paper. Scale not given. 38 × 42 cm.

In the Fitz-John Porter papers, Manuscript Division, L.C., container no. 55.

573.15

[Map of the second battle of Manassas, Virginia, showing Union and Confederate troop positions, headquarters of McDowell, Porter and Pope, and the place "Genl. Pope erroneously assigns Porter on the 29th." August 28–29, 1862] Colored ms. annotations on printed base map. Scale ca. 1:63,360. 36 × 63 cm.

In the Fitz-John Porter papers, Manuscript Division, L.C., container no. 55.

Pen and ink annotations in red, blue, and black ink on a portion of the base map by the U.S. Army Corps of Engineers entitled "Map of N. Eastern Virginia and Vicinity of Washington . . ." published after the first battle of Manassas (entry nos. 469 and 470).

573.2

Owen, William M.

[Map of the second battle of Manassas, Virginia, showing positions of the Washington Artillery, C.S.A., August 29, 1862. By William M. Owen] Colored ms. Scale not given. 29 × 22 cm.

In the Fitz-John Porter papers, Manuscript Division, L.C., container no. 55.

Imperfect; the upper right and lower left corners are missing.

Positions of the Washington Artillery at 11:30 a.m. and 1 p.m. are indicated in red ink.

Includes "Extract from Diary of Lieut W. M. Owen, Adjutant of Washn. Artillery."

Endorsed on verso: Maj. Owens of New Orleans, Washington Arty.

573.3

Plan für die schlacht bei Manassas am 28., 29., und 30. August 1862. Hannover, Germany, Helwing'sche Verlagsbuchhandlung [18–?] Uncolored. Scale ca. 1:42,500. 31 × 38 cm.

In the Fitz-John Porter papers, Manuscript Division, L.C., container no. 55.

Imperfect; the upper center and lower right and left corners are missing.

Map of Manassas battlefield showing roads, railroads, houses and names of occupants, field patterns, rivers, woodland, and relief by hachures. Troop positions are not indicated.

573.5

Pope, John.

Battlefield of Manassas, Va. close of the action August

29th, 1862. Bowen & Co., lith., Phila. Uncolored. Scale 1:25,344 ("2½ inches to one mile"). 19 × 22 cm. *From* U.S. Congress. Joint Committee on the Conduct of the War. Supplemental report of the Joint Committee on the Conduct of the War, in two volumes. Supplemental to Senate report no. 142, 38th Congress, 2d session (Washington, Government Printing Office, 1866). v. 2, fol. p. 190.

Accompanies "Report of Major General John Pope to the hon. Committee on the Conduct of the War." 217 p.

"No. 5" is in the upper right margin.

Map indicates roads, railroads, place names, drainage, relief by hachures, and troop positions.

Another copy is in the Fitz-John Porter papers, Manuscript Division, L.C., container no. 55. Handwritten note on verso reads as follows: There is very little of accuracy in this map. Porter is entirely misplaced & thrown some miles in front of his true position. Kings division of McDowell's Corps never reached the position assigned beyond Groveton. Kearney also is thrown too far forward. A map of the positions on 28″ 29″ & 30th was sent to the War Department when Gen. Belknap was there by Gen. Porter before this colored map was thought of—with the request it might be used in compiling any map of 2d Bull Run. The data on that map was verified by Confederate as well as our officers.

573.6

————————Map showing the positions of both armies August 27th, 1862 at night. [Second Manassas battle] Bowen & Co., lith., Philada. Uncolored. Scale 1:190,080 ("3 miles to 1 inch") 17 × 23 cm. *From* U.S. Congress. Joint Committee on the Conduct of the War. Supplemental report of the Joint Committee on the Conduct of the War, in two volumes. Supplemental to Senate report no. 142, 38th Congress, 2d session (Washington, Government Printing Office, 1866). v. 2, fol. p. 190.

Accompanies "Report of Major General John Pope to the hon. Committee on the Conduct of the War." 217 p.

"No. 3" is in the upper right margin.

Map indicates roads, railroads, place names, drainage, and troop positions.

573.7

————————Position of troops at sunset August 28th, 1862. [Second Manassas battle] Bowen & Co., lith., Philada. Uncolored. Scale 1:126,720 ("half an inch to the mile"). 17 × 22 cm. *From* U.S. Congress. Joint Committee on the Conduct of the War. Supplemental report of the Joint Committee on the Conduct of the War, in two volumes. Supplemental to Senate report no. 142, 38th Congress, 2d session (Washington, Government Printing Office, 1866). v. 2, fol. p. 190.

Accompanies "Report of Major General John Pope to the hon. Committee on the Conduct of the War." 217 p.

"No. 4" is in the upper right margin.

Map indicates roads, railroads, place names, drainage, and troop positions.

573.8

Proceedings of a board of army officers in the case Fitz John Porter. Maps part 4. 25 printed maps, many with annotations, 1 manuscript map, and 1 leaf.

In the Fitz-John Porter papers, Manuscript Division, L.C., container no. 55, oversize cabinet 5, drawer 8.

Title from leather label, with lettering in gold leaf, mounted on a sheet of paper.

Contents

[1] Copy of the original McDowell map . . . 38 × 54 cm.

[2] Longstreet & William's map . . . 57 × 67 cm.

[3] Charles Marshall map, Oct. 16, 1878 . . . 57 × 67 cm.

[4] Capt. Douglas Pope map, Bvt. Brig. Genl. C. B. Barnes map, Major Fox map, [and] citizen Monroe map . . . 57 × 67 cm.

[5] Charles Duffy map, Oct. 4, 1878 and E. P. Brook's map . . . 57 × 67 cm. (For another copy, see no. 19.)

[6] H. Kyd. Douglas map . . . 57 × 67 cm.

[7] Major B. S. White map . . . 57 × 67 cm.

[8] Chaplain J. Landstreet map . . . 57 × 67 cm.

[9] John H. Piatt map, Nv. 23, 1878 . . . 57 × 67 cm.

[10] Genl. Thos. L. Rosser, comd'g 5th Va. Cavalry, Maj. Genl. J. E. B. Stuart's Division [map] . . . 57 × 67 cm.

[11] Dyer map, Jan. 2nd 1879 . . . 57 × 67 cm.

[12] Illustrative map accompanying argument of petitioner's counsel. Positions of troops delineated by his counsel in 1862 & 1863. No. 2 . . . 57 × 67 cm.

[13] Illustrative map accompanying argument of petitioner's counsel. Positions of troops delineated by his counsel. No. 3 . . . 57 × 67 cm.

[14] "Illustrative map" accompanying argument of petitioner's counsel. "Positions" of the troops delineated by his counsel in 1879. No. 4 = No. 14 of maps in Board Record. 12. M. Aug. 29th '62. 60 × 71 cm.

[15] Illustrative map accompanying argument of petitioner's counsel in 1879. Position of troops delineated by his counsel. No. 5. 6, P.M. Aug. 29th '62 . . . 60 × 71 cm.

[16] Illustrative map accompanying argument of petitioner's counsel. Positions of troops delineated by his counsel, 1879. No. 6. 12. M. Aug. 30th, '62 . . . 60 × 71 cm.

[17] Illustrative map accompanying argument of petitioner's counsel of battle-field of Manassas, Va., giving positions and movements of troops August 29th, 1862 . . .[and] August 30th, 1862 . . . 2 maps on one sheet 49 × 60 cm.

[18] Letter-press descriptive of illustrative map no. 1 of counsel for the government. 33 × 39 cm.

[19] Charles Duffy map, Oct. 4, 1878 and E. P. Brook's map . . . 57 × 67 cm. (For another copy, see no. 5.)

[20] No. 2 illustrative map of the battle-field of Man-

assas, Va. showing positions and movements of troops August 29th, 1862. To accompany closing argument of counsel for the government, positions laid down by him, time of day 6 P.M. 38 × 75 cm.

[21] Board map no. 1 . . . Probable positions of the opposing forces at noon August 29th 1862, as indicated by the information then in possession of the Union generals. 76 × 68 cm.

[22] Board map, no. 2 . . . General situation at 4.30 P.M. August 29th 1862. 57 × 67 cm.

[23] Board map no. 3 . . . Supposed military situation under which the 4.30 P.M. order was issued August 29th 1862. 57 × 67 cm.

[24] Map of the battle-grounds of August 28th, 29th, & [3]0th, 1862 . . . 60 × 71 cm. (No. "23" is written in pencil at the head of the title.)

[26] Map of the three battle fields of First Bull Run, July 21st, 1861; Second Bull Run, August 28th, 29th, & 30th, 1862; Bristoe Station, October 14th, 1863. Compiled by Bvt. Maj. Gen. G. K. Warren, U.S. Army in January, 1879. Col. ms. on tracing linen. 86 × 94 cm. (Attached to entry 25 above.)

[27] Central Virginia showing Lieut. Gen'l. U. S. Grant's campaign and marches of the armies under his command in 1864–5. 79 × 80 cm.

574

Russell, Robert E. L.

Second Manassas Campaign. A series of 21 pen and ink maps showing details of battles of Gainesville, Groveton, Second Manassas, and Chantilly (August 28–September 1, 1862). Drawn by Robert E. Lee Russell. Baltimore, 1943. 1 p. l., 21 maps. Photocopy (positive). 47 × 59 cm.

G1292 .B8S5 R83 1943 folio

Bound series of maps hand-colored to show infantry and cavalry positions. Geography and Map Division also has an unbound negative photocopy.

Listed in C. E. Le Gear's *A List of Geographical Atlases in the Library of Congress* (Washington, Library of Congress, 1973), v. 7, no. 10666.

575

————Second Manassas Campaign, August 17–September 1, 1862. A series of pen and ink maps drawn by Robert E. Lee Russell. Baltimore, 1943. 2 p.l., 30 maps. Photocopy (positive). 47 × 59 cm.

G1292 .B8S5 R8 1943 folio

Bound series of maps hand-colored to show infantry and cavalry positions.

"Synopsis of Second Manassas Campaign" precedes Map 1.

Geography and Map Division also has an unbound negative photocopy.

Listed in C. E. Le Gear's *A List of Geographical Atlases in the Library of Congress* (Washington, Library of Congress, 1973), v. 7, no. 10667.

576

Sketch of 2nd Manassas, August 29th 1862 [and] sketch of 2nd Manassas, Aug. 30th, 1862. Uncolored. Scale not given. 2 maps on one sheet, each 12 × 19 cm. Over-all size 31 × 25 cm.

G3884 .M25S5 1862 .S5 Vault

Shows roads, railroads, troop positions, towns, and drainage. Names of commanders are keyed by numbers to the map, and Union headquarters are indicated by letters.

The Geography and Map Division has two copies of each map, each of which has been annotated in red ink by the same hand. One set was transferred to the Division in 1933 from the papers of Jubal Early in the Manuscript Division, L.C. The other set was received in 1905 from an unnamed source.

577

U.S. *Army. Corps of Engineers.*

Map[s] exhibiting part of the operations of the Army of Virginia under the command of Major General John Pope. Battlefield of Cedar Mountain, Aug. 9th 1862. The positions of the troops on the night of Aug. 27th and at sunset Aug. 28th 1862, and the battlefield of Manassas, Va. at the close of the action on the 29th of Aug. 1862. Published by authority of the Hon. the Secretary of War, office of the Chief of Engineers, U.S. Army. Colored. Various scales. 4 maps on one sheet, each approximately 16 × 23 cm. Over-all size 51 × 58 cm.

Maps from "Report of Maj. Gen. John Pope to the Committee on the Conduct of the War."

Each map gives troop positions, roads, railroads, towns, drainage, and relief by hachures.

577.4

Warren, Gouverneur K.

Map of battle-field of Manassas, Va., giving positions and movements of troops, August 30th, 1862. From surveys made in June 1878 by authority of the Hon. Secretary of War by Bvt. Maj. Gen. G. K. Warren, Major of Engineers, U.S.A., assisted by Capt. J. A. Judson, C.E. (A. A. Gen. "King's Division") and H. D. Garden, C.E., of Warrenton, Va. J. A. Judson, del. Julius Bien, photo lith., N.Y. Colored. Scale 1:63,360. 22 × 56 cm.

"Positions of troops were given in testimony before the Army Board at West Point, and laid down on maps by the witnesses and officers present on the field."

"The Federal troops are shown in blue; the Confederate troops in red."

"The red arrows show the route of the Confederate troops, Aug. 30th, p.m."

Map has been annotated in red ink to show "Rickett's route on 29th," "Porter 9:20 a.m. 29th," and "Porter's corps 9:30 a.m. 29."

577.5

——————Map of battle-grounds of August 28th, 29th, & 30th 1862 in the vicinity of Groveton, Prince William Co., Va. Made by the authority of the Hon. G. W. McCrary, Secretary of War. Surveyed in June 1878 by Bvt. Maj. Gen. G. K. Warren, Major of Engineers, U.S.A. assisted by Capt. J. A. Judson, C.E. (A. A. Gen. "King's Division") and H. D. Garden, C.E., (late Capt. & A.A. Gen. Confed. Army). [Washington] U.S. Army, Engineer Department [1878] Uncolored. Scale 1:21,120. 60 × 72 cm.

At head of title: Engineer Department, U.S. Army. Bvt. Maj. Gen. A. A. Humphreys, Brig. Gen. & Chief of Engineers.

Endorsed (facsim.): Official copy G. K. Warren Maj. Engrs. & Bvt. Maj. Gen. U.S.A.

Base map of the battlefield of Second Manassas showing roads, railroads, houses and names of residents, drainage, and vegetation. Troop positions are not indicated.

The following sentence below the map title has been ruled out: Note—There will be a descriptive memoir, and a sheet exhibiting hill topography, to accompany this map.

577.52

——————Another edition. Newport, R.I., Engineer Office, U.S. Army, August 27th 1878.

In the Fitz-John Porter papers, Manuscript Division, L.C., container no. 55.

2 copies. "Official copy G. K. Warren Maj. Engrs. & Bvt. Maj. Gen. U.S.A." has been ruled out on both copies.

Copy 1 has been annotated as follows: The red line on this map shows "McDowell's Ride" from 3-½ on the afternoon of Aug. 28 to midnight the same day.

"General 'McDowell's Ride' Aug. 28th '62" is written in black and red ink in the upper margin.

Annotated on verso as follows: "McDowell's Ride." Aug. 28th 1862. This original map laid before the Board at West Point—See Mr. Choate's argument.

Copy 2 has been annotated as follows: The blue line on this copy shows 'McDowell's Ride' on the afternoon of the 28th of August 1862 and during the first half of the night following. G.K.W. [i.e., G. K. Warren].

"Sheet showing 'McDowell's Ride' Aug. 28, 62" is written in blue pencil in the top margin.

577.6

——————Another edition. Colored. Scale 1:21,120. 57 × 67 cm.

G3884 .M25S5 1862 .W3 Vault

Alternate title: Illustrative map. Accompanying argument of petitioner's counsel. Positions of troops delineated by his counsel. No. 5. 6, p.m., Aug. 29th '62.

"The Federal troops are shown in blue, the Confederate troops in red."

"The contours of this map correctly represent the directions of the ridges and valleys and their approximate relative elevation. The datum plane is arbitrary . . . The h[e]ights of the principal eminences are estimated and may be in error from 5 to 20 feet."

From the papers of Joseph Roswell Hawley. L.C. copy is annotated in ink, "Porter's map no. 4—gives the correct positions at 12.M, also where Pope supposed Porter was."

577.7

——————Another edition.

Alternate title: Illustrated map. Accompanying argument of petitioner's counsel. Positions of troops delineated by his counsel. No. 6. 6, p.m., Aug. 29th [date is changed in ink to 30] '62.

In the Fitz-John Porter papers, Manuscript Division, L.C., container no. 55.

Three copies, all in poor condition. One copy is annotated in ink to show "Monroe's Hill. Where Pope erroneously put Porter on his map sent to government."

578

Webb, Willard.

[Second Manassas campaign. July 1–Aug. 30, 1862] Uncolored. Various scales. 1 pencil sketch and 6 printed maps on 5 sheets. Each 17 × 22 cm. or smaller.

Maps indicate "Jackson's flank march showing ultimate position behind R.R. grade," and positions of troops on July 1, Aug. 17, Aug. 20, Aug. 29, sunset Aug. 30, and at the "close of battle," Aug. 30.

Maps are accompanied by a list of the "organization" of the opposing forces, "approximate losses, the Rappahannock to the Potomac," and a brief description of the campaign.

579

Wells, Jacob.

Relative positions of forces at sunset, Aug. 26, 1862. [2nd Manassas campaign] Uncolored. Scale ca. 1:520,000. 10 × 9 cm. *From* Century illustrated monthly magazine, v. 31, Jan. 1886. p. 446.

Map extends from White Plains south to Kelley's Ford, and from Orlean east to Manassas Junction.

580

——————Relative positions of forces at sunset, Aug. 27, 1862. [2nd Manassas Campaign] Uncolored. Scale ca.

1:570,000. 6 × 10 cm. *From* Century illustrated monthly magazine, v. 31, Jan. 1886. p. 447.

Map extends from White Plains south to Fayetteville, and from Orlean east to Fairfax Station.

581

——————Relative positions of forces at sunset, Aug. 28, 1862. [2nd Manassas Campaign] Uncolored. Scale ca. 1:550,000. 5 × 8 cm. *From* Century illustrated monthly magazine, v. 31, Jan. 1886. p. 447.

Map of the environs of Manassas Junction.

582

——————Second battle of Bull Run. Position of troops at sunset, Aug. 29, 1862. Uncolored. Scale ca. 1:62,000. 18 × 14 cm. *From* Century illustrated monthly magazine, v. 31, Jan. 1886. p. 456.

Indicates position of troops, cavalry and skirmishes, roads, railroads, towns, rivers, houses, names of residents, hachures, and vegetation.

583

——————Second battle of Bull Run. Positions of troops Aug. 30, 1862. Uncolored. Scale 1:62,000. 17 × 14 cm. *From* Century illustrated monthly magazine, v. 31, Feb. 1886. p. 611.

"Map of the last day's fighting," showing the first and last position of the troops, roads, railroads, towns, rivers, houses, names of residents, hachures, and vegetation.

MECHANICSVILLE

584

——————Plan of the battle of Mechanicsville, June 26 [1862] Uncolored. Scale ca. 1:36,000. 9 × 9 cm. *From* Century illustrated monthly magazine, v. 30, June 1885. p. 300.

Gives troop positions, batteries, roads, rivers relief by hachures, and a few houses and names of occupants.

A brief description of the battle appears below the map.

584.1

——————Another issue.

Another issue, without title, and containing less information.

METOMKIN INLET

584.4

U.S. *Coast Survey.*

Metomkin Inlet, Virginia. From a trigonometrical survey under the direction of A. D. Bache, Superintendent of the survey of the coast of the United States. Triangulation by

John Farley, Assist. Topography by Geo. D. Wise and A. M. Harrison, Assists. Hydrography by the party under the direction of A. M. Harrison, Assist. Engd. by W. A. Thompson & J. G. Thompson. [Washington, U.S. Coast Survey] 1862. Uncolored. Scale 1:20,000. 55 × 49 cm. *From its* Report of the Superintendent of the Coast Survey, showing the progress of the survey during the year 1862 (Washington, Government Printing Office, 1864). Map 16.

"No. 16" is in the upper left corner.

584.5

——————Another issue. (*Its* no. 378)

"No. 378" is printed in the upper left corner.

Title has been changed to read "Matomkin Inlet, Virginia."

Imperfect; the lower left corner is missing.

NEW MARKET

585

Colonna, B. Allison.

New Market, Va., battlefield May 15, 1864. [Surveyed in 1910–12 by B. Allison Colonna under the direction of B. A. Colonna, Cadet Captain, D Co., Corps of Cadets, Virginia Military Institute, May 15, 1864, and late asst., U.S. Coast & Geodetic Survey in charge of office. Wm. E. Johnson, draftsman. Norris Peters Co., photo-lith., Washington, D.C. ©1914. Colored. Scale 1:15,840. 39 × 40 cm.

"This map shows the battlefield as it was May 15, 1864. It is based on the Woodstock, Va., sheet of the U.S. Geological Survey as shown in the subsketch [inset]. The woods, orchards, houses and other cultural features are by Frank J. Bushong, the best living authority, confirmed by Mr. Hupp, of Sperryville, Va., who also pointed out on the ground the Imboden-Boyd action of May 13, 1864. The places where certain ones fell are from lifelong residents of New Market, who were there on the day of the battle, and from J. H. Dwyer, of Woodson's Missourians."

Shows troop and artillery positions, roads, drainage, vegetation, and relief by contour lines and hachures. Fifty important points are keyed by number to a list to the left of the map.

Inset: [Topographic map of the Shenandoah Valley extending from Rinkerton to Melrose showing events associated with the battle of New Market.] 24 × 15 cm. (irregular shape).

586

——————Topographical sketch of the New Market, Va., battlefield of May 15, 1864, made under the direction of B. A. Colonna, Cadet Captain, "D" Co., Corps of Cadets, V.M.I. in action, and late Assistant in Charge, U.S. Coast and Geodetic Survey Office, by B. Allison Colonna, June 24 to

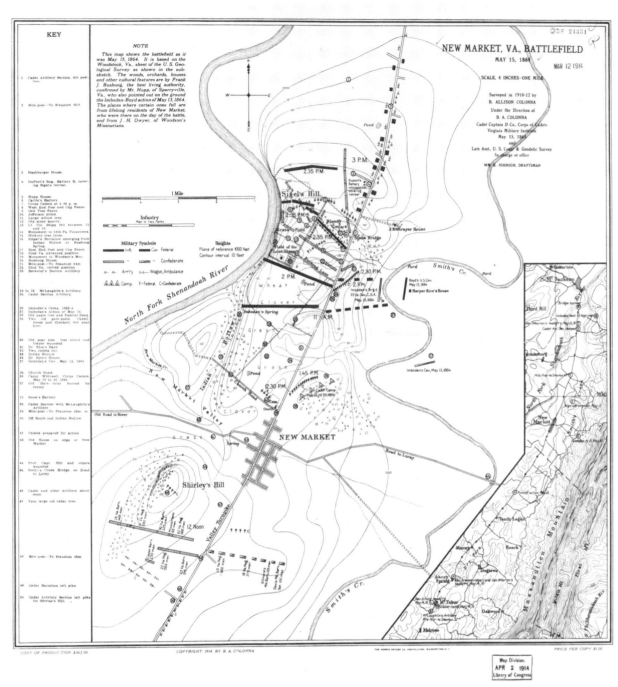

Sat., July 2, 1910, inclusive. ©1912. Uncolored. Scale 1:15,840. 54 × 37 cm.

"The sketch is of the battlefield as it was in May, 1864. The woods, orchards, houses and other cultural features and the places where certain ones fell are from lifelong residents of New Market who were there on the day of the battle."

Inset: [Sketch of part of the Woodstock, Virginia, sheet of the U.S. Geological Survey] 30 × 14 cm. (triangle shape).

Map of the Battle of New Market, Virginia, fought May 15, 1864. Included among the Confederate forces at this battle was a battalion of 247 Virginia Military Institute cadets of whom 10 were killed and 47 were wounded. Representative of the many battlefield maps published after the war, this particular one was surveyed under the direction of cadet captian B. A. Colonna who participated in the engagement. Colonna later became Assistant in Charge of Office, U.S. Coast and Geodetic Survey (now known as the National Ocean Service). (See entry no. 585.)

Indicates roads, contour lines, hachures, drainage, vegetation, and "Cadet Camp Whitwell, May 16, 1864."

587

Russell, Robert E. L.

Charge of the V.M.I. cadets. Battle of New Market, Va., May 19 [i.e., 15] 1864. Baltimore, 1933. Photocopy (positive). Scale not given. 19 × 12 cm.

"Sketch map."

Hand-colored positive photocopy. Geography and Map Division also has a negative photocopy.

NORFOLK

587.5

Owner, William.

Norfolk & environs. [1863] Uncolored ms. Scale ca. 1:205,000. 20 × 12 cm. *In his* Diary, v. 4, tipped-in at end of volume.

In the William Owner papers, Manuscript Division, L.C., container no. 1.

Map indicates the fort at Norfolk, Camp Butler at Newport News, Fort Monroe, and Fort Calhoun. Also shown are roads, railroads, and houses.

Volume 4 of the diary covers from February 13 to June 27, 1863.

588

U.S. *Coast Survey.*

[Vessels destroyed at Norfolk, 1861] Uncolored ms. Scale not given. 45 × 61 cm.

G3884 .N6S5 1861 .U5 Vault

Title from verso.

Stamped in lower right corner: U.S.C. & G. Survey. Library and archives. Feb. 24, 1902. Ass: no. 738.

Pen and ink sketch of the "U.S. Navy Yard" showing buildings, drydock, and location of the ships *Pennsylvania, Columbia, Raritan,* and *Delaware.*

NORTH ANNA

589

Howell, C. W., *and others.*

Map of the battle fields of North Anna showing the field of operations of the Army of the Potomac commanded by Maj. Gen. George G. Meade, U.S.A., from May 3d to 27th 1864. Surveyed under the orders of Bvt. Col. J. C. Duane, Major of Engineers, Chief Engineer Army of the Potomac, by Bvt. Maj. C. W. Howell, 1st Lieut. of Engineers, assisted by Messrs. L. C. Oswell, L. Bell, and R. B. Talfor,

Topographical Engineers. J. Bien, lith., N.Y. [1865?] Colored. Scale 1:15,840. 57 × 89 cm.

G3882 .N4S5 1865 .H6

Detailed map showing entrenchments, batteries, Union headquarters on May 24 and May 25–26, roads, railroads, bridges, houses, names of residents, drainage, vegetation, and relief by hachures.

Another copy is from the Orlando M. Poe papers, Manuscript Division, L.C. (G3882 .N4S5 1865 .H61)

Another copy is in the John M. Schofield papers, Manuscript Division, L.C., container no. 74. Number 6 is written in red ink on the verso of the map.

590

Michler, Nathaniel.

North Anna. [May 22–27, 1864] From surveys under the direction of B'v't. Brig.-Gen. N. Michler, Maj. of Engineers. 1867. Uncolored. Scale ca. 1:67,000. 13 × 14 cm. *From* Century illustrated monthly magazine, v. 34, June 1887, p. 292.

"Union works are marked . . .U" and "Confederate works are marked . . .C."

Shows roads, houses, names of residents, relief by hachures, drainage, mills, towns, railroads, and vegetation.

590.1

——————North Anna. [May 1864] From surveys under the direction of Bvt. Brig. Gen. N. Michler, Maj. of Engineers, by command of Bvt. Maj. Genl. A. A. Humphreys, Brig. Genl. & Chief of Engineers. Surveyed and drawn by Maj: J. E. Weyss, assisted by F. Theilkuhl, J. Strasser & G. Thompson. Photolith. by the N. Y. Lithographing, Engraving & Printing Co., Julius Bien, Supt. 1867. Colored. Scale 1:21,120. 41 × 48 cm.

In this issue, the map is printed on a yellow background with the North Anna and Little rivers colored blue.

Union entrenchments are colored blue, and Confederate entrenchments red. Indicates roads, railroads, drainage, vegetation, hachures, houses, fences, and names of occupants.

590.2

——————Another issue.

Background and water are not colored.

591

Russell, Robert E. L.

The North Anna and movement from Spottsylvania, May 21–26, 1864, between Lee, 50,000, and Grant, 100,000. Lee's famous "hog-snout" line. A series of 12 pen and ink maps drawn by Mr. Robert E. L. Russell. [Baltimore, 1931–1933] 1 p. l., 12 maps. Photocopy (positive). 43 × 59 cm.

G1292 .S6S5 R83 1933 folio

Bound series of maps with Confederate positions colored red by hand. Maps 1 to 4 are dated 1933, and maps 5 to 12 are dated 1931. Geography and Map Division also has an unbound negative photocopy.

Listed in C. E. Le Gear's *A List of Geographical Atlases in the Library of Congress* (Washington, Library of Congress, 1973), v. 7, no. 10663.

592

————Revised version. [Baltimore, 1933–1935] 1 p. l., 12 maps. Photocopy (positive). 39 × 54 cm.

G1292 .S6S5 R 1935 folio

Bound series of maps showing Confederate positions in red and Union positions in blue. Maps 1 and 4 are dated 1933, and maps 5 to 12 are dated 1935. Geography and Map Division also has an unbound negative photocopy.

Listed in C. E. Le Gear's *A List of Geographical Atlases in the Library of Congress* (Washington, Library of Congress, 1973), v. 7, no. 10664.

NORTH LANDING RIVER

592.5

U.S. *Coast Survey.*

Preliminary chart of North Landing River (head of Currituck Sound), Virginia & N. Carolina. From a trigonometrical survey under the direction of A. D. Bache, Superintendent of the survey of the coast of the United States. Triangulation by J. J. S. Hassler, Assistant. Topography & hydrography by John Mechan, Assist. Redd. drng. by F. Fairfax. Engd. by J. G. Thompson. Bowen & Co. lith., Philada. [Washington, U.S. Coast Survey] 1861. Uncolored. Scale 1:40,000. 54 × 32 cm. *From its* Report of the Superintendent of the Coast Survey, showing the progress of the survey during the year 1861 (Washington, Government Printing Office, 1862). Map 12.

"No. 12" is in the upper left corner.

OCCOQUAN RIVER

593

Fords on Occoquan and Bull Run [186–] Colored ms. Scale not given. 42 × 36 cm.

From the Jubal Early collection in the Manuscript Division, L.C.

G3883.F2S5 186–.F6 Vault

"For Col. Harrston" is written in pencil below the legend.

Map of part of Prince William and Fairfax counties, Virginia, showing "military roads to fords," "military roads from post to post," H.Q at Manassas Station, roads, drainage, and fords.

593.2

Garton, M. N.

Sketch of the Occoquan. M. N. Garton, Washington, D.C. [186–] Colored ms. Scale ca. 1:63,360. 52 × 39 cm.

G3882.O26 186–.G3 Vault

"211, L. Sheet 9."

Title is from the verso.

Pen and ink and pencil sketch map, oriented with west at the top, showing rivers and streams, fords, mills, roads, distances between selected places, villages, and houses. The map depicts the Occoquan River from Brentsville to the town of Occoquan.

Pencil note at top of sheet reads "Genl. Barnard: Mr. Garton, who acted as guide to Bull Run, requested me to call your attention to him, in case any more information should be desired concerning this country. He made this map, and has made others for me. [Signed ?] Lt. of Eng. U.S.A."

"Transferred from Office of Chf. Engr., Defenses of Washington, to Engr. Dept. Jan'y 1866."

Stamped on verso: By Transfer, Chief Engineers Office, War Department.

PENINSULA

594

Abbot, Henry L.

White House to Harrisons Landing. Prepared by command of Maj. Gen. George B. McClellan U.S.A., commanding Army of the Potomac. Compilation under the direction of Brig. Gen. A. A. Humphreys, by Capt. H. L. Abbot, Top. Engrs. Engraved by W. H. Dougal. [1862] Uncolored. Scale ca. 1:63,360. 89 × 70 cm.

At head of title: Campaign map, Army of the Potomac, map no. 3.

Shows fortifications, towns, roads, railroads, houses, names of residents, vegetation, drainage, and relief by hachures.

594.1

————Another issue. Julius Bien & Co., photo lith., N.Y.

595

————Another edition. Photographic reduction by L. E. Walker, Treasury Department. Uncolored. Scale ca. 1:95,000. 60 × 48 cm.

Principal rivers are hand-colored blue.

596

————Williamsburg to White House. Prepared by command of Maj. Gen. George B. McClellan, U.S.A., commanding Army of the Potomac. Compilation under the direction of Brig. Gen. A. A. Humphreys, by Capt. H. L. Abbot, Top. Eng'rs. Engraved by W. H. Dougal. [1862] Uncolored. Scale ca. 1:63,360. 67 × 60 cm.

At head of title: Campaign maps, Army of the Potomac, map no. 2.

Shows fortifications, towns, roads, houses, names of residents, vegetation, drainage, and relief by hachures.

597

————————Another issue. Julius Bien & Co., photo lith., N.Y.

598

————————Another edition. This map compiled by Capt. H. L. Abbot, Top. Eng'rs, September 1862. Photographic reduction by L. E. Walker, Treasury Department. Uncolored. Scale ca. 1:95,000. 46 × 41 cm.

Principal rivers are hand-colored blue.

599

————————Yorktown to Williamsburg. Prepared by command of Maj. Gen. George B. McClellan, U.S.A., commanding Army of the Potomac. Compilation under the direction of Brig. Gen. A. A. Humphreys, by Capt. H. L. Abbot, Top. Eng'rs. Engraved by W. H. Dougal. [1862] Uncolored. Scale ca. 1:63,360. 86 × 56 cm.

At head of title: Campaign maps, Army of the Potomac, map no. 1.

Shows fortifications, towns, roads, houses, names of residents, vegetation, drainage, and relief by hachures.

600

————————Another edition. This map compiled by Capt. H. L. Abbot, Top. Eng'rs., September 1862. Photographic reduction by L. E. Walker, Treasury Department. Uncolored. Scale ca. 1:95,000. 59 × 39 cm.

Principal rivers are hand-colored blue.

601

Cram, Thomas J.

Extract from "Fort Monroe, Norfolk, Suffolk, and Yorktown with their connections and surroundings for military purposes, compiled under the direction of T. J. Cram, Col. a.d.c., Lieut. Col. T. E., Maj. Genl. J. E. Wool, U.S.A. commdg. Feby. 1862." Photocopy (positive). Scale ca. 1:60,000. 65 × 58 cm.

G3882 .P4S5 1862 .C7 Vault

"Bureau of Topogl. Engineers, Washington, D.C., March 21, 1862.—D.C."

Base map covers the eastern portion of the Virginia Peninsula, from Yorktown to Fortress Monroe and indicates engagements, fortifications, roads, towns, houses and names

of a few residents, drainage, and soundings. Fortifications are colored red, woods are green, and marshes are brown.

602

Hare, J. Knowles

Hare's map of the vicinity of Richmond, and Peninsular campaign in Virginia. Showing also the interesting localities along the James, Chickahominy and York Rivers. Compiled from the official maps of the War Department. New York, W. Reid Gould, 1862. Colored. Scale ca. 1:190,080. 50 × 85 cm.

"Entered according to Act of Congress, in the year 1862, by J. Knowles Hare . . ." Copyright number "401 Jan. 22, 1863" is written in ink in the lower margin. "Copyright Library May 12, 1863" is stamped in the right margin.

Indicates location and dates of battles, forts, "line of Union advance" and route of "Union retreat," roads, railroads, county names and boundaries, towns, and drainage. Soundings are given for the York and James rivers.

Inset: A general map of the seat of war [eastern Virginia, Maryland, and North Carolina]. Scale ca. 1:2,800,000. 9 × 15 cm.

602.2

Johnson, Alvin Jewett.

Johnson's map of the vicinity of Richmond, and Peninsular campaign in Virginia. Showing also the interesting localities along the James, Chickahominy and York Rivers. Compiled from the official maps of the War Department. By Johnson and Ward. [New York, ©1862] Colored. Scale ca. 1:190,000. 45 × 68 cm.

G3882 .V5S5 1862 .J6

"Entered according to Act of Congress, in the year 1862 by J. Knowles Hare." All issues of the map carry this copyright statement.

"Geographical index, or ready reference," p. 42–43 is printed on the verso.

Map is separate.

Map is from Richard S. Fisher's *A Chronological History of the Civil War in America* (entry no. 37.8) or an edition of Johnson's *New Illustrated (Steel Plate) Family Atlas* probably published before 1864. This issue lacks printed map numbers whereas the map appearing in the 1864 and 1865 editions of Johnson and Ward's atlases (entry nos. 602.25–602.3) are numbered 35–36.

From the Benton-Jones map coll., no. 250/19. A second copy in this collection is numbered 269/21.

Map indicates county names and boundaries, place names, rivers and streams, roads and railroads, soundings in the York and James rivers, troop movements, and battle sites. The map first appeared under the title "Hare's Map of the Vicinity of Richmond, and Peninsular Campaign in Virginia . . ." (see entry no. 602).

602.25

————By Johnson and Ward. *In* Johnson's new illustrated (steel plate) family atlas. New York, Johnson and Ward, 1864. Map 35–36.

G1019 .J5 1864 fol.

"Geographical index, or ready reference," p. 47–48 is on the verso.

Listed in P. L. Phillips's *A List of Geographical Atlases in the Library of Congress* (Washington, Government Printing Office, 1909), v. 1, no. 843.

602.3

————By Johnson and Ward. *In* Johnson's new illustrated (steel plate) family atlas. New York, Johnson and Ward, 1865. Map 35–36.

G1019 .J5 1865 fol.

"Geographical index, or ready reference," p. 47–48 is on the verso.

There are no obvious differences between the 1864 and 1865 printings of this map.

For table of contents see P. L. Phillips's *A List of Geographical Atlases in the Library of Congress* (Washington, Government Printing Office, 1920), v. 4, no. 4345.

602.35

————By A. J. Johnson, New York. *In* Johnson's new illustrated family atlas of the world. New York, A. J. Johnson, 1866. Map 36–37.

G1019 .J5 1866 fol.

"Geographical index, or ready reference," p. 48–49 is on the verso.

For table of contents see P. L. Phillips's *A List of Geographical Atlases in the Library of Congress* (Washington, Government Printing Office, 1920), v. 4, no. 4346.

602.4

————By A. J. Johnson, New York. *In* Johnson's new illustrated family atlas of the world. New York, A. J. Johnson, 1867. Map 36–37.

G1019 .J5 1867 fol.

"Geographical index, or ready reference," p. 48–49 is on the verso.

There are no obvious differences between the 1866 and the 1867 printings of this map.

602.45

————By A. J. Johnson, New York. *In* Johnson's new illustrated family atlas of the world. New York, A. J. Johnson, 1868. Map 37–38.

G1019 .J5 1868 fol.

"Geographical index, or ready reference," p. 49 and "Appendix to the geographical index," p. [50] are on the verso.

For table of contents see P. L. Phillips's *A List of Geographical Atlases in the Library of Congress* (Washington, Government Printing Office, 1920), v. 4, no. no. 4349.

602.5

————By A. J. Johnson, New York. *In* Johnson's new illustrated family atlas of the world. New York, A. J. Johnson, 1869. Map 35–36.

G1019.J5 1869 fol.

"Geographical index, or ready reference," p. 35–36 is on the verso.

Listed in C. E. Le Gear's *A List of Geographical Atlases in the Library of Congress* (Washington, Library of Congress, 1973), v. 7, no. 6162.

602.55

————By A. J. Johnson, New York. *From* Johnson's new illustrated family atlas of the world. New York, A. J. Johnson, 1869. Map 35–36.

G3882 .V5S5 1869 .J6

Map is separate.

From the Benton-Jones map coll., no. 337/38.

602.6

————By A. J. Johnson, New York. *In* Johnson's new illustrated family atlas of the world. New York, A. J. Johnson, 1870. Map 49–50.

G1019.J5 1870 fol.

"Geographical index, or ready reference," p. 50–51 is on the verso.

Listed in P. L. Phillips's *A List of Geographical Atlases in the Library of Congress* (Washington, Government Printing Office, 1909), v. 1, no. 858.

602.65

————By A. J. Johnson, New York. *From* Johnson's new illustrated family atlas of the world. New York, A. J. Johnson, 1870. Map 49–50.

G3882 .V5S5 1870 .J6

Map separate.

"Geographical index, or ready reference," p. 50–51 is on the verso.

From the Benton-Jones map coll., no. 201/25.

602.7

————By A. J. Johnson, New York. [187–]

G3882 .V5S5 187– .J6

Numbered 49–50.

Similar to the preceding map, but lacks "Geographical index, or ready reference" on the verso. The map is from an edition of *Johnson's New Illustrated Family Atlas of the World* published after 1870 and before 1883.

602.75

————————Published by Alvin J. Johnson & son, New York. *In* Johnson's *new illustrated family atlas of the world.* New York, A. J. Johnson & Co., 1883, [© 1882] Map 49–50.

　　G1019.J5 1883 fol.

　　Verso of the map is blank.

　　Listed in P. L. Phillips's *A List of Geographical Atlases in the Library of Congress* (Washington, Government Printing Office, 1909), v. 1, no. 913.

602.8

————————Alvin J. Johnson & Co., New York. *In* Johnson's *new illustrated family atlas of the world.* New York, A. J. Johnson & Co., 1884. Map 49–50.

　　G1019.J5 1884 fol.

　　Verso of the map is blank.

　　Listed in P. L. Phillips's *A List of Geographical Atlases in the Library of Congress* (Washington, Government Printing Office, 1909), v. 1, no. 918.

602.85

————————Alvin J. Johnson & Co., New York. *In* Johnson's *new illustrated family atlas of the world.* New York, A. J. Johnson & Co., 1885. Map 49–50.

　　G1019.J5 1885 fol.

　　Verso of the map is blank.

　　There are no obvious differences between the 1884 and 1885 printings of this map.

　　Listed in C. E. Le Gear's *A List of Geographical Atlases in the Library of Congress* (Washington, Library of Congress, 1973), v. 7, no. 6224.

603

[Map of the part of Virginia lying between the York and James Rivers, showing battles and routes of Union forces, 1861–62] Uncolored ms. Scale not given. 56 × 75 cm.

　　G3882 .P4S5 1862 .M3 Vault

　　Railroads, towns, rivers, and county names and boundaries are given.

603.5

Owner, William.

[Map of the Virginia Peninsula. 1862] Uncolored ms. Scale ca. 1:202,500. 20 × 31 cm. *In his* Diary, v. 2, tipped-in at end of volume.

　　In the William Owner papers, Manuscript Division, L.C., container no. 1.

　　Map indicates roads, railroads, place names, rivers, and houses. Fortifications are shown at Fort Darling on the James River.

　　Volume 2 of the diary covers from February 1 to September 11, 1862.

"On to Richmond" appears at the top of the map.

604

U.S. *Army. Corps of Topographical Engineers.*

　　Part of the map of the military department of S.E Virginia and Fort Monroe, showing the approaches to Richmond and Petersburg, compiled in the Bureau of Topographical Engineers of the War Department, 1861, with additions and corrections from the map of the siege of Yorktown and the campaign maps of the Army of the Potomac, compiled by Capt. H. L. Abbot, Corps Topogl. Engrs. Engraved on stone by J. Schedler, N.Y. 1862. Uncolored. Scale 1:80,000. 73 × 126 cm. Cut in 4 parts, each approx. 37 × 63 cm.

　　Gives fortifications, towns, roads, railroads, houses, names of residents, and drainage.

605

————————Part of the map of the military department of S.E. Virginia and Fort Monroe showing the approaches to Richmond and Petersburg, compiled in the Bureau of Topographical Engineers of the War Department, with additions and corrections from Gen. Barnard's map of the siege of Yorktown, Gen. Humphrey's campaign maps of the Army of the Potomac, compiled by Capt. H. L. Abbot, Corps Topogl. Engineers, 1862, and Brig. Gen. Weitzel's sketch of the operations against Fort Darling, May, 1864. Engraved on stone by J. Schedler, N.Y. [1864] Uncolored. Scale 1:80,000. 74 × 126 cm.

　　"Transferred from Office of Chf. Engr. Defenses of Washington to Engr. Dept., Jan'y. 1866."

　　Map of the Peninsula from Richmond to Yorktown indicating fortifications, towns, roads, railroads, houses, names of residents, and drainage.

PETERSBURG

606

Campbell, Albert H.

　　Map of the vicinity of Petersburg made under the direction of A. H. Campbell, Captn. P.E.C.S.A., in charge Topl. Dept., D.N.V. 1864. Photocopy (positive). Scale 1:80,000. 50 × 63 cm. cut and mounted to fold to 19 × 11 cm.

　　At head of title: Chief Engineer's Office D.N.V. Maj. Gen. J. E. Gilmer, Chief Engineer.

　　Map of parts of Prince George, Dinwiddie, and Chesterfield counties, showing roads, railroads, towns, vegetation, houses, and names of residents. Major rivers are colored blue by hand. Fortifications at Petersburg and Drewry's Bluff are outlined in pencil.

606.5

Hunt, Henry J.

Sketch explanatory to the position of the artillery before Petersburg on the 30th of July 1864. Colored ms. Scale 1:15,840 ("4 inches to a mile"). 19 × 31 cm.

In the Henry Jackson Hunt papers, Manuscript Division, L.C., container no. 1, *Journal of Siege Operations* [Petersburg, Virginia], p. 74.

Map accompanies "List of batteries in position before Petersburg the 30th of July 1864" found on page 73 of Hunt's *Journal of Siege Operations.* The list is keyed by number to the map and indicates the military unit, commanding officer, and the size and number of guns and mortars found in each battery.

606.7

———————Sketch of the position of the artillery on the Po River, the 10th of May in the afternoon [1864] Uncolored ms. Scale not given. 21 × 14 cm. on sheet 31 × 19 cm.

In the Henry Jackson Hunt papers, Manuscript Division, L.C., container no. 1, *Journal of Siege Operations* [Petersburg, Virginia], p. 15.

Sketch indicates the following: A = 4 light 12 pdr. batteries; B = Advanced battery from A; C = Advanced section from B; D = 2 rifle batteries (3 inch); E = 2 light 12 pdr. batteries from A; F, G, & H, Enemys batteries; [and] I, Infantry columns recrossing the bridges. Hunt served as chief of artillery in the Army of the Potomac during the siege of Petersburg.

607

McCallum, Andrew.

Map shewing the position of the lines in front of Petersburg, Va., occupied by the 1st Division, 9th Army Corps, April 1st 1865. Ent. accord. to Act of Congress A.D. 1865 by Andrew McCallum in the Clerks Office of the District Court of the State of Maryland. E. Sachse & Co., Baltimore. Colored. Scale ca. 1:16,700. 24 × 34 cm.

Detailed map giving fortifications, picket lines, "Rebel chevaux de-frise," "Union abattis," "covered ways," roads, railroads, drainage, and vegetation. Each regiment of the 1st Division is identified, and the section of the line entrusted to it is delineated by broken lines.

607.2

[Map of defenses of Petersburg, Virginia, showing the position of General Lee and his staff during the attack on Fort Stedman, March 25, 1865] Col. ms. Scale not given. 110 × 79 cm.

G3884 .P4S5 1865 .P6 Vault

Anonymous pen and ink manuscript map of part of the fortifications east of Petersburg showing roads, railroads, houses, and drainage.

607.4

Map showing the position of the lines in front of Petersburg occupied by the 1st Div., 9th Corps, April 1st, 1865. Blue line print. Scale ca. 1:16,800. 25 × 34 cm.

In the Charles W. Reed papers, Manuscript Division, L.C., container no. 5 (oversize cabinet 5, drawer 5).

Map shows Union and Confederate earth works and picket lines, covered ways, roads, railroads, and rivers and creeks.

607.8

Michler, Nathaniel.

Petersburg and Five Forks. [1864–1865] From surveys under the direction of Bvt. Brig. Gen. N. Michler, Maj. of Engineers, by command of Bvt. Maj. Genl. A. A. Humphreys, Brig. Genl. & Chief of Engineers. Surveyed and drawn by Maj: J. E. Weyss, assisted by F. Theilkuhl, J. Strasser & G. Thompson. Photolith. by the N.Y. Lithographing, Engraving & Printing Co., Julius Bien. Supt. 1867. Colored. Scale 1:42,240. 55 × 85 cm.

In this issue, the map is printed on a yellow background with rivers colored green.

Detailed topographic map showing Confederate works in red and Union fortifications in blue, houses, fences, names of residents, drainage, vegetation, hachures, railroads, roads, and the street pattern of Petersburg.

607.9

———————Another issue.

Background and rivers are not colored.

608

———————Petersburg. Novbr. 2nd 1864. Photocopy (negative). Scale 1:31,680. 60 × 51 cm. cut and mounted to fold to 30 × 13 cm.

Endorsed (facsim.): Engineer Dept., Hd. Qrs. Army of the Potomac. Official [signed] N. Michler, Major [of Engrs.].

"Gilbert Thompson" is stamped in the lower right corner.

Civil War photocopy annotated in color to show the fortifications and picket lines of the 2nd, 5th and 6th Union corps situated between Fort Wadsworth and Billup's P.O. on the Weldon & Petersburg R.R.

Base map indicates roads, railroads, drainage, vegetation, forts, towns, houses and names of residents.

609

———————Sketch of the entrenched lines in the immediate front of Petersburg. [1864–5] Surveyed under the direction of N. Michler, Major of Engrs., Bvt. Col. U.S.A. Prepared expressly for the guests of Jarratt's Hotel, Petersburg, Va. A.

Hoen & Co., lith., Balto. Uncolored. Scale ca. 1:63,360. 20 × 25 cm.

Indicates Union and Confederate lines, names of forts, roads, railroads, street pattern of Petersburg, houses, names of residents, and drainage.

609.5

Reed, Charles W.

[Rough pencil sketch of the Federal entrenchments at Fort Mahone near Petersburg, Virginia, 186–] Uncolored ms. Scale not given. 24 × 18 cm. *In his* Sketch book number 1. 9th Massachusetts Battery, 1863. Sketch no. 151.

In the Charles W. Reed papers, Manuscript Division, L.C., container no. 1.

609.6

———[Sketch of Federal batteries situated between Fort Hell and Fort Davis, siege of Petersburg, Va. 186–?] Uncolored ms. Scale not given. 19 × 24 cm. *In his* Sketch book number 1. 9th Massachusetts Battery, 1863. Verso of sketch no. 158.

In the Charles W. Reed papers, Manuscript Division, L.C., container no. 1.

Pencil sketch.

609.8

[Rough pencil sketch of the Union lines at Petersburg. 1864–1865?] Uncolored ms on tracing paper. Scale not given. 43 × 55 cm.

In the Charles W. Reed papers, Manuscript Division, L.C., container no. 5 (oversize cabinet 5, drawer 5).

610

Stevens, Walter H.

Sketch of the Confederate and Federal lines around Petersburg, made under the direction of Col. W. H. Stevens, Chf. Engr., A.N.V. [186–] Photocopy (positive). Scale 1:6000. 41 × 79 cm. cut and mounted to fold to 21 × 14 cm.

This map was in the possession of Jedediah Hotchkiss at the time of his death. Major Hotchkiss served as topographic engineer with the Army of Northern Virginia. In July 1948, the Library of Congress purchased his map collection.

Indicates roads, picket lines, houses, names of a few residents, drainage, vegetation, and hachures. Union and Confederate works are hand-colored blue and red respectively. The location of the Confederate covered ways, guns, and mortars are given.

611

Stinson, J. B.

The seige [sic] of Petersburg, Va. Designed by Dr. J. B.

Stinson of Sherman, Texas. [©1908] Uncolored. Scale not given. 19 × 39 cm.

"The above map is made to conform to a diagram of the position of the opposing armies during the siege of Petersburg, Virginia, as gotten up by N. Michler, Major of Engineers of the U.S. Army. The position of Elliotts' and Gracies' brigades are mainly represented."

Map of the Richmond-Petersburg area showing forts, covered ways, "abattis," "che-val-de-frise," railroads, drainage, and roads.

Inset: Diagram of the "Crater" tunnel. 5 × 15 cm.

Description of the siege appears beneath the map.

612

The struggle at Petersburg. The lines of rebel intrenchments carried by our troops. [June 15–17, 1864] Uncolored. Scale not given. 26 × 12 cm.

Newspaper map showing "Gen Baldy Smith's line, Wednesday, June 15th," "first line of Rebel works," "line of 2nd & 9th Corps, Thursday & Friday, June 16th & 17," "seocnd [sic] line of Rebel works," and "third line of Rebel works."

613

Thompson, Gilbert.

Plan of enemy's battery no. 5 in front of Petersburg before the advance of U.S. forces, June 1864. Headquarters, Army of the Potomac, Engineer Department. October 1864. Surveyed & drawn by G. Thompson, U.S. Engrs. Uncolored ms. Scale 1:480. 39 × 47 cm.

G3884 .P4S5 1864 .T5 Vault

Pen and ink manuscript drawn on tracing cloth.

Includes a cross section of the battery, scale 1:120.

613.5

U.S. *Army. Army of the Potomac. Engineer Department.*

[Map of the environs of Petersburg, from the Appomattox River to the Jerusalem Plank Road showing entrenchments] Engineer Dept., H.Q. Army of the Potomac, June 19th 1864. Photocopy (negative). Scale 1:31,680 ("2 in. 1 mi."). 62 × 100 cm.

In the Montgomery C. Meigs papers, Manuscript Division, L.C., 10, oversize cabinet 4, drawer 3.

Very faint negative photocopy annotated to show "enemys outer line" in red and "present position, of U.S. forces" in blue. Map has also been annotated to show "depot for Genl. Butler," "depot for 18th Corps," "cattle herd," "corrals for stock," "general hospital," "general supply train park," and "depot of repairs."

Faded nature of photocopy is explained by the following note found in the lower right corner: June 26th 1864. Note—On account of the bad water used for washing these sheets, they are not as good as would be wished for. Perfect one's will be ready tomorrow.

613.8

——————[Map of the environs of Petersburg from the Appomattox River to the Jerusalem Plank Road showing entrenchments occupied by Federal forces] Engineer Department, Hd. Qrs., Army of the Potomac, July 28th, 1864. Photocopy (negative). Scale 1:7920. 75 × 100 cm.

In addition to fortifications, the map shows roads, railroads, and houses and names of some residents. Includes some pen and ink annotations.

614

——————Map of the environs of Petersburg from the Appomattox River to the Weldon rail road showing the positions of the entrenched lines occupied by the forces of the United States during the siege. Head quarters Army of the Potomoac Engineer Department. Official: [signed] N. Michler, Major of Engrs., U.S.A. [1864] Photocopy (positive). Scale ca. 1:16,100. 64 × 89 cm.

Fortifications are hand-colored as follows: Blue indicating line held by U.S. forces at date; Red indicating line previously held; Green indicating first and last lines of the enemy.

Shows roads, railroads, street pattern of Petersburg, vegetation, drainage, form lines, and houses and names of residents.

"Gilbert Thompson" is stamped beside the map title.

615

U.S. *Army. Corps of Engineers.*

[Map showing the Federal and Confederate works during the siege of Petersburg, between the Appomattox River and Hatchers Run, June 16, 1864, to April 3, 1865] Colored ms. Scale 1:7920. 5 parts, each approximately 185 × 50 cm. Over-all size 185 × 247 cm.

G3884 .P4S5 1865 .U5 Vault

Pen and ink tracing of a map formerly in the office of Chief of Engineers.

Indicates fortifications, roads, railroads, street pattern of Petersburg, and drainage.

615.4

U.S. *National Park Service.*

Petersburg National Battlefield, Virginia. Reprint 1970 [Washington] Government Printing Office, 1970. Colored. 2 maps on sheet 29 × 33 cm.

G3884 .P4:2P4 1969 .U5

Descriptive leaflet illustrated with two maps: Petersburg National Battlefield. March 1967. Rev. Dec. 1969. Scale ca. 1:38,000. 14 × 16 cm.—Petersburg siege lines. February 1969. Scale ca. 1:90,000. 13 × 16 cm.

615.5

——————Another edition. Reprint 1979 [Washington] Government Printing Office, 1979. Colored. 3 maps on sheet 29 × 33 cm.

G3882 .P47 1979 .U5

Descriptive leaflet illustrated with three maps: Petersburg siege lines. February 1969; rev. Apr. 1976. Scale ca. 1:90,000. 13 × 16 cm.—[Map of central Virginia showing troop movements and battles, May 5–7, 1864, to April 9, 1865] Scale ca. 1:2,600,000. 7 × 8 cm.—(Verso) [Petersburg National Battlefield. March 1967; rev. Apr. 1976.] Scale ca. 1:38,000. 13 × 16 cm.

615.6

——————Petersburg National Military Park, Virginia. Revised 1959 [Washington] Government Printing Office, 1959. Uncolored. Scale ca. 1:87,000. Map 13 × 19 cm. on sheet 22 × 46 cm.

G3882 .P47 1959 .U5

Descriptive leaflet illustrated with a map indicating the park boundary of the route of an auto tour. The map is dated July 1959.

615.7

——————Oct. 1960. Reprint 1962. Uncolored. 2 maps, on sheet 24 × 61 cm.

G3884 .P4:2P4 1962 .U5

Descriptive leaflet illustrated with two maps: Petersburg National Military Park. Scale ca. 1:87,000. 13 × 19 cm.—Virginia campaign of Grant and Lee, 1864–65. Scale ca. 1:970,000. 20 × 28 cm. Both maps indicate battle sites and suggested tour routes.

615.8

——————Another edition. Rev. Jan. 1965.

G3882 .P47 1965 .U5

Title of the leaflet has been changed to "Petersburg National Battlefield, Virginia."

616

Walker, L. E.

[Map of part of the Union lines during the siege of Petersburg, Virginia] Photd. for Engr. Dept. by L. E. Walker, U.S. Treasury Ext., Jan. 16th 1865. Photocopy (positive). Scale not given. 49 × 42 cm.

Shows roads, railroads, houses, fences, names of residents, drainage, vegetation, and form lines.

"Gilbert Thompson" is stamped in the lower left corner.

616.5

[Wall map showing fortifications at the time of the Battle of the Crater, Petersburg, Virginia, July 30, 1864] Colored ms. Scale not given. 184 × 194 cm. in 4 parts, each approximately 92 × 97 cm.

G3884 .P4S5 1864 .W3 Vault

Drawn with colored crayons. Map lacks place names, as well as author and title.

617

Weyss, John E.

Map of the siege of Petersburg, 1864–5. Surveyed under the direction of N. Michler, Maj: of Engrs., Bvt. Brig. Genl., U.S.A. [Surveyed and drawn by Maj. J. E. Weyss, assisted by Theilkuhl, Burchardt, Schuman, Thompson, and Graham] Photocopy (positive). Scale 1:15,840. 74 × 78 cm.

G3884 .P4S5 1865 .W4 Vault

Photocopy with title added in pen and ink.

Indicates fortifications, roads, railroads, houses, fences, names of residents, vegetation, drainage, relief by hachures, and the street pattern of Petersburg.

618

————————Another copy. Surveyed & drawn by Maj. J. E. Weyss, assisted by Theilkuhl, Burchardt, Schuman, Thompson, Graham.

G3884 .P4S5 1865 .W41 Vault

Lacks title.

Names of surveyors and draftsmen have been added by hand in the lower left corner.

619

————————[Overlay to the map of the siege of Petersburg, 1864–5. Scale 1:15,840] Colored ms. 75 × 78 cm.

G3884 .P4S5 1865 .W42 Vault

This is an overlay apparently designed to be used with the preceding maps (entry nos. 617–618). It contains brief field notes probably written by Federal engineers. The location of several camps of the U.S. Engineers and the headquarters of the Army of the Potomac on June 22 to July 11, 1864, July 12 to Oct. 1, 1864, and Oct. 2, 1864, to Mar. 29, 1865, are shown.

PRINCE GEORGE COUNTY

619.2

Confederate States of America. *Army. Department of Northern Virginia. Chief Engineer's Office.*

[Map of part of Prince George County, Virginia. 1864] Photocopy (positive). Scale ca. 1:80,000. 31 × 61 cm.

Lacks author and title.

Map consists of two sheets, each 31 × 31 cm., which have been joined together. Sheets are numbered "D. no. 3," and "D. no. 4." Depicted are towns, roads and railroads,

houses and names of residents, fortifications south of Petersburg, and woodland. The map is similar to the southern portion of Albert H. Campbell's "Map of the vicinity of Petersburg," entry no. 606.

RAPPAHANNOCK RIVER

619.4

Paine, William H.

Additions & corrections for the "Map of a part of the Rappahannock above Fredericksburg" [compiled by Capt. W. H. Paine, Dec. 1862] April 8th 1863. Uncolored. Scale ca. 1:63,360. 28 × 35 cm.

G3882 .R38 1863 .A3

Map of the Rappahannock River from Falmouth to Richard's Ferry. "The dotted parts of the river give points of reference to the original map." The map which this supplements and corrects is listed as entry no. 619.5.

"No. 34" is written in ink below the map title.

619.5

————————Map of a part of the Rappahannock River above Fredericksburg and of the Rapid Ann River & the adjacent country. Compiled under the direction of Col. J. N Macomb, A.D.C., Maj. Topl. Engrs., by Capt. W. H. Paine, A.D.C. December 1862. Autographic transfer printed at the Coast Survey Office. Uncolored. Scale 1:63,360. 2 parts, each 73 × 53 cm.

G3882 .R38 1862 .P3

"Note: This map is distributed in duplicate in order that one copy may be returned with any reliable additions and corrections that may be made upon it. Office of Surveys & Maps for the Army of the Potomac, 78 Winder's Building, Washington, D.C."

"No. 57" is written in ink in the upper right corner. A second copy in the Geography and Map Division has the number 73 in the upper right.

Reconnaissance map indicating roads, rivers, villages and towns, houses and names of residents, woodland, and some relief by hachures.

619.51

————————Another copy.

In the Abraham Lincoln papers, Manuscript Division, L.C., vol. 97, no. 20669.

"No. 81" is written in ink in the upper right corner.

Signed in green pencil "G. K. Warren, Brig. Genl. Vols."

Map has been annotated in green pencil to show "Kelly's Ford" and "Bank's Ford" across the Rappahannock River.

619.6

Vernam, John S.

Map of the Rappahannock River, from Port Royal to Richards Ferry. Drawn from surveys made by officers of the Engineer Brigade and charts of the Coast Survey of the river below Fredericksburg, under direction of Brig. Gen. D. P. Woodbury. Extensions made since March 1863 under direction of Brig. Gen. H. W. Benham. Sergt John S. Vernam Delr. Colored ms. Scale ca. 1:63,360. 41 × 88 cm.

G3882 .R38S5 1863.V4 Vault

Pen and ink manuscript map drawn on tracing linen, showing "Lines of Gen Hooker" at Chancellorsville, "Battle Field of Gen. Sedgwick" at Salem Church, roads, railroad, location of bridges across the Rappahannock River, houses, names of residents, vegetation, and relief by hachures. The area south of Chancellorsville is on a piece spliced to the main map sheet.

Endorsed on verso in two places as follows: Map of the Rappahannock from Port Royal to Kelly's Ford, showing the crossings of Gen. Hookers army and the ground occupied by our forces in and around Chancellorville [sic].

Gift: Gist Blair papers, 1936.

Printed version appears as plate 39, map 2, in the U.S. War Department's *Atlas to Accompany the Official Records of the Union and Confederate Armies* (Washington, Government Printing Office, 1891–95).

RICHMOND

619.8

Abbot, Henry L.

Sketch exhibiting the approaches to Richmond from Pamunkey River. From reconnoissances [sic] made between May 18th & June 14th 1862. By command of Maj. Gen. Geo. B. McClellan, U.S.A., commanding the Army of the Potomac. A. A. Humphreys, Brig. Gen. and Chief of Topographical Engineers, Map compiled by Lieut. H. L. Abbot, Top. Engineers. Photographed June 14th [1862] Photocopy (positive). Scale ca. 1:63,360. 56 × 68 cm.

G3884 .R5A1 1862 .A3

This field survey of New Kent County east of Richmond, Virginia, is composed of six contemporary photocopies, each measuring about 28 × 23 cm., which have been joined together to form a continuous map. The survey is based on field reconnaissances by officers Charles S. Stew-

'Drawn from Nature and Lith by John Bachmann.

In describing John Bachmann's depictions of urban America, one authority stated that "No finer artist of city views worked in America." His panoramic maps made during the Civil War also are outstanding. Displayed here is his "Birds Eye View of the Seat of War Around Richmond showing the Battle on Chickahominy River, 29 June 1862." (See entry no. 621.)

BIRDS EYE VIEW
OF THE
OF WAR AROUND RICHMOND

NG THE BATTLE ON CHICKAHOMINY RIVER

John Bachmann, Publisher

art, C. B. Comstock, M. D. McAlester, C. B. Reese, C. E. Cross, O. E. Babcock, F. U. Farquhar, W. R. Palmer, G. K. Warren, N. Bowen, George A. Custer, J. McMillan, J. W. Forsyth, W. G. Jones, James Hope, and P. C. F. West, and Messrs. F. W. Dorr, J. W. Donn, and F. A. Churchill.

Autographed in ink: Brig. Genl. J. W. Ripley, Ordnance Corps, through Bureau Topl. Engr. June 21, 1862. Drawer 48, portfolio 2, no. 5.

619.9

Babcock, John C.

Map exhibiting the approaches to the city of Richmond prepared for Maj. Gen. Geo. B. McClellan, U.S.A. Compiled from "Map of Henrico Co." and map of the "Position of Richmond, Va." with additional information and reconnoissance [sic] by E. J. Allen, S.S.U.S. Assisted by Jno. C. Babcock. Jno. C. Babcock, Del'r. J. F. Gibson, Photographer. Head Quarters, Army of the Potomac, May 31st 1862. Photocopy (negative). Scale ca. 1:76,000. 41 × 47 cm.

In the Abraham Lincoln papers, Manuscript Division, L.C., vol. 77, no. 16251.

A nearly illegible photocopy of a reconnaissance map compiled by Allan Pinkerton (alias E. J. Allen), assisted by one of his operatives, John C. Babcock. Pinkerton based his map in part on the prewar map by James Keily entitled "Smith's Map of Henrico County, Virginia" (Richmond, Robert P. Smith & C. Carpenter, 1853).

Pinkerton sent this copy, which has been annotated in blue to show "Rebel Batteries" and a small American flag denoting Federal Head Quarters, to Lincoln on June 2, 1862. (Lincoln papers, vol. 77, no. 16276).

Another copy is in the Samuel P. Heintzelman papers, Manuscript Division, L.C., container no. 11.

619.95

————————Another issue. Corrected June 6th, 1862.

In the American Institute of Aeronautics and Astronautics, Aeronautic Archives, Thaddeus Lowe papers, Manuscript Division, L.C., container 82.

This badly faded photocopy is particularly significant because it has been annotated to show the location of two Federal balloon camps and data obtained from balloon ascents. The following note appears at the bottom of the map: Balloon Camp, June 14th 1862. The red lines represent some of the most important earth works seen this morning & are located as near as possible, as is also the camps in black ink. As soon as I can get an observation from the Mechanicsville Balloon I can make many additions to this map. [Signed] T. S. C. Lowe.

620

————————Another issue. Corrected, June 20th 1862, J. F. Gibson, Phot'r. Additions July 22, 1862.

"Drawing by J. C. Babcock" is in the lower left corner.

620.2

————————Another issue. Corrected, June 28th 1862. J. F. Gibson, Phot'r.

In the Samuel P. Heintzelman papers, Manuscript Division, L.C., container no. 11.

621

Bachmann, John.

Birds eye view of the seat of war around Richmond showing the battle on Chickahominy River, 29 June 1862. Drawn from nature and lith. by John Bachmann. New York, ©1862. Colored view. 46 × 70 cm.

Perspective drawing.

622

Bailey, A. M.

Map of Richmond, Va., shewing fortifications surrounding the Confederate capital. From the latest government surveys. C. J. Culliford, lith. London [186–?] Colored. Scale ca. 1:57,000. 34 × 26 cm.

At top of map: Map of Richmond. (6^D)

A description of "The city of Richmond" and the "Forts around Richmond, with their armament" appears to the right of the map.

Important buildings are identified and the positions are located on the map by letters and numbers.

Gives the street pattern of Richmond and Manchester, forts, roads, railroads, drainage, and relief by hachures.

622.5

Blunt, Edmund, *and* **George W. Blunt.**

E. & G. W. Blunt's corrected map of the seat of war near Richmond, July 10th, 1862. Uncolored. Scale ca. 1:405,000. 37 × 47 cm.

The following label has been pasted beneath the map title: Metropolitan Book Store, Philp & Solomons, agents, Washington, D.C.

General map of the environs of Richmond showing roads, railroads, cities and towns, drainage, and soundings on the Rappahannock, York, and James rivers.

Boston publisher John H. Bufford aimed his map of "Richmond, Petersburg and vicinity" at the lucrative market comprising the officers and enlisted men serving in the Union armed forces. By using the letter-number grid reference system described by the publisher in a note, "those in the army are enabled to inform their friends of the movements of their companies and of their location and will also serve as a journal to each soldier." Bufford brazenly advertised the map as "Genl. Grant's Campaign War Map." (See entry no. 623.)

GEN^L GRANT'S CAMPAIGN WAR MAP.

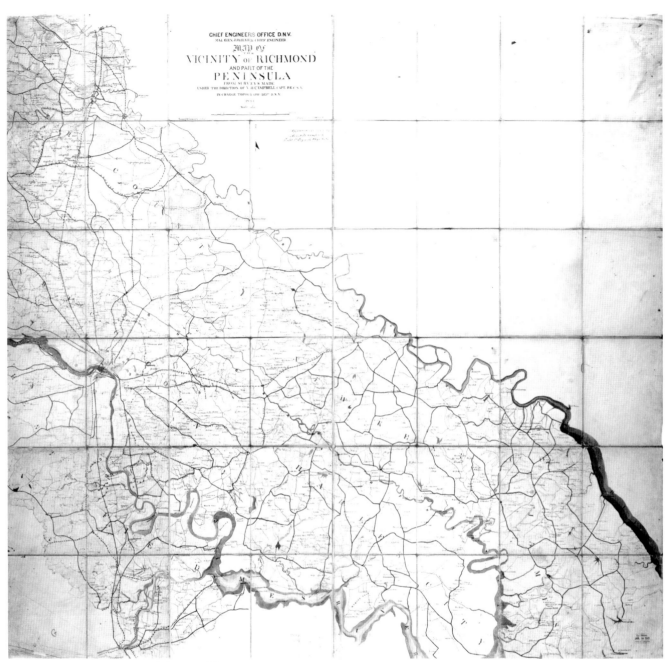

Albert H. Campbell's detailed "Map of the Vicinity of Richmond and Part of the Peninsula" is representative of the maps prepared by Confederate engineers for use in the field. Prepared in 1864, the map was photographed, hand-colored, sectioned, and mounted on cotton muslin in the Office of the Topographical Department, Department of Northern Virginia. Copies were issued to Gen. Robert E. Lee and his corps commanders in the same year. (See entry no. 625.)

623

Bufford, John H.

Richmond, Petersburg, and vicinity. Boston. [1864] Uncolored. Scale ca. 1:105,000. 59 × 47 cm.

At top of map: Genl. Grant's campaign war map.

Shows fortifications, camps, roads, railroads, street pattern of Richmond and Petersburg, towns, drainage, vegetation, hachures, and houses.

"The horizontal and upright lines represent one mile square. By refering [sic] to the number on the left and to the letter on the base, any point may be found to show the locality of the Union armies."

624

Campbell, Albert H.

Map of the vicinity of Richmond and part of the Peninsula. From surveys made under the direction of A. H. Campbell, Capt: P.E.C.S.A. in charge Topographl. Dept., D.N.V. 1864. Photocopy (positive). Scale 1:80,000. 94 × 77 cm. cut and mounted to fold to 16 × 13 cm.

At head of title: Chief Engineers Office, D.N.V. Maj. Gen. J. F. Gilmer, Chief Engineer.

Endorsed (fascim.): Approved April 26th 1864, Albert H. Campbell, Capt. P. Engrs. in chge. &c &c.

"Photographed in Off. Top. Dept., D.N.V."

"Sanxay & Gomert's patent."

Hand-colored photocopy showing roads in brown, principal rivers in blue, fortifications, railroads, street pattern of Richmond towns, houses, names of residents, bridges, fords, ferries, and relief by hachures.

This issue covers that portion of the Virginia Peninsula between Round Squirrel Church 15 miles northwest of Richmond to Old Barrell's Ferry on the Chickahominy River 35 miles southeast of Richmond.

625

————Another issue. Photocopy (positive). 94 × 102 cm. cut and mounted to fold to 16 × 13 cm.

Map of the Virginia Peninsula from Round Squirrel Church 15 miles northwest of Richmond to Williamsburg 44 miles southeast of Richmond.

Signed in ms. on verso: The property of T. Sewell Ball, Pikesville, Baltimore Co., Maryland.

This is the copy from which the following facsimile was made.

Another copy of this issue, with manuscript annotations, was acquired in 1948 with the purchase of the papers and maps of Jedediah Hotchkiss.

626

————Facsimile reproduction made from the original Confederate war map owned by T. Sewell Ball, Publisher, Pikesville, Baltimore Co., Maryland. A. B. Graham, photolith., Washington, D.C. Entered according to Act of Congress in the year 1891, by T. Sewell Ball . . . Colored. Scale 1:92,000 (not "1:80,000"). 83 × 90 cm. in 2 parts, each 83 × 45 cm.

Cover title: Fac-simile reproduction of the Confederate war map of the "Vicinity of Richmond and part of the Peninsula" which was issued to Gen'l. Robert E. Lee and his corps commanders in 1864.

This facsimile was made from the preceding photocopy (entry no. 625).

626.5

Confederate State of America. *Army. Department of Northern Virginia. Chief Engineer's Office.*

[Map of Richmond and vicinity. 1864] Photocopy (positive). Scale ca. 1:80,000. 64 × 51 cm.

Lacks author and title.

Map consists of four sheets, each 32 × 26 cm., which have been joined together. Lower sheets are numbered "Range C, no. 2" and "Range C, no. 3." Depicted are cities and towns, roads and railroads, houses and names of residents, fortifications, woodland, and relief by hachures.

For a similar map, but with author, title, and date given, see entry nos. 624–625.

627

Cross, Andrew B.

Field of war around Richmond & Petersburg, 1864–5. Lith. by A. Hoen & Co., Balto. Uncolored. Scale ca. 1:400,000. 20 × 15 cm.

Indicates "Union [and] Rebel works," "hospitals & stations of Christian commn.," roads, railroads, towns, county names and boundaries, and rivers.

Author copy is in the Abraham Lincoln papers, Manuscript Division, L.C., vol. 184, no. 39735.

628

Forbes (W. H.) and Company.

A complete map of Richmond and its fortifications within a circle of 12 miles showing the numerous forts, batteries and the range of their fire, and the various obstacles that impede the approach of the Federal army, also, the principal towns & plantations, in the immediate vicinity of Richmond, together with several of the battle fields of 1862. Publd. by W. H. Forbes & Co., Boston. Entered according to Act of Congress in the year 1863 by Forbes & Ackermann. Uncolored. Scale ca. 1:54,000. 60 × 45 cm.

"As a guide to note the approach of the Federal army, this map is invaluable, as the plan of its fortifications is taken from a correct drawing of a Southern engineer, who recently escaped to Europe."

629

Forbes, W. H. *and* **Benjamin B. Russell.**

Forbes' new and complete map of Richmond and its fortifications. Published by W. H. Forbes & B. B. Russell. Entered according to Act of Congress in the year 1864 by Forbes & Russell. Uncolored. Scale ca. 1:48,000. 61 × 45 cm.

Printed in blue ink.

Shows forts, street pattern of Richmond, towns, roads, railroads, drainage, and relief by hachures.

630

Hoffmann, J. Paul.

Map of the Confederate lines from Fort Gregg to Mrs: Price's, made under the direction of Brig. Genl. W. H. Stevens, Chief Engr., A.N.V. Copied by J. Paul Hoffman. [Richmond] Topl. Office, A.N.V., [186–] Colored ms. Scale 1:20,000. 70 × 51 cm.

G3884 .R5S5 186– .H6 Vault

Pen and ink manuscript drawn on tracing cloth, showing part of the defenses of Richmond, roads, "York River R.R.," houses, names or residents, drainage, vegetation, and relief by hachures.

631

Hotchkiss, Jedediah.

Thirty five miles around Richmond, Va. Compiled by Jed. Hotchkiss, Top. Engineer, Staunton, Virginia, from the surveys of the C.S. Engineers, U.S. Engineers, and the U. States Coast Survey. Washington, Richmond, Va., C. Bohn, 1867. Colored. Scale ca. 1:200,000. 69 × 58 cm.

Shows fortifications, towns, county names and boundaries, roads, railroads, and drainage.

Insets: Map of the city of Richmond, Va., from the U.S. Coast Survey map of 1860, with additions by Jed. Hotchkiss. . . . 1866. Scale ca. 1:52,000. 12 × 14 cm.—Map of the city of Petersburg, Va., from Lynch's map with the Confederate & Federal lines on the east from C.S. Engr. maps by Jed. Hotchkiss. Scale ca. 1:52,000. 10 × 13 cm.—[View of] the capitol of the C.S., Richmond. 9 × 10 cm.—[View of] Washington Monument, Richmond. 10 × 10 cm.

631.2

——————Another issue. 72 × 61 cm.

G3884 .R5 1867 .H6 Vault

Fortifications are not depicted on the principal map.

Signed in manuscript: To Col. A. L. Rives with the compliments of Jed. Hotchkiss, Staunton, Va. 1867.

632

Hughes, William C.

Hughes military map of Richmond & Petersburgh [sic], Va. Showing the Rebel fortifications drawn on the ground for the War Department by Major W. C. Hughes of Michigan. Willenbücher, lith. Print. by J. F. Gedney, Washn. ©1864. Colored. Scale ca. 1:105,000. 57 × 66 cm.

Copyright no. 27521. "Deposited—July 23, 1864. R. J. Meigs Clk."

"Respectfully dedicated to the Army of the Potomac."

Insets: [View of] Libby Prison. 13 × 16 cm. [View of] Belle Island. 13 × 18 cm.

Shows Confederate forts, roads, railroads, towns, vegetation, drainage, hachures, and houses.

632.1

——————Hughes topographical military map of Richmond and Petersburgh [sic] cities with adjacent country in perspective showing the rebel fortifications. [Signed] William C. Hughes. Colored. Scale ca. 1:220,000. 47 × 47 cm.

Copyright no. 27521. Deposited July 23, 1864.

Stamped in lower left corner: Copyright Library Mar. 1865.

This appears to be the work map for "Hughes military map of Richmond & Petersburgh [sic]. Va." (entry no. 632). A portion of Adolph Lindenkohl's "Military map of southeastern Virginia" (entry no. 463) has been used as a base, to which the author has added tiny drawings of houses and churches, fortifications at Petersburg, and the "Valley of death" at Fort Darling.

632.2

Magnus, Charles.

Magnus' historical war map. One hundred & fifty miles around Richmond. New York and Washington, Charles Magnus [1864] Colored. Scale ca. 1:920,000. 70 × 52 cm.

General map centered on Richmond, Virginia.

"Mirror of events [i.e., list of battles] 1861–62–63–64" has been attached to the left of the map.

Insets: Maj. Gen. Canby' base of operations [Mississippi and Red River area] 9 × 8 cm.—Maj. Gen. W. T. Sherman's base of operations [northern Georgia] 9 × 8 cm.—Fortifications around Richmond, Va. 12 × 11 cm.—Prominent battle grounds [Bethel, Bull Run, Winchester, Fair Oaks, Seven days' battles, Malvern Hill, Antietam, Chancellorsville, Mt. Crawford, and Monocacy. 1861–64] 10 maps, each 4 × 4 cm.

Includes portraits of Generals Grant and Lee.

632.3

——————One hundred & fifty miles around Richmond. 9th ed. New York and Washington, Charles Magnus [186–] Colored. Scale ca. 1:880,000. 66 × 76 cm.

G3884. R5 186– .M3

General map centered on Richmond, Virginia. Map is printed in blue with title and border in red.

"Ninth edition 3000 of Magnus' all around map."

"Dedicated to the gallant soldiers, fighting to suppress the rebellion."

Insets: 200 miles around Natchez, Miss. 18 × 17 cm.—100 miles around Chattanooga, Tenn. 18 × 17 cm.—200 miles around Montgomery, Ala. 18 × 17 cm.—100 miles around Augusta, Geo. 18 × 17 cm.—250 miles around Galveston, Texas. 12 × 19 cm.—250 miles around Charleston, S.C. 11 × 19 cm.—Memphis and surroundings. 8 × 7 cm.—Nashville and surroundings, 8 × 7 cm.

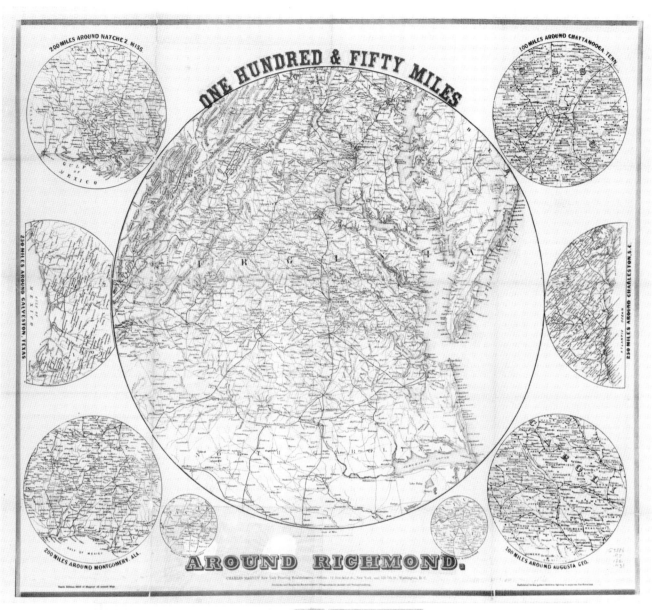

The New York and Washington publisher Charles Magnus sold the 10th edition of his popular map of "One Hundred & Fifty Miles Around Richmond" folded and inserted in an envelope captioned "Magnus' Half Dollar Portfolio. For the Army of the Potomac." Included with the map in this "Glorious Union Packet," as the publisher called it, was a "Mirror of Events [i.e., list of battles], 2 illustrated Notesheets, 1 Song Notesheet, 3 illustrated Envelopes, 6 Portraits of Army and Navy Officers, 4 plain Notesheets, 4 plain Envelopes, Penholder, [and] Pen and Lead-pencil." (See entry no. 632.4.)

632.4

————10th ed. 66 × 76 cm. folded to 13 × 21 cm.
　　G3884 .R5 186– .M31
"Tenth edition 3000 of Magnus' all around map."

Cover title of accompanying envelope: Magnus' half dollar portfolio. For the Army of the Potomac. Containing a new military map: 150 miles around Richmond and 1200 miles of southern territory in smaller circles, acknowledged for the best published, and the glorious Union packet inside . . . New York and Washington, Charles Magnus.

632.5

————12th ed.
　　G3884 .R5 186– .M32
"Twelfth edition 3000 of Magnus' all around map."

Insets: 225 miles around Vicksburg, Miss. 19 × 18 cm.—200 miles around Chattanooga, Tenn. 19 × 18 cm.—200 miles around Montgomery, Ala. 18 × 17 cm.—100 miles around Milledgeville, Ga. 18 × 18 cm.—250 miles around Galveston, Texas. 12 × 19 cm.—250 miles around Charleston, S.C. 11 × 19 cm.—Memphis and Nashville, Tenn. 9 × 9 cm.—Knoxville, Tenn., Danville, Ky. and Parkersburg, Va. 9 × 9 cm.—Fortifications around Richmond, Va. 12 × 11 cm.

Includes portraits of Generals Grant, Meade, and Hancock.

632.6

————Volunteer militia and eastern army guide. One hundred and fifty miles around Richmond. New York and Washington, Charles Magnus [186–] Uncolored. Scale ca. 1:920,000. 58 × 74 cm.

General map centered on Richmond, Virginia. The map is printed in blue ink.

Insets: Ninety miles around Nashville, Tenn.—Ninety miles around Harrisburg, Pa.—Ninety miles around Vicksburg, Miss.—Ninety miles around Baton Rouge, La. Each inset 17 × 17 cm.

632.65

Michler, Nathaniel.

Richmond, Virginia, 1865 [by Major Nathaniel Michler] From surveys by Capt. Peter S. Michie, U.S. Army Corps of Engineers. [Washington, Corps of Engineers, 1866. Richmond] Civil War Centennial Committee, 1965. Uncolored. Scale 1:9000. 2 sheets, each 126 × 75 cm.

　　G3884 .R5 1865 .M5 1965

Detailed map of the environs of Richmond showing roads and streets, property lines, buildings, names of land owners in rural areas, railroads, and fortifications.

"These reproductions of the original charts have been slightly reduced—from 30″ × 52″ to 27″ × 47″—but no

detail was lost in the reduction." The originals are on file in the Cartographic and Architectural Branch, National Archives, Washington, D.C., Record Group 77, nos. 51 and 55.

632.7

Michler, Nathanial, *and* Peter S. Michie.

Richmond [1862–1865] From surveys under the direction of Bvt. Brig. Gen. N., Michler, Maj. of Engineers and Bvt. Lieut. Col. P. S. Michie, Capt. of Engineers, by command of Bvt. Maj. Genl. A. A. Humphreys, Brig. Genl. & Chief of Engineers. Surveyed & drawn by Maj: J. E. Weyss, assisted by F. Theilkuhl, J. Strasser & G. Thompson. Photolith. by the N.Y. Lithographing, Engraving & Printing Co., Julius Bien, Supt. 1867. Colored. Scale 1:42,240. 56 × 85 cm.

In this issue, the map is printed on a yellow background with the James River colored blue.

Detailed topographic map of the environs of Richmond showing Confederate fortifications in red, Union fortifications in blue, roads, street pattern of Richmond and Manchester, railroads, towns, vegetation, drainage, hachures, houses, and names of residents.

632.8

————Another issue.
Background and river are not colored.

632.9

————Another issue.
Lacks the names of the surveyors and lithographer.

633

Prang (Louis) and Company.

Map of the battle ground near Richmond, showing plainly, every point of interest of the late & present position of the Union army. Published by L. Prang & Co., Boston [1862] Uncolored. Scale ca. 1:250,000. 50 × 65 cm.

Indicates location and dates of battles, "McClellan's present defensive line" at Harrison's Landing, principal roads, railroads, towns, and drainage.

634

Redd (J. T.) and Son.

Map showing the battle-fields around Richmond, Va. Compiled by J. T. Redd & Son. Copyrighted, 1896, by J. L. Hill Printing Co., Richmond, Va. Uncolored. Scale not given. 15 × 17 cm.

Battlefields are located by small flags.

635

Richmond, Va.

Map of present Richmond showing important Civil

War battlegrounds, fortifications, roads and points of historical interest within a twenty-five mile area. Prepared for the Richmond Civil War Centenial [sic] Committee by the Confederate Museum, the Valentine Museum, and the city of Richmond Dept. of Public Works. Copyright 1960 [by] City of Richmond, Virginia. Colored. Scale ca. 1:126,720. 83 × 59 cm.

"Roads & railroads in 1865 & points of historical interest" are colored orange, "Confederate fortifications" are red, and "Federal fortifications" are blue.

Fourteen "important battles" are listed in the lower left corner and keyed by the letters A to O to the map.

On verso: Map of the city of Richmond, Virginia, 1861–65. Colored. Scale ca. 1:7200. Map 58 × 62 cm. on sheet 97 × 64 cm. (Principal buildings and features are keyed by number to a list in the bottom margin. "Buildings outlined in blue are still in existence; those in red, no longer standing; [and] orange areas show sections burned in the evacuation fire April 2, 3, 1865.")

635.1

————Map of present Richmond showing important Civil War battlegrounds, fortifications, roads and points of historical interest within a twenty-five mile area. Prepared for the Richmond Civil War Centennial Committee by the city of Richmond Department of Public Works. Copyright 1961, City of Richmond, Virginia. Colored. Scale ca. 1:126,720. 82 × 59 cm.

G3701 .S521 1961 .R5

Revised edition of the preceding map (entry no. 635) with the map title printed in the lower left corner rather than at the bottom center of the sheet. Fifteen battles are listed below the title and are keyed by the letters A to P to the map. The verso of the map is blank.

635.2

————Map of the City of Richmond, Virginia, 1861–65. Prepared for the Richmond Civil War Centennial Committee by the Confederate Museum, The Valentine Museum and the City of Richmond Department of Public Works. Copyright 1961, City of Richmond, Virginia. Colored. Scale ca. 1:7200. 83 × 62 cm.

G3884 .R5 1865 .R5 1961

"Buildings that are still in existence" are colored blue; "Buildings that are no longer standing" are red; and yellow shaded "areas show sections burned in the evacuation fire April 2, 1865." The "Table of References" printed below the map includes 189 citations to churches, hospitals, industries, residences, banks, hotels, etc., in Richmond and 6 in Manchester. Each is keyed to the map by a number.

636

Richmond & vicinity. [186–] Colored ms. Scale not given. 60 × 85 cm.

G3884 .R5 186– .R5 Vault
Title on verso.

Indicates the general location of batteries, roads, railroads, drainage, and the names of a few landowners.

636.5

Richmond & vicinity. [186–?] Photocopy (positive). Scale ca. 1:106,000 (not 1:80,000). 27 × 34 cm.

Anonymous contemporary photocopy showing the defenses of Richmond. The map title is written in pencil.

636.7

[Richmond and vicinity. 1864] Colored. Scale ca. 1:900,000. 20 × 16 cm.

In the Abraham Lincoln papers, Manuscript Division, L.C., vol. 149, no. 31801.

A portion of an unidentified printed map is annotated to show the location of a proposed railroad between Urbanna and West Point, Virginia. The map illustrates a plan dated March 24, 1864, "To take Richmond, by Urbana [sic] & West Point." Signed by D. H. Alexander of Baltimore, Maryland, the plan was sent to Representative Robert C. Schenck, Chairman of the Committee on Military Affairs (Lincoln Papers, vol. 149, 31799–31800).

637

Robertson, H. C.

Grant's advance on Richmond. [May 5, 1864–April 2, 1865. Chicago, R. O. Evans and Co., ©1898] Colored. Scale not given. 83 × 59 cm. (Robertson's geographic-historical series illustrating the history of America and the United States)

Wall map of Richmond and vicinity showing the location and dates of engagements, and fortifications.

638

————McClellan's first advance on Richmond [May 31–July 1, 1862. Chicago, R. O. Evans and Co. ©1898] Colored. Scale not given. 82 × 59 cm. (Robertson's geographic-historical series illustrating the history of America and the United States)

Wall map of the environs of Richmond, showing the location of the Seven Days' battles.

Includes an outline of events, a view of "Capitol square at Richmond," and a portrait of General McClellan.

639

Sheppard, Edwin.

Map showing the battle grounds of the Chickahominy, and the positions of the subsequent engagements in the retreat of the Federal army towards James River and all the other points of interest in connection with the siege of Richmond from the most reliable information to be obtained by

Edwin Sheppard. Richmond, Hoyer & Ludwig [1862] Uncolored. Scale ca. 1:160,000. 42 × 52 cm.

Confederate imprint.

Map of the environs of Richmond showing location and dates of battles, roads, railroads, towns, names of counties, drainage, and the names of a few residents.

640

Sholl, Charles.

Map of Richmond, Va., and surrounding country showing Rebel fortifications. From the latest and most authentic surveys. Compiled and drawn by Charles Sholl, T. E. J. Bien, lith., N.Y. New York, D. Van Nostrand, 1864. Colored. Scale ca. 1:70,000. 48 × 48 cm.

Dedicated in ms: Maj. Genl. H. W. Halleck with the compliments of D. Van Nostrand.

Shows fortifications, street pattern of Richmond and Manchester, roads, railroads, towns, vegetation, drainage, relief by hachures, and rural houses.

640.2

————Map of Richmond, Virginia, showing its defenses and railroad connections. Drawn by Charles Sholl, Topographical Engineer. [1864] Uncolored. Scale ca. 1:52,000. 36 × 24 cm. *From* Harper's weekly, v. 8, May 21, 1864. p. 332.

"Map of Virginia, showing the military operations of Generals Grant and Butler" is on the verso. 36 × 24 cm.

640.4

————Richmond and its defences. Constructed and engraved to illustrate "The war with the South." [Compiled by Charles Sholl] Engd. by W. Kemple. ©1863. Colored. Scale ca. 1:90,000. 25 × 17 cm. *From* Tomes, Robert. The war with the South. New York, Virtue & Yorston, 1862–1867. v. 2, between p. 236 and 237.

Signed (facsimile): Charles: Sholl, Topl. Engineer.

"Entered according to act of Congress AD. 1863 by Virtue, Yorston & Co."

Caption in lower margin: A topographical map of Richmond and its vicinity, showing all batteries in existence. This is the most reliable map ever made of this vicinity.

641

Smith, William I.

Map of a part of the city of Richmond showing the burnt districts. Drawn on stone by C. L. Ludwig. Published by Wm. Ira Smith, proprietor Richmond Whig [1865?] Uncolored. Scale not given. 21 × 32 cm.

"The black markes indicates burnt."

Confederate imprint.

Another copy is in the Hubbard family papers, Manuscript Division, L.C., container no. 17.

641.2

Sneden, R. K.

Sketch of the City of Richmond, Va. December 1861. Drawn by R. H. Sneden, Topogl. H. Qrs., 3rd Corps, A. P. Baltimore Cross Roads, Va. Colored ms. on cloth. Scale ca. 1:18,500. 26 × 33 cm.

In the Samuel P. Heintzelman papers, Manuscript Division, L.C., container no. 11.

Attractive manuscript map showing Confederate camps, railroads, streets, canal and river, and selected buildings such as "tobacco warehouses," "Spotswood House," "American House," "Exchange Hotel," "Ballard House," and "Governors House."

641.5

Topographical map of Richmond, Va. from official data. [1861 or 1862?] Photocopy (positive). Scale ca. 1:87,000. 21 × 16 cm.

Contemporary Civil War photograph of an anonymous map annotated in pencil on verso: "Bro't from Richmond, Va. by an escaping Union prisoner in 1862."

Fortifications ringing Richmond are numbered 1 to 19.

From the papers of Gen. Joseph Roswell Hawley, Manuscript Division, L.C.

642

U.S. Army. Army of the James.

Copy of section of photograph map captured from the enemy showing country adjacent to Richmond and lines of defensive works surrounding the city. Headquarters, Army of the James [1864] Photocopy (negative). Scale 1:80,000. 58 × 38 cm.

Detailed map showing fortifications, roads, railroads, street pattern of Richmond and Manchester, towns, drainage, hachures, vegetation, houses, and names of residents.

The Geography and Map Division has three copies of this map, two of which have been endorsed by Lieut. Peter S. Michie, Chief Engineer, Department of Virginia and North Carolina. One endorsement is dated Oct. 17 and the other Oct. 28, 1864. The former is annotated on the verso, "'The Chamblies Map.' The property of Jos. R. Hawley, Brig. Gen. U.S.V., 10th Corps." (G3884 .R5S5 1864 .U5)

642.5

U.S. Army. Army of the Potomac.

Copy of section of photograph map captured from the enemy showing country adjacent to Richmond and lines of defensive works surrounding the city. Head Quarters, Army of the Potomac, Engineer Department, August 18th 1864. Photocopy (positive). Scale 1:80,000. 65 × 51 cm.

Signed (facsim): N. Michler, Major Engineers U.S.A.

Indicates roads, railroads, towns, fortifications, street

patterns of Richmond, Manchester, and Petersburg, drainage, vegetation, houses, and names of residents.

See entry no. 642 for another Union map based on the same captured Confederate map.

643

U.S. *Army. Corps of Engineers.*

Henrico Co., Virginia, with additions showing the defensive lines and works of Richmond. Engineer Bureau of the War Dept., 1864. Uncolored. Scale ca. 1:62,000. 82 × 48 cm.

"Authorities: From Henrico Co. map photographed by U.S. Coast Survey and captured Rebel map."

Indicates Confederate fortifications, houses, names of residents, towns, roads, railroads, relief by hachures, drainage, and vegetation.

644

————————Region embraced in the operations of the armies against Richmond and Petersburg. Engraved at the Engineer Bureau, War Dep. Bowen & Co. lith., Philada. 1865. Colored. Scale 1:80,000. 82 × 62 cm. *From* 39th Cong., 1st Sess. [1866]—Report of the Chief Engineer, U.S.A. No. 12.

"Authorities. North of James & Appomattox from photograph map captured from the enemy. South of Do. from surveys of Col. N. Michler, Corps of Engineers."

Union works are colored red and Confederate works are blue. Map includes roads, railroads, towns, street patterns of Petersburg, Richmond, and Manchester, drainage, relief by hachures, and houses and names of residents in outlying areas.

Another copy is in the Samuel P. Heintzelman papers, Manuscript Division, L.C., container no. 11 (in poor condition).

645

————————[Richmond east to Charles City C. H.] Lith. of J. F. Gedney, Wash. D.C. 1864. Uncolored. Scale 1:63,360. 64 × 89 cm.

Two printed sheets dated May 19 and 27, 1864, joined together forming a continuous map. Roads, railroads, houses and names of residents, drainage, and towns are indicated. The map has been annotated with colored pencils to show the routes of the 2nd, 5th, 6th, 9th, and 18th corps.

645.5

U.S. *Coast Survey.*

Map of the city of Richmond, Virginia. From a survey by I. H. Adams, Assist., U.S. Coast Survey, 1858, with additions from Smith's map of Henrico County, 1853. Prepared at the U.S. Coast Survey Office, A. D. Bache, Supt. H. Lindenkohl & Chas. G. Krebs, lith. 1864. Colored. Scale ca. 1:13,350. 46 × 51 cm.

G3884 .R5 1864 .U5

General map indicating streets and street names, important buildings, and relief by hachures. Water is tinted blue.

This map was acquired by the Library of Congress in 1948 with the purchase of the papers and maps of Jedediah Hotchkiss.

Longitude and latitude of the Washington Observatory added in ink in the right margin.

645.6

————————Another issue.

G3884 .R5 1864 .U51

Water is colored green and the built-up area is brown. Map has been annotated with a 1¼-inch grid.

This map was acquired by the Library of Congress in 1948 with the purchase of the papers and maps of Jedediah Hotchkiss.

645.7

————————Another edition. Published by C. Bohn, Washington, and sold by booksellers in Richmond, Va. [1864] Uncolored. Scale ca. 1:13,350. 46 × 51 cm.

G3884 .R5 1864 .U52

646

————————[Military map of Richmond and vicinity]. Projection by F. Fairfax, Coast Survey Office. [1864–65] Scale 1:7920. Photocopy (negative). 14 maps on 84 overlapping sheets. Each approximately 45 × 56 cm.

G3884 .R5S5 s7 .U5

Complete in 28 sheets. Geography and Map Division has sheets 9 to 17, 19, 20, 23, 24, and 28.

Accompanied by index "Diagram of the 8 in. to a mile maps." Base map entitled "Military map of south-eastern Virginia," 1864 (Negative photocopy in 2 parts, each 53 × 46 cm.).

Detailed map showing fortifications, towns, roads, railroads, street names, houses, names of residents in rural areas, drainage, vegetation, and relief by hachures.

Geography and Map Division also has a photocopy (positive): 14 maps on 29 sheets, each approximately 45 × 134 cm. Index map, 50 × 86 cm.

646.2

U.S. *National Park Service.*

Richmond. [Washington] Government Printing Office, 1980. Colored. Scale ca. 1:140,000. 40 × 42 cm.

G3882 .R5 1980 .U5

Map illustrates a descriptive leaflet entitled "Richmond National Battlefield Park, Virginia."

Inset: [Map of downtown Richmond showing the location of the Chimborazo Visitor Center and tour route] 8 × 15 cm.

Map indicates 1862 and 1864 battle sites, battle sites that are not part of the park, and the tour route.

646.5

————————Richmond National Battlefield Park. March 1968. Revised 1971 [Washington, Government Printing Office, 1971]. Colored. Scale ca. 1:140,000. Map 27 × 24 cm. on sheet 29 × 42 cm.

G3882 .R5 1971 .U5

Map illustrates a descriptive leaflet entitled "Richmond National Battlefield Park, Virginia" and indicates sites of 1862 and 1864 battles, roads, and tour route.

646.6

————————Another issue. 1978.

G3882 .R5 1978 .U5

646.7

————————Richmond National Battlefield Park, Virginia. Oct. 1958 [Washington] Government Printing Office, 1958. Uncolored. Scale ca. 1:250,000. Map 19 × 13 cm. on sheet 22 × 61 cm.

G3882 .R5 1958 .U5

Map illustrates a descriptive leaflet entitled "Richmond National Battlefield Park, Virginia" and shows location of Union and Confederate forces, trenches, forts, park boundary, and tour route.

647

Virginia Passenger and Power Company.

Map of Richmond-Petersburg and adjacent territory showing lines of communication and points of historical interest, compiled and brought to date from government, state, county, city, private and actual surveys by the Engineering Department of the Virginia Passenger & Power Co., January 1, 1907. P. P. Pilcher, J. M. N. Allen, and J. A. B. Gibson, delineators. Calvin Whiteley, Jr., C.E., Railway Dept. [Printed by] the Matthews-Northrup Works, Buffalo, N.Y. Copyright, 1903, by Virginia Passenger and Power Co. Copyright, 1907, by receivers, Virginia Passenger and Power Co. Colored. Scale ca. 1:135,000. 22 × 61 cm.

Union fortifications are colored purple, and Confederate fortifications are colored red.

648

Weyss, John E. *and* L. Dessez.

Richmond. [1862–65] Surveyed under the direction of N. Michler, Maj: of Engrs., Bvt. Brig. Genl. U.S.A., and P. S. Michie, Capt. of Engrs. Bvt. Brig. Genl. U.S.V. Surveyed & drawn by Maj. J. E. Weyss & L. Dessez, assisted by Theil-

kuhl, Burchardt, Schuman, Thompson, Brown [and] Collett. Photocopy (positive). Scale 1:63,360. 38 × 56 cm.

Title and names of surveyors are in the manuscript.

"No 1" is in the upper right corner.

Union fortifications are colored blue, and Confederate fortifications are red.

649

Wood, Walter B., *and* J. E. Edmonds.

Richmond & Petersburg. 1864–5. [London] Methuen & Co. [1905] Uncolored. Scale ca. 1:250,000. 20 × 28 cm. "Map VIII."

Prepared to accompany W. B. Wood and J. E. Edmonds's *A History of the Civil War in the United States, 1861–5* (London, Methuen & Co. [1905]).

Indicates Union and Confederate lines.

ROCKINGHAM COUNTY

649.5

Rockingham-Harrisonburg Civil War Centennial Commission.

Civil War action in Rockingham County, Virginia, 1861–1865. Harrisonburg, Virginia, [196–] Pamphlet, [12] p. 22 × 14 cm.

Following 8 maps drawn by Robert J. Sullivan, Jr., are included in this pamphlet:

p. [3]: Battle of Harrisonburg, June 6, 1862.

p. [4]: Battle of Cross Keys, June 8, 1862.

p. [5]: Battle of Port Republic, June 8–9, 1862.

p. [6–7]: Civil War action in Rockingham County, 1861–1865. (Map of county showing location of engagements.)

p. [8]: Cavalry action at Bridgewater, Oct. 4th & 5th 1864.

p. [9]: Cavalry action at Mt. Crawford, Oct. 4th & 5th 1864.

p. [10]: Cavalry action at Brock's Gap, October 6, 1864.

p. [11]: Night attack at Lacey Spring, December 21, 1864.

SAVAGE STATION

650

Wells, Jacob.

Plan of the battle at Savage's Station. [June 29, 1862] Uncolored. Scale ca. 1:22,500. 7 × 10 cm. *From* Century illustrated monthly magazine, v. 30, July 1885. p. 460.

Gives troop positions, names of commanders, batteries, location of field headquarters, roads, "Richmond & York River R.R.," streams, and vegetation.

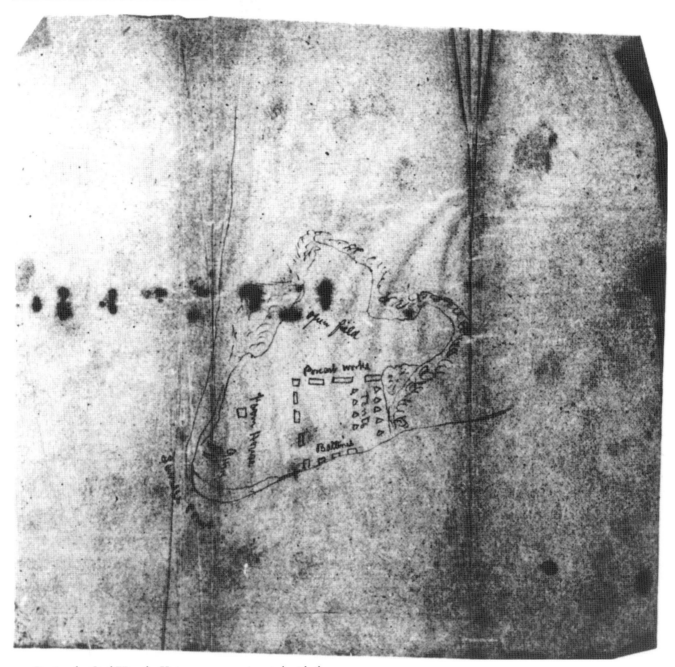

During the Civil War, the Union army experimented with the stationary observation balloon as a means for gathering intelligence data. Depicted here is Aeronaut John La Montain's sketch showing the location of Confederate tents and batteries at Sewell's Point, Virginia. Dated August 10, 1861, this is one of the earliest sketches made from the platform of a balloon. (See entry no. 654.)

SEVEN DAYS' BATTLES

650.2

The heart of the rebellion. Scene of the late Seven Days battles near Richmond. New Base of operations of the Army of the [P]otomac. Philadelphia, July 19, 1862. Uncolored. Scale ca. 1:138,000. 39 × 30 cm. *From* the Philadelphia Inquirer, Saturday, July 19, 1862, p. 1.

Map indicates battle sites, "Union redoubts abandoned," "batteries," "line of Union retreat," and the "present Rebel picket lines."

650.4

Palfrey, J. C.

Seven Days' battles. J. C. Palfrey, Dec. 8, 1876. Boston, The Heliotype Printing Co. [1876] Uncolored. Scale 1: 95,040. 46 × 32 cm.

General map of the area between the Chickahominy River and the James River indicating roads, railroads, villages, and the names of some land owners. Troop positions are not given.

Stamped "War Department Library" on the verso.

650.6

The Philadelphia Inquirer.

Field of McClellan's operations. Scene of the recent battles in front of Richmond—and the late important military operations in eastern Virginia. Philadelphia, 1862. Uncolored. Scale not given. 34 × 24 cm. *From* the Philadelphia inquirer, Wednesday, July 2, 1862. p. 1.

Map of the region east of Richmond showing the location of battlefields on June 25, 26, and 27, 1862.

650.8

The Seven Days' battles on the Peninsula. Positions and movements, June 25 to July 1 [1862] Uncolored. Scale ca. 1:168,000. 21 × 12 cm. *From,* Guernsey, A. H. "The seven days' battles on the Peninsula," Harper's new monthly magazine, v. 32, Dec. 1865–May 1866. p. 491.

651

Wells, Jacob.

Region of the Seven Days' fighting. [June 25–July 1, 1862] Uncolored. Scale ca. 1:210,000. 19 × 14 cm. *From* Century illustrated monthly magazine, v. 30, July 1885. p. 453.

Map of the environs of Richmond showing roads, railroads, fortifications, towns, rivers, bridges, and swamps.

652

Windham, Donald E.

[Seven days' battles, Virginia. June 25–July 1, 1862] Col. H. L. Landers, F.A., Historical Section, Army War College, Washington, D.C. Drawn by Donald E. Windham [1929–31] Photocopy (negative). 10 maps.

Detailed series of maps showing troop positions and names of commanders, fortifications, roads, railroads, towns, bridges, houses, names of residents, drainage, and relief by contour lines.

Map no. 1: Position of troops morning of June 25, 1862. Scale ca. 1:65,000. 32 × 34 cm.

Map no. 2: Battle of Beaver Dam Creek [Mechanicsville], June 26, 1862. Scale ca. 1:15,450. 31 × 29 cm.

Map no. 3: Battle of Gaines' Mill, Virginia, June 27, 1862. Scale ca. 1:16,100. 39 × 34 cm.

Map no. 4: The battle line, June 30, 1862, White Oak Swamp, Glendale [and] Turkey Bridge. Scale ca. 1:32,000. 37 × 34 cm.

Map no. 5: Battle of Malvern Hill, Virginia, July 1, 1862. Scale ca. 1:15,850. 51 × 45 cm.

Map no. 6: Jackson's march, June 26. Scale ca. 1:33,000. 45 × 53 cm. (Jackson's route not indicated on our photostatic copy.)

Maps 7–10: Seven days' battles, Virginia, June 25–July 1, 1862. Scale ca. 1:32,200. 4 sheets, each 49 × 44 cm. (Map of the entire theater of operations of the Seven Days' battles in 4 sheets.)

SEVEN PINES

653

[Map of the battle of Seven Pines] Relative positions at the beginning of the attack, and after dark on May 31 [1862]. Uncolored. Scale ca. 1:106,000. 10 × 14 cm.

Shows troop positions and names of commanders, roads, "Richmond and York River Rail Road," and rivers.

Brief description of the battle appears below the map.

SEWELL'S POINT

654

La Montain, John.

Aerial reconnaissance, August 10th, 1861. Photograph. Scale not given. Map 14 × 13 cm. on sheet 49 × 38 cm.

Reproduction of sketch map of Sewell's Point, Hampton Roads, Virginia ("one of the earliest aerial reconnaissance reports") together with a copy of a report to Maj. Gen. Benj. F. Butler made by John La Mountain, aeronaut. Sketch map locates Confederate tents and batteries at Sewell's Point.

SHENANDOAH VALLEY

654.2

Brown, Samuel Howell.

[Map of the lower Shenandoah Valley, Virginia] Eng. O[ffice, 2nd] Corps, A. N. Va., Sept. 9th 1864. Colored ms. Scale ca. 1:126,720. 68 × 47 cm.

G3882 .S52 1864 .B7 Vault

From the Jubal Early coll. in the Manuscript Division, L.C.

Map of the Shenandoah Valley from Front Royal and Strasburg on the south to the Potomac River on the north, showing roads in red, drainage in blue, relief in gray, and railroads, place names, and names of residents in black.

Map is similar in the area depicted and the content to S. Howell Brown's "Map of the Lower Valley" (Hotchkiss map coll. no. 144).

654.4

Hotchkiss, Jedediah

Map of the Shenandoah Valley, to illustrate the Valley Campaign of "Stonewall" Jackson, 1862. [Compiled by Jedediah Hotchkiss] Drawn by D. C. Humphreys C.E. [Philadelphia, J. B. Lippincott & Co., 1880] Uncolored. Scale ca. 1:860,000. 26 × 32 cm.

Inset: General map [of Virginia and Maryland] 11 × 12 cm.

This map was acquired by the Library of Congress in 1948 with the purchase of the papers and maps of Maj. Jedediah Hotchkiss. It is the base used to produce maps I and II in William Allan's *History of the Campaign of Gen. T. J. (Stonewall) Jackson in the Shenandoah Valley of Virginia* (Philadelphia, J. B. Lippincott & Co., 1880).

Troop positions and movements are not indicated. Includes a few annotations in red ink.

654.6

—————[Maps illustrating campaign of Gen. T. J. (Stonewall) Jackson in the Shenandoah Valley of Virginia. 1862. Compiled by Jed. Hotchkiss] D. C. Humphreys del. [Philadelphia, J. B. Lippincott & Co., 1880] Colored. Various scales. 9 maps on one sheet, 61 × 49 cm.

Proof sheet containing the maps made to illustrate William Allan's *History of the Campaign of Gen. T. J. (Stonewall) Jackson in the Shenandoah Valley of Virginia* (Philadelphia, J. B. Lippincott & Co., 1880). 175 p. Proof sheet was acquired by the Library of Congress in 1948 with the purchase of the papers and maps of Maj. Jedediah Hotchkiss.

Contents:

I. Shenandoah Valley and adjacent country, 1862. 21 × 26 cm.

II. Virginia & Maryland, 1862. 8 × 9 cm.

III. Battle of Kernstown, Sunday, March 23d, 1862. 21 × 14 cm.

IV. Battle of McDowell, May 8, 1862. 14 × 9 cm.

V. Route of Gen. Jackson from Franklin and of Gen. Ewell from Swift Run Gap in the movement against Gen. Banks. May, 1862. 14 × 13 cm.

VI. Region about Winchester showing operations against Gen. Banks. May, 1862. 27 × 20 cm.

VII. Region about Harrisonburg, Swift Run Gap and Port Republic. From surveys by C. S. Engineers. 1862. 13 × 10 cm.

VIII. Battle of Cross Keys, June 8, 1862. 13 × 10 cm.

IX. Battle of Port Republic, June 9, 1862. 13 × 13 cm.

654.8

Hunter's victory at Mount Crawford [October 2, 1864].

Scene of the operations in Shenandoah Valley—capture of Staunton [June 6, 1864] Uncolored. Scale not given. 20 × 12 cm.

Anonymous, undated newspaper map showing the Shenandoah Valley from Front Royal to Staunton. Military information is not given.

655

Lee, A. Y.

Lee's map of the Valley of Virginia. Luray, Valley Land and Improvement Co., ©1890. Colored. Scale not given. Map 16 × 42 cm. on sheet 35 × 49 cm.

Insets: [Mineral and rock deposits in the vicinity of Luray, Virginia] 13 × 11 cm.—[View of] Luray Inn. 13 × 21 cm.

Map of the Shenandoah Valley, showing roads, railroads, towns, relief by hachures, and the location of 30 Civil War battlefields.

655.5

Meigs, John R.

Map of the Shenandoah & Upper Potomac including portions of Virginia and Maryland. Compiled from surveys made under the direction of 1st. Lieut. John R. Meigs, U. S. Engrs., Chief Engineer, Dept. West Virginia and from other reliable authorities. Drawn by P. Witzel, Asst. Engr., September 1864. Cumberland, Maryland, Office of Chief Engineer, Dept. W. Va., 1864. Uncolored. Scale 1:253,440. 80 × 57 cm.

G3882 .S52 1864 .M4

General map extending from Charlottesville north to the Maryland-Pennsylvania boundary and showing roads, railroads, towns, rivers, houses and names of residents, and relief by shading.

656

Whitney, William H.

Union and Confederate campaigns in the lower Shenandoah Valley illustrated. Twenty years after—at the first reunion of Sheridans veterans on the fields and in the camps of the valley. Boston, Sept. 19, 1883. 1 p. l. 33 l. incl. 24 maps (part fold.) 41 × 37 cm.

G1292 .S5S5 W5 1883

Part blueprints and part blue line prints.

"The maps are copies of those published in 1880 in Col. Allan's 'Campaigns of Stonewall Jackson' and are there stated to be based on the United States river surveys; also they are taken from Pond's 'Shenandoah Valley in 1864' published in 1883."

Includes detailed maps of the battles of Winchester (Opequon), Fisher's Hill, and Cedar Creek.

Listed in P. L. Phillips's *A List of Geographical Atlases*

in the Library of Congress (Washington, Government Printing Office, 1909), v. 1, no. 1356.

SPOTSYLVANIA

657

Howell, C. W.

Map of the battle field of Spottsylvania [sic] C. H. Showing the field of operations of the Army of the Potomac commanded by Maj. Gen. George G. Meade, U.S.A., from May 8th to 21st 1865 [i.e., 1864] Surveyed under the orders of Bvt. Col. J. C. Duane, Major of Engineers, Chief Engineer Army of the Potomac, by Bvt. Maj. C. W. Howell, 1st Lieut. of Engineers, assisted by Messrs. L. C. Oswell, L. Bell and R. B. Talfor, topographical engineers. J. Bien, lithographer, New York. [1865?] Colored. Scale 1:15,840. 56 × 67 cm.

G3884 .S74S5 1865 .H6

"Union lines" are blue, "Rebel lines" are red, and "line captured and turned" is colored both blue and red. Union headquarters are identified by small flags. Roads, houses, names of residents, vegetation, drainage, and relief by hachures are also given.

Another copy is from the Orlando M. Poe papers, Manuscript Division, L.C. (G3884 .S74S5 1865 .H61)

Another copy is in the John M. Schofield papers, Manuscript Division, L.C., container no. 74. Number 4 is written in red ink on the verso.

657.5

King, David H., A. Judson Gibbs, *and* Jay H. Northrup.

"The salient" at Spottsylvania [sic]. [May 10–12, 1864] Uncolored. Scale not given. 15 × 8 cm. *From their* History of the ninety-third regiment, New York volunteer infantry, 1861–1865. Milwaukee, Wis., Swain & Tate Co., 1895.

Map indicates the positions of the Corps of Longstreet, Ewell and Hill, and the "charge of Barlow's Div. May 12."

658

Michler, Nathaniel.

Spotsylvania. [May 8–21, 1864] From surveys under the direction of B'v't. Brig.-Gen. N. Michler, Maj. of Engineers. 1867. Uncolored. Scale ca. 1:63,360. 15 × 19 cm. *From* Century illustrated monthly magazine, v. 34, June 1887. p. 288.

"Union works are marked . . . U" and "Confederate works are marked. . . C."

Indicates roads, houses, names of residents, drainage, vegetation, and relief by hachures.

658.1

————Spottsylvania [sic] Court House, from surveys under the direction of Bvt. Brig. Gen. N. Michler, Maj. of Engineers, by command of Bvt. Maj. Genl. A. A. Humphreys, Brig. Genl. & Chief of Engineers. [1864] Surveyed & drawn by Maj: J. E. Weyss, assisted by F. Theilkuhl, J. Strasser & G. Thompson. Photolith. by the N. Y. Lithographing, Engraving & Printing Co., Julius Bien, Supt. 1867. Colored. Scale 1:21,120. 51 × 80 cm.

In this issue, the map is printed on a yellow background with rivers colored green.

Detailed map giving Union works in blue and Confederate works in red, roads, houses, names of occupants, vegetation, drainage, and relief by hachures.

658.2

————Another issue.
Background and rivers are not colored.

659

Russell, Robert E. L.

Battle of Spottsylvania [sic] Courthouse, May 8–21, 1864, between Lee (50,000) and Grant (110,000) immediately following Wilderness battle. A series of 32 pen and ink maps drawn by Mr. Robert E. L. Russell. [Baltimore, 1933] 1 p.l., 31 maps. Photocopy (positive). 47 × 62 cm.

G1292 .S6S5 R8 1933 folio

Bound series of maps with Confederate troop positions hand-colored red. Geography and Map Division also has an unbound negative photocopy.

Listed in C. E. Le Gear's *A List of Geographical Atlases in the Library of Congress* (Washington, Library of Congress, 1973), v. 7, no. 10659.

659.2

Spottsylvania C. H. from May 8th to 21st 1864. Blue line print. Scale ca. 1:32,000. 30 × 41 cm.

In the Charles W. Reed papers, Manuscript Division, L.C., container no. 5 (oversize cabinet 5, drawer 5).

Map indicates Federal and Confederate lines, roads, woodland, houses, and names of occupants.

"From map of U.S. Engineers" is written in the left margin.

STEPHENSON'S DEPOT

660

Ruger, Albert.

Camp of the 196th Regt. O.V.I. Col. R. P. Kennedy, comdg. Stevensons Station [i.e., Stephenson's Depot] near Winchester, Va. Drawn by A. Ruger, Co. E., 196th Reg., O.V.I. Schmidt & Trowe, lith., Baltimore, Md. [186–] Colored view. 43 × 55 cm. (Ruger map coll. no. 179)

G3884 .S84A3 186– .R8 Rug 179

Bird's-eye view.

SUFFOLK

660.5

Owner, William.

Suffolk & environs. [1863] Uncolored ms. Scale ca. 1:200,000. 20 × 16 cm. *In his* Diary, v. 4, tipped-in at end of volume.

In the William Owner papers, Manuscript Division, L.C., container no. 1.

Map indicates roads, railroads, swamps, rivers, houses, and some place names.

Volume 4 of the diary covers from February 13 to June 26, 1863.

661

Soederquist, Oscar.

Military map of Suffolk & vicinity for Majr. Genl. J. A. Dix. Surveyed and drawn by Oscar Soederquist, Lieut, 99th N.Y. Vol. [1863] Colored ms. Scale ca. 1:41,000. 89 × 146 cm.

G3884 .S9S5 1863 .S6 Vault

Detailed pen and ink manuscript drawn on tracing cloth, giving fortifications, houses, names of residents, fences, roads, railroads, vegetation, drainage, and relief by hachures.

TODDS TAVERN

662

Howell, C. W.

Map of the country in the vicinity of Todds Tavern with the position of the 2nd Corps, Army of the Potomac, May 8th 1864. Surveyed under the orders of Bvt. Col. J. C. Duane, Major of Engineers, Chief Engineer—Army of the Potomac, by Bvt. Maj. C. W. Howell, 1st Lieut. of Engineers, assisted by Messers. L. C. Oswell, L. Bell and R. B. Talfor, topographical engineers. J. Bien, lith., N.Y. [1865] Colored. Scale 1:15,840. 38 × 32 cm.

Shows roads, houses, names of residents, relief by hachures, vegetation, drainage, and the headquarters of the Army of the Potomac on May 8, 1864.

Another copy is from the Orlando M. Poe papers, Manuscript Division, L.C. (G3884 .T63S5 1865 .H6)

TOTOPOTOMOY

663

————Map of the battle fields of the Tolopotomoy [i.e., Totopotomoy], and Bethesda Church. Showing the field of operations of the Army of the Potomac commanded by Maj. Gen. George G. Meade, U.S.A., from May 28th to

June 2nd 1864. Surveyed under the orders of Bvt. Col. J. C. Duane, Major of Engineers, Chief Engineer Army of the Potomac, by Bvt. Maj. C. W. Howell, 1st Lieut. of Engineers, assisted by Messrs. L. C. Oswell, L. Bell and R. B. Talfor, topographical engineers. J. Bien, lith., N.Y. [1865?] Colored. Scale 1:15,840. 61 × 72 cm.

G3882 .T6S5 1865 .H6

"Union lines" are blue, "Rebel lines" are red, and "lines captured and turned" are colored both blue and red. Union headquarters are identified by small flags. Roads, houses, names of residents, vegetation, drainage, and relief by hachures are also given.

Another copy is from the Orlando M. Poe papers, Manuscript Division, L.C. (G3882 .T6S5 1865 .H61)

Another copy is in the John M. Schofield papers, Manuscript Division, L.C., container no. 74. Number 7 is written in red ink on the verso.

663.2

Michler, Nathaniel.

Totopotomoy [1864] From surveys under the direction of Bvt. Brig. Gen. N. Michler, Maj. of Engineers, by command of Bvt. Maj. Genl. A. A. Humphreys, Brig. Genl. & Chief of Engineers. Surveyed & drawn by Maj: J. E. Weyss, assisted by F. Theilkuhl, J. Strasser & G. Thompson. Photolith. by the N.Y. Lithographing, Engraving & Printing Co., Julius Bien, Supt. 1867. Colored. Scale 1:21,120. 52 × 84 cm.

In this issue, the map is printed on a yellow background with the Pamunkey River colored green.

Detailed map giving Union works in blue and Confederate works in red, roads, "Virginia Central R. R.," houses, names of residents, vegetation, drainage, and relief by hachures.

663.3

————Another issue.
Background and river are not colored.

663.4

————Another issue.
Lacks the names of the surveyors and lithographer.

WASHINGTON

663.8

Munther, Frederick R.

Plan of camp near Washington [Virginia] by Capt. Munther. July 20, 1862. Uncolored ms. Scale not given. 40 × 33 cm.

In the papers of Maj. Gen. Nathaniel Prentice Banks, Manuscript Division, L.C., container 76.

Title is on the verso.

Pencil and pen and ink sketch drawn on lined paper showing batteries, 1st and 2nd camp lines, company wagon line, ammunition trains, supply trains, and General Banks's headquarters.

Signed "near Washington, Va. July 20th 1862 Frederik R. Munther, Captain a A.D.Ca. [i.e., Additional Aide-de-Camp]."

WAYNESBORO

664

Strauch, George B.

Battle field of Waynesboro, Va. (2d March, 1865). Prepared by Bvt. Lt. Col. G. L. Gillespie, Major of Engineers, from surveys made under his direction, by order of Lt. Gen. P. H. Sheridan, and under the authority of the Hon. Secy. of War, and of the Chief of Engineers, U.S.A. Surveyed by John B. McMaster, Civil Assistant. Drawn by George B. Strauch. J. Bien, N.Y. photo lith. 1873 Colored. Scale 1:9600. 65 × 63 cm.

Detailed map giving Union positions in blue and Confederate positions in red, street pattern of Waynesboro, houses, fences, names of residents in rural areas, roads, "Chesapeake & Ohio Railroad," bridges, fords, vegetation, drainage, and relief by hachures.

WILDERNESS

665

Howell, C. W.

Map of the battle fields of the Wilderness, May 5th, 6th and 7th 1864. Showing the field of operations of the Army of the Potomac commanded by Maj. Gen. George G. Meade, U.S.A. Surveyed under the orders of Bvt. Col. J. C. Duane, Major of Engineers, Chief Engineer Army of the Potomac, by Bvt. Maj. C. W. Howell, 1st Lieut. of Engineers, assisted by Messrs. L. C. Oswell, L. Bell, and R. B. Talfor, topographical engineers. J. Bien, lith., N.Y. [1865] Colored. Scale 1:15,840. 60 × 74 cm.

"Union lines" are blue, "Rebel lines" are red, and "lines captured and turned" are colored both blue and red. Headquarters of the Army of the Potomac is identified by a small flag. Roads, railroads, houses, names of residents, vegetation, drainage, and relief by hachures are also given.

Another copy is from the Orlando M. Poe papers, Manuscript Division, L.C. (G3884 .W49S5 1865 .H6)

Another copy is in the John M. Schofield papers, Manuscript Division, L.C., container no. 74. Number 5 is written in red ink on the verso.

665.4

King, David H., A. Judson Gibbs, *and* **Jay H. Northrup.**

The Wilderness, May 5 & 6, 1864. Colored. Scale not given. 9 × 12 cm. on sheet 22 × 14 cm. *From their* History of the ninety-third regiment, New York volunteer infantry, 1861–1865. Milwaukee, Wis., Swain & Tate Co., 1895.

Map indicates three positions of the regiment during the engagement.

665.8

Michler, Nathaniel.

The Wilderness [1864] From surveys under the direction of Bvt. Brig. Gen. N. Michler, Maj. of Engineers, by command of Bvt. Maj. Genl. A. A. Humphreys, Brig. Genl. & Chief of Engineers. Surveyed & drawn by Maj: J. E. Weyss, assisted by F. Theilkuhl, J. Strasser & G. Thompson. Photolith. by the N. Y. Lithographing, Engraving & Printing Co., Julius Bien, Supt. 1867. Colored. Scale 1:21,120. 78 × 47 cm.

In this issue, the map is printed on a yellow background with the Rapidan River colored green.

Detailed map giving Union works in blue and Confederate works in red, roads, railroads, houses, fences, names of residents, vegetation, drainage, and relief by hachures.

665.9

————————Another issue.

Background and river are not colored.

666

————————The Wilderness. [May 5–7, 1864] From surveys under the direction of Bv't. Brig.-Gen. N. Michler, Maj. of Engineers. 1867. Uncolored. Scale ca. 1:69,000. 21 × 15 cm. *From* Century illustrated monthly magazine, v. 34, June 1887. p. 279.

"Union works are marked U" and "Confederate works are marked C."

Shows roads, houses, names of residents, drainage, vegetation, and relief by hachures.

667

Russell, Robert E. L.

Battle of the Wilderness, May 5, 6 and 7, 1864, between Lee (60,000) and Grant (120,000) including the approach and the movement toward Spottsylvania [sic] Courthouse. A series of 26 pen and ink maps drawn by Mr. Robert E. L. Russell. [Baltimore, 1935] 1 p. l., 26 maps. Photocopy (positive). 42 × 57 cm.

G1292 .W5S5 R8 1935 folio

Bound series of maps. Infantry and cavalry positions, and main roads have been colored by hand.

Geography and Map Division also has an unbound negative photocopy.

Listed in C. E. Le Gear's *A List of Geographical Atlases in the Library of Congress* (Washington, Library of Congress, 1973), v. 7, no. 10660.

668

———Fifteen pen and ink maps of the battle of the Wilderness. Drawn from descriptive readings and map fragments. By Robert E. Lee Russell. Baltimore, 1931. 1 p.l., 15 maps and 2 illustrations. Photocopy (positive). 46 × 62 cm.

G1292 .W5S5 R83 1931 folio

Bound series of maps with Confederate troop positions hand-colored red. Geography and Map Division also has an unbound negative photocopy.

Listed in C. E. Le Gear's *A List of Geographical Atlases in the Library of Congress* (Washington, Library of Congress, 1973), v. 7, no. 10662.

668.5

Wilderness—May 5th and 6, 1864. Blue line print. Scale ca. 1:31,500. 41 × 29 cm.

In the Charles W. Reed papers, Manuscript Division, L.C., container no. 5 (oversize cabinet 5, drawer 5).

Map indicates Union and Confederate lines, roads, woodland, houses and the names of occupants.

WILLIAMSBURG

669

McAlester, Miles D.

Sketch of the battlefield and Confederate works in front of Williamsburg, Va., May 5th 1862, by Lt. M. D. McAlester, Chief Engr., 3rd Corps, Army of the Potomac. Publishsed [sic] by authority of the Hon. the Secretary of War, in the office of the Chief of Engineers, U.S. Army. 1876. Colored. Scale 1:7200. 29 × 31 cm.

Indicates "United States forces" in blue and "Confederate forces" in red, names of Union field commanders, hospitals, roads, houses, names of residents, drainage, vegetation, and relief by hachures.

WINCHESTER

669.5

Fortifications at Winchester, June 1861. Uncolored ms. Scale not given. 40 × 26 cm.

In the papers of Maj. Gen. Nathaniel Prentice Banks, Manuscript Division, L.C., container 76.

Title is on the verso.

Oriented with south at the top of the map.

670

Gillespie, G. L.

Battle field of Winchester, Va. (Opequon) [September 19, 1864]. Prepared by Bvt. Lt. Col. G. L. Gillespie, Major of Engineers, U.S.A., from surveys under his directions, by order of Lt. Gen. P. H. Sheridan, and under the authority of the Hon. Secretary of War, and, of the Chief of Engineers, U.S.A. George B. Strauch and E. Siegesmund, Assistants. 1873. Colored. Scale ca. 1:9600. 94 × 114 cm.

Detailed map of Winchester and vicinity showing Union positions in blue and Confederate positions in red, troop movements, names of commanders, roads, railroads, street plan of Winchester, drainage, vegetation, houses, fences, names of residents, and relief by hachures and contour lines.

671

Russell, Robert E. L.

Sheridan and Early at Winchester. Sketch map: battlefield of Winchester, Va., Sept. 19, 1864, 12 noon. Baltimore, 1932. Photocopy (positive). Scale not given. 11 × 18 cm.

Hand-colored photocopy showing the Confederate position in red and roads in brown. Geography and Map Division also has a negative photocopy.

672

———Sketch map: battlefield of Winchester, Va., Sept. 19, 1864, 3 P.M. Baltimore, 1932. Photocopy (positive). Scale not given. 11 × 18 cm.

Hand-colored photocopy showing the Confederate position in red and roads in brown.

Geography and Map Division also has a negative photocopy.

YORK RIVER

672.5

Humphreys, Andrew A.

York River and Mobajack [sic] Bay, Va. Tracing for Maj. Genl. Franklin from Maj. Humphrey's Com[mandin]g Topl. Engrs., Army of Potomac. [1862?] Colored ms. Scale not given. 66 × 69 cm.

G3882 .Y6 1862 .U5 Vault

Title is from the verso of the map.

Manuscript map drawn on tracing linen depicting the mouth of the York River and Mobjack Bay. Roads are shown in red, and place names and the names of a few residents in black. One battery is shown on a tributary to the North River.

YORKTOWN

673

Abbot, Henry L.

Official plan of the siege of Yorktown, Va., conducted by the Army of the Potomac under command of Maj. Gen. George B. McClellan, U.S.A., April 5th to May 3rd 1862. Prepared under the direction of Brig. Gen. J. G. Barnard, Chief Engr., by Lieut. Henry L. Abbot, Top. Engrs. A.D.C. Chas. G. Krebs, Engr. Lith. by J. F. Gedney, Washn. Uncolored. Scale ca. 1:13,500. 43 × 72 cm.

"This plan shows about half the line, including the point of attack. The Rebel works are laid down from reconnoissances [sic] made immediately after the evacuation, and are correctly, but very incompletely represented, owing to want of time for sketching minor details.—Our works of siege, including the approaches in the ravines of Wormley Creek, are accurately shown. Redoubts being denoted by letters, and batteries by numbers."

Contains a list of the "proposed armament of batteries."

Indicates headquarters of Generals McClellan, Porter, Woodbury, and Heintzelman, houses, names of residents, roads, drainage, vegetation, and relief by hachures and spot heights.

673.3

Humphreys, Andrew A.

Sketch exhibiting the position of Yorktown, with the approaches. From reconnoissance [sic] and survey between the 5th and 18th of April, 1862. By command of Maj. Genl. Geo. B. McClellan, U.S.A., commanding the Army of the Potomac. A. A. Humphreys, Maj. and Chief of Top'l Engineers. Photocopy (positive). Scale 1:60,000. 34 × 37 cm.

In the Abraham Lincoln papers, Manuscript Division, L.C., vol. 73, no. 15399.

Map has been annotated to show Federal positions near Yorktown, including the location of "General Head Quarters."

673.7

Worret, Ch.

The siege of Yorktown, April 1862. Drawn on the spot by C. Worret 20. N.Y.R. Lith. by E. Sachse & Co., Baltimore. Washington, D.C. and Old Point Comfort, Va., C. Bohn, ©1862. Colored view. 28 × 43 cm.

"Entered accord. to Act of Congress A.D. 1862 by C. Bohn in the Clerks Office of the District of Columbia."

Bird's-eye view of the Union siege of Yorktown, with 23 places, batteries, ship positions, troop positions, and field headquarters keyed by number to list in lower margin.

WASHINGTON, D.C.

674

Arnold, E. G.

Topographical map of the orginal District of Columbia and environs: showing the fortifications around the city of Washington. By E. G. Arnold C.E. New York, G. Woolworth Colton, 1862. Colored. Scale ca. 1:32,000. 76 × 85 cm.

G3851 .S5 1862 .A71 Vault

Detailed map indicating forts, principal buildings in Washington, street names and roads, railroads, wards, towns, houses and names of residents in outlying areas, drainage, and relief by hachures.

Population statistics are in the lower left corner.

Following handwritten note by W. C. Dodge, 116 B St. N.E., Washington, D.C. appears on the verso: This map was suppressed by the Govt. because of the information it would give the rebels. I got this copy in 1862 and have had it ever since. W. C. D.

For additional copies see G3851 .S5 1862 .A7 Vault oversize and G3851 .S5 1862 .A71 Vault copies 2, 3, and 4.

674.1

————Another copy.

G3851 .S5 1862 .A72 Vault Copy 3

This copy has been annotated in ink to show the location of hospitals. In addition, "Herewood Hospital" has been corrected to read "Harewood Hospital." Originally this copy was accompanied by a handwritten "List of Hospitals. [By] R. H. Steele, No. 406, 10th St. N.W., H & I." The list is now missing.

675

————Facsimile. [1902]

G3851 .S5 1862 .A7 1902

Published by the Capital Curio Co., for the thirty-sixth Annual Encampment of the Grand Army of the Republic, Washington, D.C., 1902.

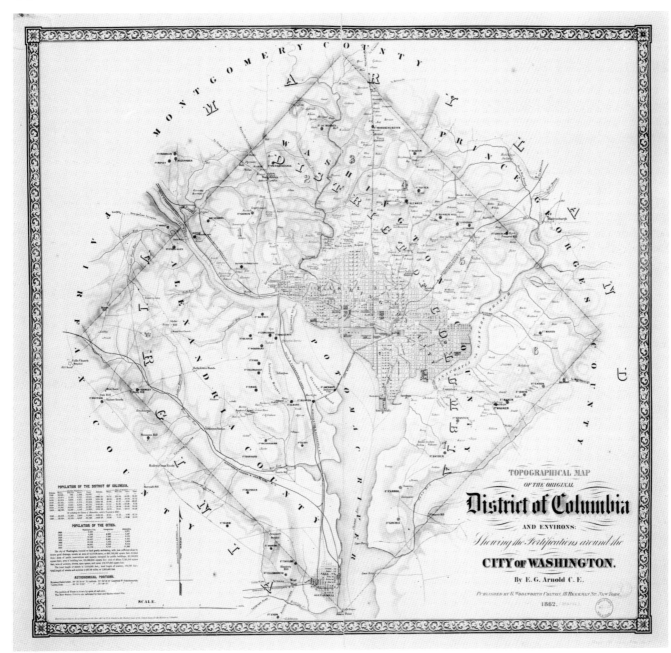

Map of Washington, D.C., and vicinity by civil engineer E. G. Arnold showing the defenses built to protect the city. In a handwritten note on the verso of one of the Library's copies, W. C. Dodge of Washington, D.C., wrote that "This map was suppressed by the Govt. because of the information it would give the rebels. I got this copy in 1862 and have had it ever since." (See entry no. 674.)

675.1

————Facsimile edition. Washington, Anne W. Ketcham/A. W. K. Designs, ©1981. Colored. Scale ca. 1:45,000. 56 × 61 cm.

    G3851 .S5 1862 .A7 1981

676

Barnard, John G.

    Map of the environs of Washington compiled from Boschkes' map of the District of Columbia and from surveys of the U.S. Coast Survey showing the line of the defences of Washington as constructed during the war from 1861 to

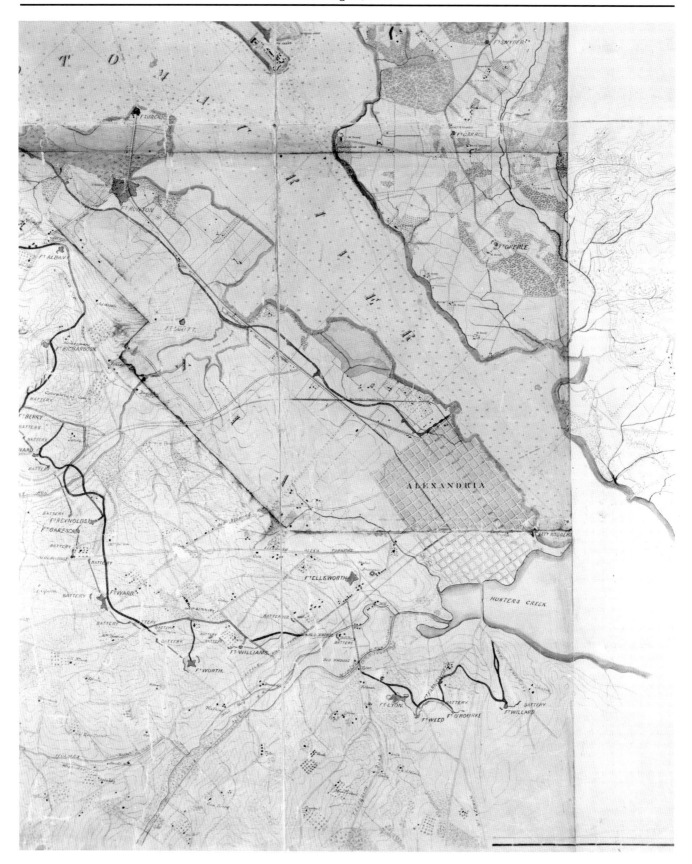

1865—inclusive. To accompany the report on the defences of Washington by Bv't. Major Genl. J. G. Barnard, Col. of Engineers, late Chief Engineer of Defences &c. Colored. Part ms. and part printed. Scale 1:15,840. 132 × 144 cm.

G3851 .S5 1865 .B3 Vault Oversize

The title and the Virginia portion of the map are entirely in manuscript, while that portion showing the District of Columbia is a printed map with manuscript annotations.

"No. 187.L" is on the verso.

Detailed map indicating forts, batteries, rifle pits, "military roads especially constructed," "military roads adopted from existing county roads," "county roads," street names, railroads, drainage, vegetation, contour lines, soundings, houses, and names of residents in outlying areas.

677

Blunt, Edmund, *and* George W. Blunt.

E. & G. W. Blunt's corrected map of Washington and the seat of war on the Potomac. [1862?] Colored. Scale ca. 1:403,000. 51 × 35 cm.

G3851 .S5 1862 .E2

Map of Washington and the adjacent portions of Virginia and Maryland, showing fortifications, towns, roads, railroads, drainage, relief by hachures, and geographic coordinates.

Another copy is in the Fillmore map coll. no. 73-A. Signed in ms. on verso: Millard Fillmore 1862.

678

Bohn, Casimir.

District of Columbia and the seat of war on the Potomac. Lithographed and printed by E. Sachse & Co., Baltimore, Md. Published by C. Bohn, Washington, D.C. [186–?] Colored view. Not drawn to scale. 24 × 38 cm.

G3851 .S5 186– .B6

Bird's-eye view of Washington and vicinity showing roads, railroads, towns, rivers, and the camps of 15 Federal army units. The units are listed below the view.

This view was in the possession of Jedediah Hotchkiss at the time of his death. Major Hotchkiss served as topographic engineer with the Army of Northern Virginia. In

Detailed manuscript and printed map compiled by the U.S. Army Corps of Engineers showing the entire interlinking network of fortifications defending the nation's capital. This remarkable map was made to accompany Gen. John G. Barnard's official report on the defenses of the city. Albert Boschke's 1861 printed map of Washington, D.C., was used as the base, and to it army mapmakers added, by hand, cultural data on Virginia, a new map title, forts, batteries, and rifle pits, as well as the military roads built to link them. Displayed here is the portion of the map showing Alexandria, Virginia, and vicinity. (See entry no. 676.)

July 1948, the Library of Congress purchased his map collection.

678.5

Boschke, Albert.

Topographical map of the District of Columbia surveyed in the years 1856, '57, '58 & '59 by A. Boschke. Washington, D. McClelland, Blanchard & Mohun, 1861. Uncolored. Scale 1:15,840 ("4 inches to one mile"). 100 × 104 cm.

G3850 1861 .B6 Vault

"Engraved by D. McClelland, Washington, D.C."

"Entered according to Act of Congress in the year 1861, by D. McClelland, Blanchard & Mohun, Hugh B. Sweeny and Thos. Blagden."

Oriented with north in the upper left corner.

Detailed topographic map of the original ten-mile-square District of Columbia showing streets, street names, houses, and public buildings in the planned portion of the city and Georgetown. In the rural areas north of the Potomac River, the map also indicates roads, property lines, houses and names of residents, woodland, orchards, and relief by contour lines. Soundings are given for the Potomac River and the Eastern Branch (Anacostia River). Because of its value to the enemy and its potential use by the U.S. Army, the copper plates from which the Boschke map was printed were seized by the Federal government. For an example of its military use see entry no. 676.

678.7

District of Columbia. *Civil War Centennial Commission*

Map of Washington, D.C.: Washington area [and] the old city. Washington, District of Columbia Civil War Centennial Commission [1961?] Colored. Not drawn to scale. 2 maps on 1 sheet 50 × 71 cm.

G3851 .E635 1961 .D5

Title on outside when folded: Civil War centennial map of Washington, D.C.

"Civil War sites of historic interest" are listed at bottom of sheet and keyed to locations on maps.

Test and illustrations appear on verso.

679

Grand Army of the Republic. Thirty-sixth National Encampment. Committee on Marking Points of Historic Interest.

Map showing location of war-time hospitals [in Washington]. Uncolored. Scale ca. 1:35,000. 18 × 24 cm.

G3851 .E58 1865 .G7

Title when folded: Catalogue of points of historic interest selected and marked by the committee on marking points of historic interest for the thirty-sixth national encampment of the Grand Army of the Republic. Washington, 1902.

Leaflet lists the "defenses of Washington," 200 "points of historic interest," 15 "important statues," and 8 "residences of President Roosevelt's cabinet." Hospitals are keyed by number to the above map. The leaflet also includes another map entitled "Map of fortifications and defenses of Washington. Taken from a map issued by the War Department in 1865," scale ca. 1:116,000, size 23 × 18 cm.

680

Hodasevich, R. A.

Topographical map, 1st Brigade, defenses north of Potomac, Washington, D.C. Executed by R. A. Hodasevich (Chodasiewicz), Private, 2d Art. P. V. Bat. G. 1st September 1863. Colored ms. Scale 1:2500. 5 irregular sheets mounted on 4 sheets, 103 × 150 cm.

G3851 .S5 1863 .H61 Vault

"189, L. Sheet 1."

"Drawn in the field with the plane table from April 17th 1863 to June 27th and from July 20th to August 25th. But from June 27th to July 20th a map of distances to principal points in range was executed for each fort of the brigade."

"This map includes 5 sheets of paper."

Detailed map of the environs of forts DeRussy, Stevens, Slocum, Totten, Slemmer, Bunker Hill, Saratoga, Thayer, Lincoln, and batteries Sill and Jameson, showing fortifications, rifle pits, roads, houses, names of residents, fences, vegetation, drainage, and relief by contour lines.

681

——————Topographical. Colored ms. Scale 1:2400. 2 parts, 94 × 220 cm. and 95 × 421 cm.

G3851 .S5 1863 .H6 Vault

"189, L. Sheet 2" and "189, L. Part of Sheet 2."

Manuscript tracing apparently made from the preceding map by R. A. Hodasevich. Lacks author statement, date, and complete title.

682

Map of fortifications and defenses of Washington. Taken from a map issued by the War Department in 1865. Uncolored. Scale ca. 1:115,000. 23 × 18 cm.

G3851 .S5 1865 .M3

"Appendix A" is in the upper left corner.

Shows fortifications, roads, street pattern of Washington, Alexandria, and Georgetown, towns, railroads, and the boundary of the District of Columbia.

682.5

Map of the defences of Washington (from atlas accompanying official records). [1865] Colored. Scale ca. 1:90,000. 30 × 23 cm.

G3851 .S5 1865 .M3

Forts and "roads used for military purposes" are colored blue. Map is based on "Defenses of Washington. Extract of military map of N. E. Virginia" (1865) reproduced in the U. S. War Department's *Atlas to Accompany the Official Records of the Union and Confederate Armies* (Washington, Government Printing Office, 1891–95), plate LXXXIX, no. 1.

682.7

Snedaw, R. K.

Map of Washington City and forts, R. K. Snedaw, Topog. [186–?] Colored ms. Scale ca. 1:63,360. 36 × 36 cm.

In the Montgomery C. Meigs papers, Manuscript Division, L.C., 10, oversize cabinet 4, drawer 3.

Title is on the verso.

Signed in ink in the lower right corner by Meigs.

Attractive manuscript map showing forts surrounding Washington, D.C. Map also depicts railroads, the boundary of the city, roads and turnpikes, the "new military road" linking Fort Stevens and Fort Alexander, and a "convalescent camp" near Fort Barnard.

682.8

Snell, T. Loftin.

Stranger's guide to Mr. Johnson's Washington—Summer 1865: the city that Mr. Lincoln knew. [Washington, Washington Post] ©1865. Colored. Scale not given. 53 × 32 cm.

G3851 .S55 1965 .S6

From Potomac (magazine), The Washington Post, June 20, 1965.

Copyright no. F 39826, June 21 1965. "©1965 T. Loftin Snell."

Map of the city center indicating points of interest and historical notes. "1965 note: buildings in black still exist."

682.9

——————Stranger's guide to Washington, D.C.: the city as Mr. Lincoln knew it. [Washington] ©1965. Colored. Scale not given. 93 × 55 cm.

G3851 .S5 1965 .S6

Copyright no. F 40356, September 10, 1965. "©1965 T. Loftin Snell."

Similar to the preceding map (entry no. 682.8), but larger in size and with a change in the title.

683

U.S. *Army. Army of the Potomac.*

[Map of the fortifications within the District of Columbia. 1862] Photocopy (positive). Scale not given. 44 × 52 cm.

G3851 .S5 1862 .U5

"Furnished for the use of the Office of the General of Ordnance by command of M. G. McClellan, [signed] J. N. Macomb, Lt. Col. & A. D. Camp, Chf. T.E., Army of Potomac, 18th March 1862"

At bottom of map in red ink: Drawer 48, Portfolio 1, no. 4.

Map indicates location and names of forts, streets, houses, and relief by contour lines.

684

U.S. *Army. Corps of Engineers.*

Extract of military map of N.E. Virginia showing forts and roads. Engineer Bureau, War Dept. 1865. Colored. Scale 1:63,360. 61 × 43 cm.

G3851 .S5 1865 .U51

"Note. The Coast Survey maps were used in the compilation north of the Potomac, outside of the Dist. of Columbia."

Forts are colored red, and roads are brown.

Indicates street pattern of Washington, relief by hachures, towns, vegetation, drainage, railroads, and houses and names of residents in the outlying areas.

685

————————Facsimile. [Kensington, Maryland, 1958]
G3851 .S5 1865 .U51 1958
Publisher of the facsimile is unknown.

685.1

————————Facsimile. [Arlington, Virginia, Cooper-Trent Operations, 1969?]
G3851 .S5 1865 .U5 1969
Similar in appearance to the facsimile listed as entry no. 685.

686

————————Another issue. *From* 39th Cong., 1st Sess. [1866]—Report of the Chief Engineer U.S.A. No. 1.
G3851 .S5 1865 .U52
In lower right corner: Bowen & Co., lith., Philada.

687

————————Another issue. Colored. Scale 1:63,360. 61 × 50 cm.
G3851 .S5 1865 .U53
This issue extends 2⅝ miles past the east corner of the District of Columbia, whereas the preceding issues (entry nos. 684–686) terminate at the east corner.

688

————————[Maps of the environs of forts Franklin, Alexander, and Ripley, in Montgomery County, Maryland. 186–]

4 maps drawn on one sheet. Colored ms. Scales not given. 55 × 68 cm.
G3843 .M6S5 186– .U5 Vault
"211, L. Sheet 4"
Four sketch maps, all covering the same area but in various stages of completion. The map with the most detail includes roads, drainage, vegetation, contours, and fortifications.

Forts Franklin, Alexander, and Ripley were part of the defenses of Washington.

688.5

————————Topographical map of the District of Columbia. [1861?] Colored ms. Scale ca. 1:253,440. 87 × 105 cm.
G3850 1861 .U5 Vault
"211, L. Sheet 3."

Incomplete manuscript on tracing linen from A. Boschke's "Topographical Map of the District of Columbia surveyed in the years 1856 '57 '58 & '59" (Washington, D.C., D. McClelland, Blanchard & Mohun, 1861). Oriented with north toward the upper left, the map indicates relief by form lines, as well as a few roads, houses, and property lines.

"Transferred from Office of Chf. Engr., Defenses of Washington, to Engr. Dept. Jan'y 1866."

Stamped on verso: By Transfer, Chief Engineers Office, War Department.

689

U.S. *National Park Service*

Guide leaflets for the tour of historic Civil War defenses—Washington, D.C. 1938. 20 l. (9 fold.) 27 × 21 cm.

Contains maps and photographs of the fortifications. The maps are as follows:

2) U.S. *National Capital Parks.* Route of forts and geological tours, District of Columbia. 1938. Scale ca. 1:46,000. 33 × 35 cm.

3) Map showing the defenses of Washington specially compiled for the photographic history of the Civil War from the official map of the Engineer Bureau of the U.S. War Department, drawn 1865. Scale ca. 1:140,000. 19 × 15 cm.

4) Arnold, E. G. Topographical map of the original District of Columbia and environs: showing the fortifications around the city of Washington. New York, G. Woolworth Colton, 1862. Scale ca. 1:130,000. 18 × 21 cm.

5) Defenses of Washington. [Forts Sumner, Mansfield, Simmons, Bayard, and Gaines] Report of Gen. Barnard. Scale ca. 1:13,500. 23 × 37 cm.

6) Defenses of Washington. Fort Bayard. Report of Gen. Barnard. Scale ca. 1:1600. 24 × 19 cm. (Plan and 8 cross sections)

8) Defenses of Washington. [Forts Reno and Kearny] Report of Gen. Barnard. Scale ca. 1:13,250. 24 × 21 cm.

9) Defenses of Washington. Fort Reno. Report of Gen. Barnard. Scale ca. 1:1525. 24 × 40 cm. (Plan and 9 cross sections)

10) Defenses of Washington. [Forts De Russy, Stevens and Slocum] Report of Gen. Barnard. Scale ca. 1:13,500. 23 × 37 cm.

13) Fort Slocum. Scale ca. 1:1225. 23 × 26 cm.

15) Defenses of Washington. [Forts Totten, Slemmer, Bunker Hill, and Saratoga] Report of Gen. Barnard. Scale ca. 1:13,200. 24 × 27 cm.

17) Defenses of Washington. [Forts Thayer, Lincoln, and Mahan] Report of Gen. Barnard. Scale ca. 1:13,200. 24 × 39 cm.

19) Defenses of Washington. Tete-DuPont—Benning's Bridge. Report of Gen. Barnard. Scale 1:1600. 24 × 18 cm. (Plan and 2 cross sections)

ANACOSTIA RIVER

689.5

Cluss, A.

Reconnaissance of "Anacostia" above Wash. Navy Yd. Aug. 18th 1861, made by A. Cluss under orders of Com. J. A. Dahlgren. Colored ms. Scale 1:12,000. 59 × 39 cm.

G3852 .A5 1861 .C5 Vault

"211, L. Sheet 16."

Map of the Anacostia River from the "Navy Yard Bridge" to a short distance above "Benning's Bridge" showing the river channel, the "flats covered with sea-weed," water depths, the "ship-house" at the Navy Yard, "Congress burying ground," powder magazine, and poor house.

BATTERY DOUGLAS

689.7

Schonborn, Harry F.

Battery Douglas [Defenses of Washington, D.C. Dec. 1861?] Uncolored pencil drawings. Scales vary. 3 p., 19 × 15 cm.

In the notebook of Harry F. Schonborn, Manuscript Division, L.C.

Measured pencil drawings.

CARVER BARRACKS

690

Magnus, Charles.

Carver Barracks, Washington, D.C. Lith. & print. by Chas. Magnus, N.Y. ©1864. Colored view. Not drawn to scale. 31 × 44 cm.

Perspective drawing.

Transferred to the Prints and Photographs Division, L.C.

FINLEY HOSPITAL

691

Seymour, Charles H.

Birds eye view of Finley U.S. Genl. Hospital. ©1864. Uncolored view. Not drawn to scale. 28 × 41 cm.

Twenty buildings are identified.

Perspective drawing.

Transfered to the Prints and Photographs Division, L.C.

FORT BUNKER HILL

691.1

Schonborn, Harry F.

Fort Bunker Hill [Defenses of Washington, D.C. Dec. 1861?] Uncolored pencil drawings. Scales vary. 12 p., 19 × 15 cm.

In the notebook of Harry F. Schonborn, Manuscript Division, L.C.

Measured pencil drawings.

FORT MAHAN

691.15

Fort Mahan—[Defenses of Washington, D.C.] Jan. 3rd, 1862. Uncolored pencil drawings. Scales vary. 10 p., 19 × 15 cm. each.

In the notebook of Harry F. Schonborn, Manuscript Division, L.C.

Measured pencil drawings.

691.2

U.S. *Army. Corps of Engineers.*

Hill no. 3 opposite Fort Mahan. [186–?] Colored ms. Scale not given. 39 × 66 cm.

G3852 .F59A1 186– .U5 Vault

Pencil and ink sketch of hill in vicinity of Fort Mahan. Contour lines at 5-foot intervals are drawn in red.

Title written lightly in pencil.

"211, L Sheet 10" noted in the lower right corner.

FORT MEIGS

691.3

————Hill between No. 1 & Fort Meigs. [186–] Colored ms. Scale not given. 52 × 77 cm.

G3852.F62A1 186– .H5 Vault

"211, L. Sheet 14."

Map shows contour lines in the vicinity of Fort Meigs. Map is oriented with north to the left.

Stamped on verso: By Transfer, Chief Engineers Office, War Department.

FORT SARATOGA

691.35

Schonborn, Harry F.

Fort Saratoga—[Defenses of Washington, D.C. Dec. 1861?] Uncolored pencil drawings. Scale ca. 1:320. 2 p., 19 × 15 cm.

In the notebook of Harry F. Schonborn, Manuscript Division, L.C.

Measured pencil drawing.

Page following plan of Fort Saratoga includes the following note: Any foreman employed by me will give Mr. Schomborn [sic] any assistance he wishes in measuring fortifications. He has permission to take his meals at any mess house he is working in the neighborhood of. [Signed] Wm. C. Grennelle [?] Egr. in chr. of forts . . .

FORT SLOCUM

691.4

U.S. Army. Corps of Engineers.

[Map showing the site of Fort Slocum and vicinity. 186–] Colored ms. Scale not given. 30 × 28 cm. on sheet 48 × 36 cm.

G3852.F624A1 186– .U5 Vault

"211, L. Sheet 18."

Map of the environs of Fort Slocum (fort not named) showing relief by form lines and hachures, roads, and the houses of Walker, Saunders, and Murphy.

"Transf'd from Office of Chf. Engr., Defenses of Washington, to Engr. Dept. 1866."

Stamped on verso: By Transfer, Chief Engineers Office, War Department.

FORT STANTON

691.6

——————Topographical sketch near Fort Staunton [i.e., Stanton] from points not under fire of its guns. [186–?] Uncolored ms. Scale 1:2400 (200 feet to 1 inch). 48 × 45 cm.

G3852 .F63A1 186– .T6 Vault

Pen and ink and pencil manuscript map indicating relief by hachures and outlines of buildings.

"211, L. Sheet 15" is noted below the title in the upper left corner.

Stamped on verso: By Transfer, Chief Engineers Office, War Department.

FORT TOTTEN

691.7

Schonborn, Harry F.

Fort Totten—from actual measurements taken by Harry F. Schonborn—Dec. 20, 1861. Uncolored pencil drawings. Scales vary. 12 p., 19 × 15 cm.

In the notebook of Harry F. Schonborn, Manuscript Division, L.C.

Measured pencil drawings.

QUEEN'S FARM

691.8

U.S. *Army. Corps of Engineers.*

Sketch of hill to be used for gov't fortification on Queen's farm. [186–?] Uncolored ms. Scale ca. 1:3000. 21 × 31 cm.

G3852 .Q4 186– .S5 Vault

"211, L. Sheet 11" appears in the upper left corner.

Stamped on verso: By Transfer, Chief Engineers Office, War Department.

Pen and ink manuscript map indicating relief by hachures. Fortification is not depicted.

WEST VIRGINIA

692

See Sherman map coll. no. 179.

693

Richardson.

Map to illustrate the report of Brigadier-General Hill. Richardson, sc., N.Y. [July 1861] Uncolored. Scale not given. 17 × 27 cm.

Map of part of West Virginia and western Maryland from Romney west to Grafton, showing the battle of Corricks Ford on July 14th, routes used by Union and Confederate columns, location of bridges burned by Confederates on July 12, 14, and 15, and the "point where pursuit was abandoned by orders of Major-General McClellan."

693.5

Wood, Walter B., *and* **J. E. Edmonds.**

West Virginia. [London] Methuen & Co. [1905] Uncolored. Scale ca. 1:2,500,000. 19 × 12 cm.

"Map II."

Prepared to accompny W. B. Wood and J. E. Edmonds's *A History of the Civil War in the United States, 1861–5* (London, Methuen & Co. [1905]).

Map indicates battle sites.

CARNIFEX FERRY

694

U.S. *Army. Corps of Engineers.*

Map of the battle field of Carnifex Ferry, Gauley River, West Va., Sept. 10th 1861. United States forces commanded by Brig. Gen. W. S. Rosecrans. Published by authority of the Hon. the Secretary of War. Office of the Chief of Engineers, U.S.A. 1876. Colored. Scale 1:5280. 47 × 44 cm.

"Copied from a map accompanying the report of Gen. Rosecrans."

Indicates Confederate works and batteries at Camp Gauley, Union positions during attack and names of units, roads, drainage, houses, fences, vegetation, and relief by hachures.

GAULEY BRIDGE

695

Raynolds, William F., William C. Margedant, *and* **W. Angelo Powell.**

Military reconnaissance in the vicinity of Gauley Bridge, Department of western Virginia, Brig. Genl. W. S. Rosecrans, comd'g., Sept. 11th to Nov. 15, 1861. By W. F. Raynolds, Capt. Top. Engr's., W. Margedant, O. V. [and] W. Angelo Powell, C. Engr. Published by authority of the Hon. the Secretary of War in the office of the Chief of Engineers, U.S. Army, 1879. Colored. Scale 1:63,360. 69 × 87 cm.

Capt. (later General) Nathaniel Michler and Maj. John E. Weyss's detailed 1863 survey of the topography and defensive works surrounding the strategic confluence of the Potomac and Shenandoah Rivers at Harpers Ferry. Until their abandonment on April 18, 1861, Harpers Ferry had been the site of the U.S. Arsenal and Armory. (See entry no. 700.)

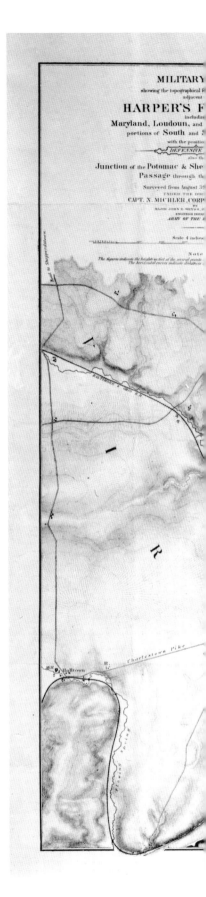

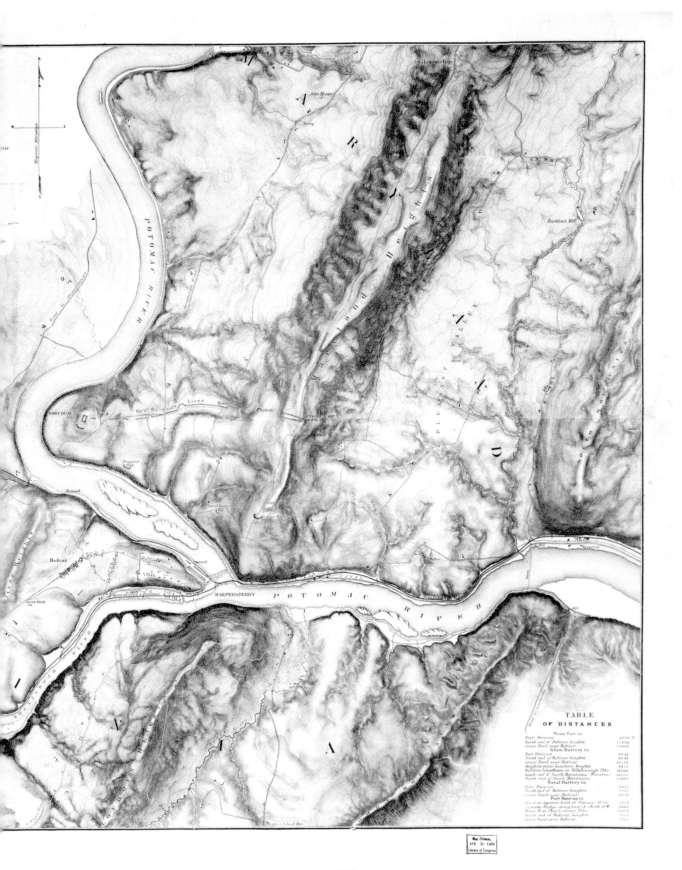

"United States forces" are colored blue, and "Confederate forces & works" are red.

Shows Union headquarters, towns, roads, houses, names of residents, drainage, and relief by hachures.

696

————Another issue. Julius Bien & co., photo lith. N.Y.

GREENBRIER RIVER

697

McRae, A. T.

Map of the battle ground of Greenbrier River, drawn and published by A. T. McRae, C.S.A., Quitman Guards, First Reg't Ga. Vol's. Engraved J. Baumgarten, Richmond, Virginia. Gary, printer, Richmond, Va. [1861?] Uncolored. Scale ca: 1:11,200. 38 × 43 cm.

Confederate imprint.

Sketch map showing Confederate camps and batteries, position of "Yankee artillery," "Gen. Jacksons quars.," "posn. of Genrl. and staff" during engagement, drawings of principal buildings, roads, and drainage.

HARPERS FERRY

697.5

Michler, Nathaniel.

Harper's Ferry [1863] Prepared by Bvt. Brig. Genl. N. Michler, Major of Engineers, from surveys under his direction, by order of Brig. Genl. & Bvt. Maj. Genl. A. A. Humphreys, Chief of Engineers, and under the authority of the Hon. Secretary of War Surveyed & drawn by Maj: J. E. Weyss, assisted by F. Theilkuhl, J. Strasser & G. Thompson. Photolith. by the N. Y. Lithographing, Engraving & Printing Co., Julius Bien, Supt. 1867. Colored. Scale 1:21,120. 58 × 70 cm.

In this issue, the map is printed on a yellow background with the Potomac and Shenandoah rivers colored green.

Map of Harpers Ferry and environs showing fortifications, roads, railroads, houses, fences, names of residents, vegetation, drainage, and relief by hachures.

697.6

————Another issue.

Background and water are not colored.

697.7

————Another issue.

Lacks the names of the surveyors and lithographer.

697.8

Owner, William.

Harpers Ferry & vicinity. [1862–1863] Uncolored ms. Scale ca. 1:620,000. 19 × 15 cm. In his Diary, v. 3, tipped-in at end of volume.

In the William Owner papers, Manuscript Division, L.C., container no. 1.

Map shows the roads linking principal towns in Northern Virginia with Harpers Ferry.

Volume 3 of the diary covers from Sept. 11, 1862, to Feb. 13, 1863.

697.9

————[Map of Harpers Ferry showing Federal and Confederate troop positions and batteries. 1862–1863] Uncolored ms. Scale ca. 1:70,000. 16 × 19 cm. *In his* Diary, v. 3, tipped-in at end of volume.

In the William Owner papers, Manuscript Division, L.C., container no. 1.

Volume 3 of the diary covers from Sept. 11, 1862, to Feb. 13, 1863.

698

Russell, Robert E. L.

Situation at Harpers Ferry, Sept. 15, 1862, 7 A.M. Baltimore, 1931. Photocopy (positive). Scale not given. 16 × 25 cm.

"Sketch map."

Hand-colored positive photocopy showing Confederate troop positions in red, rivers and woods in green, and roads in brown. Union positions, names of a few commanders, place names, and railroads are indicated in black. Geography and Map Division also has a negative photocopy.

699

Weyss, John E.

Military map showing the topographical features of the country adjacent to Harper's Ferry, Va.; including Maryland, Loudoun, and Bolivar Heights, and portions of South and Short Mountains, with the positions of the defensive works, also the junction of the Potomac & Shenandoah Rivers, and their passage through the Blue Ridge. Surveyed from August 3d to Sept. 30th 1863, under the direction of Capt. N. Michler, Corps of Engrs., U.S. Army, by Major John E. Weyss, Principal Assistant, Engineer Department, Army of the Potomac. Lettering by Wm. Hesselbach. Photocopy (positive). Scale 1:15,840. 70 × 75 cm.

"Table of distances" is in the lower right corner.

Hand-colored Civil War photograph showing fortifications, roads, railroads, contour lines, drainage, houses, fences, and the names of a few residents.

The Geography and Map Division's copy is mounted and sectioned to fold in half, but unfortunately, it lacks the portion adjacent to the fold. The missing part includes much of the town of Harpers Ferry and the fortifications to the north.

A finished copy of this map is reproduced in the *Atlas to Accompany the Official Records of the Union and Confederate Armies, 1891–95,* pl. 42, no. 1.

700

————Engraved in the Engr. Dept. Uncolored. Scale 1:15,840. 62 × 74 cm.

Printed edition of the preceding map indicating relief by hachures rather than by contour lines.

JEFFERSON COUNTY

700.5

U.S. *Army. Corps of Topographical Engineers.*

Map of Jefferson County, Va. Photographed for the Bureau of Topographical Engineers. Oct. 1862. Photocopy (positive). Scale ca. 1:26,500. 88 × 58 cm.

G3893 .J4G46 1862 .U5

Map of the eastern portion of Jefferson County, West Virginia, showing the towns of Harpers Ferry and Shepherdstown and depicting roads, railroads, houses, names of land owners, and property lines. Map was copied from S. Howell Brown's "Map of Jefferson County, Virginia," published in 1852.

Listed in R. W. Stephenson's *Land Ownership Maps* (Washington, Library of Congress, 1967), no. 1394.

This map was acquired by the Library of Congress in 1948 with the purchase of the papers and maps of Maj. Jedediah Hotchkiss.

PHILIPPI

701

Kresse, William J.

Background map; [Map of the battle of Philippi, June 3, 1861. By] W. J. Kresse. [New York] AP Newsfeatures [1961] Uncolored. Scale not given. 24 × 15 cm.

Accompanies article by Charles R. Lewis entitled "West Virginia town re-enacts Civil War's first land battle." 2 p., ea. 36 × 22 cm.

Insets: [Two location maps] ea. 7 × 7 cm.

RICH MOUNTAIN

702

Poe, Orlando M.

Plan of the battle of Rich Mountain. Drawn by Lt. O. M. Poe, Topl. Engrs. [July 11, 1861] Uncolored ms. on tracing linen. 29 × 18 cm.

From the Ezra A. Carman papers, Manuscript Division, L.C., container no. 14.

Title and author's name from sheet pinned to map.

"No. 2" at the top of the map has been marked out.

Map indicates the "crest of Rich Mountain," "Hart's house," the positions of Federal troops, skirmishers and reserves, the "trail by which Federal troops approached," the "enemy's position," and the "place where dead were buried."

Instructions for the printer are written at the bottom of the map.

ENGLISH CHANNEL

703

U.S. *Navy.*

[Map of the defeat of the Confederate ship *Alabama* by the U.S. steamer *Kearsarge* on June 19, 1864, off Cherbourg, France] Lith. of Bowen & Co., Philada. Uncolored. Scale ca. 1:41,000. 42 × 29 cm. *From.* Report on the Secretary of the Navy, with an appendix, containing reports from officers. December, 1864 (Washington, Government Printing Office, 1864). opp. p. 630.

Map shows the "Position of the Kearsarge when she received the first broadside of the enemy," the general direction of the ships during the battle, and the position of the *Alabama,* when it sank in 45 fathoms of water. Map accompanies "Captain [John A.] Winslow's detailed report of the action" dated July 30, 1864.

HOTCHKISS MAP COLLECTION

Compiled by
Clara Egli LeGear

FIELD SKETCH BOOKS

H1

Sketch book of Jed. Hotchkiss, Capt. & Top. Eng. Hd. Qurs. 2nd Corps, Army of N. Virginia. [1862–65] ms. 100, [12] leaves of maps (part col.) 25 × 16 cm.

The following annotation is written on the parchment cover:

"This volume is my field sketch book that I used during the Civil War. Most of the sketches were made on horseback just as they now appear. The colored pencils used were kept in the places fixed on the outside of the other cover.

"These topographical sketches were often used in conferences with Generals Jackson, Ewell and Early.

"The cover of this book is a blank Federal commission found in Gen. Milroy's quarters at Winchester. Jed. Hotchkiss."

A pocket sewn on the back cover has five compartments for pencils.

Maps on three yellow leaves, the size of the notebook, are inserted inside the front cover. These are followed by three leaves containing maps; 100 numbered leaves of sketches, some with maps on both sides; three leaves of sketches, some 40 blank leaves; and three leaves of sketches and notes at the end.

The sketchbook contains maps of the Battlefield of Cedar Run, dated March 23, 1862, maps of the Valley of Virginia, the Valley Turnpike from Winchester southward, the Blue Ridge, the Massanutten, Powell's Fort Valley, the regions around Strasburg, Front Royal, Port Republic, Chancellorsville, Orange, Warrenton, and Bristow Station, as well as the road between Dawsonville and Darnestown, in Montgomery County, Maryland.

The maps are finely drawn and beautifully executed, some with colored pencils, and some with lead pencil.

H2

Sketch book showing positions of Second Corps, A.N.Va. in engagements of 1864–5 by Jed. Hotchkiss, Top. Eng. 2nd Corps. ms. cover title, 34, [30] p. maps. 20 × 14 cm.

The title is written on a slip, pasted on the front cover. Page 1, inside the cover, relates to the "Battle of the Wilderness Run Thursday May 5th 1864." The latest sketch is dated Dec. 21st 1864.

The first 34 pages contain sketches; the others are blank, except for various inserted sketches. Some of the sketches are fine pen drawings, with numerous annotations, on which Federal and Confederate positions are indicated in blue and red, respectively.

H3

Sketch-book of positions of forces of 2nd Corps, A.N.Va., campaigns of 1864.—Made at or near date of their occurrence by personal observation and by conferences with officers commanding forces located. By Jed. Hotchkiss, Top. Eng. 2nd Corps, A.N.Va. ms. 1 p.l., 19 p. of maps. 16 × 9 cm.

The pages are filled with pencil sketches, dated in ink from May 8, to November 11, 1864.

The following title, written on a slip, is pasted on the front cover, "Sketches for Battle maps—Ewells & Early's campaigns of 1864–5 made at or near time of actions by Jed. Hotchkiss, Top. Eng." On the title page is this annotation, "Note. The red C's indicate that the material was used in maps in my Report to Eng. Bureau (not sent in) the 'blue' circles, that tracings of such sketches have been sent to War Records Office for publication in Atlas. J. H."

H4

Field notes on Sharpsburg Battle field. Jed. Hotchkiss, Staunton, Va. ms. [192] p. maps. 20 × 12 cm.

Measured drawings of the Antietam Battlefield area are contained on the first 11 pages; notes are on the last 3 pages; all others are blank.

H5

[Sketch book of] Jed. Hotchkiss, Top. Eng. V.D., C.S.A. 1862. ms 60, [16] p. incl. maps (part col.) 18 × 12 cm.

It includes several pages of distances on the Baltimore and Ohio Railroad and on the Western Virginia Railroad, as well as a summary of the Battle of Cedar Run, August 9, 1862. The maps include a number of sketches on various scales, the first of which is entitled "From Shenandoah Iron Works to Luray. S. Forrer." Others relate to the Valley of Virginia, the Cedar Run area, Chancellorsville, Staunton, Orange, Culpeper, Groveton, Monocacy, etc.

H6

Field note book of Wm. Luce, Eng. of Capt. J. W. Abert's

party of U. S. Top. Engs. with pass from Gen. Banks of Oct. 1861. ms. [180] p. incl. maps. 13 × 9 cm.

The title and the following are written on a slip of paper pasted on the front cover of the notebook: "Luce and his party & outfit were captured, in the Lower Shenandoah Valley in Spring of 1862, by Ashby's cavalry. This and his instruments were turned over to me by Col. Ashby. Jed. Hotchkiss, Lt. Top. Eng. A.V.D." The notebook includes sketches of roads, topographical features, etc., in Frederick and Montgomery counties, Maryland.

H7

Distances, 1862. ms. [18] p. 12 × 9 cm.

Contains 7 pages of distances, some blank pages, and several names and addresses.

The name "Henry B. Richardson" is written inside the leather front cover.

ATLAS OF THE SECOND CORPS

H8

Report of the camps, marches and engagements, of the Second Corps, A.N.V. and of the Army of the Valley Dist., of the Department of Northern Virginia; during the Campaign of 1864; illustrated by maps & sketches, by Jed. Hotchkiss, Top. Eng. V.D. ms.

1 p.l., 48 p. and atlas of 1 p.l., 38 (i.e., 59) col. maps in portfolio. 27 × 21 cm.

A number of the maps from this report are reproduced in the *Atlas to Accompany the Official Records of the Union and Confederate Armies, 1891–95.*

The paper cover of the report bears the following annotation in red ink: "The original Report, written in Dec. 1864. Jed. Hotchkiss, Staunton, Va." and this note in pencil: "The pencil changes are those made in No. (2) copy of this report. Jed. Hotchkiss. Staunton, Va. Sept. 30th 1892."

Both the report and atlas are contained in a blue paper envelope entitled: "Battle maps—Nos. 1 to 38—Campaigns of 1864–5 of 2nd Corps and of Army of Valley Dist. of Northern Virginia, C.S.A. By Jed. Hotchkiss, Top. Eng."

Contents

No. 1. Map (from Maj. A. H. Campbell's surveys) showing the positions of the camps & pickets, of the 2nd. Corps, A.N.Va., May 3rd, 1864; and the routes of march, from May 4th to May 21st, 1864, to battles of the Wilderness, and Spotsylvania C. H. to accompany Report of Jed. Hotchkiss, Top. Eng., V.D. Scale 1:160,000.

No. 1a. Map showing the positions of the camps & pickets of the 2nd Corps, Army N.Va. May 3rd 1864; the routes of march from May 4th to May 21st, 1864 to battles of Wilderness, and Spotsylvania C. H. Scale 1:160,000.

No. 2. Sketch of the Battle of the Wilderness. Position of 2nd Corps, A.N.V. Thursday May 5th 1864. S. B. Robinson. Scale 1:40,000.

No. 2a. [Similar sketch with same title]

No. 3. Sketch of the Battle of the Wilderness. Position of 2nd Corps, A.N.V., Friday, May 6th, 1864. Scale 1:40,000

No. 3a. [Similar sketch with same title]

No. 4. Sketch showing positions and entrenchments of the Second Corps, A.N.V. during the battles of Spotsylvania C. H. from May 9th to May 21st 1864. Scale 1:40,000.

No. 4a. [Similar sketch with same title]

No. 5. Map from Maj. A. H. Campbell's surveys, showing the routes and positions of the 2nd Corps., A.N.Va., from May 21st to May 27th, 1864 . . . Scale 1:160,000.

No. 5a. [Similar sketch with same title]

No. 6. Map (from Maj. A. H. Campbell's surveys) showing positions of 2nd Corps., A.N.Va. at Hanover Junction, May 22nd to May 27th 1864 . . . Scale 1:40,000.

No. 6a. [Similar sketch with same title]

No. 7. Map (from Maj. A. H. Campbell's surveys) showing the routes, camps, and positions of the 2nd Corps., A.N.Va., from May 27th to June 13th, 1864 . . . Scale 1:160,000.

No. 7a. [Similar sketch with same title]

No. 8. Map showing the routes and camps of the Second Corps, A.N.V. from Gaines Mill to Lynchburg June 13th to 18th, 1864 and of the Army of the Valley District from Lynchburg to Salem and Staunton June 19th to 27th 1864 . . . Copies by S. B. Robinson. Scale ca. 1:900,000.

No. 9. Map of engagement near Lynchburg, Saturday June 18th, 1864, from Maj. A. H. Campbell's surveys . . . Scale 1:40,000.

No. 9a. [Similar sketch with same title]

No. 10. Map of engagement at Hanging Rock, Roanoke County, Va. Tuesday June 21st 1864 . . . Scale 1:40,000.

No. 10a. [Similar sketch with same title]

No. 11. Map showing routes and camps of the Army of the Valley Dist. from Staunton, Va. to Washington, D. C. and back to Strasburg, Va. from June 27th to July 22nd 1864 . . . Copied by S. B. Robinson. Scale ca. 1:900,000.

No. 12. Map of engagement at Harper's Ferry July 4th, 1864 . . . Scale ca. 1:31,000.

No. 12a. [Similar sketch with same title]

No. 13. Map of the capture of North Mountain Depot, by McCausland's Cavalry Brigade, Monday, July 4th, 1864 . . . Scale 1:31,680.

No. 13a. [Similar sketch with same title]

No. 14. Map of action of McCausland's Cavalry Brigade at Hagerstown, Md., Thursday, July 7th, 1864 . . . Scale 1:31,680.

No. 14a. [Similar sketch with same title]

No. 15. Sketch of the Battle of Monocacy, Frederick Co. Md. Saturday July 9th, 1864 . . . Scale 1:31,680.

Jedediah Hotchkiss was one of the outstanding topographical engineers and mapmakers to serve on either side during the war. His collection of maps and papers was purchased by the Library of Congress in 1948. Hotchkiss's sketchbook clearly displays his skill at depicting the landscape. Hotchkiss noted that "most of the sketches were made on horseback just as they now appear" and that they "were often used in conferences with Generals Jackson, Ewell and Early." Reproduced here is page 28 of his sketchbook showing the "Front Royal & Winchester McAdamized Road." (See entry no. H1.)

304

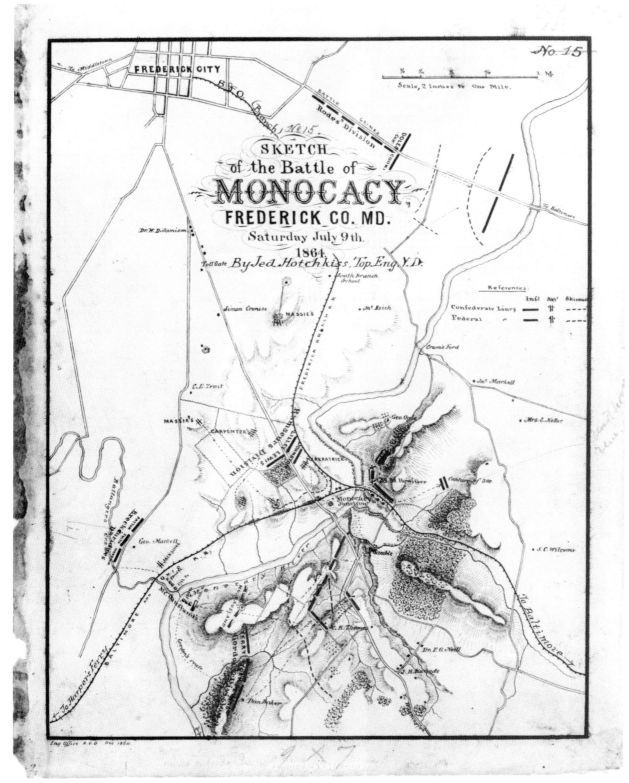

Jedediah Hotchkiss's "Sketch of the Battle of Monocacy, Frederick Co., Md. Saturday July 9th, 1864," from his unpublished Report of the Camps, Marches and Engagements, of the Second Corps, A.N.V. and the Army of the Valley Dist., of the Department of Northern Virginia: during the Campaign of 1864. *When time permitted, topographical engineers in both armies were called upon to prepare accurate, detailed maps of the fields of battle for use in official reports. (See entry no. H8.)*

No. 16. Sketch of the Battle of Rutherford's Farm, July 20th, 1864 . . . Scale 1:31,680.

No. 16a. [Similar sketch with same title]

No. 17. Map of cavalry action at Martinsburg, Va., July 25th, 1864 . . . Scale 1:31,680.

No. 17a. [Similar sketch with same title]

No. 18. Map showing routes, camps and engagements of McCausland's and Johnson's brigades of cavalry, from July 29th to Aug. 8th, 1864 (burning of Chambersburg) . . . Cop'd by S. B. Robinson. Scale 1:900,000.

No. 19. Sketch of action at Guard Hill Aug't 16th 1864 . . . Scale 1:40,000.

No. 20. Sketch of engagement at Charlestown, Sunday, Aug't 21st 1864 . . . Scale 1:31,680.

No. 20a. [Similar sketch with same title]

No. 21. Sketch of actions near Kearneysville and Shepherdstown, Va. Thursday, Aug't 25th 1864 . . . Scale 1:63,360.

No. 21a. [Similar sketch with same title]

No. 22. Sketch of engagement at Opequon Bridge and Smithfield, Monday Aug't 29th 1864 . . . Scale 1:40,000.

No. 22a. [Similar sketch with same title]

No. 23. Sketch of the Battle of Berryville, by Kershaw's Division, Saturday, Sept. 3rd 1864, and position of the Army of the Valley, Sunday, Sept. 4th 1864 . . . Scale 1:31,680.

No. 23a. [Similar sketch with same title]

No. 24. Sketch of the cavalry action of Fitz Lee's Division at Gooney run, Warren Co., Va. Tuesday, Sept. 20th, 1864 . . . Scale 1:31,680.

No. 24a. [Similar sketch with same title]

No. 25. Sketch of the cavalry engagement at Milford, Va. of Fitz Lee's Division, Wednesday Sept'r 21st 1864 . . . Scale 1:31,680.

No. 25a. [Similar sketch with same title]

No. 26. Map of the line of entrenchments at Fisher's Hill, Sept. 22nd, 1864 . . . Scale 1:40,000.

No. 27. Map of cavalry engagement, near Bridgewater, Va. Oct'r 4th and 5th, 1864 . . . Scale 1:60,000.

No. 28. Cavalry action of Gen'l Rosser near Brock's Gap, Oct. 6th, 1864 . . . Scale 1:80,000.

No. 29. Sketch of the Battle of Belle Grove or Cedar Creek, Wednesday October 19th, 1864 . . . Scale 1:40,000.

No. 30. Sketch of action of Gen. Rosser's Cavalry, near Moorefield, Va., Sunday, Nov. 27th, 1864 . . . Scale 1:63,360.

No. 31. Map of New Creek and vicinity showing position of Fort Kelley and the Federal camp captured by Maj. Gen. Rosser's Cav. Div. A.N.V. Monday, Nov. 28th, 1864 . . . Scale 1:31,680.

No. 32. Map of Gen. Rosser's night attack of Custer's Division at Lacey's Springs, Wednesday Dec. 21st 1864 . . . from Maj. A. H. Campbell's surveys. Scale 1:40,000.

No. 33. Sketch of cavalry action, at Liberty Mills, Friday Dec. 23rd 1864 . . . Scale 1:40,000.

No. 34. Sketch of cavalry engagement of Genl. Lomax near Gordonsville, Va. Dec. 24th, 1864 . . . Scale 1:40,000.

No. 35. Map showing routes of Rosser's Division to Beverly and back, Jan. 7th to Jan. 18th 1865 . . . Scale ca. 1:900,000.

No. 36. Capture of Beverly, Randolph Co. Va. by Gen. Rosser, Jan. 11th 1865 . . . Scale 1:63,360.

No. 37. Map showing positions of camps & pickets, of the Army of the Valley District, Jan. 31st 1865 . . . Scale ca. 1:900,000.

No. 38. Sketch of Gen. Rosser's attack on Federal cavalry, guarding prisoners at Rude's Hill, Tuesday, March 7th, 1865 . . . Scale 1:40,000.

No. 38a. [Similar sketch with same title]

GENERAL MAPS

H9

[Map of portions of Virginia and Maryland, extending from Baltimore to Strasburg, and from Washington to Gettysburg, with concentric circles at 5-mile intervals centering on Washington and on Baltimore. 186–] Colored ms. Scale ca. 1:185,000. 55 × 91 cm.

On tracing cloth. Drainage in blue, roads in red, culture in black. Mountains indicated by hachures.

H10

[Map of portions of Virginia, West Virginia, and Maryland, centering on Harpers Ferry and including Winchester, Hancock, Emmitsburg, and Ridgeville, Maryland.] Engineer Office, A.N.V. Drawn by Chas. G. Nauck, Ass't Eng. [186–] Colored ms. Scale 1:126,720. 48 × 75 cm.

Drawn on tracing cloth. Roads are shown in red, drainage in blue, and elevations by hachures. Drawn on a ½-inch grid.

H11

[Preliminary map of northern Virginia embracing portions of Loudoun, Fauquier, Prince William, and Culpeper Counties. 186–] Colored ms. Scale ca. 1:125,000. 86 × 57 cm.

Roads are shown in red, streams in blue, and culture in black. Elevations are shown by hachures.

H12

[Map of the northern part of Virginia and West Virginia, between the Blue Ridge and the Alleghany Front, south of the Potomac River and north of New Market. 186–] Colored ms. Scale ca. 1:250,000. 52 × 47 cm.

Roads are shown in red, streams in blue, and elevations by hachures and shading.

Annotated, "No. 21," and "The squares are miles."

H13

Part of "Map of portions of the milit'y dep'ts of Washington, Pennsylvania, Annapolis and north eastern Virginia. Compiled in the Bureau of Topographical Eng'rs, War Department &c. July 1861." Colored ms. Scale 1:200,000. 56 × 87 cm.

Roads are shown in red, drainage in blue, and elevations by shading.

H14

Map of a portion of Virginia compiled from Böye's State map under the direction of Nicolas Bowen, 1st Lieut. Top'l Eng'rs—in charge, with additions & corrections by D. H. Strother, Lt. Col. 3d. Va. Cavalry A.A.D.C. Nov. 1862. Capt. Jas. C. Duane, Chief Eng'r Army of the Potomac. Photocopy (positive). Scale 1:550,000. 48 × 45 cm.

Sun print with a few manuscript annotations, of roads and place names, namely Franklin, Monterey, McDowell, Lebanon Sps., Jenning's Gap, and Churchville.

H15

Part of "Map of portions of the milit'y dept's of Washington, Pennsylvania, Annapolis, and north eastern Virginia. Compiled in the Bureau of Topographical Eng'rs, War Department &c. Washington, D. C. Oct. 6th, 1862." Copied in Engr. Bureau C.S.A. Sept. 6th, 1864 [by] Wm. L. Sheppard Dftsmn. Forwarded to Lieut. Genl. J. A. Early Sept. 6th 1864, A. L. Rives. Col. & Asst. to Chf. Eng. Colored ms. Scale 1:200,000. 57 × 90 cm.

Drawn on tracing cloth. Roads are shown in red, drainage in blue, and elevations by hachures.

H16

[Preliminary map of northeastern Virginia embracing portions of Prince William, Stafford, and Fauquier counties. 186–] Colored ms. Scale ca. 1:63,360. 68 × 97 cm.

Roads are shown in red, streams in blue, and culture in black.

H17

[Preliminary map of northeastern Virginia, south of the Rappahannock, east of the Blue Ridge, and north of 38° N. Lat. 1864–65] Photocopy (positive). Scale 1:160,000. 67 × 99 cm.

Sun print with a number of manuscript annotations, as well as a manuscript sketch of the roads connecting the area shown in the northeastern portion of the map with Washington, D. C., and Alexandria, Virginia.

H18

Map of a portion of eastern Virginia (from a map in progress) Compiled from surveys and reconnaissances made under the direction of Capt. A. H. Campbell P.E. in charge Topl. Dept. D.N.V. Drawn by J. Houston Patton Asst. Engr.

Approved April 22nd, 1864 [by] Albert H. Campbell . . . 1864. Photocopy (positive). Scale 1:160.000. 92 × 101 cm.

Sun print with some manuscript annotations.

At head of title, "Chief Engineer's Office, D.N.V. Maj. Genl. J. F. Gilmer Chief Eng'r."

Mounted on cloth to fold to 15 × 11 cm. and annotated as follows on the back: "This map was often used by Generals R. E. Lee, R. S. Ewell, J. A. Early, and others in command during the campaigns of A.N.Va. in 1864 and 1865. Jed. Hotchkiss, Top. Eng. 2nd Corps, A.N.Va."

Another copy, mounted in two sections, likewise has a number of additional place names, as well as a ⅜-inch grid.

H19

Preliminary map of a part of the south side of James River from surveys and reconnaissances made under the direction of Maj. A. H. Campbell P. E. in ch'ge Top'l Dept. D.N.V. December 1864. J. H. Patton, Asst. Eng'r. Approved Dec. 23d 1864, Albert H. Campbell . . .[1864–65] Photocopy (positive). Scale 1:160,000. 2 sheets, 98 × 94 and 88 × 94 cm.

Sun print with a number of manuscript annotations. At head of title, "Chief Engineer's Office, D.N.V. Maj. Genl. J. F. Gilmer Chief Engr."

Sheet No. 2 is dated March 1865, and has lettered above the title, "(Vicinity of Lynchburg)."

COUNTY MAPS

H20

[Map of Albemarle County, north of the Virginia Central Railroad, and a portion of Augusta County along the south fork of the Shenandoah River. 186–] Colored ms. Scale ca. 1:150,000. 45 × 57 cm.

Fine drawing, giving roads in red, drainage in blue, and showing elevations by hachures, drawn on a ⅜-inch grid.

H21

Map of Buckingham & Appomattox Counties. Surveyed under direction of A. H. Campbell Capt. Engrs. & Chief of Topogl. Dept. D.N.V. By Charles E. Cassell, Lieut. Engrs. P.A.C.S. December 25th, 1863. Uncolored ms. Scale 1:80,000. 70 × 91 cm.

Fine drawing giving much detail. Elevations are shown by hachures and wooded areas are indicated. Drawn on a ¾-inch grid.

H22

Map of Campbell Co. Made under direction of A. H. Campbell, Maj. Engrs. in chg. Top. Dept. [186–] Colored ms. Scale 1:80,000. 71 × 72 cm.

On tracing cloth. Roads are shown in red, drainage in blue, wooded areas in green, and elevations are shown by hachures.

H23

Map of Caroline County, Va., from surveys made under the direction of Capt. A. H. Campbell, P. Engr's & Chief of Top'l. Department. Approved, Albert H. Campbell . . . 1862. Colored ms. Scale 1:80,000. 63 × 77 cm.

On tracing cloth. Shows roads in red and gives the names of some residents.

At head of title, "Chief Engineer's Office, D.N.Va. Col. J. F. Gilmer, Ch'f Eng'r."

H24

[Caroline County, Virginia. Eng. Office, 2d Corps. A.N.VA. 186–] Colored ms. Scale 1:80,000. 60 × 54 cm.

Title from the back of the map. On tracing cloth. Roads are drawn in red and elevations are shown by hachures. Gives the names of some residents.

H25

[Map of parts of Caroline, Hanover, and Henrico Counties, Va., west of the Mattaponi River and the Richmond, Fredericksburg, and Potomac Railroad.186–] Colored ms. Scale ca. 1:100,000. 28 × 33 cm.

Roads are shown in red. Some of the outer fortifications of Richmond and those along the railroad north of the South Anna River are shown. The names of a number of residents are given.

H26

[Map of the area between Fredericksburg and Hanover, Va., including Caroline County, and the eastern part of Spotsylvania County. 186–] Colored ms. Scale 1:253,440. 27 × 23 cm.

Drawn on a ¼-inch grid. Gives roads in red and drainage in blue.

H27

Survey of Culpeper and a part of Madison Counties, Virginia. Made under the direction of A. H. Campbell, Capt'n. Provisional Eng'rs. and Chief of Top'l. Dep't. By Lieu't. Dwight, C.S.P.E. Traced from a map now in progress. April, 1863. Approved April 8th, 1863, Albert H. Campbell . . . Colored ms. Scale 1:80,000. 89 × 85 cm.

On tracing cloth. Fine drawing on a ¾-inch grid, showing roads in red, and giving the names of many residents. Elevations shown by hachures.

H28

Map of Dinwiddie County, Va. Surveyed under the direction of A. H. Campbell, Capt. Engr's, P.A.C.S. in ch'ge Top'l Dep't. D.N.Va. by S. L. Sommers & H. M. Graves, Ass't Engr's. . . . Approved July 1, 1864, J. Innes Randolph, 1st Lt. Engrs. . . . 1864. Colored ms. Scale 1:80,000. 57 × 60 cm.

Fine drawing on tracing cloth. Shows roads in red, gives names of residents, and indicates much wooded area.

H29

Map of part of Essex, King and Queen, and King William Counties made under the direction of Capt. A. H. Campbell, Chief Topographical Dep't . . . Traced from a map now in progress. Approved April 21st 1863 by Abert [sic] H. Campbell Cap. P. Eng. & Chief Top. Dep. D.N.Va. Copy certified Oct. 22nd 1863 Eng. Office 2nd Corps, Jed. Hotchkiss Capt. & Top. Eng. Colored ms. Scale 1:80,000. 77 × 83 cm.

Spattered with ink in the upper left portion.

Drawn on a ¹³⁄₁₆-inch grid. Roads are shown in red, drainage in blue, and forests in green. The names of some residents are given.

At head of title, "Chief Engineers Office, D.N.V. Col. J. F. Gilmer Chf. Eng."

H30

[A map of Fairfax County, and parts of Loudoun and Prince William Counties, Va., and the District of Columbia. Copied by J. Paul Hoffmann, Top'l. Office, A.N.Va. Approved S. Howell Brown . . . March 29th 1864. Colored ms. Scale 1:126,720. 62 × 35 cm.

On tracing cloth. Shows fortifications west of Washington. A fine drawing giving drainage in blue, roads in red, elevations by hachures, and the names of some residents.

H31

A map of Fauquier Co. Virginia, compiled by various sources, including a reconnoisance [sic] by Capt. J. K. Boswell, Chf. Eng. 2d C., surveys of the O[range] & A[lexandria] and the M[anassas] G[ap] Railroads, state maps, &c., with personal reconnoisances [sic]. By Jed. Hotchkiss, Act'g Top. Eng. 2nd Corps A.N.V. March 1863. Colored ms. Scale 1:126,720. 65 × 49 cm.

Unfinished with roads in red, drainage in blue, and the names of some residents. Drawn on a ½-inch grid.

H32

[Map of Fauquier County, Va. 186–] Colored ms. Scale ca. 1:80,000. 33 × 43 cm.

Drawn on a ½-inch grid. Roads are shown in red, drainage in blue, and elevations by hachures in pencil.

H33

Map of Fauquier & Loudon [sic] Co's. Va. By order of L't. Col. Wm. P. Smith Chf. Eng'r. Topog'l. Office A.N.V. Copied by A. S. Barrows Ass't Eng'r. [186–] Colored ms. Scale 1:126,720. 49 × 40 cm.

On tracing cloth. A fine drawing giving drainage in blue, roads in red, elevations by hachures, and names of many residents.

H34

[Map of parts of Fauquier, Prince William, and Rappahannock Counties, Va. 186–] Colored ms. Scale ca. 1:126,720. 39 × 45 cm.

On tracing cloth. Roads are drawn in red, drainage in blue, and elevations are shown by hachures. The names of some residents are given.

The reverse side is annotated, "Part of Loudon Co., Va. ½-inch scale."

H35

Frederick Co., Va., from Wood's map. [186–] Colored ms. Scale 1:160,000. 42 × 46 cm.

Shows roads in reds, drainage in blue, and mountains by hachures. Drawn on a ⅜-inch grid.

H36

[Map of Greene County, Va. 186–] Colored ms. Scale ca. 1:40,000. 87 × 86 cm.

Drawn on a ¾-inch grid on an irregular sheet of tracing paper, giving considerable detail. Roads are shown in red, drainage in blue, wooded areas in green, and elevations are indicated by hachures.

H37

[Map of Hanover County, Va. 186–] Colored ms. Scale ca. 1:80,000. 56 × 95 cm.

Drawn on tracing cloth on a ¾-inch grid. Roads in red, drainage in blue, wooded areas in green, and elevations by hachures. The names of a number of residents are included.

H38

[Map of the northern portion of Hanover County, Va., showing fortifications on the South Anna River near Taylorsville. 186–] Colored ms. Scale ca. 1:80,000. 36 × 27 cm.

Fine drawing on tracing cloth. Roads are in red, drainage in blue, wooded areas in green, and elevations are shown by hachures.

H39

[Map of Hanover County, Va. 186–] Colored ms. Scale ca. 1-160,000. 51 × 53 cm.

Describes several bridges across the Chickahominy River as destroyed.

Drawn on a ¾-inch grid. Roads are shown in red and drainage in blue. The names of a number of residents are included.

H40

Map of part of Henrico and Chesterfield Counties, July 12th, 1862. Albert H. Campbell Capt. P. Engrs., & Chf. Top. Dept. Colored ms. Scale 1:40,000. 105 × 77 cm.

Drawn on tracing cloth. Roads and some wooded areas are drawn in red. Includes the names of a few residents.

Annotated on the reverse in pencil, "Gen. Lee's."

At head of title, "Chief Engineer's Office, D.N.V. Maj. W. H. Stevens Chief Eng."

H41

[Map of Henrico County, Va., showing fortifications around Richmond, north and east of the James River. 1864] Colored ms. Scale 1:40,000. 64 × 133 cm.

Shows roads in red, drainage in blue, and elevations by hachures. Includes the names of a number of residents. Drawn on a ⅜-inch grid.

H42

Map of King William County, Va., surveyed & under the direction of Captain John Grant, P.A.C.S. A.S. Barrows Principal Assis't Eng. Made under the direction of A. H. Campbell Capt. P.E. & Chf. Top. Dept. . . . Approved by him Jan. 22nd 1863. Reduced from above by Jed. Hotchkiss Capt. Top. Eng. 2nd Corps, August 27th 1863. Colored ms. Scale 1:80,000. 51 × 53 cm.

At head of title, "Chief Engineer's Office, D.N.V. Col. J. F. Gilmer, Chf. Eng."

Drawn on a ¾-inch grid. Roads are shown in red, drainage in blue, wooded areas in green, and elevations by hachures. Includes the names of a number of residents.

H43

[Map of Loudoun County and part of Clarke County, Va., Jefferson County and part of Berkeley County, W. Va., and parts of Montgomery and Frederick Counties, Md. 1864] Colored ms. Scale 1:126,720. 44 × 41 cm.

"Copied by J. Paul Hoffmann, Top'l. Office, A.N.Va."

"Approved S. Howell Brown. 1st Lt. Engs. Troops in chg. Top'l. Dep't. A.N.Va. March 23rd 1864."

On tracing cloth. Roads are shown in red, drainage in blue, and elevations by hachures. The names of a number of residents are included.

H44

[Map of Loudoun County, Va., and parts of Fairfax County, Va., Jefferson County, W. Va., and Washington and Frederick Counties, Md. 186–] Colored ms. Scale ca. 1:120,000. 49 × 76 cm.

Unfinished map on tracing cloth. Roads are shown in red, drainage in blue, and elevations by hachures. Gives the names of a few residents.

H45

[Map of Louisa County and part of Hanover County, Va. 186–] Colored ms. Scale ca. 1:160,000. 41 × 56 cm.

Drainage and roads are shown only in the Hanover County area. Drawn on a ⅜-inch grid.

H46

[Map of Madison County, Va. 186–] Colored ms. Scale ca. 1:160,000. 28 × 22 cm.

Drawn on a ⅜-inch grid. Drainage is shown in blue and roads in red. Includes the names of a number of residents.

H47

Map of Montgomery County, Virginia. Taken from actual survey made by topographical party in charge of Lieut. C. S. Dwight Engineer Corps P.A. C.S. A. M. Smith, Asst. Eng. . . . S. W. Hill C.E. del. June 1864. Colored ms. Scale 1:40,000. 86 × 112 cm.

Drawn on tracing cloth, on a ⅜-inch grid. Roads are shown in red, drainage in blue, wooded areas outlined in green; elevations are shown by crude contour lines. Includes the names of a number of residents.

H48

[Map of Montgomery County, Va. 186–] Colored ms. Scale ca. 1:80,000. 59 × 57 cm.

Drawn on tracing cloth, on a ¾-inch grid which is in red; drainage in blue. Includes the names of a number of residents.

H49

[Map of Nelson and Amherst Counties, Va. 186–] Colored ms. Scale 1:80,000. 79 × 96 cm.

Drawn on tracing cloth on a ¾-inch grid. A large ink spot covers part of the map. Roads are given in red. Elevations are shown by hachures and wooded areas by symbols.

Signed "Lt. C. S. Dwight."

H50

[Map of Orange County, Va., 186–] Colored ms. Scale ca. 1:80,000. 41 × 75 cm.

Drawn on a ¾-inch grid, giving roads in red, drainage in blue, elevations by brown hachures, and the names of many residents.

H51

Orange County, Va. By Lieut Walter Izard P.E. [186–] Colored ms. Scale ca. 1:40,000. 78 × 152 cm.

Unfinished, with title in pencil, it shows roads in red, drainage in blue, elevations by hachures, and wooded areas in green. Drawn on a 1½-inch grid.

H52

Survey of Orange County, Virginia made under the direction of A. H. Campbell Capt. Prov. Eng. & Pr. Top. Dep. by Lieut. Isard [sic] C.S.P.E. Traced from a map now in progress, April 1863. Approved April 8th 1863 by Albert H. Campbell . . . Colored ms. Scale ca. 1:80,000. 44 × 88 cm.

Drawn on a ¾-inch grid. Roads are in red, drainage in blue, woods in green. Elevations are shown by hachures.

At head of title, "Chief Engineers Office, D.N.V. Col. J. F. Gilmer, Chief Eng." Annotated, "Loaned to the War Records Office by Maj. Jed. Hotchkiss, Sept. 17, 1892."

H53

[Map of Prince Edward County, Va. 186–] Colored ms. Scale ca. 1:60,000. 25 × 31 cm.

On tracing paper, drawn on a ⅜-inch grid. Township names in red ink are the only ones given on the map.

H54

Map of Prince George Co., Va. made under the direction of A. H. Campbell P. E. in charge of the Top. Dept. D.N.Va. by S. L. Sommers Asst. Engr. App. July 18, 1864 by Albert H. Campbell. Colored ms. Scale 1:80,000. 48 × 56 cm.

On tracing cloth, drawn on a ¼-inch grid. Gives roads in red, drainage in black, and wooded areas in blue and green. Includes the names of many residents.

H55

Rappahannock Co., Virginia. Engr. Office, 2nd Corps. Novr. 1863. Colored ms. Scale ca. 1:160,000. 32 × 35 cm.

Fine drawing on a ⅜-inch grid, giving roads in red, drainage in blue, and elevations by hachures.

H56

Roanoke County, Virginia. [186–] Colored ms. Scale ca. 1:160,000. 26 × 31 cm.

Fine drawing on a ⅜-inch grid, with roads in red, drainage in blue, and elevations by hachures. Includes names of many residents.

H57

Rockbridge Co., Va. [186–] Colored ms. Scale ca. 1:160,000. 45 × 57 cm.

Fine drawing on a ⅜-inch grid, with roads in red, drainage in blue, and elevations by brown hachures. Includes the names of many residents.

"No. 25" is in the upper left corner.

H58

Map of Spotsylvania County surveyed by and under the direction of Captain John Grant P.A.C.S. S.T. Pendleton, Principal Asst. Engr. 1862. Colored ms. Scale 1:40,000. 108 × 117 cm.

Finely drawn on a 1½-inch grid, with a number of pencil annotations. Roads are in red, drainage in blue, and terrain by appropriate symbols.

H59

[Map of Spotsylvania County, Va. 186–] Colored ms. Scale ca. 1:80,000. 63 × 45 cm.

On brown paper. Roads are shown in red, drainage in blue, and elevations by green form lines.

Fortifications are shown in the Chancellorsville area. Includes the names of many residents.

H60

[Map of Spotsylvania County, Va. 186–] Colored ms. Scale ca. 1:80,000. 60 × 43 cm.

Drawn on a ¾-inch grid. Roads are shown in red, drainage in blue, and elevations and forested areas by hachures and symbols in black.

Fortifications are shown in the Chancellorsville area. Includes the names of many residents.

H61

[Map of Spotsylvania County, Va. 186–] Colored ms. Scale ca. 1:80,000. 61 × 43 cm.

Roads are shown in red, drainage in blue, and elevations by green form lines.

Fortifications are shown in the Chancellorsville area. Includes the names of many residents.

H62

[Map of Spotsylvania and Caroline Counties, Va. 186–] Colored ms. Scale ca. 1:126,720. 41 × 68 cm.

Drawn on a ½-inch grid. Roads are shown in red, drainage in blue, and wooded areas in green. Includes the names of some residents.

H63

[Map of Stafford County, Va. 186–] Colored ms. Scale ca. 1:126,720. 34 × 55 cm.

Drawn on a ½-inch grid. Unfinished map giving roads in red and drainage in blue. Includes the names of some residents.

H64

Field map of the north part of Wythe County. Surveys by Mayhew's party under command of 1st Lieut. Walter Izard, [186–] Colored ms. Scale ca. 1:40,000. 51 × 123 cm.

A pencil correction in the title inserts the name of "Lt. Magill Smith, Topl. Engr." above that of Lt. Izard.

Roads are shown in red, drainage in blue, elevations in brown hachures, and wooded areas in green. Includes the names of residents.

H65

[Map of part of Wythe County, Va. 186–] Colored ms. Scale ca. 1:80,000. 47 × 76 cm.

On tracing cloth, drawn on a ¾-inch grid, which is in red. Incomplete map with drainage in blue and elevations shown by contours.

CAMPAIGN AND BATTLE MAPS

West Virginia Campaign—July 1861

H66

[Sketch of western Virginia and eastern West Virginia, between Staunton and Clarksburg. 1861] Uncolored ms. Scale ca. 1:550,770. 41 × 26 cm.

Drawn in ink with many pencil annotations. Mountains are shown by coarse hachures. A list of distances between Monterey, Huntersville, Warm Springs, and various other places is given.

H67

[Map of part of eastern West Virginia, extending from Romney westward to Clarksburg, centering on the Rich Mountain Battle area. 1861.] Colored ms. Scale ca. 1:700,000. 27 × 42 cm.

Roads are shown in red, drainage in blue, and mountains by green hachures. Locates "Camp Bartow" and "Yankee Camp on Cheat Mt."

H68

[Map of portions of Hampshire and Mineral Counties, W. Va., and Garrett County, Md. 1861] Colored ms. Scale ca. 1:126,720. 45 × 30 cm.

Roads are shown in red, drainage in blue, and mountains by form lines. Railroads are shown as well as the location of Fort Kelley at the site of present Keyser, West Virginia.

H69

Averill's map of western Va. [including Randolph, Upshur, and parts of adjoining counties, W. Va. 1861] Uncolored ms. Scale ca. 1:341,925. 81 × 62 cm.

The title is written in pencil on the reverse.

The map shows roads, streams, and mountains (by form lines), as well as the names of some residents.

H70

Camp Garnett and vicinity, Rich Mountain, Randolph Co., Va. By order of Lt. Col. J. M. Heck, commanding post, July 1861. . . . By Jed. Hotchkiss, Top. Eng. Uncolored ms. Scale 1:63,360. 21 × 13 cm.

Elevations are shown by form line.

Finished drawing on tracing paper, similar to the map reproduced in the *Atlas to Accompany the Official Records of the Union and Confederate Armies, 1891–95,* pl. 2, no. 6.

H71

[Map of the Rich Mountain battlefield, W. Va. July 11–12, 1861] Colored ms. Scale ca. 1:63,360. 21 × 14 cm.

Dotted lines are marked respectively. "Route of enemy," and "Route of J. Hotchkiss & Co."

H72

[Sketch of the battle of Rich Mountain, July 11–12, 1861] Uncolored ms. Not drawn to scale. 25 × 19 cm.

Rough sketch on blue paper. It shows "Garnett's Camp Friday night," and the following annotation, "Up Horse Shoe 19 miles to Red House on N.W.T.—Then down to N. Br. Bridge 7."

H73

[Area of the battle of Rich Mountain, July 11–12, 1861] Uncolored ms. Not drawn to scale. 14 × 20 cm.

Rough pencil sketch on blue paper. Shows "Big Run," the "Main Cheat," "White's," and "Red Bridge."

H74

Battle of Rich Mt. [Randolph Co., Va. July 11, 1861] Uncolored ms. Scale ca. 1:200,000. 20 × 31 cm.

A rough sketch on blue paper, similar to a portion of the map in the *Atlas to Accompany the Official Records of the Union and Confederte Armies, 1891–95*, pl. 2, no. 6.

Shows fortifications, "Camp of enemy," "Cavalry Camp," "Dr. Hillary," and "Hart's house," as well as "Route of the enemy to the rear."

H75

[Sketch of the area of the battle of Rich Mountain, July 11–12, 1861] Uncolored ms. Not drawn to scale. 19 × 25 cm.

Rough pencil sketch on blue paper, of the area between Kaler's Ford, and "Red H." A list of some 13 distances between Garnett's Camp and Kaler's Ford is given on the reverse.

H76

[Rough sketch of the battle of Rich Mountain, July 11–12, 1861] Uncolored ms. Not drawn to scale. 19 × 23 cm.

Pencil sketch on blue paper. It shows fortifications, near "Crouch," and "Stalnaker's," along Tygart's Valley River in the battle of Rich Mountain. Annotations in red name several of the fighting units.

H77

[Rough sketch of the roads between Beverly, W. Va., Leadsville, Bealington, and Philippi, and Bealington and Meadowville, in the Rich Mountain area. 1861] Uncolored ms. Not drawn to scale. 25 × 20 cm.

Pencil sketch on blue paper.

H78

[Rough sketch of the Rich Mountain battle area, extending from Beverly, W. Va. to Clarksburg. 1861] Uncolored ms. Not drawn to scale. 21 × 26 cm.

Pencil sketch on blue paper. Annotated as follows, "Natty Creek in NW of Co. & joins the waters of Big Run, Pecks run & goes down the Clarksburg road."

H79

[Two sketches on one sheet of the road from Huntersville, W. Va. along Knap Creek to the Greenbrier River, and from the Greenbrier River across Brushy Ridge. 1861] Colored ms. Not drawn to scale. 21 × 14 cm.

Pencil sketch on blue paper, giving roads in red, and drainage in blue. There are two pencil sketches on the reverse side, one of which also shows a road from Huntersville.

Distances from Beverly to Leadsville to New Interest, etc., are noted.

H80

[Pencil sketch of the route of scouting party from Monterey, Highland County, Va. toward Beverly, Randolph County, W. Va. 1861] Uncolored ms. Not drawn to scale. 32 × 20 cm.

The party's report on the conditions of roads, probably made during the Tygart Valley Campaign, is written on the reverse.

H81

[Pencil sketch of the road from Slaven's Cabin to the top of Cheat Mountain in the area of the battle of Rich Mountain, July 11–12, 1861] Uncolored ms. Scale ca. 1:31,680. 59 × 10 cm.

Gives distances along the road, from 76 to 85 miles. The only names on the map are "Slaven's Cabin," "Matthias W. White," and "The Red Bridge."

H82

[Map of parts of Highland County, Va., and Pendleton County, W. Va. 1861] Colored ms. Scale 1:316,800. 24 × 19 cm.

On brown tracing paper, the lower right corner of which is wanting, leaving part of the title which reads "Highla" and "5 mi to." Roads are shown in red, drainage in blue, and mountains by form lines.

H83

Highland Co. & notes at foot of North Mt. [1861] Colored ms. Scale ca. 1:40,000. 27 × 20 cm.

Two colored field sketches on a sheet, giving names of residents along the road.

H84

[Sketch of roads and streams in Highland County, Va., and Pendleton County, W. Va. 1861] Colored ms. Scale ca. 1:500,000. 21 × 27 cm.

Sketch of the South Branch of the Potomac, North Mountain, Hevener's Mountain, etc.

H85

[Sketch of parts of Highland County, Va., and Pendleton County, W. Va., 1861] Uncolored ms. Not drawn to scale. ca. 36 × 20 cm.

Two sketches on an irregular sheet, one with notes on the reverse.

Manassas Campaign—1861

H86

First Manassas. [July 21, 1861] Colored ms. Scale 1:63,360. 40 × 41 cm.

Map on tracing cloth with title in pencil. It shows some troop positions, and includes a list of Confederate regiments engaged in the battle of Manassas, with the names of their commanders.

Southeastern Virginia Campaign—1861

H87

Gloucester Point Fort. Richmond, 20 September 1861. Uncolored ms. Scale ca. 1:2500. 26 × 21 cm.

An outline of the fort, giving dimensions.

H88

[Outline map of Hampton Roads, and the vicinity of Norfolk, Va. 1861] Uncolored ms. Scale ca. 1:126,720. 31 × 25 cm.

On tracing cloth, without names.

Valley Campaign—1862

H89

[Map of the Shenandoah Valley by Jed. Hotchkiss. 1862] Colored ms. Scale 1:80,000. 254 × 111 cm.

This map was made at the request of General Jackson early in 1862, and is one of the outstanding maps in the collection. It includes the Shenandoah Valley from Winchester to Staunton, and from the Blue Ridge to the Alleghany mountains.

Drawn on tracing cloth on a ¾-inch grid, roads are shown in red, drainage in blue, and contour lines in black. The names of many residents are given.

H90

Battle of Kernstown, Sunday, 23 March, 1862. Jed. Hotchkiss, Top. Eng. Valley D. Colored ms. Scale 1:31,680. 39 × 30 cm.

Includes a list of the regiments and brigades in the Valley Division. A pencil annotation at the lower edge reads, "Hd. Qrs. of Maj. Gen. Jackson in a fence corner, Sunday night."

H91

Sketch of the Battle of Kernstown, Sunday, March 23d 1862, by Jed. Hotchkiss, Top. Engr. V.D. Colored ms. Scale 1:31,680. 29 × 21 cm.

A fine drawing giving Confederate positions in red ink, and listing the brigades and regiments of the Valley Division and Colonel Ashby's Cavalry. Includes a number of pencil annotations.

H92

[Sketch of the vicinity of Kernstown, Va. 1862] Uncolored ms. Scale ca. 1:80,000. 26 × 20 cm.

An incomplete pencil sketch, a small portion of which has been traced in ink.

H93

Sketch of the battle of McDowell on Thursday, May 8th, 1862 (Jackson) by Jed. Hotchkiss Top. Eng. Valley Division. Colored ms. Scale 1:31,680. 24 × 30 cm.

An unfinished drawing of the map with same title in *Atlas to Accompany the Official Records of the Union and Confederate Armies*, 1891–95, pl. 116, no. 1.

H94

[Sketch of the vicinity of McDowell, Va. 1862] Uncolored ms. Scale ca. 1:31,680. 23 × 31 cm.

Except for the fact that this map shows no troop movements, it is similar to the foregoing sketch.

Drawn on tracing paper.

H95

[Sketch of the vicinity of Cross Keys, Va. 1862] Uncolored ms. Scale ca. 1:40,000. 14 × 20 cm.

Pencil sketch of the roads and streams in the area of Cross Keys. The names of several residents are given.

H96

Topographic map of the battle-field of Port Republic, Virginia, June 9, 1862. By Jed. Hotchkiss, Top. Eng., Valley Dist. A.N.Va. . . . Eng. Office of Jed. Hotchkiss, Staunton, Va., May, 1886. Uncolored ms. Scale 1:25,000. 28 × 27 cm.

Annotated, "The squares are square miles."

Peninsula Campaign—1862

H97

Position of Richmond, Va. prepared by order of Maj. Gen. Geo. B. McClellan U.S.A. A. A. Humphreys, Brig. Gen. & Chief of Topl. Engrs. May 27th 1862. Compiled from "Map of Henrico Co." and "Sketch exhibiting the approaches with additional reconnaissances. Henry L. Abbot, Lieut. Topl. Engrs. Colored ms. Scale 1:75,000. 76 × 69 cm.

Map on tracing cloth, showing positions of Federal and Confederate armies in June and July 1862; also roads, railroads, and wooded areas, in parts of Henrico, Hanover, and Chesterfield counties.

Annotated, "Copied from a map captured from the enemy June 27th 1862."

H98

Position of Richmond, Va. prepared by order of Maj. Gen. Geo. B. McClellan, U.S.A. A. A. Humphreys, Brig. Gen. & Chief of Topl. Engrs. May 27th, 1862. Compiled from "Map of Henrico Co." and "Sketch exhibiting the approaches" with additional reconnaissances. Henry L. Abbot, Lieut. Topl. Engr. Uncolored ms. Scale 1:75,000. 46 × 52 cm.

Map on tracing cloth, showing roads, railroads, and wooded areas in parts of Henrico and Hanover counties.

H99

Sketch of McClelland's [sic] position, July 7th, 1862 [at Harrison's Landing] Wm. W. Blackford, Capt. Corps Eng'rs del. Colored ms. Scale ca. 1:40,000. 36 × 77 cm.

On tracing cloth. Shows McClellan's army between Kimmages Creek and Herring Creek on the James River, with some detail of the roads, residents, and terrain in the surrounding area.

H100

[Map of the James River Valley from the vicinity of Richmond to Chesapeake Bay, including parts of Henrico, Chesterfield, Charles City, and James City counties, Va. 186–] Colored ms. Scale ca. 1:80,000. 67 × 103 cm.

An unfinished map on an irregular sheet of tracing paper. The lower half shows roads in red, drainage in blue, and includes names of many residents. The upper left portion in the vicinity of Richmond shows only roads and railroads, and the upper right portion is wanting. A number of fortifications, both Confederate and Federal, are given. In the area of Malvern Hill is the notation, "Battle of July 1862."

H101

[Sketch of the Rapidan River Station and Racoon Ford in

On March 26, 1862, Gen. Thomas J. "Stonewall" Jackson ordered his topographical engineer, Jedediah Hotchkiss, to "make me a map of the Valley, from Harper's Ferry to Lexington, showing all the points of offence and defence in those places." The resulting comprehensive map measuring 254 by 111 cm. was of significant value to Jackson and his staff in planning and executing the Shenandoah Valley Campaign in May and June 1862. Depicted here is a small portion of the map showing the northern part of the Shenandoah Valley in the vicinity of Front Royal, Woodstock, and Strasburg, Virginia. The map is part of the Hotchkiss Map Collection in the Geography and Map Division, Library of Congress. (See entry no. H89.)

Orange County, Va. 186–] Colored ms. Scale ca. 1:100,000. 21 × 17 cm.

Rough sketch drawn on ruled paper with black and colored pencil.

H102

[Sketch of a portion of Orange County, north and west of Gordonsville to Rapidan Station. 186–] Colored ms. Scale ca. 1:250,000. 16 × 24 cm.

Sketch on an irregular piece of ledger paper. Roads are shown in red, drainage in blue, and wooded areas in green. Names of some residents are given.

H103

[Sketch of a portion of Orange County, Va. showing roads between Orange Court House, Gordonsville, and Liberty Mills. 186–] Colored ms. Scale ca. 1:125,000. 10 × 17 cm.

Roads and railroads are shown in red, drainage in blue, and elevations by brown hachures.

H104

[Map of parts of Orange, Louisa, and Spotsylvania counties, Va. 186–] Colored ms. Scale ca. 1:200,000. 15 × 21 cm.

Roads are drawn in red, drainage in blue, names and some roads in pencil. The signature of J. K. Boswell appears twice on the map.

H105

[Sketch of the road from Madison northward to Dulaney's in Madison County, Va. 186–] Uncolored ms. Scale ca. 1:63,360. 14 × 36 cm.

Pencil sketch with names of residents along the road.

H106

[Sketches of portions of Madison County, Va. 186–] Colored ms. Scale ca. 1:200,000. 40 × 28 cm.

Drawn with colored pencils, these sketches on both sides of the sheet show considerable detail. Roads are drawn in red, drainage in blue, and elevations are shown by hachures.

Manassas Campaign—1862

H107

[Sketch of a portion of Orange County, north and east of Orange showing the Rapidan River from Rapidan Station to Germanna Mills and the Plank Road to Robertson's Tavern at Trap. 1862] Colored ms. Scale ca. 1:126,720. 20 × 28 cm.

Pen sketch on an irregular sheet of brown paper, showing roads in red and drainage in blue. Distances are given between road junctions.

H108

[Sketch of the Manassas battlefield. 1862] Uncolored ms. Scale ca. 1:63,360. 22 × 27 cm.

On tracing paper, drawn on a 1-inch grid. Map centers on Groveton, and extends from Haymarket on the west, to Bethlehem Church on the south, to the Stone Bridge on the east, and Catharpen and Bull Runs on the north. Includes the names of a number of residents.

H109

[Sketch showing positions of Second Corps, A.N.Va., August 26th to September 2, 1862, embracing engagements at Bristoe Station, Manassas Junction, Groveton or Second Manassas, and Ox Hill or Chantilly, Va. Prepared to accompany report of Lieut. Gen. Thos. J. Jackson by Jed. Hotchkiss, Top. Eng. Jan. 1863] Colored ms. Scale ca. 1:63,360. 44 × 36 cm.

A printed reduction of this map is in the *Atlas to Accompany the Official Records of the Union and Confederate Armies,* 1891–95, pl. 111, no. 1.

H110

Surveys of the military defences, vicinity of Washington, D.C. Compiled at Division Hd. Qrs. of Gen. Irvin M'Dowell U.S.A. Arlington, Jan. 1st, 1862. Colored ms. Scale 1:63,360. 51 × 41 cm.

Probably a copy of a captured map.

Drawn on tracing cloth, with roads in red, drainage in blue, and elevations shown by hachures. Some of the fortifications around Washington are named. A numbered list refers to public buildings in Washington.

Maryland Campaign—1862

H111

Northwest, or no. 1 sheet [and Southwest, or no. 2 sheet] of preliminary map of Antietam (Sharpsburg) battlefield. Enlarged from the "Michler" map of the War Records Atlas, with corrections and additions Nov. 1894 [and Jan. 1895] . . . [Washington] Antietam Battlefield Commission [1894–95] Colored. Scale 1:10,500. 123 × 78 cm.

Printed copies of sheet 1 and 2 are mounted as one map to fold to 16 × 10 cm. with manuscript additions of names of residents and topography. Title on the reverse, "Map of Antietam battlefield, Sharpsburg, Md. By Jed. Hotchkiss, Staunton, Va., 1894–5."

H112

[Northwest, or no. 1 sheet of preliminary map of Antietam (Sharpsburg) battlefield. Enlarged from the "Michler" map of the War Records Atlas, with corrections and additions Nov. 1894. Antietam Battlefield Commission] Uncolored ms. Scale 1:10,500. 64 × 80 cm.

On tracing cloth. The above title is taken from the printed map, of which this is the fair drawing.

H113

Antietam battlefield. Preliminary map no. 3. Jed. Hotchkiss. July 1895. Uncolored ms. Scale 1:5040. 92 × 52 cm.

Drawn on tracing cloth, the map indicates elevations by hachures, drainage, fields, houses, etc., in the area north of Sharpsburg.

H114

[Preliminary map of the Antietam battlefield area, including Sharpsburg and the adjacent territory. 1895] Colored ms. Scale ca. 1:31,680. 41 × 36 cm.

On tracing cloth. The map gives only the principal roads and drainage, and the names of residents at the time of the battle.

H115

[Sketch of a portion of the Antietam battlefield, north of Sharpsburg, in the area of the West Wood, North Wood, and East Wood. 1895] Uncolored ms. Scale ca. 1:10,000. 30 × 29 cm.

Unfinished drawing on tracing cloth, giving houses, roads, field boundaries, etc. The only name, "Nicodemus," is lettered in pencil.

H116

[Sketch of a portion of the Antietam battlefield, north of Sharpsburg, in the area of the West Wood, North Wood, and East Wood. 1895] Colored ms. Scale ca. 1:10,000. 25 × 24 cm.

Unfinished drawing on tracing cloth, giving houses, roads, field boundaries, etc. Worm fences are shown in red; post and rail fences are shown by dashed lines. The "North Wood" and "Ea[s]t Wood" are indicated; also D. R. Miller, Samuel Poffenberger, Simon Morrison, the Dunkard Church, and a Toll Gate.

H117

[Preliminary field sketch of part of the Antietam battlefield, in the area north of Sharpsburg. 1895] Uncolored ms. Scale ca. 1:5040. 20 × 25 cm.

Several sketches, giving distances and elevations along roads north of Sharpsburg, on both sides of note paper of the Antietam Battlefield Commission. The names D. R. Miller and Mumma are given on adjacent sketches.

H118

[Preliminary field sketch of part of the Antietam battlefield, in the area north of Sharpsburg. 1895] Uncolored ms. Scale ca. 1:5040. 20 × 25 cm.

A number of spot elevations are given along roads and fences. The names of Nicodemus and D. R. Miller appear in the upper right portion of the map. The sketch is on note paper of the Antietam Battlefield Commission.

H119

[Preliminary field sketch of part of the Shepherdstown Road east of Sharpsburg. 1895] Uncolored ms. Scale ca. 1:10,000. 19 × 14 cm.

Sketch on yellow line graph paper. Shows elevations and distances along the road and a short stretch of the railroad where it is near the road. The only names given are "Antietam Div.," "3rd La.," and "2nd La." Annotations give distance of the "Town wood" from "2nd lane" etc.

H120

[Preliminary field sketch of part of the Antietam battlefield, north of Sharpsburg near the Toll Gate and Adam Michael's field. 1895] Uncolored ms. Scale ca. 1:10,000. 19 × 14 cm.

Sketch on yellow line graph paper. Shows streams, fences, and roads south of Adam Michael's field.

H121

[Survey of the property of George Poffenberger and Mrs. Nicodemus in Washington County, Md., surveyed by] S. S. Downin S.W.C. 1883. Uncolored ms. Scale 1:5940. 21 × 29 cm.

Property in the Antietam battlefield area, north of Sharpsburg.

H122

[Survey plat of the property of Joseph Poffenberger in Washington County, Md., surveyed by] S. S. Downin, S. W. County, December 16th, 1851. Uncolored ms. Scale 1:5940. 28 × 21 cm.

Property in the Antietam battlefield area, north of Sharpsburg.

Fredericksburg Campaign—1862

H123

Sketch of battle of Fredericksburg, December 13th 1862, by Wm. W. Blackford, Capt. Corps. Engrs. C.S.P.A. Colored ms. Scale 1:31,680. 39 × 35 cm.

Drawn on gray tracing paper on a 2-inch grid. Gives a list of nine Confederate divisions whose positions are indicated by numbers.

H124

[Map of Fredericksburg, Va., and vicinity. 1862] Uncolored ms. Scale ca. 1:31,680. 20 × 40 cm.

A finely drawn map, on a 2-inch grid, giving roads, railroads, some elevations by hachures, and names of a few residents. "Quarters," and "Alsops Quarters" are located.

H125

[An unfinished drawing of the battle of Fredericksburg, Saturday December 13, 1862] Colored ms. Scale ca. 1:20,000. 64 × 36 cm.

Roads are shown in red, drainage in blue, wooded areas in green, and elevations by hachures. Gives the names of several residents in the area; locates "Gen. Lee's Hd. Qrs.," "Hamilton's Crossing," and "Deep Run."

This map bears a similarity to the map in the *Atlas to Accompany the Official Records of the Union and Confederate Armies,* 1891–95, pl. 31, no. 4.

H126

[Sketches of roads west of Fredericksburg, Va. 1862] Uncolored ms. Scale ca. 1:20,000. 26 × 19 cm.

Two pencil sketches on either side of a sheet, giving measurements, drainage, elevations by hachures, and the names of several residents.

H127

[Map of the vicinity of Fredericksburg, Va. 1862] Colored. Scale ca. 1:125,000. 21 × 31 cm.

This map comprises portions of two U.S. Geological Survey quadrangles, in which roads have been drawn in red ink, streams in black, and a number of names have been added.

H128

[Map of the Rappahannock River below Fredericksburg, showing Port Royal, Moss Neck, Corbin's Neck, etc. 1862–3] Colored ms. Scale ca. 1:20,000. 61 × 141 cm.

An irregular map on tracing paper, drawn with colored and lead pencils, on a 3-inch grid. Shows the headquarters of Generals Jackson, A. P. Hill, and Early during the winter of 1862–63.

Chancellorsville Campaign—1863

H129

[Sketch of the battles of Chancellorsville, Salem Church, and Fredericksburg, May 2, 3, and 4, 1863. Prepared by order of General R. E. Lee, by Jed. Hotchkiss, Topogl. Engr. 2d Corps, A.N.V.] Colored ms. Scale ca. 1:63,360. 59 × 107 cm.

A similar map, somewhat reduced, with the above title is contained in the *Atlas to Accompany the Official Records of the Union and Confederate Armies,* 1891–95, pl. 41.

H130

[Pencil sketches of Confederate troop positions along the Furnace Road south of Chancellorsville, on the "night of May 1st" and "May 2nd" 1863] Uncolored ms. Not drawn to scale. 16 × 21 cm.

A list of several troop movements is given in pencil at the right of the sketches.

H131

Map of the battle of Chancellorsville, Saturday, May 2nd 1863. Colored ms. Scale 1:31,680. 28 × 47 cm.

Finely drawn map, with a number of annotations in pencil. Positions and movements of both Union and Confederate forces are indicated.

H132

The battle of Chancellorsville, or "The Wilderness" Saturday May 2nd 1863. Colored ms. Scale 1:63,360. 20 × 27 cm.

The positions of the divisions of A. P. Hill, Trimble, and D. H. Hill are indicated by red numbers, and explained in the legend. A number of pencil notes are in the right margin.

H133

[Preliminary field sketches of parts of the Chancellorsville battlefield, May 2–4, 1863] Colored ms. Scales ca. 1:63,360, 1:24,000, etc. 38 × 26 cm.

Several pencil sketches on both sides of a sheet of ledger paper, one of which is annotated, "Saturdays Position."

H134

[Preliminary field sketches of parts of the Chancellorsville battlefield, May 2–4, 1863] Colored ms. Scale ca. 1:63,360. 26 × 20 cm.

Two pencil sketches, one of which is annotated, "Position Friday P.M.—Gen. McLaws."

H135

The battle of Chancellorsville Sunday May 3rd 1863. Drawn by S. B. Robinson. Colored ms. Scale 1:31,680. 21 × 32 cm.

Fine drawing of terrain, roads, lines of defense, etc. Shows no troop positions.

H136

[Map of the battle of Chancellorsville] Sunday May 3rd [1863] Colored ms. Scale 1:50,000. 25 × 32 cm.

Fine drawing of terrain, roads, lines of defense, etc., centering on Chancellorsville, with no names, except those of Union and Confederate army units. A pencil list of 29 names of Confederate commanders corresponds to numbers on the map.

H137

[Preliminary field sketches of parts of the Chancellorsville battlefield, May 2–4, 1863] Uncolored ms. Scale ca. 1:63,360. 20 × 26 cm.

Pencil sketches on both sides of the sheet, one side of which contains the following annotation, "Sunday P.M. Mohone [sic] & Semmes were moving to position at first of fight. The Division swung on the left on Monday & Mohone [sic] then retired to the rifle pits."

H138

[Map of Chancellorsville battlefield, May 3–4, 1863] Colored ms. Scale ca. 1:63,360. 29 × 21 cm.

Fine drawing of terrain, roads, lines of defense, etc., south of the Rapidan River and extending a mile south of Chancellorsville. The only place name is "United States Mine or Bark Mill Ford." Troop positions are numbered in pencil 1 to 9, with explanations, also in pencil, in the lower margin. The only other annotation reads, "Sunday P.M. & Monday."

H139

Sketch of Banks Ford [on the Rappahannock above Fredericksburg, held by the Confederates under McLaws and Anderson during the battle of Chancellorsville, May 3, 1863] Colored ms. Scale ca. 1:63,360. 10 × 14 cm.

Shows fortifications, roads, elevations, and names of residents in the vicinity of the ford.

H140

[Sketch of the United States Ford on the Rappahannock River, 1863] Colored ms. Scale ca. 1:80,000. 11 × 10 cm.

Roads are shown in red, drainage in blue, wooded areas in green, and elevations by hachures.

H141

[Three sketches on one sheet of fortifications, roads and streams in the vicinity of Salem Church and Banks Ford in the battle of Chancellorsville, May 1863] Colored ms. Scale ca. 1:63,360. 20 × 26 cm.

Drawn with colored pencils on a sheet of ledger paper. Roads are drawn in red, drainage in blue, wooded areas in green, and elevations by hachures.

H142

Memoranda of J. Hotchkiss, Top. Eng. Hd. Qrs. 2nd Corps A.N.Va. [Sketches and notes relating to the battle of Chancellorsville, 1863] Uncolored ms. Various scales. 6 leaves, 26 × 9 cm. each.

H143

[Sketch of the roads south of Bowles's Shop near Salem Church, Virginia, showing "Early's line" probably in May 1863] Uncolored ms. Scale ca. 1:63,360. 20 × 14 cm.

Pencil sketch on a sheet from a notebook. On the reverse side is a diagram giving the distances of Bowles's Shop from Charlottesville, Gordonsville, etc.

Gettysburg Campaign—1863

H144

Map of the lower [Shenandoah] Valley by 1st Lt. S. Howell Brown. Copied by J. Paul Hoffmann, Topl. Office, A.N.Va. [1863] Colored ms. Scale 1:126,720. 68 × 48 cm.

A finely drawn map on tracing cloth that includes parts of Warren, Frederick, and Clarke counties, Virginia, and Morgan, Berkeley, and Jefferson counties, West Virginia. Roads are shown in red, drainage in blue, and elevations by hachures. The names of many residents are given in the upper portion of the map.

H145

[Map of the Shenandoah Valley from Mt. Jackson to Midway, including parts of Shenandoah, Page, Rockingham, and Augusta counties, Virginia. 186–] Colored ms. Scale 1:160,000. 72 × 48 cm.

On tracing cloth. Roads in red, drainage in blue, elevations are shown by form lines. Dots are shown for many houses, without names of residents.

H146

[Map of the Shenandoah Valley from Harrisonburg to Mt. Jackson, with topographical detail along the principal roads from Thornton's Gap to Swift Run Gap, and along several valley roads in northwestern Virginia. 186–] Colored ms. Scale 1:80,000., 78 × 96 cm.

Unfinished map on tracing cloth. It is annotated on the back, "Harrisonburg to Mt. Jackson. Hotchkiss."

H147

[Map of Shenandoah Valley from Winchester to New Market, Virginia and from Millwood to Waverly P.O. including parts of Frederick, Clarke, Warren, Shenandoah, and Page counties, Virginia. 186–] Colored ms. Scale ca. 1:160,000. 54 × 41 cm.

Incomplete map. Roads are drawn in red, drainage in blue, and elevations are shown by brown form lines and hachures. Drawn on a 3/8-inch grid.

H148

[Map of the Shenandoah Valley, from Front Royal and Middletown to Staunton, etc. 186–] Colored ms. Scale ca. 1:250,000. 56 × 71 cm.

An unfinished map. Roads are shown in red, drainage in blue, and elevations by brown hachures. The Massanutten Range and Little North Mountains are shown, but only part of the Blue Ridge between Manassas Gap and Swift Run Gap. The road from Warrentown to Gordonsville is shown, with some detail on either side. Much of the intervening area is blank.

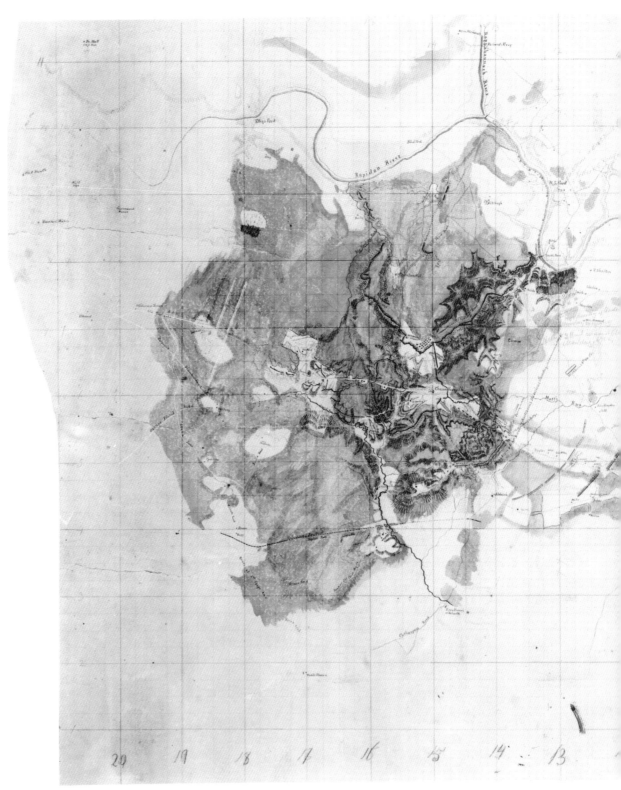

Jedediah Hotchkiss's manuscript map prepared by order of Gen. Robert E. Lee of the Battles of Chancellorsville, Salem Church, and Fredericksburg, Virginia, fought May 2, 3, and 4, 1863. It was at the

320

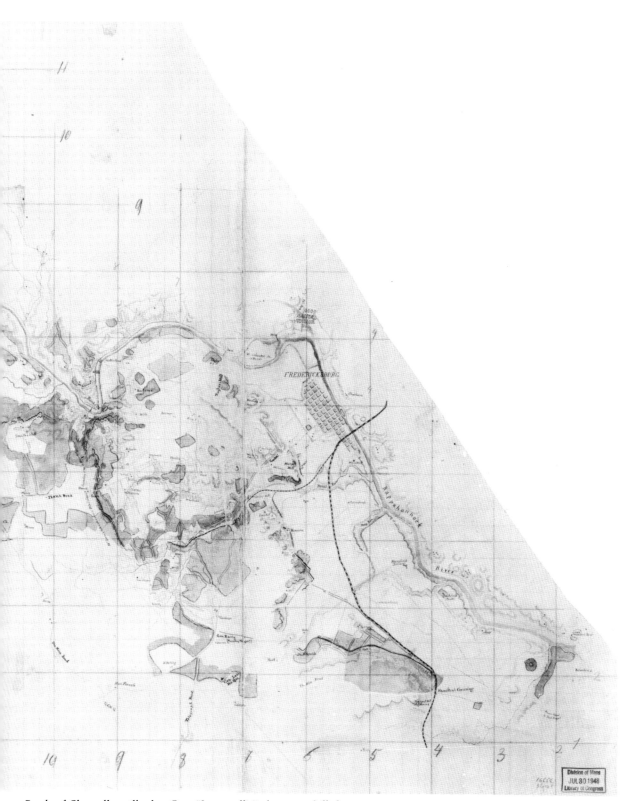

Battle of Chancellorsville that Gen. "Stonewall" Jackson was killed.
(See entry no. H129.)

H149

Topographical sketch of a portion of the North Mountain Range & the Valley of Virginia. Jed. Hotchkiss (del.) Stribling Springs, Va. [1863] Colored ms. Scale 1:316,800. 41 × 35 cm.

An unfinished map on graph paper.

This map may have been drawn before the war. Hotchkiss was in Stribling Springs in 1858–1859.

H150

[Map of Shenandoah County between Mt. Jackson and New Market, Virginia. 1863] Colored ms. Scale 1:126,720. 21 × 13 cm.

Ink drawing, showing the "B. & O. R.R. Valley Branch," the Shenandoah River, Smith Creek, and Helman Creek.

H151

[Sketches of roads in the Shenandoah Valley between Winchester and Woodstock, Virginia. 1863] Colored ms. Scale ca. 1:40,000 and 1:80,000. 44 × 36 cm.

Maps on both sides of a sheet give drainage, elevations, woods, and names of residents along several roads, mostly between Woodstock and Spring Hill, Virginia.

H152

[Map of parts of Rockingham and Shenandoah counties, Virginia, including Harrisonburg and Orkney Springs. 186–] Colored ms. Scale 1:126,720. 35 × 35 cm.

Pencil drawing on brown paper. Roads are shown in red, drainage in blue, elevations by faint brown hachures.

H153

[Sketch of the Shenandoah Valley in the vicinity of Mt. Jackson. 186–] Colored ms. Scale ca. 1:63,360. 23 × 21 cm.

Pencil sketch with road in red and drainage in blue, drawn on a 1-inch grid. It shows the Valley Turnpike and part of the North Fork of the Shenandoah River from about Hawkinstown southward past Mt. Jackson to the mouth of Smith Creek.

H154

[Sketch of roads south and west of Mt. Jackson, Virginia. 1863] Colored ms. Scale ca. 1:63,360. 25 × 22 cm.

Names the "Middle Road," and gives names of some residents. Roads in red, drainage in blue, and wooded areas in green. Drawn on a 1-inch grid.

H155

Sketch of the second battle of Winchester, June 13th, 14th, and 15th 1863, to accompany report of Lieut. Gen. R. S. Ewell, commanding 2nd Corps, by Jed. Hotchkiss Top. Engr. 2nd Corps. Colored ms. Scale ca. 1:31,680. 44 × 48 cm.

On tracing paper. A printed reduction of this map is in the *Atlas to Accompany the Official Records of the Union and Confederate Armies,* 1891–95, pl. 43, no. 3. It shows positions of Confederate troops and names their commanders.

H156

[Map of parts of Pennsylvania, Maryland, and Virginia, covering areas from Harrisburg to Leesburg, and from Hancock to Baltimore. 1863] Photostat of colored ms. Scale 1:160,000. 88 × 116 cm.

One of the finest maps of the collection; the manuscript original is in the Handley Library at Winchester, Virginia. Two cards attached to the original read as follows, "Map made by Capt. Jed. Hotchkiss at Moss Neck—by order of Gen. T. J. Jackson," and "Used by Gen. R. E. Lee in the famous Gettysburg campaign."

The names of many residents are included throughout the area covered, namely that part of Pennsylvania south of Harrisburg, west of the Susquehanna River and east of Tuscarora Mountain; that part of Maryland west of Monocacy and the Patapsco but including Baltimore, and parts of Loudoun County, Virginia, and Jefferson and Berkeley counties, West Virginia.

H157

[Map of Pennsylvania and part of New Jersey. 186–] Colored ms. Scale ca. 1:300,000. 95 × 178 cm.

Drawn on tracing cloth. Mountains are shown by hachures; roads are in red.

H158

Sketch of routes of the 2nd Corps A.N. Virginia from Frederickburg, Va. to Gettysburg, Pa. and return to Orange C.H. Va. June 4th to August 1st 1863, to accompany report of Jed. Hotchkiss Top. Eng. 2nd Corps. Prepared by order of Lt. Col. Wm. Procter Smith, Chief Engineer, A.N.V. Colored ms. Scale 1:633,600. 41 × 35 cm.

Roads are shown in red and green, drainage in blue, and mountains in brown hachures.

H159

[Preliminary sketch of the Battle of Gettysburg showing troop positions July 2, 1863] Colored ms. Scale ca. 1:28,000. 47 × 40 cm.

Annotated in pencil as follows, "Walker remained here until 1 A.M. of the 2nd July, then near Benners 2 hours, then supported Stewart. The advance to enemys works was made by 3 Brigades on the night of 2nd of July."

H160

[Preliminary sketch of the battle of Gettysburg showing troop positions, July 2, 1863] Colored ms. Scale ca. 1:28,000. 29 × 40 cm.

Similar to the foregoing map, without annotation.

H161

Map showing the routes of Brig. Gen. J. B. [sic] Imboden's command during the Pennsylvania campaign of 1863. By Jed. Hotchkiss Capt. & Top. Eng. . . .[1863] Colored ms. Scale 1:316,800. 54 × 46 cm.

Incomplete map on thin tracing paper, somewhat torn, with title in pencil. The area covered extends from Brock's Gap, Virginia to Cumberland, Maryland, to Bloody Run, Pennsylvania, to Gettysburg, to Harpers Ferry, to New Market, to Brock's Gap. The following annotation appears in the lower left corner, "Gen. Imboden started from Churchville, Augusta Co—30 S.W. of this point June 9th, 1863." The dates of successive encampments are given along the route between Romney on June 15, 1863, to Cashtown near Gettysburg on July 3–4, 1863.

H162

[Sketch of the battlefield of Gettysburg, July 1st and 2nd 1863] Colored ms. Scale ca. 1:28,000. 48 × 38 cm.

Shows troop movements on July 1 and 2, 1863. Confederate divisions and corps are named, but Federal commands are not named.

Bristoe, Virginia, Campaign—October 1863

H163

[Five sketches on one sheet of areas in Culpeper County, Virginia, in the vicinity of Liberty Mills, Germanna, Ely's Ford, etc. 1863] Uncolored ms. Scale ca. 1:25,000. 21 × 13 cm.

Sketches and tables of distances appear on both sides of the sheet.

H164

[Sketch of Flint Hill, Virginia, and the roads to Gaines X Roads, F. Eastham, and the Hermitage. 1863] Uncolored ms. Scale ca. 1:80,000. 15 × 20 cm.

Pencil sketch on blue paper. Battle Run Church, Cooksie's Mill Road, and Toucett's are also named.

H165

Sketch of the battle of Bristoe, Wednesday October 14th, 1863; by Jed. Hotchkiss, Capt. & Top. Engr. 2nd Corps, A.N.Va. Colored ms. Scale 1:40,000. 34 × 23 cm.

Names the Confederate commands.
Drawn on a 1 1/2-inch grid.

Rapidan to the James River Campaign—1864

H166

Map showing position of the brigades of 2nd Corps, C.S. Army of N. Va. May 5, 1864. By Jed. Hotchkiss, Top. Eng. 2nd Corps. Campaign of "The Wilderness." Uncolored ms. Scale ca. 1:160,000. 11 × 16 cm.

The data on this map is included on a similar map in the *Atlas to Accompany the Official Records of the Union and Confederate Armies,* 1891–95, pl. 83, no. 1.

H167

Campaign of "The Wilderness." Position of brigades of 2nd Corps, A.N. Va. May 6th, 1864. By Jed. Hotchkiss Top. Eng. 2nd Corps. Uncolored ms. Scale 1:39,000. 8 × 12 cm.

The data on this map is included on a similar map in the *Atlas to Accompany the Official Records of the Union and Confederate Armies,* 1891–95, pl. 83, no. 2.

H168

Sketch showing positions and entrenchments of the Army of N. Va. Made by Jed. Hotchkiss, Top. Eng., 2nd Corps, A.N. Va. from sketches during and after the engagements. Uncolored ms. Scale 1:40,000. 17 × 21 cm.

Shows Federal and Confederate lines. Uncolored version of a map with similar title in the *Atlas to Accompany the Official Records of the Union and Confederate Armies,* 1891–95, pl. 83, no. 3.

H169

[Col. William Allen's map of the vicinity of Hanover Junction. 1864] Colored ms. Scale ca. 1:90,000. 24 × 28 cm.

The title is on the back of the map. Roads are shown in red. The names of a number of residents are included.

H170

Map showing the lines of entrenchments of the C.S. Army of Northern Va., [exten]ding from the Totopotomoy to the Chickahominy, and the positions of the brigades of the 2nd Corps, A.N. Va., from May 23rd to June 10, 1864. By Jed. Hotchkiss, Top. Eng. 2nd Corps. Uncolored ms. Scale ca. 1:40,000. 37 × 33 cm.

On tracing paper.

H171

Map showing the line of entrenchments of the Army N. Va. from Totopotomoy to the Chickahominy and the positions of the 2nd Corps, A.N.V. from May 28th to June 10th 1864 in Hanover Co., Va. Colored ms. Scale 1:40,000. 22 × 35 cm.

Finely drawn map giving roads in brown, drainage in blue, forests in green, and elevations by hachures. Confederate troop positions are in red.

H172

[Sketch of the Rapidan River Valley, covering parts of Madison, Greene, Orange, Culpeper, Spotsylvania, and Stafford counties, Virginia. 1864] Uncolored ms. Scale ca. 1:350,000. 32 × 38 cm.

Pencil sketch on blue lined writing paper.

H173

[Map of portions of Orange, Louisa, Spotsylvania, and Culpeper counties, Virginia. 1864] Colored ms. Scale ca. 1:400,000. 29 × 34 cm.

An unfinished drawing in pencil, showing roads in red, drainage in blue, and cultural features in ink and pencil.

H174

[Sketch of the cavalry engagement of General Lomax near Gordonsville, Virginia, Dec. 24th, 1864. By Jed. Hotchkiss, Top. Eng. V. D.] Colored ms. Scale ca. 1:40,000. 23 × 25 cm.

A similar map with the above title is in the *Atlas to Accompany the Official Records of the Union and Confederate Armies,* 1891–95, pl. 84, no. 8.

The following annotations in pencil appear on the face of the map, "Fight at G occurred Dec. 24th—two divisions of the enemy commanded by Torbert. My force was 1100 men in the works," and "Jackson was withdrawn from center, when the enemy threatened his left. Gap filled by extending the line of other two Brigades." Confederate troop positions and movements are also shown in pencil.

H175

Map of Pr. George, Surry, Sussex, and Southampton Counties. Top. Eng. Office, V.D. Feb. 7th, 1865. Copies by J. A. Wilson. Colored ms. Scale 1:240,000. 50 × 51 cm.

Drawn on tracing paper.

Richmond Campaign—1864–65

H176

Map of vicinity of Richmond, made under the direction of A. H. Campbell, Capt P. E. in charge Topl. Dept. D.N. Va. [1864] Colored ms. Scale 1:40,000. 91 × 73 cm.

Finely executed map on tracing cloth, with annotations in the lower left corner, "Gen. R. E. Lee's." Covers parts of Henrico and Chesterfield counties and shows many fortifications.

At head of title, "Chief Engineer's Office, D.N.V. Maj. Gen. J. F. Gilmer, Chief Engineer."

H177

Map of the city of Richmond showing its defences. [1864] Colored ms. Scale 1:40,000. 37 × 29 cm.

Finished drawing on tracing cloth; shows fortifications surrounding the city, numbered 1 to 16.

H178

[Map of the vicinity of Richmond, north and east of the James River. 1864] Colored ms. Scale ca. 1:40,000. 94 × 61 cm.

An unfinished map on tracing cloth. It bears the following annotation, "Nerly [sic] all the streams are marshey [sic]. Indistinct roads are marked with fine lines or dots sketched and drawn by D. E. Henderson."

Some fortifications and troop positions are shown.

H179

Map used by Jed. Hotchkiss, Top. Eng. 2d Corps A.N. Va. in campaign of 1864. Colored ms. Scale 1:160,000. 23 × 26 cm.

On an irregular piece of tracing cloth, the map includes the area north and east of Richmond to the Pamunkey River, in Henrico and Hanover counties, giving the names of many residents. The title is on the reverse.

H180

Map of the Confederate lines from New Bridge road to Chafins Bluff, made under the direction of Brig. Genl. W. H. Stevens Chf. Eng. A.N.V. Topl. Office, A.N.V. Copied by J. Paul Hoffmann. [1864] Colored ms. Scale 1:20,000. 86 × 63 cm.

Confederate fortifications shown in red are similar to those on the map entitled "Map of Hanover, Henrico and part of Chesterfield Counties, Va. . . . 1864," in the *Atlas to Accompany the Official Records of the Union and Confederate Armies,* 1891–95, pl. 135, no. 3.

Drawn on tracing cloth.

Shenandoah Valley and Maryland Campaign— 1864

H181

Battle of Monocacy [July 9, 1864] Colored ms. Scale ca. 1:19,760. 18 × 13 cm.

Gives Confederate troop movements only. A pencil sketch on the reverse indicates "Doles," "Cook's (Doles) crossed Monocacy," and "Skirmishers went 2 miles beyond River."

H182

[Topographical map of the District of Columbia and adjacent areas in Virginia, showing fortifications] Top'l Office, April 2nd, 1864. Colored ms. Scale 1:63,360. 37 × 28 cm.

A finished drawing on tracing cloth, showing roads in red, drainage in blue, and elevations by hachures.

H183

Sketch of the battle of Rutherford Ian [Rutherford's Farm]

July 20th 1864. By Jed. Hotchkiss Capt. Top. Eng. V. D. Uncolored ms. Scale 1:126,720. 15 × 19 cm.

Preliminary sketch with title in pencil of map in the *Atlas to Accompany the Official Records of the Union and Confederate Armies,* 1891–95, pl. 83, no. 6.

H184

[Sketch of the region west of Charlestown, West Virginia, showing fortifications, 1864] Colored ms. Scale ca. 1:31,680. 28 × 23 cm.

Fine pencil drawing showing topography by brown form lines, also roads, fences, etc., and giving names of several residents. It is similar to a portion of a map entitled "Sketch of engagement at Charlestown, Va., Sunday, Aug. 21st 1864. To accompany report of Jed. Hotchkiss . . ." in *Atlas to Accompany the Official Records of the Union and Confederate Armies,* 1891–95, pl. 82, no. 6.

H185

[Sketch of the Battle of Winchester, September 19, 1864] Colored ms. Scale ca. 1:85,000. 34 × 34 cm.

Evidently a Federal sketch, as it shows "Rebel line of battle," and "Line of Rebel retreat," as well as Federal troop positions.

H186

Map of vicinity of Winchester & Kernstown. Approved Dec. 17, 1864. J. Innes Randolph, 1st Lt. Engrs. for Maj. A. H. Campbell Engr. in chg. Top. Dept. Colored ms. Scale 1:40,000. 55 × 38 cm.

Unfinished sketch on tracing cloth, drawn on a 1 1/2-inch grid, with topographical detail only along the roads. Annotated "No. 23" in the upper left corner.

H187

Map of vicinity of Fisher's Hill. 1864. Colored ms. Scale 1:40,000. 44 × 37 cm.

Annotated, "Approved Dec. 17th 1864, J. Innes Randolph, 1. Lt. Engrs for Maj. A. H. Campbell, Eng. in chg. Top. Dept." Drawn on tracing cloth. Roads are shown in red, wooded areas in green, and mountains by form lines. Hachures are added in the area of Fishers Hill, southwest of Strasburg. Drawn on 1 1/2-inch grid.

H188

[Five sketches along the Valley Pike in the vicinity of Fishers Hill, Strasburg, Cottontown, Mount Hope, Toms Brook, etc. 186–] Colored ms. Scale ca. 1:40,000. 44 × 36 cm.

Drawn with colored pencils, giving roads in red, drainage in blue, wooded areas in green, and hachures in brown. Names of settlements and of residents are in black pencil.

H189

Map of the vicinity of Strasburg and Fisher's Hill from sur-

vey's by Lieut. Koerner P. E. under direction of Maj. A. H. Campbell Chf. Topl. Dpt. D.N.V. Approved Jny 27th 1865, Albert H. Campbell, Maj. Engrs. in chge Top. Dep. D.N.Va. Colored ms. Scale 1:80,000. 36 × 58 cm.

Incomplete map drawn on tracing cloth, covering portions of Frederick, Clarke, Shenandoah, and Warren counties, Virginia. Roads are shown in red, drainage in blue, and elevations by hachures. The names of many residents are given.

H190

[Map of the vicinity of Strasburg, Virginia. 186–] Colored ms. Scale ca. 1:126,720. 33 × 43 cm.

Finely executed unfinished drawing showing the roads, streams, mountains, etc., south and west of Strasburg. No names appear on the map. Drawn on a 1/2-inch grid.

H191

[Topographic map of the vicinity of Harpers Ferry, West Virginia. 1864] Colored ms. Scale ca. 1:65,000. 21 × 16 cm.

Unfinished drawing, without place names. Elevations are indicated by brown hachures.

H192

[Map of Harpers Ferry and vicinity, West Virginia. 1864] Colored ms. Scale ca. 1:27,000. 57 × 53 cm.

An unfinished map on an irregular piece of tracing cloth. Property lines and owners' names are given in the Jefferson County area.

H193

[Map of cavalry engagement near Bridgewater, Va., Oct. 4th and 5th, 1864, by Jed. Hotchkiss, Top. Eng., A.V.D.] Colored ms. Scale 1:80,000. 21 × 16 cm.

Finished drawing, without names, of the map reproduced in the *Atlas to Accompany the Official Records of the Union and Confederate Armies,* 1891–95, pl. 82, no. 12.

H194

Sketch of the battle of Belle Grove or Cedar Creek, Wednesday, Oct'r. 19th, 1864. By Jed. Hotchkiss &c. Uncolored ms. Scale 1:63,360. 21 × 26 cm.

Fine drawing of the battle area giving elevations by hachures, wooded areas, drainage, roads, railroads, and the names of some residents. It shows a few fortifications. Drawn on a 1-inch grid.

H195

Sketch of the battle of Belle Grove or Cedar Creek, Wednesday Oct'r. 19th, 1864. By Jed. Hotchkiss &c. Colored ms. Scale 1:40,000. 26 × 31 cm.

Fine drawing of the battle area, mostly north of the north fork of the Shenandoah, showing some fortifications. Drawn on a 3/8-inch grid.

H196

[Preliminary sketch of a portion of the Belle Grove or Cedar Creek battlefield area. 1864] Uncolored ms. Scale 1:23,500. 21 × 26 cm.

Two pencil sketches on a sheet of blue lined writing paper of areas north of Belle Grove. One sketch locates the residences of Jas. D. Tabler, Hen. Walters, Milton Taylor, Dan Miller, and Wm. Dinges; the other sketch names W. Dinges and Dinges.

H197

[Preliminary sketch of a portion of the Belle Grove or Cedar Creek battlefield area. 1864] Uncolored ms. Scale ca. 1:20,000. 21 × 26 cm.

Two pencil sketches on a sheet of blue lined writing paper of areas around Belle Grove. One sketch locates the residences of Sam Breedlove and Dan Ritenour; the other sketch names Belle View.

VALLEY CAMPAIGN—1864–65

H198

[Preliminary map of the battlefield of Waynesborough, Virginia, March 2, 1865. Uncolored ms. Scale 1:9,600. 63 × 59 cm.

A finished colored version of this map appears in the *Atlas to Accompany the Official Records of the Union and Confederate Armies,* 1891–95, pl. 72, no. 7.

H199

Rude's Hill & vicinity, Shenandoah Co. Va. [1865] Colored ms. Scale ca. 1:80,000. 21 × 24 cm.

This map, drawn on a 3/16-inch grid, is somewhat similar to one entitled, "No. 38. Sketch of Gen. Rosser's attack on Federal cavalry, guarding prisoners at Rude's Hill, Va., Tuesday, March 7th, 1865, by Jed. Hotchkiss," in *Atlas to Accompany the Official Records of the Union and Confederate Armies,* 1891–95, pl. 84, no. 11.

MAPS RELATED TO THE POSTWAR ACTIVITIES OF JEDEDIAH HOTCHKISS

General Maps

H200

[Map of the world on the Mercator projection. 1875] Colored ms. Scale ca. 1:130,000,000. 14 × 30 cm. on sheet 19 × 36 cm.

Annotated in the upper left corner, "No. 4". Also "Latitude of Virginia" designates a line drawn in red across the map at about 38° N. Lat.

H201

[Base map of Alabama, 1893] Uncolored ms. Scale ca. 1:1,470,000. 51 × 60 cm.

This map and the following six were "prepared for the purpose of illustrating a proposed report by Hotchkiss on the geology of all States and counties represented in the mines and mining exhibits at the Columbia Exposition, 1893." They are drawn on tracing cloth, showing drainage and county boundaries, and giving county names and those of the principal cities and towns.

H202

[Base map of California. 1893] Uncolored ms. Scale ca. 1:750,000. 172 × 76 cm.

H203

[Base map of Georgia. 1893] Uncolored ms. Scale ca. 1:1,350,650. 46 × 38 cm.

H204

[Base map of Kansas. 1893] Uncolored ms. Scale ca. 1:1,620,000. 41 × 71 cm.

H205

[Base map of Maryland. 1893] Uncolored ms. Scale ca. 1:514,000. On sheet 54 × 89 cm.

H206

[Base map of North Carolina. 1893] Uncolored ms. Scale ca. 1:1,231,000. 40 × 71 cm.

H207

[Base map of Pennsylvania. 1893] Uncolored ms. Scale ca. 1:375,000. 87 × 146 cm.

H208

[Five small maps of Virginia and parts of adjoining States showing forest regions, distribution of forests in 1870, faunal regions, distribution and density of population in 1870, and density of Negro population in 1870] Colored printed maps with ms. annotations. Scale ca. 1:10,000,000. 5 maps on sheet 35 × 28 cm.

H209

Map of Appalachian Virginia (& parts of W. Va. & Ky.) by Jed. Hotchkiss Top. Eng. Staunton, Va. 1873. D. C. Humphreys del. Uncolored ms. Scale 1:1,500,000. 24 × 27 cm.

Fair drawing giving county names, principal settlements, railroads, canals, and drainage.

H210

Map of Piedmont Virginia, by Jed. Hotchkiss, Top. Eng.

Staunton, Va. 1873. D. C. Humphreys del. Uncolored ms. Scale 1:1,500,000. 24 × 21 cm.

Fair drawing giving county names, principal settlements, railroads, canals, and drainage.

H211

Map of Tide-water Virginia, by Jed. Hotchkiss, Top. Eng. Staunton, Va., 1873. D. C. Humphreys del. Uncolored ms. Scale 1:1,500,000. 25 × 16 cm.

Fair drawing giving county names, principal settlements, railroads, canals, and drainage.

H212

Map of Middle Virginia, by Jed. Hotchkiss, Top. Eng. Staunton, Va. 1873. Uncolored ms. Scale 1:1,500,000. 24 × 16 cm.

Fair drawing giving county names, principal settlements, railroads, canals, and drainage.

H213

[Outline map of eastern Virginia and the Chesapeake Bay region] 1882. Uncolored. Scale ca. 1:1,000,000. 41 × 27 cm.

Annotated in pencil, "Copy of Map No. 4 U.S.C. & G. Survey Report, 1882."

H214

A centennial map of Lexington Presbytery of the Synod of Virginia of the Presbyterian Church in the United States, organized Sept. 26, 1786; centennial, Sept. 26, 1886; at Timber Ridge Church. By Jed. Hotchkiss, Top. Eng. Staunton, Va., 1886. Uncolored ms. Scale ca. 1:500,000. 46 × 54 cm.

Includes a list of the Virginia and West Virginia counties in the Lexington Presbytery.

H215

Map of the location of the North-western-Turnpike-road. Made under direction of C. Crozet, Pr. Eng. by Chas. B. Shaw Ast., 1831. Colored ms. Scale 1:126,720. 38 × 106 cm.

"This copy made by Fr. Koch, Richmond, Va. Jan. 27th 1862." It shows the road with some detail on either side, from Winchester westward to the Cheat River in Preston County, West Virginia.

H216

[Sketch of Central West Virginia, showing drainage between Clarksburg and Charleston. 18—] Uncolored ms. Scale ca. 1:341,925. 62 × 78 cm.

Pencil drawing on blue lined sheets of letter paper.

H217

Plats of the Wilson Cary Nicholas surveys (from the origi-

nals) made in Wythe and Russell Counties, Virginia, now Mercer, Raleigh, Wyoming, McDowell, and Logan Counties, West Virginia. Eng. Office of Jed. Hotchkiss, Staunton, Va., July 1st, 1884. Uncolored ms. Scale 1:430,000 (not "2,000 poles to 1 inch"). 35 × 42 cm.

Drawn on tracing cloth.

Geology

H218

Geological map of Virginia & West Virginia showing their chief geological sub-divisions by Prof. William B. Rogers on basis of the physical & pol. map of A. Guyot. [18—] Colored. Scale ca. 1:3,250,000. 28 × 21 cm.

Colored to show surface geology, with the legend in the upper right margin. The printed map is entitled, "Middle Atlantic States & North Carolina. By A. Guyot."

H219

Hotchkiss' Geological map of Virginia and West Virginia. The geology by Prof. William B. Rogers, chiefly from the Virginia State survey, 1831–41. "With later observations in some parts." Richmond, Va., Lith. by A. Hoen & Co., 1875. Colored. Scale 1:1,520,640. 34 × 51 cm.

Printed map, annotated and colored to show "The Great Limestone Valley," and the "Lower Coal Measures Coking Coals." Concentric circles show 25, 50, 75, and 100 miles around Buchanan; principal railroads are outlined in green.

H220

Geological map of the Potomac basin west of Blue Ridge, Virginia and West Virginia, showing the relations of its Upper Potomac Coal Basin and the iron-ore bearing areas in reference to the West Virginia Central and Pittsburg [sic] R.R., and its connections and extensions. Compiled from surveys by W. B. Rogers and others by Jed. Hotchkiss, Consulting Eng., etc. Staunton, Va. 1882. Uncolored ms. Scale 1:500,000. 40 × 61 cm.

Inset shows a "Geological section across Georges Creek Coal Basin and eastward. By Prof. I. C. White, May 1881. Trans. Am. Phil. Soc."

H221

Geological section across Potts Creek Valley.—Section along Potts Creek Valley [from Paint Bank to Helmentollers. 18—] Colored ms. Horizontal scales, 1:36,000 and 1:70,000 respectively. 23 × 33 cm.

Vertical scales 1 inch to 750 feet and 1 inch to 600 feet, respectively.

H222

Geological section crossing Blue Ridge at White's Gap,

Rockbridge Co. Va. & extending 10 miles beyond Hunterville [sic], Pocahontas Co., W. Va. Surveyed by W. H. Ruffner & J. L. Campbell. Constructed by J. L. Campbell. [18—] Colored ms. Scale 1:31,680. 28 × 390 cm.

Vertical scale 1 inch to 600 feet.

H223

[Profile showing geological structure of a section in Virginia from Mill Mountain in Rockbridge County to Blue Ridge Mountain in Augusta County. 18—] Colored ms. Scale 1:31,680. 21 × 163 cm.

Vertical scale 1 inch to 1000 feet.

H224

Section from Little North Mountain to Big North Mountain crossing S. W. of Ferrol Furnace; constructed by Prof. J. L. Campbell of Washington & Lee Un'vty from survey made jointly with Profr. Thos. Egleston of New York and Major Jed. Hotchkiss of Staunton, Va. [1879?] Uncolored ms. Scale 1:12,800. 16 × 94 cm.

Vertical scale 1 inch to 1000 feet.

H225

Geological section of Great and Little No. Mountains near Ferrol, Va. By J. L. Campbell. [18—] Uncolored ms. Scale 1:39,600. 27 × 30 cm.

Vertical scale 1 inch to 6000 feet.

Eight pencil sketches and a small location map on a sheet of blue lined paper. Annotated at the top, "Teste [sic] H. Bowyer C. B. C."

H226

Geological section from S. Fork of Shenandoah R. to Lost R. (across Shenandoah Co.) by Prof. Jos. Lesley. [1860] Colored ms. Not drawn to scale. 7 × 19 cm.

H227

[Geological section] from Cold Mt. in Amherst across Rockbridge & Bath Cos., Va. & part of Pocahontas Co., W. Va. by Dr. W. H. Ruffner & Prof. J. L. Campbell [1861–77] Drawn by Prof. C. Colored ms. Scale 1:126,720. 15 × 59 cm.

Vertical scale 1 inch to 2400 feet.

H228

[Chart of geological time and formations, from Archaean to Quaternary, or Age of Man] Colored ms. 183 × 61 cm.

An incomplete chart of five columns, giving (1) geological time; (2) the color designations; (3) names of geological formations; (4) blank; (5) pencil annotations.

H229

[Profiles of 17 cross sections of various parts of Virginia, drawn on 11 sheets] Uncolored ms.

Vertical and horizontal scales vary. Sheets vary in size, 11 × 31 cm. to 19 × 28 cm.

Mining Properties

H230

Map of the N. C. Morse patent of eighty-six thousand acres of coal, timber, iron, etc. lands in Pike County, Kentucky. Eng. Office of Jed. Hotchkiss, Staunton, Va. July 7, 1884. Uncolored ms. Scale 1:126,720. 25 × 36 cm.

Insets of (1) Geological section across "Elkhorn" lands, from Ky. Geol. Survey, 1884; and (2) Map of part of Kentucky and Virginia, W. Va. and Ohio—showing location of coal and timber lands. Scale ca. 1:750,000.

H231

[Sketch of the southwestern portion of Rockingham County, Va. 18—] Colored ms. Scale 1:160,000. 16 × 18 cm.

Roads are drawn in red, drainage in blue, and elevations are shown by brown form lines. The only annotation on the map is "1:160,000. Abbott Iron Co. survey."

H232

Map of "Big Hill" Iron Lands 592 1/2 acres, Botetourt Co., Virginia. Jed. Hotchkiss, Feb. 15, 1881. Colored ms. Scale 1:19,800. 22 × 15 cm.

H233

Topographical map showing the location of Big Hill Iron Lands, Botetourt Co., Va. By Jed. Hotchkiss, Top. Eng. Staunton, Va. Mar. 1882. Uncolored ms. Scale 1:80,000. 22 × 21 cm.

Insets of (1) Title map of "Big Hill" Iron Lands, 592 1/2 A. Botetourt County, Va., and (2) Geological section of Big Hill, on line A-B . . .

H234

Map showing locations of iron properties on and near Chesapeake and Ohio Railway, Virginia. By Jed. Hotchkiss, Consulting Engineer. Staunton, Va. Septr. 1879. Colored ms. Scale 1:160,000. 24 × 66 cm.

Map on tracing cloth of the area from Buffalo Gap west of Staunton along the mountains to Covington.

H235

Plat "B", Charter Oak Lands, Clifton Forge, Alleghany Co., Va. showing the Clifton Forge Tract of 1695 acr's—1 to 15 . . . Surveyed 12th to 15th of July 1893. Uncolored ms. Scale 1:12,000. 41 × 47 cm.

Annotated, "Copy of C. W. Switzer's map."

H236

[Map of mineral lands in Culpeper County, Virginia, on the

Rapidan River. 18—] Colored ms. Scale ca. 1:19,800. 44 × 39 cm.

H237

A topographical map of the Elizabeth Furnace Iron Property, Augusta Co., Va. Containing about 6250 acres, Aug. 1867. Colored ms. Scale ca. 1:23,500. 56 × 43 cm.

Drawn on tracing paper. Insets show (1) Map showing the general location of Elizabeth Furnace, Augusta Co., Va. by Jed. Hotchkiss . . . 1867, and (2) Profile of the road from Elizabeth Furnace to ore banks &c. From surveys by Jed. Hotchkiss July 1867.

H238

Map of part of the Great Flat-top Coal-field of Va. & W. Va. showing location of Pocahontas & Bluestone collieries. Eng. Office of Jed. Hotchkiss, Staunton, Va. May, 1886. Uncolored ms. Scale ca. 1:31,680. 22 × 22 cm.

H239

Coal section of Flat-top Mountain. Jed. Hotchkiss, Staunton, Va., 1896. Uncolored ms. Scale ca. 1:150,000. 26 × 40 cm.

On tracing cloth. Vertical scale 1 inch to 450 feet.

Annotated "No. 2," the cross section extends from Pineville or Castle Rock to Bluestone River, and the mouth of Crane Creek.

H240

Section of coal beds in Flat-top Mountain. Jed. Hotchkiss. Staunton, Va., 1896. Uncolored ms.

Annotated "No. 3" and "The lower coal measures. No. XII."

H241

[Map of] "Kennedy" Iron Lands, 4,500 acres [in Augusta County, Virginia.] Jed. Hotchkiss, Cons. Eng. Staunton, Va., June, 1882. Uncolored ms. Scale: 1:63,360. 16 × 20 cm.

Inset shows a section of Kennedy Mountain with location of an ore bed. On tracing cloth.

H242

Map of Little North Mt. Land (Collat to S G C 20 M Ap. 1, 1879.) Compiled from plats &c. by Jed. Hotchkiss, Consulting Eng. Staunton, Va., Feb. 12, 1876. Colored ms. Scale 1:63,360. 27 × 29 cm.

On tracing cloth.

H243

Map of Little North Mountain or Preston & Wilson Iron Lands, compiled by Jed. Hotchkiss, Cons. Engineer. Staunton, Va. Sept. 1883. Uncolored ms. Scale 1:63,360. 28 × 25 cm.

H244

The Am. Manufacturer's map of the New River & the Flat-top Coking Coal Fields of the Virginias, by Jed. Hotchkiss, Cons. M. E. Staunton, Va. Sept. 1886. Uncolored ms. Scale ca. 1:360,000. 31 × 25 cm.

Profile shows "Partial section of Kanawha Coals by Prof. I. C. White."

H245

[Map showing the location of] Roaring Run Furnace [lands in Alleghany County, Virginia, nearing Covington. 18—] Colored ms. Scale ca. 1:160,000. 17 × 21 cm.

On tracing cloth.

H246

[Map showing the location of the Shenandoah Iron Works at Shenandoah, Virginia. 18—] Colored ms. Scale ca. 1:80,000. 17 × 9 cm.

Drawn on graph paper.

Map shows drainage, roads, and railroads between the Blue Ridge and the Valley Turnpike. The only names on the map are "Shenandoah Iron Works," and "Iron Ore."

H247

[Sketch of the vicinity of the Shenandoah Iron Works on the South Fork of the Shenandoah River at Shenandoah, Virginia. 18—] Uncolored ms. Not drawn to scale. 13 × 9 cm.

Pencil sketch of the immediate vicinity of the Shenandoah Iron Works, between the Blue Ridge and the river.

H248

Topographical map of the cultivated land at Shenandoah Iron Works, Page County, Va. showing the location of the furnace, forge, mill, mansion house &c. &c. belonging to the same. The property of Messrs. Dan'l & Henry Forrer. By Jed. Hotchkiss, Top. Eng. Staunton, Va. July 1865. Colored ms. Scale 1:5148. 70 × 74 cm.

H249

Topographic map of the Vesuvius Furnace Iron Estate, Rockbridge Co., Va. 8,000 acres. Reduced from W. A. Donald's map, made in 1874. By Jed. Hotchkiss, T. E., Staunton, Va. Mar. 1882. Uncolored ms. Scale 1:63,360. 26 × 21 cm.

Inset shows geological section along Dogwood Hollow, by Jed. Hotchkiss.

H250

Map of 11,000 acres of iron and coal lands in Wythe Co., Va. from map of C. R. Boyd, 1888. Colored ms. Scale 1:63,360. 28 × 37 cm.

H251

Topographical map of the Cabin Creek coal lands, situated

in Boone and Kanawha Counties, West Virginia, containing 15,532 acres, from surveys by M. A. Miller. Engineer Office Jed. Hotchkiss, Staunton, Va. [18—] Colored ms. Scale 1:15,800. 97 × 105 cm.

Drawn on tracing cloth.

H252

A topographical map of the lands of the Cabin Creek Coal Co. of W. Virginia embracing 14,307 acres in Kanawha and Boone Counties, West Virginia from actual surveys, by M. A. Miller, 1873. Colored ms. Scale 1:63,360. 46 × 41 cm.

H253

[Dr. Hale's Map of Cabin Creek lands. 1893] Uncolored ms. Scale ca. 1:20,000. 50 × 51 cm.

Title is on the back of the map.

The lands are located in Kanawha County, West Virginia.

H254

Map showing location of Flat-top—New River—Gauly Lower Measures Coal Field, West Virginia. [18—] Colored ms. Scale ca. 1:1,500,000. 23 × 31 cm.

Title is in pencil. The map contains several instructions to the draftsman.

H255

Map showing location of the "Gallego" forty thousand acres of coal and timber lands, Fayette County, W. Va. Eng. Office of Jed. Hotchkiss, Staunton, Va., 1885. Uncolored ms. Scale 1:200,000. 28 × 27 cm.

Drawn on tracing cloth.

H256

Map of the Loup-Piney Divide coal lands in Fayette and Raleigh Cos., West Virginia. Eng. Office of Jed. Hotchkiss, Cons. Eng. Staunton, Va., Nov. 1879. Colored ms. Scale 1:63,360. 41 × 25 cm.

H257

Map of the Loup-Piney Divide coal lands in Fayette and Raleigh Cos., West Virginia. Eng. Office of Jed. Hotchkiss, Staunton, Va., Oct. 25th, 1879. Uncolored ms. Scale 1:63,360. 33 × 25 cm.

Drawn on tracing cloth.

H258

[Survey of a tract of 9,138 acres of coal lands on the New River in Raleigh County, West Virginia, west of Quinnimont. 18—] Colored ms. Scale ca. 1:28,500. 38 × 53 cm.

Includes a list of 10 tracts of land as well as a geological column of coal measures, scale 1 inch to 300 feet.

H259

Map of the New River Coalfield on C. & O. R. R. by Jed. Hotchkiss, C. E. [18—] Colored ms. Scale 1:200,000. 27 × 21 cm.

An inset cut from a larger map. Drainage is shown in blue; the railroad is shown in red.

H260

[Sketch of the Riverside Iron Works and other properties, in Kanawha County, West Virginia.] 1870. Colored ms. Scale 1:19,920. 47 × 64 cm.

Annotated as follows, "Riverside Iron Works vs. John B. Kelty & others. Report of Com's Nov. 5, 1870. Deed Book 27, p. 614–619, Kanawha Co. W. Va."

H261

Map showing location &c. of "Middleton" coal lands, Fayette County, W. Va. From surveys by County Surveyor Settle. Eng. Office of Jed. Hotchkiss, Staunton, Va. Feb. 1882. Uncolored ms. Scale 1:39,600. 36 × 42 cm.

Drawn on tracing cloth.

H262

Map showing land holdings in Muddlety Cr. Coal Field in Nicholas Co., W. Va. W. C. Reddy, C. E. Nicholas C. H., W. Va. Feby 25, 1895. Colored ms. Scale 1:126,720. 20 × 27 cm.

H263

Map of the "Slaughter's Creek" coal and timber lands—2,907 acres, Kanawha County, West Virginia. Engineer Office of Jed. Hotchkiss, Staunton, Virginia, Jan. 1875. Colored ms. Scale 1:63,360. 24 × 15 cm.

Drainage in blue; elevations shown by brown form lines.

Railroads

H264

Railroad map of South Carolina. By Jed. Hotchkiss, T. E. Drawn by C. Haile, Jr. Staunton, Va., 1880. Uncolored ms. Scale 1:1,250,000. 33 × 39 cm.

Drawn on tracing paper.

H265

[Route of the New River R. R. 188–] Colored ms. Scale ca. 1:180,700. 47 × 38 cm.

Dashed red line across the map indicates the "Proposed New River R. R. 68 miles from Central [Virginia] to Hinton [West Virginia.]"

H266

Potomac, Fredericksburg, & Piedmont R. R. from Fredg

[Fredericksburg] to O. C. H. [Orange Court House] 38 miles. By C. M. Braxton [187–] Colored ms. Scale 1:48,000. 34 × 138 cm.

Sketch map on tracing paper.

H267

Map of Royal Land Company's Railroad (narrow gauge) from their anthracite coal fields to deep water. Carter M. Braxton, C. E. [18—] Colored ms. Scale 1:316,800. 49 × 108 cm.

Drawn with colored pencils on tracing paper, the map covers central Virginia from the Allegheny Mountains to Chesapeake Bay.

H268

Profile, Royal Land Co. R. R. C. M. Braxton C. E. [18—] Colored ms. Scale ca. 1:316,800. 14 × 83 cm.

Colored to show locations of mineral deposits along the profile which extends from Matthias' Point to Briery Branch Gap.

"Scale 50 horizontal to 2 vertical."

H269

[Map of Royal Land Company of Virginia lands in Rockingham, and Augusta counties, Virginia, and Pendleton County, West Virginia.] C. W. Oltmanns C. E. Harrisonburg, Va., Jan. 1877. Colored ms. Scale 1:63,360. 104 × 44 cm.

H270

Map of central Virginia showing proposed southern extension of the Shenandoah Valley R. R. from Waynesboro to Consack's to accompany report of Jed. Hotchkiss, Cons. Eng. Staunton, Va. Nov. 15, 1880. Colored ms. Scale 1:500,000. 28 × 43 cm.

H271

Map showing the preliminary line of the East River Railroad. May 1881. Engineer Office of Jed. Hotchkiss, Cons. Eng. Staunton, Va. Nov. 15, 1880. Colored ms. Scale 1:500,000. 28 × 43 cm.

H272

[Sketch of the "Proposed route of Virginias Railway" to Flat-top and Guyandot coal fields, West Virginia. 188–] Uncolored ms. No scale given. 20 × 63 cm.

Unfinished drawing on tracing cloth.

County Maps

H273

[Sketch of the road from Charlottesville to Afton, and from

Browns Cove to Afton, Albemarle County, Virginia. 186–] Uncolored ms. Scale ca. 1:675,000. 10 × 15 cm.

Pencil sketch giving names of settlements.

H274

[Sketch of parts of Albemarle and Nelson counties, Virginia, showing roads from Charlottesville to Scottsville, Lovingston, Howardsville, Afton, etc. 186–] Uncolored ms. Scale ca. 1:200,000. 10 × 13 cm.

Pencil sketch giving the names of a number of settlements. Annotation on the reverse, "Foot of Blue Ridge."

H275

Albemarle County, Virginia, by Jed. Hotchkiss, Top. Eng. Staunton, Va. 1867. Colored ms. Scale 1:126,720. 52 × 65 cm.

Fine drawing, giving roads in red, drainage in blue, and elevations by hachures.

H276

Map of Amherst Co. Virginia, prepared by Hotchkiss and Robinson, Topographical Engineers, Staunton, Virginia. 1866. Colored ms. Scale 1:63,360. 76 × 98 cm.

Finished topographical drawing but lacking all names. Shows roads in red, drainage in blue, and topography by hachures.

H277

Amherst County, Virginia, by Jed. Hotchkiss, Top. Eng. Staunton, Va. 1867. Colored ms. Scale ca. 1:126,720. 53 × 65 cm.

Unfinished map giving roads in red, drainage in blue, but lacking names.

H278

Map of Augusta Co., Virginia, 1738–1770. By Jed. Hotchkiss, Staunton, Va. [1886] Uncolored ms. Scale ca. 1:9,000,000. 10 × 17 cm.

H279

Map of part of Augusta County, Colony of Virginia, 1755–1760. By Jed. Hotchkiss, T. E. Staunton, Va. 1886. Uncolored ms. Scale 1:1,450,000. 16 × 18 cm.

H280

[Part of Augusta County, Va. 186–] Colored ms. Scale ca. 1:80,000. 99 × 25 cm.

An incomplete map of an area 12 miles wide through Augusta County, including Staunton. Roads are shown in red, elevations by form lines, and wooded areas in green. The name "Tye River Gap" is written in pencil near the bottom of the map, which shows by blue dashed lines, parts of the surveyed lines of the Valley R. R. and the Shenandoah Valley R. R.

H281

[Sketch of the road from Waynesboro toward Staunton, in Augusta County, Virginia. 186–] Colored ms. Scale ca. 1:63,360. 26 × 21 cm.

Sketch is drawn on both sides of the sheet with colored pencils, showing roads in red and drainage in blue.

H282

Augusta County, Virginia, prepared by Jed. Hotchkiss, Top. Engineer, Staunton, Va. 1867. Colored ms. Scale ca. 1:126,720. 53 × 69 cm.

Unfinished map, giving roads in red and drainage in blue. Some elevations are shown by hachures, but coverage is incomplete.

H283

Map of Augusta County, Virginia, 1886. Autographed by Jed. Hotchkiss, Top. Eng. Staunton, Va. Oct. 1886. Uncolored ms. Scale 1:264,000. 29 × 27 cm.

A list of six magisterial districts in the lower left corner corresponds to numbers on the map.

H284

Map of Botetourt [and Roanoke] Co. from surveys and reconnoisance [sic] by L'eut. Walter Travd [i.e., Izard] Engr. P.A.C.S. under direction of Major A. H. Campbell, Engr. P.A.C.S. Engr. Office of Jed. Hotchkiss, Staunton, Va. By Sev. P. Ker. [1885] Uncolored ms. Scale 1:80,000. 110 × 56 cm.

On tracing cloth. The map has a separate title for the Roanoke County portion of the map, with dates of 1865 and 1885.

H285

Brunswick County, Virginia. By Jed. Hotchkiss, Top. Eng. Staunton, Va. 1867. Colored ms. Scale ca. 1:126,720. 53 × 68 cm.

Unfinished map, with roads in red, drainage in blue.

H286

Buckingham County, Virginia. By Jed. Hotchkiss, Top. Eng. Staunton, Va. 1867. Colored ms. Scale ca. 1:126,720. 53 × 66 cm.

Unfinished map, lacking all names.

H287

Caroline County, Virginia. By Jed. Hotchkiss, Top. Eng. Staunton, Va. 1867. Colored ms. Scale ca. 1:126,720. 52 × 65 cm.

Unfinished map giving roads in red and a few place names.

H288

Charles City, Pr. George and Surry Counties, Virginia. By Jed. Hotchkiss, Top. Eng. Staunton, Va. 1867. Colored ms. Scale 1:126,720. 53 × 85 cm.

Finished drawing, giving roads in red, drainage in blue, and names in black.

H289

Map of Charlotte County, Virginia. By Jed. Hotchkiss, Top. Eng., Staunton, Va. [186–] Uncolored ms. Scale ca. 1:80,000. 79 × 51 cm.

Unfinished map in pencil, with a few names in ink.

H290

[Sketch of the road from Somerville to Jonas Run, beyond Stevensburg, in Culpeper County, Va. 186–] Uncolored ms. Scale ca. 1:63,360. 32 × 21 cm.

Pencil sketch in three sections.

H291

Culpeper and Orange Counties, Virginia. By Jed. Hotchkiss, Top. Eng. Staunton, Va. 1867. Colored ms. Scale ca. 1:126,720. 52 × 65 cm.

Unfinished map giving roads and drainage, but few place names.

H292

Hanover County, Virginia. By Jed. Hotchkiss, Top. Eng. Staunton, Va., 1867. Colored ms. Scale ca. 1:126,720. 52 × 65 cm.

Unfinished map giving roads and drainage, but few place names.

H293

Preliminary map of Hanover County, Virginia. By Jed. Hotchkiss, Top. Eng. Staunton, Va. 1871. Uncolored ms. scale 1:165,000. 35 × 42 cm.

Title in pencil.

H294

[Map of Hanover County, Virginia.] Eng. Office of Jed. Hotchkiss, Staunton, Va. May 1, 1886. Uncolored ms. Scale 1:124,000. 42 × 50 cm.

Inset: Geologic map of Hanover Co. after W. B. Rogers.

H295

James City, York, Warwick, and Elizabeth City Counties, Virginia. By Jed. Hotchkiss, Top. Eng. Staunton, Va. 1867. Colored ms. Scale ca. 1:160,000. 56 × 66 cm.

Unfinished map with a number of pencil annotations.

H296

[Map of Louisa County, Virginia.] Jed. Hotchkiss, Staunton,

Va. [186–] Colored ms. Scale ca. 1:80,000. 55 × 68 cm.

On tracing cloth. Roads are shown in red, drainage in blue, township boundaries in green, elevations by hachures, and forested areas by symbols.

Annotated in pencil as follows, "I have corrected the location of Trevilians Depot on this map." Also, "Voting places" are given in the margins.

H297

Map of Louisa County, Virginia; by Jed. Hotchkiss, Top. Eng. Staunton, Va. 1871. Uncolored ms. Scale 1:160,000. 31 × 36 cm.

"The map is based on the surveys of the C. S. Engineers."

H298

Map of Lunenburg County, Virginia; by Jed. Hotchkiss, Top. Eng., Staunton, Va. 1871. Uncolored ms. Scale 1:80,000. 60 × 65 cm.

H299

Map of Mecklenburg County, Virginia. By Jed. Hotchkiss, Top. Eng., Staunton, Va. [186–] Uncolored ms. Scale 1:80,000. 51 × 83 cm.

Unfinished map, in pencil, except for the title and a few names which are in ink.

H300

Virginia. Mecklenburgh [sic County, 187–] Colored. Scale ca. 1:500,000. 13 × 21 cm.

This printed map is cut from a larger one and mounted on a sheet of ledger paper. It is annotated in red ink as follows, "If you will send me the names of the P. M.'s at these places I think I can locate them exactly—I think all that I have located are correct. Jed. Hotchkiss, Staunton, Va. Sept. 11 / 75."

H301

Map of Nelson County, Virginia; prepared by Hotchkiss & Robinson, Topographical Engineers, Staunton, Va. 1866. Colored ms. Scale 1:63,360. 91 × 86 cm.

Roads are given in red, drainage in blue; elevations are shown by hachures. Six townships numbered in Roman numerals are colored in outline.

H302

Preliminary map of Orange County, Virginia. By Jed. Hotchkiss, Top. Eng. Staunton, Va. 1871. Uncolored ms. Scale ca. 1:160,000. 24 × 37 cm.

Title in pencil.

H303

Preliminary map of Prince Edward County, Virginia from

survey by Washington & Lee University. By Jed. Hotchkiss, Top. Eng., Staunton, Va. 1871. Uncolored ms. Scale ca. 1:160,000. 33 × 38 cm.

H304

Rappahannock, Madison and Greene Counties, Virginia. By Jed. Hotchkiss, Top. Eng. Staunton, Va. 1867. Colored ms. Scale ca. 1:126,720. 47 × 52 cm.

Unfinished map giving roads in red, drainage in pencil, and a few place names.

H305

[Map or Rockbridge County, Virginia. 18—] Uncolored ms. Scale 1:380,160. 23 × 19 cm.

Unfinished map, the only names in the county being "Lexington," and the "North R." Middlebrook and Greenville in Augusta County are the only other names given. The hachuring is in pencil.

H306

Preliminary map of Surry County, Virginia, from survey by Washington & Lee University. By Jed. Hotchkiss, Top. Eng., Staunton, Va., 1871. Uncolored ms. Scale 1:126,720. 30 × 39 cm.

Title in pencil.

H307

Sussex [and] Southampton Counties, Virginia. By Jed. Hotchkiss, Top. Eng. Staunton, Va. 1867. Colored ms. Scale ca. 1:126,720. 65 × 55 cm.

Unfinished map giving roads in red, drainage in pencil, and a few place names.

H308

[Sketch of parts of Warren, Rappahannock, and Culpeper counties, Virginia, including the area between the Rappahannock River the the Blue Ridge, from Front Royal to Culpeper. 186–] Colored ms. Scale 1:253,440. 27 × 20 cm.

Drawn on tracing cloth, showing roads in red, drainage in blue, and elevations by hachures.

H309

[Rough sketch of roads and streams in Pocahontas and Greenbrier Counties, West Virginia. 18—] Colored ms. Scale ca. 1:300,000. 40 × 25 cm.

Real Property Maps

H310

Copy Sept. 1879 (G.R.F.) of map [of a tract of land on Little North Mountain in Alleghany County, Virginia] compiled in the Top. Eng. Office of Jed. Hotchkiss, by C. W. Oltmanns.

Staunton, Va. Dec. 1872. Colored ms. Scale ca. 1:25,000. 55 × 65 cm.

Drawn on tracing cloth in colored inks, showing red for roads, blue for draininage, and brown form lines for elevations.

H311

[Peters Mountain] Alleghany Co. [Virginia] 780 a. A. J. Huddleston dec'd.—D. Y. Huddleston, J. B. Biers . . .[18—] Colored ms. Scale ca. 1:63,360. 69 × 23 cm.

Roads are shown in red, elevations by form lines.

H312

Map of Dr. Dellinger's mill property with 153 acres of land showing proposed changes of public roads, bridge site &c. from surveys by Jed. Hotchkiss, Top. Engineer. Staunton, Va. Aug. 1867. Colored ms. Scale ca. 1:7,900. 36 × 32 cm.

Land located in Augusta County, Virginia, on Middle River.

H313

Map of 360 acres of land, lying in Bath County, Va., the property of W. Ramsey, Esq'r [18—] Colored ms. Scale 1:14,940. 37 × 49 cm.

Inset: Map showing the location of the 360 acres of land in Bath County, Va. owned by Wm. Ramsey, Esq'r. Scale 1:253,440.

H314

Map of Walker's Mtn. land [in Bath County, Virginia] compiled from title papers. Eng. Office of Jed. Hotchkiss, Staunton, Va., Nov. 4, 1879. Colored ms. Scale 1:20,000. 33 × 89 cm.

Drawn on tracing cloth.

Inset: Map of Walker's Mountain and vicinity, scale 1:160,000.—Probable geological section on line A–B.

H315

[Plat of the "Dan T. Nelson Tract" of land on Long Branch. [18—] Uncolored ms. Scale 1:126,720. 17 × 23 cm.

The location of this tract has not been established. Besides "Long Br.," "Pigeon-roost Fork," and "Emily Fork" of "Wolf Cr." are named, as well as "Sang Gap" and "Pike Co."

Drawn on tracing cloth.

H316

A topographical map of that portion of "The Manor of Leeds" belonging to Col. M. G. Harman of Staunton, Va., from surveys by Jed. Hotchkiss, Top. Engineer. Staunton, Va., August, 1865. Uncolored ms. Scale 1:25,000. 18 × 26 cm.

A survey of 3,000 acres in Fauquier County, Virginia.

H317

Plat of the James Barbour patent of 5,012 a[cres in Page County, Virginia. 18—] Uncolored ms. Scale 1:100,000. 27 × 20 cm.

On tracing cloth.

Includes a list of the lots and their acreage entitled "Summary of 'Hume' tract."

H318

Survey of I. R. Houston, deputy surveyor of Rockbridge Co., Va. of lands in dispute between Wm. B. McNutt & D. & H. Forrer, being Nos. 1, 2 & 3 of this plat (Nos. 14, 15 & 16 of the bill.) [18—] Colored ms. Scale ca. 1:1440. 57 × 47 cm.

H319

Map of lands lying between Mann's and Kenney's Creeks in Fayette Co., West Virginia owned by Echols, Bell & Catlette. January 1880. Uncolored ms. Scale 1:9900. 34 × 57 cm.

Drawn on tracing cloth.

H320

Tract No. 1. Plat of Wm. T. Mann. 1,147 a[cre] patent, according to patent calls, corrected by lat. & dep. [18—] Colored ms. Scale 1:31,680. 35 × 22 cm.

The tract is located on the New River in Fayette County, West Virginia.

H321

Map of Gauly Farm, 1722 acres. 1868. Uncolored ms. Scale 1:7920. 55 × 76 cm.

Drawn on tracing paper. The farm is located at the mouth of New River, at Gauley, Fayette County, West Virginia.

H322

Map showing the location of the "Herr" lands, Grant County, W. Va. Compiled from 1855 map of W. Va. C.& Pg. Rv., by Jed. Hotchkiss, Cons. Eng. Staunton, Va., May 1892. Uncolored ms. Scale 1:126,720. 26 × 22 cm.

A "Geological section across Upper Potomac Coalfield," is attached.

H323

Sketch map showing location of 5,007 acres of Elkhorn Fork, W. Va. coal & timber lands. [18—] Uncolored ms. Scale 1:63,360. 25 × 27 cm.

The lands are located in McDowell County, West Virginia.

H324

Copy of map of Ellen Smith 10,000, Raleigh Co., W. Va.

from actual transit survey. M. E. Miller & others. [18—] Colored ms. Scale 1:18,000. 97 × 73 cm.

Drawn on tracing cloth.

H325

Map showing location lot no. 10 of Moore & Beckley Patent, Raleigh Co., W. Va. (10,000 a[cres] included) [18—] Colored ms. Scale ca. 1:126,720. 28 × 23 cm.

H326

Moore & Beckly [sic] Patent, lot no. 10, Atlantic & North Western R. R. land. [18—] Uncolored ms. No scale given. 94 × 58 cm.

A tract of 4,000 acres on the Fall Branch of the New River, Raleigh County, West Virginia.

H327

Plat of the partition of Moore & Beckley survey of 170,038 a[cres] in the counties of Giles & Logan, Virginia (Surveyed for Andrew Moore & John Beckley, Nov. 2nd, 1794) . . . Filed Nov. 23rd 1829 . . . Uncolored ms. Scale 1:126,720. 36 × 28 cm.

In the lower left corner, "Sev. P. Ker."

"Plat copied from bundle of 'cases ended.'"

H328

[Survey of a tract of land on Twelve Pole Creek, Wayne County, West Virginia. 18—] Uncolored ms. Scale ca. 1:7920. 51 × 29 cm.

Rough sketch drawn on tracing paper, on an 8-inch grid.

H329

Map showing the location of Mount Rogers, Augusta Co., Va. By Jed. Hotchkiss, Top. Eng. Staunton, Va., Aug. 1886. Uncolored ms. Scale 1:1,000,000. 16 × 22 cm.

Circles at 25-, 50-, and 75-mile distances centered on Mount Rogers.

H330

[Sketch map of the vicinity of Roanoke, Virginia. 18—] Colored ms. Scale ca. 1:80,000. 35 × 52 cm.

Shows roads in red, drainage in blue, and cultural features in black. Elevations are shown by form lines. Drawn on a 3/4-inch grid.

On the same sheet is a detailed survey, on the scale of about 1:20,000, of several properties, notably McClanahan between the Roanoke River and Back Creek and along the Franklin Turnpike.

H331

[Two hundred miles around Staunton, Va. [18—] Colored ms. Scale ca. 1:2,500,000. 16 × 27 cm.

An unfinished map on an irregular sheet, giving concentric circles at 50, 100, 120, 150, 190, and 200 miles.

H332

Map showing the location of Staunton, Va. [and] showing the railways leading to the Staunton Opera House. Top. Eng. Office of Jed. Hotchkiss, Staunton, Va. 1886. Uncolored ms. Scale 1:3,800,000. 13 × 24 cm.

A fair drawing of a map issued by "Croscup & West Eng. Co. Phila." Concentric circles show 100- to 200-mile radii from Staunton.

H333

Map of the drainage and catchment basin of Asylum Creek to illustrate a report on a water supply for the W. L. Asylum of Va. by Jed. Hotchkiss, Cons. Eng. Oct. 1879. Colored ms. Scale 1:12,000. 37 × 28 cm.

The elevated land around the drainage basin is indicated by hachures, and is described as "Approximate outline of the catchment and drainage basin of the Asylum Creek— a tributary of Lewis Creek in Staunton, Virginia."

H334

Map of the drainage & catchment basin of Asylum Creek to illustrate the question of a water supply for the Western Lunatic Asylum, Staunton, Va. [1879?] Uncolored ms. Scale 1:12,000. 35 × 27 cm.

An unfinished sketch in pencil and ink.

H335

Oak Hill lots [Staunton] Jed. Hotchkiss, Staunton, Va., 1874. Uncolored ms. Scale 1:600. 56 × 76 cm.

Drawn on tracing cloth. The title is on the back of the map.

H336

Map of Huntington, W. Va., and vicinity, the Ohio River terminus of the Virginias Railway. [18—] Uncolored ms. Scale 1:30,000. 20 × 73 cm.

Drawn on tracing cloth. Shows Huntington, Central City, Kellogg, Kenova, and Ceredo, West Virginia, as well as Catlettsburg and Hampton, Kentucky.

H337

Map of the "Kanawha City" estates, Kanawha County, West Virginia . . . Engineer Office of Jed. Hotchkiss, Staunton, Virginia, Jan. 1875. Colored ms. Scale 1:40,000. 29 × 44 cm.

Annotated as follows: "This is the map of the Kanawha City Estates, approved of by me, to accompany report. J. P. Hale. Feb. 9th, 1875."

Drainage in blue, elevations indicated by brown contour lines.

H338

[Map of the vicinity of White Sulphur Springs and Chaly-
beate Springs, West Virginia. 18—] Uncolored ms. Scale ca.
1:63,360. 15 × 16 cm.

    Pencil drawing.

H339

[Outline map of Canada. 1893] Uncolored ms. Scale ca.
1:2,855,420. 2 sheets, each 67 × 103 cm.

H340

[Map of Ulster County, Ireland. 18—] Colored ms. Scale ca.
1:250,000. 97 × 140 cm.

Coat-of-arms of Ulster County, Ireland, is in the upper
left section.

H341

[Sketch map of Palestine. 18—] Colored ms. Scale ca.
1:1,325,000. 37 × 26 cm.

    Coastline and drainage in blue, roads in red, form lines
in brown. Includes a list of 45 place names which corre-
spond to numbers on the map.

SHERMAN MAP COLLECTION

S1

Lindenkohl, Henry.

    Historical sketch of the rebellion. [Drawn by H. Lin-
denkohl. Chas. G. Krebs, Lith.] Published at the Office
of the U.S. Coast Survey. [1863] Colored. Scale ca.
1:5,850,000. 47 × 45 cm.

    Margins of maps have been cropped thereby eliminat-
ing the names of the cartographer and lithographer.

    Blue lines denote the "limits of loyal states in July,
1861," red lines denote the "limits occupied by United
States forces July 1863," and small ships indicate the extent
of the naval blockade.

    "Population census 1860" is in the lower right corner.

    For another copy see entry no. 40.

S2

Lloyd, James T.

    Lloyd's new map of the United States, the Canadas and
New Brunswick, from the latest surveys showing every railroad & station finished to June 1862, and the Atlantic and
Gulf coasts from the United States Superintendent's official
reports of the Coast Survey by order of Congress. New
York, 1863. Colored. Scale ca. 1:2,250,000. 95 × 129 cm.
cut and mounted to fold to 20 × 12 cm.

    General map of the United States showing state and
county names and boundaries, cities and towns, fortifications, railraods, and roads.

S3

D'Avignon, F. *and* C. D. Elliot.

    Map of the military department of the Gulf, prepared
by order of Maj. Gen. N. P. Banks. Major D. C. Houston,

Chief Engineer. Jany. 1864. Drawn by F. D'Avignon &
C. D. Elliot. Photocopy (positive). Scale ca. 1:2,000,000.
63 × 116 cm.

    Coast line and principal lakes and rivers are colored
blue, and roads, railroads, and distances are red.

S4

Riemann, H.

    Map showing the army-movements around Chatta-
nooga, made to accompany the Report of Maj. Genl. U. S.
Grant, by direction of Brig. Genl. Wm. F. Smith, Chief
Engr., Mil: Div: Miss: Compiled and drawn by H. Riemann,
44th Ills. Vols. Chattanooga, Topogl. Engr. Office, Hd. Qrs.
Army of the Cumbd., Jan. 4th 1864. Photocopy (positive).
Scale ca. 1:274,000. 32 × 48 cm.

    At head of title in ms: No. 2.

    Map of parts of Tennessee, Alabama, and Georgia,
showing roads, railroads, towns, rivers, and hachures.

    Troop movements are not indicated.

    For a larger version, see entry no. 401.3.

S5

Ruger, Edward.

    Map prepared to exhibit the campaigns in which the
Army of the Cumberland took part during the War of the
Rebellion. [1861–65] By order of Maj. Gen. Geo. H.
Thomas, U. S. A. Compiled under the direction of Bvt. Ma-
jor Genl. Z. B. Tower, Chief Eng'r., Military Div. of the
Tenn., by Ed. Ruger, Sup't., Top'l. Eng'r. Office at Nashville.
Colored. Scale 1:1,267,200. 2 parts measuring 66 × 44 cm.
and 66 × 35 cm.

    Map of South Carolina, Kentucky, and Tennessee, and

parts of Georgia, Alabama, Mississippi, North Carolina and Virginia, showing roads, railroads, towns, rivers, names and boundaries of states, and relief by hachures. Lines of march are indicated by colors and symbols. Includes "Jeff. Davis' line of flight."

For another copy see entry no. 84.

S6

Kossak, William *and* John B. Muller.

Military map showing the marches of the United States forces under command of Maj. Genl. W. T. Sherman ... during the years 1863, 1864, 1865. Compiled by order of Maj. Genl. W. T. Sherman ... at Head Quarters, Military Division of the Mississippi, under the direction of Bvt. Maj. W. L. B. Jenney ... Drawn by Capt. William Kossak ... and John B. Muller, draughtsman. Engraved at Head Qrs., Corps of Engineers ... by H. C. Evans & F. Courtenay. Printed by Joseph F. Gedney. St. Louis, Mo., 1865. Colored. Scale 1:1,267,200. 70 × 117 cm.

Detailed map of southeastern United States showing fortifications, "movements of Gen. J. H. Wilson's Cavalry Corps," "pursuit of Hood," "movement on Atlanta, Ga.," and the routes of the 4th, 14th, 15th, 16th, 17th, and 20th Corps and the cavalry.

For another copy see entry no. 72.

S7

U.S. *Army, Corps of Engineers.*

Map showing route of marches of the army of Genl. W. T. Sherman from Atlanta, Ga. to Goldsboro, N.C. [1864–65] To accompany the report of operations from Savannah, Ga. to Goldsboro, N.C. Engineer Bureau, War Department. Prepared by order of the Secretary of War for the officers of the U.S. Army under the command of Maj. Gen. W. T. Sherman. Colored. Scale ca. 1:1,900,000. 28 × 39 cm.

Indicates roads, railroads, towns, and rivers. The routes of the cavalry and the 14th, 15th, 17th, and 20th Army Corps are shown by colors and symbols.

A copy of "Gen'l. Sherman's farewell to the armies of Georgia & Tennessee," special field orders no. 76, dated May 30, 1865, is attached to the bottom of the map.

For another copy of the map, see entry no. 90.

S8

Freyhold, Edward.

Military map of the United States, compiled and drawn by E. Freyhold. 1869. Colored. Scale 1:5,000,000. 71 × 102 cm.

At head of title: Office of the Chief of Engineers, War Department.

Indicates names and boundaries of states and military districts, forts, towns, rivers, "military & wagon roads," railroads, and relief by shading.

S9

Lindenkohl, Adolph.

Northern Alabama and Georgia. Compiled and engraved at the U. S. Coast Survey Office, from state maps, postoffice maps, local surveys, military reconnoissance [sic] and information furnished by the U. S. Engineers attached to the Military Division of the Miss. Drawn by A. Lindenkohl. H. Lindenkohl & Chas. G. Krebs, lith. [1864] Uncolored. Scale 1:633,600. 67 × 55 cm.

Printed on cloth.

General map of northeast Alabama and northwest Georgia, showing roads, railroads, towns, drainage, state boundaries, and relief by hachures.

S10

——————Another copy.

S11

——————Another copy.

S12

——————Another issue. Similar to the preceding cloth maps (entry nos. S9–11) but printed on paper.

Includes red overprint, highlighting state boundaries and railroads.

For another copy see entry no. 102a.5.

S13

——————Another issue.

Map lacks red overprint.

In the Vinnie Ream Hoxie family papers, Manuscript Division, L.C., container no. 10 (oversize).

Note on verso reads "Field map carried by General Sherman on his famous march from Atlanta to the Sea, presented by him to Vinnie Ream soon after the close of the Civil War and bequeathed by her to her husband. [Signed] R. L. Hoxie Brig. Gen., U. S. A."

"Genl. Sherman" appears in ink in two places on the verso.

For another copy of this map see entry no. 102a.5.

S14

[Map of northwest Alabama and northeast Mississippi. 1863] Colored ms. Scale not given. 33 × 58 cm.

Pen and ink manuscript map drawn on tracing cloth. Indicates roads in red, drainage in blue, and railroads and names of counties and towns in black.

S15

[Map of northeastern Alabama and northwestern Georgia

showing movement of Union troops under the command of Gen. Edward M. McCook. 1864] Colored ms. Scale ca. 1:390,000. 36 × 42 cm.

"Traced from La Tourrettes state map of Alabama, 1856."

Ink drawing on tracing cloth giving "McCooks routes," "McCooks cavalry," roads, drainage, towns, and relief by hachures.

Crossed swords shown near Cedar Bluff, Alabama, denote "Straights captured" [i.e., Col. Abel B. Streight].

S16

Hyer, N. F., F. D'Avignon, *and* B. Von Reizenstein.

Mobile and vicinity. Prepared by order of Maj. Gen. N. P. Banks, D. C. Houston, Major & Chief Engineer. N. F. Hyer, C. E., F. D'Avignon, [and] B. Von Reizenstein, delrs. Photographed by Brown & Ogilvie. July 1863. Photocopy (postive). Scale ca. 1:125,000. 80 × 85 cm.

At head of title: Department of the Gulf. Map no. 11.

Shows roads, towns, "Mobile and Ohio rail road," drainage, township and section lines, vegetation, and soundings. Fortifications, batteries, and obstructions are indicated in red ink.

Pen and ink tracing of the defenses of Mobile (12 × 11 cm.) attached in the upper left corner.

S17

Ruger, Edward.

Selma, Al'a., and vicinity. Compiled from information by Cap't. E. Ruger, Top'l. Eng'r., staff of Maj. Genl. Rousseau. Cap't. Merrill, U.S. Eng'rs., Chief Top. Eng'r. Drawn by Waggoner. Chattanooga, Top: Eng'r. Office, Hd. Qu'rs. Dep't. Cumb:, Feb. 1864. Uncolored. Scale 1:12,672. 31 × 21 cm.

Map indicates fortifications, streets, important buildings, railroads, telegraph lines, drainage, vegegation, and relief by hachures.

"Remarks" to the right of the map describe the fortifications surrounding Selma, the militia, and the industry of the town.

S18

[Map of the environs of Arkansas Post, Ark. January 1863] Colored ms. Scale 1:253,440. 32 × 21 cm.

Pen and ink sketch map showing drainage in blue, entrenchments at Arkansas Post in red, and roads and names of towns in black.

S19

Pitzman, Julius.

[Map of Arkansas Post, Ark.] Surveyed January 12th &

13th 1863 by Julius Pitzman, Capt. & Topographical Engineer. Colored ms. Scale not given. 56 × 44 cm.

At bottom of map: For General W. T. Sherman, General of the Army.

Pen and ink manuscript showing "Post of Arkansas," rifle pits, hospitals, "log huts," "Steuarts route Jan. 10th," "Steeles route night of Jan. 10th," roads, vegetation, drainage, and relief by hachures.

S20

[Map of part of Georgia and South Carolina. 186–] Uncolored. Scale ca. 1:357,000. 54 × 81 cm.

Portion of an unidentified printed map showing roads, railroads, towns, and drainage.

Handwritten note in lower right corner: From Chf. Engrs. Off., Mily Divn. Miss., O. M. Poe, Bvt. Col. & Chf. Eng[r.]

S21

[Map of part of Catoosa, Whitfield, and Walker counties, Georgia. 1864] Colored. Scale not given. 55 × 42 cm.

Reconnaissance map showing roads, rivers, railroads, towns, relief by hachures, and the names of a few residents.

Railroads and principal towns are colored red by hand.

S22

Merrill, William E.

Part of northern Georgia. No. 2. Compiled under the direction of Capt. Wm. E. Merrill, Chief Top'l Eng'r, D.C. Lithographed Topo'l Eng'r Office, Head-quarters, Dep't of the Cumberland. [1864] Uncolored. Scale 1:253,440. 50 × 32 cm.

Printed on cloth.

Endorsed (facsim.): Official issue. Wm. C. Margedant, Capt. & Supt.

Sheet "no. 2" of three sheets printed on cloth for the use of cavalry officers during Gen. W. T. Sherman's Atlanta campaign. This sheet extends from Rome on the north to Franklin on the south and indicates towns and villages, roads, railroads, drainage, and some relief by hachures. Troop positions and movements are not indicated. See Sherman map coll. no. 31 and 32 for copies of the first sheet and entry no. 129.75 for sheet 3. For another copy of sheet 2, see entry no. 129.74.

S23

[Troop positions in Georgia. 1864?] Colored ms. Scale not given. 23 × 32 cm.

Area and engagement not identified.

Pen and ink manuscript drawn on tracing cloth, showing "Hookers line," "Hookers old works," "Gen. Newtown's right, Stanley's left," and "Rebel works."

S24

U.S. *Army. Department of the Cumberland. Topographical Engineers.*

Map of part of Fulton, Fayette, and Campbell counties, from surveys, state map, and information. Topl. Engr. Office, Army of the Cumbd. [1864] Uncolored. Scale ca. 1:65,000. 55 × 44 cm.

Printed map on a 9/16-inch grid, showing roads, railroads, streams, towns, and names of a few residents. Includes pencil annotations.

Map includes an overlay covering the East Point-Rough & Ready area. It measures 18 × 24 cm. and contains information not shown on the original map.

S25

————Another copy.

S26

————Another issue.

"Extra copies to be filled up and returned for second edition" is added to the map title.

S27

Hergesheimer, Edwin.

Map showing the operations of the national forces under the command of Maj. Gen. W. T. Sherman during the campaign resulting in the capture of Atlanta, Georgia, Sept. 1, 1864. Drawn by E. Hergesheimer. Chas. G. Krebs, lith. Washington, Coast Survey Office [1864] Colored. Scale 1:380,160. 55 × 36 cm.

"Prepared at the Coast Survey Office, Washington, D. C. from information furnished by Capt. O. M. Poe, Chief Engr., Gen. Sherman's staff, and from Gen. Sherman's published report."

Shows entrenchments, Union troop movements, towns, roads, railroads, drainage, and relief by hachures.

Brief statement concerning "National" and "Rebel" forces is in the lower left corner.

For another copy see entry no. 128.

S28

————Another issue.

G3921 .S5 1864 .H4 Sher 28

Similar to preceding map (entry no. S27) but lacking the statement in the lower left corner concerning "National" and "Rebel" forces.

S29

Merrill, William E.

Map of northern Georgia, made under the direction of Capt. W. E. Merrill, Chief Topl. Engr. Lith. and printed in

Topl. Engr. Office, Dept. Cumbd., Chattanooga, Tenn., May 2d, 1864. Colored. Scale 1:253,440. 94 × 88 cm. cut and mounted to fold to 16 × 23 cm.

Signed in ink on verso: W. T. Sherman, Maj. Genl. Map used by General Sherman in the campaign of 1864.

Map also signed in ink on verso: Corse [i.e., Maj. Gen. John M. Corse].

The Topographical Department of the Army of the Cumberland, under the direction of Col. William E. Merrill, was responsible for providing the maps necessary for the 1864 Atlanta Campaign. Their first assignment was to prepare an accurate field map, the result of which was this "Map of Northern Georgia," which was lithographed at the field headquarters of the Army of the Cumberland and distributed to every commanding officer before the Army engaged in combat.

Map prepared "from the Cherokee land maps and from information compiled by N. Finegan draughtsman, from surveys of the Topl. Engrs., Army of the Cumbd. compiled by H. Riemann draughtsman, [and] from the state map of Georgia."

Map indicates roads, railroads, towns, drainage, and relief by hachures. A few additions have been made in pencil.

S30

————Another copy.

Signed in pencil on verso: W. T. Sherman, Maj. Genl.

S31

————Part of northern Georgia. Compiled under the direction of Capt. Wm. E. Merrill, Chief Top'l Eng'r, D.C. Printed in the field, Chattanooga, Tenn., May 5th 1864. Uncolored. Scale 1:253,440. 52 × 34 cm.

Printed on cloth.

Endorsed (facsim.): Official issue. Wm. C. Margedant, Capt. & Supt. Topl. Eng'r. Office, D.C.

General map extending from Chattanooga, Tennessee, on the north to Dallas, Georgia, on the south and showing roads, railroads, towns, drainage, and relief by hachures. Troop positions and movements are not indicated. This is the first of three sheets printed on cloth for the use of cavalry officers during the Atlanta Campaign. See Sherman map coll. no. 22 for sheet 2 and entry no. 129.75 for sheet 3.

S32

————Another copy.

S33

Brooks, A. F.

Map illustrating the operations of the army under com'd. of Maj. Gen. W. T. Sherman in Georgia, from May 5th 1864 to Sept. 4th 1864; Compiled under the direction

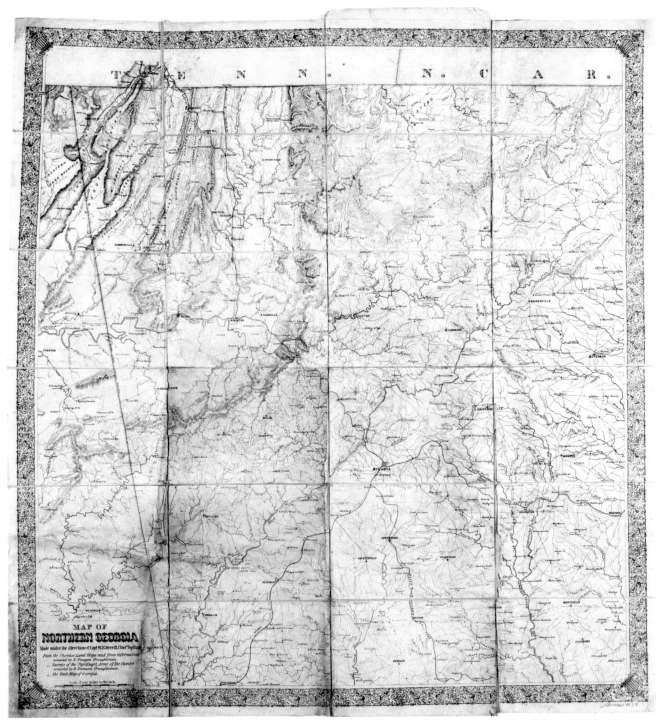

"Map of Northern Georgia," prepared under the direction of Capt. (later Colonel) William E. Merrill, Chief Engineer, Department of the Cumberland. Printed at field headquarters in Chattanooga, Tennessee, on May 2, 1864, the map served as the principal reference map for all field commanders in the initial stage of the Union campaign to capture Atlanta, Georgia. Reproduced here is one of two copies of the campaign map owned by William T. Sherman, commanding general of the Military Division of the Mississippi. (See entry no. S29.)

For ease of carrying in the field, the campaign map was cut into 24 sections and mounted on cloth to fold to 16 by 23 cm. Pasted to the cloth mounting were cardboard covers to protect the map when folded. The cover shown here bears the signature of "W. T. Sherman, Maj. Genl." as well as that of Major General John M. Corse who led the 2nd Division, XVI Corps during the Atlanta Campaign. (See entry no. S29.)

of Capt. O. M. Poe, Chief Eng'r. from maps and data furnished by the Eng'rs. of the Armies of the Cumberland, Tennessee & Ohio, and drawn by Lt. A. F. Brooks. Photographed at Chief Engrs. Office, Mily. Divn. Miss., Atlanta Ga. Photocopy (positive). Scale 1:253,440. 75 × 47 cm.

Photocopy of a manuscript map.

Union and Confederate works are colored blue and red, respectively.

Indicates roads, railroads, towns, drainage, and relief by hachures.

S34

U.S. *Army. Corps of Engineers.*

Portion of a map being compiled in the Engr. Bureau, July 1864. Photocopy (positive). Scale 1:350,000. 111 × 83 fold. to 18 × 21 cm.

Map title and state names added in blue ink.

"Personal & confidential" is written below the title.

Following handwritten notes appear on verso: W. T. Sherman, Maj. Genl., 1864 & 5. Campaign in Georgia & South Carolina.—Part of Georgia & South Carolina, July 1864.—Map used by him in the Georgia & Carolina Campaign. Sherman.

Map of part of Georgia and South Carolina, showing roads, railroads, towns, houses, names of residents, and drainage.

S35

U.S. *Army. Department of the Cumberland. Topographical Engineers.*

Parts of Fulton, Fayette, Clayton, and Campbell counties, Georgia, from surveys and information at Top. Eng. Office, Dept. Cumb., before Atlanta, Ga. August 23rd 1864. Colored. Scale not given. 56 × 49 cm.

Printed map on a ⁹⁄₁₆-inch grid, showing roads, rail-

roads, towns, drainage, houses, and names of residents.

Map contains many pencil annotations, and roads have been colored red by hand.

S36

[Pen and ink sketch map drawn on tracing cloth, showing roads, streams, bridges, ferries, fords, houses, names of residents, and towns between Atlanta and the Chattahoochee River. 1864] Uncolored ms. Scale ca. 1:77,000. 52 × 68 cm.

Lacks title and authority.

Oriented with south at the top of the map.

S37

Finegan, N.

Atlanta & vicinity. Compiled from state map and information under the direction of Capt. W. E. Merrill, Chief Top'l. Eng'r. Sergt. N. Finegan, del. Chattanooga, Topl. Eng., Hd. Qrs., Jan. 30th 1864. Uncolored. Scale ca. 1:63,360. 51 × 33 cm.

1-inch grid.

Indicates fortifications, roads, railroads, drainage, street pattern of Atlanta, towns, hachures, and a few spot elevations along the Chattahoochee River.

S38

————Another copy.

S39

Poe, Orlando M.

Map illustrating the siege of Atlanta, Ga. by the U.S. forces under command of Maj. Gen. W. T. Sherman, from the passage of Peach Tree Creek, July 19th 1864, to the commencement of the movement upon the enemy's lines of communication south of Atlanta, August 26, 1864. Reduced and engraved in the Engineer Bureau, War Dept., from an original prepared under the directions of Cap. O. M. Poe, Corps of Eng's. and senr. engr. on Gen'l. Sherman's staff. Edw. Molitor, lith. Colored. Scale ca. 1:47,520. 31 × 52 cm.

"Proof sheet."

Signed in ms: Richd. Delafield, Bvt. Major General Chief Engineer; Engineer Bureau, War Department (December 28/'65).

Indicates entrenchments, relief by hachures, vegetation, drainage, roads, railroads, towns, and the names of a few residents in the environs of Atlanta.

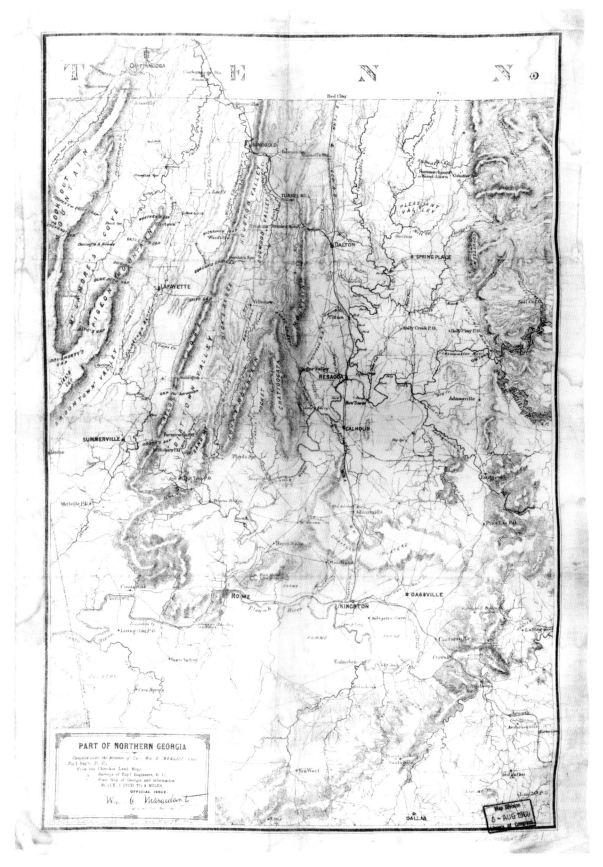

PART OF NORTHERN GEORGIA

Compiled under the direction of Capt. Wm. E. MERRILL, Chief Top'l Eng'r, D. C.
From the Cherokee Land Maps,
Surveys of Top'l Engineers, D. C.
State Map of Georgia and information
SCALE, 1 INCH TO 4 MILES
OFFICIAL ISSUE.

"The red figures indicate the surface elevation at these points, above the plan [sic] of reference, which is taken at 50 ft. below the water-table of the City Hall."

S40

————————Another issue. 31 × 52 cm.
Slightly revised issue of the preceding map.

S41

[Map of the battle of Atlanta, Georgia. July 22, 1864] Uncolored ms. Scale 1:63,360. 10 × 11 cm.

Pencil sketch of the environs of Decatur, Georgia, showing the "line of the enemy," and the position of a Union battery and the 15th and 17th Army Corps.

Copy of this map appears in the *Atlas to Accompany the Official Records of the Union and Confederate Armies,* 1891–5, pl. 45, no. 3. A note on the printed copy states that "McPherson handed me this sketch a few moments before he was killed, July 22, 1864 (W. T. Sherman)."

S42

[Position of Army of Tennessee near Atlanta, Georgia, July 22, 1864] Uncolored ms. Scale not given. 28 × 40 cm.

At bottom of map: McPherson.

Pencil sketch showing the position of the 15th, 16th, and 17th Army Corps to the east of Atlanta. "Rebel Conscr. Camp" is indicated to the southwest of Decatur, Georgia.

A printed copy of this map appears in the *Atlas to Accompany the Official Records of the Union and Confederate Armies,* 1891–95, pl. 90, no. 3.

S43

Position of the Army of the Tenn. July 23d 64. Colored ms. Scale 1:63,360. 17 × 22 cm.

At bottom of map: McPherson.

Pen and ink sketch of part of the country between Atlanta and Decatur, Georgia, showing "old works" in black and "new works" in blue.

S44

U.S. *Army. Department of the Cumberland. Topographical Engineers.*

Atlanta. From Vincent's subdivision map, published by the City Council. Drawn and printed at Topl. Engr. Office, Hd. Qrs. A. C., in the field. July 25th 1864. Uncolored. Scale 1:15,840. 40 × 26 cm.

In addition to the standard edition of the campaign map lithographed on paper, the Topographical Department, Department of the Cumberland, also issued it on muslin in three parts. Cloth maps were printed mainly for the convenience of cavalry officers. This particular map was "Printed in the field, Chattanooga, Tenn., May 5th 1864," only three days after the full campaign map was issued. (See entry no. S31.)

Printed on cloth.

Contains an index to important buildings.

The Geography and Map Division has a copy of the map on which this is based. It is entitled "Vincent's subdivision map of the City of Atlanta" (Savannah, Edward A. Vincent, [185–?]), colored, scale 1:4800, size 72 × 73 cm.

S45

Atlanta. [July 25, 1864] Uncolored ms. Scale not given. 34 × 26 cm.

Unfinished pen and ink map drawn on tracing paper. It appears to be a tracing of the map of Atlanta "drawn and printed at Topl. Engr. Office, Hd. Qrs. A. C., in the field, July 25th 1864" (see Sherman map coll. no. 44).

S46

Augusta, Ga., 1864. Uncolored ms. Scale not given. 34 × 24 cm.

Pen and ink sketch showing the defenses of Augusta. Date written in pencil.

A printed reduction of the map appears in the *Atlas to Accompany the Official Records of the Union and Confederate Armies,* 1891–95, pl. 132, no. 6.

S47

Plan of fortifications at Augusta, Ga. [1864] Colored. Scale not given. 22 × 31 cm.

Pen and ink sketch map.

Savannah River is colored blue.

"Augusta Georgia 1864" is added in pencil.

S48

Sketch of roads from Gen. McCooks Hd. Qrs. near junction of Ackworth & Dallas & Marietta roads, to Ackworth & Big Shanty & R.R. Rebel lines of battle as they retired before McCooks Cavalry, June 3, 1864. Uncolored ms. Scale not given. 25 × 20 cm.

Pencil sketch on stationery of "Head-quarters First Cavalry Division, Department of the Cumberland." Letterhead on verso.

S49

Reese, Chauncey B.

[Map of the vicinity of Browning's Court House, De Kalb County, Georgia. July 1864] C. B. Reese, Capt. Engrs. Uncolored ms. Scale not given. 19 × 13 cm.

Pencil sketch.

Printed copy of this map appears in the *Atlas to Accompany the Official Records of the Union and Confederate Armies,* 1891–95, pl. 45, no. 4.

S50

[Map of part of the counties of Fulton and Cobb, Georgia,

showing fortifications on the Chattahoochee River at Isoms Ford and Phillips Ferry. 1864] Additions by 3d Division, 23d A.C. Uncolored ms. Scale 1:63,360. 43 × 35 cm.

Pen and ink sketch indicating roads, railroads, towns, drainage, hachures, and the names of a few residents.

S51

Schofield crossing the Chattahooche. [sic] [July 1864] Colored ms. Scale ca. 1:25,500. 19 × 30 cm.

Sketch map indicating Union troop positions and fortifications, location of field headquarters, roads, relief by hachures, vegetation, houses, and names of residents.

A printed reduction of this map appears in the *Atlas to Accompany the Official Records of the Union and Confederate Armies,* 1891–95, pl. 65, no. 4.

S52

[Schofield crossing the Chattahoochee. July 1864] Colored ms. Scale ca. 1:25,800. 19 × 30 cm.

At bottom of map: Schofield.

Similar to the preceding map but lacks troop positions and the location of field headquarters.

A military camp is indicated west of the Chattahoochee River near the Ulrich farm.

S53

[Map of the environs of the Chattahoochee River at Sandtown, Georgia. July 5–17, 1864] Uncolored ms. Scale not given. 18 × 13 cm.

At bottom of map: Stoneman.

Pencil sketch indicating roads, towns, and drainage.

Similar to a printed map in the *Atlas to Accompany the Official Records of the Union and Confederate Armies,* 1891–95, pl. 45, no. 5.

S54

[Map of the environs of Powers and Isoms ferries, Cobb County, Georgia. 1864] Colored ms. Scale 1:63,360. 20 × 19 cm.

Pencil sketch indicating creeks, roads, railroad, houses, and names of residents.

S55

U.S. *Army. Department of the Cumberland. Topographical Engineers.*

[Map of southern portion of Cobb County, Georgia, from Marietta to the Chattahoochee River] Compiled from the Cherokee land map and resent [sic] surveys and information at Topl. Engineers Office: Head quarters, Army of the Cumberland. Official. [1864] Colored ms. Scale ca. 1:64,000. 47 × 60 cm.

Signed in ms: O. M. Poe, Capt., Engrs.

Pen and ink manuscript drawn on tracing cloth, showing surveyed roads and located points, houses and names of residents, drainage, towns, and relief by hachures.

S56

————Additions & corrections to the map of Cobb Co., Ga. Printed at the Top. Engr. Office, D. C., in the field, June 10th 1864. Photocopy (negative). Scale 1:63,360. 19 × 18 cm.

Map of part of Cobb County north of Lost Mountain, showing roads, drainage, vegetation, houses, names of residents, and relief by hachures. Note on map reads "Unable to locate Lost Mt."

S57

————Another copy with roads colored red.

S58

[Map of part of Cobb County, Georgia, showing roads to the west of Marietta, in the vicinity of Powder Springs. June 10–July 3, 1864] Colored ms. Scale 1:63,360. 26 × 20 cm.

At bottom of map: Garrard

Sketch map, oriented with south at the top, showing roads in red, drainage in blue, and the names of towns, residents, and creeks in black.

Printed copy of this map appears in the *Atlas to Accompany the Official Records of the Union and Confederate Armies,* 1891–95, *pl. 62, no. 10.*

S59

U.S. *Army. Department of the Cumberland. Topographical Engineers.*

Part of Cobb Co., Ga. Compiled & printed at the Top. Eng. Office, D. C., in the field. Big Shanty, June 12th 1864. Photocopy (negative). Scale 1:63,360. 33 × 49 cm.

Map of the environs of Marietta, showing roads, railroad, relief by hachures, drainage, houses, and names of residents.

Photocopy contains annotations in red and black.

S60

————Another issue with an attachment (19 × 12 cm.) pasted to the left side of the map. Attachment labeled "Additions & corrections to the map of Cobb Co., Ga. Printed at the Top. Engr. Office D. C. in the field, June 10th 1864."

S61

Finegan, N.

Part of Cobb County, Georgia, from surveys made by the Topl. Engrs. of the Dept of the Cumb . . . Dept. and Army of the Tenn . . . [and] 23d Army Corps. Compiled by

Sergt. N. Finegan, draughtsman. Printed at Topographical Engr. Office, Head Quarters Department of the Cumberland, June 26th 1864. Photocopy (negative). Scale ca. 1:64,000. 34 × 34 cm.

Endorsed (facsimile): Official issue. H. C. Wharton, Lt. Engrs.

Map of northwestern Cobb County, showing roads, railroad, towns, houses, names of residents, streams, hachures, and the location of the headquarters, Department of the Cumberland.

S62

————————Another copy.

S63

————————Another issue showing location of "H. Q. A. C." and additional roads and names of residents.

S64

————————Another copy.

S65

Columbus, Ga. [1864] Uncolored ms. Scale not given. 29 × 35 cm.

Pen and ink sketch map showing the defenses at Columbus, Georgia.

S66

Plan of fortifications at Columbus, Ga., 1864. Uncolored ms. Scale not given. 22 × 31 cm.

Pen and ink sketch map with "Columbus Geo. 1864" written in pencil.

A printed copy of this map is in the *Atlas to Accompany the Official Records of the Union and Confederate Armies,* 1891–95, pl. 132, no. 7.

S67

[Union troop positions at Dallas and New Hope Church, Georgia. May 25–June 5, 1864] Uncolored ms. Scale not given. 25 × 20 cm.

At bottom of map: McPherson.

Pencil sketch on stationery of "Head-quarters Department and Army of the Tennessee." Letterhead on verso.

A printed copy of the map appears in the *Atlas to Accompany the Official Records of the Union and Confederate Armies,* 1891–95, pl. 48, no. 3.

S68

[Union troop positions east of Dallas, Georgia. May 25–June 5, 1864] Uncolored ms. Scale ca. 1:15,750. 26 × 13 cm.

At bottom of map: McPherson.

Pencil sketch drawn on a 300-yard grid.

A printed copy of this map appears in the *Atlas to Accompany the Official Records of the Union and Confederate Armies,* 1891–95, pl. 43, no. 9.

S69

[Union troop positions east of Dallas, Georgia. May 25–June 5, 1864] Uncolored ms. Scale ca. 1:32,500. 13 × 12 cm.

At bottom of map: McPherson.

Pencil sketch.

A printed copy of this map is in the *Atlas to Accompany the Official Records of the Union and Confederate Armies,* 1891–95, pl. 43, no. 5.

S70

[Union troop positions north of Dallas, Georgia. May 25–June 5, 1864] Uncolored ms. Scale not given. 25 × 20 cm.

At bottom of map: McPherson.

Pencil sketch.

A printed copy of this map is in the *Atlas to Accompany the Official Records of the Union and Confederate Armies,* 1891–95, pl. 43, no. 6.

S71

[Union troop positions at Dallas, Georgia. May 27, 1864] Uncolored ms. Scale not given. 20 × 25 cm.

Marked "McPherson" and "May 27."

Pencil sketch on an irregularly shaped piece of paper.

A printed copy of this map is in the *Atlas to Accompany the Official Records of the Union and Confederate Armies,* 1891–95, pl. 48, no. 4.

S72

[Fortifications west of Dalton, Georgia. 1864] Uncolored ms. Scale not given. 26 × 20 cm.

Pencil sketch on stationery of "Head-Quarters Department of the Cumberland, Office Provost Marshal General." Letterhead has been marked out.

Shows roads and relief by hachures.

S73

[Positions of the Army of the Ohio in front of Dalton, Georgia. May 8 and 9, 1864] Colored ms. Scale not given. 26 × 24 cm.

At bottom of map: Schofield.

Sketch map drawn with colored pencils. Troop positions are red and blue, railroads are blue, roads are red, and relief, towns, and names of residents are black.

A printed copy of this map is in the *Atlas to Accompany the Official Records of the Union and Confederate Armies,* 1891–95, pl. 55, no. 6.

S74

Skinner, C. W.

[Map of part of De Kalb and Gwinnett counties. 1864]
Colored ms. Scale 1:63,360. 51 × 21 cm.

"This platt I have made from survey and information
and it is as correct as I can make without traveling over the
ground held by the rebels . . . [Signed] C. W. Skinner, Major
& Topgl. Eng., 2d Cav. Div."

Pencil sketch of the country between the Chattahoochee River and Stone Mountain, showing roads, railroad,
houses, and names of residents.

At top of map: View of McAfees Br. from north side
Chattahoochee Riv. Sargt. H. S. Heywood, del., 4th M. C.

S75

**U.S. *Army. Department of the Cumberland. Topographical
Engineers.***

Part of De Kalb and Fulton County, Ga. Compiled for
the use of the Topographical Engrs. from the original land
map & surveys of De Kalb County. Compiled & printed at
the Topl. Engr. Office, Department of the Cumberland. Marietta, Ga., July 5th 1864. Uncolored. Scale 1:63,360.
47 × 32 cm.

"Note. The topographical Engineers are directed to return as soon as possible one copy of this land map with all
the information they are able to obtain, to this office. Corps
Engineers will cause a speedy compilation."

Base map printed on a ⁹⁄₁₆-inch grid.

S76

————————Another copy.

Roads have been added in red, and fortifications are
indicated north of "Turners Fy. Road," 3 miles northwest of
Atlanta.

S77

————————Part of De Kalb and Fulton County, Ga. Compiled for the use of the Topographical Engrs. from the original land map & surveys of De Kalb County. Compiled &
printed at the Topl. Engr. Office, Department of the Cumberland, Marietta, Ga., July 5th, 1864. Land map of De Kalb
County from the original drawn and printed at Topogr.
Engr. Office, Dept. of the Cumberland. Marietta, Georgia,
July 11th 1864. Uncolored. Scale 1:63,360. 49 × 61 cm.

Two lithographed maps with separate titles, joined together forming one continuous map. The map has been annotated in pencil and red ink, apparently by Lt. Harry C.
Wharton, topographic engineer with the Army of the Cumberland. A note on the verso written in pencil by Wharton
reads as follows: Dear Bill [probably Col. William E. Mer-
rill], This is the only map I have of the country you want—
If you have any way to have it traced to night please do so

*During the march on Atlanta, field parties were provided with
lithographed base maps on which to plot new data. Instructions on
the map of "Part of De Kalb and Fulton County, Ga." direct the topographical engineers "to return as soon as possible one copy of this
land map with all the information they are able to obtain, to this
office. Corps Engineers will cause a speedy compilation." Formerly in
the possession of General Sherman, this copy contains annotations
apparently made by Lt. Harry C. Wharton, an engineer in the Army
of the Cumberland. (See entry no. S77.)*

and either return this or the tracing. My office is in Marietta.
No one here with me or I would have it traced my self. If
you cannot trace it keep it.

S78

————————[Part of De Kalb and Fulton County, Georgia.
Compiled for the use of the Topographical Engineers from
the original land map and surveys of De Kalb County. Com-
piled and printed at the Topographical Engineers Office,
Department of the Cumberland. Marietta, Georgia. 1864]
Second edition. Uncolored. Scale 1:63,360. 49 × 63 cm.

First edition published July 5–11, 1864.

Base map printed on a ⁹⁄₁₆-inch grid. Indicates "rebel
works" southeast of "Isoms ford and ferry."

S79

[Map of part of De Kalb County, Georgia, from the Chattahoochee River south to Peach Tree Creek. July 17–18, 1864]
Uncolored ms. Scale not given. 34 × 40 cm.

Pencil sketch indicating the location of Headquarters,
Department of the Tennessee, on July 17th and 18th, and
the position of the 15th 16th, and 17th Army Corps on
Peach Tree Creek.

Roads, drainage, towns, and the names of a few residents are given.

S80

[View of fortifications near the ruins of the Western and
Atlantic Railroad bridge across the Etowah River in Georgia. 1864] Uncolored ms. 15 × 26 cm.

Pencil sketch.

S81

[Map of the Etowah River from Rome to Cartersville, Georgia. 1864] Colored ms. Scale not given. 26 × 58 cm.

Pen and ink manuscript on tracing cloth, showing
roads in red, drainage in blue, and relief in black. Houses,
names of residents, towns, fords, bridges, and ferries are indicated. Fortifications are shown at Caldwell Ford.

S82

[Pencil sketch showing the location of the Headquarters,
Department of the Tennessee, on Flint River near Jones-

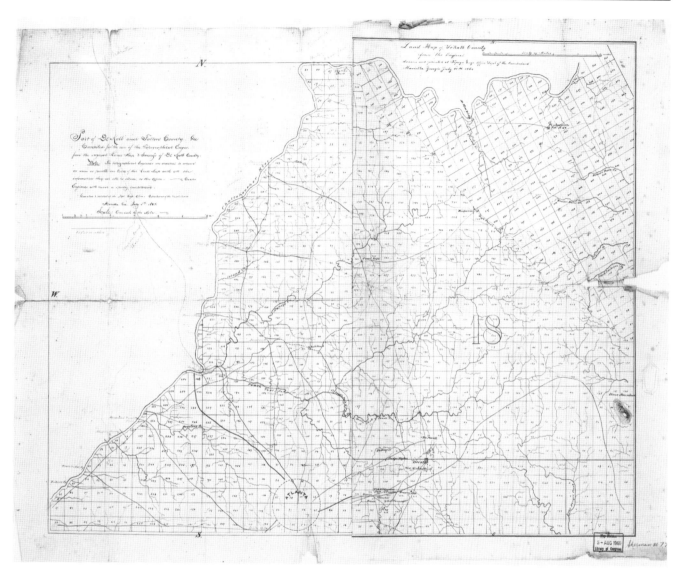

boro, Georgia] Hd. Qrs. D. and [A. Tenn.] Aug. 30, 1864. 8 A.M. Uncolored ms. Scale not given. 25 × 20 cm.

"Jonesboro 1864" is written on the verso.

At bottom of map: Logan's Corps is across the Flint River—the 16th is on the right of the main Jonesboro road—and the 17th Corps is now going into position on the left of this road.

S83

Skinner, C. W.

[Map of part of Fulton County, Georgia, from Roswell south to Atlanta. July 13, 1864] Colored ms. Scale not given. 50 × 30 cm.

Handwritten note on verso: Hd. Qurs. 2 Cav. Div., July 13, 64. Sketched by Maj. Skinner, 3 Ohio Cav., T. E. 2 Cav. Div. Respt. furnished to Maj. Gen. Sherman, comdg. army. [Signed] K. Garrard, Brig. Gen. comdg. div.

Pencil sketch indicating roads, railroads, bridges, ferries, drainage, and towns. "Confederate camp" shown northeast of Atlanta.

S84

[Map of the country northwest of Jonesboro, Georgia. Aug.–Sept. ? 1864] Uncolored ms. Scale not given. 41 × 42 cm.

Pen and ink manuscript drawn on tracing cloth, showing roads, railroads, towns, and streams. Troop positions and names of commanders are added in pencil.

"Roads from best information."

S85

[Map of the northwestern part of Cobb County, Georgia, showing Union works near Kenesaw Mountain. June 1864] Colored ms. Scale not given. 34 × 35 cm.

At bottom of map: (Thomas)

Pen and ink manuscript on tracing cloth "compiled from surveys made by the Topl. Engrs. of the Dept. of the Cumb. . . . Dept. and Army of the Tennesse[e], . . . [and the] 23d Army Corps, under the direction of the [Topl. Engrs.] at Head Quarters, Dept. Cumb."

Roads are red, streams are blue, and towns, names of residents, and relief are black. The map indicates the locations of the Headquarters of the Department of the Cumberland on the 19th and 24th of June.

S86

Macon, Geo., 1864. Uncolored ms. Scale not given. 44 × 31 cm.

Pen and ink sketch of the defenses at Macon. Title and date are written in pencil. A printed copy of this map is in the *Atlas to Accompany the Official Records of the Union and Confederate Armies,* 1891–95, pl. 135, no. 4.

S87

Map of Macon, Ga. and vicinity. [1864] Uncolored ms. Scale ca. 1:16,000. 38 × 37 cm.

Title on verso.

Pen and ink sketch map showing the defenses at Macon, Georgia.

S88

[Union troop positions northwest of Marietta, Georgia. June ? 1864] Colored ms. Scale not given. 20 × 29 cm.

At bottom of map: Thomas & Schofield.

Sketch map showing the 20th Army Corps' 1st Division in red, 2nd Division in green, and the 3rd Division in blue. The position of the 4th Corps is given in black ink and that of the 23rd Corps in purple ink. Map also includes roads, towns, relief by hachures, creeks, railroad, houses, and names of residents.

A printed reduction of this map is in the *Atlas to Accompany the Official Records of the Union and Confederate Armies,* 1891–95, pl. 65, no. 2

S89

[Union troop positions west of Marietta, Georgia. June? 1864] Uncolored ms. Scale not given. 12 × 21 cm.

Rough pencil sketch showing the position of troops under Schofield and Hooker.

A printed copy of this map appears in the *Atlas to Accompany the Official Records of the Union and Confederate Armies,* 1891–95, pl. 65, no. 5.

S90

[Map of the environs of Marietta, Georgia. June 10–July 3, 1864] Colored ms. Scale not given. 10 × 16 cm.

At bottom of map: Garrard's cavalry.

Pencil sketch showing roads, railroad, hachures, and a few towns.

Troop positions are not given.

Similar to a map in the *Atlas to Accompany the Official Records of the Union and Confederate Armies,* 1891–95, pl. 43, no. 4.

S91

[Map of the Union troop positions southwest of Marietta, Georgia. June 10–July 3, 1864] Colored ms. Scale not given. 25 × 20 cm.

At bottom of map: Garrard.

Pencil sketch giving roads in red, drainage in blue, and place names in black. Indicates the position of Schofield and Hooker on Noses Creek.

Printed copy of this map appears in the *Atlas to Accompany the Official Records of the Union and Confederate Armies,* 1891–95, pl. 65, no. 3.

S92

Skinner, C. W.

[Map showing the position of troops to the north of Marietta, Georgia, June 10–July 3, 1864] Colored ms. Scale not given. 30 × 32 cm.

Sketch map drawn with colored pencils. Union positions and drainage are colored blue and Confederate positions and roads are colored red. Map also includes towns, houses and names of residents, railroad, and relief by hachures.

A printed reduction of this map appears in the *Atlas to Accompany the Official Records of the Union and Confederate Armies,* 1891–95, pl. 49, no. 4.

S93

[Union troop positions northwest of Marietta, Georgia. June 10–July 3, 1864] Colored ms. Scale not given. 30 × 35 cm.

At bottom of map: (Schofield)

Pencil sketch showing the position of the 20th and 23rd Army Corps. Roads are in red and drainage in blue. Map also includes the names of residents and relief by hachures.

A printed copy of the map is in the *Atlas to Accompany the Official Records of the Union and Confederate Armies,* 1891–95, pl. 62, no. 13.

S94

Garrard, Kenner.

Sketch of the roads &c near the position of this Div. on the left of the Army. The red represent the Rebels & the black the Union. Tysons, Hd. Qurs. 2 Cav. Div., June 12, 1864. Colored ms. Scale not given. 31 × 43 cm.

Pencil sketch extending from Marietta north to Canton, Georgia, giving troop positions, picket lines, towns, roads, and the names of a few residents.

A report, written and signed by "K. Garrard, Brig. Gen., Comd'g. Div.," appears to the left of the map. It describes the 2nd Cavalry Division's clash with the Confederates.

A printed reduction of this map is in the *Atlas to Accompany the Official Records of the Union and Confederate Armies,* 1891–95, pl. 62, no. 14.

S95

[Map of the environs of Olley Creek near Marietta, Georgia] June 28th [1864] Uncolored ms. Scale 1:31,680. 25 × 31 cm.

Pencil sketch showing roads, creeks, houses, names of residents, and vegetation.

Union positions are given in black ink and Confederate positions in red ink.

S96

[Map of the environs of Olley Creek near Marietta, Georgia. July? 1864] Uncolored ms. Scale 1:63,360. 25 × 20 cm.

Pencil sketch giving the position of "Adams' Cavalry," fortifications, roads, streams, houses, and names of occupants.

Drawn on a ½-mile grid.

S97

Part of Paulding County [Georgia] showing the position of the Left Wing 16th A.C., June 4th 1864. Uncolored ms. Scale 1:31,680. 41 × 39 cm.

Drawn in ink on tracing cloth. Includes roads, vegetation, drainage, relief by hachures, houses, and names of residents. The position of the 15th Army Corps is also shown.

S98

[Union troop positions at Peach Tree Creek, Georgia. July 20, 1864] Colored ms. Scale not given. 18 × 19 cm.

At bottom of map: Thomas.

Sketch map showing railroads in blue and red, creeks in blue, roads in brown, and troop positions, headquarters, and place names in black.

A printed copy of this map appears in the *Atlas to Accompany the Official Records of the Union and Confederate Armies,* 1891–95, pl. 47, no. 5.

S99

[Union and Confederate works astride the Dallas and Marietta Road near Pine Hill, Georgia. June 1864] Colored ms. Scale 1:31,680. 25 × 32 cm.

At bottom of map: [Sch]ofield.

Pencil sketch indicating houses, names of occupants, vegetation, streams, and relief by hachures. Union works are shown in black ink, and Confederate works in red ink.

A printed copy of this map appears in the *Atlas to Accompany the Official Records of the Union and Confederate Armies,* 1891–95, pl. 47, no. 4.

S100

U.S. *Army. Department of the Cumberland. Topographical Engineers.*

Information map of part of Georgia. Printed at Top: Engr. Office, Head -Q'rs. Dep't. of the Cumberland in the field, May 30th 1864. Photocopy (negative). Scale 1:31,680. 28 × 40 cm.

Map of the vicinity of Pumpkin Vine Creek, Bartow County, Georgia, showing roads, creeks, vegetation, houses, and names of residents.

S101

McPherson [at] Snake Creek Gap. [May 8–13, 1864] Uncolored ms. Scale 1:63,360. 39 × 33 cm.

Pen and ink sketch showing Confederate works at Resaca ("location not accurate") and the Union position in Snake Creek Gap.

A copy of this map is printed in the *Atlas to Accompany the Official Records of the Union and Confederate Armies,* 1891–95, pl. 63, no. 4.

S102

[Map of the environs of Resaca, Georgia] Printed at Head Quarters, Dept. Cumb., May 13th 1864. Photocopy (negative). Scale 1:63,360. 44 × 28 cm.

Indicates Confederate works at Resaca, the Union position in Snake Creek Gap, roads, railroad, towns, drainage, houses, names of residents, and relief by hachures and contours.

S103

Garrard, Kenner.

Sketch of vicinity of 2 Cav. Div. camp. [Signed] K. Garrard B.G. The proposed camp is where the 3 Brig. now is. [June? 1864] Colored ms. Scale not given. 25 × 20 cm.

Pencil sketch of Roswell and vicinity, giving roads in red and mountains and streams in blue. Title, signature, and the following note are written in ink: Roswell is a very pretty factory town of about four thousand inhabitants. Mills & private property are not injuried [sic] by me. [The word "mills" has been marked out.]

S104

McPherson—crossing at Rosswell [i.e., Roswell, Georgia. July 1864] Uncolored ms. Scale not given. 28 × 27 cm.

Pencil sketch showing the fortifications of the 15th and 16th Army Corps on the bluffs along the Chattahoochee River, location of the "H.Q., Army of the Tenn." near "Ros-

Sherman Map Collection

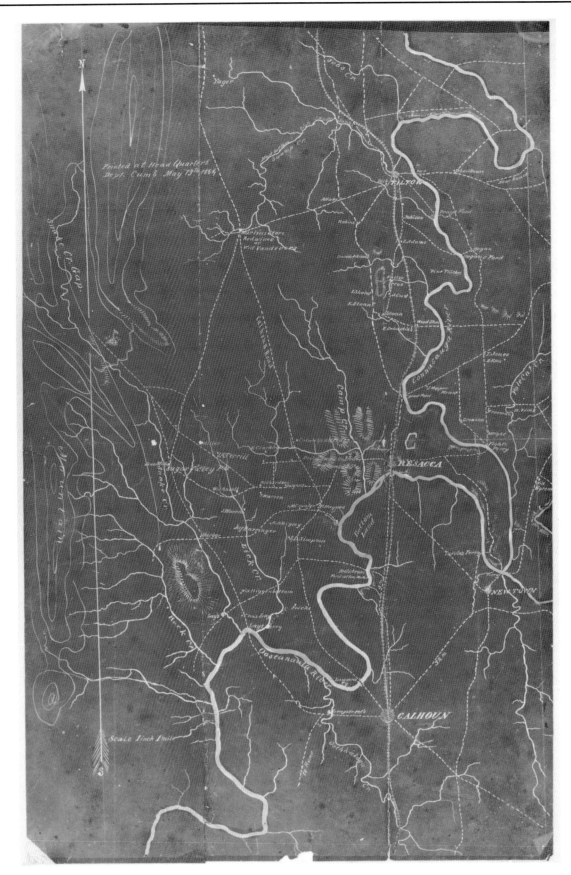

swells Factory," roads, and a few houses and the names of their occupants.

A printed copy of this map appears in the *Atlas to Accompany the Official Records of the Union and Confederate Armies,* 1891–95, pl. 49, no. 3.

S105

[Plan of the fortifications on Causten's Bluff, Georgia. 1864] Uncolored ms. Scale 1:2000. 28 × 47 cm.

Pen and ink manuscript drawn on tracing cloth.
Part of the defenses of Savannah.

S106

Fort Lee. [1864] Uncolored ms. Scale 1:2000. 33 × 33 cm.
Pen and ink manuscript drawn on tracing cloth.
Part of the defenses of Savannah, Georgia. Includes five profiles of the works, each at the scale of 1:666.

S107

Fort McAllister. [1864] Uncolored ms. Scale 1:2000. 35 × 35 cm.
Pen and ink manuscript drawn on tracing cloth.
Part of the defenses of Savannah, Georgia.

S108

Fort Tattnall. [1864] Uncolored ms. Scale 1:2000. 42 × 28 cm.
Pen and ink manuscript drawn on tracing cloth.
Part of the defenses of Savannah, Georgia. Includes three profiles, each at the scale of 1:666.

S109

Fort Thunderbolt. [1864] Uncolored ms. Scale 1:2000. 36 × 32 cm.
Pen and ink manuscript drawn on tracing cloth.
Part of the defenses of Savannah, Georgia.

S110

Battery on Turner's Rocks. [1864] Uncolored ms. Scale 1:2000. 35 × 34 cm.
Pen and ink manuscript drawn on tracing cloth.
Part of the defenses of Savannah, Georgia.

S111

Works at eastern point of Whitmarsh Island [and] bastion on the line of defences across Whitmarsh Island. [1864] Uncolored ms. Scale 1:2000. 41 × 30 cm.

Map of the environs of Resaca, Georgia, May 13, 1864, showing the position of the Army of the Tennessee at Snake Creek Gap, Georgia, in the early stages of the Atlanta Campaign. The map was produced by a relatively quick photoreproduction process invented by Capt. William C. Margedant, a topographical engineer with the Army of the Cumberland. (See entry no. S102.)

Part of the defenses of Savannah, Georgia.
Pen and ink manuscript drawn on tracing cloth. Includes profiles of "Bastion on line of defences across Whitmarsh Island" and "Bastion at eastern point of Whitmarsh Island," each of which is at the scale of 1:666.

S112

Position of the 15th, 16th & 17th A.C.s, July 5th [1864] evening. Uncolored ms. Scale not given. 23 × 29 cm.
Pencil sketch of the environs of Turner's Ferry in Cobb County, Georgia. Indicates "Rebel works" and "Rebel works taken this morning," roads, railroad, and drainage.

S113

Lederle, O.

Kentucky and Tennessee. Memphis, O. Lederle, 1862. Uncolored. Scale ca. 1:1,200,000. 44 × 65 cm.
Indicates towns, roads, railroads, and drainage.

S114

[Map of the Big Black River, Mississippi, in the vicinity of Bush and Birdsong's ferries. 1863] Uncolored ms. Scale not given. 20 × 25 cm.
Pencil sketch showing drainage, roads, houses, and names of residents. Small flags apparently indicate campsites.

S115

Matz, Otto H.

Map of the country between Monterey, Tenn: & Corinth, Miss: showing the lines of entrenchments made & the routes followed by the U.S. forces under the command of Maj. Genl. Halleck, U.S. Army, in their advance upon Corinth in May 1862: Surveyed under the direction of Col. Geo. Thom, A. D. C. & Chief of Topl. Engrs., Department of the Mississippi, by Lieuts. Fred. Schraag and C. L. Spangenberg, Asst. Topl. Engrs., and drawn by Lieut. Otto H. Matz, Asst. Topl. Engr. Colored. Scale 1:31,680. 77 × 57 cm.
Gives Union and Confederate entrenchments, houses, names of residents, fences, roads, railroads, vegetation, fields, drainage, and relief by hachures.
For another copy, see entry no. 267.

S116

[Map of the environs of Vicksburg and Jackson, Mississippi. 1863] Uncolored ms. Scale not given. 25 × 39 cm.
Pencil sketch showing towns, railroads, roads, and drainage.

S117

[Map of the environs of Vicksburg and Jackson, Mississippi. 1863] Colored ms. Scale 1:380,160. 20 × 29 cm.

Pen and ink sketch map drawn on tracing cloth. Indicates roads in red, drainage in blue, and railroads, towns and names of residents in black.

S118

[Map of the environs of Vicksburg, Mississippi. 1863] Uncolored ms. Scale not given. 16 × 21 cm.

Pen and ink sketch map indicating drainage.

The "new channel" of Steel's Bayou is depicted.

S119

[Map of the environs of Vicksburg, Mississippi. 1863] Colored ms. Scale 1:63,360. 42 × 64 cm.

Pen and ink sketch map drawn on tracing cloth, showing roads in red, principal rivers in blue, and "Vicksburg & Jackson R.R.," streams, towns, and names of residents in black. Fortifications are indicated at the "R.R. Bridge" across the Big Black River.

S120

Spangenberg, Charles.

Map of the siege of Vicksburg, Miss. by the U.S. forces under the command of Maj. Genl. U. S. Grant, U.S. Vls. Maj. F. E. Prime, Chief Engr. Surveyed and constructed under direction of Capt. C. B. Comstock, U.S. Engrs. and Lt. Col. Js. H. Wilson, A. I. Genl., 1st Lt. Engrs. Drawn by Chs. Spangenberg, Asst. Engr. Vicksburg, Miss., Head Qrs. of the Dept. of the Tenn., Aug. 20th 1863. Photocopy (positive). Scale ca. 1:16,800 (not "four inches to one mile"). 75 × 70 cm.

Dedicated in ms: To Thomas E. Sherman to keep forever, from his father, W. T. Sherman, Maj. Genl. Jan. 20, 1864.

Union and Confederate entrenchments are hand-colored blue and red respectively.

Detailed map showing roads, streets, railroads, hachures, vegetation, houses, and drainage.

Contains five topographic profiles, six cross sections of artillery batteries, and one cross section of a "rebel rifle pit."

This is a photocopy of a manuscript map. The original manuscript was probably used in producing the printed map described in entry no. 285.

S121

U.S. *Army. Corps of Engineers.*

Eastern portion of the Military Department of North Carolina, compiled from the best and latest authorities in the Engineer Bureau, War Department, May 1862. Uncolored. Scale 1:350,000. 85 × 55 cm.

Incomplete copy of printed map. For a complete copy see entry no. 306.

Shows roads, railroads, towns, drainage, and swamps.

Following handwritten statement appears to left of map

title: Engineer Department, Washington, Dec. 24th/ 64. For Major Genl. Sherman. [Signed] Richd. Delafield, Genl. & Chief Engineer, U.S. Army.

S122

Colton, Joseph H.

New topographical map of the eastern portion of the State of North Carolina with part of Virginia & South Carolina, from the latest & best authorities. New York, 1864. Colored. Scale 1:506,880. 100 × 67 cm.

Inscribed on verso: Compliments of Capt. A. S. Kimball, AQM [illegible].

Indicates principal coastal forts, towns, state and county boundaries, roads, railroads, and drainage.

Inset: Plan of the sea coast from Virginia to Florida. 12 × 63 cm.

"Entered according to Act of Congress, in the year 1860, by John H. Colton . . ."

S123

[Map of part of North and South Carolina. 1864–5?] Colored ms. Scale 1:350,000. 39 × 51 cm.

Pen and ink manuscript drawn on tracing cloth. "Tracing from map in Chf. Engrs. Office, M. D. M."

"For Genl. Sherman."

Map extends from Fayetteville west to Monroe, North Carolina, and from Reedy Branch, North Carolina, south to Allen's Bridge P. O., South Carolina.

Indicates roads, railroads, drainage, towns, mills, and the names of a few residents. A few roads have been emphasized by red lines.

S124

Comstock, Cyrus B.

Plan and sections of Fort Fisher carried by assault by the U.S. forces, Maj. Gen. A. H. Terry commanding, Jan. 15th 1865. Engraved in the Engineer Bureau, War Dept. E. Molitor, lith. Uncolored. Scale 1:3840. 28 × 40 cm.

"Head Qurtrs., U.S. forces, Fort Fisher, Jan. 27th 1865. Forwarded to Engineer Dept. with letter of this date. C. B. Comstock, Lt. Col., A. D. C. & Brvt. Brig. Gen. &&."

Detailed plan of the fort showing the position, type and size of guns, rifle pits, and electric wires leading to a "line of torpedoes."

Three cross sections of ramparts are given in inset.

For another copy see entry no. 310.

S125

Schultze, Otto Julian.

Sketch of vicinity of Fort Fisher surveyed under the direction of Brvt. Brig. Gen. C. B. Comstock, Chief Engineer, by Otto Julian Schultze, Private, 15th N. Y. V. Eng.

Engraved at the Engineer Bureau, War Dept. [1865] Uncolored. Scale 1:12,000. 37 × 25 cm.

"Ft. Fisher, Feb. 9th 1865. Forwarded to Engineer Department with letter of this date. C. B. Comstock, Lt. Col. A. D. C. & Brvt. B. Gen."

Map of Federal Point showing forts Buchanan, Fisher, and Lookout, roads, commissary, hospital, headquarters, vegetation, drainage, and relief by hachures.

Inset: Fort Buchanan. Scale ca. 1:2400.

For another copy see entry no. 314.

S126

[Map of the coast of South Carolina, from Charleston to Savannah. 186–] Uncolored. Scale ca. 1:355,000. 55 × 42 cm.

Portion of an unidentified printed map showing roads, railroads, towns, and drainage.

Handwritten note in lower right corner: From Chief Engrs. O[ff.] Mil'y. Divn. Miss: O. M. [Poe] Bvt. Col. & [Chf. Engr.] 67.

S127

Lindenkohl, Adolph.

Sketch of sea coast of South Carolina and Georgia, from Bull's Bay to Ossabaw Sound. Drawn by A. Lindenkohl. E. Molitor, lith. 1863. Uncolored. Scale 1:200,000. 41 × 96 cm.

At head of title: U.S. Coast Survey A. D. Bache, Supdt.

Indicates forts, towns, roads, and railroads.

For another copy see entry no. 364.

S128

[Pencil sketch of the Atlantic Coast from Charleston, South Carolina, to Savannah, Georgia, 1864?] Uncolored ms. Scale not given. 39 × 47 cm.

S129

Mills, Robert.

Abbeville District, South Carolina. Surveyed by Wm. Robertson, 1820. Improved for Mills' Atlas, 1825. Uncolored ms. Scale 1:126,720. 48 × 59 cm.

"Approved, Chas. R. Suter, 1st Lt., U.S. Engrs., Chf. Engr., D. S."

Pen and ink tracing of a map in Robert Mills's *Atlas of the State of South Carolina* . . . Baltimore, F. Lucas, Jr. [1825].

S130

————Barnwell District, South Carolina. Surveyed by Thos. Anderson, D. S., 1818. Improved for Mills Atlas, 1825. Uncolored ms. Scale 1:126,720. 56 × 76 cm.

"Approved, Chas. R. Suter, 1st Lt., U.S. Engrs., Chf. Engr., D. S."

Pen and ink tracing of a map in Robert Mills's *Atlas of the State of South Carolina* . . . Baltimore, F. Lucas, Jr. [1825].

S131

————Beaufort District, South Carolina: Surveyed by C. Vignoles & H. Ravenel, 1820. Improved for Mills' Atlas. 1825. Uncolored ms. Scale ca. 1:126,720. 84 × 56 cm.

"Approved, Chas. R. Suter, 1st Lt. & Chf. Engr., D. S."

Pen and ink tracing of map in Robert Mills's *Atlas of the State of South Carolina* . . . Baltimore, F. Lucas, Jr. [1825]. Savannah & Charleston R.R. has been added.

S132

————Charleston District, South Carolina. Surveyed by Charles Vignoles & Henry Ravenel, 1820. Improved for Mills' Atlas, 1825. Uncolored ms. Scale 1:126,720. 88 × 86 cm.

"Approved, Chas. R. Suter, 1st Lt., U.S. Engrs., Chf. Engr. D. S."

Pen and ink tracing of map in Robert Mills's *Atlas of the State of South Carolina* . . . Baltimore, F. Lucas, Jr. [1825].

S133

————Christ Church Parish, So. Ca. [Charleston District] From Mills' Atlas of South Carolina. Traced at the Coast Survey Office for the Engineer Dept., April 1863. Uncolored ms. Scale 1:126,720. 40 × 49 cm.

"No. 71" is in the lower right corner.

Pen and ink tracing of part of the map of Charleston District in Robert Mills's *Atlas of the State of South Carolina* . . . Baltimore, F. Lucas, Jr. [1825]

S134

————Chester District, South Carolina. Surveyed by Charls Boyd, D. S., 1818. Improved for Mills' Atlas: 1825. Uncolored ms. Scale 1:126,720. 36 × 51 cm.

"Approved Chas R. Suter, 1st Lt., U.S. Engrs., Chf. Engr., D. S."

Pen and ink tracing of map in Robert Mills's *Atlas of the State of South Carolina* . . . Baltimore, F. Lucas, Jr. [1825].

S135

————[Chesterfield District, South Carolina. Surveyed by John Lowry, 1819. Improved for Mills' Atlas, 1825] Uncolored ms. Scale ca. 1:126,720. 44 × 44 cm.

Incomplete; the left portion of the map containing the title is wanting.

Pen and ink tracing of a map in Robert Mills's *Atlas of the State of South Carolina* . . . Baltimore, F. Lucas, Jr. [1825].

"Approved, [C.] R. Suter, Lt. & Chf. Engr., D. S."

S136

——————Colleton District, South Carolina: surveyed by Saml. A. Ruddock, 1820. Improved for Mills' Atlas, 1825. Uncolored ms. Scale 1:126,720. 70 × 61 cm.

"Approved, Chas. R. Suter, 1st Lt., U.S. Engrs., Chf. Engr., D. S."

Pen and ink tracing of a map in Robert Mills's *Atlas of the State of South Carolina* . . . Baltimore, F. Lucas, Jr. [1825].

S137

——————Darlington District, South Carolina. Improved for Mills' Atlas: 1820. Uncolored ms. Scale 1:126,720. 51 × 51 cm.

"Approved, C. R. Suter, 1st Lt., U.S. Engrs., Chf. Engr., D. S."

Pen and ink tracing of a map in Robert Mills's *Atlas of the State of South Carolina* . . . Baltimore, F. Lucas, Jr. [1825].

S138

——————Edgefield District, South Carolina. Surveyed by Thos. Anderson, 1817. Improved for Mills' Atlas: 1825. Uncolored ms. Scale 1:126,720. 58 × 77 cm.

"Approved, C. R. Suter, 1st Lt., U.S. Engrs., Chf. Engr., D. S."

Pen and ink tracing of a map in Robert Mills's *Atlas of the State of South Carolina* . . . Baltimore, F. Lucas, Jr. [1825].

S139

——————Fairfield District[t], South Carolina. Surveyed by John Allen Tharp, 1820. Improved for Mills' Atlas, 1825. Uncolored ms. Scale 1:126,720. 40 × 44 cm.

"Approved, C. R. Sute[r], 1st Lt., U.S. [Engrs], Chf. Engr., [D. S.]"

Pen and ink tracing of the eastern three-fourths of a map in Robert Mills's *Atlas of the State of South Carolina* . . . Baltimore, F. Lucas, Jr. [1825].

S140

——————Georgetown District, South Carolina. Surveyed by Wm. Hemingway, 1820. Improved for Mills' Atlas, 1825. Uncolored ms. Scale 1:126,720. 66 × 53 cm.

"Approved, Chas. R. Suter, 1st Lt., U.S. Engrs., Chf. Engr., D. S."

Pen and ink tracing of a map in Robert Mills's *Atlas of the State of South Carolina* . . . Baltimore, F. Lucas, Jr. [1825].

S141

——————Greenville District, South Carolina. Surveyed

by George Salmon, 1820. Improved for Mills' Atlas, 1825. Uncolored ms. Scale 1:126,720. 64 × 49 cm.

"Approved, Chas. R. Suter, 1st Lt., U.S. Engrs., Chf. Engr., D. S."

Pen and ink tracing of a map in Robert Mills's *Atlas of the State of South Carolina* . . . Baltimore, F. Lucas Jr. [1825].

S142

——————Horry District, South Carolina. Surveyed by Harlee, 1820. Improved for Mills' Atlas, 1825. Uncolored ms. Scale 1:126,720. 51 × 59 cm.

"Approved, C. R. Suter, 1st Lt. & Chf. Engr., D. S."

Pen and ink tracing of a map in Robert Mills's *Atlas of the State of South Carolina* . . . Baltimore, F. Lucas, Jr. [1825].

S143

——————Kershaw District, South Carolina. Surveyed by J. Boykin, 1820. Improved for Mills' Atlas, 1825. Uncolored ms. Scale 1:126,720. 45 × 56 cm.

In lower right corner: B. Burkhardt, Comp. H., 103 N. Y. V. Reg.

"Approved, Chas. R. Suter, Lt. & Chf. Engr., D. S."

Pen and ink tracing of a map in Robert Mills's *Atlas of the State of South Carolina* . . . Baltimore, F. Lucas, Jr. [1825].

S144

——————Lancaster District, South Carolina. Surveyed by J. Boykin, 1820. Improved for Mills' Atlas, 1825. Uncolored ms. Scale 1:126,720. 51 × 40 cm.

"Approved, Chas R. Suter, Lt. & Chf. Engr., D. S."

Pen and ink tracing of a map in Robert Mills's *Atlas of the State of South Carolina* . . . Baltimore, F. Lucas, Jr. [1825].

S145

——————Laurens District, South Carolina. Surveyed by Henry Gray, D. S., 1820. Improved for Mills' Atlas, 1825. Uncolored ms. Scale 1:126,720. 45 × 57 cm.

In lower right corner: Traced by A. Cheville, 47 N. Y. V., Compagnie K.

"Approved, Chas. R. Suter, 1st Lt., U.S. Engrs., Chf. Engr., D. S."

Pen and ink tracing of a map in Robert Mills's *Atlas of the State of South Carolina* . . . Baltimore, F. Lucas, Jr. [1825].

S146

——————Lexington District, South Carolina. Surveyed by M. Coate, 1820. Improved for Mills' Atlas. 1825. Uncolored ms. Scale 1:126,720. 50 × 43 cm.

"Traced by O. Enz, Co. G. 48."

"Approved, Chas R. Sut[er], Lt. & Chf. Engr."

Pen and ink tracing of the eastern two-thirds of a map in Robert Mills's *Atlas of the State of South Carolina . . .* Baltimore, F. Lucas, Jr. [1825].

S147

————————Marion District, South Carolina. Surveyed by Thos. Harlee, D. S., 1818. Improved for Mills' Atlas: 1825. Uncolored ms. Scale 1:126,720. 69 × 56 cm.

"Approved, Chas. R. Suter, 1st Lt. & Chf. Engr., Dept. of the South."

In lower right corner: Traced by B. Schelten, Comp. A, 103 N. Y. S. V.

Pen and ink tracing of a map in Robert Mills's *Atlas of the State of South Carolina . . .* Baltimore, F. Lucas, Jr. [1825].

S148

————————Marlborough District, South Carolina. Improved for Mills' Atlas, 1825. Uncolored ms. Scale 1:126,720. 39 × 49 cm.

In lower right corner: B. Burkhardt, Comp. H, 103 N. Y. V. R.

"Approved, Chas. R. Suter, Lt. & Chf. Engr., D. S."

Pen and ink tracing of a map in Robert Mills's *Atlas of the State of South Carolina . . .* Baltimore, F. Lucas, Jr. [1825].

S149

————————Newberry District, South Carolina; Surveyed by M. Coate, 1820. Improved for Mills' Atlas: 1825. Uncolored ms. Scale 1:126,720. 39 × 42 cm.

"Approved, C. R. Suter, 1st Lt., U.S. Engrs., Chf. Engr., D. S."

Pen and ink tracing of a map in Robert Mills's *Atlas of the State of South Carolina . . .* Baltimore, F. Lucas, Jr. [1825].

S150

————————[Orangeburgh District, South Carolina. Surveyed by B. Busby, 1820. Improved for Mills' Atlas, 1825] Uncolored ms. Scale ca. 1:126,720. 54 × 40 cm.

Incomplete; the eastern and western portions of the map are wanting.

Pen and ink tracing of part of a map in Robert Mills's *Atlas of the State of South Carolina . . .* Baltimore, F. Lucas, Jr. [1825].

S151

————————Pendleton District, South Carolina. Surveyed by Scribling, 1820. Improved for Mills' Atlas: 1825. Uncolored ms. Scale 1:126,720. 76 × 65 cm.

"Approved, Chas. R. Suter, Lt. & Chf. Engr., D. S."

"Traced by B. Schelten, Comp. A, 103 Reg., N. Y. S. V.

Pen and ink tracing of a map in Robert Mills's *Atlas of the State of South Carolina . . .* Baltimore, F. Lucas, Jr. [1825].

S152

————————Richland District, South Carolina. Surveyed by Marmaduke Coate, 1820. Improved for Mills Atlas, 1825. Uncolored ms. Scale ca. 1:126,720. 47 × 45 cm.

"[A]pproved, Chas. R. Suter, 1st Lt., U.S. Engrs., Chf. Engr., D. S."

Pen and ink tracing of a map in Robert Mills's *Atlas of the State of South Carolina . . .* Baltimore, F. Lucas, Jr. [1825].

S153

————————Spartanburgh District, South Carolina. Surveyed by J. Whitten, 1820. Improved for Mills' Atlas, 1825. Uncolored ms. Scale 1:126,720. 59 × 55 cm.

In lower right corner: Traced by A. Cheville, Compagnie K, 47 N. Y. V.

"Approved, Chas. R. Suter, Lt. & Chf. Engr., D. S."

Pen and ink tracing of a map in Robert Mills's *Atlas of the State of South Carolina . . .* Baltimore, F. Lucas, Jr. [1825].

S154

————————Sumter District, South Carolina. Surveyed by S. H. Boykin, 1821. Improved for Mills Atlas, 1825. Uncolored ms. Scale 1:126,720. 77 × 60 cm.

"Approved, C. R. Suter, 1st Lt., U.S. Engrs., Chf. Engr., D. S."

Pen and ink tracing of a map in Robert Mills's *Atlas of the State of South Carolina . . .* Baltimore, F. Lucas, Jr. [1825].

S155

————————Union District, South Carolina; Surveyed by R. Thompson, 1820. Improved for Mills' Atlas. 1825. Uncolored ms. Scale 1:126,720. 50 × 47 cm.

"Approved, Chas. R. Suter, 1st Lt., U.S. Engrs., Chf. Engr., D. S."

Pen and ink tracing of a map in Robert Mills's *Atlas of the State of South Carolina . . .* Baltimore, F. Lucas, Jr. [1825].

S156

————————Williamsburgh District, South Carolina. Surveyed by I. Harlee, 1820. Improved for Mills' Atlas, 1825. Uncolored ms. Scale 1:126,720. 50 × 62 cm.

"Approved, Chas. R. Suter, 1st Lt., U.S. Engrs., Chf. Engr., D. S."

Pen and ink tracing of a map in Robert Mills's *Atlas of*

the State of South Carolina . . . Baltimore, F. Lucas, Jr. [1825].

S157

————York District, South Carolina. Surveyed by Gordon Moore, 1820. Improved for Mills' Atlas, 1825. Uncolored ms. Scale 1:126,720. 39 × 61 cm.

"Approved, Chas. R. Suter, 1st Lt., U.S. Engrs., Chf. Engr., D. S."

Pen and ink tracing of a map in Robert Mills's *Atlas of the State of South Carolina . . .* Baltimore, F. Lucas, Jr. [1825].

S158

Michler, Nathaniel.

New map of Tennessee by Capt. Michler, Topl. Engineers, U.S.A. Lith. of J. Bien, New York. [186–] Uncolored. Scale not given. 57 × 86 cm.

No. "10" is at the head of the title.

Map of the environs of Nashville showing roads, distances, railroads, towns, and drainage. Small flags apparently indicate campsites.

S159

Lyell, G. A.

[Map of part of the counties of McNairy and Hardin, Tennessee, and Alcorn and Tishomingo, Mississippi. 1862] G. A. Lyell, del. Uncolored ms. Scale ca. 1:254,000. 30 × 21 cm.

Pen and ink manuscript map indicating troop positions near Corinth, towns, mills, railroads, roads, and drainage.

S160

[Map of part of the counties of McNairy and Hardin, Tennessee, and Alcorn and Tishomingo, Mississippi. 1862] Uncolored ms. Scale ca. 1:254,000. 31 × 21 cm.

Unsigned pen and ink manuscript, similar in content to the preceding map signed by G. A. Lyell.

S161

[Map of part of the counties of McNairy and Hardin, Tennessee, and Alcorn and Tishomingo, Mississippi. 1862] Colored ms. Scale 1:253,440. 32 × 21 cm.

Anonymous pen and ink manuscript map.

Troop positions at Corinth and Shiloh are colored blue and red, and contour lines are brown. Map includes the names of some residents.

S162

Michler, Nathaniel

Map of middle and east Tennessee and parts of Ala-

bama and Georgia. Compiled from various authorities for the use of the Arm[ies] of the Ohio and Cumberland, by [Capt.] N. Michler, Corps of Topographical Engineers, U.S.A., assisted by Major John E. Weyss, U.S. Volunteers, Principal Assistant, and C. S. Mergell, Draughtsman, from March 1862 to December 1862. Photocopy (positive). Scale not given. 115 × 177 cm. Cut and mounted to fold to 29 × 22 cm.

Railroads are colored red, drainage is blue, and some roads are brown. A few corrections in ink are indicated in the vicinity of Chattanooga.

For another copy see entry no. 393.5.

S163

U.S. *Army. Department of the Cumberland. Topographical Engineers.*

Information map. [Southeastern Tennessee] Topographical Engineer Office, Head qrs., Army of the Cumber[land]. Chattanooga, Nov. 26th 18[63] Colored. Scale 1:63,360. 88 × 59 cm.

Incomplete; part of the title is wanting.

Reconnaissance map of parts of Hamilton, Bradley, McMinn, Meigs, and Rhea counties, Tennessee, showing houses, names of residents, roads, railroads, drainage, and relief by hachures. The map is lithographed on four sheets of blue paper which have been joined together.

S164

Smith, William F.

Battlefield of Chattanooga with the operations of the national forces under the command of Maj. Gen. U. S. Grant during the battles of Nov. 23, 24 & 25, 1863. Published at the U.S. Coast Survey Office, from surveys made under the direction of Br. Genl. W. F. Smith, Chief Engr., Mil. Div. Miss. . . . Colored. Scale ca. 1:42,500. 46 × 40 cm.

Indicates troop positions, Union and Confederate headquarters, roads, railroads, drainage, vegetation, relief by shading, and the names of a few residents in the outlying areas.

See entry nos. 402 and 403 for editions with different blue overprinting indicating Union positions and headquarters.

S165

[Map of the environs of Chattanooga, showing roads, railroads, towns, houses, names of residents, drainage, and relief by hachures. 1864?] Colored. Scale not given. 96 × 132 cm.

Lacks title and author.

"Chattanooga" is written in pencil on the verso.

Reconnaissance map is lithographed on 16 sheets of paper (each 24 × 33 cm.) which have been joined together.

S166

Smith, William F.

Map of the battlefield of Chattanooga. Made to accompany report of Major General U. S. Grant. By direction of Brigadier General W. F. Smith, Chief Engr., Mil. Div. Miss. [1864] Photocopy (positive). Scale ca 1:29,800. 55 × 43 cm.

At head of title (in manuscript): No. 9.

Drainage and Union fortifications are in blue, and Confederate positions are in red. The map includes roads, railroads, towns, street pattern of Chattanooga, houses, names of a few residents, vegetation, and relief by contour lines.

S167

Rockwell, Cleveland, *and* R. H. Talcott.

Topographical map of the approaches and defences of Knoxville, E. Tennessee, shewing the positions occupied by the United States & Rebel forces during the siege. Surveyed by direction of Capt. O. M. Poe, Chf. Engr. Dept. of the Ohio during Dec., Jan. and Feb. 1863–4, by Cleveland Rockwell, Subasst. U.S. Coast Survey. R. H. Talcott, Aid Photocopy (positive). Scale ca. 1:20,400. 33 × 37 cm.

"This copy made for Lieut. Gen. U. S. Grant by order of Maj. Genl. J. G. Foster."

"Rebel works & lines" and "Rebel rifle pits" are red; "Federal works & lines" and "rifle pits" are blue; and "rifle pits, held first by one party, and afterwards by the other" are blue and red.

Map includes roads, railroads, contour lines, vegetation, drainage, and houses.

S168

Pitzman, Julius, *and* Frick.

Memphis and vicinity. Surveyed and drawn by order of Maj. Genl. W. T. Sherman, by Lieuts. Pitzman & Frick, Topographical Engineers. [186–] Uncolored ms. Scale 1:31,680. 55 × 71 cm.

Finished pen and ink map drawn on tracing cloth.

"For General Sherman, General of the Army."

Indicates fortifications at Fort Pickering and Fort Harris, roads and streets, railroads, vegetation, drainage, relief by hachures, houses, fences, and the names of a few residents in the outlying areas.

S169

Hebard, H. S.

Map of Mission [sic] Ridge showing the position attacked by the forces under command of Maj. Gen. W. T. Sherman, Nov. 24th & 25th 1863. H. S. Hebard, draftsman. Colored ms. Scale ca. 1:20,500. 29 × 33 cm.

Finished pen and ink manuscript.

Oval-shaped map of the battle of Missionary Ridge, Tennessee, showing roads, railroads, vegetation, drainage, houses, fences, and relief by hachures. Names of Union commanders are underlined in red.

S170

Peseux, M.

Battlefields in front of Nashville where the United States forces commanded by Major General Geo. H. Thomas defeated and routed the Rebel army under General Hood, December 15th & 16th 1864. Surveyed and drawn under the direction of Gen: Tower by M. Peseux. Reduced and engraved in the Engineer Bureau. Uncolored. Scale 1:42,240. 33 × 39 cm.

From "39th Cong., 1st Sess. [1866]—Report of the Chief Engineer, U.S.A."

Legend in the upper left corner contains a brief résumé of each day's action while the map shows troop positions, roads, railroads, hachures, drainage, vegetation, and rural houses. Streets and houses of Nashville are not indicated.

For another copy see entry no. 433.

S171

U.S. *Army. Army of the Tennessee.*

Map of the field of Shiloh. April 6 [1862] Colored ms. Scale 1:14,400. 49 × 63 cm.

Finished pen and ink manuscript on tracing cloth. Shows Federal position the "morning of April 6th" in blue, and Federal position the "night of April 6th" in red.

Map includes names of Union commanders, roads, relief by hachures, vegetation, houses, fences, and drainage.

S172

Matz, Otto H.

Map of the field of Shiloh, near Pittsburgh Landing, Tenn., shewing the positions of the U.S. forces under the command of Maj. Genl. U. S. Grant, U.S. Vol. and Maj. Genl. D. C. Buell, U.S. Vol. on the 6th and 7th of April 1862. Surveyed under the direction of Col. Geo. Thom, Chief of Topl. Engrs., Dept. of the Mississippi. Drawn by Otto H. Matz, Asst. Topl. Engs. Lith. of J. Bien, N.Y. Colored. Scale 1:14,400. 44 × 62 cm.

Shows relief by hachures, vegetation, drainage, houses, and roads.

For another copy see entry no. 437.

S173

Bien, Julius.

Topographical sketch of the battlefield of Stone's River near Murfreesboro, Tennessee, December 31st 1862 to Jan. 3d 1863. Lith of J. Bien, N.Y. Uncolored. Scale ca. 1:16,200. 48 × 62 cm.

At head of title: 9.

Shows troop positions, names of commanders, Confederate works, roads, "Nashville and Chattanooga R.R.," vegetation, houses, fences, names of residents, and rivers.

S174

[Map of part of Virginia, West Virginia, and Maryland. 186–] Uncolored. Scale ca. 1:203,300. 55 × 42 cm.

Portion of an unidentified printed map showing roads, railroads, towns, drainage, and relief by hachures. It extends from Hagerstown south to Warrenton, and Strasburg east to Leesburg.

S175

Lloyd, James T.

Lloyd's official map of the State of Virginia from actual surveys by order of the Executive, 1828 & 1859. Corrected and revised by J. T. Lloyd to 1862, from surveys made by Capt. W. Angelo Powell, of the U.S. Topographical Engineers. Colored. Scale ca. 1:650,000. 76 × 121 cm. Fold. to 26 × 16 cm. in covers.

"Entered according to Act of Congress in the year 1861 by J. T. Lloyd . . ."

Indicates forts, towns, mills, factories, iron works, drainage, relief by hachures, county names and boundaries, roads, and railroads.

Part of a military map of North Carolina (Scale 1:350,000) is mounted on the verso.

"Sherman, March, 1865" is written in pencil inside the cover.

For another copy of Lloyd's map see entry no. 465.1

S176

[U.S. Coast Survey.]

[Military map of south-eastern Virginia. Compiled at the U.S. Coast Survey Office. Drawn by A. Lindenkohl. H. Lindenkohl & Chs. G. Krebs, Lith. 1862] Colored. Scale 1:200,000. 72 × 56 cm.

Incomplete copy of printed map (for complete copy see entry no. 474).

Map indicates fortifications in the Richmond area, towns, roads, railroads, drainage, and some vegetation.

S177

U.S. *Army. Corps of Engineers.*

Portions of Virginia and North Carolina, embracing Richmond & Lynchburg, Va. and Goldsboro & Salisbury, N. C., compiled in the Engineer Bureau, War Department, for military purposes, 1864. J. Schedler, N. Y. Uncolored. Scale 1:350,000. 83 × 101 cm.

General map showing roads, railroads, towns, drainage, and relief by hachures.

S178

U.S. *Army. Corps of Topographical Engineers.*

Central Virginia, compiled in the Bureau of Topographical. Engrs. of the War Department for military purposes. July 1862. Corrections and additions, Oct. 27, 1864. Uncolored. Scale 1:350,000. 55 × 79 cm.

General map indicating towns, mines, mills, roads, railroads, drainage, and relief by hachures.

S179

[Map of part of Pocahontas, Randolph, and Webster counties, West Virginia. 1865?] Colored ms. Scale not given. 61 × 41 cm.

Pen and ink sketch with additions in pencil.

Map shows the approximate position of the "enemy" south of Mace and the location of two camps southeast of Huttonsville, one of which is named "Camp Summit Cheat."

Map also includes "turnpikes," "common roads," "horse paths," towns, drainage, houses, and names of residents.

S180

Bell, C. J.

"Atlanta campaign." Left wing, 16th Army Corps. May 4th to Sept. 8th 1864. Maj. Genl. G. M. Dodge, comdg. Genls. Corse and Burke, comdg. divisions. From the original official map used on the march. Property of J. E. Meqinn, 66th Ills. Copied and presented by C. J. Bell, 81st Ohio. June 1890. Blue print. Scale 1:253,440. 76 × 42 cm.

Indicates dates, positions and campsites, roads, railroads, towns, and drainage.

S181

Glümer, J. von.

Map illustrating the operations of the army under command of General W. T. Sherman, in Georgia. From May the 5th to September the 4th 1864. Compiled and drawn under the direction of Bvt. Brig. Gen'l. O. M. Poe, Corps of Engineers, Col. & A.D.C., late Chief Engineer, Military Division of the Mississippi. Compiled and drawn by J. v. Glümer. Julius Bien & Co., lith., N.Y. Colored. Scale ca. 1:253,440. 2 parts, each 40 × 70 cm.

3 copies.

"Lines of works erected by the United States forces" are shown by the color blue and those of the Confederate forces by the color red. Indicates towns, churches, mills, roads, railroads, drainage, hachures, and geographic coordinates. Broken lines represent the area covered by each of "the five maps of the Atlanta campaign." For a description of the five maps see entry no. 131 and Sherman map coll. entry no. S200.

S182

Hamel, P. W.

Map showing detailed topography of the country traversed by the reconnaissance expedition through southern and southeastern Nevada in charge of Lieut. Geo. M. Wheeler, U.S. Engineers, assisted by Lieut. O. W. Lockwood, Corps of Engineers, U.S.A., 1869. P. W. Hamel, Chief Topographer and Draughtsman. Photolith. by the N.Y. Lithg. Engrg. & Prtg. Co. Head Quarters, Dept. of Cal., Oct. 26th 1870. Colored. Scale 1:760,320. 94 × 51 cm.

At top of map: Reconnaissance maps; Department of California; Military map no. 1.

"Officially compiled and published at the Engineer Office, Head Quarters Department of California in 1869 and 70, by order of Brigadier General E. O. C. Ord, Commdg. [Signed in facsimile] Geo. M. Wheeler, Lieutenant of Engineers in charge. Head Quarters Dept. of Cal., Oct. 26th 1870."

Detailed map of Elko, White Pine, Lander, Nye, and Lincoln counties, Nevada, showing mining districts, camps, astronomical stations, good and bad wagon roads, trails, the Central Pacific Railroad, settlements, drainage (including the "dividing line of watershed between Humboldt & Colorado Basin"), and relief by hachures and spot heights.

No. "23" is written in red ink on the verso.

S183

Johnston, Alexander Keith.

The physical atlas. A series of maps & notes illustrating the geographical distribution of natural phenomena by Alexander Keith Johnston . . . Based on the Physikalischer Atlas of Professor H. Berghaus, with the co-operation in their several departments of Sir David Brewster, K. H. &c. &c., Professors J. D. Forbes, Edward Forbes and J. P. Nichol, Dr. Ami Boue, G. R. Waterhouse, Esqr., J. Scott Russell, Esqr., and Dr. Gustav Kombst . . . Edinburgh and London, William Blackwood & sons, 1848. 5 p. l., [94] p., 30 col. maps. 57 × 38 cm.

G1046 .C1J57 1848b Vault

S184

Ludlow, William.

Map of a reconnaissance of the Black Hills, July and August, 1874, with troops under command of Lt. Col. G. A. Custer, 7th Cavalry, by Capt. Wm. Ludlow, Corps of Engineers. American Photo-Lithographic Co., N.Y. (Osborne's Process). [1874] Uncolored. Scale 1:760,320. 64 × 54 cm.

At top of map: Brig. Genl. A. A. Humphreys, Chief of Engineers, U.S.A. [and] Brig. Genl. A. H. Terry, comdg. department.

Reconnaissance map showing routes of exploring par-

ties, drainage, and relief by hachures and spot heights.

No. "3(2)" is written in red ink on the verso.

S185

Mahon, Charles.

Map of the alluvial region of the Mississippi. Prepared to accompany the report of Capt. A. A. Humphreys and Lieut H. L. Abbot, Corps of Top'l. Engrs., U.S.A. to the Bureau of Topl. Engrs., War Dept. Drawn by Chs. Mahon. 1861. Colored. Scale 1:1,500,000. 73 × 46 cm.

At head of title: U.S. Miss. Delta Survey. Plate II.

Map of the Mississippi River from Cape Girardeau to the delta showing the extent of the alluvial region.

No. "16" is written in red ink on the verso.

For another copy see entry no. 14.4.

S186

Mitchell, Samuel Augustus.

A new universal atlas containing maps of the various empires, kingdoms, states and republics of the world, with a special map of each of the United States, plans of cities &c. comprehended in seventy sheets and forming a series of one hundred and seventeen maps, plans and sections . . . Philadelphia, S. A. Mitchell, 1849, 2 p. l., 73 pl. Incl. 72 col. maps. col. front. 45 × 36 cm.

G1019 .M64 1849 Copy 2 Vault

Printed at bottom of title page: Entered according to Act of Congress in the year 1846, by H. N. Burroughs. . . .

Bookplate of Gen. W. T. Sherman was lost when the atlas was rebound in 1946.

Maps 20, 22, 23, 27, 28, 32, and 72 contain pencil annotations.

S187

Niox, Gustave Leon.

Carte du Mexique. Dressée au Depôt de la Guerre, par Mr. Niox, Capitaine d'Etat Major, d'après les levés des officiers du Corps Expéditionnaire et les renseignements recueillis par le Bureau Topographique. Paris, 1873. [Washington] Published by authority of the Hon. Secretary of War in the office of the Chief of Engineers, U.S. Army, 1881. Colored. Scale 1:3,000,000. 2 parts, each 71 × 53 cm.

Prepared by the Office of the Chief of Engineers from a map originally published in Paris in 1873. This copy has been annotated in various colors to show railroads in operation and "rail roads whose charters are still valid. Data obtained from 'the Republic and its Rail Roads' . . . by Rob't. Gorsuch, published by Hosford & sons, New York. 1881. Palmer Sullivan route located from map of 'Mexican National R.R.'."

Inset: Carte des divisions politiques. 26 × 39 cm.

Base map indicates place names, roads, drainage, and relief by spot heights.

"Map of Mexico" is written in ink on the verso.

S188

————————Map of the Mexican National Railway showing the lines granted by the Mexican government to the Mexican National Construction Company (Palmer-Sullivan concession). From the map of Captain Nioux [i.e., Niox] published in the office of the Chief of Engineers, U.S.A. 1881. Colored. Scale 1:3,000,000. 2 parts, each 72 × 53 cm.

Inset: Map showing the political divisions [of Mexico], 26 × 39 cm.

Map indicates cities and towns, roads, drainage, and relief by shading and spot heights. The Mexican National Railway is depicted by red lines.

Pencil note in the bottom margin reads "Printed by Julius Bien."

S189

Poe, Orlando, M.

Map illustrating the defence of Savannah, Ga. and the operations resulting in its capture by the army commanded by Maj. Genl. W. T. Sherman. Dec. 21st 1864. Compiled 1880–81 under the direction of Bvt. Brig. Genl. O. M. Poe, Maj. Corps. of Engs., Col. & A.D.C., late Chief Engineer, Military Division of the Mississippi. Am. Photo-litho. Co., N.Y. (Osborne's process). Colored. Scale ca. 1:85,000. 75 × 64 cm.

Detailed map of Savannah and vicinity, showing "Union works in blue," "Confederate works in red," roads, railroads, vegetation, drainage, houses, names of a few residents in outlying areas, fences, and geographic coordinates.

Includes plans of the following fortifications: works at the eastern point of Whitmarsh Island; Fort Thunderbolt; bastion on the line of defense across Whitmarsh Island; Fort Tattnall; Battery on Turner's Rocks; Fort McAllister; Causten's Bluff; and Fort Lee.

S190

Roeser, C.

Montana Territory. Compiled from the official records of the General Land Office and other sources by C. Roeser, Principal Draughtsman G.L.O. Photo lith. & print. by Julius Bien, N.Y. 1879. Colored. Scale 1:1,267,200. 58 × 81 cm.

At head of title: Department of the Interior, General Land Office, J. A. Williamson, Commissioner.

Map indicates range and township lines, cities and towns, county names and boundaries, county seats, military and Indian reservations, railroads, and relief by hachures. The map has been annotated in ink to show "Wolf Pt. Agency," and "Poplar Cr. Agency" on the Missouri River.

Mileages from these agencies are indicated to the right of the map.

S191

Ruger, Edward.

Map of the battlefield of Chickamauga, September 19th and 20th 1863. Compiled under the direction of Col. W. E. Merrill, Chief Eng'r., Dep't. of the Cumberland, by Edward Ruger, Sup't. Top'l. Engineer Office D.C. Redrawn by Louis Boedicker, top'l. draughtsman, 1867–1868. Corrected and positions of troops located by Captain S. C. Kellogg, 5th Cavalry, 1889. ©1892. Julius Bien & Co., lith. Colored. Scale 1:20,000. 10 maps, each 56 × 93 cm.

Maps were originally published loose in two paper folders entitled "Chickamauga, Sept. 19th and 20th 1863." The folder for the "First day" included "Sheet no. A: Preliminary movements, Sept. 18th" and sheets 1 to 4. The "Second day" folder (missing from this copy) contained sheets 5 to 8 and "Sheet no. Z: Movements of Sept. 21st and 22nd (after the battle)."

Each map gives troop positions and movements, names of commanding officers, a legend describing the action depicted, roads, houses, names of residents, fences, relief by hachures, vegetation, drainage, and fords.

For another copy see entry no. 159.

S192

Switzerland. *Landestopographie.*

Topographischer Atlas der Schweiz im Massstab der Original-Aufnahme. [Bern, 1870–] Colored. Scale 1:25,000 and 1:50,000. Each sheet 31 × 41 cm.

Relief shown by contours at intervals of 10 meters on 1:25,000 sheets, 30 meters on 1:50,000 sheets.

The Sherman collection includes the following two sheets from this series:

Blatt 383. "Röthenbach." Eidg. Stabsbureau, 1886. Scale 1:25,000.

Blatt 482. "Sierre." Eidg. Stabsbureau 1886. Scale 1:50,000.

S193

Tanner, Henry Schenck.

A new universal atlas, containing maps of the various empires, kingdoms, states and republics of the world, with a special map of each of the United States, plans of cities, &c., comprehended in seventy sheets and forming a series of one hundred and seventeen maps, plans and sections, by H. S. Tanner. Philadelphia, Carey & Hart, 1844. 3 p. l., 72 pl. (col. maps, col. diagrs.) 46 × 37 cm.

G1019 .T2 1844b Vault

Cover title: Tanner's universal atlas. 1844.

Bookplate: W. T. Sherman General.

Signed in ink on end paper: Sherman 1844.

Includes numerous ink and pencil notations on maps and in the margins. Lengthy notes pertaining to proposed railroad and canal routes across the Isthmus of Panama are written on blank pages opposite map [36] "Mexico & Guatemala" and map [39] "Venezuela, New Grenada & Equador" [sic]. The atlas also includes the following pencil and pen and ink sketch maps:

> Opposite map [35]. Aransas and Corpus Christi Bays, Texas, showing location of "U.S. Camp Aug. 1845" north of the town of Corpus Christi.
>
> Margin, map [43]. Unidentified area containing the place names Macomadas and Zoara."
>
> Opposite map [48]. Part of the regions of Catalonia and Aragon, Spain, showing roads, drainage, relief by hachures, and place names.
>
> Margin, map 50. Danube River in the vicinity of "Ratisbonne" [i.e., Regensburg] Germany.
>
> Margin, map 57. Two sketches of the environs of Verona, Italy.
>
> Margin, map [61]. Northern coast of Crete.

S194

U.S. *Army. Corps of Engineers.*

Dakota Territory. Prepared by order of Brig. Gen'l A. H. Terry, Commanding the Department. 3d. ed., 1878 revised & corrected under Lieut. Edward Maguire, Corps of Engineers, by Pr'vt. Julius J. Durage, Topogl. Ass't. Originally compiled under the direction of Capt. D. P. Heap, Corps of Engrs. by W. H. Wood, 1872. Uncolored. Scale 1:760,320. 2 parts, 54 × 94 cm. and 51 × 94 cm.

Map indicates the extent of the public land surveys, roads, railroads, towns and villages, Indian tribes and reservations, rivers and streams, forts, routes of exploring expeditions, and some relief by hachures.

No. "8" is written in red ink on the verso.

S195

————Map illustrating the military operations in front of Atlanta, Ga. From the passage of Peach Tree Creek, July 19th 1864, to the commencement of the movement upon the enemy's lines of communication, south of Atlanta, August 26th 1864. Compiled by authority of the Hon. the Secretary of War in the Office of the Chief of Engineers, U.S.A., 1875. Facsimile reproduction by the Graphic Co., N.Y. Colored. Scale ca. 1:32,000. 2 parts. 73 × 50 and 73 × 29 cm.

Insets: A portion of the Confederate defenses of Atlanta. Scale ca. 1:1300. 16 × 14 cm.—A portion of the U.S. defensive works erected after the capture of Atlanta. Scale 1:1200. 21 × 25 cm. Confederate and Union defenses shown in the insets are keyed to the map by the letters A to G and the numbers 7 to 12 respectively.

Detailed map showing fortifications, headquarters, location and dates of battles, street outline of Atlanta, roads, railroads, vegetation, drainage, relief by hachures, towns, mills, churches, and the location of rural houses and the names of residents.

For another copy see entry no. 143.

S196

————Map of the region between Gettysburg, Pa. and Appomattox Court House, Va. exhibiting the connection between the campaign and battle-field maps prepared by authority of the Hon. Secretary of War, under the direction of Brig. & Bvt. Maj. Gen'l A. A. Humphreys, Chief of Eng'rs. U.S.A. by Bvt. Brig. Gen'l N. Michler, Major of Eng'rs. from surveys by Bvt. Brig. Gen'l N. Michler, Maj. of Engs. and others, and from data in the Engineer Department. Compiled and drawn by Major John E. Weyss, C. [i.e., G] Thompson and J. De la Camp. [Washington] War Department, Office of the Chief of Engineers, 1869. Colored. Scale ca. 1:290,000. 2 parts, each 56 × 69 cm.

Index map made to accompany the U.S. Army, Corps of Engineers' *Military Maps Illustrating the Operations of the Armies of the Potomac & James. . . .* ([Washington] War Dept., Office of the Chief of Engineers, 1869). For a complete description of this atlas see entry no. 518.

Map indicates the area covered by each sheet in the atlas, as well as defensive works in the vicinity of Richmond and Petersburg, place names, roads, railroads, drainage, and relief by shading.

Another copy is in the James A. Garfield papers, Manuscript Division, L.C., series 8, container no. 1.

S197

————Map of the United States. Prepared by authority of the Honorable the Secretary of War, in the office of the Chief of Engineers under the direction of Brig. General A. A. Humphreys, Chief of Engineers & Bvt. Maj. Gen'l, U.S. Army. 1877. Colored. Scale 1:5,000,000. 2 sheets, each 88 × 66 cm.

Insets: West Indies and Isthmus of Darien. Scale 1:20,000,000. 16 × 21 cm.—Territory of Alaska. Scale 1:20,000,000. 21 × 26 cm.

"Originally compiled and drawn by E. Freyhold."

General map showing "military & wagon roads," canals, telegraph lines, and cities and towns. "Rail roads corrected and revised to 1877." Military camps and forts identified by red flags.

S198

————Map of the United States showing the limits of the military departments and the positions of the military posts. Prepared by authority of the Honorable the Secretary of War, in the office of the Chief of Engineers under the direction of Brig. General A. A. Humphreys, Chief of Engineers & Bvt. Maj. Gen'l, U.S. Army. 4th ed. 1877. Colored. Scale 1:5,000,000. 4 sheets, each 44 × 66 cm.

Insets: West Indies and Isthmus of Darien. Scale 1:20,000,000. 16 × 21 cm.—Territory of Alaska. Scale 1:20,000,000. 21 × 26 cm.

"Originally compiled and drawn by E. Freyhold."

Map indicates military departments and posts, "military & wagon roads," canals, telegraph lines, and cities and towns. "Rail roads corrected and revised to 1877. The rail roads designated as land grant roads [marked blue on the map] are from a list furnished by the Quarter Master General."

S199

————————Map of the Yellowstone and Missouri Rivers and their tributaries explored by Capt. W. F. Raynolds, Topl. Engrs., and 1st Lieut. H. E. Maynadier, 10th Infy. Assistant, 1859–60. Revised and enlarged by Major G. L. Gillespie, U.S. Engr's., Bvt. Lt. Col., U.S.A., Chief Engr., Military Division of the Missouri, 1876. Published by authority of the Hon. the Secretary of War, Office of the Chief of Engineers, U.S. Army, 1876 [i.e., 1877] Uncolored. Scale 1:1,200,000. 83 × 104 cm.

Statement in lower left margin reads: Western sheet. Map of Yellowstone and Missouri Rivers. From Capt. Raynolds exploration 1859–60, with additions by Major Gillespie. Published by authority of the Hon. the Secretary of War, Office of the Chief of Engineers, U.S. Army. 1877.

"Engraved in the Office of the Chief of Engineers."

Map of the Yellowstone and Missouri river basins from 96° to 114° longitude and 41° to 49° latitude showing rivers and streams, towns, forts, Indian tribes and reservations, roads, railroads, relief by hachures, and routes of exploring expeditions.

No. "38" is written in red on the verso.

S200

————————Map[s] illustrating the military operations of the Atlanta campaign . . . 1864. Compiled by authority of the Hon. the Secretary of War in the office of the Chief of Engineers, U.S.A. American Photo-Lithographic Co., N.Y. (Osborne's Process). [1874–1877] Colored. Scale ca. 1:87,000. 5 maps.

Detailed maps showing roads, railroads, drainage, vegetation, hachures, houses, names of residents, towns, churches, mills, fortifications, and the "lines of march pursued by the separate [Federal] armies."

The area covered by each of the following five maps is indicated by broken lines on the *Map Illustrating the Operations of the Army under Command of General W. T. Sherman in Georgia* (entry no. S181).

Map I: This map embraces the region extending from the Tennessee River to the Oostanaula River and exhibits the works of the United States and Confederate forces . . . 1875. 89 × 52 cm.

Map II: This map includes the region from Resaca on

the north to Ackworth on the south, and exhibits the works of the United States and Confederate forces . . . 1877. 71 × 64 cm.

Map III: This map includes the region extending from Rome, Kingston, and Cassville on the north to include Dallas and Marietta on the south and exhibits the works of the United States and Confederate forces . . . 1876. 58 × 80 cm.

Map IV: Embracing the region from Pine, Lost, and Kennesaw Mountains south to include Atlanta, and its environs, exhibiting the lines of operations at Pine, Lost, and Kennesaw Mts., at Smyrna camp ground, along the Chattahoochie [sic] River, and in the investment of Atlanta . . . 1874. 63 × 67 cm.

Map V: This map includes the region from the Chattahoochee River south to Jonesboro and Lovejoy's Station, and exhibits the works of the United States and Confederate forces . . . 1877. 65 × 67 cm.

For another copy see entry no. 131.

S201

U.S. *Army. Corps of Topographical Engineers.*

Map of the State of Florida compiled in the Bureau of Topogl. Engrs. from the most recent authorities, and prepared by order the Honorable Jeff. Davis, Secretary of War, in conformity with a resolution of the Senate of the 11th Feby. 1856, calling for "a general map of the Peninsula of Florida, illustrative of the recent surveys for a canal, executed by virtue of the appropriations made for that purpose." 1856. Reproduced in 1875. Uncolored. Scale ca. 1:850,000. 2 parts, each 92 × 49 cm.

General map of Florida showing "rail roads in operation to 1873," railroads under construction, "proposed line of canal," rivers and swamps, township and range lines, county names and boundaries, and towns and villages.

No. "9" is written in red ink on the verso.

S202

U.S. *Coast and Geodetic Survey.*

Pacific coast from San Francisco Bay to the Strait of Juan de Fuca. The reduced drawing was compiled by C. Junken and A. Lindenkohl. Engraving by H. M. Knight, J. G. Thompson and W. A. Thompson. Issued December 1888, F. M. Thorn, Superintendent. Verified: B. A. Colonna, assistant in charge of office. [Washington, 1889] Uncolored. Scale 1:1,200,000. 109 × 74 cm.

U.S.C.& G.S. 602.

At top of map: No. 602 price 50 cents; plate no. 2029; Electrotype copy no. 2 U.S.C. & G.S.

Stamped in red ink in bottom margin: Printed Sep. 18, 1889.

Nautical chart showing shore line configuration, place names, lighthouses, buoys, magnetic variation at seven locations, elevations of principal mountain peaks, and water depths by soundings.

S203

——————Puget Sound, Washington Territory. Compiled and drawn by A. Lindenkohl. Issued in June 1878, C. P. Patterson, Superintendent. Verified, J. E. Hilgard, assistant in charge of office. [Washington, 1889] Uncolored. Scale 1:200,000. 73 × 44 cm.

U.S.C. & G.S. 662.

At top of map: No. 662 price 40 cents; Plate no. 1144; Electrotype copy no. 1 by G. Mathiot U.S.C.S.

Stamped in red ink in bottom margin: Printed Oct. 11, 1889; Corrected to Nov. 4, 1889.

Nautical chart showing shore lines of Puget Sound, place names, lighthouses, buoys, and water depths by soundings and the 50 fathom curve.

S204

U.S. Geological Survey.

Georgia—Dahlonega sheet. Henry Gannett, Chief Geographer. Gilbert Thompson, Geographer in charge. Triangulation by U.S. Coast and Geodetic Survey. Topography by Chas. M. Yeates. Surveyed in 1885. [Washington] 1886. Colored. Scale 1:125,000. 47 × 38 cm.

Topographic map indicating contours at intervals of 100 feet.

S205

——————Georgia–Dalton sheet. Henry Gannett, Chief Geographer. Gilbert Thompson, Geographer in charge. Triangulation by S. S. Gannett. Topography by F. M. Pearson. Surveyed in 1886. Colored. Scale 1:125,000. 47 × 38cm.

Topographic map indicating contours at intervals of 100 feet.

S206

——————Georgia–Marietta sheet. Henry Gannett, Chief Geographer. Gilbert Thompson, Geographer in charge. Triangulation by U.S. Coast and Geodetic Survey. Topography by M. Hackett. Surveyed in 1887–8. Colored. Scale 1:125,000. 47 × 38 cm.

Topographic map indicating contours at intervals of 50 feet.

S207

Warren, Gouverneur K.

Map of Nebraska and Dakota, and portions of the states and territories bordering thereon, compiled by Bv't Maj. Gen. G. K. Warren, Maj. Engineers. March, 1867. Uncolored. Scale 1:1,200,000. 111 × 82cm.

At head of title: Engineer Dep't U.S. Army. Bv't Maj. Gen. A. A. Humphreys, Chief of Engineers.

Map indicates roads, railroads, rivers and streams, towns and villages, Indian tribes, and routes of exploring expeditions. Map has been annotated in blue pencil to show the location of Fort Meade, Dakota Territory, and Fort Hartsuff, Nebraska.

The following items, once owned by General William T. Sherman, were presented to the Library of Congress in 1942, by his granddaughter, Miss Eleanor Sherman Fitch. Sherman's copies, however, are no longer included in the Library's map collections.

S208

[Corps badges of United States Army, 1865. Engineers Department, Washington, D.C.]

Description from memorandum dated June 29, 1942, from Library's Chief, Division of Maps, to Chief, Accessions Division.

S209

Kossak, William, *and* John B. Muller.

Military map showing the marches of the United States forces under command of Maj. Genl. W. T. Sherman, U.S.A., during the years 1863, 1864, 1865. Compiled by order of Maj. Genl. W. T. Sherman, U.S.A., at Head Quarters, Military Division of the Mississippi, under the direction of Bvt. Maj. W. L. B. Jenney . . . Drawn by Capt. William Kossak . . . and John B. Muller, draughtsman. Engraved at Head Qrs., Corps of Engineers, U.S.A., by H. C. Evans & F. Courtenay. Printed by Joseph F. Gedney. St. Louis, Mo., 1865. Colored. Scale 1:1,267,200 (20 miles equal 1 inch). 72 × 118 cm.

Other copies of this map, as well as the reduced versions at the scale of 1:1,584,000 (25 miles to 1 inch), are included in the collections of the Geography and Map Division. See entry nos. 72–75.

S210

[Plans and elevation for 4 houses (New York), on tracing linen, five sheets.]

Description from memorandum dated June 29, 1942, from Library's Chief, Division of Maps, to Chief, Accessions Division.

S211

Switzerland. Landestopographie.

Topographischer Atlas der Schweiz in Massstab der Original-Aufnahme. [Bern, 1870–] Colored. Scale 1:25,000 and 1:50,000. Each sheet 31 × 41 cm.

Sheets: 180, "Ursenbach;" 235, "Hochalp;" 254,

"Wildhaus;" 269, "Weisstannen;" 279, "Noiraigue;" 344, "Matran;" 345, "Marly;" 370, "Signau;" and 422, "Lenz."

Other copies of these sheets are included in the collections of the Geography and Map Division. Sheet 422 is at the scale of 1:50,000; the remainder are 1:25,000.

S212

Symons, Thomas W.

Map of the Department of the Columbia projected and compiled at the Engineer Office, Department of the Columbia, by Lieut. Thomas W. Symons, Corps of Engineers, assisted by Alfred Downing and C. C. Manning, Topographical Assistants, U.S. Army. Drawn by Alfred Downing, Topographical Assistant. Prepared and published under the direction of Brig. Gen. H. G. Wright, Chief of Engineers, U.S. Army, 1881. Colored. Scale ca. 1:1.000,000. 79 × 107 cm.

At head of title: Brevet Brig. Gen. Frank Wheaton, commanding department.

Other copies of this map are in the collections of the Geography and Map Division.

S213

U.S. Geological Survey.

[Topographic maps of the United States] Scale 1:125,000.

Sheets: Atlanta, Cartersville, Ellijay, Rome, and Tallapoosa, Georgia; Chattanooga, Cleveland, Murphy, Ringgold, Tennessee.

Other copies of these sheets are included in the collections of the Geography and Map Division.

TITLE INDEX

Mountain, Kenesaw Mountain, and Little Kenesaw Mountain], 164.5

[Map of the environs of Powers and Isoms ferries, Cobb County, Georgia], S54

[Map of the environs of Resaca, Georgia], S102

[Map of the environs of Savannah, Georgia], 206

[Map of the environs of the Chattahoochee River at Sandtown, Georgia], S53

[Map of the environs of Vicksburg and Jackson, Mississippi], S116–S117

[Map of the environs of Vicksburg, Mississippi], S118–S119

Map of the environs of Washington, 676

[Map of the Etowah River], S81

Map of the field of operations of Gregg's (Union) & Stuart's (Confederate) cavalry at the battle of Gettysburg, 327, 357.3

Map of the field of Shiloh, S171

Map of the field of Shiloh, near Pittsburgh Landing, Tenn., 436–437, S172

Map of the field operations of the Army of Virginia during the months of July and August 1862, 465.67, 573.8 (25)

Map of the fortifications and defenses of Washington, 679

[Map of the fortifications at Port Hudson, Louisiana], 239.3

Map of the fortifications of Columbus, Ky., 218

[Map of the fortifications within the District of Columbia], 683

[Map of the Fredericksburg and Chancellorsville battlefields], 550.8

Map of the front of Kearney's [sic] command, 559.14

Map of the Gettysburg battlefield, 351.7–351.8

[Map of the James River Valley from the vicinity of Richmond to Chesapeake Bay], H100

Map of the "Kanawha City" estates, Kanawha County, West Virginia, H337

[Map of the lines of march of the Army of the Potomac from Culpeper to Petersburg, Virginia], 500–501

Map of the location of the North-western-Turnpike-Road, H215

Map of the Loup-Piney Divide coal lands, H256–H257

Map of the lower Mississippi River, 28, 41

Map of the lower [Shenandoah] Valley, H144

[Map of the lower Shenandoah Valley, Virginia], 654.2

Map of the main battlefields, routes, camps and head qrs., in the Gettysburg, Wilderness and Appomattox campaigns, 512

[Map of the Manassas battlefield area in Northern Virginia], 564.5–564.6

Map of the marches and battles of T. J. "Stonewall" Jackson, 483

Map of the Maryland campaign, 244

Map of the Mexican National Railway, S188

Map of the military department of the Gulf, S3

Map of the military division of the West, 52.5

Map of the military operations during the war of 1861–1865, 62.2

Map of the Mississippi at Island no. 10, 298

Map of the N. C. Morse patent of eighty-six thousand acres of coal, timber, iron, etc. lands in Pike County, Kentucky, H230

Map of the New River Coalfield on C. & O. R. R., H259

[Map of the northern part of Virginia and West Virginia, between the Blue Ridge and the Alleghany Front], H12

[Map of the northern portion of Hanover County, Va.], H38

[Map of the northwestern part of Cobb County, Georgia], S85

[Map of the part of Virginia lying between the York and James Rivers], 603

Map of the positio[n] occupied by the Second Division, 15th A.C., 153.4

[Map of the position of the Confederate steamer Antonica when she ran aground on Frying Pan shoals], 309.2

Map of the positions of the fourth Alabama Regt. during the battle of Stone Bridge, 564.8

[Map of the positions of the North Atlantic Blockading Squadron off New Inlet and Cape Fear, N.C.], 316.76

Map of the present seat of war in Missouri, 296.5

[Map of the Rappahannock River below Fredericksburg], H128

Map of the Rappahannock River, from Port Royal to Richards Ferry, 619.6

Map of the Rebel fortifications at Columbus, Ky., 216.95–217

Map of the rebellion, as it was in 1861 and as it is in 1864, 51.3

[Map of the Red River campaign], 241.2

Map of the region between Gettysburg, Pa. and Appomattox Court House, Va., 508.8, S196

[Map of the Rich Mountain Battlefield, W. Va.], H71

Map of the Sea Islands, 365.2

Map of the seat of war!, 16–17

Map of the seat of war exhibiting the surrounding country, 451.2

Map of the seat of war, in South Carolina, and Georgia, 359

Map of the seat of war in Virginia, 451.5, 454, 457, 508.6

Map of the seat of war [in Virginia and Maryland], 449.6–449.7

Map of the seat of war in Virginia showing minutely the interesting localities in the vicinity of Richmond, 456

Map of the seat of war. Maryland & Delaware with parts of Pennsylvania. Showing the railroads, 77.2

Map of the seat of war, positions of the rebel forces, batteries, entrenchments and encampments in Virginia, 450.3

Map of the seat of war showing the battles of July 18th & 21st 1861, 563–563.4

Map of the seat of war showing the battles of July 18th, 21st, & Oct. 21st 1861, 564

Map of the seat of war. Supplement to P. S. Duval & Son's military map, 449.4

Map of the seat of war. To accompany the American conflict, 59–60

Map of the seat of war with the lines of r. roads leading thereto, 12

[Map of the second battle of Manassas, Virginia], 572.45, 573.1–573.2

Map of the Shenandoah & Upper Potomac including portions of Virginia and Maryland, 655.5

Map of the Shenandoah Valley, 654.4, H89

[Map of the Shenandoah Valley, from Front Royal and Middletown to Staunton, etc.], H148

[Map of the Shenandoah Valley from Harrisonburg to Mt. Jackson], H146

[Map of the Shenandoah Valley from Mt. Jackson to Midway], H145

Map of the siege of Petersburg, 617–619

Map of the siege of Vicksburg, 275

Map of the siege of Vicksburg, Miss., 285–285.1, S120

Map of the "Slaughter's Creek" coal and timber lands—2,907 acres, Kanawha County, West Virginia, H263

Map of the southern and border states, 6

Map of the southern states, including rail roads, 14.55, 32.9, 37

Map of the southern states of North America with the forts, harbours & military positions, 36.5

Map of the southern states, showing all the railroads, their stations & distances, 29

Map of the State of Florida, S201

Map of the State of Virginia, 465.45

Map of the surveys made for the U.S.M.R.R., 1863 & 4, from Kentucky to East Tenn., 216

Map of the Tennessee River, 95

Map of the territory between Corinth, Miss. and Pittsburg Landing, Tenn., 439

Map of the three battle fields of First Bull Run . . . Second Bull Run . . . Bristoe Station, 573.8 (26)

[Map of the Union troop positions southwest of Marietta, Georgia], S91

Map of the United States, S197

Map of the United States, and territories, 14.6

Map of the United States of America showing the boundaries of the Union and Confederate geographical divisions and departments, June 30, 1861, 3.5

Map of the United States of North America, 11.5

Map of the United States showing the limits of the military departments and the positions of the military posts, S198

Map showing the site of Fort Slocum and vicinity, 691.4

Map showing the system of Confederate fortifications on the Mississippi River at Island no. 10 and New Madrid, 300–301

Map showing the system of rebel fortifications on the Mississippi River at Island no. 10 and New Madrid, 299.8

Map showing the war operations, in Virginia & Maryland, 449

Map to illustrate report of Brigadier-General Hill, 693

Map used by Jed Hotchkiss . . . in campaign of 1864, H179

Map[s] exhibiting part of the operations of the Army of Virginia under the command of Major General John Pope, 577

[Maps for history of 20th Army Corps], 77.1

[Maps illustrating campaign of Gen. T. J. (Stonewall) Jackson in the Shenandoah Valley of Virginia], 654.6

Maps illustrating Gen'l. Sherman's "march to the sea" and through the Carolinas and Virginia, 77

[Maps illustrating the Gettysburg campaign], 356

Map[s] illustrating the military operations of the Atlanta campaign, 131–132, S200

[Maps of the environs of forts Franklin, Alexander and Ripley, in Montgomery County, Maryland], 688

Marion District, South Carolina, S147

Marlborough District, South Carolina, S148

Matomkin Inlet, 584.5

May 17 to 23, 1864, Adairsville to Euharlee, Ga., 147.5

Memoranda, April 9, 1865. 10 o'clock A.M. Clover Hill (Appomattox Court House), Virginia, 525

Memoranda of J. Hotchkiss . . . [Sketches and notes relating to the battle of Chancellorsville], H142

Memphis and vicinity, S168

Metomkin Inlet, Virginia, 584.4

Middle Georgia & South Carolina, 129.1

Middle Tennessee, 389.7

The middle Tennessee and Chattanooga campaigns, 396

The military campaigns of Nathan Bedford Forrest, 62

The military campaigns of Stonewall Jackson, 479

Military charts, 18

Military map, Baltimore Co., Md., 254.5

Military map no. 54, prepared as basis for additional surveys, 102.8

Military map of America, 24

Military map of middle Tennessee and parts of East Tennessee, 393

Military map of part of Louisiana, 232.5

Military map of Philadelphia, 1861–1865, 358.1

Military map of Richmond & Petersburgh [sic] Va., 632

[Military map of Richmond and vicinity], 646

Military map of south-eastern Virginia, 463, 472–475, 489–492

Military map of Suffolk & vicinity, 661

Military map of the middle and southern states showing the seat of war during the great rebellion in 1861, 17.4–17.45

Military map of the States of Kentucky and Tennessee, within eleven miles of the 35th parallel of latitude or southern boundary of Tennessee, 216.7–216.8

Military map of the United States, 19, S8

Military map of the United States & territories, 10

Military map of the United States shewing the forts & fortifications, 24

Military map of the vicinity of Frankfort, Kentucky, 220.5

Military map refering [sic] to the campaigns of the Army of the Potomac in Virginia, 486

Military map refering [sic] to the campaigns of the Army of the Potomac in Virginia, Maryland and Pennsylvania, 502

Military map showing the marches of the United States forces under command of Maj. Genl. W. T. Sherman, 72–75, S6, S209

Military map showing the topographical features of the country adjacent to Harper's Ferry, Va., 699–700

Military maps, 92

Military maps illustrating the operations of the armies of the Potomac & James, 518–520

Military maps. Illustrating the operations of the armies of the Potomac and James against Richmond, 517

Military maps of the United States, 93

Military maps of the War of the Rebellion, 100

Military reconnaissance in the vicinity of Gauley Bridge, 695–696

Military reconnaissance of Virginia, 536.6

Military topographical map of eastern Virginia, 499

[Miscellaneous lithographed proof sheets of areas in Virginia], 483.5

The Mississippi [Alton to the Gulf of Mexico] as seen from the hurricane deck, 17.5

Mississippi River from Cairo Ill. to St. Marys Mo. in VI sheets, 95.2

Mississippi River, Grand Gulf, Turner's Pt., New Carthage, 48.4–48.42

Mississippi River, Rodney, St. Joseph, Bruinsburg, 48.5–48.52

Missouri, 296.7

Mobile and vicinity, S16

The model war map giving the southern & middle states, with all their water & railroad connections, 31.7

Monitor map, showing the whole seacoast from Chesapeake Bay, down to Savannah harbor, 45

Montana Territory, S190

Monumental guide to the Gettysburg battlefield, 338.2

Moore & Beckly [sic] patent, lot no. 10, Atlantic & North Western R.R. land, H326

Mountain region of North Carolina and Tennessee, 43.4–43.5, 53, 79a.6

Mouths of Roanoke River, North Carolina, 317.3

Nashville—Tenn. and vicinity, 1863, 429.4

New and complete map of Richmond and its fortifications, 629

New army map of the seat of war in Virginia, 452

A new bird's eye view of the seat of war, 449.8

New county map of the United States and Canadas, 47

New Haven Harbor, 117.1–117.15

New map of Charleston Harbor, 376

New map of Kentucky and Tennessee from authentic reports of county surveyors, 215.7–215.8

New map of Port Hudson, 240

New map of Tennessee, S158

New map of the seat of war in Virginia and Maryland, 477–478

New map of the United States, the Canadas and New Brunswick, 50

New map of Vicksburg, 286

New Market, Va., battlefield, 585

New military map of the border & southern states, 27, 38, 71

A new military map of the seat of war, 13.8

The new naval and military map of the United States, 32.5–32.7

New Orleans to Vicksburg, 229.5

A new universal atlas, S186, S193

The new war map of Maryland, part of Virginia & Pennsylvania, 242.5

New war map of Virginia, 464

Newberry District, South Carolina, S149

No. 1. First Vicksburg campaign or Chickasw [sic] Bayou, 265.5

No. 2 illustrative map of the battle-field of Manassas, Va., 573.8(20)

(No. 2) Map of the battlefield of Antietam, 250.1

No. 2 plan of fort for Sta. Rosa Id., Pensacola Harbour, 118

No. 2. The battle fields of Virginia. Map of a portion of the Rappahannock River and vicinity, Virginia, 481

Norfolk & environs, 587.5

North and South in 1861, 13.9

North Anna, 590–590.2

The North Anna and movement from Spottsylvania, 591–592

[North Carolina], 305a.5

North Carolina & South Carolina, 305a.4

North Carolina coast line, 305a.8

[North Carolina, with adjacent parts of Virginia and South Carolina], 305a.6–305a.7

the turnpike between Nolensville and Chapel Hill, Tenn., 396.25

Topographical sketch of the environs of Murfreesboro, Tennessee, 445–446

Topographical sketch of the environs of Nashville, Tennessee, 433.4

Topographical sketch of the line of operations of the Army of the Ohio, 395

Topographical sketch of the New Market, Va., battlefield, 586

Topographical sketch of the vicinity of Kingston, Tennessee, 426.2

Topographischer Atlas der Schweiz, S192, S211

Topography of the north side of Hunting Creek near Alexandria, Va., 520a.9

Totopotomoy, 663.2–663.4

Tour route, Chickamauga Battlefield, Chickamauga and Chattanooga National Military Park, Georgia and Tennessee, 162.6

Tract no. 1. Plat of Wm. T. Mann 1,147 a[cre] patent, H320

The Tribune war maps, 6.2

Troop movements at the battle of Cold Harbor, 531.5

[Troop positions at Dallas, Georgia], 168.5

[Troop positions at the battle of Resaca, Georgia], 201.8

[Troop positions in Georgia], S23

Two hundred miles around Staunton, Va., H331

[Two sketches on one sheet of the road from Huntersville, W. Va. along Knap Creek to the Greenbrier River, and from the Greenbrier River across Brushy Ridge], H79

[An unfinished drawing of the battle of Fredericksburg], H125

Union and Confederate campaigns in the lower Shenandoah Valley illustrated, 656

[Union and Confederate works astride the Dallas and Marietta Road near Pine Hill, Georgia], S99

Union District, South Carolina, S155

[Union troop positions at Dallas and New Hope Church, Ga.], S67

[Union troop positions at Dallas, Ga.], S71

[Union troop positions at Peach Tree Creek, Georgia], S98

[Union troop positions east of Dallas, Ga.], S68–S69

[Union troop positions north of Dallas, Ga.], S70

[Union troop positions northwest of Marietta, Georgia], S88, S93

[Union troop positions west of Marietta, Georgia], S89

The United States in 1861, 9.5

United States property on the Gettysburg battlefield, 351.9

United States shewing the military station's, forts &c., 7

Upper Potomac from McCoy's Ferry to Conrad's Ferry and adjacent portions of Maryland and Virginia, 245.15–245.2

[Vessels destroyed at Norfolk], 588

Vicinity of Alexandria, La., 232.86

Vicksburg, 293

Vicksburg and its defences, 283.2–283.3

Vicksburg & vicinity, 282.44

Vicksburg and vicinity, 279, 282.3, 291.9

The Vicksburg National Military Park and vicinity showing lines of siege and defense of the city, 282.5

Vicksburg National Military Park and Vicksburg National Cemetery, 291–291.2

Vicksburg National Military Park, Miss., 290.5

Vicksburg National Military Park, Mississippi, 291.4–291.8

Vicksburg National Military Park. Topographical survey, 292

View of Fort Hindman, Arkansas Post, 115.2

[View of fortifications near the ruins of the Western and Atlantic Railroad bridge across the Etowah River in Georgia], S80

View of Fredericksburg, Va., 554

View of Johnson's Island, 320

View of Vicksburg and plan of the canal, fortifications & vicinity, 294

Virginia campaign map, 498

Virginia, Maryland, Delaware, and part of Pennsylvania, 47.8

Virginia. Mecklenburgh [sic] County, H300

Volunteer militia and eastern army guide, 632.6

[Wall map showing fortifications at the time of the battle of the Crater, Petersburg, Virginia], 616.5

War between the states, 58

The war between the states campaigns of Stonewall Jackson, 482

The War between the States, 1861–1865, 80.7

The war in North Carolina, 307

War map, showing the vicinities of Baltimore & Washington, 241.5

War maps and diagrams, 14.65–14.8

War of Secession, 366

War telegram marking map, 465.7–465.8

The West Point atlas of American wars, 97

The West Point atlas of the Civil War, 97.2

West Virginia, 693.5

Western border states, 12.7

Western Tennessee, and part of Kentucky, 396.2

Western territory of the present war, 30.3

[Western Virginia from Petersburg to Warm Springs], 458

White House to Harrisons Landing, 594–595

The Wilderness, 665.8–666

The Wilderness, May 5 & 6, 1864, 665.4

Wilderness—May 5th and 6, 1864, 668.5

Williamsburg to White House, 596–598

Williamsburgh District, South Carolina, S156

Winter quarters 1864, 428.4

Works at eastern point of Whitmarsh Island, S111

A world atlas of military history, 55.5–55.6

Wreck chart: [showing the shipwreck location of Confederate ships *Georgiana* and *Mary Bowers* off the coast of Isles of Palms, South Carolina], 389.1

Wyld's military map of the United States, 19

Yazoo Pass & vicinity, 43.55

Yazoo River defences at Walnut Hills, 279

A year of maneuvers to topple a fortress, 43.2

York District, South Carolina, S157

York River and Mobajack [sic] Bay, Va., 672.5

Yorktown to Williamsburg, 599–600

INDEX